C000219698

3303350229

HENRY III

Henry III

The Great King England Never Knew It Had

Darren Baker

For my mother, who shared a birthday with Henry.

First published 2017

The History Press
The Mill, Brimscombe Port
Stroud, Gloucestershire, GL5 2QG
www.thehistorypress.co.uk

British Library Cataloguing in Publication Data.
A catalogue record for this book is available from the British Library.

ISBN 978 0 7509 6814 0

Typesetting and origination by The History Press
Printed in Great Britain

CONTENTS

PREFACE

Tell anybody you're writing a biography of Henry III and chances are they have heard of Henry VIII, the king with all the wives. Henry IV, V and VI enjoy less, but some, familiarity thanks to title works by Shakespeare, who also rendered Henry VII, the first of the Tudors, for the stage. Going all the way back to the beginning, Henry I was the king of the bastards, fathering at least twenty of them, and his equally licentious grandson Henry II was the father of Richard the Lionheart and King John, whom he cursed as bastards on his deathbed. But the third Henry always draws a blank.

'Henry who?'

That's what a guard at Westminster Palace asked after I explained, at his urging, what I was doing lingering around the grounds one sunny morning. I told him I was trying to imagine what all this must have looked like during the reign of this particular Henry, adding offhandedly that he was the greatest king of medieval England. He smugly drew back and directed the attention of this obviously ill-informed North American towards the statue of Richard the Lionheart just off in the distance.

'There's our greatest king,' he declared.

The message was clear. I could take my Henry whoever wherever and leave history to the statues.

It was a fitting send-off given all the debate and anxiety then going on in Britain about invasive foreigners, which happened to be the same issue that dominated Henry's reign eight centuries earlier. An ambitious and visionary king, he was determined to keep his increasingly insular country inside Europe. He welcomed people and ideas from the Continent and was keen to replace the greed and dull projection of power of his predecessors with a more humane and open-hearted monarchy. The pageantry of English royalty today is his creation, as is the centrepiece of national heritage, Westminster Abbey.

Parliament next door is also his contribution. It was under his rule that it became a legislative body and sat elected representatives for the first time. If Henry is remembered at all, it's because of that institution, although for reasons he might not appreciate. The barons and clergy, fed up with all the foreigners, the spending and the king's cooperation with the papacy, the Brussels of its day, conspired to rein him in. In the civil war that followed, he was defeated and subjected to the first ever parliamentary state. Henry became a captive of his own government and his reputation never recovered.

It should not have been that way. His uncle Richard the Lionheart endured a far more humiliating captivity and yet there he sits atop a horse outside Parliament with his sword raised up high. Other warrior kings like Edward III and Henry V are similarly glorified because they won great victories and stamped the authority of England wherever they went. They commanded fear and respect as a great king should.

Henry was never cut out to be a warrior. He wasn't even cut out to be a king if we judge him by their manly pursuits. Instead of hunting and killing, he liked to build and decorate. Instead of making war, he fed the poor. As he had no mistresses, he had no bastards. He loved his children dearly, and his devotion to his wife Eleanor of Provence allowed queenship to flourish in England. Hearing all that, our guard might say he sounds like one swell fellow, but lacks the qualities most people expect in a great king. It's all about him chopping heads and the women he beds, you understand.

These men ruled in a harsh age, and nearly all of them came to sorry ends. Henry III, again, was the exception. He died in his exquisitely painted chamber after the longest reign of any English monarch until the modern age, one that gave his people peace and prosperity for nearly fifty years. He had his faults and miscues to be sure, all of them described to devastating effect by his contemporaries, who vented their xenophobic rage on the man they held responsible for England's wealth going into the hands of scroungers from abroad. Modern historians have been less withering, but still unimpressed with his legacy, at least in comparison to the men he shared the stage with: the saintly Louis IX of France, the charismatic Frederick II of the Holy Roman Empire and Henry's own brilliant adversary Simon de Montfort. They too, by the way, came to sorry ends.

I was inclined to see Henry in this manner when I set out to write a biography of Montfort. Indeed, the introduction to this volume has been construed to convey this image of him. The circumstances that brought him to the throne certainly point in that direction. Young boy at the time, nation at war with itself, regency dominated by powerful men like William Marshal, forced to govern under the restrictions of Magna Carta. Excuses for failure can be easily made with a political education of this sort, but it speaks little of Montfort's own greatness if the king was truly so weak and misguided for decade after decade. In undertaking this biography, I went in search of a worthier opponent. By the time I finished, eighteen months later, I had found much more than that. Henry III was not just a dynamic and capable king, even a great one all things considered, but also a colourful and complicated personality.

He was, for example, witty, eloquent, and well informed, had a phenomenal memory and mischievous sense of humour, but he could also be temperamental, devious and prone to making hasty judgements. While he had a mystical side that drew him, not surprisingly, to the number three, he wasn't as superstitious as some supposedly steelier kings. Some of the chances he took appear positively reckless, but also understandable given what he hoped to achieve, and more or less had to in order to revive the Plantagenet dynasty. He took pride in being the first king since the Norman Conquest to be born and raised in England, but he never longed to see more of it, or the rest of Britain and Ireland for that matter, the way he did for France. Although abandoned by his mother and manipulated by the ministers of his minority, piety and charity led him to forgive them and everybody else who betrayed his trust. The insecurity and loneliness of his youth made him needy and emotionally driven, something most men in his position would try to conceal, but not Henry. With him, everything was out there, in his speeches, letters, and documents. It might just as well be, for deep down he knew everything was part of a plan that would turn out well in the end. It's little wonder then that as that very end approached, he embarked on his boldest quest yet, to set the creation of the universe in stone. And date it for good measure.

It's the biographer's supreme good fortune that Henry's reign coincided with another big bang, this one in official recordkeeping. This makes it possible to vet the history documented by the chroniclers and so arrive at a reasonably sober portrait of the man and his times. That has been done, admirably and painstakingly, by scholars starting in the Edwardian era and continuing to this day. There are too many to name here, but those who have provided me with assistance include Nick Barratt, Julia Barrow, Richard Cassidy, Joseph Creamer, David D'Avray, and Marc Morris. Others who have undertaken invaluable research in this field are Sophie Ambler, Paul Binski, Paul Brand, Stephen Church, Sara Cockerill, David Crook, David Crouch, John Paul Davis, Anne Duggan, Katherine Harvey, Margaret Howell, Paul Hyams, Adrian Jobson, Julie Kanter, Lars Kjær, Clive Knowles, Simon Lloyd, Michael Prestwich, Michael Ray, John Sadler, Scott Waugh, Björn Weiler, Benjamin Wild and Louise Wilkinson. It should be noted that many of them have contributed to the online Henry Fine Rolls Project, far and away the most ambitious and successful attempt to make Henry III and his reign accessible to a modern audience.

There is a core group of historians and scholars whose dedication and groundbreaking work deserve special mention. First and foremost is David Carpenter, the chief investigator of the Fine Rolls Project and author of two books on Henry, with a third currently in the works. His immense output is indispensable for any biography, indeed any understanding, of the king and his reign. Michael Clanchy, who has encouraged me in this endeavour from the beginning, was among the first to call for a re-examination of Henry's policies, rightly suspecting that what he said was just as important as what he did. Two inescapable topics when discussing Henry III are Simon de Montfort and Parliament, and John Maddicott has greatly enhanced our knowledge of both. Any biography of this king that doesn't consult the work of Robert Stacey first is simply incomplete, and few words can describe the incredible insight and depth which Nicholas Vincent applies to practically everything in the thirteenth century. Finally, there is Huw Ridgeway, whose own outstanding research has given us a whole new way of looking at Henry and the events of the reform period. He kindly read parts of this book and offered helpful suggestions and corrections throughout. He and his colleagues have my heartfelt gratitude and thanks.

For the views and information contained in this book, I myself am responsible.

My final word of thanks goes to those who provided the background for an undertaking of this sort. They include my wife Eva and children Dagmar and Michal here in the Czech Republic, and my sister-in-law Jana Veyres and friend Milan Hrabec on the ground in England. It goes without saying that I could not have completed this book without their support.

TIMELINE

1199 John, the youngest son of Henry II and Eleanor of Aquitaine, becomes king at the death of his brother Richard I

1200 Marriage of John and Isabella of Angoulême

1204 Philip II of France completes the seizure of Normandy, Maine and Anjou

1205 Peter des Roches becomes the Bishop of Winchester

1207 Henry Plantagenet born in Winchester, Stephen Langton becomes the Archbishop of Canterbury

1208 Probable birth year of Simon de Montfort; the Albigensian Crusade in southern France begins; England placed under interdict

1209 Richard of Cornwall born

1210 Joan future Queen of Scots born

1213 John reconciles with the pope, makes England and Ireland fiefs of Rome

1214 Battle of Bouvines, England loses Normandy forever; the future Louis IX is born; future Empress Isabella born

1215 Magna Carta enacted; Eleanor Plantagenet born

1216 Beginning of the Barons' War with French intervention; Pope Innocent III dies, succeeded by Honorius III; King John dies, Henry crowned in Gloucester

1217 Prince Louis surrenders, the French invasion force leaves England

1218 Isabella of Angoulême goes back to France; the legate Guala to Italy

1219 William Marshall dies; the struggle over the regency commences between Hubert de Burgh and the Poitevin faction under Peter des Roches

1220 Henry crowned second time in Westminster Abbey; Isabella of Angoulême marries Hugh Lusignan

1221 Joan marries Alexander II of Scotland; Pandulf's legateship ends; first friars arrive in England
1223 Plot by the Poitevins fails; Hubert de Burgh becomes Henry's supreme adviser; Philip II of France dies, his son becomes Louis VIII
1224 Siege of Bedford; Louis VIII seizes Poitou from Henry; William Marshal II marries Eleanor Plantagenet; Eleanor of Provence born
1225 Henry reissues Magna Carta for a tax; Richard of Cornwall leads an expedition to save Gascony
1226 Louis VIII dies of dysentery, his son becomes Louis IX
1227 Henry declares himself of age; Pope Honorius III dies, succeeded by Gregory IX; minor rebellion by Richard of Cornwall
1228 Stephen Langton dies, Richard Grant becomes the Archbishop of Canterbury; Llywelyn ap Iorwerth defeats an English force near Montgomery
1230 Henry's failed invasion of Brittany; Simon de Montfort arrives in England
1231 Richard of Cornwall marries Isabel Marshal; William Marshal II dies; Peter des Roches returns; Montfort acquires Leicester
1232 Hubert de Burgh falls from power; the Poitevins again in control at Henry's court; Ranulf of Chester dies
1233 Baronial party under Richard Marshal rises up against Henry and the Poitevins
1234 Edmund of Abingdon becomes the Archbishop of Canterbury; Richard Marshal killed; downfall of the Poitevins; Henry's sister Eleanor takes a vow of celibacy; Louis IX marries Margaret of Provence
1235 Henry's sister Isabella marries Frederick II of the Holy Roman Empire; Henry of Almain born; Robert Grosseteste becomes Bishop of Lincoln
1236 Henry marries Eleanor of Provence, her uncle William of Savoy becomes his principal adviser; Statute of Merton enacted
1237 Henry confirms Magna Carta in return for a tax; treaty with Scotland
1238 Simon de Montfort marries Eleanor Marshal, outcry throughout England, Simon goes to Rome to ask for a dispensation; an assassin tries to kill the king; Peter des Roches dies; Joan, Queen of Scotland dies
1239 Henry makes Simon the Earl of Leicester; the future Edward I born in Westminster; Henry denounces Simon and Eleanor and drives them from the country; William of Savoy dies
1240 Richard of Cornwall's wife Isabel dies, he and Montfort leave on crusade; Henry's daughter Margaret born; Edmund of Abingdon dies; Llywelyn dies
1241 Peter of Savoy comes to England; Boniface of Savoy elected Archbishop of Canterbury; Gilbert Marshal dies; Pope Gregory IX dies; Empress Isabella dies; Eleanor of Castile born
1242 Henry invades Poitou, it turns into a rout, he goes to Gascony, his daughter Beatrice born there

1243 Henry, Eleanor and the Montforts return to England; Richard of Cornwall marries Sanchia of Provence; the new pope, Innocent IV, confirms Boniface of Savoy as the Archbishop of Canterbury and William Raleigh as the Bishop of Winchester; Hubert de Burgh dies

1244 War with Scotland averted; the 'Paper Constitution' proposed; major Jewish tallage; Jerusalem falls to the Turks; Louis IX vows to go on crusade

1245 Henry's son Edmund born; reconstruction of Westminster Abbey commences; the Council of Lyon; Frederick deposed; inconclusive war in Wales; the two remaining Marshal sons die

1246 Charles of Anjou marries Beatrice of Savoy, takes Provence; standoff over papal exactions; Isabella of Angoulême dies

1247 Treaty with Wales; the Lusignans come to England; the ceremony of the Holy Blood; Richard of Cornwall undertakes the re-coinage

1248 Simon appointed Viceroy for Gascony; Louis IX embarks on crusade

1249 Louis takes Damietta; Hugh Lusignan dies on crusade; Alexander of Scotland dies, his son becomes Alexander III

1250 Louis' army destroyed in Egypt, survivors taken prisoner and ransomed; Henry vows to go on crusade; William Raleigh dies; Aymer Lusignan elected Bishop of Winchester; Henry's exchequer speech; Frederick II dies

1251 Shepherds' Crusade in France; situation in Gascony deteriorates; Henry's daughter Margaret marries Alexander III of Scotland

1252 Simon acquitted at trial over his administration in Gascony; clash between the Savoyards and Lusignans; Blanche of Castile dies

1253 Statute of Jewry; Henry confirms Magna Carta for a second time, goes to Gascony, reconciles with Montfort; Queen Eleanor regent; Henry's daughter Katherine born; Robert Grosseteste dies

1254 Start of the Sicilian business; first Parliament with elected representatives; the queen and children go to Gascony; Edward marries Eleanor of Castile; Louis returns from crusade, he meets Henry for the first time; reunion of the Provencal sisters in Paris; Pope Innocent IV dies, succeeded by Alexander IV

1255 Intervention in Scotland; Jews of Lincoln are condemned; Edmund declared King of Sicily

1256 Distraint of knighthood; papal collections accelerate; Welsh uprising under Llywelyn ap Gruffudd

1257 Richard of Cornwall elected King of the Romans; councillor's oath; Katherine dies; gold coin issued; war in Wales called off

1258 Onset of famine following rains; barons march on the king; reform period begins; the Provisions of Oxford drawn up; Lusignans are expelled

1259 Richard of Cornwall returns to England; Simon and Richard de Clare fall out; the bachelors march on Parliament; the Provisions of Westminster enacted; Simon and Edward become allies; Henry goes to Paris to sign a peace treaty with Louis

1260 Beatrice marries John of Brittany; Henry's return to England delayed; Simon and Edward threaten rebellion; Simon to stand trial for sedition, interrupted by Welsh incursion; Simon, Clare and Edward reach power-sharing agreement; Aymer Lusignan dies

1261 William de Valence returns to England; Henry absolved of his oath to the Provisions of Oxford, barons unite against him; Edward won back to father's side, his household purged; Clare and other barons defect; Simon goes into exile in France; Pope Alexander IV dies, succeeded by Urban IV

1262 Henry and Eleanor go to France for third visit; Richard of Cornwall goes to Germany; arbitration between Henry and Simon before Queen Margaret; Welsh uprising; royal couple returns in December to unrest

1263 Westminster Palace burns; Simon returns, leads army that targets Savoyards; Edward robs the New Temple; Mansel, Boniface and Peter of Savoy flee; Queen Eleanor's escape thwarted by a mob at London Bridge; Henry accepts the Montfortian government; Louis approves of the Provisions; Henry and Edward win over Simon's supporters, they nearly capture him in Southwark and Simon breaks his leg; Urban cancels the Sicilian business

1264 Louis nullifies the Provisions, civil war breaks out; Henry takes Northampton, he and Edward are captured at Lewes; Simon summons Parliament that approves a constitutional monarchy, he fortifies the south-east coast against invasion; arbitration through the papal legate fails; the invasion force melts away; Urban IV dies

1265 The legate becomes Clement IV; Simon summons a Parliament that includes representatives of the towns, he marches west to deal with his disaffected partner Gilbert de Clare; Edward escapes and joins Clare, defeats Simon's army at Evesham; Simon and his son Henry are killed; the king orders the disinheritance of the Montfortian survivors; Queen Eleanor returns to England, accompanied by the new legate Ottobuono; Edmund becomes the Earl of Leicester; Eleanor de Montfort and her children go into exile

1266 War of the Disinherited continues; the Dictum of Kenilworth; the Montfortians are slowly reabsorbed; Walter Cantilupe dies, the other bishops are suspended; Hugh Bigod dies

1267 Gilbert de Clare turns against Edward and the king, seizes London, stands down; Treaty of Montgomery with Llywelyn; Statute of Marlborough

1268 Edward and other nobles take the cross; Ottobuono leaves England; Peter of Savoy dies; Peter d'Aigueblanche dies; Clement IV dies

1269 Translation of Edward the Confessor to a new shrine at Westminster Abbey
1270 Louis leaves on crusade to Tunis and dies shortly after arriving; Edward continues the crusade to the Holy Land; Roger Bigod dies; Boniface of Savoy dies
1271 Henry of Almain hacked to death in a church in Italy by Guy de Montfort
1272 Richard of Cornwall dies; Norwich riots; Henry III dies at Westminster Palace
1274 Edward returns to England and is crowned
1275 Henry's daughters Margaret and Beatrice die; Eleanor de Montfort dies
1291 Eleanor of Provence dies
1296 Edmund of Lancaster dies
1307 Edward I dies

England, Wales and Scotland during Henry's reign, 1216–72.

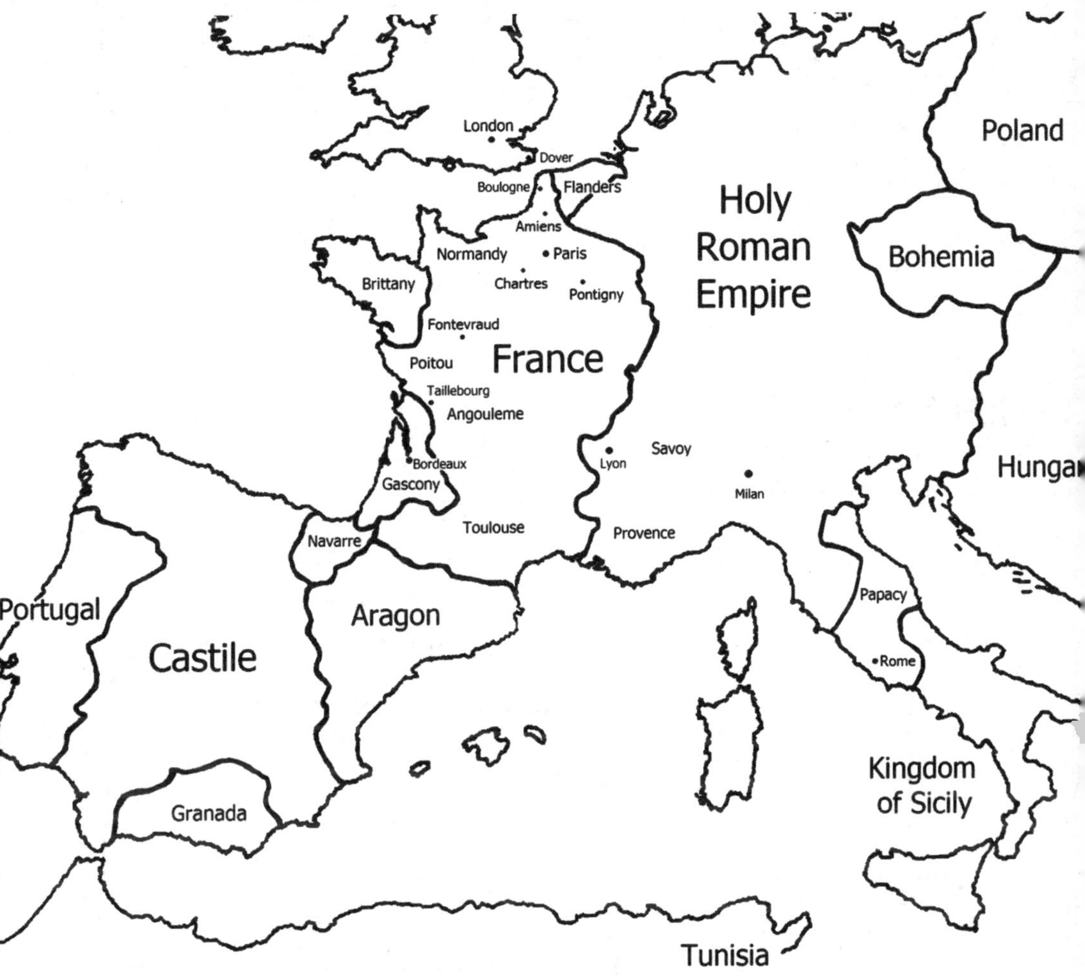

Europe around 1260.

Aldersgate
Moorgate
Newgate
Bishopsgate
Guildhall
Fleet St.
CHEAPSIDE
St. Paul's
Aldgate
New Temple
Strand
Savoy Palace
River Thames
Charing
Bishop of Durham's Palace
The Tower
London Bridge
Bishop of Winchester's Palace
SOUTHWARK
Westminster Palace
Westminster Abbey
Lambeth Palace

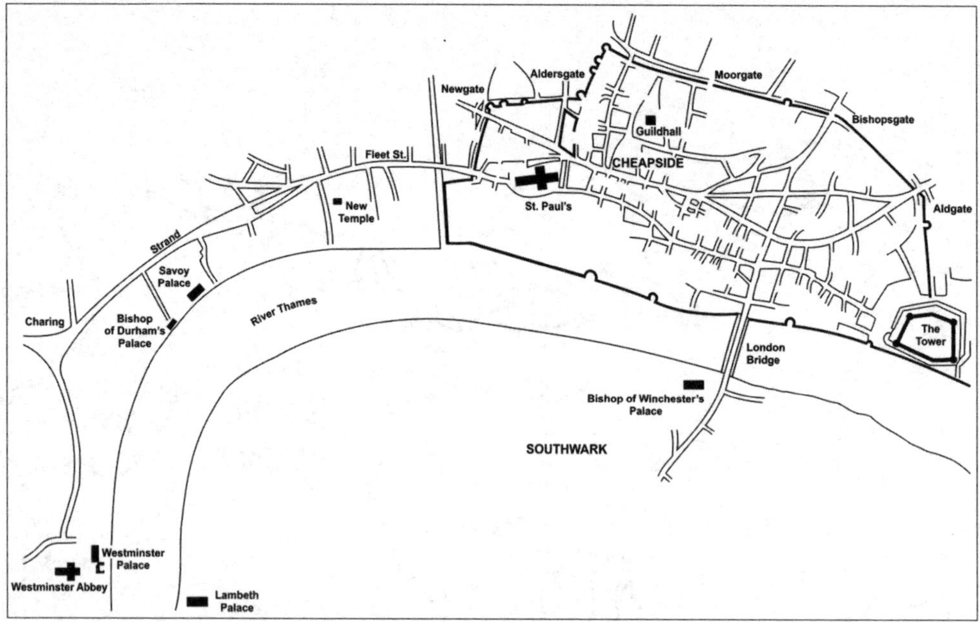

London in the thirteenth century.

River Thames
Present waterline
Modern Houses of Parliament
Medieval waterline
Pier
King's Chapel
Chapel
Watergate
Cloister
St Stephen's Chapel
Painted Chamber
Queen's Chamber
Lesser Hall
Exchequer
Westminster Hall
Lady Chapel of Westminster Abbey

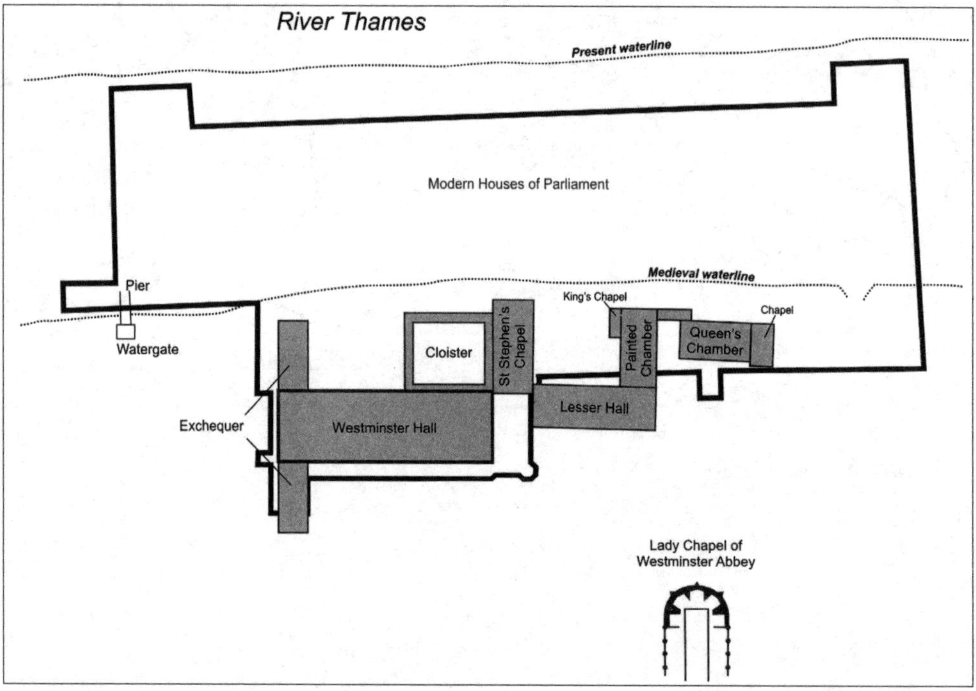

Westminster Palace in the thirteenth century.

INTRODUCTION

Theatre Royal

If history were judged in the eye of the beholder, then this Parliament would be remembered as the most impressive gathering of state ever held in England. Not so much because of the great men of the realm assembled on that occasion, or even because of the business they had come to discuss. Rather it was the venue itself, the new Chapter House of Westminster Abbey.

It had been lovingly designed by the monarch himself, Henry III, the first king since his Norman ancestors conquered the land nearly two centuries earlier to show any appreciation for architecture and craftsmanship. So certain was he of the beauty of the Chapter House that he had it inscribed with words to the effect that, as the rose is the flower of flowers, this was the house of houses.[1]

He chose it as the setting for Parliament in the spring of 1257 because he needed all the help he could get to win funding for his latest, grandest and most outrageous project yet. Three years earlier he had agreed to fund a papal war in Sicily in return for making his son Edmund the king of that island. The cost was immense: the pope already claiming arrears well over three times Henry's annual income. Unless he got his barons and clergy to sign on, the project was doomed, and Henry, a most pious man, faced excommunication.

The king knew it was going to be a hard sell. Parliament had not approved a tax for him in almost twenty years. That's because he spent that money without consulting them. He never consulted them anyway, they complained, but as far as he was concerned, they had only themselves to thank for that. They had rebelled against him three times on account of the bad advice he was getting from his councillors. Each time Henry felt humiliated and betrayed, by both his barons and the councillors.

He was determined from that point on to rule as he saw fit, and just so there would be no more misunderstandings, he vacated the offices of chancellor and justiciar, the one meant to keep the use of his seal in check, the other his justice. More ominously, he created a court of his own making, dominated by his relatives from abroad. They backed his personal rule and were lavishly rewarded as a result.

The problem with this style of kingship is that Henry was no leader of men. Although he had been king for as long as any of them could remember, they knew he had ascended the throne as a boy and not some great warrior like his uncle Richard the Lionheart. He removed any doubt about that after his two military expeditions in France ended in failure, all because of his inability to rise to the occasion. On the other hand, they were grateful he was nothing like his father John, who could do nasty things to people who opposed him – and to those who didn't, for that matter.

If the barons had to describe their king today, the word 'simple' came to mind. It described that frankness of speech, innocence of character and whimsical ambition they had so often witnessed throughout his reign – qualities that were endearing in children, maybe in ordinary adults, but the last thing they expected or wanted in a king. And now, the earls, lords, bishops and abbots who gathered in the Chapter House were about to see another brazen display of that simplicity.

They knew all about the Sicilian business. Besides knowing that it was financially and logistically impossible, they were still angry at the king for allowing himself to be duped into this scheme by one of the alien factions at court. Had he consulted them on this and other matters of state, they could all be admiring the Chapter House together now instead of wearily wondering what new antics were in store for them.

Parliament in that day met only occasionally and then for a few weeks at most. As the one that spring was coming to an end, Henry could sense that the beauty of the interior, replete with statues of the Archangel Gabriel and Virgin Mary, was having no effect on the mood of the assembly. They were as obstinate as ever. It was time to bring out his showstopper. It was a boy dressed in the costume of an exotic land. Sicily, it turned out. 'My faithful subjects,' he declared. 'I present to you my son Edmund, upon whom the Lord has bestowed kingly dignity. How evidently worthy he is of your favour, and how tyrannical and inhuman it would be of you to deny him it.'[2]

Just when they thought they had seen it all. Only their king could have concocted such a silly demonstration in the hope of getting his way. In the end, the clergy, fearing the pope's wrath, agreed to give him some money, but the barons, beholden only to the king, still refused. The only thing his shabby theatre accomplished was to increase their contempt for his authority and the way he did business. The next time Parliament met, in a year's time, they staged a bit of their own theatre when they marched up to him in full armour. The king was startled and asked if he was their prisoner.[3] Not exactly, but they had come to put their foot down. There would be no more capricious rule, hare-brained schemes or aliens calling the shots. They demanded reform and, just like those earlier rebellions, the king gave in. It had always been his way. Humbly offer concessions, then claw them back and go on ruling as before. This time, however, he had a real fight on his hands, one that would take almost a decade to resolve and leave the country devastated. Yet he emerged the victor because they had underestimated him again. Experience should have told them that the word that best described Henry wasn't 'simple', but 'survivor'.

PART I

THE PLENITUDE OF POWER

1

RECLAIMING A SCARRED KINGDOM 1199–1219

The people of England could be thankful that Henry III was no Richard I or John, for neither of them had done the realm any good. Richard had spent nearly all of his ten years on the throne abroad, some of it as a captive following his crusade. His English subjects, whom he derided as timid, had to pay a fortune to obtain his release, and even then he went on warring and making them pay for it.[1] He might have justified it all as self-defence, because King Philip II of France was determined to drive the English out of the Continental lordships they had accumulated under Richard and John's fabled parents, Henry II and Eleanor of Aquitaine. Richard was laying siege to yet another castle when a crossbowman cut short his reign in 1199. The king was interred in Fontevrault Abbey next to his father, against whom he had rebelled to the end of the old man's life.

Leaving behind no legitimate children, Richard named John as his successor, but Philip threw his support behind Arthur, the son of John's deceased older brother Geoffrey. John had managed to secure the loyalty of his French provinces, and everything might have turned out well had he not met Isabella, the beautiful heiress of Angoulême. He was married at the time, to another Isabella, but she was older and they had no children, and because they were distant cousins, he had no trouble getting an annulment from her and making the new Isabella his wife.

It wasn't just for her youth and allure that John wanted her. Angoulême was in Poitou, smack between his other major provinces of Normandy and Gascony, and being the lord of that land in right of his wife would give him a firmer grip on whatever trouble the French might give him. It came quickly enough, because Isabella had been betrothed to Hugh (IX) Lusignan, another lord of Poitou. John not only dispossessed him of his intended, but intended to dispossess him of his land as well.[2] Hugh appealed to Philip, who ordered John to appear before him to explain his conduct.

As the price for allowing John to ascend the throne in the first place, Philip had demanded and got £14,000, a deal that invited scorn back in England when it was remembered how Richard used military and diplomatic skill to keep Philip at bay.[3] By paying up, John recognised Philip as his overlord and was therefore bound to obey his summons. When he didn't appear, Philip declared all his fiefs in France forfeit and gave them to Arthur. John was going to have to fight for them after all.

Everyone knew that he was no warrior like his brother, but he fooled them in a lightning strike that bagged the rebellious nobles of Poitou and his nephew Arthur. This victory put him in an extremely good position to cut a new, more favourable deal, but John's myriad flaws included an almost perverse arrogance and vindictiveness. He starved to death twenty-two of his captives at the castle of Corfe in Dorset and had Arthur disappear, probably murdered.[4] Horrified by his cruelty, John's vassals in Normandy deserted him and he was forced to abandon the province in the face of a French invasion. By 1204, only Gascony and Poitou remained of his Continental possessions.

The loss of Normandy deprived John of a valuable source of income, making it hard for him to amass the fortune he would need to get it back and live large as was his custom. Inflation caused by poor harvests compounded the problem, but he got an unexpected windfall when the Archbishop of Canterbury died in 1205. The monks tried to choose one of their own as his replacement, but the king forced them to back his man. This caused the pope to step in with his own candidate, the learned Stephen Langton, but John was incensed that he would get no say in the appointment and refused to allow Langton even to enter England.

The pope was the equally contentious Innocent III, and in 1208, right around the time he was launching the Albigensian Crusade in the south of France, he placed England under interdict, meaning that Christian rites like mass and burial could not be performed, a very damning prospect in that pious age. John was content to call his bluff even after the pope upped the ante by excommunicating him. All the Church's revenue in England went to his treasury during the standoff, as much as £100,000.[6]

In 1212, John was ready to invade France, but had to change plans unexpectedly when Wales revolted. He raged even more than usual, because in 1205 he had married his natural daughter Joan to Llywelyn, the self-proclaimed prince of the northern part of that land, to secure his allegiance. Before John could teach him a lesson, Joan informed her father of a baronial conspiracy to murder him. It was centred in the north of the country close to Scotland, which he had punished two years earlier when there were hints of an alliance with France. At that time John forced the Scots to pay him £7,000 and deliver up two princesses for his safekeeping. Holding hostages for compliance was a serious business with him, and in his fury against Wales, he had several of their children maimed and executed.

John moved north to break up the conspiracy and assess his standing with the barons. He knew they had every reason to want to get rid of him. His boundless energy enabled him to stay on the move and harass them to no end. He held their lands and titles for ransom and taxed them pitilessly to pay for his failures abroad. Some of his actions make amusing anecdotes, like his demand that one mistress pay him 200 chickens as the price for letting her spend one night with her husband.[7] Others clearly do not, the most notorious being how he locked up and starved to death the wife and son of a nobleman after she made an off-hand remark implicating John in Arthur's murder.[8]

Some of these abuses he inherited from Richard, who had made no secret that he viewed England only as a cash cow. One chronicler noted how 'everything was for sale, counties, sheriffdoms, castles and manors'.[9] Both brothers sold the king's justice, and the fees they set for inheritances and wardships were arbitrary and excessive. Not all the money was expected to be paid. The whole point was to keep the barons in debt to the crown and therefore in their place.

The way John saw it, they had it coming. They had refused to sail with him when he first aimed to retrieve Normandy in 1206, rightly, he suspected, because some of his leading men held lands on the Continent and were worried that Philip would confiscate them if they supported his efforts.[10] In an increasingly paranoid state, John began inviting foreigners into his administration, not just because he could trust them, but knew they had no qualms about doing dirty work in a strange land.

The plot against his life was reinforced by a hermit's prediction that he would die soon.[11] Sufficiently worried, John promised some reforms as a way of thwarting dissent and getting the barons to sail with him to France, but his invasion was further delayed when a papal nuncio named Pandulf arrived to inform him that Philip was going to invade him, with Innocent's blessing no less. The king cracked under all these pressures and accepted not only the pope's authority over Church appointees, but over his kingdom as well. He declared that England and Ireland were henceforth fiefs of Rome, owing £700 a year in tribute.[12]

Since John now came under papal protection, Pandulf ordered the French to stand down. Philip was not of a mind to comply after spending £60,000 on preparations, but his ally the Count of Flanders was, so Philip attacked him instead. John came to the count's aid with a battalion led by his half-brother William Longespee, the Earl of Salisbury.[13] When Longespee chanced upon the entire French fleet unprotected at harbour in Damme in May 1213, he put it to the torch.

Emboldened by this turn of events, John launched his invasion and landed at La Rochelle in early 1214. With a war chest of £130,000, he planned to split the French by striking from the south while a consortium of allies moved in from the north.[14] He was initially successful in winning over Hugh Lusignan and other local barons, but they deserted him as an army under Philip's son Louis approached. Philip himself routed the northern allies at the battle of Bouvines on 27 July 1214, definitively settling any chance of Normandy returning to England.

John lamented that since becoming a vassal of Rome, nothing had gone right for him. His barons would say that about his entire reign, but they never had one leader to unite them in opposition. That changed with the arrival of the new Archbishop of Canterbury. Stephen Langton saw right through the supposedly humbled king and his new friendship with the papacy. John was not only weaselling out of making full restitution to the Church, but was planning to continue his repressive ways. Chronicler Roger of Wendover reports that at an assembly of prelates and barons held at St Paul's Cathedral on 25 August 1213, Langton took a few of them aside to show them what appeared to be an ancient charter.[15]

It was the coronation oath of John's great-grandfather Henry I. When in 1100 this youngest son of William the Conqueror moved to secure the crown, he promised to stop the oppressions of his brother William Rufus, who had just been killed in a suspicious hunting accident. That first Henry promised to respect the rights of the barons and clergy and implored them to do the same to their own subjects. In his embellished account, Wendover has Langton suggest that the barons might want to use this document as the basis for getting John to mend his tyrannical ways.

Nothing would have come of it had John returned from the Continent sufficiently chastened by his defeat. Instead he tried to impose another tax, and that was it. Just after Christmas of 1214, a group of barons approached the king in 'gay military array' to demand that he confirm the liberties contained in the oath of his forebear. When John was later informed of the specifics, Wendover has him asking, 'Why did they not ask for my kingdom as well?' The only oath he was interested in was that of the barons' loyalty to him. As negotiations faltered, his opponents assembled an army and won the backing of the mayor of London. John realised he would have to sue for peace. He met them at Runnymede, a meadow close to the Thames, and hammered out the details of a new charter of liberties.[16]

Magna Carta, as it became known, started off as twelve general concessions of the king to the rule of law, even those laws derived from custom.[17] The final document had sixty-three articles meant to anticipate and resolve future disputes between the crown and subjects. Some of the clauses are so fundamental for protecting the rights of individuals that they remain on the books today, like number 40: 'To no one will we sell, to no one will we deny or delay right or justice.' To make sure the king observed this and the other articles, a security clause was added at the end empowering twenty-five barons to use force if necessary to ensure his compliance.[18]

John was disgusted by what had indeed turned out to be the barons asking for his kingdom, but he sealed the charter on 15 June 1215 as a way of buying time. His patron Innocent III was as big an autocrat as he was and would surely agree that this was no way to treat a king. Sure enough, reforms were well underway when the pope issued a bull annulling the charter. He was within his rights from a legal standpoint, inasmuch as England was now his fief, but he made it clear to the barons that what bothered him was the way they had gone about it. Using coercion against one's lord was never a good thing.[19] By September, the barons realised that John's rule was beyond remedy. They raised an army, installed their own administrators, and looked around for someone else to be their king.

They settled on Philip's 29-year-old heir Louis, who justified his claim to the throne through his wife Blanche of Castile, the daughter of John's older sister. Louis was pious and austere, nothing like the foppish and clownish John, but what really worked in his favour was the men and money available to him in France. John knew better than most that nobody puts an invasion force together just like that and aimed to destroy the barons before Louis was ready. Leaving them to cower in London, he ravaged their lands in unspeakable fashion, terrorising their people who, after all, were his subjects as well.

In May 1216, Louis landed with 1,200 knights, and it was John's turn now to run scared.[20] He was deserted on all sides, including by his half-brother William Longespee, who had only recently done much of the ravaging for him. Louis marched into London in triumph and made great gains in the east, but couldn't take Dover. While he hammered away there, John sped north to reinforce his base of operations. Perhaps his greatest defeat of the war occurred when the baggage train carrying his treasure and jewels near the coast was washed away by the fast-rising tide. Losing his crown was no longer a metaphor or even a threat but the real thing. By then he was sick with dysentery anyway and could go no further after reaching Newark.[21] He wrote to the pope that he was dying and begged him to secure the succession for his family. He died in the early hours of 19 October 1216 as a storm lashed overhead.

★ ★ ★

If the civil war was all about John, his removal from the scene did nothing to end it. As far as Louis was concerned, the throne was his, and the sooner they all got on with it the better. The rebel barons would have jettisoned him then and there if they could have. Besides not being a very pleasant person to work with, Louis had let it be known that he considered anyone who rebelled against their king to be traitors, and he was ready to give their lands to his French supporters.[22] But they couldn't just go back to the English side, either. They had their honour to think of, and many of them had personal quarrels with the loyalist barons. All they could do was sit and wait for events to play out.

The loyalists themselves wasted no time. John had named his eldest son Henry as heir, and it was urgent to crown him as soon as possible. Normally this was done at Westminster Abbey by the hand of the Archbishop of Canterbury, but Louis held London and Stephen Langton was being held in Rome. He had gone there to explain why he had not excommunicated the rebel barons as ordered by Pope Innocent and found himself forbidden to return to England until peace had been established. The pope had sent a legate named Guala Bicchieri to France to stop the invasion, and when Louis sailed in spite of his efforts, Guala followed him across the Channel, determined to punish him and the rebels for their disobedience. Dressed in red robes atop a white horse, this Italian cardinal turned the ouster of the French prince into a crusade.[23]

Guala was named as one of John's thirteen executors and his authority was supreme, but he lacked the prestige of the other major executor, William Marshal, the Earl of Pembroke. Marshal was another baron who had been treated shabbily by John, but played it safe by allowing his son William II to do the rebelling for the family. He was universally lauded as the greatest knight with, by his own reckoning, some 500 victories in tournaments.[24] There was no question that he should lead the regency council to govern the realm in the interim. But he was an old man now, tired of all the strife of recent years, and whatever energy he had left to restore order in the country would depend in part on his impression of young Henry.

The boy was at Devizes Castle, where John had put him for his safety after the war broke out. When Isabella learned of her husband's death, she left her residence at Exeter to bring Henry to the executors at Gloucester. Devizes was 45 miles to the south, so Marshal and his men rode out to meet them halfway, on a plain near Malmesbury.

Henry had only just turned 9 years old. He was by all accounts a fine-looking lad, and his first words to Marshal, spoken from the horse he rode on together with his retainer Ralf of Saint-Samson, indicated that he understood the gravity of the situation.

'Welcome, sir. I commit myself to God and to you. May God give you grace to guard over us well.'

Even if he had been trained to say that by his mother, the old man was clearly moved.

'Sire, on my soul I will do everything to serve you in good faith as long as I have the strength.'[25]

At that point it all became too much for the boy and he burst into tears. Far from being taken aback, Marshal and the other hardened men in his train began to shed tears themselves. On solemn occasions John had always been apt to clown around and say something embarrassing. No one could ever tell if he was serious or not. It was one of the many ways he kept them on edge throughout his reign. Now that he was dead, they could all let their emotions out. It was little wonder that so many barons, both loyalists and rebels, left on crusade after hostilities ceased. They needed a holiday.

Then of course there was the reason why they were there in the first place. The party made for Gloucester with all due haste. The first order of business was knighting the young prince. Since Marshal was the most eminent knight in the land, it was obvious he should have the honour. The next morning, on 28 October 1216, the 'pretty little knight' as Henry was called was led to the abbey church to recite the coronation oath after Jocelin of Wells, the Bishop of Bath. In his high voice he proclaimed that he would maintain peace and honour, reverence for God and the Church, do justice to his people, observe good laws and customs, and abolish all the bad and evil ones.[26]

He then took a fateful step, one over which he had no control, and did homage to the Church and pope for England and Ireland, swearing so long as he held them that he would pay the £700 in tribute promised by his father. After that he was anointed and crowned with the best prop they had available, an ornamental chaplet for a woman's hair supplied by his mother. Peter des Roches, the Bishop of Winchester, performed this part of the ceremony with the bishops of Worcester and Exeter.[27]

The ceremony was missed by the only major baron who could match Marshal in terms of wealth and power. He was 46-year-old Ranulf de Blondeville, the Earl of Chester, and there was some concern that he might be angered that they had gone ahead with the coronation without him. On the contrary, when he arrived the next day, he approved all that had been done. Moreover, like the others, he was insistent that Marshal head the regency council to rule in the boy's name, but the Earl of Pembroke again balked. 'The child has no money and I am an old man,' he complained.

His squire John of Earley appealed to something higher than mere money and age. No matter what course Marshal took or what the outcome, his reputation would only be enhanced: 'All men will say that never did a man win such honour upon earth. Is it not worth winning?' Guala then threw in a remission of his sins, which finally roused Marshal to action. He declared that he would carry the young king on his shoulders from country to country, begging for bread if that's what it took. That said, he had a war to win and asked that Henry be placed in the charge of somebody else so he didn't have to drag him all over the country.[28]

Henry's mother Isabella wasn't even considered for the role of guardian. John had never allowed her any active role due to his controlling nature and the fact that she was just a child herself when he absconded with her. It was reported that she was 12 when she came to England, the legal age of consent for girls in that era, but she could have been as young as 8. If she still needed to do some growing, it would explain the gap between her arrival in 1200 and Henry's birth on 1 October 1207 in Winchester.[29] On the other hand, Wendover insinuates that they were already sleeping together in 1203 when he castigates the king for not hauling himself out of bed with Isabella to thwart Philip's designs on his territory.[30] That would have made her a lithesome 15 to his stocky 36.

John was certainly lust-bound most of his life, fathering several illegitimate children with noblewomen as well as wenches. Not the least of the grievances against him had to do with his roving eye for the wives and daughters of his barons. Isabella wouldn't have seen any of this first-hand. John kept her on the move from residence to residence, maintaining strict control of her household and income. What she did know, at least about his first wife, couldn't have made her happy. He maintained that first Isabella with gifts and money and at one point had both women sharing Winchester Castle. It was only because of the impending birth of Henry that John moved his first wife to new accommodation.[31]

They had four more children after Henry: Richard in 1209, and three girls, Joan, Isabella and Eleanor, between 1210 and 1215. All grew up in separate households, presumably to keep any one guardian from having excessive influence over the royal brood. Richard was at Corfe Castle together with the high-born children of opponents whom John retained as hostages, including two sisters of Alexander II of Scotland. Of greater tragedy was Eleanor of Brittany, Arthur's older sister, who had been captured together with her brother. Since she had the best claim of anyone to the throne of England, hers was a life to be spent under guarded if comfortable confinement.

In Marshal's opinion, the logical guardian for Henry was the one he already had, Peter des Roches, who first took the boy into his household when he was 4. He came from Touraine, around modern-day Tours, and entered John's service as a holdover from the military operations of Richard's chamber.[32] If John had a best friend, Peter was likely it. They liked to hunt, enjoyed bawdy humour and of all the exiles who followed the king to England, Peter received the greatest reward when John succeeded in getting him elected Bishop of Winchester in 1205.[33] He didn't let John down, either, standing by him during the interdict while other bishops fled. John made him justiciar, the chief judicial officer of the country, in 1213, and left him in charge the next year during his final campaign in Poitou. His alien background, arrogant demeanour and single-handed determination to do the king's bidding made Peter unpopular with the barons, and his removal as justiciar in 1215 was seen as another concession made at Runnymede. Ever the soldier at heart, Peter liked to be in the thick of the action and would have preferred to work with Marshal and Guala to get rid of Louis, but he understood that his position at court was now wholly dependent on his proximity to the young king.

Henry safely off with the bishop, Marshal and Guala decided that their first weapon against Louis would be political. Since Magna Carta was at the heart of all the strife, they could only benefit by reissuing it in a form everybody liked. Loyalist barons had as much to gain from a charter of liberties as the rebels, but the restrictions on royal prerogative had to be removed if the new pope, Honorius III, was to go along with it.[34] For starters, there could be no security clause implying that the king was not to be trusted. Also to be removed was the ban on levying scutage without the barons' consent. John had been merciless with this tax, which was imposed upon every lay and clerical tenant-in-chief for the number of knights he was obliged to provide in times of war. If he owed sixty knights, but only thirty turned up, he was required to pay the king cash for the other half. At £2 per knight, he owed £60, an immense sum in an age where earning £10 a year was enviable among the people who actually did work. Since the barons taxed their tenants much the way the king taxed them, they could easily live without the consent clause.[35]

The first major council of Henry's minority was convened in Bristol on 11 November. The barons and clerics in attendance took oaths of fealty and homage to him and approved the revised charter the next day. Since the young king didn't yet have a seal, Marshal and Guala attached theirs to Magna Carta, and it was once again official.[36] It was perhaps on this occasion that Henry met for the first time Hubert de Burgh, the castellan whose defence of Dover had been a major factor in halting Louis's initial juggernaut. Hubert was also the justiciar and his endorsement of the revised charter, while not mandatory, was at least encouraging. This son of the Norfolk gentry, then not quite 50 years old, was the medieval version of a mixer, a man who always seemed to be wherever the action was. While the siege of Dover had forced him to forgo the coronation, he arranged a truce with Louis so that he wouldn't miss this all-important council.

Since he couldn't take Dover, Louis positioned his forces around London for a strike at the Midlands. Marshal let him take a string of castles, knowing Louis had no hope of ever taking the throne from a king who had the full backing of the Church and, equally important, had never done anyone any harm. Back in France, King Philip was of the same mind, and in February 1217 summoned his son homeward to discuss the situation. Just getting to the coast turned out to be a struggle as guerrilla bands in the woods cut off stragglers and Louis's supplies. He finally crossed the Channel, only to hear his father tell him he had shot his bolt and would do well to make peace with the best conditions he could get. If he was determined to proceed, he would have to do it without any more help from him.[37]

Blanche of Castile dismissed this defeatist attitude and went about collecting reinforcements for her husband. Louis returned to England at the end of April and went back to besieging Dover. By then, several major rebels had defected, including Marshal's son William II and the already once-flipped William Longespee. But surrender was out of the question for the main instigators of the rebellion. Robert Fitz-Walter had taken the lead in forcing John to Runnymede, declaring himself to be the 'Marshal of the Army of God', and his cousin Saer de Quincy, the Earl of Winchester, was said to be one of the main drafters of Magna Carta. Both men were among the twenty-five sureties for the charter, and their inability to force the king to comply with it led them to the sorry state they were in now, on the receiving end of contempt from both sides. They were as much outcasts in their own land as John's alien mercenaries.[38]

Tired of all the petty sorties in and around London, they hit upon the idea of joining up forces in Lincoln to take the castle held there by the hereditary custodian Nicola de la Haye. Already in her sixties by this point, Lady Nicola had been withstanding sieges from the northern barons and their Scottish allies for two years.[39] When Marshal heard the news, he knew this was the pitched battle he needed to wrap things up. He arrived with his forces on 20 May, but the besiegers took themselves behind the walls of the city instead of facing them in the open.

That would have left Marshal in the awkward position of besieging the besiegers. Fortunately, he had Peter des Roches, who could not resist putting on the chain mail again and left Henry in the care of Guala in Nottingham. He risked capture by reconnoitring Lincoln from within, where he discovered an unused gate. Marshal couldn't be contained when informed of the news and raced towards it without his helmet on. The French and rebels were routed in what was a mostly bloodless street battle.[40]

Marshal was ecstatic that he had won such a complete victory and was said to have ridden immediately to Nottingham to brag about it, never minding his men plundering the city in the meantime. Nobody could begrudge him the victory, or using it to relive the glory of his tournament days. Indeed, seeing Isabella of Angoulême for the first time before Henry's coronation might have stirred memories of how Isabella's beautiful mother Alice de Courtenay had captivated him at a tournament nearly four decades earlier.[41]

The haul of prisoners included Fitz-Walter, Quincy and 300 knights, and 150 more came over to Henry before the summer was out. Louis agreed to peace talks, but the negotiations broke down when he refused to hand over the churchmen who had defied Rome and backed his cause, including Stephen Langton's brother Simon. Guala wanted to make examples of them, but Louis held different standards of loyalty for barons and clergy. This refusal also bought him time while Blanche got her reinforcements together.[42]

On 24 August 1217, they left from Calais under the command of Alice's brother, Robert de Courtenay. Guiding the flotilla of ten troopships and seventy support craft was Eustace the Monk, a notorious privateer who had served John well before switching sides and securing the Channel for Louis. The plan was to head straight for the Thames and London, but Marshal and Philip d'Aubigny, who was in charge of defending the coast, prepared to meet them at Sandwich. Marshal was so fired up by this time that he had to be prevented from going to sea to lead the assault himself. As the line of French ships passed their position on shore, Hubert de Burgh led out a squadron of eighteen ships that sailed by them as if fleeing to avoid battle. Once they got behind them, however, they turned to attack with the wind at their backs.

Two ships rode up alongside Eustace's flagship and tossed pots of lime into the air to blind and choke the crew. A volley of arrows later, it was over. Courtenay and his knights were captured, but a search had to be conducted for Eustace. Found in a bilge hold, he was forced topside, where he offered to pay a ransom like the others, but he had offended too many people in his lifetime. The most he got was choosing where on the ship to have his head chopped off.

The other troopships got away safely to France because the English sailors saw easy pickings in the smaller supporting craft. They later set up a hospital with some of the booty seized from them, but spoiled any honour in it by tossing the crews overboard as 'food for fishes'.[43] This first great victory at sea for the Royal Navy was blighted by its use of chemical warfare and the slaughter of defenceless seamen, but it proved decisive. Louis would have to settle for being just the King of France.

Henry was at Windsor with his mother Isabella when peace negotiations began again. She was a party to the confirmation of the treaty concluded with Louis at Kingston on 18 September 1217. Nine days later Henry entered London as king for the first time. The rebels were given amnesty and their lands back, but the churchmen would have to take their chances with Guala, who sent them grovelling to Rome. Louis was allowed to leave unmolested, with £7,000 to cover his expenses and dignity.[44]

He took the money but reneged on his agreement to work on his father to return Normandy. Marshal came under criticism then and later on for not forcing him to surrender. Since he still held land in France from Philip, he was accused of offering generous terms as a way of staying on everyone's good side. But the most important thing to him and the legate was to bring peace to the realm as quickly as possible. To show his good faith, Marshal placed his Norman lands as surety for the payment to Louis. That wasn't good enough for John's exiles, who had much to gain from the recovery of their homelands. They were disgusted by the lost opportunity, and Peter des Roches for one refused to pay any part of the tax needed to buy off the French.[45]

★ ★ ★

The previous civil war in England lasted far longer and was more destructive, but the victor in 1154 had been Henry II, a young man full of energy and determination, married to a formidable woman in Eleanor of Aquitaine. Their grandson Henry III was not even 10 years old when peace was established after this second civil war, and his regency council was headed by a man old enough to remember that first one. Both wars had been fought over the crown, but the second had had the redeeming feature of the charter of liberties being at stake. It was therefore imperative that, before any reconciliation and reconstruction could begin, everyone knew where they stood. At a meeting of the council held on 6 November 1217 at St Paul's Cathedral, the charter was revised again, and a new charter was issued alongside it to regulate the forests. The charter of liberties thus became the Great Charter of the two, or Magna Carta in Latin.[46]

Henry spent Christmas 1217 in Northampton as the guest of Fawkes de Bréauté, a Norman who had served John so well that the king had married him to the widow of the Earl of Devon and gave him custody of several jurisdictions. Officially, Fawkes was given the honour of hosting the court because of the vital role he had played at Lincoln, but it was no secret that Henry was broke and couldn't afford the festivities. Where John had as many as 100 household knights, Henry could only afford seven in a diminished entourage of thirty-nine, including two trumpeters and a nurse.[47]

As the sheriff of seven counties, Fawkes was charged with collecting the revenue due to the crown in those areas. Since the exchequer was closed during the fighting, he and the other sheriffs, who were typically magnates like him, spent the money as they saw fit, on ordinary expenses, for the war effort or to enhance their wealth and prestige. Peter des Roches for one wasn't just the Bishop of Winchester, but also the sheriff for surrounding Hampshire county. In his nearly seven years in the post, he accounted for just £7 in royal revenue, a pound a year on average.[48]

When the exchequer reopened in November 1217, none of the sheriffs were in any rush to account for their incomes, or to give up control of the castles they held. They were equally cavalier about enforcing the king's justice. In the counties controlled by Ranulf, the Earl of Chester, it was his name that ran on the writ, not Henry's. The war had allowed him to add three adjacent sheriffdoms to his portfolio, none of which was accounted for with the exchequer, and he even issued his own local charter of liberties. The rebellion had made potentates out of him and the other magnates, and they rejected any notion that they were subordinate to the regents. The foreign ones were speaking for all of them when they declared that they had been put there by a king and only a king could remove them.[49]

Their smug attitude compounded the biggest problem facing the regency. After two years of pillage and plunder, restoring land and property to the rightful owners was a daunting task. Some of the claims even went back to John's illegal seizures before the war. It was a slow, arduous process, involving the chancery issuing writs and the sheriffs convening juries to attest to the authenticity of the claims. In some cases, the sheriffs, all loyalists during the war, had axes to grind with former rebels and didn't care what amnesty had been proclaimed. They would get their land back when the sheriff got around to it, if at all.

The regents also had to contend with Wales and Scotland, both of which had thrown in their lot with Louis. Alexander II had made very little gains in the north, so it was easy for him to go back to the status quo. Llywelyn had had more success but wanted to have Guala's excommunication of him lifted. In the treaty concluded at Worcester in March 1218, he agreed to terms that made Henry the overlord of

Wales, but otherwise allowed him to exploit the post-war period to tighten his custody over disputed castles and areas.[50]

By the summer of that year the regency had been frustrated in repeated attempts to reassert royal authority over castles and sheriffdoms. Marshal knew a stand had to be made somewhere and chose Newark, where John had died. The castle belonged to the Bishop of Lincoln, but Robert de Gaugi, an alien captain installed there by John, refused to give it up despite repeated summonses. In July 1218 Marshal gathered a force that included former rebels, and, with Henry alongside him, laid siege to the place. The standoff ended peacefully, but it took eight days for Gaugi to walk out of the castle, and there were still dozens more strongholds to be reclaimed or else destroyed.[51]

This show of unity belied the regency's weakness and its failure to get the barons to help relieve Henry's poverty. Many of them were planning to go on crusade and were squirreling away their funds for that adventure, but the truth was that they didn't pay up because they didn't feel threatened by a king who was just a boy, and some of them said as much. Henry was 11 now and attending meetings of the council, but he was still growing and learning and mostly removed from the day-to-day business of governing. In November 1218, he was finally given a seal. It was cast from £3.5 worth of silver and showed the king as a grown man enthroned on one side, and on horseback on the reverse.[52] The custody of the seal was given to the chancellor, Ralph Neville, a protégé of Roches who was also the Bishop of Chichester. The seal was first used to stipulate that none of the king's charters conferred permanence until he came of age. This was the first real measure of his power, for it reminded everyone that some day he was going to take stock of all the decisions made while he was a boy. In simple terms, whatever he gave today might be taken away tomorrow.

That tomorrow was still a long way off, but a further improvement in the clout and solvency of the crown took place when a general eyre, or judicial circuit, was launched at the end of 1218. Itinerant judges were sent across the realm, hearing criminal and civil pleas and levying fines as part of dispensing justice. This generated nearly £1,000 in revenue, more than four times what the sheriffs brought to the exchequer at this time.[53] Not everyone was pleased with the verdicts, the sheriffs least of all when they went against them, and some, like Fawkes, tried to ignore or obstruct them. Nevertheless, the reassertion of royal authority in the counties was a sure sign that a corner had been turned in the young king's reign.

Less hopeful was the inevitable change in the regency. Guala was worn out by his labours and longed to return to Italy.[54] His request was granted towards the end of 1218, but his replacement as legate was none other than Pandulf, the nuncio who had sparred with Stephen Langton in Rome and was probably behind his suspension. The archbishop had been reinstated and returned to England earlier that year, fuelling concerns that the two might resume their quarrel. Langton, however, found that his archdiocese needed all his attention and withdrew from direct involvement in the kingdom's affairs for the time being.

Then, in April 1219, William Marshal resigned when it was clear he didn't have long to live. He was moved by boat to his manor of Caversham upriver from Windsor, where a final conference was held with the king, Pandulf, Peter des Roches, Hubert de Burgh and assorted officials. Only a truncated baronage was present. Men like Ranulf of Chester and Robert Fitz-Walter, opponents in the recent war, were abroad together on crusade.

Marshal intended for the barons to choose his successor as Henry's guardian, but Peter saw no need for it. In his view, Marshal had named him guardian at the outset so that he could focus on the war and settlement. The king was already in his custody and things should stay that way. His presumption not only aggravated the old warrior's discomfort, but confirmed his belief that no country was 'more divided by passion than England'. Whoever was named guardian, he declared, would only inflame jealousy in the others, so he decided to commit Henry to God, which was to say to Pandulf. His last words to the young king implored him not to follow the example of 'any evil ancestor' lest his life be cut off short.

'Sire, I pray God that if ever I have done anything pleasing to him, he may give you grace to be a good man.'

'Amen,' replied the king.

Marshal died on 14 May 1219 and was buried at the New Temple Church just outside the London city walls. Stephen Langton eulogised him as the greatest knight of the era.[55] He left behind a country on the mend after years of conflict and war, but Peter's scene at his deathbed showed how fragile the situation still was. At first, the bishop worked in tandem with Pandulf and the justiciar, Hubert de Burgh, who was beginning his rise in the regency. Together they formed a triumvirate but, as Marshal had predicted, they began squabbling almost immediately.

2

COMING OF AGE 1220–1224

John died almost 150 years to the day after the battle of Hastings which had put William, Duke of Normandy on the throne of England. To consolidate his position, William had replaced the Anglo-Saxon nobility and prelates with his Norman and Continental supporters, giving about 250 people control of a land with just under 2 million inhabitants.[1] That works out to roughly 0.01 per cent of the population holding 99.99 per cent of the wealth in their hands, a figure not vastly different from modern trends. William found much about the organisation of the country that he liked and so kept the institutions of shires, sheriffs and taxes in place. The difference now was the language of communication, as English was replaced by French in the courts and administration and by Latin, the first common language of Europe, in official paperwork.

The natives weren't expected to learn French, just work hard and not murder their new masters. The safest way for the Normans to dig in was by introducing feudalism, which collectivised the people and land around manors scattered throughout the country. The king parcelled out the estates he didn't keep for himself and his family to his tenants-in-chief, as the leading barons were called. In return, they owed him a number of knights for service based on their holdings. These knights were their tenants, middling lords or affluent freeholders who could afford the costs of knighthood (horse, armour, squire, trips abroad). Their service might involve a military campaign, manning a castle or running a special errand. Whatever the assignment, chances were that the knight grumbled when he received the summons. He had his own estates and tenants to look after and it was a hassle breaking out all that equipment. It was easier to send cash in lieu of service and, more often than not, the king was happier to receive it. He could outsource the assignment for a better price and pocket the difference.

By the thirteenth century, there were between five and six thousand knights in a country grown to something over three and a half million inhabitants, or nearly double the population when the Normans arrived. The vast majority, upwards of 90 per cent, were peasants. They toiled the fields and tended the flocks and basically did all the work that fed and clothed the nation. More than half of them were stuck in serfdom, meaning that they owed their lords some kind of menial service in addition to rent, like fetching his firewood and bringing in his harvests. Unlike free peasants, they were completely at the mercy of their lords. They had to ask his permission to leave the estate and face his justice when accused of an offence. The serf, however, was theoretically covered in times of poor harvests or upheaval, whereas the free peasant had to tough it out on his own.[2]

At the death of a tenant-in-chief, the king naturally had a say in what became of his dominions. If the lord was childless and his widow stood to inherit, he insisted that she remarry a man of his choosing, and if she didn't like that idea, he made her pay to choose her own husband or remain single. The same rule applied if the lord left behind an heiress. The king had lots of family members or allies who were grateful to marry above their circumstances and he counted on reaping support from that gratitude.

William Marshal was an obvious example of this practice. He acquired his great estates in Wales, Ireland and England after Richard I gave him the hand of the heiress to those lands, when he was 43 and she 17. They had ten children together, five of them sons, and when William II inherited the earldom of Pembroke from his father, he had to pay the king a tax called a 'relief', which was fixed at £100 by Magna Carta. This cap was instigated in response to the way Richard and John had arbitrarily exploited reliefs and other feudal incidents to the hilt.

The king had to dole out patronage regularly to keep his barons loyal and happy. Since the wardship of minors was both lucrative and politically contentious, three of the first five clauses of Magna Carta were devoted to it. Whoever bought a wardahip got all the benefits of the estates until the minor came of age, and sometimes his marriage rights came in the package.[3] It was all indicative of a very intricate system of rights and privileges ingrained in feudal society. Even lords with just a few manors got a say, and possibly a cut, in every property settlement that came under their control, mindful of course that their own overlords were watching.

The king himself being a minor had no precedent, but John had inadvertently simplified matters by submitting to the papacy. His action meant that Henry was automatically the ward of the pope and, by extension, his legates. The only point lacking clarity was at what age to end his minority. The pope and Continental custom preferred 14, the accepted age of puberty in boys, but in England 21 was the tradition. This difference of seven years was a big deal to people whose grants from the king would become permanent, or reversed entirely, when he came of age.[4]

The coming of age at 14 coincided with the accepted end of a pupil's education. Nothing is known about Henry's schooling, but he was likely taught the basic building blocks of medieval learning, including grammar, rhetoric, geometry, arithmetic and music.[5] A Latin poet then in the service of the court dedicated a long verse grammar to him and his brother Richard, indicating that the boys acquired some mastery of that language.[6] Like his forebears, Henry grew up speaking French, but what variety is hard to say. His mother and many of the aliens at John's court, including Peter des Roches, were from south of the River Loire, where the French was similar to Occitan. The English nobility generally spoke an anglicized version of the northern French brought over by the Normans, but having grown up with wet nurses and servants from the local population, they were probably comfortable in English as well. What English Henry learned certainly came from members of his household, including his nursemaid Ellen Dun. His brother Richard is on record as being able to speak English, and the evidence suggests that Henry could at least make conversation in it.[7] He washed and fed the poor with such frequency that it's improbable that no words passed between him and his less fortunate subjects during those occasions.

One of John's best knights, Philip d'Aubigny, was charged with teaching him to ride a horse, personal combat and the more assertive pursuits of being a king. Philip seems to have had limited success, for Henry never did grow up to be like his father and uncle, always in the saddle, constantly whipping up a storm in front of them. He showed no great love for falconry, hunting or other blood sports. His lifelong passion was the arts, encompassing design, painting, architecture, fashion and organising festivities. While John had enjoyed wenching and watching people squirm in his youth, Henry probably passed the time sketching new churches and clothes for his wardrobe.

Even his famous piety owed to the visual forms that went with it. He liked to gaze at the church, the altar, the priest holding the chalice, the paintings and statues that worked on his imagination. He became almost obsessed with mass, despairing if he had to miss one, and later had a small chapel built adjacent to his private quarters so he could watch the service through a slit in the wall without having to rise from bed. Not that Henry was overtly slothful. He was simply wedded to spectacle and comfort and didn't see any reason why he couldn't enjoy both at the same time.

His entire reign would be marked by a love of pageantry and the theatrical, perhaps in response to the spare, almost dreary atmosphere of his coronation, where even a comical element may have been present ('Crown? Anybody got a crown?'). Sensing it had lacked proper dignity and authority, the pope instructed Pandulf to have the ceremony performed for a second time in Westminster Abbey under the guidance of the Archbishop of Canterbury. On 17 May 1220, all the regalia fitting for the occasion were brought out, and Henry, seen in one contemporary image in bright red and blue robes, was crowned King of England again. The ceremony was followed by a great feast in Westminster Hall, for which at least forty oxen and 4,000 chickens were roasted.[8]

The crown used for the second ceremony was said to be the same one worn by Edward the Confessor. The connection was important, because William the Conqueror claimed that Edward, a distant relative of his, had named him successor before he died in 1064. His propaganda promoted the notion that Harold, the Saxon king who followed Edward, was the real usurper, and William was only setting things right by killing him at Hastings. That was all well and good, but none of the kings who followed the Conqueror had any use for the Confessor, with his ghostly appearance, unwarlike ways and insistence on celibacy. One can almost imagine John doing mocking imitations of him at binge gatherings of his barons.

There was no chance of that happening with Henry. The Confessor would become his idol, the king he revered above all others. It would be years before he actually developed a cult around him, which some saw as a cynical excuse for not being more like his fierce Norman ancestors. But if there was any English king susceptible to an epiphany, Henry was it, and he would have known that the king whose crown he received on his head had been buried on the day of the Epiphany (6 January) there in the abbey itself. And if he had an inkling that his mother would cause as much trouble in his life as the Confessor's mother caused him, perhaps there was some link there as well.

Isabella was not present at her son's second coronation. Despite being queen dowager, she had been shut out of the regency and denied any direct influence on Henry. It couldn't have been because of her connection to John or her alien background. The country was dominated by people who owed their careers to John, and many of them were aliens. Rather, England was a land where women were at best politically marginalised, where civil war had raged in the previous century because the nobility didn't want to accept Henry I's daughter Matilda as his successor. The best she could do was claim the crown for her son Henry II, who later locked up his queen, the most famous woman in Europe, for sixteen years until his death. Their son Richard treated his queen Berengaria shabbily, as John had done to Isabella. Nicola de la Haye, the castellan of Lincoln, was the only woman with any real authority, and she was now coming under pressure from William Longespee to vacate her place for him.[9] Isabella knew that she would have to go back to Angoulême in order to play the major role she coveted.

Fortunately, John provided her a way out with his last bit of diplomacy in Poitou. During his abortive campaign there in 1214, he had Isabella bring their daughter Joan to him so that he could betroth her, then 4 years old, to Hugh Lusignan's son. He did not mean to make up for swiping Isabella from Hugh, rather he wanted to secure the count's loyalty against Philip.[10] Hugh ended up abandoning him, but the marriage between Joan and his son was still on when John died. In the summer of 1218, Isabella left England, ostensibly to check up on her daughter, who, as was the custom of the time, was being raised by Hugh's family. She found that the son, then in his thirties, was in no rush to marry a girl still years away from the wedding bed. The next year he succeeded his father as Hugh X and began bullying neighbouring lordships like Angoulême. Isabella was soon complaining that he was out to get her, which turned out to be literally the case, because when he finally did marry in the spring of 1220, the mother was the bride and not the daughter.[11]

It was certainly a surprise, but the union had all kinds of advantages going for it. First and foremost, it was a marriage of equals, a rare thing in that era. They were about the same age. She was a countess, he a count. As a couple, they were now a political force to be reckoned with, ironically what John was trying to prevent by eloping with Isabella twenty years before. As the stepfather of the King of England, Hugh would watch over and protect his interests in the area. That was how Isabella sold her marriage back in England, and the news was in fact welcomed. The council was just then in negotiations for a matrimonial alliance with Scotland, and Joan would make a nice bargaining counter. Five days after his coronation, Henry sent congratulations to the man he called 'father' and asked him to ensure the safe return of his sister.[12]

The only detail to work out was the property settlement. A widow was entitled to a dower, a share of her husband's estate, and Isabella wanted her dower lands in England to go to Hugh as her dowry, which was also known as a marriage portion. Sign them over, she said, and she would send her daughter on the next ship. It sounded like extortion, and Hugh only confirmed it by his intention to keep the lands in Poitou given to Joan as her marriage portion. He wanted it all, and Isabella warned her son not to do anything to upset his new stepfather.[13]

Beyond the political implications, Isabella's decision to stay abroad and start a new family basically made an orphan of Henry. Many noble children in that age grew up apart from their families, whether for marriage or education, but he was clearly a sensitive type, preferring to draw, we can assume, angels on wing instead of knights on horseback. Her abandonment must have left him bereft of the emotional support he craved, even if Isabella was capable of offering that much. What is certain is that he wasn't going to find any in all the gruff and greedy men who were constantly making noise around him and telling him what to do.

That included hurrying him up north to York after the coronation for a meeting with Alexander II, the King of Scotland whose sisters were still in English custody. The treaty made between Alexander's father and John more than a decade earlier had called for Henry to marry the eldest of these sisters, Margaret, who was twice his age.[14] With Joan now available, Henry's councillors proposed instead that the two kings become brothers-in-law, but by Alexander marrying Joan, and they would work on finding high-born husbands for his sisters. Of course, they didn't actually have their hands on Joan, and Alexander was informed that he might have to settle for Henry's next oldest sister, Isabella, who was brought north so he could have a look at her.

To facilitate Joan's return, Henry invited Hugh to be his guest at an event even more lavish than his second coronation, the translation of St Thomas Becket's remains to a new shrine at Canterbury Cathedral on 7 July 1220.[15] It had been fifty years since Becket, the Archbishop of Canterbury, was murdered in the cathedral by men who understood that it was what Henry II wanted. The king was not only humiliated and debased in the ensuing uproar, but the Church was rubbing it in even now by scheduling the new internment of the martyr's remains on the anniversary of Henry's own burial. Luminaries from as far away as Hungary attended the ceremony, marking it as Henry III's debut on the international stage. The grandeur and spectacle of the solemn procession, coming so soon after his second coronation, could only have endeared him more to the majesty of the Church, and reminded him never to mess with it.

Hugh didn't come, but sent representatives who ruined the vibe by still insisting on the swap with Joan. Henry could have her as soon as Hugh got everything else. To facilitate their decision from his end, he went on a rampage again against his neighbours in Poitou. The council had no choice but to give in to his demands, and three months later agreed to release Isabella's dower in England without first securing Joan's marriage portion.[16] The only thing Henry had to offer Alexander with his bride was some debt relief and the custody of Fotheringhay Castle, about 37 miles east of Leicester. It was a lame deal all round, and not least because Henry wasn't even in control of Fotheringhay.

★ ★ ★

Anyone with doubts about whether the Normans were in charge after 1066 needed only look off into the distance at the gloomy hulk of stone on the hill. Like feudalism, the English castle was a Norman invention, and they dotted the landscape with them, a projection of their power and organisation. At the beginning of Henry's minority, a little over thirty royal castles formed the centre of administration in the shires. Following the second coronation, the barons swore to surrender any royal castles still in their hands or help force their surrender.[17] A month on and nothing had happened, so a test case was required. All agreed there was no better candidate than William de Forz, the Count of Aumâle.

This son of a Poitevin father and Norman mother had become something of a public menace since peace was proclaimed, engaging in a banned tournament and refusing to hand over properties to their rightful owners. He was already on probation for the two royal castles he was holding. When the court left York, the council moved to prise them from his control. He was told to just walk away. This he did, with all the stores inside, but he was still invited to spend Christmas with Henry at Oxford in 1220. Then, without warning, he left the festivities, went on a tear through the countryside and seized several castles. It took all the available law enforcement to suppress him and his men, who were once again forgiven on their promise to go on crusade. To some it seemed like a bad example to set, and it took Forz twenty years to fulfil his crusading vow, but he mostly settled down after that.[18]

One of the castles which Forz had seized was Fotheringhay, but that's getting ahead of the story. Fotheringhay was not a royal castle, rather it had belonged to David, Earl of Huntingdon. He had fought together with William Marshal II for the rebels in the recent war, but when Marshal switched sides, he was given David's castle. He was still in possession of it when David died in 1219 and was in no hurry to hand it over to David's 12-year-old son, John the Scot, who like his father was a vassal of Alexander. Marshal saw little reason to fall in line with castle reclamation until the other potentates did as well.

Marshal's wife had died several years earlier. He was just then considering several marriage prospects on the Continent, all of which the council was eager to thwart to ensure that his vast holdings remained free of foreign influence. Alexander's sister Margaret also made a tempting bride because, as a princess, she would more or less ennoble his wealth and status. But he was too powerful a baron for his sympathies to be allowed to drift north, so the only way the council could avoid that union was by offering him a princess of their own, and they had one among Henry's other two sisters. Since Isabella was on standby for Alexander until Joan returned, 5-year-old Eleanor was put forward.

With Margaret, Marshal could start cohabitating immediately, but he would have to wait almost a decade for Eleanor to grow up, and he was already in his thirties. Still, becoming the brother-in-law of the king had obvious advantages. There was also the matter of his irascible neighbour Llywelyn, who in the summer of 1220 had ravaged his lands and caused all kinds of destruction. Marshal needed help turning him back, and the council proposed to do just that as soon as he agreed not only to marry Eleanor, but hand over Fotheringhay and the two royal castles he was holding in the meantime.

He had to wonder if he was getting a lame deal the same as Alexander. Marshal would surrender the castles, but watch all his patience waiting for Eleanor come to naught when a more useful royal alliance presented itself to the court and she ended up overseas somewhere. The justiciar Hubert de Burgh gave him his word that the betrothal would take place, and if the other magnates didn't relinquish their castles, then he could have his back. Marshal consented to the match, but still held on to Fotheringhay until finally, in September 1220, Henry ordered him to surrender it before it caused him 'great damage and shame'.[19] He complied the next month, but the castle went into the hands of Ranulf, Earl of Chester, who had just returned from crusade and was holding it for the rightful owner, his nephew John the Scot. When

Forz occupied it after Christmas, Ranulf got together with Marshal to oust him.[20] It was an unlikely pairing between these two neighbours. Their earldoms edged up against Wales, and Marshal suspected there was a reason why only he got the worst of Llywelyn's depredations. He had also resigned his two royal castles, but Ranulf was still holding on to his. On top of that, he was lukewarm to the proposal of his marriage to the king's sister.[21]

It was difficult enough trying to dislodge English barons from the castles, but the alien captains were absolutely resolute that they were staying put. In this atmosphere of mistrust and lack of cooperation, an idea was born to frame one of them. He was Peter de Maulay, one of John's henchmen from the Continent who allegedly carried out the killing of Arthur. He was the current warden of the coastal stronghold of Corfe, where Arthur's sister Eleanor of Brittany was in her third decade of internment. In May 1221 Maulay was accused of hatching a plan to put Eleanor on a boat to France so she could press her claim to the English throne. He found this out when he arrived in Winchester for a celebration and was clamped in irons after the feast.[22]

The arrest was most likely the work of Hubert de Burgh. Ironically, he too had once had Arthur in his custody, but refused to carry out John's order to blind and castrate the boy.[23] He concocted the conspiracy charge against Maulay as a way not only of clearing him out of the castle, but getting his friend Peter des Roches out of government as well. Roches had left the country after he and Hubert fell out over the direction of the regency, but he was not the kind of man to take defeat lightly. He said he was going on a pilgrimage to Santiago de Compostela in Spain, but he could just as easily be going somewhere else to await the arrival of Eleanor of Brittany. So read the charge.[24]

In addition to several royal castles, the council also recovered Joan, who had been put on a ship in La Rochelle some time after the agreement was reached with Hugh the previous October. It had been nearly three years since Henry had seen his sister and, judging by their later relationship, their reunion was heartfelt and affectionate. Duty called, however, so in June 1221 the court progressed north to York, where the 10-year-old girl was given in marriage to the 22-year-old King of Scotland.

There was nothing like a wedding to talk about other weddings, and one that was long overdue was apparently decided on this occasion. Alexander's sister Margaret, now approaching 30, would finally get to marry, and the bridegroom was Hubert himself. He was certainly on a roll that season, though not to everyone's liking. They pointed out that he had been married twice before, in each case with an eye towards his own advancement. Margaret may have been past her prime, but she was still a princess and the sister of a king. Hubert was a commoner, just like Marshal, only without his prestige. To be constrained to marry someone of inferior social rank was considered disparagement, and a clause had been inserted in Magna Carta to prevent this from happening. Magna Carta wasn't our problem, the Scots might have replied, and whatever the obscurity of Hubert's background, his power in England made him a man worth courting.[25] Currently, his only rival in the regency was Pandulf, but that too was about to change.

One important person who had been missing from the excitement of late was Stephen Langton. After the translation of Thomas Becket, which put his diocese in debt for many years, he left for Rome on a variety of tasks, one of which was to ask the pope to remove Pandulf as legate. This was partly personal, given their history, but what he really wanted was no legate at all, because the Archbishop of Canterbury would always be subordinate to whoever filled that office. Langton got a sympathetic hearing and was back in July 1221. Rather than wait to be recalled, Pandulf turned in his resignation at the end of the month.[26]

No sooner was Hubert rid of him, however, than Peter des Roches reappeared, and he wasn't alone. The first Dominican friars arrived in England that summer and were accompanied by Roches to Canterbury, almost as if he were their tour guide. Always ready to take on all comers, Roches immediately jumped into the fray surrounding Maulay, and got him cleared of all charges of treason at a meeting of the council. He couldn't get him reinstated at Corfe, but he did win him the equivalent of damages. Maulay still owed the crown £6,000 for his accounts as the Sheriff of Somerset and £4,900 for the heiress given to him in marriage by John. He was now told to forget about it, the money would be written off as upkeep for the castle while it was under his watch.[27]

The justiciar probably felt he could afford to be magnanimous. He knew that his rival was about to suffer another setback on 1 October 1221, when Henry turned 14 and his education came to an end. Without any immediate influence over the king, Peter was powerless to affect the course of the regency, which should not have been the case given that nobody had been more of a father figure to him.[28] Henry might have forever remembered Peter as the parent he never really had, but the bishop was militant and methodical in everything he did, capable of great action and loyalty but of little personal affection. The bond that had developed between them was strictly businesslike.

Henry spent Christmas that year as Peter's guest in Winchester, the city of his birth, but the atmosphere of the court was fraught with tension. Now it was Ranulf's turn to fall out with Hubert, principally over the latter's open alliance with his two major adversaries, Longespee and Marshal. Hubert's overweening ambition, with his princess wife and determination to reclaim castles and sheriffdoms for the king, was a threat to potentates like Ranulf. Nor did it help that the justiciar was an upstart, a complete nobody who owed his rise to royal service, not to family lineage. He dared presumed to tell Ranulf and the rest of the ancestral nobility what to do. Langton intervened to avert a brawl from breaking out at court, if not a general disturbance throughout the land.[29]

The rift opened the floodgates of an issue that would dominate Henry's reign. An undercurrent of anti-alien factionalism had seeped into English politics in the wake of Richard and John filling key positions in government with men who were born and raised on the Continent. The English baronage were generally jealous of the power and patronage accumulated by these aliens and tried to stir up local resentment against them. It didn't help the aliens' cause that they were an arrogant and intemperate lot who couldn't resist adding personal invective to the quarrel, as when Fawkes de Bréauté declared that all Englishmen were traitors who only wished and desired war. He would have them know that he was prepared to give them all they could stomach on that front.[30]

Remarks like that were widely reported, so when Ranulf was seen to be taking a stance against the government, it could only mean that he was being led astray by these name-calling foreigners.[31] The argument was largely superficial, since they all spoke French, worshipped Christ and were equally determined to exploit the English-speaking population for all they were worth. In the summer of 1222, the people of London got a harsh reminder of just how superficial the argument about foreigners was.

It started as a wrestling match between the young men of the city and those of the suburbs, which Westminster was at that time. One of those licked by the city boys was the Abbot of Westminster's steward, who called for a rematch the following week, with the offer of a prize ram for the winning team. The steward recruited a group of strong men to redeem his honour, but when the subsequent match proved to be a draw, he and his men suddenly produced weapons and beat and chased their opponents back inside the city walls. The infuriated Londoners returned in force, led by a hothead named Constantine, and ransacked Westminster.

Hubert was in the west of the country when the riot broke out and didn't arrive until over a week later, but he instituted an immediate crackdown with an armed contingent under Fawkes. Constantine confessed his role as agitator, was even proud of it, so Hubert had Fawkes lead him and two accomplices away the next day to be hung. In vain, the condemned man offered £10,000 to spare his life, but Fawkes merely scoffed and ordered his men to start pulling on the ropes.

Afterwards Hubert and Fawkes, the native and the alien, rode through the city together, picking up those accused of taking part in the riot and having their hands or feet chopped off. The mayor and aldermen had tried to prevent the disturbance, but they were turned out of office. The city was fined, ordered to hand over hostages and informed that it would have to win back the king's goodwill.[32] Hubert would deservedly find London a most uncongenial place when his own day of reckoning came.

When Constantine bragged about stirring up the populace, he couldn't imagine it would lead to his summary execution. He was no nobleman like William de Forz and therefore could not expect the same forgiveness for flouting the law, but due process was so commonplace as to be taken for granted. And yet it was still an era in which mutilation or death was meted out in special cases. Ordeal by fire and water had only been banned by the Church in 1215, at the Fourth Lateran Council organised by Innocent III, but didn't disappear in England until trial by jury became the accepted form four years later.

In April 1222, the full work of the Lateran Council was published at a synod convened in Osney near Oxford by Stephen Langton. Rather than sweep away other superstitions, the decrees were more concerned with housekeeping within the Church and the right of the clergy to administer justice to their own. This had been at the heart of the quarrel that got Becket slain in his cathedral back in 1170. Priests who committed murder and other felonies were usually defrocked and tossed out. Henry II wanted them to face the civil authorities as well, but Becket considered that double jeopardy and risked exile and eventual death in defence of the principle. At the Osney synod, Langton upheld Becket's position and allowed a priest charged with murder to be simply expelled, whereupon he reportedly continued his crimes. But the archbishop then went to the other extreme by having a deacon who converted to Judaism turned over to lay judges for burning at the stake. The contradiction here seemingly owes something to the influence of the newly arrived Dominican friars, whose founder, Dominic de Guzman, had been one of the spiritual guides in the mass burnings of heretics during the recent Albigensian Crusade.[33] Langton, however, was committed to the Lateran Council's intention of suppressing Jewish communities throughout the Christian world. The one in England had arisen after the Norman Conquest and numbered around 5,000 in the thirteenth century, settled almost entirely in towns.[34] They were now under the threat of various decrees, one of which demanded they distinguish themselves by their outer dress, ostensibly to prevent cohabitation between the faiths.

This decree was first mandated in England in March 1218, while Langton was still abroad. Henceforth all Jews were ordered to wear the mark of two white tablets on their garments when in public. Guala may have been behind it, but the writ itself was sealed by William Marshal, suggesting that it was a ploy to raise money for the cash-strapped regency. Exemptions from wearing the tablets were offered at a price, which many Jews bought because they didn't want to get beaten up or harassed on sight. The decree was seldom enforced, so after the synod, Langton took it upon himself to prohibit any interaction with the Jews of Canterbury, including the selling of food and other daily essentials to them. Under Hubert's guidance, Henry countermanded the order, even hinting at something unpleasant in store for those who persisted in it.[35]

Langton didn't see any inconsistency between letting priests get away with murder and denying basic human decency to some members of society. An Englishman educated at the University of Paris, where he later taught for many years, he was narrowly focused on the meaning of kingship and its relation to the Church. He believed that a king must rule within the law and proceed in accordance with good judgement, for once he stepped beyond those bounds he became a tyrant, oppressing his people and, no less important, interfering with churchmen like himself. John had been the worst example of that, but his son wouldn't be, whether he inherited the same disposition or not, because Magna Carta would always be there to anticipate his every move.

At a council meeting held at Westminster at the beginning of 1223, the 15-year-old king was asked by Langton and several of the barons in attendance to confirm the rights contained in the charter of liberties. William Brewer, one of John's faithful adherents, unexpectedly declared that since Magna Carta had been extracted by force, it was invalid and was therefore in no need of confirmation. Perhaps he was thinking that Henry, now that he had his own seal, might like to hammer out a version that took his own opinions into account. Langton was having none of it and snapped at Brewer that he was threatening the peace of the realm with such comments. Henry quickly stepped in, showing, as he would throughout his reign, that he was never at a loss for words.

'We have sworn to observe all these liberties, and what we have sworn we are bound to abide by.'

The confrontation, however, got him thinking about the liberties of the kingdom that existed before his father's reign. He had a writ sent out to each sheriff ordering them to assemble a committee of twelve knights or liegemen for each county to investigate this matter. Langton could not have been happy about Henry taking an initiative that might lead to a revision of the charter, and in April 1223, just before the sheriffs were to publish their findings, they were told to forget about it. If asked, they were only to say that the king had no desire to resurrect 'any evil customs'.[36]

In fact, Langton preferred to have a charter of liberties with the king's seal of approval. He wanted a strong king, believed there should be one, to keep the peace and protect the Church.[37] It's just that now wasn't the time, not until Henry was the complete master of his realm. The government's resumption of the royal demesne, which is to say the king's estates, had been a success and brought in an extra £600 to the exchequer, but the ultimate power in the land, the castles, were still not reclaimed, six years after the end of the war.[38] The only way to put an end to this state of affairs was to fully empower the king, otherwise he might some day want to quash a certain charter of liberties that seemingly protected everybody's rights but his.

Pope Honorius III put it into motion with three letters. The first one he addressed to Hubert, Roches and Brewer, informing them that he was elated to hear that Henry was far more mature than his age suggested. He should therefore be given the free disposal of his kingdom, and the pope expected these three ministers to make sure that happened. The second letter went to Ralph Neville, the keeper of Henry's seal, instructing him to ensure that the king's letters went out only 'at his will'. The baronage got the third one, encouraging them to support the king and reminding them that a failure to do so could earn them the sentence of excommunication. These letters were probably procured by Roches, not because he felt that Henry had come of age and wanted the pope to act on it, but because he saw no other way to emancipate him from Hubert.[39]

* * *

Henry was still shy of his sixteenth birthday when the pope got involved in the final reclamation of his kingdom. Apart from the cartoonish figures drawn in medieval manuscripts, no portrait or drawing of him survives to tell us what he looked like on the verge of manhood or at any other point in his life.[40] Judging by his tomb, he grew up to be about 5ft 7in (174 cm), which was an average height for men of that day. He is represented as having fair to sandy hair, with a smooth complexion and the general high colouring of his ancestors, nearly all of whom came from France. Henry was the first king after the Norman conquest to be born, raised and spend practically all his life in England, and yet were it not for his Saxon great-great-grandmother Matilda, his blood would be all French.

It was little wonder that a man who loved Christmas so much would become fond of handing out gifts, as he began to do around this time. It was a small but important part of the patronage the king had to dispense in order to keep his barons and their families happy. Nothing made their day more than receiving wine or deer from him, not merely as a sign that they were in his favour, but also just knowing that the lord king was thinking about them. Even his incarcerated cousin Eleanor of Brittany was not forgotten and received delicacies like raisins, almonds and figs from time to time. Henry would prove to be a man of great personal attachments, and nothing gave him more joy than making the day of those people who really were in his favour. This was the case with two nuns at a convent who received steady gifts from him. Once when he found out that a cartload of firewood he sent them had still not arrived, he ordered Brewer to see to it immediately or else he was going to send him the bill for it.[41]

His strongest political attachments just then were to Hubert de Burgh and Stephen Langton, two Englishmen who spearheaded the final drive against the potentates. Their biggest help came from William Marshal II, another Englishman on the face of it, but who in fact was born in Normandy. On the opposite side stood nearly all the alien captains, but they were led by another Englishman, Ranulf of Chester. Ranulf was friends with Llywelyn of Wales, Marshal's biggest enemy and the only true foreigner of the lot, and these two sealed their alliance the year before when Llywelyn's daughter Helen married Ranulf's nephew and heir John the Scot.

Marshal started things off in the spring of 1223, when the truce with his Welsh neighbour expired. Fresh from Ireland with men and supplies, he quickly overran the castles of Cardigan and Carmarthen. By summer he had conquered most of south Wales, and Henry congratulated him by sending him ten deer from Windsor Forest.

This was Hubert's chance to put Llywelyn and Ranulf in their place, so he mustered an army under Marshal and Longespee at Worcester. Everything changed, however, when Philip of France died in July and the country's military resources were suddenly directed south to bolster Henry's demand that the new king return Normandy to him. A delegation under Langton was sent to Louis VIII to remind him of his promise to do so. Louis asked for time to think about it, which he only used to make sure of his hold over the duchy. When Pandulf next arrived to hear his answer, he was basically told to get lost before Louis resurrected his claim to the English throne.[42]

The outcome was more favourable in Wales. On 8 October 1223, a week after he turned 16, Henry received Llywelyn's submission at Montgomery. Worried that they might be next, Ranulf and the other malcontents tried to tell the king that Hubert was out of control and should be dismissed, but the justiciar turned it into a plot and whisked Henry away to Gloucester for his own protection. Ranulf then played into his hands by seizing the Tower of London. That brought Hubert and Henry back to London with an armed battalion. The malcontents retreated to Waltham Forest, 8 miles to the northwest, where Langton found them when he and the other bishops went to organise a peace conference at the beginning of December.

Men like Ranulf, Fawkes and Maulay swore that their only problem was Hubert. Get rid of him and there would be peace in the land. Hubert took it personally and knew exactly who was behind it. Looking at Peter des Roches, he called him a traitor and blamed him for all the evils that beset the kingdom. The Bishop of Winchester, the warrior monk who loved a good scrap, returned 'evil for evil' by declaring that if it cost him everything he had, he would ruin Hubert some day. With that, he led Ranulf and the others out of the room 'murmuring and complaining'.[43]

The archbishop managed to work out a six-week truce, but agreed with Hubert that Henry was going to need greater authority to prevent eruptions like these from happening again. On 10 December, the king was finally given full control over his seal as urged in the papal letters. Hubert and Langton, however, weren't prepared to go further and give him the free disposal of his kingdom, and so no official proclamation was made that the king had come of age. Henry's letters from now on would be attested by himself and not the regent but, as before, no grants were to be permanent for the time being.[44]

This latest move towards empowering Henry was behind the malcontents holding their own Christmas gathering in Northampton. This was Fawkes country, in the heart of the Midlands, as good a staging area as any to make a show of force. Henry, Langton and Hubert decided to show them by taking the Christmas court to Northampton as well. Like a bunch of scrooges, the malcontents packed up and moved 32 miles north to Leicester, also within Fawkes country, but they knew they had been checkmated. Henry's guest list included ten earls, among them Ranulf's brother-in-law William de Ferrers, the Earl of Derby. With a solid showing of the baronage behind him, Henry summoned Ranulf and the others to join him. They grudgingly appeared and must have gritted their teeth when invited to make the greatest gift in their power to the king and hand over his castles. The letter from Pope Honorius beseeching them to do so was produced, but even then Ranulf wanted confirmation that the pope hadn't changed his mind in the meantime.[45]

In fact, he had, and Ranulf knew it. During the summer, when it looked as if recovering Normandy might unite them all, Hubert and Peter agreed that now was not the time to let the ongoing squabble over castles disrupt that unity. They sent a proctor to Rome to ask Honorius to revoke his earlier letters demanding Henry's empowerment, which he did, but with no great pleasure. But by the time that new letter arrived in November, Hubert and Peter were at war again and it was quickly filed away.[46] In making his appeal, Ranulf was demanding to see the letter, but Langton had enough of all the evasiveness and griping and ordered the malcontents to resign their castles forthwith, else he would excommunicate the lot of them on the spot.

Ranulf's loyalty to the crown went back to the reign of Henry's grandfather, when that king, Henry II, anxious to maintain his hold over Brittany, nudged him into marrying Constance, the widow of his son Geoffrey and mother of Arthur and Eleanor. It didn't matter that Ranulf and Constance loathed each other, a feeling that apparently went back to their days as wards of the court. Henry II knew all about loveless marriages and simply would have told Ranulf to stick it out, the kingdom came first. He did, and now, some twenty-five years after Constance got an annulment from him, Ranulf was swallowing his pride and doing the same. He surrendered the three castles he was holding, plus the sheriffdoms that went with them, and his associates followed suit.[47]

To soften the blow, Langton acquiesced to their condition that all the castles be redistributed fairly. Hubert and his supporters complied and turned over theirs to their local bishops, but before long they were reconfirmed with them. If it seemed like a betrayal on Langton's part, the malcontents had only themselves to thank for it. In asking for the pope to get involved, they had suggested that what England needed was another legate. Nothing could have infuriated the archbishop more, and his coming out completely on Hubert's side may have been his response to this.[48] For his part, Fawkes saw something more sinister and claimed that Langton's real aim was to force all foreigners like him out of the country.

According to Fawkes, Langton was of the mind that the aliens were 'the scourge of all native men', whom they treated as 'booty'. Even if Fawkes himself had made disparaging remarks in this vein, he and the rest of the aliens were nevertheless settled in their adopted land, having married into the local population and started families. They had nothing to go back to on the Continent. It was no less important that all of them had stood by John and Henry as Louis attempted to take the throne from them. Meanwhile, those who had aided Louis, including Marshal and Longespee, were now sitting comfortably in their castles, and Marshal was on the verge of getting his princess bride after all. If that weren't bad enough, Langton was at that very moment arranging permission for his brother Simon to return to England after his exile, he who had served as Louis's chancellor and was one of the French king's most vehement supporters.[49] There was nothing fair in this settlement, Fawkes asserted, and he was right.

He and the others were being disingenuous with their profusions of loyalty, however. As sheriffs, they were responsible for collecting revenue due to the king from the royal demesne, fines, taxes and the 'farm' of the county, which consisted of various traditional payments like the sheriff's aid, view of frankpledge, ward penny and so on. The sheriff farmed the county, which is to say he paid the king a fixed sum for running it and keeping whatever was extra. The farms were aptly called 'ancient' because their values had been set decades ago and so lagged far behind inflation. It was the opportunity to pocket this huge difference, aptly called 'profit', that enticed magnates to take up the post in the first place.

Seeing just how much profit was being made, the exchequer began tacking on surcharges, called 'increments', to allow the king to enjoy more of his own income. John had followed his brother's lead in increasing increments to boost his income, but then went one better by demanding everything. He wanted farm, increments and profit. With John on the ropes, the magnates saw their chance to relive the good old days by having an article included in Magna Carta that prohibited increments. It was subsequently removed in the 1216 version as part of an admission by the barons and prelates that they had infringed the rights and revenues of the crown.[50]

Following the war, sheriffs like Fawkes, Ranulf and Peter not only kept the profit, but the farm as well, accounting for next to nothing at the exchequer. Their lack of interest in solving the government's persistent financial crunch was a major impetus behind Hubert's drive to bring local administration firmly under central control. The sheriffs who were now appointed, whether old or new at the job, were required to account for everything.[51] As with the castles, it was the determination of Fawkes and the other potentates to look after themselves first and the king as an afterthought that had brought them to their present predicament. Of course, the way they saw it, it was just Hubert wanting to keep all the money and power for himself.

Their only hope was for the pope to get involved and dispatch a legate. Honorius was by now confused and disturbed by the conflicting reports he was receiving and sent Henry a letter advising him not to play favourites. Learning what was afoot in Rome, and perhaps worn out by the ever-elusive pursuit of peace, Langton organised a great council in London in April 1224. There, Ranulf's party was restored certain manors in return for exchanging the kiss of peace with Hubert.[52] They were still hoping for a legate to come to their rescue, but were willing to take what they could get in the meantime. Hubert's former ally Fawkes went along, but he was still refusing to hand over one castle, in Bedford. In what was an eerie replay of the scheme to remove Maulay from Corfe, Fawkes suddenly found himself charged with breach of the peace, a capital offence. The complaint was eight years old, but a finding of guilt could still get him outlawed and hung.

As an alien, sheriff, braggart and keen manipulator of ransoms and inheritances, Fawkes had innumerable enemies, but none more powerful than Marshal, who considered him 'capricious and evil'. Marshal's success in Wales led to his appointment as the justiciar of Ireland, with the task of going there and crushing another rogue, Hugh de Lacy. Before his departure, he was finally given the hand of Henry's sister Eleanor after a wait of three years. Since she was only 9, he would have to wait a few more years to consummate their marriage, but being the king's brother-in-law gave him extra clout overseas. He was happy to leave his child bride behind with her governess, but since the government expected him to thrash Lacy, he expected them to do the same to Fawkes.[53]

Fawkes insisted that he was being framed and began garrisoning Bedford Castle, then under the command of his brother William. He refused to answer any summons on the charge against him, so the government commissioned a court in Dunstable to hear more complaints against him. One of the judges, Henry of Braybrook, was a personal enemy of William de Bréauté. On 17 June, William kidnapped Braybrook as he was on his way to a council meeting convened in Northampton, Fawkes' former seat of power. The main purpose of the council was to deal with an even more urgent matter that had come up, and the actions of the Bréauté brothers made a mess of that and everything else. The result was to force Henry to show for the first time his mettle when pressed too far.[54]

In April 1224, the truce with France expired, but there was every reason to expect Louis to renew it. He had built up an army, it was true, but he was planning to use it at the instigation of the pope against Raymond VII of Toulouse, who was again succouring Albigensian heretics in the south. Louis had already been on crusade against them, and in 1218, smarting from his defeat in England, he massacred the several thousand residents of Marmande. The thought of what this humourless man might do now was enough to force Raymond to capitulate. With the crusade suddenly called off, Louis announced on 5 May that there would be no renewal of the truce with England. He clearly intended to use his army to seize Poitou from Henry.[55]

The government had taken steps to avert this by appeasing Hugh Lusignan, whose castles blocked any advance to the ultimate prize of La Rochelle. He was offered £800 for the arrears of Isabella's dower, to be paid up front, and he could keep Joan's marriage portion for at least the next four years. Louis brushed these terms aside, offering Hugh Joan's marriage portion for life, land in Poitou equal to Isabella's dower and Bordeaux in Gascony if Hugh could take it. In the first of many acts that would blacken the Lusignan name in England, Hugh signed on with Louis in June 1224. Isabella's role in the betrayal was probably negligible, as she was confined for much of the decade with non-stop pregnancies.[56]

What to do about Poitou dominated the agenda of the great council in Northampton, which opened with a proposal to reinstate Peter, Ranulf and their group into government, both because the pope wanted it and the threat posed by Louis demanded unity more than ever. A tax was going to be needed to raise money for the defence of La Rochelle and that required the consent of all the magnates. Fawkes was at the meeting, where it was also decided to shelve the old charge against him. Then his brother went and pulled his kidnapping stunt.

Saying he had nothing to do with it, Fawkes nevertheless fled, finding shelter in Wales with Llywelyn. The Bedford garrison refused to surrender, insisting that under feudal law they could only take orders from their lord, Fawkes. While it was brazen defiance of the king, Henry made an attempt to retrieve the fugitive so that they could hear it from him. When the posse returned empty-handed, Henry demanded they surrender lest he hang the lot of them. No way, was their answer. Fawkes' engineering additions to the fortress gave them confidence that they could hold out indefinitely.

Henry was faced with the most difficult decision of his reign so far. The situation in Poitou demanded immediate action, but the days of men like Fawkes having free run of the realm had to end. While impulsive and quick to temper like his father and grandfather before him, Henry forever put his trust in peaceful outcomes, and it's possible the garrison could have escaped his wrath had they come to their senses once the siege engines were rolled into place. But their snipers with crossbows began picking off his men, killing six knights and scores of soldiers and supporting personnel, and they went so far as to cut off all communication with him, which was tantamount to thumbing their noses at him. The castle had to be taken by inches, the siege lasting all summer, and the garrison still had to be smoked out in the end.[57]

They were sorely mistaken if they thought that releasing Braybrook and their other prisoners beforehand would win them any mercy. Henry warned the eighty survivors they would swing and that's exactly how they ended up. The only mercy he showed was to allow three of the eleven knights among them to be cut down before strangling on condition that they joined the Templars and left for the Holy Land. Ranulf and Alexander Stavensby, the Bishop of Coventry, convinced Fawkes to go to the king directly at Bedford and plead for his life. No doubt it was arranged to give him the best view of his brother and the other corpses dangling on their ropes. Henry left his fate to the council, which spared his life but seized all his possessions and banished him for eternity. He wandered on the Continent for the next two years, first being arrested by Louis, then held for ransom by a Burgundian whom he had held for ransom after the civil war. He succumbed to poisoning in 1226. At the time of his banishment, he swore to Henry that he had only £3 to his name, but he raised that figure to £7,700 on his deathbed.[58]

Since it was money he never reported to the exchequer, Henry tried to claim it through the pope, but Honorius was less than sympathetic to the course of action he had taken. He nevertheless saved his lashing for Langton: 'Where is that abundant wisdom of yours, if it is by your advice that the king is making war on his own subjects, whilst he sees foreign enemies preparing war against him!'[59] But Henry was adamant that he 'had to go there' and told the pope as much in a letter. 'It would have been worse had we not,' he assured him.[60]

Some of the pope's ill will was due to what Henry lost as a result of the siege. On 24 June Louis made his move, securing the way to La Rochelle and beginning his own siege there on 15 July. The town surrendered less than three weeks later, and so Poitou, like Normandy before it, now belonged to the French. Honorius, whose bungled crusading fervour had contributed to its fall, meekly asked Louis to withdraw, but that only earned him a rebuke to stay out of it. Henry had spent £1,311 on besieging Bedford, money that could have gone to reinforcing La Rochelle, but in fact the town was lost more through the will of its citizens, who felt they had never really had much support from England.[61] But money was always a big matter where lordships were at stake, and here the King of France had four times more royal income than his English counterpart. They were hardly in the same league, he sneered, adding that Henry was a mere 'boy and pauper'.[61]

Having exacted his revenge, Louis returned to Paris and left Hugh Lusignan to conquer Gascony by himself. After some initial progress, he was stopped cold well before Bordeaux. While he retreated to contemplate his next move, Hubert used the occasion of the Christmas feast at Westminster to lobby the barons and prelates for a tax to outfit and dispatch an expeditionary force to the province. The king's dignity was at stake, he informed them. The King of France had treated him with contempt, and if they did nothing to stop him, he might just get around to making good his claim to the English throne after all.[63]

3

SILKY WHITE GLOVES 1225–1230

For better or worse, medieval England was considered the land of milk and honey. It was an island of fabled wealth that made it a top destination for marauders and fortune-seekers. William the Conqueror seemingly confirmed that this was the case when he opened up the royal treasury after his victory at Hastings and discovered a wardrobe spun of gold and precious jewels, just the thing to wear the next time he and his men went home to show off the spoils of their cross-Channel venture.[1]

In 1194, England didn't pay all of the £100,000 needed to ransom the captive King Richard, he of the Lionheart fame, but enough of it to convince his brother John that there was more where that came from. In 1207, he asked his magnates for a special aid, which was a nice way of saying 'tax'. At that time, there were three commonly accepted aids for every king to take, namely for the ransoming of his royal person, the knighting of his eldest son and marriage of his eldest daughter. John proposed a new one, a 'gracious aid for the defence of our kingdom and recovery of our rights' on the Continent. But that wasn't the precedent that scared the magnates most. He wanted more than just scutage, where he taxed them directly and they passed the burden along to their tenants. He was after a tax on movables, making every individual household subject to the king's collectors. Under this form of national taxation, there was nowhere for the magnates to hide, and they weren't happy about it.[2]

Officially they were, though, because John claimed to have got the consent of the realm to levy the tax. What he meant was he had the consent of cronies like Roches and Brewer, but the mere fact that he mentioned it establishes that taxation implied consent long before it was taken up in Magna Carta. Hubert, another one of those cronies, knew that in the current political climate, he was going to have to get real consent in order to get a similar aid, which was the only kind that could raise the money needed to save Gascony. Naturally this was not consent from the knights or freeholders, let alone women or serfs, but from their lords gathered around for the king's Christmas feast.

After some discussion, they agreed to a tax on movables, 15 per cent to be exact, but with a caveat. They wanted something, too. John had got his tax without giving anything in return, not even a lull in exerting pressure on the kingdom, but now there was no way the magnates were going to pass up an opportunity to impose conditions, to set the standard for all future taxation. Led by Stephen Langton, they demanded that Henry attach his seal to Magna Carta, thereby making it official once and for all. It was a quid pro quo arrangement, which indicated that mere consent no longer sufficed. The king would have to give something in return if he wanted their money.[3]

Henry must have wondered what had become of chivalry and feudal solidarity. Here his rights were under threat, but instead of rising to the standard, his barons and clerics were equivocating their support. Even if Langton hadn't meant it intentionally, he was spearheading a transformation of taxation that meant the king could never again expect aid out of simple loyalty. From now on, they would answer all his requests with their hands outstretched, perhaps with a smug look on their faces. That was not the best of prospects for any king with grand ambitions and a lavish sense of generosity.

Having undergone two revisions in the two years since its inception as a peace treaty, the charter itself would remain unchanged from the last version approved in 1217. The only difference was the preamble. The preceding charters had declared that the king conceded the following liberties with the counsel of his barons. Now he was doing it of his own goodwill. The idea was to remove the stigma of coercion, which Brewer had pointed out two years earlier and got a nasty rebuke from Langton for his trouble. While the quid pro quo nature of the agreement implied coercion of a benign sort, Henry was in fact all for the protection of the rights enshrined in Magna Carta. A constant theme throughout his long reign was his insistence that the barons do justice to their tenants much the way he was expected to do justice to them.

Since this was the way they had decided to go, the final chapter of the charter was reserved for Henry's declaration that he was granting these liberties in return for a fifteenth part of the nation's movable wealth. Those who didn't pay up couldn't expect to enjoy these liberties.[4] Of course, he had the barons and clergy in mind, the people foisting the charter on him in this fashion. Most peasant families were too poor to pay any tax. They were getting by eating only bread and pottage, which was a type of porridge with just about anything thrown in to give it robustness and bite, including nettles and other weeds. At this level of subsistence, their few possessions were generally exempt from the collection. When Henry received word that some of his commissioners were being overly zealous with the poor, he ordered them to stop. In the end, most of the 15 per cent tax came from farm produce and goods destined for sale, yielding just under £58,000, or about the same as John amassed with a 13 per cent rate eighteen years earlier.[5]

The Gascons knew it was going to take more than money to hold off Hugh and Louis. They advised Henry to come in person to deal with the situation or, more realistically, send his brother at the head of the expedition. Richard had only just turned 16, but as second in line to the throne he was bound to inspire more respect than any of the king's deputies. So Henry knighted him, gave him the county of Cornwall at his pleasure, and titled him the Count of Poitou as an incentive to take back that territory if the opportunity presented itself. Given Richard's youth and inexperience, that decision would be left up to the two famed warriors who accompanied him, his uncle William Longespee and Philip d'Aubigny. Together with several dozen knights, they set sail on 23 March 1225.[6]

They made headway initially, but got bogged down when they went to retake the strategic castle of La Réole on the River Garonne. Hubert stepped up by dispatching immediate funds, £37,000 in all from the tax collected. Louis was sufficiently worried to order Hugh Lusignan to relieve the castle, but when he got there, Richard was waiting in ambush. According to Wendover, he gave his stepfather a thorough thrashing, complete with the sound of blaring trumpets. He chased him off the field and seized the remnants of his baggage train. By November the castle had fallen and Poitou lay beyond the river to the north.[7]

The situation stalemated after that. Richard was also pursuing a marriage for himself, and Longespee's inability to keep his nephew in line on this matter led to the old man's recall. Worn out by the struggles of the last twenty years, he was happy for it until his boat foundered after setting off. He and the crew had to seek refuge on an island controlled by Louis. After three days of keeping their heads down, Longespee was recognised and told that he had till dawn to be gone or else face capture. It cost him £20 to make sure he got that much time, and his ship was again tossed about as soon as they departed.[8] They were long overdue by the time they pulled in off the Cornish coast after Christmas. These events put Longespee in a grim mood and it grew grimmer when he learned what Hubert had been up to in the meantime.

Convinced that the ship had been lost at sea, Hubert went to Henry for permission to give the marriage rights to Longespee's now presumed widow, Ela, to his nephew Raymond. Henry agreed on condition that Ela was willing, which she most certainly was not after the young man shined up his armour and showed up asking for her hand. Not only had she learned that her husband was alive, but the much younger Raymond was nowhere near her class. She had been the heiress of the Earl of Salisbury, which is where Longespee got his title from. She told the confused suitor he would realise what a waste of time this charade was the moment he sought a bride elsewhere.

When Longespee appeared at Marlborough Castle, where Henry was recovering from a dangerous but unspecified illness, he brushed aside the king's joy and immediately complained about how Hubert had sent some lowlife to beseech his wife with base intentions. He demanded satisfaction from the justiciar or else he would make sure the whole kingdom heard about his wounded pride. Hubert was mortified to find that he had overplayed his hand in such an unseemly manner and followed up an apology to Longespee with several valuable horses and other expensive gifts. Apparently he was worried Longespee would continue to use the affair against him because, according to Wendover, he slipped some poison into his food at a dinner meant to celebrate their reconciliation. The chronicler admits that the charge is hearsay, but cannot resist going with it after Longespee went home and took to his bed. He did, in fact, die a little over a month later.[9]

Hubert was lucky the king didn't sack him then and there. As he would show on later occasions, Henry hated when people put him in embarrassing situations. Dignity was a word he used often in association with kingship, and nothing aroused his temper more than someone taking advantage of him or making him look like a fool. It was especially painful in this case because Henry was close to his uncle. Indeed, Wendover says that he was still grieving over his loss at sea when Hubert made his silky suggestion about who Ela should marry next. But he could also see that Hubert was the ablest man he had, who had reclaimed his castles and sheriffdoms, increased his revenues, got through his tax and saved his lone remaining overseas province. There was still much work to be done, and since Hubert had been willing to hang his head on the spot and make amends, it was better they put the episode behind them.

After Longespee's death, Ela never did remarry as rich widows were expected to. With Hubert's humble backing, she eventually succeeded her husband as the Sheriff of Wiltshire, first at Henry's pleasure, then for life, and finished her days in a nunnery she had founded.[10] Raymond didn't let her admonition to find somebody of low birth stand in the way of his ambitions, however. The widow of the Earl of Essex was more susceptible to his advances, and Henry showed that there were no hard feelings by making him the gift of several manors. While this could sound like Hubert was again in full favour and intervening with the king for his family, Raymond was called a 'brave and noble knight' in his own time, whatever Ela might have thought.[11]

Events on the Continent also made any shake-up of the council impractical at this time. The Albigensian Crusade was set to ignite again after Honorius, fed up with Raymond VII's lack of vigour in persecuting heretics in the south, told Louis that Toulouse was again his for the taking. The last time that happened, he had taken Poitou instead. To Henry, it seemed only right that he take it back while the French were making war elsewhere. Louis suspected as much and asked Honorius to cover for him with a stern letter to Henry not to interfere with the work of a crusader.

Now 18 years old and full of the vigour which the Count of Toulouse supposedly lacked, Henry had every reason not to trust Louis. He could easily veer off course with his army and end up in Gascony instead. Without Longespee at his brother's side, Henry was worried that Richard might not be able to thwart such a move, so he threw himself into making plans to go there himself. It took the combination of his illness, a letter from the pope and another from Richard assuring him that everything was fine to finally put him off. The only good news about these developments was an astrologer's prediction that Louis would face either death or ruin from his crusade.[12]

He was also needed at home to deal with Otto, a papal nuncio sent by Honorius to ask for clemency for Fawkes and for payment of the tribute. Henry gave him just over £1,000, but declared that Fawkes had been justly banished and that was that. Otto then brought up the real reason for his visit. The pope wanted English churches and religious houses to provide paid positions, collectively known as benefices, for his army of clerks, lawyers and notaries. As a global corporation, the Catholic Church required an immense bureaucracy, more than Rome could afford. Until now, they had been supported by the buying and selling of favours among officials. The only way to combat corruption of this sort was for the local clergy to pitch in. They could certainly afford it. In England alone, the Church owned a quarter of all the land. Sharing the wealth in this manner would restore transparency and integrity in the faith. Honorius wasn't trying to be funny when he said benefices were beneficial for everyone.[13]

The bishops, abbots and priors were all for restoring transparency and integrity, but they were no fools. Benefices were equally corrupt. They often went to family members and friends, who might easily land on the payrolls of multiple churches. The money could be better spent on hospitals and feeding the poor, they said. That was true, but the pope was no fool either. He knew they were doing the same thing. They were all doing it because getting on the gravy train was the surest way to make a good living in those days. The practice wasn't being condemned, merely made more inclusive so that the Mother Church could get the piece of the action she surely deserved. Just the thought of how much action moved one archbishop to pine for the good old days when all he had to do to get something done was bribe somebody.[14]

Henry made no commitments, but the pope got the impression that he was working on his behalf and so authorised the clergy to pay the king a tax on a sixteenth of their revenues as his reward. The clergy got the opposite idea, that Henry was on their side, and so they gladly paid it. Although they managed to secure Otto's recall, the process of bestowing English church offices on Italian clerks had been going on for a while now, at least since Guala was regent. Otto was just there to step up the process.[15]

Around this time Henry began exploring the marriage market as a means of gaining diplomatic leverage on the Continent. When Louis proposed marrying his daughter to the son of Holy Roman Emperor Frederick II, Henry countered with his 11-year-old sister Isabella. He proposed to marry himself to the daughter of Leopold, Duke of Austria, but in the end it was she who married the German prince. That infuriated King Ottokar I of Bohemia, who wanted Frederick's son for his own daughter Agnes. He next tried to lure the widowed Frederick himself with Agnes and sought to raise her profile by offering her first to Henry, who seemed interested, but she refused all suitors, including Frederick, and entered a convent.[16]

A more realistic prospect for Henry's Continental designs was 8-year-old Yolanda, the daughter of Alice of Thouars, the deceased Countess of Brittany. Alice was the half-sister of Arthur and Eleanor through their mother Constance, who had married Guy of Thouars after the annulment of her marriage to Ranulf. Alice had died in 1221, leaving her husband Peter of Dreux as the caretaker Duke of Brittany in right of their underage son. The dukes of Brittany held an ancestral claim to the earldom of Richmond, which Henry dangled before Peter in return for a marriage alliance with Brittany.[17] This would give him a foothold next to Normandy and Anjou for whatever recovery operations he mounted there in the future.

His plans to recover English lands got that much closer to happening when Louis, as the astrologer predicted, succumbed to misfortune after rampaging through southern France. He died of dysentery on his way home in November 1226, just over ten years to the day after John's death from the same illness. Like John, Louis had spent his last hours fretting about leaving his kingdom to an underage heir, 12-year-old Louis. Unlike him, he named the boy's mother guardian and regent and ordered the bishops attending him to swear that he did it while yet 'sane of mind'.[18] Blanche of Castile had already shown that she had the ability and steeliness to get things done. By giving her the role John had denied Isabella of Angoulême, Louis ensured that his son had it much easier on the road to kingship than Henry ever did.

★ ★ ★

That rare meeting between two outstanding figures of different centuries occurred when Eleanor of Aquitaine journeyed to Castile in 1200 to accompany her granddaughter Blanche to France for her marriage to Louis. It was part of an agreement worked out between John and Philip to ensure peace over Normandy, by having Philip's son marry one of John's nieces, the daughters of his sister Eleanor and Alfonso VIII of Castile. There were two to choose from, one 13, the other 12 years of age. The eldest was reportedly the better looking of the two, but her name, Urraca, didn't go down well with the emissaries who came to view her. They supposedly picked the younger Blanche on this basis, proving how a name in itself can affect the course of history.[19]

Eleanor of Aquitaine was 78 years old and it was the dead of winter, but off she went over the Pyrenees for her last adventure abroad. While John and Philip valued her prestige for such a mission, she had a wanderlust that must have been unbearable during all the years she was imprisoned by her husband Henry II. In that age of difficult travel, she had journeyed to the Holy Land on the crusade of her first husband, Louis VII, Philip's father; to Navarre to find for a bride for her son Richard the Lionheart; and later to Germany to retrieve him from his own imprisonment. No doubt Eleanor imparted lots of advice and wisdom to her granddaughter on the way back, and may have detected a bit of herself in the young girl who would one day leave her mark on the affairs of Europe much the way she had in her own heyday.

Although Henry III and Blanche of Castile were first cousins, she was nearly twenty years older and had done her best to help her husband try and take the throne from him. He would not go that far in taking advantage of her son, but he did want his father's French lordships back and was ready to encourage an uprising against her regency. The advice of his astrologer, who had evidently been right about Louis, wasn't needed to make that happen, rather lots and lots of grants, and he started making them to his mother, stepfather and other lords around Poitou.[20] If he had been waiting until he reached 21 to declare himself of age, he forgot about it now and announced in January 1227, at 19 years old, that his seal henceforth had full effect. He was clearly in a hurry now that he saw his best opportunity to revive English fortunes on the Continent.

It wasn't just to reassure his new allies that he was in full possession of royal authority that he rushed out of his minority. He was also going to need money, and there was no hope of getting his council to approve another nationwide tax so soon after the last one. Coming of age, however, meant that the chancery would begin enrolling his charters. All subjects and institutions holding lands or privileges were therefore invited to prove by what right, or *quo warranto* in the legalese of the age, they were granted. Charters were to be either reaffirmed or issued for the first time, in both cases with his seal, in exchange for a handsome fee. It was no precedent, as Frederick II, another ward of the pope, had instituted the same policy after his coronation in 1220. Henry could also make the case that it would clear up a lot of uncertainty over who owned what in the decade following the civil war.[21] He did reap a windfall from it, nearly £4,000 by the end of the year, but the expense and tediousness of the bureaucratic process naturally aroused a lot of opposition.[22]

Even more resentment came from the way he taxed various towns, as was his right as their nominal overlord. He demanded £3,500 from London because that was the same amount the city had given Louis when he left in 1217, not quite a going away present but distasteful enough to Henry.[23] Fundraising drives like these would earn him a reputation for grubbiness he was never able to shake off, but at this stage he still had his chief minister to take the flak. Hubert gladly did so because of what the king could offer him now that he was in full control of his seal. The following month Henry bestowed the prestigious title of earl upon him. Of the hundreds of lords who might be called barons, barely a dozen held this rank, and not too many of them were happy seeing it go to a glorified civil servant.

In creating the earldom of Kent for Hubert, Henry was more concerned about the projection of dignity. He felt it unbecoming for a princess such as Margaret of Scotland to be married to a commoner with no landed title. He was doing it as much for her and, by extension, his relationship with his brother-in-law Alexander II. He made it clear that all the lands connected to the earldom were to pass on only to her children and not to Hubert's son from his first marriage. Being a great honour, it came with conditions attached, and another one no doubt was to continue the success that had got him this far.

That meant recovering Plantagenet territories in France, but Hubert knew it would always come down to a bidding war there and Henry could never hope to match the resources of the French monarchy. Still, having a minor on the French throne was about their best chance to realign local loyalties. Hubert threw himself into the fray, dispatching a delegation under Walter Gray, the Archbishop of York, with 'soft speeches and large promises' for Hugh Lusignan and other disaffected nobles.[24] Henry's brother Richard did his part in Gascony by signing a treaty with Raymond of Toulouse and advancing into Poitou with Welsh reinforcements and barrels of silver pennies.

The coalition of the disaffected fell apart when Blanche appeared with an army at Tours. It was just for show, for behind the scenes she offered plenty of largesse to wean them away from Henry's feelers. Hugh and Isabella got royal marriage alliances for their numerous children and a handsome pension. Peter of Dreux got Blanche's third son John for his daughter Yolanda, whom Henry had intended for his own bride, plus control of John's endowment lands until he grew up. They had all sold out. Henry felt the betrayal deeply, but all he could do to vent his anger was to give temporary custody of Richmond, which Peter had been hoping for, to Ranulf in compensation for the lands in Brittany he had lost under King John.[25]

Another unhelpful development was the death of Honorius in March 1227. While he never met his benefactor, personal loss tended to affect Henry deeply, and all his life he would remember how Honorius had stood behind him from the beginning, securing his throne and exhorting his minders and barons to let him be king in more than just name. Now that he was, he wanted the rest of his inheritance back, but it was going to take time and money to bring the new pope Gregory IX around to his side of the argument. Perhaps by then the pacified French barons would realise what a mistake they had made and beseech Henry for help again. Experience should have told him to steer clear of this undependable lot, but ambition and the need to prove himself, combined with a report that an invasion of

England was still being entertained in French circles, meant that, as with Bedford three years earlier, he had to go there.

It would definitely be some time before he went, because in the summer of 1227 Henry had his own little rebellion to deal with, started by his brother of all people. Richard had come home to great pomp following his two years abroad and received the title of Earl of Cornwall as his reward. It seems to have gone to his head, because he went right to Berkhamsted and evicted a stout German fellow named Walerand from a manor belonging to that earldom. King John had given it to Walerand in recognition of his services, which included watching over Isabella of Angoulême. Walerand went to complain about his rough treatment to Henry, who agreed that Richard had acted presumptuously and told him to return the manor. He refused, and if the king thought about giving him any trouble in the matter, he was ready to take his case all the way up to the judgement of his fellow barons.

Henry exploded when he heard this. His brother was insinuating that anyone unhappy with his decisions need only convince a quorum of barons to overturn it, as if they constituted a medieval supreme court. According to Wendover, Henry adopted an 'imperious and indiscreet tone' and ordered Richard to return the manor forthwith or else leave the country. 'Hah,' said Richard, 'I will neither return it nor leave the country without a decision from my peers.' With that, he left. Hubert was equally indignant at the young man's snarly insolence. He stoked Henry's fury by suggesting that Richard be kept under house arrest lest he stir up a revolt. It's not known if Henry gave such an order, because Wendover again admits he's leaning on hearsay, but Richard got the message that he had better run for it, and he did.[26]

This was the first of many quarrels between the brothers and the template for how to solve them in the future. It's fair to say that neither brother really knew the other one very well. The turmoil of John's reign and Henry's early minority had left little opportunity for them to grow up together. Where the king's guardian was the urbane Peter des Roches, Richard was reared under the coarser Peter de Maulay. As with Henry and all these other characters, we don't know what Richard looked like. A roof boss reputed to represent him suggests that he was a full-bearded redhead later in life, in contrast with Henry's sandier features. Whatever the differences in their outward appearance, they were nothing alike in their values and personalities. Henry was a dreamer with the big picture always in mind. Richard was narrowly focused on the bottom line and his portfolio. The one motif that best describes the two of them is Richard liked making money, and Henry spending it. If they sat down together to commission a project, Richard would roll his eyes and sigh the minute Henry excitedly unfurled his wish list.

Although far shallower in character than Henry, Richard had a cooler head and better grip on reality. Instead of turning around and grovelling for forgiveness, he knew right away what to do and headed to Marlborough, the residence of his brother-in-law William Marshal II. Marshal had always been an ally of Hubert, but the year before Hubert had him replaced as the Justiciar of Ireland with his nephew Richard de Burgh and he took it as an affront. It's incredible to see how in that one year of 1226 Hubert so flippantly alienated his two most steadfast allies, Marshal and Longespee, all to set up his own nephews. And he hadn't forgotten about Raymond, either, the nephew he sent to woo Longespee's wife. Hubert suggested that Henry might want to retaliate against his brother by taking Berkhamsted from him and maybe giving it to a loyal knight like Raymond.[27] That's exactly the course Henry took three days after Richard's outburst, probably to show him that, the barons be damned, he alone would decide the outcome of this little feud.

Richard reckoned that Marshal could rally support for him, but in fact almost any baron could have since they were all angry at Hubert. They didn't like the way he was bleeding them for money, accumulating lands and favours for himself and his family, acting for the council alone, and pretending that he was somebody important now that he had an earldom. Marshal proved what a hollow ring his new title had by rounding up six other earls and their retinues, including his old nemesis Ranulf, to let the Earl of Kent know that he was not welcome in their club. They gathered at Stamford and sent a warning to the king that, although they blamed everything on Hubert, he had better make good the insult to his brother or they would march. Henry agreed to meet them in Northampton in early August and, while he refused to back down over Walerand, he did give Richard their mother's dower lands, plus some other property seized from the French. And like that, says Wendover, they all went home.[28]

The earls certainly didn't go to all that trouble and expense for Richard's benefit. They were also disturbed that Henry was lately trying to roll back the Forest Charter in violation of his confirmation of it only two years earlier. This charter was in many ways more contentious than Magna Carta. The royal forest was another invention of the Normans, designed to give the king a monopoly over the best game and timber and mineral rights in the land and to deny the woods as havens for outlaws and degenerates. He also enjoyed a lot of revenue from the fines slapped on the people regularly caught harvesting a bit of firewood or grazing their animals within its boundaries.

Henry II took advantage of the chaos following the civil war under King Stephen to increase the amount of forest reserved for his private use, until it covered nearly a quarter of the country.[29] His son Richard the Lionheart created more resentment by ordering the blinding and castration of poachers of his venison.[30] The Forest Charter removed this barbaric punishment, relaxed controls and used county surveys to reverse much of the afforestation. Worried about the massive loss of income and control this represented, the government refused to accept the surveys and continued to crack down hard on infringements. When the Bishop of Salisbury was caught hunting in the royal forest, he received a writ to explain where he came off taking such liberties, 'and then we will do to you what is just'.[31]

The reissue of the Forest Charter in 1225 gave the counties their chance to redraw the boundaries again, basically telling the government 'no forest charter, no tax'. Henry realised they were taking advantage of his position, trading on their willingness to help him retain Gascony, but he gritted his teeth and looked away. The result was open season on the forests, as villagers moved in to clear land for wood and ploughing and bagging as many animals as they could take. Henry was well aware of what was going on but waited until he had assumed full regal powers to challenge the demarcations of the knights who conducted the surveys. Errors were admitted, pardons made and several tracts of land again brought under his control. He was aiming for a compromise, but the earls could see no end to the reclamations and decided to use Richard's defiance to put a halt to them. Henry agreed that they could discuss their grievance over the forest at a major assembly with the sheriffs and wardens, but it doesn't seem to have taken place. Once Richard got his way, the rest just sort of forgot about it.[32]

As the rebellion against Blanche in France had shown, buy off one and the rest melt away. That's the lesson Henry took away here. It was better to chip away at any opposition, to work with individuals than with groups. Since Richard always had a price, Henry should talk to him first. It was possible that veteran grumblers like Ranulf and Marshal weren't prepared to go the whole distance in any case. It was important to draw the king's attention to that bad influence over him. If that was the main point of mustering their men in a show of force, their strategy was terrible, because Henry went on rewarding Hubert and reclaiming the forests.

It was, however, a forest that marked the end of Hubert's string of successes. These peaked in April 1228 when Henry made him several life grants, including the office of justiciar. Life and hereditary offices were nothing new in England; Henry had made Ralph Neville his chancellor for life just the year before. But the grant to Hubert declared that the king was acting on the advice of his magnates, which was surely not the case.[33] The real problem, however, was all the castles that came into his custody, a complete reversal of the redistribution policy which had averted civil war. Hubert was now in possession of Dover, Rochester, Canterbury and, most importantly, Montgomery in Wales. In August, he ordered the garrison of Montgomery to begin clearing a nearby forest that stretched into Ceri, presumably to drive out Welsh bandits. The bandits responded by driving the woodsmen back and besieging the castle.

Still anxious to get into any real action, Henry led a small force that quickly raised the siege and marched 5 miles further inland through the dense forest, burning and cutting it along the way. They came across a house of the Cistercian order, and when Henry learned that it was used as a depository for Welsh plunder, he ordered it burned to the ground.[34] Llywelyn had been most patient up until then, but when Hubert decided to build a new fortress there and received Henry's permission, that was it. If the king was looking for a proving ground for his future military expedition in France, the Welsh were happy to oblige.

The English army of nearly 500 knights was mainly led by local lords called 'Marchers', men like William Marshal II, Gilbert de Clare and William de Braose, but their hearts were never really in it.[35] They knew it was all Hubert's fault, that he was only interested in carving out a lordship for himself there. On the other hand, the Welsh were fired up and consistently cut the enemy supply lines, forcing them to resort to foraging and plunder. Braose was captured during one such foray, and Henry realised he had better cut his losses while he still could. In the 'disgraceful peace' that followed, the king agreed to tear down the half-built fortress and clear out. From Llywelyn he got an apology and a face-saving contribution of £2,100 towards dismantling it. Llywelyn could easily afford it: he had demanded the same sum from Braose for his freedom.[36]

The king was derided for wasting time, money and men on the widely ridiculed 'Hubert's folly', but he blamed his first real loss in the field on the lacklustre response of his army commanders. Some he suspected of colluding with the Welsh out of desire to see the justiciar humiliated and kicked out of the Marches. All they got for their intrigue was Hubert gaining two more castles in the area. Far from punishing or even sacking Hubert, Henry probably felt that the outcome might have been different had Hubert had an even larger lordship to keep watch over the border. This was rewarding failure in the minds of the other barons. Whatever lay behind Henry's continuing trust in the man, Hubert was now more isolated than ever, and the king could not have failed to notice it.

★ ★ ★

Hubert owed no small part of his previous success to Stephen Langton, but the Archbishop of Canterbury died in early July 1228, two months before the fiasco in Wales. He had mostly withdrawn from the political scene, but before his death did get into a row with Henry over the Church offering sanctuary to criminals, even giving him £2,100 to confirm this liberty and others by charter. Henry returned the money and did him the great favour of reconciling with his brother Simon so he could be named Archdeacon of Canterbury.[37] In ecclesiastical matters, Langton remained intolerant as ever and followed up his persecution of the Jews with sanctions against clerical mistresses. These 'concubines', he declared, were not to enjoy mass, church burial or see their children baptised unless they repented and offered security for it. And if a betrothed woman indulged in the carnal pleasures with a priest, she was to be punished twice for adultery. As for the offending priest, he was warned to report her or else face suspension.[38]

If we believe the bishops, Langton's monks had forgotten this injunction when they gathered to elect his successor. The man they chose was one of their own, a certain Walter of Eynsham who, according to the bishops, had violated a nun and had children by her. Henry had his own reasons for considering Walter unfit for the post. He had joined the interdict against his father John, his own father had been hung for thievery and he was just plain useless.[39] Walter didn't see why any of that should stand in the way of a free election and went to Rome to face off the king's representatives, led by Alexander Stavensby, the Bishop of Coventry and Lichfield, before the pope.

The only thing Gregory wanted to hear from Stavensby was whether Henry planned to make any fuss if the churches of England donated a tenth of their revenues to his crusade chest. When the bishop assured him he wouldn't, Gregory agreed that Walter had to go, but he couldn't just quash a free election in the Church. To do so would legitimise interference from the king. Instead, he would toss Walter into the grinder of formality, in this case the test of Scripture that candidates like him normally underwent from a board of cardinals. The questions were usually routine, but Walter suddenly found himself facing three cardinals asking him the most ambiguous and rigorous of nonsense, like whether Jesus descended into hell in the flesh or not. Wendover doesn't report what answer the monk gave, only that it was unsatisfactory.[40] He was indeed deemed useless and Gregory annulled his appointment. Henry's nominee, the scholarly Richard Grant of Lincoln, was then named archbishop without an election, formalities or, according to the Dunstable annalist, Grant having the strictest of moral fibres.[41]

It took Gregory a while to actually turn his attention to the affair because he had been caught up in what was to become one of the great scandals of the thirteenth century. The background was the Fourth Crusade preached in 1204 by Innocent III, which ended with Christians sacking other Christian cities in the east. Four years later he preached another crusade against the Albigensians of southern France, who were also Christians but intent on worshipping in their own way. Innocent's successor Honorius had tried to redirect efforts back to the Holy Land and was counting on his former pupil Frederick II to make it happen. The emperor was married to the daughter of the nominal King of Jerusalem and was told he could add that title to his portfolio if he took the city. Not until Gregory became pope did he finally set sail, but then turned back, claiming illness. Gregory suspected it was a ruse to stay in Italy to expand imperial power over areas controlled by the papacy. So that he 'might not seem like a dog unable to bark', the pope excommunicated him, but that didn't stop Frederick from eventually arriving in the Holy Land and recovering Jerusalem through diplomacy.[42] His bargaining with infidels instead of shedding their blood only infuriated Gregory more, while the local Christian lords, jealous of his success, waited until he left to launch a war against the retinue he left behind. Meanwhile, the pope was preparing his own war against Frederick in Italy upon his return, under the leadership of Frederick's father-in-law no less, and was expecting the churches of England to contribute to this more personal style of crusading.

Frederick put a glowing spin on his crusade in a letter to Henry, who then heard a completely different version when a papal chaplain arrived at court. He had come to England to inform the prelates that there was no collection plate too big to restore the pope's authority. He wanted a tenth of everything, no deductions allowed, payment due even while the crops were still in the field. Ranulf, who had been on crusade, was outraged and specifically barred any papal agents from entering his earldom.[43] Henry himself was silent on the matter. He admired Frederick, who was thirteen years older. His ease in recovering Jerusalem, which had stumped even the mighty Richard the Lionheart, could only have encouraged him to win back his Continental lands.

Among the guests welcomed by Henry at his Christmas court of 1228 in Oxford were the Archbishop of Bordeaux and several messengers from Normandy. Their tidings were all the same. If the king came to them in person, they would guarantee him plenty of men and horses to regain his possessions. That's the kind of news Henry liked to hear, but of course nothing could be done in the dead of winter. It was best to wait till summer, when the truce with France would expire anyway.[44] He nevertheless sent Stavensby and his team to negotiate an extension of it as a means of exploring a peaceful settlement. They were to say that Henry was willing to give up Normandy if he got Maine, Anjou and Poitou back, or the new King Louis IX could keep those provinces, but return Normandy and marry Henry's sister Isabella.[45]

Unfortunately, Blanche scored her biggest victory yet with the Treaty of Meaux in April 1229, which brought the Albigensian Crusade to an end after more than twenty years. The only marriage she was interested in, and got, was between the daughter and only child of Raymond VII, another grandchild of Henry II and Eleanor of Aquitaine, and her fourth son at that time, Alphonse of Poitiers. The deal all but guaranteed that the county of Toulouse would come under the control of the French monarchy some day. Henry could have the extension of the truce, but nothing more.[46]

Undeterred, he announced a general muster for the autumn. Before that, on 27 July, Peter of Dreux arrived to do homage to Henry for Brittany and repeated the description of all the acclaim that awaited his landing. The king was elated and prepared just the right uniform for the occasion, a flowing silk cloak with gloves and sandals.[47] His confidence was further boosted by the thousands of barons, knights and foot soldiers who assembled in Portsmouth from as far away as Scotland, Wales and Ireland. Those who saw them were awestruck. Invasion forces of this size were nothing new in England, but always arriving, never departing.

And like that, all of Henry's hopes were shattered when the launch date of 13 October 1229 came and he found there were not enough boats in the fleet to transport even half of his army. He was beside himself with fury. Somebody had screwed up, and he knew exactly who to blame. According to Wendover, he turned to Hubert in front of the other magnates and accused him of taking a bribe from Blanche to thwart the invasion. He was probably grasping for any charge, for his next move showed just how furious he had become. Unsheathing his sword, he rushed at him, but the other magnates, led by Ranulf, quickly shuffled Hubert out of the room.

It was no case of temporary insanity, rather the wool being lifted from Henry's eyes. He had lavishly rewarded Hubert, but not only had he let him down but made him look like a fool, standing there in a silky white suit with nowhere to go. Fortunately Henry was better than most Plantagenet kings in being able to take disappointment in stride and agreed that the only option was to postpone the invasion until spring.[48]

Hubert wasn't taking any chances and made sure there were plenty of ships when the army embarked with nine earls, 450 knights and several thousands of men-at-arms. Henry left his chancellor Ralph Neville and royal justice Stephan Seagrave in charge and sailed on 30 April 1230.[49] They arrived at St Malo on the Breton coast a couple of days later, only the king wasn't with them. During the passage, Henry had diverted to the island of Jersey with thirty ships after his 15-year-old sister Eleanor became seasick. He didn't just leave her there, but waited for her to recover before catching up with the fleet.

Eleanor had joined the expedition because her husband was William Marshal II, one of Henry's commanders, and there was an immediate political need for her to come along. Henry had little chance of success unless Hugh Lusignan finally threw in his lot with him. Since his wife presumably had the most influence over him, Henry planned to meet his mother and bring Eleanor along. Isabella of Angoulême hadn't seen her daughter since she was three years old and it's possible Henry was hoping a family reunion might induce her to act.[50] Then there was Eleanor herself, who was probably already the wilful and determined woman she became later in life. She might have insisted on accompanying her husband and seeing her mother, and if her brother reaped some political benefit out of it, so much the better.

At the time of the landing, many French nobles were at war with Theobald, the Count of Champagne, who had been the first to sell out when they rose up against Blanche. They had come to intensely dislike the queen dowager, for being both a woman and foreigner, and sneered that what really got Theobald to defect were the passionate charms of the forty-year-old austere regent who had given birth to twelve children. This while she was supposedly sleeping with a papal legate. The nobles were forced to put their war aside when Blanche called out the army to meet the English threat. They marched to Anjou, to await whatever drive Henry had in mind.[51]

Given his pious and humanistic nature, Henry knew exactly what his first order of business should be after stepping ashore. Kneel, deliver thanks, indulge in a welcoming party, and get ready for the banquet that evening. All the while he would cast a keen eye about at what clothes the people were wearing, how they built their houses and churches, how their French was distinctly different from his, how they prepared their meals. Never was an invading king more suited for the role of tourist than conqueror, and yet in many ways it was understandable. He was young, impressionable, a bit overwhelmed by the fact that he was even there, and wholly inexperienced in warfare. He would naturally defer to Hubert, who had defended Chinon on the Loire for John during the war with Philip and spent two years as a captive after the fortress was destroyed.[52]

His recent go at the Welsh, however, should have been an indication that Hubert had no more stomach for war. A group of sixty Norman knights came to swear fealty to the king in the expectation of him leading his army into Normandy. Henry was all for it, but Hubert cautioned otherwise. Far too dangerous, he insisted. The Normans must have been dumbstruck to hear such faintheartedness, but since they had come this far, they asked Henry to give them just half his knightly force and they would get the job done for him. Hubert refused to hear any more of it. The king shouldn't risk the lives of his men to support what was essentially another private war. So the Normans returned empty-handed, and when Blanche found out what they had done, she had the lot of them disinherited.[53]

If Hubert had a strategy at all, it was to march to Nantes and let the French make the first move. They were unwilling to oblige for the reason why there were so few pitched battles during the Middle Ages: no matter how big the army, fortified the position, or talented the commanders, victory was ultimately up to a higher force, and few rulers were willing to risk an open battle on where they stood with the Almighty at that moment. Strategy was all about wearing the enemy down one castle at a time and buying off his supporters. There were roughly 50 miles separating the two camps, and in all that time Henry and Hubert held meetings and prayers in their camp, and Louis and Blanche did the same in theirs. But the English did have one trump card in the standoff. The French knights only had to serve forty days to fulfil their feudal obligation. After that, they left and went back to fighting Theobald again.[54]

Hubert seems to have counted on this, because he brought along £5,200 in cash to keep the English army paid in the meantime.[55] By July the French had disbanded, and the way seemed open to march south to Poitou. Henry's meeting with his mother at Dinan prior to that, however, had failed to bring Hugh Lusignan on board. The Count of La Marche refused to switch his allegiance. He did not impede his stepson's progress through Poitou, but the most support Henry was able to obtain came from minor lords, none of whom came cheap. Altogether, he promised subsidies worth £2,800 a year for what was in effect the shakiest of holds.[56]

It was a bargain compared to the £50,000 it had cost him to retain Gascony, but he was warned he might still lose that region unless he put in an appearance. The army marched south of the Loire, encountering resistance only from the stronghold of Mirambeau, and reached Bordeaux in August. There they held more meetings, prayers and feasts, then returned to Nantes for more of the same. Wendover acidly comments that it had all the splendour of one long Christmas parade.[57]

At some point Henry realised that he had no chance of stepping up with Hubert constantly in the way. In desperation, he wrote to the papacy asking for a legate to join him. He would have remembered that Guala and Pandulf were men of action who took his interests to heart and got things done. The English clergy, however, were adamant about keeping a legate out of their business and put pressure on him until he recalled the appointment.[58] Disappointed they were never going to do more on this expedition beyond negotiate and cut deals, Henry decided to play the tourist for real and visit several shrines in Brittany. He even ambled along the rocks of Armorica for a look at the Atlantic Ocean.[59]

By September, the futility of it all became apparent when Blanche concluded a peace agreement between her warring factions. Peter of Dreux refused to sign on, insisting that his loyalty still lay with Henry, but at a cost of £4,200 up front.[60] Henry was just then down with dysentery, and when informed about Peter's demand, he probably waved a hand from his sick bed and muttered 'pay it'. When his brother and other members of the expedition fell ill as well, Henry knew the game was up. Leaving behind Marshal and Ranulf to salvage what they could from the expedition, he departed and arrived in Portsmouth on 28 October 1230. It had been a costly disappointment.

That it might have been different was immediately shown when the French mobilised to drive out the remnants of the army. As they neared Brittany, Ranulf led his men from behind and destroyed their convoys and siege equipment. They later sallied forth and razed three castles, including one in Normandy.[61] It's debatable whether Henry would have had similar success had he disregarded his chief minister's almost paranoid determination to keep him out of harm's way. Hubert's whole world depended on the king's survival, and he was too much of a realist to see any good coming out of the expedition. Unable to prevent the undertaking any longer, the best he could do was make it as benign as possible.

He was certainly right if he acted on the belief that Henry did not fully appreciate the consequences of success there. First, there was the whole problem of this Angevin Empire. Hubert knew from experience that it required constant attention and resources to maintain, and yet all the kings who had managed it before Henry came to bad ends. Henry II died broken and embittered, on the run after being forced to conclude a humiliating peace with Philip and his own son Richard. The Lionheart himself spent the last five years of his reign galloping from one end of France to the other trying to hold it all together and ended up dying an agonising death from gangrene during the last of his many sieges. And John's ill-fated history with the empire was of course well known. Henry had spent the first years of his reign coddled in comfort, and all the indications were that he liked it. Being on permanent campaign in France was probably the last thing he expected.

There was also the problem of doing justice to everyone for their inheritance, not just his own. The loss of Normandy had allowed John to seize the English lands of those Normans who swore allegiance to Philip. These lands were a windfall of patronage for him to dole out to his supporters at home, but any recovery of Normandy meant that they would have to be given back. At the same time, the English barons who had lost lands in Normandy would demand theirs back, which is the reason why the ancestral nobility like the Marshals and Ranulf were all for the military operation. It would be a nightmare of swaps if somehow Henry pulled it off, and Hubert was sure that he couldn't and made sure that he didn't. He for one had nothing to gain abroad, but plenty to lose in all the grants of these 'lands of the Normans' that Henry had made to him. For him, the failure of the expedition meant personal success.

Finally, there was one outcome that had repercussions for the rest of Henry's reign. While Ranulf was literally holding the fort at the castle of St James-de-Beuvron near present-day Mont Saint-Michel, he was approached by a young knight who asked him to hand over the earldom of Leicester, which was then in Ranulf's custody. It was due him by inheritance, he claimed. He was the son of Ranulf's cousin, and he did indeed have a better right to it. Normally the old Earl of Chester might not have cared otherwise, but this man's father was no ordinary cousin. He was the greatest warrior in Europe during his time, and his son's audacity in approaching him suggested that he got more from his father than just his name. Duly impressed, Ranulf agreed to take the young Simon de Montfort to see the king upon his return to England.[62]

4

EXCHANGING THE OLD FOR THE OLD 1231–1232

Despite the lack of fighting, there were plenty of casualties during the Breton campaign, mostly from disease or accidents, and two incidents affected Hubert directly. His nephew Raymond drowned after his horse stumbled along the banks of the Loire, and Gilbert de Clare, the Earl of Gloucester, died of dysentery just before sailing home. Gloucester was one of the richest earldoms in the land, and since Clare's heir Richard was only 8 years old, Hubert was eager to obtain the wardship of the boy. Henry showed there were no hard feelings about the campaign and sold it to him, albeit for the huge sum of £5,000, a quarter up front. He even spent Christmas that year as Hubert's guest at Lambeth Palace. Hubert always arranged the Christmas courts, usually lavish affairs hosted by one of the magnates, but the sojourn in France, which is what the campaign really was, suggested the king might want to keep a low profile that season.

In any case, they were stuck with each other as they laid plans to hold a great council in January for the unpleasant business of asking for money to cover the campaign and the promises that resulted from it. In all, £7,000 was raised from the magnates and £5,800 from the Jews, far short of the £20,000 they were looking for, and they almost didn't get that much when the clergy initially refused to pay.[1] Archbishop Grant felt that churchmen shouldn't be taxed for military undertakings abroad; more importantly, he had recently joined the opposition against Hubert.

At issue was Tonbridge Castle, which was built by the Clare family about 40 miles from Canterbury.[2] In 1163 Thomas Becket had tried and failed to exert lordship over the castle in one of his bids for more power. Now, since the king wanted church money, Grant thought the time was right to revive that claim. Henry reminded him that the Clares held Tonbridge from the crown directly and he was just going to have to accept that fact. Grant didn't think it was the king talking, rather Hubert, because, as the custodian for the Clare estate, it was his men occupying the castle. Fed up, he excommunicated the garrison and left for Rome to complain about Hubert. He had other issues gnawing at him as well, like his churchmen becoming too embroiled in secular affairs, but Hubert's control of everything had become intolerable. And if that weren't bad enough, he was married to a woman who was distantly related to one of his former wives, and he knew about it all along.[3]

In fact, had Hubert not been married, he might have tried to snap up Clare's widow in addition to his son. She was Isabel, the second daughter of William Marshal. The old knight had captured Gilbert de Clare at the battle of Lincoln and so was entitled to a ransom for his release. Since Gilbert happened to be single, Marshal told him he could go just as soon as he married his daughter. She was 30 years old and the mother of six children at his death. In the old days, a woman of her rank would have been forced into a remarriage of the crown's making.[4] If the king said, 'Marry my brother', that was it, she was stuck with the oaf.

Magna Carta now protected baronial widows like her from such coercion. Isabel was technically free to marry whomever she pleased, and for her second husband she did in fact choose the king's brother, Richard of Cornwall. He was nine years younger than her, but had been looking to marry well for some time. Henry wasn't invited to their wedding on 30 March 1231 because he didn't approve of it. Baronial widows had the freedom to remarry, but the king's assent was still required and he didn't remember giving it in their case.[5] He also thought it was a wasted opportunity. Their sister Eleanor was already married to the head of the Marshal family. Richard should have kept himself available for another useful alliance. Then there was the fact that Henry was still unmarried after several attempts to find a wife and he was going to be 24 that year.

William Marshal II was at the wedding, having returned from the Continent the month before. He must have let himself go at the feast, because he was suddenly dead within a week. There is no word on what caused it, just that he up and died. He was buried next to his father at the New Temple Church, his tomb today adorned by an effigy of a cross-legged knight with a cherubic grin. He and Eleanor never did succeed in having a child. The principal heir to his vast estate was his brother Richard, who lived in Normandy on lands inherited from their father. That made him a vassal of the King of France, which in turn made Henry reluctant to accept his homage for the earldom of Pembroke. He promised William that Richard would be allowed to succeed him, but now delayed it by saying Eleanor could be pregnant. When it turned out that this was not the case, he followed Hubert's advice and declared Marshal to be in league with his enemies, meaning the French. He ordered him to abjure the realm within fifteen days or risk imprisonment.[6]

The king's doubts about Marshal's loyalty came at a time when Llywelyn was on the rampage again. Henry had done his best to maintain good relations with him, even taking no action after he had William Braose strung up on 2 May 1230 before a large crowd of onlookers.[7] Llywelyn had let him go after he paid his ransom, but then discovered him on errant business in his wife's bedchamber. At the time Braose was married to Eva, the fourth daughter of William Marshal, and had four young daughters with her. The wardship of his lands eventually ended up in Hubert's hands. Combined with the Gloucester estates, that made Hubert the greatest lord in the region and a threat as far as Llywelyn was concerned. The Welsh began raiding the Braose lands, but withdrew when Henry approached with a small army. When the king next went north to tend to other matters, they started up again and a number of them were captured by the English garrison. Hubert knew what to do with them. In the London riot eight years earlier, he had chopped off the limbs of the troublemakers. With the Welsh he went further and chopped off their heads.[8] He then sent the gruesome collection of orbs to the king. This way of his boasting that he was getting the job done was a gross display of cruelty that could only have appalled Henry.

It certainly infuriated Llywelyn, who quickly overran the area with all the wrath he could muster. According to Wendover, he even burned to the ground churches that were harbouring women and girls inside. The indignation was now all Henry's, and he mobilised a large force at Oxford to march on Wales. Llywelyn enlisted a monk to trick the advance force into an ambush, where his men slaughtered them in the marsh and thickets. When Henry arrived on the scene, he was ready to burn down the monk's monastery in retribution, but was moved by the abbot's entreaties to levy a fine of £200 instead. After that, he set his men to work rebuilding the fortress of Painscastle to block further incursions in the future.[9] It took almost two months to complete and during that time things got worse for Hubert.

First, there was Richard Grant denouncing him in Rome with such insistence that the pope didn't want to hear anything more when the royal proctor showed up to give the other side of the story. The archbishop had been wronged, clear and simple. Gregory may only have been trying to make amends for all the money he had siphoned out of the English clergy for his war against Frederick, but Grant was emboldened to take on the king and his minister upon his return. But no sooner had he set off on the journey homeward than he fell ill and died on 3 August, having never left Italy.[10]

While word of his death wouldn't reach England for a month, it coincided with the arrival of Peter des Roches after an absence of four years. The Bishop of Winchester had left somewhat in disgrace but was now a celebrity for marching into Jerusalem at the side of the emperor. He took part in the peace negotiations between Frederick and Gregory in 1230, which led to an uneasy accommodation between them. On his way home through France, Peter assisted Ranulf in concluding a three-year truce with Blanche, which brought the rest of the English contingent home.[11] He met up with Henry on the Welsh border in early August 1231 and happily recounted these achievements. The king could only have listened in awe before turning to Hubert and asking, 'And you, Sir?'

All Henry could see from him was a mess everywhere. He preferred to greet his guests in style, not in the mud and din of the building works going on around him. It was time to put an end to all this belligerence and disorder and reach his own accommodation with his subjects. First up was Richard Marshal. The Welsh uprising reaffirmed that Henry needed a strong baronial presence in the Marches, stronger than Hubert, and if Marshal was anything like his father and brother before him, than he was his man. He was granted a safe conduct pass in June to come to the king and do homage, but took his time and the ceremony didn't take place until 8 August. To allay any lingering bitterness, Marshal was exempted from paying the customary £100 relief for inheriting the estate.[12]

Two days later Henry received his brother Richard and granted him the county of Cornwall in fee. This gave Richard land to back up his title and, importantly, control of its profitable stannaries. He was made several other grants and received confirmation of their mother's dower lands.[13] Finally, on 13 August, Henry welcomed Ranulf and listened to his petition that the earldom of Leicester should go to this fine young man with him, Simon de Montfort.

Henry and Simon had already met, just before the expedition to France, when the Frenchman arrived to ask the king in person to give him the earldom. As with Ranulf, he seems to have made an immediate impression. Henry agreed he could take custody of Leicester upon Ranulf's death and offered to take him into his service at the very respectable sum of £267 a year. It's unclear what role Montfort played during the expedition or what means he used to get Ranulf to relinquish his claim. He might have bought him out, since he acquired a debt of £200 to the older man. Whatever arrangement they came to, Henry accepted Simon's homage for Leicester, but withheld the title of earl for the time being.[14]

In fact, Simon was only getting half of the earldom. It had been split between the two sisters of Robert Beaumont, the fourth Earl of Leicester, after he died childless in 1204. The oldest sister claimed the half of Leicester that came with the title for her son Simon de Montfort III, who later rose to become the leader of the Albigensian Crusade. His very capable and vigorous generalship earned him a mixed reputation before he was killed outside the walls of Toulouse in 1218. In the meantime, his half of the earldom came into the custody of his cousin Ranulf, probably as a reward from John for his loyalty during the baronial crisis. Of the two sons left behind by Simon III, the oldest, Amaury, had no chance of becoming earl. He was already the Constable of France, and it would hardly do to allow him to parlay the secrets of both courts. His brother Simon IV, however, held no land or title in France.[15] Amaury told him to go forth and claim Leicester if he could, and, if successful, to pay him £500 for his rights.

All told, Montfort took on at least £700 of debt to acquire an estate generating only £500 a year, a meagre income compared to an earldom like Gloucester, which was worth seven times that amount. He immediately got caught up in the politics of the court when Ranulf, in making his petition on Montfort's behalf, complained about two grants made by Henry while he was in France. Both were in Leicestershire and both went to more relatives of Hubert. Ranulf considered this a snub, but Henry confirmed the grants. A furious Ranulf stormed out of court and took Montfort with him.[16] In alienating a newcomer like Simon so quickly, Hubert had outdone even himself.

Another reason for Ranulf's outburst was the whole Welsh fiasco. He had always been on good terms with Llywelyn and despaired to think of the losses incurred just so Hubert could secure a lordship for himself in the area. Moreover, the truce he worked out with Blanche came with recognition of Henry as the overlord of Brittany and parts of Poitou, which meant that the expedition had limited – but still some – success. But keeping it all together was going to require a lot of focus and subsidies, not tramping around on another fruitless campaign in Wales. Henry seems to have been of the same mind. In an effort to woo Ranulf and Simon back to court, he reversed the controversial grants. A great council was to meet in October and he needed men aligned to his Continental policy to help get things back on track.[17]

★ ★ ★

By the autumn of 1231, Hubert knew he was losing his grip on Henry. The court was now stacked with men opposed to him, including Ranulf, Richard of Cornwall, Richard Marshal, Peter des Roches and Simon de Montfort. Also at the council meeting were Philip d'Aubigny and Peter of Dreux, men equally committed to consolidating what gains there were on the Continent. The topics for discussion included the successor of Richard Grant as Archbishop of Canterbury and peace with Llywelyn, but the overriding topic was the king's impending marriage. Seemingly out of nowhere, he had decided to marry a Scottish princess after all.

Margaret, it will be remembered, had been married to Hubert, but her sister Isabella was sent back to Scotland after they failed to find a good match for her. Then in 1225 came the death of Hugh Bigod, the Earl of Norfolk. His heir Roger, whose mother was Maud, the oldest of William Marshal's daughters, was technically underage at 16. His wardship eventually went to King Alexander for £4,000. Since the boy was on his way to Scotland, the council decided to marry him to Isabella, who was more than a decade older than him.[18]

But there was a third Scottish princess, Alexander's youngest sister Margery. She hadn't been part of the original treaty, but its whole point was to get the Scots to relinquish claims to northern English territory in return for a royal marriage. When the two kings celebrated Christmas together at York in 1229, Alexander may have brought up these claims, and the fact that Margery was still single. At 30, she was several years older than Henry, but there was no reason to suppose she couldn't bear children. The king's illness in France, moreover, must have reminded Hubert that if Henry died, the crown would go to Richard of Cornwall, and that would spell the end of his career.[19]

Henry was all for marrying Margery and began making plans for a wedding in York. He may have been anxious about those Scottish territorial claims or just plain lonely. Unlike his father and grandfather, he didn't wench and was overly fond of nuns, but whether this was out of piety or the disruptive conditions of his childhood is hard to say. That he craved affection is clear in his relationship with his family, his squabbles with Richard notwithstanding. He had been king for fifteen years, shuffled from one crisis to the next, and all the time constantly surrounded by old men. He needed something resembling personal warmth and a home life before he went insane.

The magnates didn't care about his emotional state. They saw the wedding as more of Hubert trying to insinuate himself ever closer to the king by becoming his brother-in-law. It would be all the more undignified because, of the Scottish sisters, Henry's wife would be younger than Hubert's. Led by Richard Marshal, they were firmly opposed, but Wendover says it was Peter of Dreux who eventually got him to drop the idea. If Henry needed a wife, he should marry his daughter Yolanda. Of course, that match had already been arranged once before, until Peter had reneged on the deal.[20]

In another bid for greater independence, Henry decided to forgo Hubert's traditional Christmas court and spend it instead as the guest of Peter des Roches in Winchester. He was curious whether the bishop could live up to the imperial lavishness he had been talking about since his return. He certainly wasn't disappointed if there were as many presents of silver and gold as claimed by the Dunstable annalist.[21] Peter was intent on showing the king that all this could be his if he got rid of that scoundrel Hubert. After Christmas, Henry named him one of his barons at the exchequer and charged him with the task of fixing his deplorable finances.

To do that, Peter would first have to rein in the king himself. He told Henry flat out that he had only himself to thank for his poverty. He had immediately given away every bit of baronial land and inheritance that came his way without sitting on it first and letting it generate revenue for the crown. His father and grandfather had been rich kings because they greedily held on to everything, were loath to make people happy by the gift of their beneficence. They always had enough money to thrash the Welsh, he boasted. Henry, by contrast, was complaining that he barely had enough to afford 'common food and clothing'.[22]

He was right, the king should stop to think about how many wardships and escheats (property reverting to the crown) had ended up in Hubert's hands. He probably didn't want to think about it and just told Peter to do what he had to do. Meanwhile the council refused Hubert's request for a tax to pay the subsidies due Peter of Dreux and other French lords. Ranulf spoke for the rest when he said the magnates had fulfilled their obligations by serving in France. He was all for maintaining Henry's modest gains on the Continent, but couldn't resist the opportunity to make Hubert look bad in the king's eyes. He succeeded insofar as Henry was forced to pawn his crown jewels to the Templars to meet his commitments. He also had to take loans from Italian merchants and tax the Jews again, all of it a rather unseemly business.[23]

It wasn't just the money of the Jewish community that Henry was after. He wanted their souls as well. In January 1232, he founded a home for converted Jews not far from the New Temple. This move may have been a response to the Bishop of Winchester's admonishment that he should keep up with the French. Peter had just been in France, where a school of thought was flourishing under Louis IX that engendered hostility towards Jews, both for their faith and high interest rates. Indeed, one of the first acts of newly ennobled Frenchman Simon de Montfort in Leicester was to expel the Jewish families there. He declared that he was doing it for the good of his soul, not for the good of the people of Leicester who owed the Jews money.[24]

Montfort was also acting under the guidance of the Archdeacon of Leicester, Robert Grosseteste. Like the French, Grosseteste was obsessed with the money-lending practices of the Jews and insisted they go out in the world and earn their bread. Since religious bigotry meant that they would starve in that case, he figured a bit of despair might lead them to conversion.[25] Henry's missionary work was generally not fanatical but, like Montfort, there may have been an element of cynicism in this case. The convert's property went to the crown, and he would need it if he had any hope of supporting the home. Ever beset by money problems, he struggled to come up with the impressive £490 endowment, which was more than he gave to any of the Christian houses he founded in London.[26]

Henry's desire for a change from the style of kingship thrust upon him by his minority got a boost on 19 May 1232 when the body of King John was translated to a new tomb in Worcester. Henry attended the ceremony with his sister Eleanor, who would have been too young to remember her father, but of his five children she was the most like him in terms of energy and wilfulness. Richard of Cornwall wasn't there, but had named his recent newborn son after the late king. This was no beginning of a revision of the reviled king, however. Wendover forgoes mention of the occasion in favour of a long and ludicrous tribute to the virtues of John's brother, Richard. In proclaiming that the Lionheart 'never allowed justice to be subverted by bribery', the chronicler was pining for the glory days of an English king who never existed.[27] Henry was a firm believer in glory days past and may have decided then and there that he would have to be more like his father if he ever hoped to match him in wealth and luxury.

Although he was one of John's most trusted advisers, Peter des Roches was, at 60, too old to take on any major overhaul of the king's administration. But he had someone ideally suited for the task, a fellow native of Touraine named Peter de Rivallis. Reported to be a son or nephew of the bishop, he had started out in King John's service and worked in the royal wardrobe during Henry's minority. He left with the other aliens in 1223 and more or less came out of nowhere again in May 1232. His rise after that was spectacular. By the middle of June, he had obtained numerous grants, sheriffdoms, escheats and wardships. Henry put Rivallis in a position to both rival the old guard and take a close look at why his finances were in such a lamentable state. He hadn't forgotten Hubert in the meantime and continued to show him marks of favour, like appointing him justiciar of Ireland for life.[28] But something had to give, and Hubert was going to do everything in his power to make sure his position was secure when it did.

The opportunity came when Henry took his entourage to East Anglia to visit Bromholm Priory on the coast, where a fragment of the true cross was held. The fragment had been peddled first around other priories by a chaplain who said he stole it while serving in Constantinople. He wasn't looking for money for it, just a home for himself and his two sons, but got no takers until he reached Bromholm in 1223. The priory quickly grew famous with the relic, and Henry was among the worshippers apt to stop by whenever they could. Knowing this, Hubert arranged for the royal party to stay at his ancestral home in nearby Burgh the day after their visit on 1 July 1232. There, he and his wife Margaret and son John entertained the king, Peter de Rivallis, Ralph Neville, royal steward Godfrey of Crowcombe and other household officials.[29] It was on this occasion that Henry swore an oath on the gospels that the justiciar and his wife, the chancellor and steward, would maintain their offices and possessions for life. They could all feel secure in their positions and go to bed easy that night.

Imagine the scene: they are sitting around the hearth with goblets of wine and talking about the true cross when Hubert suddenly unfurls a charter and asks if Henry would be so good as to attach his seal to it. It says that the king will 'observe all the charters which he has granted to Margaret, countess of Kent, and all the grants, gifts and confirmations therein contained'.[30] Hubert then unfurls another oath, whereby he swears to do everything in his power to keep the king from going back on his word. The others in the entourage also receive their own charters with the king's oath, but they are nevertheless surprised by what appears to be another of the justiciar's devious schemes. The king never swore oaths to his grants, particularly an oath with no appeal on the face of it. And the idea that one of his subjects would swear an oath at the same time to compel him to abide by it reminds the older members present of the former security clause in Magna Carta. Hubert's rise to power started with Magna Carta, and now, seventeen years later, he's clearly desperate to hold on to it.

Henry has always had a soft spot for people who turn to him in need, and this is the man who has been his mentor for the past decade. On the other hand, he dislikes being put in awkward situations, and this is about as awkward as they get. They have just visited his favourite shrine, had a lovely meal and wine, and suddenly his hosts are telling him in front of the others to sign this. Of course, the others don't raise any doubts because they don't know what to make of it on the spur of the moment, and besides they stand to benefit as well. Hubert and Margaret have it all planned out, and Henry, right on cue, orders his attendants to seal the oath. After that, they go back to their banter about the cross.[31]

In fact, there is no background story to accompany the enrolment of these oaths in the chancery. That's because the dinner party had unwittingly established a whole new precedent of royal prerogative without the council discussing it first. If the other bishops and earls found out about it, they would be scandalised, demand the dismissal of the justiciar and shake their heads at the king's gullibility. Perhaps while still at Hubert's home, Neville told the king that what they had done was irresponsible and wrong and should be reversed. Henry, it will be seen, was not at all adverse to admitting mistakes after being caught in the act. In this case, he didn't share the same fears as his chancellor, but nor did he attempt to bring him around. Some time after the oaths were enrolled, Neville quietly scratched his name off the list.[32]

This is all speculation, but it should be noted that Neville was dissatisfied with the way a lot of things were going lately. This included Rivallis getting his hands on the privy seal, which was a direct challenge to his authority as chancellor, and his not succeeding Richard Grant as Archbishop of Canterbury. He had in fact been elected by the monks, but only because of his political connections, exactly the thing Grant had been complaining about to his dying breath. There were too many churchmen in government. Simon Langton also complained that Neville lacked the required learning for the post. Now that the pope was into quashing free episcopal elections, he did the same to Neville's on these grounds. Hubert tried to punish Langton for his interference, but was rebuffed.[33] His gesture did little to appease Neville, who knew that all of Canterbury's revenue went to the crown while the archbishopric remained vacant. Hubert's little trick with the oath only confirmed that everything he was up to these days had greed and menace written all over it.

The chancellor may have already lost faith in him prior to Bromholm, but Henry probably did want to reassure Hubert and Margaret of his trust and affection. His childhood had been characterised by manipulation and abandonment, and his proximity to this couple during the last ten years suggests that they were the closest thing he would ever have to surrogate parents. Despite the recent failures, Henry was determined to stick by them. Hubert had to be thankful that Henry was no John, who would have thrown him in prison long ago with a single rasher of bacon. But the king did have his father's temper, and Hubert had to know that if he ever violated that trust, then, oath or no oath, the rupture wasn't going to be pleasant.

★ ★ ★

The lavishness of the Christmas court in Winchester was muted by the 'great excitement', as Wendover describes a series of robberies and kidnappings that began around that time. They were aimed at the Italian priests and clerks installed in English benefices, which was the medieval version of taking jobs away from the natives. This practice of papal provisions was all the more insulting because some of the Italians hadn't bothered to come to England at all to take up their plum positions, just had the money sent to them. This compounded the resentment already felt over Gregory's exactions of tithes to fund his turf war with Frederick. As the attacks accelerated, an anonymous writer warned that anybody who interfered with the depredations or did business with these foreigners would have their property seized and burnt and their persons subject to the same bodily harm.[34]

Riding with their heads covered in sackcloth, the bandits struck in several parts of the country. They carried out the worst of their threats when two papal messengers were assaulted, one of them fatally. A sheriff's posse caught up with a group of them, but incredibly let them go after they were shown letters of authorisation from the king himself. The sheriff was either stupid or in on it, but the outcry was just the same when details reached Gregory's ears. He wrote a furious letter to Henry, denouncing him for complacency at best and demanding that he find and punish the perpetrators to 'strike fear and dread in others'.[35] The pope himself appointed a commission of clerics to get to the bottom of the matter, and their findings couldn't have embarrassed Henry more.

The attacks had been organised by a secret society known as *Universitas*, led by a Yorkshire knight named Robert Tweng. He had recently won a suit to a church benefice, only to watch the papacy snatch it from him. His group was eighty strong, but they had lots of support from bishops, deacons, clerks and knights with similar grievances. Those identified were dismissed, imprisoned or went on the run. Tweng was ordered to face the pope in person, but received absolution for his crime spree. Eager not to apply the 'rod of apostolic punishment' too much, Gregory realised that reform was overdue and ordered that the Canterbury district, where most of the attacks occurred, be given special attention. He may have also felt a twinge of guilt because there was still no archbishop there. He had rejected the latest candidate for being too old and simple, but realised that having anyone in the post might have helped suppress the outrages after they began.[36]

For all the trouble Tweng caused, Henry sympathised with his feeling of injustice and gave him letters of support. But he was far less merciful when he received the results of the inquiry in mid-July. Two of Hubert's associates were charged, seemingly validating the suspicion that the justiciar himself was involved. Presumably he was trying to repeat his earlier success in ousting Peter des Roches with an anti-alien campaign. It didn't work this time because the disturbances were clearly anti-papal and not directed against foreigners in general. Having realised this, and knowing how in deep he was, he thrust the oaths at Burgh in front of the unsuspecting Henry as a last-ditch effort to protect himself and his family from the royal wrath.[37]

It certainly had to be a blow to Henry not only to learn that his chief judicial officer was promoting outlawry throughout the realm, but to realise that it was Hubert, the father figure who had guided him into manhood and kingship. Few had done as much to deserve the keys to the kingdom, and Henry implicitly trusted him because he felt he had his best interests at heart. But, like William Marshal and Stephen Langton, Hubert was only interested in himself. The king was there for him, not the other way around. And yet Henry craved personal attachment like no other, put great store in whatever relationships he could count on. Cutting ties with Hubert would be as much an emotional purge as an official one.

There is no record of how Hubert got the axe. The court had moved to Woodstock in Oxfordshire and within two weeks he was gone. Henry later hinted that it had been a nasty affair, that Hubert even tried to kill him. He allegedly rushed at the king with a knife, determined to cut his throat, and in the ensuing struggle the king had to call for his attendants to pull him off. Both Henry and Matthew Paris, the chronicler who described the incident, were inclined to melodrama, for if such a scene had happened, Hubert might well have faced the gallows.[38] In all likelihood, he had dropped the façade of professionalism in the face of disgrace and physically threatened his former protégé, maybe even attacked him in a moment akin to Henry coming after him with a sword three years earlier. Like two co-dependents whose shared world had finally crashed around them, it was inevitable that their relationship would end in violence. And the worst was yet to come.

By 1 August 1232 Hubert was banished from court. Later that month Henry seems to have considered banishing him from the realm as well, but never dispatched the order.[39] Instead he demanded that Hubert account for every transaction he ever made while in office. This included all the money paid into the treasury, all debts owed to the crown, all taxes imposed and collected, a list of all his domains in England, Wales and Ireland, all his liberties in forests, warrens and counties, all scutages, marriage portions, taxes, gifts and presents that passed through his hands, and all losses incurred because of his waste and negligence. Hubert declared that King John had given him immunity from rendering accounts of this sort, and he had a charter to prove it. But Roches wasn't about to let a technicality like that stop him from ruining Hubert as he swore he would. What was issued by John, he argued, died with John.[40]

The problem was that all of Hubert's charters had been either issued or confirmed by Henry, and Magna Carta prohibited him from annulling royal charters at will as his father and ancestors had done. The only way to legally retrieve the seventeen castles and more than 100 properties which Hubert had accumulated was by arraigning him before a panel of his peers.[41] He had enough enemies among them to ensure the outcome Henry wanted, and some of them were eager for more than just forfeiture.

They had been waiting for this day for a long time and began putting together a dossier of charges against the justiciar that could only have inflamed Henry's anger even more.

Hubert, they claimed, had sabotaged the king's marriage plans with Austria, sabotaged his military expedition to France and seduced Margaret of Scotland. The more outrageous charges had him conspiring to hang William Braose, poisoning several notables, like William Marshal II and Archbishop Grant, and giving Llywelyn a certain jewel from the treasury that made him invincible in battle. The reality check came from the people of London, who hadn't forgotten how Hubert executed the rabble-rouser Constantine and mutilated several of their own without trial. They demanded justice, and Henry declared his intention to give it to them. This was more than Hubert could handle. Summoned to appear before a meeting of the council at Lambeth on 14 September 1232, he fled to the Priory of Merton and claimed sanctuary.[42]

Now Henry was really furious. When he first heard the charges, the more reasonable ones anyway, he demanded an immediate reply from Hubert, but granted his request for time to prepare a defence. Even if Hubert had good reasons to worry about his fate, the king had so far proceeded against him in accordance with due process, despite Peter's insistence that he take a harsher line. By seeking sanctuary, Hubert was taking advantage of his goodwill, making him look bad again, and that, he should have known, was unforgiveable. Henry gave him one more chance to appear, and when instead he received a message that his former minister was too much in fear of his life to obey, Henry decided to justify that fear.

The story as told by Wendover and Paris is full of dramatic flair. Henry sent orders to the Mayor of London to take matters into his own hands. The mayor responded by ringing the bell as twilight fell and reading out the king's order to bring Hubert before him 'dead or alive'. By daybreak, 20,000 people were on the road to Merton 6 miles to the southwest, while Hubert, forewarned of their coming, said his final prayers. Several citizens had woken up Roches in the night to intervene, only to be told that the king's commands should always be their top priority. Ranulf had no love for Hubert, but found the whole thing disgraceful. He went to Henry himself and told him bluntly that unleashing a mob to do his bidding would make him a laughing stock before the world. That mob, moreover, might not be so easily dispersed once its bloodlust was worked up. Regaining his senses as it were, Henry had Neville dispatch two riders to recall the crowd, which grudgingly returned to London in a 'state of astonishment'.

Henry had been further enraged by Hubert's action because he was supposed to be going to the Welsh Marches to conclude a peace treaty with Llywelyn, and perhaps retrieve that magic jewel of invincibility while he was there. In order to get back on track, Henry agreed to put off a hearing on Hubert's case until early the next year. Hubert left Merton to visit his wife Margaret in Bury St Edmunds and then headed further north to see the Bishop of Norwich. Learning of his progress, however, the king got it into his head that Hubert was up to no good, perhaps making a run for his brother-in-law, the King of Scotland. He sent his steward Godfrey of Crowcombe and a body of household knights to bring him back and imprison him in the Tower of London. Again, Hubert somehow found out and sought sanctuary in another church, this one in Brentwood. Godfrey had known and worked with Hubert since John's reign, but he dragged him from the altar after the king warned him that it was his head otherwise.[43] Wendover also states that Henry supposedly waited up all night to listen for their arrival, and upon being assured that Hubert was finally in his hands, went to bed and had a nice, fitful sleep.

The next morning he was aroused by the Bishop of London protesting against the violation of sanctuary. Henry agreed that his men had seized Hubert illegally and ordered him taken back to Brentwood on 26 September. But they didn't just leave him there, rather they established a perimeter around the chapel to wait out the nominal forty days accorded to sanctuary. And just so that Hubert would realise he was only making it worse for himself, Henry ordered his supply of food and drink to dwindle to one large beer and half a loaf of bread per day.[44]

The council had gone ahead in Hubert's absence and ordered his lands, castles and custodies to be seized and put in trust under the care of Peter de Rivallis. His seventeen years as justiciar came to an end when Stephen Seagrave assumed the post. As a leading jurist, Seagrave finally brought judicial expertise to an office that had always been occupied by magnates and cronies. His appointment was nevertheless political insofar as Henry wanted an Englishman in the post to quell rumblings about Roches importing foreigners into government. Seagrave was also a protégé of Ranulf, and Henry may have wanted to do him a good turn for again intervening after his temper got the better of him.[45]

Roches succeeded where Hubert failed that spring and obtained a tax on a fortieth of movables from the council. It ultimately brought in £16,475, enough to keep subsidising Henry's Continental allies.[46] With Hubert out of the way, the court was now dominated by men who wanted to pursue this policy. Ranulf still held lands in Brittany, Richard of Cornwall was the titular Count of Poitou, Richard Marshal had a French wife and Norman inheritance, and Simon de Montfort was French. Peter of Dreux was still hanging around, still asking for handouts, but again put off the marriage planned between the king and his daughter Yolanda.[47] Now turning 25 and still bereft of intimate companionship, it was little wonder Henry was in a peevish mood that season.

Declaring that it was better to take a chance on the king's mercy than die of starvation, Hubert finally emerged on 5 November. He went back willingly to the Tower of London, where he was met by Rivallis and officials from the exchequer. They explained that the king had learned that he had amassed a nice treasure horde at the New Temple. Whether it had been pilfered from the treasury or not, Rivallis urged him to placate the king and allow the Templars to open the vaults. According to Wendover, the stash included £8,000 in pennies, 140 silver and gold goblets, and a large quantity of precious stones. The inventory provided by the Templars lists fewer pennies (£150) but nineteen more goblets worth nearly £600 in total. The only really incriminating evidence was a gold circlet with sapphires that had indeed been lifted from the crown jewels.[48]

For Hubert's enemies, this alone was enough to condemn him to death. Henry, however, was inclined to be merciful and couldn't deny that Hubert had been loyal for most of his career. 'He faithfully served first my uncle king Richard, next my father king John, and although he has acted ill towards me, he shall never by my means suffer an unjust death; for I would rather be considered a foolish and remiss king than a cruel and tyrannical one.'[49]

A panel of four earls was convened on 10 November 1232 for the purpose of passing judgement on one of their peers in accordance with article 39 of Magna Carta. The trial, held at Cornhill between St Paul's Cathedral and the Tower of London, was something of a sensation, with Seagrave and other justices, city aldermen and at least eight bishops in attendance.[50] Hubert made no defence, refused to accept the legitimacy of the proceedings and asked only for the king's mercy. Henry gave it to him in a statement that mentioned the attacks on the Italian clerics as the main reason for his arrest. In an arrangement that was probably worked out beforehand, he was to be held in close confinement in the Castle of Devizes, with the four earls acting as surety for his whereabouts and behaviour.[51] The lands he held from the king were confiscated, but he was allowed to keep those that came to him through purchase or inheritance.

The four earls did not include Ranulf. He died on 26 October 1232 in Wallingford, aged around 60. Since he had been in ill health and had no children, arrangements had been made to split up his huge estate. His nephew John the Scot became the Earl of Chester, while the earldom of Lincoln was revived for his sister Hawise. She immediately resigned her claims to it in order to allow her son-in-law John de Lacy to become earl by right of his wife.[52] The scramble for other properties and custodies held by Ranulf, as well as those by Hubert, would be an infinitely messier affair. For Henry, it represented a windfall in terms of the reliefs and fees paid for this major redistribution of land, but the simultaneous departure of the two most powerful magnates in the land created a power vacuum that the king, still too trusting for his own good, was ill-prepared to grapple with in the coming months.

For one thing, Rivallis used his position as the custodian of Hubert's portfolio to retain much of it for himself and Roches. By not sharing the spoils, they were courting the same enmity that dogged Hubert. Worse, they were encouraging Henry not to stop with Hubert in making a fresh start. Godfrey of Crowcombe, the loyal knight who had yanked Hubert from the altar at his orders, was deprived of the county of Oxford to make room for their affinity.[53] They also began a purge of offices, starting with Walter Mauclerk, the Bishop of Carlisle, at the treasury. He was told to begin accounting for everything, always the first step towards dismissal.

Since Walter and Godfrey were beneficiaries of Henry's Bromholm oath, their charters were technically unassailable, but Roches had a plan for that. In late October he sent two clerks to Rome to have the pope declare that no king could swear away the liberties of the crown as Henry had done. His oath was therefore annulled and, because he had been so presumptuous in sealing it in the first place, the king was ordered to undergo a mild penance.[54]

The court spent Christmas at Worcester because Henry had gone to the Welsh Marches in late November to conclude a three-year truce with Llywelyn. According to Wendover, Roches had Henry replace all the Englishmen at court with foreigners. He did this in order to get his hands on 'all the baronies and youths of the nobility, both male and female, who were foully degraded by ignoble marriages'. The king went along because, 'simple man that he was', he believed the foreigners' lies.[55] Of course, it was more complicated than that. The 'English' barons Richard Marshal and Simon de Montfort were newcomers from France, whereas the 'foreign' bishop Peter des Roches had lived in England for more than a quarter of a century.[56] Wendover knew all that, but, simple man that he was, preferred to see the emergence of two factions at court only in terms of geopolitics.

The king didn't prefer one faction to the other because it was more foreign, just more familiar. He had known Roches all his life, had been raised and tutored by him, and became estranged from him only because of Hubert. Had he listened to him back then, his court would have been able to live large like it had in his father's day and not have to scrape by all the time. He was willing to give Roches a chance to prove it, and if the other faction was for it, then they could all do business together. It's true that he had got off on the wrong foot with their leader, Richard Marshal, but since that time Marshal had been one of the most active members of the court, and Henry liked men with ambition.

Unfortunately, Marshal also had a chip on his shoulder and was constantly complaining about something or other. His sense of grievance may have been justified to some extent, but he nevertheless represented that type of baron which Henry was forever finding irksome, and would plague him for the rest of his reign: the grumbler. Contrary to the king's natural cheeriness and predisposition to sympathy, charity and beneficence, grumbling magnates like Marshal always had some beef to air under the thin veil of a threat, and that was guaranteed to sour the atmosphere of the court with quarrels, ill will and the need to take these things outside.

5

HENRY'S HARSH LESSON IN KINGSHIP 1233–1234

The unfree peasant looking at his lord in the thirteenth century might have wondered what on earth he had to grumble about. He didn't have to till the fields and chop the wood and milk the cows and do the laundry, all that for the same slop morning, noon and night. He spent his day hunting and hawking before sitting down to a meal of braised venison either supplied from his private reserve or as a gift from the king. Hospitality was very important for the reputation of the lord and lady of the manor, so they might be joined by the local abbot or another lord related to them by birth or marriage. After the meal they would gather by the hearth and guzzle goblets of wine as they gossiped and griped, mainly about the king and his capricious favouritism. Hearing this from the house servants, the peasant would roll his eyes and shake his head, because he truly had a lot to grumble about, mostly because of his lord and lady.

In the early days of the manorial system, the Norman lord usually farmed out his properties for a set fee, leaving him free to spend as much time across the Channel as he liked. Some time in the twelfth century, he realised his estates were much more profitable if they were managed directly. Using a steward and team of bailiffs and reeves, he got richer by having them collect money rents from his tenants and working his farms to support both generous consumption at home and fat profits at the market. He drove his peasants ever harder with new labour obligations that were unjust, but since they had no recourse to justice outside his court, all they could do was grumble about it.[1] He could also hire out cheap labour to cut and thresh his wheat with the vigour that yielded really big margins. This put money in his hands to buy whatever his estate needed but didn't produce, like textiles, forgings and candles, and whatever he and his family wanted but didn't need, like wine, spices and the latest fashions.

Helping to fuel this prosperity, oddly enough, was the castle. In the beginning it was meant to be menacing and strike fear into the natives. Now the natives swarmed around its walls for the security and opportunity it represented, and in the process they set up trades and markets that evolved into urban centres much the way villages sprang up around the manor.[2] People working in crafts, commerce and services were also subject to rents and lordships, but generally depended on cash rather than in-kind payments for their transactions. That was no problem, because the cash supply was also growing at an incredible rate, mostly due to inflation and the massive export of wool to Flanders. The only coin in circulation was the silver penny, but there were so many millions of them that terms of account like the pound, which was worth 240 pennies, had to be used to keep track of their sums.*

Losing a castle, manor or custody was as much a blow to the lord's revenue as to his power and prestige. In that season of the king overturning his charters in violation of Magna Carta, nobody was ready to call him to account as long as they got in on the action. So it was with Richard Marshal when the old case of Walerand the German came up again. He was the household knight who had clashed with Richard of Cornwall five years earlier, resulting in Henry's first rebellion. He seemed to have made even more enemies since then, because Henry dispossessed him of a Norman escheat at the time of Hubert's fall and gave it to Marshal. There was no question it was an illegal act, but Marshal was happy to go along.[3]

Marshal didn't have much use for Magna Carta anyway, at least not article 7, which guaranteed a widow her marriage portion and inheritance within forty days of her husband's death. He had prevented that from happening for his sister-in-law Eleanor, presumably because of the furore surrounding his succession to the earldom of Pembroke, but he continued to make problems for her after that was settled, and it was easy to see why. His dead brother's estate in England, Wales and Ireland was worth in the neighbourhood of £3,000 in annual income, and she was entitled to a third of it. The idea of losing £1,000 a year to a 16-year-old, even the sister of the king, was hard to bear.

She demanded her rights just as much as he demanded his and kept after him about paying up. In July 1232, after more than a year of contention, he offered her £400 a year to be done with it, a far from fair deal, but one Henry insisted she take. The king might have argued that it was a rather decent income and it spared her the hassle of having to manage so large an estate.[4] He didn't stop to consider that

* The term of account most widely used in Europe at the time was the mark, which was worth 2/3 the value of the pound. The seemingly odd figures given in this book are the results of converting marks to pounds, e.g. 10,000 marks = £6,667.

maybe she wanted to be hassled, for she later threw herself into estate management with gusto. To their eternal regret, she took the sum offered.

The settlement did nothing to mollify Marshal, however. He even missed the first payment. Henry must have found his behaviour bizarre. William Marshal II had been so affable and cooperative. When he died, the king was said to have been so inconsolable that he contemplated being buried next to Marshal and his father at the New Temple.[5] Some of Richard's coolness may have been just circumstance. Having lived in France for so long, he came to the court a complete stranger, and he evidently lacked the charm that allowed someone in a similar position, like Simon de Montfort, to hit it off with Henry from the start. But there was also the problem of expectations. The Marshal family name and holdings made him the obvious leader of the barons following Ranulf's death. They looked to him to turn back this tide of foreigners out to purge the court and settle a few scores.

The first to go was the treasurer Walter Mauclerk. His life charters and grants, formerly protected by the now defunct Bromholm oath, were all revoked. He was replaced by Rivallis, although the actual work in the treasury went to Robert Passelewe, another foreigner formerly banned from the country. Mauclerk's accounts were audited, and in February 1233 he was ordered to pay a fine of £1,000 to recover the king's goodwill.[6] He was being railroaded, but nobody noticed because of a more sensational case that was just then about to tear the realm apart.

On 6 February the manor of Upavon in Wiltshire was seized from household knight Gilbert Basset and returned to Peter de Maulay, who was also back on the scene. Maulay had been dispossessed of Upavon in 1229, but refused to vacate it until Hubert warned him to do so or he would put him in a special place where he would see 'neither his hands nor his feet'.[7] Hubert had arranged to have Henry give the manor to Gilbert by royal grant, thus making him the owner. Now, at the urging of Roches, Henry annulled that charter and gave Maulay a new one to the manor. It was an act of arbitrary disseisin, which is to say Gilbert was deprived of the property without due process. The Bassets were from the ancestral nobility with close ties to the Marshals. Gilbert knew exactly where to go with this affront.[8]

Even though Marshal had also benefited from Henry's abrogation of charters, he was reportedly 'incited by his zeal for the cause of justice'. He went to the king to demand an end to the lawlessness of all these foreigners, now lumped together as Poitevins to suggest that they all came from Poitou. Roches and Rivallis were actually from Touraine and Maulay from Normandy (just like Marshal), but that was beside the point. Poitou was that infernal place where so much good English money had been wasted in the last twenty-five years. Since the clamour was all about the man who had 'perverted the king's heart', Wendover has Roches make the reply to Marshal, as if Henry were too dumb to do it himself: 'His lord the king is surely allowed to summon as many foreigners as he chooses for the protection of his kingdom and crown, and as many and such men as would be able to reduce his haughty and rebellious subjects to their proper obedience.'[9] That type of inflammatory rhetoric recalled what Fawkes said during the minority about the English being natural troublemakers who needed a firm hand from abroad. Marshal is not on record disagreeing with that opinion, it is just reported that he left the court a few days after Basset did and never returned. He went to Wales, then to Ireland. Meanwhile, Henry took his court to Canterbury in April 1233 to find a way to mend the rift between crown and bishops over a variety of issues, not least of which was the post of archbishop which had stood vacant for more than eighteen months. A third candidate had been dispatched to Rome, but for now the government hoped to placate the bishops with something they always welcomed, a bit of anti-Jewish legislation.[10]

As in any age, money was needed to make money, but in the absence of a banking system, it was the Jewish moneylenders who helped propel the English economy forward. They had first got into the money trade as more and more high-quality silver was needed to monetise wool exports. Their expertise with precious metals and contacts all over the Continent made them ideal for transacting foreign business for Christian moneyers. As the latter left the trade under pressure from the Church, the Jews took their place in towns that had either a mint or a market, but always a castle for protection.[11]

Unlike on the Continent, the Jewish population belonged to the crown. This meant that the king was free to take however big a cut he wanted from their profits in the money trade. The practice had made a convenient political tool by the time John became king. He could use the bonds held by Jewish creditors to force their Christian debtors to pay up at once. Since they couldn't, he would have them do his bidding and, failing that, seize the land they had used to secure the loan. It was all very legal, but the lord still felt aggrieved and saw the Jews as accomplices in the king's oppressions. This left them open to spontaneous acts of violence during political upheavals, as happened during the conflict over Magna Carta.[12]

Jewish communities mostly flourished during the first years of Henry's reign, despite Stephen Langton's best efforts against them, but now the king had a bishop at his side who fondly remembered the days of intrusive royal policy. Roches knew from experience that heavily taxing the Jews was an effective way of keeping pressure on the barons and at the same time raising much-needed funds. In March, a tallage of £6,667 was demanded in various instalments. The next month, a Statute of Jewry was published after the court arrived in Canterbury to again reflect the anti-Semitic measures being pushed by Louis IX in France.[13] It capped weekly interest rates on loans at two pennies per pound, or 43 per cent annually. The statute also declared that only those Jews who could be of service to the king were allowed to stay. The others had six months to pack up and leave the realm.[14]

The bishops were by and large Langton's disciples, but Roches was still wasting his time. No amount of legislation against the Jews would make them happy because he was the primary source of their disaffection. They were angry at him for inciting Gregory to come down hard on them over the anti-papal attacks the year before. He was suspected of implicating Roger Niger, the Bishop of London, in the scandal because he supported Hubert during his downfall. Poor Roger was forced to go to Rome to plead his innocence and was robbed in Parma on the way.[15] The bishops were almost guaranteed to frown on any candidate he promoted to become Archbishop of Canterbury, and he made it easy for them in the case of John Blund of Oxford.

The first thing Blund had going against him was his work in the secular sphere, namely the exchequer. Then there was his enthusiasm for Aristotle, which ran counter to their more conservative beliefs.[16] Finally, there was the fact that Roches supported him, not only politically and academically, but also in the form of gifts and loans for £1,400. Under pressure from the Langtonians, Gregory rejected him and worked behind the scenes to elect the candidate put forward by the bishops, Edmund of Abingdon.[17]

Having got nowhere appeasing the bishops, Henry tried to lure the younger generation of barons to his court when it moved on next to Gloucester in May 1233. There he belted three new earls: Hugh de Vere (Oxford), Thomas de Beaumont (Warwick) and Roger Bigod (Norfolk). He had little chance of winning over Bigod, and not just because he was Marshal's nephew. Henry had made him and the other two wait three years to receive their earldoms, and Bigod was a classic grumbler. But at least he was there. Several barons failed to attend the ceremony, and Henry found nothing quite as offensive as somebody ignoring his summons. And if it was true that they had chosen instead to attend a tournament organised by Marshal in nearby Worcester, then they were really in trouble.

⋆ ⋆ ⋆

Tournaments in that age involved mounted knights charging and battling it out in a general melee before a viewing public. They were naturally very popular and justified in the sense that they kept men on horseback fit for war, but the authorities didn't like them because of the rowdiness and hell-raising they stirred up, among both participants and spectators. Getting maimed or trampled to death was always a risk, but the real killing was in the collecting of ransoms for captured opponents, an only slightly more chivalrous pursuit than the personal scores settled on the pitch or political intrigues devised off of it. Tournaments were often prohibited to keep disgruntled or scheming groups of armed men from getting together to forge unholy alliances. William Marshal was the most famous knight of them all, but as

Henry's boyhood regent, he banned one tournament for fear it might disturb the 'tranquillity' that had finally come to the land.[18]

As king, Henry was nominally the supreme knight, and while he may have got little thrill from action like that, he undoubtedly enjoyed the ritual and spectacle that went with it. He also understood that knights needed training for battle, and on one occasion ordered his personal retinue to attend a tournament at Northampton in 1228 in anticipation of landing in France the following year.[19] But he had no use for tournaments that played on rivalries, discontent or hinted at larger conspiracies, and the one organised by William Marshal's son was just that type. He banned it and tried to head off the rogue knights in Worcester, but they quickly had their tourney and fled before he arrived. Henry had to settle for fining the city instead.

Where he could strike at Marshal was making him pay up under the agreement worked out for his sister's dower. He distrained his lands, which is to say temporarily seized them, and did the same to several other grumblers who defied his orders to cancel the tournament and attend court. He followed up by demanding hostages from certain Marcher lords to prevent them from endangering the truce with Wales. Marshal knew all about this practice of using children as surety for good behaviour. He was 15 years old in 1207 when he was made a hostage for his father's difficult relationship with King John.[20] He and the grumblers saw it as further evidence that the mindset of the former reign had been resurrected by Peter des Roches. They wanted nothing to do with the court as long as Peter had any influence over it and ignored another summons to meet the king in Oxford on 24 June.

And it wasn't just them, either. A Dominican scholar preached to Henry that he would never have peace until he got rid of the Bishop of Winchester and Rivallis. He was something of a clever man, for he chose to make a pun on the name Peter des Roches to get his point across.

'My lord king, what do sailors fear the most?'

Henry could sense something tiresome coming his way and advised him to ask a sailor, but the Dominican would not be denied.

'I will tell you. It is stones (*pierres*) and rocks (*roches*).'

His message was that the ship of state was in danger of foundering unless the king tossed the helmsman overboard. Henry wasn't prepared to do that, but he did agree to give the malcontents another chance to answer his summons to meet in Westminster on 11 July. They not only ignored it, but warned him to dismiss Roches and Rivallis or they would take matters into their own hands, including choosing a new king if it came to that.[21] Henry dared them to try it and ordered more seizures. He used an uprising by the Irish to order the feudal host to muster in Gloucester at the end of August. From there, he could choose to proceed to Ireland or go after the malcontents if they continued to defy him.

Far from backing down, Marshal made his most provocative move yet. In answer to a second summons for 1 August, he convened his own assembly at the Basset manorial home in High Wycombe, about 35 miles from Westminster. They had hatched a plan to march on the council to carry out their threat, but many of the grumblers decided it wasn't a good idea and stayed away. Marshal's nephew the Earl of Norfolk attended, but three other earls, Cornwall, Warenne and Derby, all his brothers-in-law, were absent.[22] Henry packed up the court and began heading westward, ultimately to Gloucester but ready to turn off towards High Wycombe if necessary. By the time he reached Windsor, Marshal and Bigod had sued for peace and received safe conduct passes to go home. Neither did, however. For all their anger at the king and Roches, they were angrier still at those who made them look like fools, who deserted the cause of justice, and they were determined to make them pay for it.[23]

At the top of the list was Richard of Cornwall. He and Marshal had teamed up six months earlier to drive Llywelyn out of Radnor, but then in the fight over Upavon, Marshal had backed his man Basset, and Cornwall his former tutor Maulay. Henry knew his brother could always be enticed away from rebellion with a handsome gift and made him one in the form of the wardship of Baldwin de Redvers, the future Earl of Devon. Cornwall had deserted William Marshal II during their confrontation with the king six years earlier, but had been forgiven and went on to marry into the Marshal family. There would be no forgiving him now. Marshal decided to seize one of his castles in the Marches. Bigod risked forfeiting his new earldom by following his uncle into rebellion, but he too had a score to settle over a castle, and so both were seized at the same time.[24]

By this act, Marshal had declared war. Henry renounced him as his liegeman, ordered his estates confiscated and changed his course for Hereford. He recaptured the two castles and had moved on to besiege Marshal's own castle of Usk when a truce was reached on 7 September 1233.[25] Bigod made his peace and was restored to favour; he even got to witness his first royal charter. Still, he lost one of his castles as a warning against future disobedience. Marshal may not have deserved special consideration, but he was who he was, so Henry offered him leniency and another chance to air his complaints before a council meeting on 2 October 1233.[26]

As much as Marshal may have wanted to make peace, the hotheads in his camp were set on full vengeance. Gilbert Basset was backed by his brothers Fulk and Philip and their volatile brother-in-law Richard Siward. They dismissed the truce and intensified their campaign of guerrilla warfare.[27] They had a lot of sympathisers, including members of the garrison at Devizes, where Hubert de Burgh was being held. Unfounded rumours that Roches was seeking custody of the castle so he could put Hubert to death led two attendants loyal to Marshal's party to organise his escape to a nearby church. Since Henry had ordered precautions to prevent something like that from happening, the garrison knew they risked getting hung for sleeping on the watch. They quickly tracked Hubert to the church, dragged him back to the castle and the whole farce of sanctuary was set to play out again.[28]

Two bishops, Roger Niger of London and Richard Poer of Salisbury, went to Henry in Hereford to demand that Hubert be restored to the church. 'Fine, whatever', was about all he had to say to them. He was hoping to exile Hubert for this latest escapade anyway and planned to bring it up at a council meeting. The bishops, however, got the jump on him by demanding that he make peace with Marshal and the other malcontents.[29] That only worked Henry up into a fury, because he had tried to make peace, no less than twice already, and all he got for it was Marshal thumbing his nose at him. Marshal and the others were traitors, Henry declared, and deserved whatever punishment he could inflict on them. That was the whole problem, according to the bishops. Whatever one thought of their insurrection, they had been banished without trial by peers as enshrined in article 39 of Magna Carta.

Roches interjected at this point to argue that there were no peers in England. His comment was twisted to reflect a stuffy, superior attitude, but it was meant to show that in France, for example, judgement was passed by a small circle of people from one's rank and class. England was different in that a peer was any free man the king saw fit to appoint to his court to mete out justice. The way Roches saw it, Marshal was going on and on about trial by peers because he wanted the special treatment indicative of being a peer in France, and he was refusing to submit himself to any process until he received assurances of it.[30]

This was all very academic for the bishops and they couldn't care less anyway. Roches was the source of all the problems as far as they were concerned and they threatened to excommunicate him, Rivallis, Seagrave and all the others they felt were corrupting the kingdom. Henry had to wonder why they had not included the malcontents in their list, but he still offered concessions in the hope of removing Marshal from the fight and isolating ruffians like Basset and Siward. This hope was shattered when he received word in mid-October that Marshal had joined up with Llywelyn to retake Usk, thus confirming that he was in league with the Welsh. Giving full vent to his Angevin temper, Henry demanded that the bishops excommunicate Marshal, but they excused him, saying he had only retaken his own castle.[31] They could defend him all they wanted, the king ordered Marshal's estates confiscated and called out the host to muster in Gloucester by 2 November.

Before that, Siward struck in what was the greatest propaganda triumph of the war. On 29 October he led a band of Welshmen into Devizes, grabbed Hubert at the church altar and crossed the Severn to join Marshal at his castle of Chepstow. The raid was clearly designed to humiliate the king, to let him know that they could go anywhere they wanted and do anything they pleased. Henry declared them outlaws, and Hubert too, for going along with them. Perhaps more enraged now than he had ever been in his entire life, Henry ordered the destruction of their properties and began planning an offensive against them.[32]

But this was the Welsh Marches, a hilly, foreboding terrain where it was next to impossible to keep an army on the move and supplied for the purpose of guerrilla warfare. Henry couldn't even muster a full army because the threat of rebellion had now spread elsewhere, particularly in the north. His brother-in-law Alexander of Scotland had been none too happy over what he saw as the harsh treatment of his own brother-in-law Hubert. Henry's failure to marry his other sister Margery was another sore spot and offered further incentive for Alexander to press his claim for the northern counties. Henry's own subjects in neighbouring Cumberland were equally offended by the high-handed treatment of their local bishop, Walter Mauclerk of Carlisle. All this meant that the king had to spend more money but got fewer men where he actually needed them.[33]

His campaign was doomed from the outset. At last free to conduct the military drive he had been denied in France, Henry could see for himself that he was no soldier at heart. He didn't like to be in the saddle all day long, riding up and down the lines, squaring men in their formations and barking out orders, always vigilant against the enemy. While the host was mustering at Hereford, he set out for the castle of Grosmont without realising that Marshal had stripped the area of provisions. Also, nobody asked whether the fortress could accommodate the entire court. Of course, it couldn't, so the baggage train and foot soldiers had to remain on the plain below, exposed to attack by Marshal's men, which took place the next morning in full view of the courtiers on the walls. Wendover almost takes delight in listing them by name. There was Peter des Roches and Peter de Rivallis and Ralph Neville and Stephen Seagrave ....[34]

Knowing there was little he could do with winter approaching, Henry went back to Hereford to await the host. Marshal and his men moved on to a castle held by John of Monmouth, another former member of the Marshal affinity, now considered a traitor. Flemish mercenaries from the castle set upon them on 25 November while they were still not at full strength. Marshal refused to retreat and ended up fighting off a dozen of them single-handedly until the Flemish commander was felled by a cross-bolt to the chest. The rest of Marshal's men then arrived and proceeded to slaughter the 'Poitevins'. The countryside was 'tainted by numbers of dead foreigners'.[35]

Monmouth held, but other castles fell as Marshal and the Welsh continued their advance. The king had moved on to Gloucester for his Christmas court in the meantime. The severe frost that year added to the scarcity brought on by the war and the poor harvest before it. The magnificent feast Roches had given Henry two years before in Winchester, intended to show the king what he could have every Christmas if he, Peter, and not Hubert were his guiding hand, made a striking contrast to this gloomiest holiday in memory.[36] The bishop had some explaining to do, but for now all Henry could do to extricate himself from this mess was to try to appeal to Marshal yet again. He needed an emissary to seek him out with some offer of a settlement. He wasn't going to let him off scot-free, just make him somehow understand that he was going to have to make peace with the king some day if he ever hoped to have peace at all.

It was best to have a churchman convey his offer, but it was clear he couldn't trust the bishops. He chose the Italian Agnellus of Pisa, the provincial of the Franciscans in England, who had led his order there in 1224.[37] He was highly regarded by everyone and, being a real foreigner, Henry probably wanted Marshal to realise that all this anti-alien talk he was using to bolster his image was ridiculous and unhelpful. Agnellus found Marshal in Wales at the Abbey of Margam in Glamorgan a few days before Christmas and told him that the king was willing to grant him life and limb despite his treasonous actions. He would, moreover, allow him to keep a portion of his estates in any reconciliation.

That alone doomed the mission. If Marshal agreed to even partial confiscation, it would forever brand him a disloyal subject, something no son of the vaunted Greatest Knight could bear to live with. He then launched into a long justification for his rebellion, blaming everything on the king and his advisers. He was not at all worried what the ultimate judgement might be because God was on his side. So not only did the gentle friar also fail, but he contracted a disease around that time from which he never recovered.[38]

To prove their war was just, Marshal and his men claimed that their depredations were aimed only at courtiers or defectors. Their guerrilla bands under Siward or Basset would strike a manor belonging to Seagrave or Richard of Cornwall and burn the houses, the woods, even the farm animals. That changed in 1234, the year 'Satan was at work', says the Dunstable annalist. On 7 January, Marshal, Llywelyn and their men road into Shrewsbury and put the town to the torch. In describing the aftermath, Wendover spares no details: 'It was a dreadful sight for travellers to see the corpses of the slain, which were almost numberless, lying unburied and naked in the roads, affording meals for the beasts and birds of prey, the stench from which had so corrupted the air that the dead killed the living.' Despite this atrocity, Wendover still insists that Marshal only fought to obtain justice. If he blames anyone, it's the king for going back east and leaving the region at the mercy of his enemies.[39]

★ ★ ★

Henry's decision to return to London wasn't so much an abandonment of the war in Wales, rather an invitation for Marshal to take it to Ireland. Marshal's extensive holdings in Leinster had been left vulnerable with so many of his tenants serving in his guerrilla campaign in Britain. Across the sea, Henry was able to cobble together an alliance between his justiciar for Ireland, Maurice Fitz-Gerald, the former justiciar Richard de Burgh, who lost his position when his uncle Hubert fell from power, and the Lacy clan of Ulster, long-time enemies of the Marshals. As their attacks against Leinster grew, Marshal used the king's departure from the Marches to cross over in February to try to reverse the tide.[40]

While that had the desired effect of inducing Llywelyn to negotiate a peaceful settlement, the other rebel bands were still unpacified. Throughout the conflict Henry had hoped that the bishops might step in to get them to lay down their arms, but they had constantly directed their threats towards him and the court instead. Now those threats were only going to get worse as the new Archbishop-elect of Canterbury prepared to take up his post.

Edmund of Abingdon was another staunch Langtonian, a Paris-trained lecturer at Oxford who took priestly orders late in life, but made up for it with a scrubbed-down, ascetic lifestyle that included crumbs and water for subsistence and wearing a hairshirt clamped to his torso.[41] He was the complete opposite of Henry, who liked good food, fine wine and the snug comfort of soft, silky garments against his skin. Although still awaiting his consecration as archbishop, Edmund was invited to a council meeting scheduled for Westminster on 2 February. Since he was expected to come out against Roches like the other bishops, Henry made a point of stopping in Winchester on his way to London to reassure his beleaguered adviser.[42]

The meeting started off acrimoniously when Roger Cantilupe, the court legist, charged Alexander Stavensby, the Bishop of Coventry and Lichfield, of being in league with Marshal and therefore seeking to depose the king. An embarrassed and furious Stavensby responded by putting on his robes and excommunicating whoever had put that slur into Henry's head. He then took a shot back at Cantilupe by reminding everybody that his father had been hung over a breach of the peace.[43] It was into this atmosphere of hissing and bad blood that the cadaverous Edmund looked at Henry and launched his attack against Roches and Rivallis:

> In the first place, they hate the English people. They estrange your affections from your people, and those of your people from you, as is evident from the conduct of [Marshal], who is the best subject in your dominions. By the wicked lies which they tell you about your people, they pervert all their words and deeds.

And that was just his opening. It was because of Roches that King John had lost the affections of his people, lost his territories and nearly England itself. The Peters controlled everything in the country, from castles, wards and marriages to escheats, the treasury and the privy seal. Edmund ended by begging the king, then warning him, that unless he governed by the advice of his native subjects, 'we shall proceed, by means of the censure of the Church, against you and all other gainsayers'.[44]

Unlike his father, Henry took the threat of excommunication seriously and didn't dare arouse Edmund's vehemence any further with a defence of his advisers. He merely asked for time to weigh his complaints, saying that he couldn't just dismiss his court like that. But there was also pressure coming from the pope, who was beginning to sympathise with Hubert de Burgh.[45] Henry ignored the pope's suggestion that he be more lenient with him, but he was merciful to his wife Margaret. After the council meeting, he set off on another visit to Bromholm Priory and on the way granted her eight manors from her husband's estate. The only person with him as he knelt before the shrine of the true cross and made his devotions was Peter de Rivallis. Doubtless Rivallis kept one eye on the king as he prayed, knowing as he did that Hubert was in that exact same spot right before his fate took a nasty turn.

From the coast, the royal entourage headed westward into the Midlands. A guerrilla band must have been dogging their progress, because they struck one of Seagrave's manors close to where the court was staying in Huntingdon on 24 February. Seeing the flames from afar, Seagrave set off with an armed posse to track down the insurgents, but took fright when he heard they were being led by Siward. Henry and his attendants nearly rolled with laughter when he returned looking like he had seen a ghost.[46]

The court turned south to be in Canterbury for Edmund's consecration on 2 April 1234. As the Bishop of Winchester, Roches had to be there whether the other bishops wanted him or not, and they made it clear that they didn't by leaving him to sit alone with the king before the altar. A council meeting followed in Westminster to discuss a truce worked out with Llywelyn in March. Edmund used that occasion to warn the king again to get rid of Roches and Rivallis or risk damning his soul. Wendover reports that Henry finally caved and ordered Roches to go back to Winchester and keep his nose out of his affairs in the future.[47] It couldn't have been as simple as that, because Roches was heading the commission to renew the truce with France, which was set to expire in June.[48] By the following month, however, he was gone for good, just as word came from Ireland that Richard Marshal had been mortally wounded in a skirmish.

It happened on 1 April, when negotiations with the justiciar Fitz-Gerald turned into a brawl and Marshal was deserted by all of his men. That's according to Wendover, who shows Marshal single-handedly beating off his enemies, chopping the hands off of one and cutting another completely in half, until locals with pitchforks and axes finally brought him and his horse down. They then removed his armour and stabbed him in the back. He was taken to one of his own castles and recovered for a spell, but the wound became infected and no amount of intervention by the physician could prevent a fever from setting in. Marshal died on 16 April 1234, leaving behind no children, just a French wife who, ironically, was distantly related to Peter des Roches.[49]

The Dunstable annalist portrays Henry as distraught over the passing of so great a knight, but he probably felt that Marshal got what he deserved.[50] He had raised rebellion in the kingdom, ignored all attempts to negotiate and was a fool to think he could fight his way out of a peace conference where he was outnumbered to begin with. The chroniclers, however, were not about to let posterity see it in those terms. He was idolised as the leader of a movement that protected the rights of all Englishmen against a hateful group of foreigners out to despoil their land. It didn't matter that Marshal himself was a foreigner to all intents and purposes. He died for the cause of justice and that alone obscured any hypocrisy that might otherwise blight his enduring sacrifice. When the next uprising to expel all foreigners broke out in thirty years' time, no one thought there was anything amiss about it too being led by a Frenchman.

For the bishops, Marshal's death was their chance to ruin Roches and Rivallis, and they wasted no time going about it. At a council in Gloucester, Edmund said he had copies of letters that were reportedly sent to Ireland under the king's seal to encourage the nobles there to kill Marshal or send him to Henry in chains. Their reward would be a division of his lands. Since no letters have been found, the archbishop likely used the well-known suspicion that Rivallis had illicit access to the royal seal to pin Marshal's death on him and embarrass Henry in the process.[51] 'Examine your conscience, my king,' he warned, 'for all those who caused those letters to be sent and were aware of the treachery intended are just as guilty of the murder of the marshal, as if they had slain him with their own hands.'[52]

They were clearly being made scapegoats, but what condemned Roches was the failure of the peace initiative with France, which had been Henry's overriding concern that spring. The French were poised to invade Brittany after the truce expired, and Henry had no money to fend them off. He was on the verge of bankruptcy again, partly due to Marshal's rebellion, but also because he had never learned the lesson imparted to him by Roches. He hadn't sat on all the bounty that came his way after the death of Ranulf and fall of Hubert. Instead of letting it make money for the crown, he gave it away again, most of it to Roches and Rivallis.

Yet there was a purpose in allowing them to monopolise so much royal favour and offices. Henry expected them to carry out reforms to put an end to his perennial poverty. Rivallis was given control of a staggering twenty-two counties to increase and speed up the increments and profits reported at the exchequer. He was made keeper of the royal wardrobe, which covered the king's household expenses, the keeper of escheats and wardships, which were the real nuggets of patronage, and was made the treasurer of the exchequer. No one was in a better position to overhaul the king's financial administration. Unfortunately, Roches made sure that task was subordinated to a redistribution of wealth designed to reward his friends and allies and punish those who had ousted him earlier.[53]

Roches and Rivallis were supposed to make Henry rich and enviable. Now, barely two years later, the king had no money and very little dignity to show for it.

There wasn't much Henry could do about his indigence just then, but he sought to recover his dignity by allowing the bishops to seize the initiative at the Gloucester council. He doubtless felt stung by the way they had blatantly favoured the other side, to the point of threatening him, but he was willing to humble himself before them if that's what it took. At their urging, and supposedly because it was one of the terms demanded by Llywelyn, Henry welcomed the rebels to his peace and knighted and belted Richard Marshal's brother Gilbert as the new Earl of Pembroke.[54] Basset, Siward and even Hubert were restored their lands and pardoned for their outlawry because, as Henry informed the Sheriff of Berkshire, 'it had been proclaimed against them unjustly and contrary to the law of the land'.[55]

In full penitent mode, Henry stood by as his justices overturned his controversial acts as part of a general overhaul of the legal code. This was thorny ground they were treading on. As Henry de Bracton's law book commented at the time, no one but the king could stand in judgement of his charters because he had no equal in the realm. His authority was supreme, answerable only to God. The only way to keep him from acting in an arbitrary and despotic manner was to fall back on the law that created his authority. If he stepped outside that law, the barons should 'put a bridle on him'. That way, they preserved his honour before God.

Under leading jurist William Raleigh, the Upavon case was cited as an example of a situation where the king needed a bridle, and the magnates of the realm proceeded to apply it retrospectively by giving the manor back to Gilbert Basset in May 1234. Thirteen similar cases came up over the course of the next two years, and the king even admitted that he acted unjustly in a suit brought forward by Hubert.[56] This triumph of justice, as it were, culminated in an order to the sheriffs to proclaim Magna Carta in every county court.[57]

The gesture of conciliation that proved the most controversial had to do with Henry's sister Eleanor. Gilbert Marshal had inherited his brother's problem with her dower and may have informed Edmund that he would like it to form part of any settlement. The arrears owed to her was one thing, but there was also the fate of all those properties. Since Eleanor had no children, they would revert back to the Marshals after her death. But if she married again, that would change everything.[58]

Edmund probably conveyed these concerns to the king and suggested that Eleanor might want to offer her widow's chastity as a concession to peace. Henry doubtless dismissed the notion, knowing that as far back as her first marriage that he had no 'greater treasure' than his sisters for the useful alliances they created.[59] But he also knew that Eleanor was independent and headstrong and might seize the opportunity for perpetual widowhood at 19 years old just to get out of having to remarry and end up a miserable wretch in a foreign land like her sister Joan.

Just then, Eleanor's former governess entered the picture, a pious and learned woman who was very much a mother figure to her. She was also a widow and had decided to make it her life's calling. They could do it together, she offered. Some time during the peace negotiations the two ladies knelt before Edmund and took a vow of chastity. He then placed a ring on their fingers, making them widows for life. It's fair to say Eleanor came to regret it almost immediately.[60]

Reprisals at court were now inevitable and no one was identified with the fallen regime more than Roches. As a bishop, however, he was entitled to protection from the Church, the same as the bishops who were out to get him. His long familiarity with the king likewise helped him to steel himself against the latter's displeasure. Henry had a fearsome temper, but the trick was to weather it, to let him vent his rage until his inherently pious nature reasserted itself. In the end, Roches lost a handsome pension, had to pay a fine of £100 for an unrelated default and faced a slew of pleas but, all in all, he emerged from the purge much better off than Rivallis and Seagrave.[61]

Seagrave decided to follow Hubert's example and run for it. He had survived Roche's ouster by several weeks, but when his dismissal came, he sought sanctuary at the church of St Mary in Leicester. When he eventually appeared before the king on 14 July, he blamed everybody else, especially Rivallis. Passelewe also fled, but it was some time before he was discovered hiding in London at the New Temple, holed up in a secret cellar. While he claimed that he was too ill to come out, the charges against him began to mount, especially his pilfering at the Jewish exchequer. Both men lost most of their grants and had to pay a fine of £666 for grace.[62]

It was Rivallis who came closest to incurring the king's wrath. If Wendover's successor Matthew Paris can be believed, Henry was almost ready to pluck his eyes out. He mostly brought it on himself by attempting to weasel out of his day of reckoning. He had been ordered to render accounts on 19 June, but it wasn't until 14 July that he appeared before the king, together with Roches and Seagrave, and then made only excuses. Paris says that he was tonsured with a dagger dangling from his belt, as if to give the impression that he was a warrior monk ready to defend himself. Henry had him thrown in the Tower and kept there until Edmund made bail for him three days later.

Rivallis should have known from what happened to his enemy Hubert that messing Henry about only made it worse in the end. But he tried to bargain away some possessions and offices in order to keep others, then blamed his misdeeds on Henry himself: 'Lord king, I was made rich by you. Do not destroy the man you have made.'[63] The more Henry remained unmoved, the more galling Rivallis became. He insisted his lands be returned to him because the king should not act out of love or hatred for any of his subjects. He was clearly referring to protection from arbitrary will, which must have had the whole court snickering, considering how he had encouraged the king to do exactly that against others. Hypocrite though he was, the council agreed that only the law of the land would henceforth prevail, and the most Henry could demand of Rivallis was an account of his actions while in charge of so many crown offices. His case was adjourned to the following year.[64]

There was yet one more Peter to fall from grace. For three years Peter of Dreux had been leeching money off Henry to maintain Brittany as a Continental fief. He had spent it all making war on his Breton nobles and had no hope of keeping the French at bay without more. All Henry could send him was a force of ninety knights and some Welsh infantry, who did an admirable job of repulsing the French and buying Peter time, but in November, without even informing Henry, he submitted to a humiliating peace with Louis. Henry's pseudo-lordship collapsed and, all told, nearly £14,000 completely wasted.[65] Louis didn't stop there, either, and seized a barony from the Marshal family. And so Richard's rebellion and death had the further effect of finishing off the Plantagenets and Marshals in Normandy for good, making Louis all the more powerful and richer for it.

Now 20 years old and newly married, Louis was still a mummy's boy, but Blanche had put her considerable abilities to good use on his behalf. By contrast, the 27-year-old Henry was single and dominated by men left over from his father's administration, who were only interested in pursuing their private agendas. If he found it hard to let go of them, it was because he found it hard to let go of anything. He was in many ways the clingy type, owing not just to the insecurities of his youth but to an innate tenacity that made him stick to his course in the face of adversity. Fortunately, he had what his father always lacked, the saving grace of pulling back in time to avert disaster. The magnates demanded he change course by getting rid of his ministers of state – first Hubert, then Peter – and he duly complied. From now on, there would be no ministers directing the course of the realm, just him.

Clearly the bishops and barons hadn't thought their little rebellion through. When they insisted that Henry get rid of his ministers of state, they meant the personalities, not the positions themselves. In good hands, they were sureties for good government. Too late, said the king. Henceforth he would govern alone. He was finally rid of the old guard from his father's rule, the men who had bossed him around and taken advantage of him since he was a boy. It was because of them that people were still sneering he was *rex puer*, the boy king.[66] Now he would give his court a makeover and at last become the undisputed ruler of the land.

PART II

PERSONAL RULE

6

A COMPLETE MAKEOVER 1235–1237

The first sign that the king was planning to go it alone as the middle years of his reign began was his decision not to name anyone to replace Stephen Seagrave as justiciar. This office went back to the early days of Norman rule, developed initially, as the name implies, for judicial affairs, but was now identified with too much power in the wrong hands. Since the legal system hummed along without one, Henry could afford to keep the position vacant. He might have thought the same could be said of the chancellorship, as Ralph Neville had been compromised by the spate of illegal charters issued during the recent upheaval. His retirement from the scene would have removed another member of the old guard, but Henry took no action lest the bishops get the idea he was taking too much power into his own hands. But his new course was evidently clear. No more would he allow any one minister to exalt himself at his expense.

One of the officials harried by the defunct regime but since restored to favour was Walter Mauclerk. He didn't get his job as treasurer back, but was forgiven his £1,000 fine and sent on a special assignment.[1] Henry wanted him to go to Germany as his envoy. The emperor had put aside his differences with the pope and was working with him to preach a crusade. Both saw peace between France and England as vital for this enterprise, and thought that a marital alliance between England and the empire would induce France to put a halt to its expansionist policy. In November 1234 Frederick announced his intention to marry Henry's sister Isabella, and Gregory encouraged the proposal.[2] A German delegation led by Peter de Vinea, Frederick's chief minister, arrived the following February to hear the king's answer.

The spirit of the new consensus in government can be seen in how the members of the council needed three days to consider it. The main issue was the exorbitant £20,000 dowry demanded by the emperor. It would require a special tax, always a point of contention among the magnates, but Wendover says they were unanimous in their approval. Isabella was at the Tower in anticipation of this outcome and brought to Westminster to be viewed and vetted by the German party. She was reportedly so beautiful and adorned with such 'virgin modesty' that the men couldn't take their eyes off her. A wedding ring from the emperor was placed on her finger, shouts of 'Long live the empress' were proclaimed, and Henry went to work on planning an elaborate ceremony for her departure.[3]

Apart from the marriage negotiations, Henry also wanted Mauclerk to clear the air about a certain other matter. Peter des Roches had gone abroad in January 1235 and would probably be calling on his friend the emperor. Henry wanted to make sure that Frederick heard from him first what lay behind the recent troubles in England. In a letter carried by Mauclerk, he lashed out at his 'spiritual father' for leading him astray from the rule of the righteous. He had put his trust in him and the result was war and calamity. In all of this, Roches had stressed the 'plenitude of power', meaning that the authority of the king was absolute, and his subjects got what they deserved whether they deserved it or not. In choosing this term, Henry was also needling Frederick, because it was the same one used by the pope to justify his authority over the emperor. If Roches was indeed talking like that, he might find his friend Frederick not so happy to see him.[4]

Henry's busy itinerary that spring included planning his own marriage. Nothing ever came of the match with Peter of Dreux's daughter Yolanda. He had been talking to Henry while trying to marry her to Theobald, the puffy Count of Champagne. It was while still dealing with Marshal's insurrection that he began negotiating to marry Joan, the heiress of the county of Ponthieu around modern-day Calais.[5] The wedding took place on 8 April 1235 with Mauclerk exchanging vows for him. Since bride and groom were related within the degrees, a papal dispensation was required to make the marriage binding. Henry dispatched a set of proctors to Rome to get it by 27 May so she could be crowned on the feast of Pentecost. That was lightning speed in the Middle Ages, but he felt so secure in his relationship with Gregory that he also asked him to stand surety for the enormous dowry he owed Frederick.[6]

This particular date was also the first anniversary of the marriage between Louis IX and Margaret of Provence. That match came about after Raymond VII of Toulouse, still fuming over the way Blanche had bullied him into submission, began bullying his neighbour to the east, Raymond Berenger V of Provence. Both France and Provence saw a marital alliance as the best way to keep Toulouse in line. Raymond and his wife Beatrice had four daughters, and the eldest, Margaret, was said to be a 'girl of pretty face but prettier faith'. That made the 12-year-old an ideal bride for the overly pious Louis. They too needed a dispensation since they shared a great-great-grandfather in Alfonso VII of León and Castile.[7]

As emperor, Frederick was the overlord of both Provence and Savoy, the Franco-Italian province home to Margaret's mother Beatrice, but neither had asked for his blessing. Since Savoy controlled the Alpine passes, it was vital for Frederick to keep France from making too many inroads in that part of the world. The marriage of Louis and Margaret may have stirred him to look to England for a marital ally, but it definitely drew Henry's attention to the fact that Raymond and Beatrice's next daughter, Eleanor, was only a year or two younger than Margaret. Blanche had given every indication that she was not happy about his marriage to Joan: he would acquire Ponthieu, which was too close to Normandy. If she succeeded in blocking his dispensation, he could always marry this Eleanor. He could frustrate whatever designs Blanche had on Provence and Savoy by marrying into the same ruling family.[8]

First, he had to see his sister off to her new life as the emperor's third wife. He arranged a spectacular ceremony for it, starting in Westminster on 8 May and concluding with her departure three days later. Henry had her bedecked with rings, necklaces, jewels and a gold crown engraved with the four English martyr and confessor kings. Her silk robes and garments, beds, cushions and furniture, everything was over the top. The only thing Wendover found excessive were the silver pots and pans. Isabella's attending party was outfitted in blue trimmed with lamb fur, as opposed to the green worn by the king and his household. Gifts were lavished on the German delegation that arrived to escort her, and a party said to number in the thousands rode with her to the coast. There, brother and sister said goodbye, forever it turned out, which made the tears that passed between them all the more poignant.[9]

Isabella couldn't have had any illusions about the sacrifice she was making in becoming the wife of a man who was twenty years older, had children by his two deceased wives and acted more like an oriental *pasha* than a Christian emperor. He had imprisoned his last wife, Yolanda of Jerusalem, after she took exception to him making a mistress out of her cousin. In Germany, Isabella's ceremonial wedding had to be delayed because the crown prince, the man she might have married a decade earlier, had risen up in revolt. Frederick wanted to secure his domains before setting out on crusade and that meant sharing as little power as possible with his heir, who was the titular King of the Romans. By early July it was over and his son was in chains on his way to prison in Apulia, where he would die seven years later. On 20 July 1235, Isabella and Frederick were married in person in Worms. After four days of feasting the Bishop of Exeter led the bridal delegation homeward with many gifts for Henry, including three leopards in honour of the English royal arms.[10]

By then her brother had still not seen Joan, nor would he. Henry's proctors had been busy in Rome trying to get the dispensation, but so had the French side, trying to prevent it, and Blanche was turning up the heat on Joan's parents. In the end, it was Henry himself who recalled his men on 16 July and the marriage was allowed to lapse without validation. But because Blanche had denied Joan a king for a husband, she was obliged to find a suitable replacement and did so two years later in her widowed nephew Ferdinand III of Castile. He was twenty years older and had ten children, but their marriage was a success.[11]

Although Henry had decided on Eleanor of Provence by then, a story has come down that it was she who pursued him. Growing up in the land of troubadours and poets, she tried her hand at a romance called *Blandin of Cornwall* and sent it to Richard of Cornwall in the hope of making a good impression. Indeed, Richard was just then trying to get out of his marriage. He and Isabel's first two children had died in infancy, and her brother's war had doubtless strained their relationship. He sought an annulment on the grounds that he and her late husband Gilbert de Clare were related in the fourth degree. Gregory thought that was going too far and encouraged him to hang in there. When the pope's letter arrived, Isabel was pregnant again and in November 1235 gave birth to a son, Henry, who would grow to full manhood.[12]

Eleanor wasn't out to snare Richard in any case. The story has it that he was supposed to show her poem to his brother, who would be so enraptured with the knightly exploits of Blandin that he'd fall madly in love with the author and demand her hand, even without a dowry. Henry might have preferred it to have happened like that, because he found himself in the awkward position of having to inform her parents that he was already married. They should be patient, he was working on it. But the switch in brides was seen favourably by Blanche. Even if Henry was doing a little intriguing of his own, trying to insinuate himself into the family of her daughter-in-law, the important thing was that he no longer had any interest in Ponthieu.[13]

There was one more high-profile wedding to arrange that summer. Relations with Scotland had still not recovered from the Hubert saga and Marshal war. To ease tensions, 40-year-old Gilbert Marshal agreed to marry Alexander's 35-year-old sister Margery, whom Henry had almost married four years earlier.[14] It nearly didn't happen, because on 13 May 1235, just five days after Isabella's splendid farewell, Westminster was shocked by a murder committed in a boarding house just opposite the palace gates. A group of horsemen rode up in the night and killed one of the occupants, a clerk named Henry Clement. He had come on business for Maurice Fitz-Gerald, the Justiciar of Ireland, who was accused of complicity in Richard Marshal's death. Clement had been heard to brag that Marshal was a no good traitor who got what was coming to him. Gilbert Marshal was suspected of ordering the clerk's killing as revenge, but was cleared after a long process.

The actual killer was identified as William de Marisco, whose father Geoffrey was a former Justiciar of Ireland himself. Geoffrey and his family were also said to have betrayed Richard Marshal in the negotiations that led to his death, but Henry and most everybody else rather thought they had aided and abetted him during the struggle in Ireland. The Mariscos were imprisoned after hostilities ceased and forced to pay fines for their release. Father and son had come to Westminster to seek rehabilitation, and William came to believe that Clement was there to block it. He went berserk, slew him with a party of men, and went into hiding on Lundy Island in the Bristol Channel, where he took up pirating.[15]

★ ★ ★

The English delegation that arrived in Provence to negotiate a dowry settlement carried six sets of letters with them, each dated 15 October 1235. Henry was hoping to offset some of the £20,000 he owed Frederick with Eleanor's dowry and asked for £13,334 in the first letter, double what Louis got for Margaret. Raymond Berenger was just then so poor that he paid only a fifth of Margaret's £6,667 dowry, all of it borrowed, and had to pledge several of his fortresses as security for the rest.[16] Henry thought it was worth trying anyhow and drew up five other letters, each lowering the amount sequentially from £10,000 down to £2,000. His proctors were ordered to get the best deal they could and then produce the letter that most closely matched the figure. But no sooner had they set off than he realised he was tempting fate and rushed off a letter dated four days later telling them, in typical Henry fashion, that the amount didn't matter, they were to procure her even without a dowry. That's what he got in the end, but Raymond eventually squared things by giving Eleanor a marriage portion of £6,667 as well.[17]

It wasn't just past disappointments that made Henry eager not to lose this bride. His proctors would have given him a full report about Eleanor, her appearance, manner, bearing, and elocution skills. Even in an age where aristocratic women were invariably described as beautiful, the four sisters of Provence apparently really were. In Eleanor's case, hers was a graceful and elegant beauty.[18] Given Henry's flair for showmanship and spectacle, she would also have to be charming and light on her feet, be able to glide in and out of all the pageantry that he adored. All that she supposedly had, and her Occitanian accent would have piqued his desire further.

On 23 November 1235 Eleanor and Henry were married by proxy at Tarascon Castle in Provence. Her maternal uncle, William of Savoy, the Bishop-elect of Valence, led her party of escort, which included 300 horsemen if Matthew Paris can be believed. Theobald, a distant relative of Henry, paid their way for the five days it took them to pass through his territories. A French royal party was sent by Louis, Margaret and Blanche to escort them the rest of the way to the Channel. Henry was at Winchester for the Christmas court and proceeded to Canterbury to receive them after they reached Dover. What first impressions Henry and Eleanor had of each other, we don't know. Paris only says that Henry rushed into the arms of the messengers, and then, 'having seen the girl, he accepted her and married her'. The date was 14 January 1236.[19]

Henry was 28, gregarious, generous and sensitive to matters of taste and dignity. Unlike his father and grandfather, he fathered no illegitimate children, hordes in their cases, and there is no evidence he had even been with a woman prior to Eleanor. They had to consummate their marriage to make it binding, but given their lack of experience in these matters, it was likely that neither was in any rush after their wedding bed was blessed. The depth of their first intimacy together probably lacked the stress of Louis and Margaret's, who had to wait three days on the advice of his priests, and Frederick and Isabella's, whose act of consummation was determined by his astrologers telling him when the moment was right.[20]

Five days later the newlyweds left for Westminster in preparation for Eleanor's coronation the following day. Not even the king's second coronation fifteen years earlier rivalled the spectacle of this occasion. The streets of London were cleaned of filth, mud and odorous debris. Banners, garlands, candles and lamps were hung everywhere, and the outdoor entertainment put on for the throngs of people dressed in their Sunday best included a frenzy of horse racing. Afterwards the riders got into formation and rode out to meet the royal couple. They were decked out in costly silk garments and carried 360 gold and silver cups to be used at the coronation banquet. Their progress was announced by a troop of trumpeters whose playing further bedazzled the onlookers crowding the route.[21]

A special blue cloth was laid out between Westminster Palace and the abbey church for the royal procession. The three earls in the lead were John the Scot of Chester, carrying the sword of St Edward, John de Lacy of Lincoln waving a staff for crowd control and Gilbert Marshal of Pembroke with his own staff to make sure the way in front of Henry was kept clear in the church, banquet hall and everywhere else that day. Then came the king wearing his regalia, looking solemn and reverential under a canopy of purple silk held aloft by four barons with silver lances. Eleanor followed him, also beneath a silk canopy, her hair falling to her shoulders. She had a bishop walking on each side of her to offer support. Archbishop Edmund conducted the ceremony of the anointing and crowning, reciting prayers throughout that were naturally focused on biblical women who bore sons to succeed their fathers.[22]

And that was, after all, what she was there for. She would have known at that point that her sister Margaret was already a year and a half into her marriage with no baby in sight. While that could not have endeared her to her mother-in-law, some of it was Blanche's fault. Her domineering presence and Louis's submissiveness to her made Margaret's first years of marriage a miserable plight. One pitiful story has the young couple having to fraternise secretly in a stairwell that connected their rooms. At the first sign of the queen dowager approaching, the ushers posted outside their doors would knock so they could quickly get back to their rooms before she came barging in on one or the other.[23]

Margaret, however, was still only 14 years old, and many aristocratic brides, Blanche included, failed to have children in their teens. Henry's sister Eleanor was childless with William Marshal II, and their mother Isabella of Angoulême didn't have Henry until she was around 20, after nearly eight years of marriage to the lascivious John. More ominous was the case of their sister Joan, who at 25 was still childless after fifteen years of marriage to Alexander II. Some of the ill feeling just then between Henry and his brother-in-law was doubtless explained by the inability of the Scottish royal pair to beget an heir.

Nobody dared to talk about such things at the queen's coronation banquet. The feast was lavish, as it was meant to be, the citizens of London taking care of the wine and those of Winchester preparing the meal of venison and fish. Perhaps unknown to Eleanor was the absence of the presiding officer, Hugh de Albini, who had been excommunicated in a fit by Edmund because Hugh would not allow him to hunt in his forest.[24] Another squabble played out there cast Simon de Montfort against Roger Bigod for the right to be the king's steward. The office consisted of holding a water basin for Henry to wash his hands in during the meal – not the most glamorous of jobs, but the whole point was to be seen in close proximity to the king. Both the earls of Leicester and Norfolk had held the office in the past and neither Simon nor Roger was the type to back down. Somehow Montfort came out on top and wore his ceremonial robe as he carried himself with deference and kindness for Henry's pleasure throughout the evening.[25]

It's possible the men who came to fetch Eleanor from gloriously sunny Provence mentioned something about the weather in England. Nothing, however, could have prepared her for the rains that fell that winter of 1235–36. The rivers became swollen and destroyed mills and bridges and inundated cropland and marshes. The Thames burst its banks and flooded the palace at Westminster, forcing people with business there to get around by horse or boat. There were signs before her arrival that a deluge was imminent, such as a 'spurious sun seen by the side of the true sun', an omen of natural and spiritual powers that were best appeased before these things got out of hand.[26]

Since the leading men of the realm were going to be gathered for his wedding, Henry scheduled a meeting of the great council to take place following it on 23 January. The flooding forced them to relocate to the Priory of Merton, near today's Wimbledon, where Hubert had first sought sanctuary three and a half years earlier. The purpose of the meeting was to codify the work of judges performed since Magna Carta came into force in 1225, especially those rulings and discoveries following the civil war. This 'Statute of Merton' enacted laws that essentially formed the foundation of the later legal system. They included protecting the accused from dispossession unless convicted; imprisoning a person who ejects somebody from a property, loses the case but then ejects them a second time; allowing widows to recover the full value of their dower after winning a suit to recover it; and permitting landowners to make enclosures as long as they do not infringe the right of access of tenants. This last law was controversial because it approved the growing tendency of the wealthy to build their own private parks and fish ponds. The lords actually wanted to take the law further to demand direct involvement in the punishment of trespassers caught fishing or pissing in their ponds, but Henry refused, stating that breaches of the peace remained under his authority.[27]

Probably the hottest topic of debate at Merton was the secular view that children born out of wedlock whose parents married later on were still illegitimate. In the mind of churchmen, they were legitimate because they were solemnised during the wedding ceremony. Led by Robert Grosseteste, the new Bishop of Lincoln, they urged the magnates to bring English common law in line with canon law and end this nonsense.[28] Grosseteste personally appealed to his friend and chief justice of the king's court, William Raleigh, but did himself no favours by forcing Raleigh to read a tortuous fourteen-page letter where he even describes the dilemma of what to do if a child is born in the middle of his parents saying 'I do'. This is possible, he says, because 'giving birth is not an instantaneous action but a successive one, whose movement may even be interpreted by a period of inaction'.[29] Raleigh was more amused than impressed, and the law remained unchanged, doubtless to keep from upsetting untold numbers of probate transactions.

These meetings of barons, prelates, judges and clerks were hard to organise because they required a lot of travel, expense and coordination of everybody's time. In addition, these men were all busy with something or other and had to drop it for the few or several days it took to discuss what were generally petitions, law cases and other mundane matters. It was because of all the discussion involved that these assemblies gradually took on another name to distinguish them from the smaller king's council. One word that failed to take off was *colloquium*, but *parliament* had more luck because what they were doing was 'parlaying'. Later that year of 1236, the term entered the official record for the first time when a law case was deferred to 'parliament' for the following January.[30] But because Merton was an actual legislative process, where laws were debated and passed or rejected by a broad spectrum of the realm, it could easily be considered the first English parliament as the word is understood today.

If Henry and Eleanor didn't get much of a honeymoon because of government business, the one between Henry and the magnates following Marshal's insurgency was coming to an end. In April 1236 the council was reorganised into a body politic of twelve members, each sworn to serve the king faithfully as he in turn was sworn to follow their counsel. Eleanor's uncle, William of Savoy, had made such a good impression on Henry that he was asked to stay on after the wedding and become the head of his council.[31] It was known that William had tried to ingratiate himself at the French court after escorting Margaret to her marriage, but Blanche quickly dispensed with his services. She probably saw in him what the English magnates did, a glorified parasite, but the handsome, urbane, ambitious and worldly Bishop-elect of Valence was the kind of man Henry wished he had more of in his baronage.

As the second of seven sons, William had been forced by his father into clerical service as a way of securing his future. Henry had long known about him because the Count of Savoy had written to him in 1220 requesting a benefice for him.[32] So even back then William was freeloading off England, or at least that's how the barons saw somebody like him hanging around long after he should have left. Although a skilled diplomat and sometime warrior, he was the archetypal foreigner with his finger in every pie, and what bothered them most was that he had his eye on their pies.

But Henry was still hoping to reform his financial administration and needed someone like William to make it happen, not so much because of his executive abilities, rather his very newness to the land, his lack of any personal history with the magnates that would influence his decisions. In this case, it involved a complete overhaul of the sheriffdoms. To start with, there would be no more filling the office with barons, clergy or household knights. In the past this had worked because they were a symbol of strong royal authority in the counties, which was good for collecting the king's revenue. But then, as power went to their heads, the money to the exchequer dried up. The plan now was to appoint local gentry or knights as sheriffs, to serve only as custodians of the counties at the king's pleasure, and to make them answerable for all revenue in return for a salary and moderate 'entertainment'.

Pocketing the profits of the county farms had always been one of the perks of being a sheriff. With that gone, there was only the authority of the office, but even that was diminished with this new role of a salary-drawing custodian for revenue collection. Prelates and barons couldn't be bothered to serve under these conditions and gave way to minor officials appointed by the exchequer. The issue was more contentious with household knights like Godfrey of Crowcombe and Ralph Fitz-Nicolas, who had to be squeezed out of their sheriffdoms.[33] It was little wonder that William of Savoy generated so much hostility. Once again, a foreign bishop in the mould of Peter des Roches was cleaning house.

The political ramifications were only too obvious and came out in the open at a Parliament held at the end of April. Matthew Paris has the magnates wondering aloud, 'Why doesn't this fine fellow go to France and manage affairs there?'[34] Nothing irritated Henry more than his barons telling him whose advice he should follow. If they wanted to discuss it further, he would meet them at the Tower of London, and off he went. He was hoping to intimidate them with this sinister change of venue, and the barons balked at going there, afraid as they were that he would unleash his temper on them. Thinking better of their quarrel, the king reappeared at Westminster and Parliament continued, but he was insistent on William of Savoy staying. The reforms at least were working, evident from the fact that the value of the royal demesne alone was increasing by £800 a year.[35]

The mistrust continued to linger unabated from the latest conflict, however. In May Henry pardoned Peter de Rivallis, Stephen Seagrave and Robert Passelewe, but had Richard Siward, their former enemy, banished to Scotland. Siward had been rehabilitated and admitted to the council, he even carried a sceptre at Henry's wedding, but Richard of Cornwall hadn't forgotten how he rampaged through his lands during the insurrection. Richard told his brother it's either him or me. Siward was soon reinstated after his banishment, but then was imprisoned, this time at the connivance of Rivallis and Simon de Montfort. The harassment ended when Edmund of Abingdon secured his release on the grounds that he had taken the cross, as had Montfort, Cornwall and other nobles.[36] Doubtless they wouldn't be crusading together.

Still determined to consolidate his power, Henry cashiered long-serving steward Fitz-Nicholas and ordered Ralph Neville to turn over the seal, but here he was rebuffed. The chancellor said he had been given the seal by the common consent of the kingdom and could only give it up with similar consent. Henry must have found that excuse presumptuous, because he was still a minor when Neville was given the seal, but he backed off for the time being. Matters came to a head in June, when a group of nobles confronted the king at Winchester, where he had gone to stay with his bride. They charged him with colluding with the pope to get some of his charters revoked, again more allusions to the Roches regime. Henry denied it, but their suspicions were based on an embassy he had sent to Rome, on a mission most of them were guaranteed to view even less favourably.[37]

* * *

All the sniping at court didn't prevent Henry from paying attention to Eleanor and being sensitive to her needs. A natural tourist and guide, he chose to bring her to Winchester because it was both his birthplace and steeped in history associated with the Saxons and Alfred the Great. Eleanor knew all about the Saxons, but the king she was most familiar with was Arthur, the great Saxon slayer. Arthurian romances depicting this mythical king defending Britain from invading Germanic tribes had swept through Europe long before she was born.[38] How familiar she was with them before she arrived in England can only be imagined, but their honeymoon that summer of 1236 included a visit to Glastonbury. Two graves uncovered in the rebuilding of the abbey there in 1184 had been proclaimed by the monks to be those of Arthur and Guinevere, his unfaithful consort.[39] Whether it was Henry's idea or hers to go to see them, he was clearly being considerate of his young wife in what might be described as 'the little things', something unimaginable in his father, uncle or grandfather.

Eleanor got to see more of Britain when the court moved north in September to Newcastle, where Henry hoped to mend relations with Scotland. Alexander, emboldened by a secret alliance with Llywelyn and his new brother-in-law Gilbert Marshal, was again demanding Northumbria as his wife Joan's long overdue marriage portion. For the sake of peace, says Paris, Henry offered him £53 a year to keep the northern counties intact as they were.[40] He went further and made a more lucrative grant to his sister, perhaps in appreciation for her help at that time, but significantly it was made to her alone and not as a marriage portion for her husband's benefit. Providing Joan with an income of this sort made her more independent of Alexander, which was probably the intent given her evident unhappiness up north.[41]

Other events which touched Henry personally at this time were the death of Philip d'Aubigny, his first instructor as a boy, and the return of Peter des Roches. Philip had gone to Jerusalem the year before with the express intention of dying there, and his tomb can still be seen today at the Church of the Holy Sepulchre. Peter, who worked in tandem with Philip on Henry's education, arrived in England after an absence of nearly eighteen months. He was initially worried that Henry was still angry at him and asked Gregory to explore the possibility of him returning to Winchester. The king replied that the bishop had left of his own free will and was welcome to return any time. According to Paris, he was wracked by disease, and one of his first acts was to ask Henry for permission to draw up his will.[42]

Hubert also cropped up again that season, but under more scandalous circumstances. His daughter Megotta was 14 years old and the sole heir to her mother and father's lands. When several barons expressed an interest in her marriage prospects, word leaked out that she was, in fact, already married. It happened four years earlier, after Hubert fell into disfavour and Margaret sought refuge at Bury St Edmunds with Megotta and their ward Richard de Clare who, like Megotta, was then 10 years old. Some time around then, the two children were secretly married. Margaret told Hubert about it, but he didn't believe her. That's what he told Henry after he was ordered to appear before him with an explanation. Henry didn't believe him and suggested that Hubert had violated the oath he had taken to surrender all rights to the Clare wardship, including the boy's marriage, as part of the deal to get his lands back. Hubert again played dumb and said he knew nothing about a link between his lands and the oath. So Henry had to go through the whole process of having their agreement fetched from the chancery and shown to him. Hubert's response now was along the lines of, 'Oh, that one. I never liked it.' Doubtless with the king glaring at him, he asked for time to prepare a defence and was obliged with a hearing early the next year.[43]

More of the usual trouble from Hubert wasn't going to spoil the elaborate feast Henry had scheduled for 13 October. This day marked the translation of St Edward the Confessor and it was the first time he and Eleanor celebrated it together. Henry's interest in Edward may have gone back to his youth and the similarities in their lives, including abandonment by their parents and their preference of peace to war. His interest was doubtless encouraged by Peter des Roches, who cultivated Anglo-Saxon saints in his diocese despite all the flak he got for supposedly being anti-English. Henry had been left reeling by the violence of the last insurrection and the accusations that he had allowed it all to happen.[44] But he didn't just turn to Edward the Confessor for spiritual solace. Henry was also making a political statement, because whatever the truth of the Confessor's reign, he was seen as a good king. If Henry aspired to emulate him, then at least his critics couldn't accuse him of not trying. That was just the defensive part. The sharper edge of developing a cult around Edward was meant to remind all the grumblers that he, Henry III, was resurrecting the glory and durability of Norman and Saxon traditions embodied in the saint. The Confessor had withstood the treachery of his barons and the misfortunes of fate, and so would he. Three years before, he had had the monks of Westminster sing the *Laudes Regiae*, the ancient hymn in praise of the king, on the Confessor's feast day, and the practice had continued ever since.[45] Those barons who joined in the chant and those who didn't would be duly noted.

It's unlikely that he explained all this to Eleanor, or the one uncomfortable aspect about the Confessor he most certainly would not try to emulate. The married Edward had died childless, reportedly because he wished to remain chaste his whole life, which led to the Norman invasion and destruction of the Anglo-Saxon realm.[46] That, of course, was ancient history. Castles, mounted knights, feudalism and the French language had long been commonplace in everyday English life. But it was true in Henry's day, as it had been in Edward's, that a secure succession was the surest guarantee of peace and prosperity when a ruler died. Edward was only thinking of himself and not his people in refusing conjugal relations with his wife, and the result was calamity. Henry would not make that mistake, but nor was he going to rush things with his young wife. Even in those days it was well known that the older a girl was, the better chance she had a delivering a healthy heir.[47] He and Eleanor could wait till she was at least 14 or 15.

Eleanor would have seen for herself Henry's devotion to the Confessor in the great chamber he had modelled for himself at the Palace of Westminster. It occupied the ground where Edward reportedly died at the end of 1064, just as his rebuilding of the abbey next door in the Romanesque style was coming to completion. These quarters consisted of a long, narrow room running twenty-five metres from east to west, eight metres side to side, and ten metres to the ceiling. The foot of Henry's bed was set against the north wall at the east end, giving him a view of the Thames through two bay windows on his right. The posts supporting the canopy were painted green, his favourite colour, with gold stars sprinkled throughout, and in keeping with this theme, he had the chamber painted in a 'good green colour' to resemble a curtain. With the addition of murals, which Henry closely supervised, this hall eventually acquired the fabled name of the Painted Chamber.[48]

Opposite the head of the bed was a squint, or opening, in the wall that allowed Henry to follow the services in his private chapel next door without having to rise too early, and above that, for further inspiration, a life-size painting of Edward's coronation. The majestic bed and painting were meant to be centrepieces. The king regularly received visitors and held meetings in the chamber, even sessions of the council. In that year of 1236, he had a phrase inscribed over the entrance that said, 'He who does not give what he has, will not get what he wants.' The magnates who arrived there ready to deny him a tax were to be reminded that largesse worked two ways.[49]

The palace itself was not the orderly, coherent construction it appears today, rather various halls connected in no apparent order. The king's chamber was south of the great hall built by King William Rufus in 1097, and just south of it, running perpendicular from the east end, was the queen's own narrow bedchamber, also with a private chapel. Henry took care to make it comfortable and pleasing to the eye, intending as always that others should see it, too. Eleanor was fortunate that her husband was nothing like his father or grandfather, who were always on the move and therefore gave little thought to making this place or that one a home. Their escorts and retainers usually had to put up with whatever lodgings were available.[50] Westminster was ideally suited to become the main residence of the royal family because it housed the exchequer and the abbey that Edward had built. It was from this period that it essentially became the capital of the English nation.

Henry also lavished presents on Eleanor – something John would never have thought of doing for Isabella of Angoulême – including gold and jewelled rings, girdles and brooches. But everything came at a cost and Henry never could spend within his means. By the end of 1236 his debts could no longer be ignored and he had a summons sent from his Christmas court at Winchester for Parliament to convene at Westminster. On 20 January, perhaps in the Painted Chamber, the assembly was told that poor accounting at the treasury had left the king destitute, and a tax on movables (ultimately worth £22,500) was needed to get him on his feet again.

They murmured and growled, because of the previous taxes they had paid, including the recent collection for Henry's sister's dowry, but mostly because the recent reforms threatened to take back various properties that belonged to the crown. Those fears should have been allayed by William Raleigh appearing as the king's spokesman, he the jurist who had done the most to reverse the disenfranchisements under Roches. The magnates still asked for time to think about it. Gilbert Basset, the former insurrectionist and now one of Henry's boosters on the council, hinted that the grumblers were being disloyal. One of the nobles heading off into the other room rebuked him for this claim, insisting that they were all the king's friends.[51]

After four days, these friends came back with an affirmative answer, but with several conditions attached. First, they wanted a token purge of the council. Though they would have preferred removing William of Savoy or even Basset, they settled for Crowcombe. They also wanted to enlarge the council by three men of their choosing, one of them John Fitz-Geoffrey, the son of King John's long-serving justiciar, and one of the nobles originally disenfranchised under the reforms. Next, the magnates demanded that the tax revenue be kept by four knights in a safe place to ensure that it was only used for the benefit of the kingdom. And finally, to alleviate any thought that he had fallen under the spell of excommunication for failing to observe Magna Carta, the king was to order Edmund to renew the sentence against anyone who violated or improperly interpreted the charter.[52] On 28 January 1237 Henry took the extra step of confirming the document again, because he had been a minor when he issued it under his seal in 1225.

In addition to being the first 'parliament' recognised by that name, this may have been the most democratic assembly yet summoned to treat with the king. The Tewkesbury annalist says that 'citizens and burgesses' were present, and chronicler Thomas Wykes agrees that 'the people' were there.[53] It's likely that they were representatives of London or other towns where mercantile wealth easily rivalled the great estates. They would have been oligarchs, as anxious as the magnates not to pay any tax at all, and so the democratic innovation here only went so far.

Some time after the meeting broke up, William of Savoy left the realm to attend to other matters, but he was soon back. Matthew Paris uses his return to heap more venom on the king, saying he had abandoned the example set by Frederick and Louis, who 'did not permit their backs to be trodden upon by their wives and their relatives'. Like many of his monastic contemporaries, Paris was educated in France and wrote in Latin, so when he despaired of foreigners 'fattening themselves on the good things of the country', his sympathy was going to monks like himself, not to the English-speaking population toiling in the fields to keep him and the other monks clothed and fed.[54]

William's departure was probably related to the ongoing uncertainty on the Continent at this time over Frederick's war against the city states of northern Italy, causing Gregory all kinds of worry. Insisting that he was only after peace, the emperor summoned the monarchs of Europe to a conference at Vaucouleurs, neutral ground between the empire and France. Henry decided to send a delegation to represent him, including his brother Richard of Cornwall and Peter des Roches, but the bishop declined to go because of the way Henry had defamed him to Frederick. It would be most unseemly, he said, to show up with credentials from the same king who had lately said that he was not to be trusted under any circumstances. The conference was cancelled at any rate, presumably because

Louis intended to turn up with an army as his credentials, which unnerved Frederick.[55]

Henry had his own uncertainties about peace closer to home. In Wales, his half-sister Joan died that year and Llywelyn suffered a stroke. They had intended the succession to go to their son Dafydd, but Llywelyn's older, illegitimate son Gruffudd thought otherwise. Llywelyn wanted a treaty with England to secure Dafydd's position, but Henry fobbed him off, saying his most trusted advisers, Richard of Cornwall, William of Savoy and Simon de Montfort, were unavailable for the negotiations. Henry had also planned to send William and Simon to Scotland to bargain with Alexander, but that embassy too had to be called off. Naturally, the busyness of foreign councillors in all of this met with disapproval by Paris, who especially upbraids Montfort for being an 'infamous' influence after he joined John de Lacy and councillor Geoffrey the Templar in helping Henry arrange to have a legate arrive in England in June 1237.[56]

That had been the aim of the secret mission to Rome the previous year. The papacy liked dispatching legates as a means of exerting its authority from the centre, and the time was especially opportune with everything going on, from the preaching of a crusade and collecting money for it to the nagging mistrust of Frederick's intentions. Henry's request, however, was met with scepticism because it was remembered how he had asked for a papal legate but then retracted the request the last time he asked for one, when he was making no headway in France in 1230.[57]

Pope Gregory wanted to make sure that Henry was serious this time, not least because his Archbishop of Canterbury and other bishops were not going to like it. The official reply of his proctors probably included a wink that said, 'That's the point.' In bringing the last insurgency to an end, Edmund and his suffragans had subjected the king to all kinds of indignities, including complicity in the 'murder' of Richard Marshal.[58] They were going around presenting themselves as men of justice and protectors of Magna Carta, when in fact they clawed and scratched over money and power just like the barons and presumed to tell him what to do. The presence of a legate would subject the bishops to greater scrutiny and allow the king the freedom to act without Edmund glaring at him all the time.

The legate turned out to be the same Otto who had stirred up so much resentment on his last mission to England a decade earlier to collect a clerical tax. Perhaps hoping to put all that behind them, he got off to a good start by refusing all gifts and acting in a humble manner unusual for the office. In his first task, he succeeded in having the most fervent of enemies exchange the kiss of peace. These included Peter des Roches, Hubert de Burgh, Stephen Seagrave, Gilbert Basset and Richard Siward. He also managed to calm the situation after a tournament at Blythe between knights of the north and the south turned into an ugly brawl after the southerners got the best of their opponents.[59] He next accompanied Henry to York to conclude a treaty with Scotland in September. When Otto asked about paying a visit north of the border, Paris has Alexander advising him against it, saying that no legate had ever set foot on Scottish soil because many 'wild men dwell there, who thirst after human blood'. Alexander added frankly that he himself was unable to tame them. Otto was willing to take his chances and later convened a council at an abbey near Edinburgh to raise funds for the crusade.[60]

The terms of the treaty called for England to give Scotland 24 square miles of land with a yearly value of £200 as a marriage portion for Joan, for which Alexander would do homage to Henry. The continued lack of an heir up north was felt all the more keenly with the death in June of Alexander's distant relation John the Scot, the Earl of Chester. He was only 30 at the time and Paris claims that he was poisoned by his wife Helen, daughter of Llywelyn.[61] Like his uncle Ranulf, John had only sisters for heirs, thus leaving the succession to the earldoms of Chester and Huntington and the throne of Scotland all in doubt. It was agreed in York that Joan would accompany her new sister-in-law the Queen of England on a pilgrimage to Canterbury, doubtless to pray for an heir, maybe even one for Eleanor now that she was approaching the end of her second year of marriage.[62]

In November that year, Otto summoned a synod at St Paul's in London to enact various canons governing clerical conduct, among them revisiting the issue of concubines. Where Langton had been ready to punish the women, Otto gave priests one month to get rid of them or face suspension. He also spelt out the duty of the bishops, to be the 'model of the flock' and watch over their dioceses, with no mention at all about becoming involved in political affairs. But it was the issue of benefices that caused the most consternation among the prelates. Otto wanted to end pluralism, but the new Bishop of Worcester, Walter Cantilupe, the son of Henry's steward during his minority, used himself as an example of a holder of multiple benefices who would resort to anything to keep them. He therefore advised Otto to consult the pope first, 'for his own safety'. Suspecting that tempers might fray, Henry sent an armed guard to accompany Otto throughout the course of the synod.[63]

Edmund decided to bring these matters directly to the pope's attention. He was fed up with Otto anyway, as any archbishop forced to sit next to an enthroned legate would be, especially one like this, who wasn't even a bishop, but a mere archdeacon. It was outrageous that the Archbishop of Canterbury had to bow and defer in all matters of the English Church to this pretentious nobody. Otto was clearly enjoying his status and tried to keep him from going, but Edmund wouldn't listen and sailed the week before Christmas.[64]

The king was probably happy to be rid of him. Edmund was a dyspeptic old grouch who was guaranteed to cast a pall over his Christmas court, and the one this year at Westminster would be extra special. Forever the family man, he would be welcoming his sisters Joan and Eleanor, the first time all of them had been together in more than fifteen years. They would be joined by their cousin Eleanor of Brittany, still under confinement at 53 years old and no doubt happy to get away for occasions like these.[65]

Henry would be more generous than usual because he had a lot to be thankful for. At 30 years old, with more than twenty years on the throne behind him, he was finally in firm control of his life, with a loving wife and a court suited to his idea of kingship. The only sour note was his brother Richard, who was jealous of men like William of Savoy and Simon de Montfort and their hold over the council, and he didn't care for Otto, either. As far as Richard was concerned, the king was growing 'worse and worse in the madness he has conceived'.[66]

7

WAXING HOT AND COLD 1238–1240

Of all the councillors in the 1230s, none was more faithful than Simon de Montfort. He was almost destined to be a man Henry III would like, if only because he had the loyalty the king found more and more wanting in his native-born baronage. Nothing is known about Montfort's background in France except that his mother and father were famous crusaders who left him orphaned before he reached adolescence. In a youth dominated by war and destruction, he somehow emerged well educated and ready to make his mark in the world. The fact that he was even there owed to daring, ambition and a knack for getting things done. Like Henry, he was sharp-witted, short-tempered and a gifted speaker. Each was fiercely protective of his rights and privileges and had an almost insatiable drive to achieve his goals, but where Henry had the majesty of his office behind him, Simon had charisma and dedication. The dissimilarities between them only grew from that point on.

For example, their attitude towards faith. Henry saw religion as something for the senses, to be seen, heard, felt, smelt and touched, an outward expression of devotion that was good for the soul and offered incidental economic and political benefits. It was about incense and ritual and feeding hundreds of paupers on a daily basis, thousands for grand occasions. Simon was a more introspective sort, a lone man praying by candlelight in the middle of the night rather than kneeling in a cathedral glittering with gold. The pastoral preaching of the friars that stressed simplicity and good works had more appeal for him and softened his natural crusading ardour. But when the cause was at stake, he was hard as steel, not to be deterred and always leading with the edge of his commitment and sword. Henry was wax by comparison, but that made him equally formidable, in that he was able to form and reform himself with a capacity for resilience rarely matched in any age. In the final analysis, both men were tough, wilful and prepared to go the distance. The circumstances that brought them together or wrenched them apart ensured that no matter who came out on top, their contemporaries were witnesses to one of the great political duels of history.

The fall of the Roches regime provided the opportunity for a closer relationship to develop between these two. Simon had escaped the enmity that drove the Poitevins from court because he came from a different part of France and had become the lord of Leicester through inheritance rather than as a freeloading immigrant trading on loyalty to the king. But the barons were a resentful and envious lot who looked for any excuse to undercut anyone they saw as monopolising the king's counsels and favours. Like William of Savoy, Simon had no roots in the realm and that made him just another foreign interloper. He was going to need Henry if he hoped to succeed in his adopted country.

The estates that came into Simon's possession were in a dilapidated state and not likely to help him pay back the money he had borrowed to acquire them. The easiest way out of his morass of debts was to marry well, and Henry might have liked to make him the gift of an English heiress, but that would only fuel more resentment. A bride on the Continent was another matter, and in 1235 Montfort sought the hand of Mahaut, the Countess of Boulogne. She was several years older and had two children, but apparently she rebuffed him at Blanche's insistence. He fared no better with Joanna, the Countess of Flanders. That pursuit had reached the stage where Simon, according to a French chronicler, had to flee the Continent for fear of Blanche, who made Joanna swear in April 1236 that she had not married him nor ever would.[1]

Boulogne lay just across the straight from Dover, and Flanders, just east of Boulogne, was the destination of England's wool exports. Had Simon succeeded against the odds in marrying either countess, Henry would have had a baron strategically placed on the Continent to further his interests. He had to know that Blanche would never permit this any more than she did his own proposed marriage to Joan of Ponthieu, but Simon's marriage schemes reiterated to the French that the issue of his inheritance wasn't going away. If Henry was behind what were essentially two hopeless suits from the start, he may have hinted to Simon that he would remember his willingness to oblige. One mark of Henry's thanks can be seen in October 1236, when Simon took the liberty of issuing a charter as the 'Earl of Leicester' for the first time, even though the title was not yet his.[2] The king may even have promised to compensate him with a valuable match at home as soon as he could arrange something.

One widow who wished she was available was his sister Eleanor. Since taking her vow of perpetual widowhood three years earlier, she had busied herself with the management of her estates and wasn't afraid to turn to Henry for help when men like the Marshals tried to ignore or bully her. But he also took a sober view when she overreached and didn't hesitate to rule against her. Just the same, he made plenty of gifts of venison and oak to her, and for her twenty-first birthday gave her the royal manor and castle of Odiham, situated between Winchester and London.[3]

It was clear, however, that all the kindness and attention from her brother had to be curtailed now that he had started a family and children would be coming along soon. Or so they all hoped, because the royal pair were now approaching their second anniversary without any sign of impending parenthood. The queen was just 14, but her sister Margaret was 16 and still waiting to conceive after almost four years of marriage to Louis. One of the reasons for Joan's prolonged stay south of the border was so that the queens of England and Scotland could make a pilgrimage to Canterbury together in the hope of finding spiritual support for their dilemma.

According to Matthew Paris, the king's sister Eleanor also wished to become a mother at this time.[4] If she wanted to do something about it, her position as a princess sworn to chastity made it impossible. There was her honour and reputation to think of, not to mention finding a man of equal rank ready to come to her rescue. He would have to be a brave and audacious fellow indeed to risk the wrath of the king, archbishop and baronage all at once. But then, that was the kind of man Simon de Montfort was.

There is no record of when or where he and Eleanor met, but they certainly crossed paths during any number of state functions. He was seven years older than her, a 'handsome and strenuous knight' who was tall and beardless if his seal is any indication. She was described as beautiful and elegant, as might be expected for a daughter of Isabella of Angoulême. The physical attraction aside, both saw advantages in marriage to the other. Eleanor would get a husband from a renowned family, who had high standing at court and wasn't afraid of people like the Marshals. Simon would have a wealthy wife from a royal background, who was also related by marriage to the King of Scotland and the emperor. They were young enough to start a family and could go places with all the ambition that drove them.[5]

It's unlikely they risked sleeping together before informing Henry of their desire. He was a romantic who liked to be helpful, but he detested people taking advantage of him. The idea that they couldn't be absolutely sure she wasn't pregnant when one or both of them went to talk to him would have infuriated him. It would not just have been that she had broken her vow of her own volition, or had been seduced, but that he was forced to go along because it was a done deal, as if his permission didn't matter any more. Henry could be easily accommodating, frighteningly so it seemed to some, but the thought of a crossbow wedding wasn't likely to endear him to the nuptials.

Of course, marriage between the virtuous princess and foreign favourite was going to invite all kinds of speculation, none of it flattering. But there was nothing in Magna Carta stopping the king from agreeing to the match, save perhaps for the article on disparagement. But that had already been dealt with sufficiently when Eleanor was married to William Marshal II.[6] Simon may have lacked Marshal's rank of earl, but that could be fixed, and the Montfort family was at least the equal of the Marshals in the eyes of Europe.

The real problem was Eleanor's vow. The papacy would be happy to issue them a dispensation for a price, but Edmund would take it personally if she repudiated it, for a foreigner no less. He would definitely throw a fit, but then again maybe that was another incentive for Henry to give his approval. Allowing Eleanor to marry, on top of bringing in the legate, would further undercut the archbishop's authority. The old man did, however, like to hurl excommunications as if they were thunderbolts, so it was better for them to bide their time. It came when he left for Rome just before the Christmas court. Perhaps some time during those festivities Henry told Simon and Eleanor to meet him in his chamber on 7 January. In 1238, that was a Thursday.

On the appointed day, at the appointed hour, Henry led Eleanor and Simon into the small oratory that adjoined his chamber through a door next to his bed. There stood Walter, the chaplain of St Stephen's Chapel on the palace grounds. The ceremony was accompanied by mass and afterward the king gave the bride away. Paris describes the wedding as 'clandestine' because nobody knew about it except those four present.[7] Henry might have liked to have asked their brother to attend, but he didn't even consult him. Richard would only have come out against the marriage and rally the other barons to do the same. So Henry decided not to bring it up before the council, figuring that they could simply go ahead and let the others find out on their own. Then they would see. And did they ever.

For the first few days, nobody seemed to know anything. Then suddenly Richard of Cornwall was up in arms, and he was joined by Gilbert Marshal, who was naturally worried that Eleanor now had a husband to help press her claims against him. Richard was angry not just because Eleanor was his sister too, but he had also been shut out of the remarriage plans for his 15-year-old stepson Richard de Clare. It will be remembered that Clare had been married in secret to Hubert and Margaret's daughter Megotta. In October the previous year, she was on her deathbed. Since the boy was Henry's ward, he decided, with the council's approval, that he should next marry Maud, the daughter of John de Lacy, Earl of Lincoln. The price was £3,333, later lowered to £2,000. To Richard, it seemed as though Lacy and Montfort were always teaming up on the council to earn the king's favours. Megotta died in November and Clare and Maud were married on 26 January 1238.[8] By then, the rebellion was in full swing.

There was no fighting, just a lot of sabre rattling as Richard incited the barons to anger against the regime. The Channel ports remained loyal, but London, as usual, was ready to come out against the king. The legate tried to intervene, telling

Richard that he had a duty to stand by his brother in times of unrest, but he responded with a tirade that basically came down to the foreigner thing again. Instead of enriching the realm with his marriage, the king was squandering what wealth was left on all these outsiders who arrived with his queen. He should have sent them packing as Blanche had done in France and the emperor with their sister Isabella's retinue. Rogue councillors like Lacy and Montfort were reaping ample benefits for allowing Henry to pursue this misguided policy. England was a vineyard where all who chanced upon it gathered the grapes.[9]

Henry sent new councillor John Fitz-Geoffrey to negotiate a deal, but the barons wanted nothing less than an end to his personal rule. Since his oath to abide by Magna Carta seemed insufficient, they wanted to appoint four 'discreet' barons to the council with at least two in constant attendance, each sworn to impartiality and ready to offer redress. These 'conservators of liberties' as they were called were to include a justiciar and chancellor and have full knowledge of the workings of the government. They could be appointed or removed only by common assent, and if one of them died, the other three were to arrange his replacement. Parliament was only to convene at their insistence. And finally, all those who were a bad influence on the king were to be dismissed.

The terms were part of what became known as the 'paper constitution'. There is a debate over whether it actually belongs to this episode or to a later confrontation in 1244 when similar terms were revealed, but the intent of the barons to obtain a more active role in government was the same in both cases.[10] Henry's initial response might have been the same as his father's: 'Why not just ask for my kingdom?' What they were proposing was nothing less than a constitutional monarchy with the king shorn of real power. No matter what he did, these four officers would always dog his steps and sit in judgement over his acts as if they were his equals. Equally distasteful was their presumption to assume his prerogative of summoning Parliament. They would make Parliament a state institution and govern the kingdom through it as if he were simply a figurehead. He would rule at their pleasure.

The previous rebellion had been brought to an end with no thought of abrogating the king's natural and customary powers, just reminding him of what the law was. This was far worse, but even an absolutist like Roches was significantly unnerved by the united front to advise Henry to accept their terms. As the barons continued to collect arms to force a showdown, he asked for time, but not even Otto could get them to soften their stance. On 22 February the legate sealed the agreement on behalf of the king, but Henry wasn't through yet. Everything depended on his brother, or rather his price, and so he had Montfort and Lacy go to work on Richard while he moved to the Tower of London in case the situation got out of hand. In the end, Richard of Cornwall deserted after being offered presents and promises that included £4,000 for his upcoming crusade. The barons were confused and angry, probably at themselves because they should have known he would pull a stunt like this. Without him, however, they felt rudderless and gradually went home to continue their grumbling there. Paris says that Cornwall's fame was greatly 'clouded' by his indiscreet action, but that was just because the others didn't understand business as well as he did.[11]

There may have also been a more personal reason for Richard leaving the uprising he started in the lurch. His sister Joan fell ill in the midst of this excitement and was confined in Havering, northeast of London. Henry did his best to make her comfortable and after some time her health improved, but by 21 February she was drawing up her will. She died on 4 March 1238 in her brothers' arms. Henry had a marble tomb built for her at Tarrant, a convent in Dorset that had passed to Queen Eleanor's patronage. The choice probably reflected the friendship that had developed between the two queens in those last months they spent together. In memory of his sister, Henry spent £21 for silk altar cloths for the twenty-six churches between Tarrant and London. Alexander made no memorial offerings to her, nor did he make any effort to bring her body back to Scotland.[12]

Close as Henry was to his family, the recent events could only have taken a toll on him. He might have been inclined to take it out on the people at the centre of the dispute, yet he was lending money to Simon and Eleanor as the paper constitution was being drafted. They weren't out of the woods yet, and Simon made ready to journey to Rome to buy the dispensation for breaking Eleanor's vow. Henry furnished him with letters to the pope and more than £1,500, an extraordinary amount. Simon added £333 of his own, which an alderman of Leicester accused him of extorting from him.[13] It would take six weeks to get there as a horse gallops, but Henry also instructed Simon to meet the emperor along the way since he was now his brother-in-law, too. Given the anger they had stirred up among the other nobles, they both understood that he was free to take as much time abroad as he needed.

News had arrived that spring from Frederick that Isabella had given birth to a baby boy they named Henry in honour of her brother. The emperor was still trying to woo the king and Richard of Cornwall into greater cooperation in his war with the Lombard League of northern Italy. He wanted to stamp imperial authority on all his lands before departing on crusade, but the Milanese refused to buckle even after he trounced them at the battle of Cortenuova. As a good brother-in-law, Henry dispatched a regiment of English troops to assist Frederick in his siege warfare that summer. They were led by his former seneschal of Gascony, Henry de Trubleville, and included the king's protégé John Mansel.[14]

Savoy was a fief of the empire, so William had to join the campaign too and left with the regiment. The departure of him and Montfort from the council did nothing to calm the recent spate of anti-alien hysteria. Otto found that out when his household got into a scuffle with some students at Oxford, leaving one of his kinsmen dead. A riot ensued as the students next demanded Otto's blood, that 'plunderer who perverts the king and enriches foreigners with spoils'. He hid out in the church tower until darkness fell, then made his escape. Henry was livid when he heard what had happened and ordered the Earl of Surrey to march in and suppress the university.[15] Thirty students were imprisoned and Otto put the city under interdict, but Grosseteste was the bishop with authority over Oxford and threatened to retaliate with his own ecclesiastical penalties if the students weren't released. A compromise was worked out that had the perpetrators humble themselves before the legate, and in return the university was allowed to reopen, at least until the next spring riot.[16]

★ ★ ★

Peter des Roches had evidently put aside the hurt he felt over Henry badmouthing him to Frederick and helped him resolve the crisis with both the barons and students. Now well into his sixties and worn out by a life lived at full throttle, he retreated to his manor at Farnham, not far from Odiham, and died there on 9 June 1238, bringing more than forty years of service to the crown to an end. In his obituary, Matthew Paris called Roches's death an irreparable loss, a surprising lament given that Roches had been the most conspicuous of the foreign influences despised outside the court. But relations between the pope and emperor were on the verge of unravelling again, and Paris remembered that it was Peter who had worked diligently to restore peace between them.[17]

The loss was understandably more personal for Henry. He had grown up in Peter's household, got all his first impressions of life under his tutelage and was crowned by him as a 9-year-old boy. Peter could never be a foreigner to Henry the way others saw him, but then he never quite became a real father figure, either. Their relationship was well past its prime by the time Peter gained his former ward's unwavering trust, but then threw it away just to exact revenge on Hubert. In doing so, he plunged Henry into a painful and embarrassing affair from which neither fully recovered. But he had been a very capable man, whether in clerical robes or armour, and as the embodiment of the quintessential European courtier, Henry could only wish he had more men of his stamp at court. William of Savoy was that type, and when the monks gathered to choose a new Bishop of Winchester, Henry informed them that he would like to see William replace Peter. They didn't need to be reminded that Roches had been foisted on them in 1205 by King John, or that Henry had been born in Winchester and so expected extra consideration in their choice.

William was already the Bishop-elect of Valence, between Lyon and Avignon in southern France, but like Peter he was a warrior and diplomat at heart. He was just then engaged in Frederick's war against Milan, and this was reason enough for the monks to reject him as a 'man of blood'.[18] They proposed the eminent justice William Raleigh instead, but that just made Henry laugh. Raleigh, he said, had killed more men with this tongue than William had done with a sword. When the king persisted with William of Savoy, the monks forgot about Raleigh, but settled on Ralph Neville for the post, thinking rather innocently that Henry would be happy to reward his faithful chancellor in this fashion. Neville was the bishop of nearby Chichester, but that was small potatoes compared to Winchester, whose £3,000 in annual revenue put it on par with the richest earldoms. He happily accepted, but again they had all read the king wrong. He called the monks fools and heaped abuse on the 'impetuous and perverse' Neville. In August, he went further and took the great seal away from him after more than twenty years in his possession. He then sent a team of clerks and lawyers to Rome to get Neville's election quashed.[19]

The monks' opposition to William of Savoy as a soldier and foreigner was rather petty considering the relatively good relations they had had with Peter des Roches. The same could not be said of the relations between Edmund and his monks of Canterbury, who quarrelled endlessly about their functions and jurisdictions. His mission to Rome was all about getting the papacy to back his ultimate authority and to remove Otto at the same time, but the monks of Canterbury got there first with some sharp lawyers. A bitter debate ensued, with Simon Langton doing his best to accuse the monks of committing shameless forgeries and burning incriminating documents. Pope Gregory wished to remain neutral and referred their bickering back to the judges in England. He did invite Edmund and the other prelates then in Rome to a splendid banquet, but the archbishop had a bad feeling about it and stayed away. Some time during the feasting, a cardinal's nephew was assassinated in front of the pope and other merrymakers. Edmund put it down to divine providence that he had not been there to witness the brutal act.[20]

Matthew Paris also put it down to providence that another assassin failed around this time. The court was at Woodstock on 9 September 1238 when a 'certain learned esquire' raved like a lunatic that Henry had usurped the kingdom from him and should now give it back. Several attendants rushed upon him, intending to beat and drive him away, but Henry took mercy on the fool and ordered them to desist. That night the man crawled through a window into the king's bedchamber with a knife, but went into a frenzy when he found it empty. One of the queen's chambermaids heard the racket and alerted the attendants. They had to break down the door to seize the intruder, who admitted after a struggle that he had been sent there to kill the king. Henry set aside all mercy and ordered him dragged, drawn and quartered, perhaps the first known recorded case of this type of execution in England.[21]

The would-be assassin had been sent by William Marisco, who was still at large on Lundy Island after murdering Henry Clement three years earlier. Orders were given to apprehend him and his pirates on the island, but it wasn't until 1242 that they were captured and brought to London to be tried, dragged and hanged. In the aftermath of this attempt on his life, Henry ordered iron bars fitted across the windows to all his bedchambers. Even the outflow of his latrine at Westminster was fitted with a grille, not so much an indication of paranoia, rather his usual attention to detail. Henry may even have started sleeping with the queen more, because it was being in her chamber that night that saved his life. They were almost certainly locked in a snug embrace when the madman struck. She soon discovered that she was pregnant and would give birth nine months and eight days after this harrowing call.[22]

To believe Paris, there were worries that the queen might be barren, and that made the birth of a son to her sister-in-law Eleanor on 26 November welcome news. The succession was assured, he proclaimed, even though Richard of Cornwall's son was already 3 years old at the time. Montfort had returned from the Continent in October with the dispensation for his marriage and headed to Kenilworth Castle to be with Eleanor in the final stages of her confinement.[23] Since the court was only 42 miles away at Woodstock, the king gathered up his retinue and journeyed to see the newborn Henry, the third nephew named after him. He may have been one of the godfathers at the baptism conducted by Alexander Stavensby, who was still trying to make amends to the king since opposing him during the Marshal insurgency. The bishop reportedly fell ill during the ceremony itself, but recovered sufficiently to leave Kenilworth and go about his functions. He was in Andover the day after Christmas when he died of a stroke.[24]

The court moved to Winchester for Christmas that year, and Paris cynically suggests that Henry chose this venue just so he could plunder the profits of the vacant see to use for an extravagant celebration. Only his charity and almsgiving made him worthy in the monks' eyes, it was said, but the king was definitely in no giving mood when Gilbert Marshal and his knights invited themselves for breakfast. They were refused entrance and had to be driven back by the doorkeepers when they insisted on crashing the royal party. Suspecting that Henry was behind the snub, Gilbert returned to his abode and invited everybody within shouting distance to join him at his breakfast table. He would teach the king what Christmas was all about. Yet he was bothered by Henry's apparent ill will towards him and resolved to find out what was behind it. Savvy courtiers knew that it was best not to approach too soon after falling out, but Gilbert either didn't know or didn't care and sent his lieutenants the next day to inquire about it.

Henry denounced this as more impudence. 'What's this now? Where does Earl Gilbert come off threatening me in this manner?' He told them to remind Gilbert that his brother had been a 'bloody traitor' who deserved his wretched end, and it was only through the intercession of the archbishop that Gilbert was allowed to succeed him as the Earl of Pembroke.[25] He could have added that Gilbert had been stirring up aggression in the Marches, had made common cause with the King of Scotland against him and had recently joined the rebellion sparked by the Montfort marriage, the idea being that he was infused with the same disloyalty as Richard Marshal. On top of all this, Gilbert had defaulted on the dower payments to Eleanor de Montfort. As surety for the money, Henry was forced to cover the arrears from the treasury.[26] He was fed up with Gilbert's insubordination and free-loading and so had told him to go find his breakfast elsewhere that festive season.

As a parting shot, Henry might have noted that Gilbert should think about emulating Simon de Montfort if he hoped to win back his favour. Simon had arrived in England nine years earlier with a single knight on loan and the most tenuous of claims. Now he was the king's brother-in-law and could look forward to spending many a happy Christmas in his company. On 2 February 1239, as the court was gathered in the great hall of Winchester for the feast of Candlemas, Henry invested Montfort with the title of Earl of Leicester. He had withheld it up to that point because he was wary of creating further resentment over Simon's spectacular rise, especially among those who saw him as a foreigner reaping the rewards that might otherwise come to them. But now that he was married to Eleanor, he needed a title more becoming to the husband of a princess. On that occasion Montfort could not have missed the painting of the Wheel of Fortune on the eastern gable of the hall. Henry had had it commissioned in 1236 during the construction of the great hall, probably a manifestation of his belief in charity. Fortune was fickle, and those without 'give' might find a bitter lesson in store for them come the next spin of the wheel.[27]

Nobody was more aware of this than Ralph Neville. Around that time, the pope quashed his election to become the new Bishop of Winchester. He had done the same to him a decade earlier when he aspired to be the Archbishop of Canterbury, only this time it had nothing to do with his fitness for the post. The king didn't want Ralph there and Pope Gregory obliged him, nothing more. The monks were forced to hold another election, but it took almost a year to obtain what should have been routine permission. They would have been justified in accusing the pope of more pandering to the king.[28] Henry was obviously trying to buy time for William of Savoy to return from abroad, and for himself to continue enjoying the revenue of Winchester while its episcopal seat remained vacant. The monks could see the king spending the next Christmas in their midst as well, living and entertaining lavishly and making them pay for it.

The pope was playing along because he had his own difficulties to deal with. He was well into his eighties, but determined as ever to launch a crusade while still in command of his faculties. He had counted on Frederick to make it happen, but realised that he had been deceived when his offer to mediate the conflict in northern Italy was spurned. The emperor was using that war not, as he claimed, to fortify his position at home before leaving on crusade, but rather as a prelude to conquering all of Italy. When he next married his illegitimate son Enzio to the heiress of Sardinia, which the papacy considered part of its dominions, that was it. In March 1239 Gregory excommunicated and anathematised Frederick, for the second time. Frederick replied by declaring that if anyone needed to be deposed, it was the pope.[29]

The rupture could not have come at a worse time. The crusader states in the Holy Land were coming under increasing pressure as the Saracens fled before the Mongols. The Latin Christian Empire was losing ground to the Greek Christian Empire and needed help as well.[30] With the Holy Roman Empire now an avowed enemy, Gregory needed crusaders in Jerusalem, Constantinople and Rome all at once. Henry hoped the pope and emperor could settle their differences, but he was prepared to choose sides. So far, his marital alliance with the empire had brought him no advantage in regaining his Continental lordships. The one time Frederick made a show of force against Louis, he backed down when the King of France refused to be intimidated.[31] Gregory, on the other hand, had shown that he could be quite useful. He was helping Henry get the kind of bishop he wanted in Winchester and had allowed Otto to prolong his legateship, thereby ensuring that the cantankerous Archbishop of Canterbury remained marginalised.

With the queen about to give birth, Henry was mindful to spend these days in Westminster. He wanted the child to be born there, on the ground hallowed by the venerated Edward, and if it was a boy, he would be named after the Confessor as well. It was a bold move, resurrecting an English name for an English king, something unheard of since the Conquest. It would also dispel all the grumbling about his wife's relations having too much influence at court. Giving him a name more common in her family, like Amadeus or Boniface, would confirm the barons' worst fears.

The main thing is it had to be a boy, and on the night of 17–18 June they all got their wish. For the queen, not quite 16 years old, it was the greatest relief, producing a healthy heir as she was expected to do. Not until the following year did her sister in France finally give birth. It was a girl, and so terrified was she of Louis's reaction that she asked the Bishop of Paris to intervene for her.[32] In London, there was nothing but rejoicing at the thought of having a future king they could call their own, Edward of Westminster. Four days later the infant was taken to the abbey next door and baptised in a grand ceremony. Normally the Archbishop of Canterbury would have had the honour, but the legate outranked him and so he had to settle for merely confirming him. Assisting Otto at the font was Roger Niger, the Bishop of London, and Walter Mauclerk, the Bishop of Carlisle. The seven nobles chosen to serve as Edward's godfathers included his uncles Richard of Cornwall and Simon de Montfort, William Raleigh and Richard's old guardian Peter de Maulay.[33]

While it was important for Edward to be born in Westminster, Henry and Eleanor had planned all along to raise their family 24 miles upstream at Windsor

Castle. Founded by William the Conqueror on a bluff overlooking the Thames, it was far more secure than Westminster Palace, or even the Tower of London for that matter, and it offered something of a country retreat away from the noise and grime of the city. It was also on the way to other royal palaces like Clarendon, Marlborough and Woodstock. Coming back from one of their stays in the west of the country, Henry might leave the family at Windsor and continue on to Westminster, deal with a host of government business and receive visitors, then head back there for a few days, five on average, and continue with his family upcountry or return to Westminster alone.[34]

Work had begun on making the castle environs more homely shortly after their marriage. New apartments were built with tiled floors, fireplaces, en-suite toilets, beautifully painted walls and windows that opened into the garden. Eleanor's chamber was adorned with a stained-glass window depicting the Tree of Jesse, a clear reminder to her to be 'fruitful and multiply'. Although Eleanor was also determined to be a nurturing mother, during these crucial child-bearing years the infant Edward was mostly cared for by two wet nurses, Alice and Sarah, and by Sybil Giffard, who had stayed with the queen during her confinement and acted as midwife. Having done her job so splendidly, Henry made Sybil the impressive gift of a £10 annual pension.[35]

* * *

Gifts started pouring into Westminster in honour of the newborn. The king quibbled over the value of some and ordered the couriers to return them for something more befitting the occasion. 'God gave us this child, but the king sells him to us,' was the wry comment of one court observer.[36] Notorious as Paris is for embellishing his accounts, Henry's actions over the next few months suggest that there may have been some truth in this claim. Becoming a father at 31 seems to have left him feeling insecure about how he was going to pay for everything. A figurehead king could easily live off his income, but not a king whose ambition included massive building and renovation projects, almsgiving and an endless cycle of foreign policy initiatives.[37] Two rather unseemly episodes illustrate the anxiety Henry must have felt.

First there was old Hubert de Burgh. Suddenly, out of nowhere, he was ordered to stand trial again on all the charges dating back to his dismissal in 1232. He had seduced Margaret of Scotland, engineered the fall of Poitou, tried to kill Henry at Woodstock and so on. The most revealing charge had to do with Henry's marriage negotiations while Hubert was justiciar. Hubert was alleged to have told one prospective bride's family that Henry was 'squinty-eyed, silly, and impotent; had a sort of leprosy; was deceitful, perjured, weak, and more a woman than a man; he only vented his rage on his own followers, and he was entirely incapable of enjoying the embraces of any noble lady'. It's not just incredible that he would describe the king in this fashion, hinting that he was deformed, monstrous, effeminate and homosexual, but that Henry had no qualms about it becoming, as it were, public record.

As for why the king decided to go after his old mentor again, Paris asserts that it was money. If Hubert died under indictment, his entire estate would revert to the crown. In the end, an agreement was reached in August that called for Hubert to transfer four of his castles to the king in return for dismissal of the case. Hubert lived another four years, dying at his manor in Surrey on 12 May 1243 and taking the title Earl of Kent with him. What, if anything, Henry had to say about the passing of the man who had been most instrumental in the formative years of his kingship is unrecorded, but Paris lauds him as one who 'preserved England for the English'.[38]

Somewhere in the middle of Hubert's latest tribulations, on 9 August 1239 to be exact, the court gathered for the queen's churching, the ceremonious act of blessing and purification following childbirth. Never would Henry put on a more embarrassing display of his temper than the scene that followed the arrival of Simon and Eleanor de Montfort among the guests. He inexplicably rounded on Simon, calling him an excommunicated man and forbidding him and Eleanor from attending the ceremony. Not knowing what to think, the couple left and crossed the water to Southwark, where they were staying at the palace of the late Bishop of Winchester. Henry, remembering he had lent it to them for their stay in London, now sent orders for their eviction. That must have left the Montforts feeling more confused and hurt than ever, and, going against the well-known prescription to let the king cool off first, they went back to the ceremony to find out what was behind his outburst.

Now Henry really went berserk. He accused Simon of seducing his sister, bribing the pope to make their marriage lawful and naming him, Henry, as security for his outstanding debts. He worked himself up into such a fury that he even ordered Simon taken to the Tower and locked up. By then, Richard of Cornwall had had enough and refused to allow it. The Montforts weren't taking any chances and fled to stay with his kin in France.[39] And like that, Simon de Montfort had tumbled from favour like Peter de Roches and Hubert de Burgh before him, only without any hint that it was coming. But because he was family, and the king regained his composure as always, he would inevitably be back. There was no denying, however, that the excruciating incident, which played out in front of their friends and peers, was a turning point in their relations, and the warmth of their early years was gone forever.

Why this happened can be explained by the impending arrival of another important visitor. Thomas of Savoy was William's brother and so another of the queen's uncles. Like William, Thomas had been destined for a career in the Church, but he too was a mixer by birth, always angling somewhere for political and financial advantage. Some time that summer, Thomas had acquired the debt long owed by Montfort for his earldom. Originally, the debt was £200 for Ranulf, and when he died in 1232, the amount was assigned to Peter of Dreux through their Breton connection. That money had increased over the years, either through interest or new loans, to £1,900. The irony here is that whatever money Simon had been borrowing from Peter came from the subsidies Henry was providing. The king was giving money to one sponger, who lent it to another, who named him as security. This meant that if Simon didn't pay up, Henry would have to give Peter the same amount all over again. Peter certainly needed all the money he could get for the crusade he was planning, but rather than call in the loans through Henry, who might have told him to go to hell, he brought suit at the papal court. Simon was threatened with excommunication, but in the end a deal was worked out to put Thomas in possession of £1,340 of the debt, probably bought at a discount from Peter.[40]

After all Henry had done for Simon, and not just giving him the earldom and his sister in marriage, but also making various loans and gifts over the years to him, he couldn't help but see his part in this transaction as shameless. But that alone probably didn't set him off on the day of the queen's re-entry into public affairs. Archbishop Edmund had refused to accept the Montfort marriage and tried to prevent Gregory from legalising it. According to a later story, he even cursed Eleanor and all her children.[41] Since he was presiding over the ceremony of the churching, he might have whispered some innuendo that scandalised the king, or at least made him regret all the problems he had had on account of the marriage. With the seediness surrounding the money and Simon taking advantage of him like this, it all came together at a point sure to provide the maximum exposure and number of witnesses. Henry may have even wanted it that way, to make such a violent eruption against a trusted courtier that none of them ever forgot it or tried something like that again.

A week later he received Thomas of Savoy in great state, again ordering the filth of the streets of London to be cleaned up. Thomas was a man well worth courting, because he had recently married Joanna of Flanders, the countess whom Montfort had pursued earlier. The wool trade with Flanders was vitally important for England's prosperity, and Henry agreed to a £333 subsidy to Thomas in support of it. Although Flanders technically fell within the French sphere of influence, Thomas owed allegiance to Frederick. The enmity between pope and emperor was forcing the Savoyard brothers to take sides like everyone else, and over the course of that summer they were edging towards the papal camp. When the bishopric of Liège in Flanders fell vacant, Thomas tried to promote his brother William for the post over the imperial candidate and he got Gregory's backing for it.[42] Henry still wanted William for Winchester, meaning he had the pick of three bishoprics at his disposal. In the end, he got none of them, because he died around 1 November 1239 at Viterbo, where it was said that he had gone to make arrangements to lead the papal army against his former lord Frederick. The suddenness of his death gave rise to rumours he had been poisoned, which wasn't altogether a bad thing to someone like Paris, who called William of Savoy a 'spiritual monster and beast with many heads'.[43]

Where Henry's money worries took on the form of policy concerned England's Jewish community. The booming economy had accelerated the need for ready capital and they supplied it through loans denoted on bonds kept in *archae*, or chests. By this time, the Jewish community controlled approximately £135,000, almost a third of the liquid assets in the kingdom, and there was a separate Jewish exchequer for managing all this business. They had always paid the king a moderate tax averaging about £1,700 a year, but on 21 June 1239, Henry ordered their leaders imprisoned and not released until a third of the value of their bonds and possessions were handed over to the crown. In November the council adopted more legislation enforcing the cap of 43 per cent annual interest on their loans and putting a moratorium on accumulating interest charges.[44]

The crackdown coincided with a papal bull of 9 June calling for the seizure of the Talmud, allegedly for inspiring blasphemy. With his crusading fervour worked up, Gregory ordered secular rulers to take action, but realistically expected only the King of France to respond with any conviction. Louis, who believed a good thrust of the sword was the best way for laymen to deal with blasphemy, did not disappoint. French rabbis were arrested and their books confiscated, culminating in the condemnation of the Talmud by the University of Paris. At first Louis was restrained by the Archbishop of Sens, but when that learned man suddenly died, it was seen as divine judgement, and the French king publicly burned every copy of the Talmud he could find.[45]

Henry preferred extortion to destruction as his gesture to papal-inspired anti-Semitism. Instead of burning the Talmud, he seized copies and sold them back to their owners. But hard times were certainly ahead for the Jews of England. Henry's move against them was no one-off blow as it had been in the past. He set out to exploit the Jews as a stop-gap measure in his finances.[46] He may have convinced himself that it was part of his mission to convert them, by throwing their livelihood into turmoil, but the sheer volume of their assets could have only made him wonder why he hadn't thought of siphoning off their wealth before. Over the remaining twenty years of his personal rule, Henry raised his income by almost a third in this fashion, far more than from any other source.[47]

Another controversial source of income came from vacant sees. Unlike his Norman forebears, Henry did not deliberately set out to deprive England of bishops just to add more Church money to his treasury, but he did insist on having a voice in who his magnates were, whether spiritual or lay. Throughout his reign,

Henry appealed eight episcopal elections, or 11 per cent of the vacancies, to the papacy. Sometimes all it took was a little manipulation to get his way, as in the case of Hereford. A local praiseworthy canon had been elected in 1239, but was persuaded to resign, according to Grosseteste, amidst bribery and intimidation. Elected in his place the following year was Peter d'Aigueblanche who, as the name shows, was another foreigner. He had come to England with William of Savoy and impressed the king with his facility of language and administration. Henry doubtless sensed the skilled diplomat he was to become and knew he needed to find a bishopric to reward him for his services and add prestige to his authority. Hereford was nowhere near as wealthy as Winchester, but it could provide adequate provision for the family members and friends sure to follow Peter.[48]

In finding positions for newcomers, Henry was careful not to upset the patronage queue. The diocese of Coventry and Lichfield fell vacant before Hereford, but Hugh Pattishall had been serving as treasurer since the shake-up of 1234, long before Aigueblanche began his rise, and got the post. The public servant who stood at the absolute head of the queue was William Raleigh, and the canons of Coventry and Lichfield originally wanted him. He declined, obviously preferring to be the bishop of a more lucrative diocese like Winchester, but since the king blocked his way there, he took the next best opening, at Norwich. And then William of Savoy died, meaning Winchester might be available to him after all.

Not if Henry could help it. He already had another candidate in mind: William's younger brother Boniface, the Bishop of Belley near the French Alps. He had never met him, but all indications suggested that he was another very able fellow like his brothers. To clear the way for his election, Henry installed another foreigner, Prior Andrew of Brittany, to run the convent at the head of a royalist party of monks. Their brethren resented the intrusion and claimed that strong-arm tactics were used to soften them up. Apparently not enough, because when the committee-to-elect came together, they voted three in favour of Boniface, but four for William Raleigh. Henry was livid. The monks were only doing it to spite him, and he immediately asked Gregory to quash this second election as well. He even got nine of the earls to write letters of support for his position.[49]

Senior primates like the Archbishop of Canterbury and Bishop of Lincoln were outraged by the king's interference. After Christmas court, again celebrated in Winchester, the bishops assembled in London on 13 January 1240 to demand an end to what they called oppression. They gave Henry a list of thirty complaints prefaced by a reference to Magna Carta which, they said, obliged him to respect ecclesiastical liberties.[51] Indeed, the first clause of the charter specifically guaranteed the rights of the Church, in particular free elections, but that was in the original version of 1215, the one forced on King John. It had been removed in the 1216 version to keep Louis VIII from using it to elevate his supporters during the civil war.[52] If Stephen Langton had tried to get it reinserted into the charter sealed by Henry in 1225 and confirmed in 1237, he failed. The prelates could argue for no more protection under Magna Carta than whatever was enjoyed by all free men of the realm, and that was the point. The bishops had given up any hope of getting the pope or legate to back them up in their quarrels with the king. From now on, they would appeal not to Scripture or canon law to maintain their rights, but to Magna Carta. The struggle between the sceptre and mitre in England would be an English-only affair if they could help it.

Henry appeared to sympathise, but he had a pretty clear idea about his own rights. When Edmund asked Gregory to allow him to fill clerical positions that had been vacant for more than six months, Henry countered that this was contrary to his royal dignity, and the pope, of course, sided with the king. Gregory was preparing to impose a clerical tax for his crusade against Frederick and wanted to ensure Henry did nothing to impede it. The abbots and bishops protested against extortion like this, and for making war against another Christian no less, but Edmund was worn out by the endless strife in his life and quickly capitulated. He turned over £530 and advised his brethren not to resist. Their only comfort was some *schadenfreude* in knowing that the foreigners beneficed in England had to pay the most, up to a fifth of their earnings.[53]

They weren't the only ones dismayed by what they saw as the king's 'infatuated obedience' to the papacy. Frederick reproached him for allowing the publication of his excommunication in England and the collection of gold and silver for the papal war chest. He demanded the expulsion of Otto and a complete turnaround in Henry's attitude, otherwise he might be inclined to repay him in kind. But Henry was already in deep. Thomas of Savoy had again arrived for his subsidy and to raise money for a planned attack against the imperial party in Flanders. That ignited a conflict involving the empire and Toulouse against Flanders, Provence and France, which was only diffused when Thomas retreated and Frederick gave Louis assurances of his goodwill. Once again, the emperor was cowering in front of the King of France, and it had to make Henry wonder if their alliance was ever going to pay dividends.[54]

The only indication that there was opposition in the council to Henry's entanglement in these affairs comes from his dismissal of Simon the Norman in April 1240. His service to the king went back a decade, and so high had he risen in his confidence that Henry gave Simon control of the seal after taking it from Neville. He was chosen as one of the godfathers to Edward and represented the king at the papal court in the disputes over episcopal elections. The latter alone, together with being a foreigner, made him anathema in the eyes of Matthew Paris, who attributed his fall to his insolence and alienation of practically everyone.[55]

The one member of the nobility who still had any traction with the king made ready to depart on crusade during these unsettled times. Richard of Cornwall spent the Christmas of 1239 with the court in Winchester, where he got Henry to admit his ward Baldwin de Redvers to the earldom of Devon. Tragedy then struck when his wife Isabel died in childbirth on 17 January 1240. Richard had just renewed his crusading vow, and in June headed for Dover in the company of Henry and Otto. He left with a party that included Baldwin, William Longespee II, Philip Basset and about sixty knights. Other nobles departing on crusade, presumably with the intention of dying in the Holy Land, were King John's old captains Peter de Maulay, who got his wish, and William de Forz, who died at sea on the way. Richard met Louis in Paris for the purpose of extending the truce between England and France, then continued down to Marseille, where a papal legate unsuccessfully tried to get him to change course for Romania to fight for the Latin emperor instead. He arrived in Acre three months after departing.[56]

Simon de Montfort led a separate party of crusaders overland. He had come back to England in April 1240, the first time since his disgrace, and while reportedly received in state by Henry, he was there to sell woodland in Leicester to finance his crusade and to bring his son Henry to his mother. In France Eleanor gave birth to another boy, named Simon naturally, and bundled up both boys to leave with her husband for Italy. Frederick lent them a palace in Brindisi on the southern tip of the Adriatic coast, where she waited more than a year for Simon to return from the east. She may have given birth to their third son, Amaury, while there and found some opportunity to visit her sister the empress.[57]

The last major figure to depart that year was the Archbishop of Canterbury. Still at war with his monks and forever undercut by Otto, Edmund resolved to go to Rome in search of the long-elusive satisfaction of becoming the pre-eminent Church authority in England. He was received by Blanche upon his arrival in France, but took ill and died on 16 November 1240, aged about 65. He requested to be buried at the Abbey of Pontigny, where everyone knew Thomas Becket and Stephen Langton had stayed during their years of exile at the hands of oppressive kings. Although most of Edmund's unhappiness had to do with struggles in his own diocese, a legend quickly formed that he had been forced into exile as well. Dying there made him a martyr, a fictitious but useful one when the time came for the next showdown between the bishops and king.[58]

He left in the autumn, right around the time Queen Eleanor was delivered of a second child, a daughter named Margaret after her sister. She was born on 29 September, and as the birth neared, Henry had the great hall of Westminster filled with paupers for a feast in his wife's honour. He even had a candle holder worth the incredible sum of £3 made for the queen to carry at her churching, and perhaps more significantly, didn't make any scenes at it like the previous year. What to get her for Christmas seems to have slipped his mind, however, causing him considerable anxiety as he placed his order for a golden cup for his 'beloved consort' with less than a week to go.[59]

That Christmas, spent in Westminster, was to be Otto's last in England. He had managed to extend his legateship several times, but now Gregory was summoning a council of leading churchmen to deal with Frederick and wanted him there. Henry was perhaps not as broken up to see him go as was reported, for he didn't need him any more with the passing of Edmund. He certainly valued Otto's services and all he had done to mediate the constant disputes and bickering that must have struck Otto as weirdly English in nature. As a mark of his appreciation, Henry knighted Otto's nephew and gave the young man a wardship, which he turned around and sold to the Bishop of Carlisle. The king then invited Otto to take his seat at the table for the feast, while he sat at his right and the Archbishop of York to his left.[60]

For Henry, humility was just as important as majesty, but some around the table thought he was belittling himself. They were probably the abbots and bishops who had borne the brunt of the papal exactions and thought Otto deserved no deference for his part in it. Seeing their scowls, the legate would have reminded them that, like their late, revered archbishop, he was a firm believer in the plenitude of power that emanated from Rome. The pope commanded, he obeyed and they should do so too without squawking.

8

NOT THE USUAL RETIREMENT AND PLEASURES 1241–1244

There were two more feasts for Otto to enjoy before he left England on 7 January 1241. The first was held two days earlier on the anniversary of the death of Edward the Confessor, which Henry now celebrated in Westminster with the same regularity as the feast of translation on 13 October. He marked this occasion by knighting more than a dozen initiates. One of them was the guest of honour at the feast held the following day, Epiphany, which marked the official end of Christmas. He was Peter of Savoy, the fourth of the Savoyard brothers to enter the royal orbit. Born around 1203, he too was a skilled administrator and soldier but, like Thomas, he married well to escape a career in the Church.[1] He loved nothing better than wheeling and dealing and was completely in the thick of things between the papacy and empire.

Naturally Henry appreciated a man of his calibre at court, and to entice him to stick around and work for him, in May he gave him custody of the earldom of Richmond. He did not, however, confer the title of earl upon him, and Peter had the good sense not to go around calling himself one. But he was anxious to see what the English nobility were made of and challenged Roger Bigod, the Earl of Norfolk, to bring out his best. They would see who was superior, the natives or foreigners. When they lined up on the field at Northampton, however, the English found themselves outnumbered. Men like Gilbert Basset, thinking to please the king, or else being susceptible to a bribe, decided to join the foreign party for the tournament. Henry banned it from going forward at the last minute, but instead of getting credit for saving the English knights from a good thrashing, he was blamed for trying to stage it in favour of the foreigners in the first place.[2]

Gilbert Marshal had joined his nephew Roger Bigod's side at Northampton. He had earlier sworn to go on crusade if only he could be reconciled with the king, but even then Henry was seeking an unusually high £6,666 in damages from him. The case was thrown out as groundless, but it informed Gilbert that reconciliation was going to cost him, and in the end he was forced to surrender the castle of Pevensey in Sussex. He also had to enter a separate reconciliation with Maurice Fitz-Gerald, the justiciar of Ireland, whom he held responsible for the death of his brother Richard. He still didn't sail, however, and probably never intended to after Llywelyn died in April 1240. The succession conflict in Wales provided him with opportunities to consolidate his lordship in the region, and he knew he would have to submit to Henry if he hoped to get various Welsh princes to submit to him. Things were going well when he got together with other Marchers to sponsor a tournament in Hertford on 27 June. Henry banned it, but Gilbert and the others threw themselves into the melee anyway. He lost control of his horse, was thrown and dragged for some distance. He died later that evening.[3]

Henry had banned the tournament because a march on Wales was in the offing and he didn't need his magnates to get killed in a mock battle when a real one might be awaiting them. Dafydd had assumed primacy among the princes after he invited his half-brother Gruffudd to negotiate, only to seize and imprison him before he got a word in edgewise. Although Dafydd was his nephew, Henry wasn't about to let him throw his weight around the way Llywelyn had. He summoned the feudal host to muster at Chester in August, but Dafydd capitulated within a month. He surrendered the homage of the Welsh nobility to Henry and handed over Gruffudd, who was taken to the Tower of London along with his wife Senena. They became hostages for Dafydd's good behaviour in the sense that they would be released to wreak vengeance on him if he acted otherwise.[4]

The Tower itself had just undergone major reconstruction to give it more or less the form it has today. A new curtain wall with eight towers, the western gateway and moat were all added at a total cost of £5,000. Henry had decided that these improvements were necessary after spending a week there during the rebellion following the Montfort marriage. The living quarters were also refurbished, but Henry only intended to live there if he had to. There was no point making it a residence when he had Westminster and Windsor to shuttle between. He wanted the Tower to project power over London while serving as a fortress, repository, arsenal and prison. Gruffudd and Senena were among the first occupants of the new Tower and would find out in time just how good a job Henry had done in restoring it.[5]

The turmoil in Wales had a direct effect on the Marshal inheritance in the south. Since Gilbert Marshal left behind only an illegitimate daughter, his brother Walter was next in line to become the Earl of Pembroke, but he knew he had a problem because he had also been present at the banned tournament. After burying his brother at the New Temple in London, next to the two William Marshals, Walter kept out of sight until the court came to Gloucester in mid-July. His confrontation with the king was a stormy one, as might be expected. Matthew Paris says that Henry rehashed the old charges against Richard Marshal, this time to include a shot at his and Walter's father William by declaring that he had treacherously let Louis VIII escape when he had him in his grasp. In his own version of the encounter, Henry was indeed angry at Walter, but it was because he defied him when told to turn over Gilbert's castles until the succession was settled. Walter eventually got the queen and her former steward Nicholas Farnham, now the Bishop of Durham, to intercede and was made the Earl of Pembroke in October, but it cost him two castles.[6]

It was a time of notable deaths. Eleanor of Brittany died in August 1241 in Bristol after nearly forty years of close confinement. While Henry made her gifts and invited her to court celebrations, her final years were a lonely endurance test without the companions she had had during the early years of her incarceration. She was buried in Amesbury, a convent that would attract the interest of the queen in her own later years.[7]

Gilbert Basset was next after he went out hunting and was crushed when his horse stumbled. Left paralysed, he died shortly afterwards. The rebel firebrand was followed to the grave by his former nemesis and last justiciar Stephen Seagrave in November.[8] It is indicative of Henry's mercy and forgiveness that both men, perpetrators of gross misconduct against the realm, not only escaped imprisonment and execution but were politically rehabilitated, something unimaginable under later rulers like the Tudors. Dying between them on 29 September was Roger Niger, the Bishop of London who had openly opposed the king during the Roches regime. For his successor, Henry had hoped to translate Peter d'Aigueblanche from remote Hereford, but didn't make an issue out of it when Fulk Basset, Gilbert's brother, was elected instead.[9]

The death that had the biggest impact was Gregory's on 22 August. He was at least 90 by that time, having been born as far back as the reign of King Stephen, but it can be said that his life was cut short on account of the reversals in his fight against Frederick, a man half his age. The imperial army was advancing on Rome, and many of the prelates summoned by Gregory for a council to depose the emperor, including Otto, were captured in a huge sea battle on 3 May 1241 by Enzio of Sardinia and imprisoned in a squalid summer palace. When negotiations for a settlement outlasted the life of the pope, a conclave was convened to elect his successor. The process bogged down, so Frederick sent Otto there under guard with instructions to get on with it. Finally, after two months, the oldest cardinal among them emerged as Celestine IV. He died less than three weeks later. Now more bitterly divided than ever, several of the cardinals fled for fear of another gruelling election, and Otto wasn't freed until August 1242.[10]

The death of Gregory deprived Henry of a valuable ally in his attempt to control episcopal appointments. Fortunately, he was still around when another important piece of business came up earlier in the year with the election of a new Archbishop of Canterbury. Henry's choice was Boniface of Savoy, lately rejected by Winchester. He was reportedly the best-looking of the Savoyard brothers and, as the youngest, was the closest to the king in age. None of that would have mattered to the monks, who probably would have barely considered him were it not for Edmund. Their deceased archbishop had so blackened their names in Rome that they told Henry he could have whoever he wanted if he helped them win absolution. They got it, but when their other archenemy, Simon Langton, learned of it, he launched an appeal. He desisted after Henry warned him he might feel his displeasure 'in more ways than one' if he persisted. But while the chapter got a clean slate, after further reflection, some of the monks became convinced they had sold their souls and left for another order.[11]

The election of Boniface to Canterbury should have cleared the way for Raleigh to move to Winchester from the bishopric of Norwich, but Henry refused to drop his appeal against his election. Gregory had not acted on it, and now that he was dead and no successor was forthcoming, the vacant see remained in crown hands. While the king deplored what he saw as insolence on the part of the monks and his former chief justice, he certainly wasn't averse to exploiting the resources of Winchester for a while longer. With the fortune he was spending on construction, renovations, entertainment, papal appeals and keeping England tied to the Continent, money again dominated the royal agenda. Five years earlier Henry had instituted a new council to enact reforms of his financial administration, and while successful at first, it seemed nothing could keep up with the king's spending.

Drastic measures were needed to raise funding, and two had severe consequences for the rest of Henry's personal rule. In January 1241, a writ went out to each Jewish community to send representatives to meet the king at a Parliament in Worcester on 10 February. The only item on the agenda for the 109 men who showed up was to draw up an assessment for distributing the recent £13,334 tax levied by the council. It was hoped that doing it in an open assembly would prevent the bribery and favouritism that had allowed the wealthiest among them to evade earlier taxes. When it was over, the five richest were assessed 64 per cent of the tax, with Aaron of York tallaged the most at £2,634. Broken down by community, the Jews of York had to pay the heaviest burden, roughly 50 per cent, followed by London at 20 per cent and Oxford at 13 per cent. To make sure the collection got off to a good start, fourteen hostages were taken to the Tower to stand as surety until the payments started coming in. This new approach to taxation wasn't just about making it fair, but also efficient, as learned by the chaos that accompanied the collection of the Third. The proceedings of this 'Jewish Parliament' were handed over to the exchequer, whose officials now knew how much wealth was out there, who had it and what sheriff to contact to go pick it up.[12]

The other drastic measure to raise revenue meant rethinking the role of the sheriff again. The days of the bishop, earl or household knight serving as sheriff ended five years earlier when the post was filled with a minor, local official given custody of the county in return for an allowance. Like the aristocratic sheriff, he was charged with collecting revenue and making payments, only he had to account for everything during the biannual audit at the exchequer. He or his clerk would arrive with pouches full of transaction orders, whether writs or tally sticks for the less literate, and silver pennies, sometimes cut into halves or quarters. He sat at a long table opposite the 'barons' of the exchequer, the high officials like the treasurer who did the auditing. The actual calculations involved exchequer clerks placing counters on a chequered cloth with squares denoting denominations so that everyone could see with their own eyes where the sums received from the sheriff stood in relation to the sums he owed.[13] The results were recorded on parchment rolled up to resemble pipes, later to be used not just to hound debtors but to set new targets for the county farms.

Giving the sheriff an allowance in return for full accounting was meant to impede corruption, but it also stifled whatever ambition and diligence he might bring to the post. He was sure to react to any announcement of higher targets much the way a modern sheriff would: 'What's in it for me?' Only by going back to the profits system could he be induced to work harder than he already did. But there was one more problem. Squeezing more money out of the counties was bound to provoke resistance. The aristocratic sheriff could always ignore the indignation of the locals, whom he didn't know and didn't care about, but it was an altogether different story when the sheriff himself was local and lacked baronial rank and connections to back up his authority. The way around this was to recruit knights and minor officials from other counties to come in and throw their weight around. It was hoped that being a complete stranger might make the sheriff more inured to the hostility of the community as he and his bailiffs went about eyeballing and touching everything of value. The incentive of a quick profit, and equally quick exit if necessary, also meant there would be no shortage of takers for the job.[14]

For the first year of the new programme, the target was set at just under £4,000. It was a huge increase, almost 75 per cent over the ancient farms, but still a small portion of the £24,000 in revenue that typically went to the crown every year. Jewish tallages and vacant bishoprics helped push income past £30,000 for the first time that year, but these too were temporary windfalls. The only other staple of royal revenue was the demesne itself, but this brought in barely £6,000, five times less than what it might have been worth had Henry's ancestors not given away so much land as patronage.[15] His uncle Richard and father John also had incomes of about £24,000, but inflation made his feel more like half that. He could also thank them for the precarious state of his finances in the first place. Their stripping of unsustainable resources had led to Magna Carta and the resulting restraints on any ambitious fundraising schemes he might dream up in a similar vein.[16]

What was even more galling was the fact that the royal income had been as high as nearly £50,000 when Normandy was still under English control. The province had accounted for nearly half of that money, all of which was now going to the French monarchy.[17] Louis was rich by comparison and could indulge in the flights of generosity and lavishness that were so much part of Henry's nature. He could even afford a shopping spree of holy relics Henry could only dream of, starting with the crown of thorns. Since first coming to light in AD 409, the crown had been worshipped at the basilica of Mt Sion in Jerusalem until it was moved to Constantinople as the Saracens closed in. In his fight against the Greeks, the Latin emperor pledged it to Venice for a loan of £2,500. He told Louis that if he could redeem that pledge, the crown was all his. The transaction was completed in 1239 and, with great pomp and reverence, the thorns arrived at the royal chapel of Saint Nicholas in Paris.[18] Two years later, Louis acquired a piece of the true cross, evidently made of the same wood that Henry had admired in Bromholm Priory, for £6,250. To house these and other relics, the French king shelled out another £25,000 to construct shrines encrusted with gold and jewels. He started work on a new chapel, Sainte-Chapelle, to house his collection and saw it built in record time for just £10,000.[19]

An undertaking of this scale would have set Henry back two years' revenue but, not to be outdone, he ordered the construction of a shrine for his patron Edward the Confessor to be made of the purest gold and adorned with costly jewels. In taking on the expense himself, it would not be finished for nearly three decades, and at one point he had to pawn some £1,200 of the jewels in the shrine just to keep his household afloat. He got them back two years later and lived to see the elaborate work finished at a cost of £5,000, making it as good an illustration as any of not just the difficulty he faced in finding funding for his projects, but how he always seemed to pull them off in the end.[20] The more reasonable ones, anyway.

The prickly sensation of the crown of thorns did nothing to stoke guilt in Louis over his father taking Poitou from Henry while he was a minor. Quite the opposite, he bestowed the province on his brother Alphonse of Poitiers in June 1241 in honour of him reaching his majority. He could rightly insist he was only executing the instructions of his father's will, but it was a *faux pas* nevertheless given that the official Count of Poitou, Richard of Cornwall, had just then helped secure the release of the French nobles, including Simon de Montfort's brother Amaury, who were being held captive following the battle of Gaza in November 1239. Richard took on enormous expense in clothing and feeding them, and burying the unlucky ones, only to have their king embarrass him in this unseemly fashion.[21]

Actually, the money wasn't Richard's. With papal blessing, Richard had employed an army of friars in the English countryside to encourage people from all walks of life to take up the cross in return for a remission of their sins. Since none of these people could afford the costs of crusading, they were then sold an indulgence that allowed them to stay at home, but still free themselves of their sins. In this way, invalids, imbeciles and children all got to become honourable crusaders for the cost of whatever meagre earnings their families had to redeem their vows.[22] Richard of Cornwall became a hero among the French captives, but it was England's poor and destitute who paid for their freedom.

He stopped in Sicily on the way home that summer to meet Frederick, a fellow redhead whose short, stout body, red face and beady eyes were probably not the features he imagined in a man bearing the title of emperor. Richard was treated to Frederick's oriental fetishes with a series of bloodlettings, baths, and entertainment by spry Saracen girls doing orbital gymnastics. A visit was arranged with his sister Isabella, the first time they had seen each other in six years. Interestingly, they needed her husband's permission first. Seeing the emperor's overbearing and controlling nature up close must have made Richard glad he never accepted any of his invitations to serve under him. He had gone to Rome to plead on his behalf before the papal Curia, but found Gregory, just weeks away from death, more hostile to the emperor than ever. After four months he left for England, while Isabella went back to her harem to await another child. On 1 December 1241 she died giving birth to a daughter, aged just 27. Frederick, who was not there, had her interred in Andria with all the honours accorded to an empress.[23]

* * *

The Isabella on everyone's mind when Richard of Cornwall returned in January 1242 was his mother and the insult meted out to her during the investiture of Alphonse of Poitiers as Count of Poitou. She and Hugh were from two of the oldest, most distinguished clans in the region, and she had been Queen of England, but when they went to do homage to Alphonse, Louis and his mother Blanche forced them to wait three days for an interview. They then left Isabella standing in front of everyone as if she were just another servant in the room.[24] The two queen dowagers were rivals going back to the days of Blanche's husband trying to seize the English throne from Isabella's husband and nothing had been forgotten. Louis may have chosen to humiliate Isabella only out of fear of his mother, but it was shabby treatment that could not go unanswered. At Alphonse's Christmas court, Hugh appeared as summoned, but only to defy him with a coalition of other disaffected nobles, and added the *coup de grâce* of burning his lodgings to the ground before leaving.[25]

Hugh felt he could afford to act tough because he had most of the nobility of Poitou behind him. They too were independent-minded lords who didn't want Louis and his brothers presuming to tell them what to do. He had more serious backing from Raymond of Toulouse, still desperate to keep his county from falling into the hands of his son-in-law Alphonse, and James I of Aragon, who had his own claims in southern France. But the real heavyweight would be his stepson Henry, who was sure to arrive with an expeditionary force now that his dream of recovering Poitou was within grasp. In November they reached an agreement and Henry called for Parliament to meet on 28 January 1242 so he could ask for funding.

The magnates already knew what was in the works and came prepared to stonewall the discussion. They had no interest in Poitou and generally viewed the province with disdain, a land of traitors and troublemakers. Indeed, any foreigner who landed on the bad side of an Englishman in those days was likely to be called a Poitevin regardless of his true origins. It was true that their king was three-quarters Poitevin himself and Hugh was his stepfather, but it was still inconceivable that they should trust the same man who had helped Louis VIII overrun the province in the first place. And their opinion about Henry wasn't much better. When Richard of Cornwall and Walter Gray, the Archbishop of York, made his request for the aid, they only talked about how he taxed and oppressed them mercilessly despite his oath to uphold Magna Carta.

Gray was one of the very few in attendance who remembered what it was like to serve under a king like John and must have found their griping immature and theatrical. Henry tried to break up their united front by summoning them for some individual persuasion, but all he heard was that the truce with France had a couple more years to run and he should respect it. He was amazed that they were not 'more eager to reclaim the rights of the kingdom and try the fortune of war against those who injure us', but they remained unmoved.[26] In the end, all Henry got was £6,000 in scutage from the barons and knights who declined to go with him overseas. Together with funds from the Jewish tallage and other sources, he collected £35,000 for his expedition, or 8,400,000 pennies loaded into barrels.

Despite denying him the aid, six earls and their retinues accompanied him. He also had his household knights, about seventy-five men he kept on retainer at an annual cost of £1,000, and a similar number of sergeants, some of them mounted, and squad of crossbowmen. His last bit of business to wrap up was a visit to the shrine of Bromholm where, in front of his brother and Roger Bigod, he swore not to break the truce. If he did, may Louis invade England at his invitation. Leaving Gray in charge of the kingdom, Henry moved down to Portsmouth and set sail on 5 May with his pregnant wife and a force of 200 knights. They landed at the mouth of the River Gironde a little over a week later.[27]

Well before then, Henry had dispatched his Continental diplomats Peter of Savoy and Peter d'Aigueblanche to the Spanish kingdoms, to Toulouse, Provence and Burgundy to add as much weight as possible to the coalition. Louis was already aware that something was afoot, mainly thanks to Peter of Dreux snitching Hugh's plans to him before any actual movements had taken place. Attempts were made to intercept the two envoys, but both escaped and completed their missions. Louis wasn't about to wait for Henry to land with whatever force he was putting together and immediately called out his host to march on Poitou and have it out with the Lusignans and their supporters. As Henry was being greeted by his stepfather, whom he was meeting for the first time, Hugh's castles in La Marche were already under assault.

On 24 May Henry appointed commissioners to discuss violations of the truce, which could be anything from seizing English merchants to encroachments in Gascony. We are told that Louis's answer was everything Henry could have hoped for. He was not only willing to honour and extend the truce, but to cede Poitou and the greater part of Normandy to Henry as his father swore he would. Had that truly been the case, Henry would have packed up immediately and gone home. But it was another fabrication from Matthew Paris designed to show that, in refusing the offer, Henry provoked the war. In the king's own version of events, the commissioners scheduled a second meeting after the first broke off. His men then arrived prepared to give ground, but the French didn't bother to show up.[28]

Two weeks later he wrote home that France had violated the truce and war was imminent. Summonses were sent to all men owing Henry service, including Simon de Montfort, who was in Burgundy following his return from crusade. Like Richard of Cornwall, Simon had done no fighting in the Holy Land other than the political kind. The imperial authorities of Jerusalem were at constant odds with a baronial faction that included Philip de Montfort, the Lord of Tyre and Simon's cousin. Given Simon's connection to the emperor, Philip promoted him as the one crusader who could unite the Christian forces in what was becoming an ever more precarious position for all of them. In June 1241 a letter was sent to Frederick from the 'barons, knights and citizens' of Jerusalem asking him to appoint Simon governor, but nothing came of the request.[29]

Montfort obediently answered Henry's summons, but instantly raised all kinds of complaints to the king about how he distrained his lands to pay back Thomas of Savoy. Henry agreed to make good the money because he needed all the military expertise he could get.[30] Louis had overrun Hugh's castles and was now heading towards the River Charente to bag the English invader. His object was the town of Taillebourg and its stone bridge across the river. Henry was encamped about 10 miles to the south near Saintes, trusting the lord of Taillebourg not to just open the gates to Louis, but that's exactly what he did. Henry dispatched a force to contest the crossing of the bridge, but they couldn't prevent the enemy's superior numbers from securing a perimeter on their side or from building a makeshift bridge further up the river with the intent of encircling them. The English had to buy time if they were to escape, and for that they had Richard of Cornwall, whose redemption of French prisoners in Egypt had bought him plenty of goodwill on the other side. Dressed in a pilgrim's robe with staff in hand, he received enthusiastic cheers as he walked into the French camp to ask for a truce. Louis had only half a mind to grant it but, it being a Sunday, he agreed they could have twenty-four hours to contemplate the error of their ways and then he was going after them.[31]

The French crossed the river during the night and the next day set off in pursuit. The only fighting of the campaign took place on 22 July 1242 after Hugh, stung by the disgraceful reputation he now enjoyed on both sides, fell upon the French foragers who had got ahead of their army. That led to a fierce engagement in the vineyards outside of Saintes, where Montfort, Bigod and William Longespee II were said to have distinguished themselves. But Louis was relentless and kept snapping at Henry's heels as one Poitevin lord after another deserted him. Not until they reached Blaye, nearly 50 miles to the south, were they able to regroup and cross into Gascony, but at the loss of much of their equipment and dignity.[32]

By that time Hugh was no longer with them. Through Peter of Dreux, he let Louis know he was genuinely sorry for the sad state of affairs he found himself in and appealed for mercy. Louis was willing to receive his and Isabella's submission on 1 August, but at the cost of all his castles taken outright plus their £1,000 annual pension. If Louis had hoped the investiture of his brother in Poitou would lead to rebellion and ultimately to the proud Lusignans grovelling at his feet, then he could easily call it a day and head back to Paris. But he was an expansionist very much in the mode of his father and grandfather and now aimed to sweep down all the way to the Pyrenees.

For Henry, these days had to be a complete nightmare. He had hoped to reclaim Poitou, now he could well lose the rump remainder of the Angevin Empire. Just keeping his hold on Gascony had been difficult enough for the past decade and addressing that situation had been part of the agenda for the expedition. Louis's behaviour had taken them all off guard. Whether it owed to Margaret recently giving birth to another girl or he saw the campaign as an opportunity to emancipate himself from his mother's clutches, the delicate, effeminate Louis was showing a spirited aggressiveness in the field that Henry could never hope to match.[33] If he could capture the English king and hold him for ransom, which seems to have spurred him on, he could legally deprive him of his claims in France and make him pay the costs of his punitive campaign and victory celebration afterwards.

It wasn't like they could just set sail from Bordeaux at any time, either. On 25 June, in the midst of the negotiations for the truce, Eleanor gave birth to Henry's second daughter, Beatrice, named pointedly after her mother and not his. Eleanor had not had an easy time of it and a sea voyage could have been perilous for mother and infant.[34] John wouldn't have hesitated to put them on a boat if that was what it took to save his skin. Fortunately, Henry didn't have to make any choice, because one defensive measure taken by the Poitevins was just then decimating the French army. They had stripped the land as they retreated and polluted the wells with offal and latrine matter. As summer bore down in August, thousands of French knights, foot soldiers and as many as eighty barons died of heat, hunger and dysentery, including some who had been rescued by Richard of Cornwall. Louis himself fell seriously ill and, worried of meeting the same fate as his father, broke off hostilities and returned north.[35]

The surviving French troops kept going south in the direction of Toulouse, where Raymond had finally stirred at Henry's insistence. His attempt to drive out the French garrison meant to keep an eye on him was half-hearted at best, but that didn't stop Louis from wanting to make an example of him as he did of Hugh. Louis even put Hugh at the head of the army sent to crush him. Raymond forgot the treaty he made with Henry in late August and asked Blanche to intercede for him. In January 1243 he got off with only a reaffirmation of his original terms with the French monarchy and a promise to Blanche to root out any remaining heretics in his county.[36]

Hugh must have seethed at the leniency shown to Raymond, especially since he himself returned from Toulouse despised as ever by his peers. A year after his submission, he was accused of treason and challenged to a duel. Tradition allowed a younger man to stand in for him, and his son eagerly volunteered, but Alphonse of Poitiers overruled the arrangement and ordered Hugh to pick up the mace. The other peers, however, were troubled by this bit of Capetian arrogance and pleaded with Louis and his brother to come to their senses.

They eventually did and the charge and challenge were dropped, but the persecution continued. Humiliated by their submission, Isabella swore off Hugh and her second brood of children and entered the nunnery of Fontevrault. She needed the sanctuary, because a rumour started going around that she had paid two cooks to poison the royal brothers. It could have been an innocent case of using too much vinegar, but Louis had the hapless cooks executed, and the French, no doubt with Blanche's blessing, were happy to cover Isabella with more infamy. Matthew Paris, always the first to call names, says she was seen as 'Jezebel rather than Isabel for having sowed the seeds of so many crimes'.[37]

Raymond would have preferred no war in the first place if only he could beget an heir to keep his county from falling into Alphonse's hands. One solution was an annulment of his union with Sanchia of Aragon and marriage to another Sanchia, the third daughter of his enemy Raymond Berenger of Provence. A son from that union would inherit both Toulouse and Provence, forming a conglomerate strong enough to keep the Capetians at bay. The annulment was granted by Gregory in 1241, but he died before issuing a dispensation for the marriage contract.[38] So Raymond married Hugh and Isabella's 12-year-old daughter Margaret as part of their new alliance, thus becoming Henry's brother-in-law and cousin. Since all these European noble houses were interrelated, a dispensation was required here as well, but the papacy remained vacant throughout the course of the rebellion. Although Raymond's heart had never been in it, Louis was in a mood to punish him and would have, had Blanche not demanded restraint.[39]

Henry ranted about Raymond's desertion in a letter to Frederick, following an earlier one he sent bemoaning the same lack of fidelity in Hugh and the Poitevins. Raymond came to see him while he was in Bordeaux, along with King James of Aragon, another conspirator whose help never materialised. Their visit only created dissent, because neither had forgotten how their fathers had been thrashed by Simon de Montfort's father at the battle of Muret in September 1213 and tried to turn Henry against him. Simon had already aroused Henry's displeasure after he called his intention of making a stand at Saintes foolish. He even suggested he should be locked up just like the tenth-century Frankish king Charles the Simple after the battle of Soissons. They should find a house with iron bars on the windows, like the ones they have in Windsor, to keep him 'securely within'. What was foolish was to say such a thing to the king. Simon, who evidently knew his history, had to know that if he had said something similar to John, he would have been in one of those houses in Windsor soon enough and lucky if he ever got out. He later admitted he had said it in the passion of the moment. To make amends, and notwithstanding the jibes of Raymond and James, he agreed to stay with the king in Bordeaux long after most of the senior nobility had left.[40]

These included Richard of Cornwall, who fell out with his brother soon after they made their escape. Apparently Henry had promised to give him Gascony as his reward for pulling off the one-day truce, a mission which a man of Richard's vanity could not have had any desire to undertake. He would look ridiculous approaching the French in a pilgrim's robe with staff in hand. He could easily be taken prisoner and held for ransom while Henry and the other earls slipped away. The only way he was going to do it was if his brother gave him something big. He made Gascony his price, and probably felt he deserved it because he had saved it back in 1225. Plus, the king owed him compensation for the loss of Poitou. Henry had agreed on the spot, because if any mantra best described the way the Plantagenets did business when the heat was on it was 'promise anything'.[41]

No doubt Henry waited until they reached Bordeaux before telling Richard that the deal was off. The whole point of retaining Gascony was to give it to his son Edward some day. Henry had so little royal demesne left in England that he had practically nothing to give him when he grew up and began demanding a principality of some sort to rule over. He wanted to avoid having Edward mope around the court, restless and carping about how useless and miserable it was to be a prince, and getting into a rebellious spirit like his grandfather's older sons. The episode was another reminder to Richard, who had been the heir apparent for more than twenty years, that his nephew would one day eclipse him in influence, as Queen Eleanor already had.

This new disappointment came at a bad time because Richard's crusade had made him something of a celebrity on the Continent. He had met Louis, Blanche, Frederick, the late pope, had seen Paris, Rome and Jerusalem, and thoroughly enjoyed the attention he received for being the brother of the King of England. On his way home from crusade, he had been feted by the dignitaries of every town he passed through in Italy, and in Cremona the emperor's elephant led the welcoming party, complete with trumpeters riding on its back.[42] The only way to build on his reputation as a power broker in European circles was to be based close to where the action was, and Cornwall was a long way from it.

Recognising his new-found status, and long familiar with his ego, Henry had better prospects for him anyway. Sanchia of Provence was still available after her betrothal to Raymond of Toulouse fell through, and since her two older sisters were queens, she might easily inherit the province when Raymond Berenger died. If she wed Richard, he could rule Provence in right of her, thus becoming the international statesman he aspired to be. Sanchia was said, moreover, to be extraordinarily beautiful, but Richard would have seen her for himself when he stopped in Provence on his way to the crusade.

The pre-campaign mission of Peter of Savoy had included arranging their marriage. Sensing this was on the agenda must have been the impetus for Louis to try and capture Peter before he made it to Provence. But as with her sisters, Sanchia would have to come without a marriage portion. It was up to Henry to make his brother land grants and a cash settlement of £3,000. Richard proposed to go to Provence for his bride, but the hostilities with France and lingering bitterness over the lordship of Gascony caused him to leave the court abruptly and head home with the earls of Pembroke and Gloucester. Their ship nearly foundered in a storm at sea, and when they arrived on 18 October, Richard vowed to build an abbey in thanks for his deliverance.[43]

★ ★ ★

The desertion of Henry's allies left him with no alternative but to conclude a new truce with Louis in April 1243. He was forced to cede the ground he lost and pay £1,000 a year on top of the enormous expenses he had already incurred, nearly £80,000 by the time it was over.[44] The campaign had been a failure from the start. The Poitevins launched their revolt too early, with Henry still months away from putting an expedition together, and this gave Louis all the initiative. Once Henry landed, more time was lost as he went through the formalities of negotiating the truce. He may have hoped the show of strength would get Louis to make concessions and so avoid a war, but the French were on a roll by then and he had little chance of stalling their advance even had he crossed the Charente first. The Poitevin lords were running scared by that point and thinking only of surrender. Henry may not have been much of a soldier, but the men he had with him who were lauded for their military skills, Montfort and Bigod to name two, apparently didn't have a clue what to do either except retreat. Had they been captured, it would have been a calamity in terms of the ransom money, easily £100,000 at the minimum. As it was, they got away with just an ignoble defeat.

Poitou was lost for good. Good riddance in the eyes of Matthew Paris. In describing these events, he doesn't try to hide his contempt for the Poitevins or for the king lingering on the Continent as if he were on an extended holiday in the south of France. Henry remained abroad for a full year after hostilities ceased, dispatching what seemed like endless orders for supplies and money. Since he was in the area, he had decided to take what measures he could to bring Gascony firmly under control. He undertook the municipal reorganisation of southern cities like Dax and Bayonne and courted the biggest fomenter of discord in that area, Gaston de Béarn, who was a first cousin of the queen. Rebel pockets were systematically reduced, and in the action at Vérines his protégé John Mansel was struck by a stone that crushed one of his legs. So concerned was Henry for his full recovery that he advised the surgeons attending him that if ever there was a time to shine in their profession, now was it.[45]

His base of operations was Bordeaux, then dominated by two families, the Colombines and Solers. It was while the king was in town that the Colombines won the mayoral election, ending six years of Soler rule. The Solers had been loyal in the brief war with Louis, but Henry viewed the change of power as key to getting both factions to cooperate. The Colombines advanced him loans during his stay, not just in the hope of taking over city hall, but to protect their interests in the wine trade with England.[46] Most Englishmen at that time drank beer, to excess as the rest of Europe noted even then, but wine imports were steadily growing. Home-grown varieties needed additives to mask their acidity and lack of fragrance, and the booming economy meant more families could afford the French stuff. Henry was eager to promote the trade and to do business with the merchants who ran it because the duties on exports offset the expenses of governing the province. As with many of his projects, the real benefits of this policy lay in the future.[47]

Henry himself consumed copious amounts of wine and rarely did he arrive anywhere ahead of an order for which wines to buy and in what quantity. Wine was the occasion for a practical joke he once played on his purchasing agent, a man by the name of Peter the Poitevin. They were on the return voyage to England in late September 1243 when he presented Peter with a list of debts the agent owed. The items were all outlandish, like 8,000 gallons of wine supposedly bought on the same day that Peter claimed he had a dream about an emperor named Otto. They couldn't be true, yet there they were, officially enrolled in the accounts.

As Peter was probably considering whether to jump overboard or not, he was shown another part of the roll where these same items were cancelled. Henry had concocted the whole scene to get him to pull the longest, dumbest face possible in front of the gang. The king liked to mix it up with his clerks in this fashion, but whether he might have imbibed before this particular bit of fun, the record doesn't say.[48]

They could laugh now, but back in 1236 the royal wine chamber was a scandal. A shortage that year led to skyrocketing prices and the refusal of merchants to allow the king's purveyors to take their wine at prise, which was a preferential price well below the market. The purveyors might pay £1 for a cask that normally fetched £2, but that's when there was plenty of stock. Now prices were almost double that. It was suspected that some of these prise purchases were being resold on the market to enrich the purveyors, maybe the king himself. The testimony of the chamberlain showed how messy the situation had become when he told exchequer officials that he kept no accounts, nor, incredibly, could he be bothered to. They wanted to arrest him on the spot, but because he was a cleric, they allowed him to go to Henry to seek his grace.[49]

Arriving in Portsmouth after an absence of nearly eighteen months, the king and queen proceeded to Winchester, where he insisted that, whatever they thought of his latest Continental campaign, the magnates receive them in state. A month later Beatrice landed with her daughter Sanchia. The royal party had already met them in Bordeaux, the first time Eleanor had seen her mother and sister in more than seven years. Sanchia was by now 17, a woman compared to the child Eleanor had been when she came to England to get married. Her wedding to Richard of Cornwall on 23 November 1243 surpassed all feasts before it, if there were indeed 30,000 dishes prepared as Paris claims.[50]

Where the feasting really did run into the thousands was on 1 January 1244, the day of the Circumcision, and Henry's order that 6,000 of the poor be fed in Westminster Hall and the Painted Chamber while the children were fed in the queen's chamber. Almsgiving was central to his piety and in that year alone 240,000 meals were dispensed to the poor. As a norm, he fed around 500 paupers a day at an annual cost of more than £700. His relief for the poor was also a way of eliciting prayers for the souls of those dearest to him. Learning of the death of his sister Isabella, he ordered meals for 100,001 paupers, followed by 4,000 every year to mark the anniversary of her passing.[51] For all his desire to run Henry out of France, even Louis was impressed by his adversary's charity, and forbade his court to mock him over his recent misadventure in Poitou.

While both kings sometimes also served up the food at these feedings, Henry missed this particular one because the royal family was spending Christmas that year at Richard's castle residence in Wallingford. Henry was reportedly gracious to Sanchia throughout the occasion and made an effort to make her feel at home.[52]

Something less wholesome could have been read into this had it been one of the lecherous kings of England of the same name, but courtesy and affability towards young ladies seem to have been the hallmarks of this Henry.

Acerbic commentators nevertheless took exception to what they saw as more of the king fawning over foreigners. He might have been forgiven the gifts of robes and jewels he lavished on his mother-in-law, but the £400 pension he gave her was put down to Beatrice working her charms on him. A loan of £2,700 made out to his father-in-law at this time, secured against five strategic castles in Provence, rather points to Henry buying loyalty against France.[53] But there was no denying that Beatrice had the same considerable skills that made her brothers famous diplomats throughout Europe, and Simon de Montfort for one recognised this. He approached her to patch up relations with the king, which remained strained because his wife Eleanor was still waiting all these years for a marriage portion. Beatrice told Henry that she found it scandalous that he had bestowed so many favours on her family while neglecting his own sister. He ultimately awarded the couple a yearly grant of £350 and forgave nearly £2,000 of their debts, although his action owed as much to political reality as to his mother-in-law's intervention. Henry had several fights before him, and having Montfort on his side was, if nothing else, the practical way to go.[54]

In June 1243, the cardinals finally settled on Sinibaldo Fieschi of Genoa as their new pope, Innocent IV. He had a backlog of petitions to consider, including the confirmation of Boniface of Savoy as Archbishop of Canterbury and the translation of William Raleigh from Norwich to Winchester. Both men had been rivals for Winchester. The pope innocently thought that by giving Boniface Canterbury, he would remove any objection to Raleigh taking over at Winchester.[55] Since there was no appeal against the pope, the best Henry could do was to ask Innocent to reconsider his decision given that his objections were never taken into account. Raleigh not only refused Henry's entreaties to draw up the petition together, but appeared barefoot before the gates of Winchester on Christmas Eve ready to take up his duties. Knowing it was coming, Henry had the mayor bar his entrance. Raleigh placed the entire city under interdict, put on his shoes and after a period of harassment by the king (says Paris), left for France to get backing from Louis.[56]

As proof of his humility, Henry offered to submit his case to the masters of Paris for their opinion, but Raleigh scoffed at any such idea and used his reply to take a swipe at the king. Henry II, he recalled, was so learned in the law that he was asked to arbitrate international disputes, which was unthinkable in his grandson, who, by the way, was also a poor soldier by comparison. Just look at what happened in Poitou, he all but declared. That a bishop and jurist of Raleigh's stature chose to belittle and insult the king in this manner was a mark of how personal their feud had become. Now proclaimed an 'enemy', Raleigh was advised to keep his distance.[57]

In a letter to Boniface, Grosseteste deplored the king's actions, saying they were against the pope and, more interestingly, Magna Carta. He asked the new archbishop to get his niece the queen to work on softening her husband's stance. If she made any progress on that front, it occurred at the same time that Henry received the pope's reply. Making no mention of his objections, Innocent told Henry that his decision was final and he must allow Raleigh to receive the temporalities (assets) of Winchester. Henry yielded as he knew he would have to in the end, and Raleigh returned in April 1244. It took another five months of haggling about the interdict before the new bishop was allowed to enter the cathedral and receive the kiss of peace. Although Henry didn't win this fight, he had profited from it nevertheless, by as much as £20,000, the sum generated in Winchester during the nearly six years the see was in his hands.[58]

The queen might have exerted more influence in the matter of episcopal appointments when Ralph Neville, the former chancellor and Bishop of Chichester, died in February 1244. To succeed him, Henry wanted Robert Passelewe, the treasurer who fell into disgrace under the Roches regime, but who, like Seagrave and Rivallis, had been rehabilitated and was then serving as a justice for the forest. His vigorous pursuit of fines and punishment for forest offences made him as unpopular as ever, but to please the king, the Chichester chapter went along with his wishes and elected him.[59]

Boniface arrived in England for the first time that very month, and it was his job as primate to ensure that Passelewe was qualified for the post. He turned the task over to a panel led by Grosseteste, who disliked the whole idea of interchanging royal administrators and churchmen, his friend William Raleigh notwithstanding. Passelewe was found to be wholly ignorant of Scripture. Boniface not only took their advice and rejected him, but accepted the candidate they put forward, Richard Wyche, another protégé of Edmund of Abingdon.

The archbishop was on shaky ground in not consulting the king first, and Henry let him know it. He called him an impossible ingrate and refused to allow Wyche to succeed as bishop. He had some choice words for his wife as well. She felt compelled to write him a letter to assure him that the bonds of kinship to her uncle did not exceed her affection for him. That soothed his ego, as did her observation that Boniface had, in fact, done him a favour. Few people were as adept at collecting money as Passelewe and so it was better to keep him where he was. Even so, the case went to Rome the following year. Innocent backed Boniface, but reiterated that he, as pope, had final authority on postulation, not the archbishop. As a sop to Henry, he agreed that Passelewe, who was already the Archdeacon of Lewes, might become a bishop at a later time.[60]

For Henry, the issue was no longer about promoting his clerk, but a battle of wills with Grosseteste over the king's insistence on having a say in church appointments. They had clashed before, notably in 1241 when Henry gave John Mansel a benefice claimed by Grosseteste. Henry backed down when the bishop threatened Mansel with spiritual penalties, and found him another plum. Then, to make amends to the king, Boniface gave Passelewe a benefice in Northampton, which also fell under Grosseteste's jurisdiction. The bishop refused to have him, again pointing to his worldly credentials. This led Henry to fire off a letter to Grosseteste, asking him to explain the whole point of royal unction, that is the anointing of a new monarch with oil, if it did not impart spiritual as well as temporal power unto the king, doubly so in his case since he had been anointed twice.

In a typically long-winded reply, Grosseteste drew a fine line between church and state, and Henry would do well to observe it. While unction endowed the king with the sevenfold gift of the Holy Spirit (wisdom, understanding, counsel, knowledge, fortitude, piety and fear of the Lord), it only dignified his rule, only commanded him to 'excel in godlike and heroic virtues'. Under no circumstances did it make him equal to or greater than any priest, much less confer priestly powers on him. Henry was indignant that Grosseteste should lecture him in this manner and advised him to reconsider his tone. Grosseteste refused to back down on clerical superiority, but he did fall over himself apologising to him in his next letter. He was eager to secure the goodwill of 'your royal magnificence' and 'your royal serenity' and so was prepared to 'correct and amend anything you consider wrong'.[61] Passelewe didn't get this appointment either, but Grosseteste, like the queen, understood that the best way to get along with the king was to talk to him like one.

The bishop was no doubt flattered that Henry was paying him so much attention, given that tensions were especially fraught that year at home and abroad. Wales was again a flashpoint after Gruffudd made an attempt to escape from the Tower of London on 1 March 1244 and fell to his death when his makeshift rope of linen snapped. Henry had used his potential release from custody as incentive for Dafydd to abide by the terms imposed three years earlier. He now sent Gruffudd's oldest son Owain to Chester to remind Dafydd he was going to have more family infighting if he got it into his head to use the death of his brother to raise rebellion. But Dafydd was two steps ahead of him. He made a direct appeal to Innocent for papal protection and had gained the support of Gruffudd's youngest son Llywelyn, who would prove every bit as able as his namesake grandfather.[62] Unstable as the situation in Wales was becoming, Henry left it to the Marcher lords to keep Welsh ambitions in check. There was trouble brewing on his other border and he decided a more important showdown was required there.

A little over a year after his wife Joan died, Alexander II of Scotland married Marie de Coucy, the daughter of a French nobleman. In 1241 his long hoped-for son, also named Alexander, was born. Henry was still interested in binding their kingdoms through marriage and, before departing for France, suggested his daughter Margaret, born a year earlier, for the newborn heir. Intrigue at the Scottish court, however, led a family of exiles to accuse Alexander of a great many things before Henry, especially of plotting an alliance with France. When questioned about it, the King of Scotland declared that he held nothing of his realm from the King of England, not now, not ever. Finding this snub intolerable, Henry ordered his troops to mobilise at Newcastle on 1 August in preparation for a massive invasion, and orders were issued for the construction of siege engines and 30,000 crossbow bolts.

On 17 June 1244 another order pertaining to military operations went out, one where Henry could put his real talents to good use. He commissioned the creation of a royal battle standard to be made of red samite (heavy silk fabric) with a dragon stencilled in gold. Saxon kings had used the dragon standard before, as had his father and uncle, but Henry being Henry, his had to really look like a dragon. Sapphires were used to make glowing hot eyes and the tongue of burning fire was shaped so that it appeared to flick in the wind. The dragon was meant to strike fear into the hearts of the enemy and if this didn't do the trick, nothing would. Until that time, it was to be kept at Westminster Abbey, much as the French had their Oriflamme at Saint-Denis.[63]

Alexander was unlikely to have been moved had he seen this dragon approaching. He was the first to advance with his troops, as far as 7 miles from Newcastle. He then stopped and asked for a negotiated end to the confrontation. Within days it was over. Through Walter Gray and Richard of Cornwall, Alexander promised not to enter any foreign alliance against Henry, his liege lord, unless he was 'unjustly oppressed' by him, and he confirmed the future marriage between their children. There were enough subtleties in the provisions to make it look like the King of Scotland had more independence in his relationship with England than his forebears had, which Henry could live with for the sake of peace.[64]

The treaty was ratified on 13 August 1244 and the army quickly disbanded after that. Matthew Paris savages Henry at this point for not marching straight to Wales to deal with the fighting there. Instead he followed the 'woman's plan' by hurrying to Westminster for 'his usual retirement and pleasures'. While Henry may have preferred the comfort of home and family to warfare, the avoidance of fighting in Scotland meant he could take no scutage to defray the cost, including a body of foreign knights brought over by Thomas of Savoy. The quickness of the treaty reflects Henry's inability to afford the army longer than was needed to force Alexander to terms. He did dispatch two bodies of household knights to assist the Marchers, but the northern force was annihilated in an ambush. Their commander, Herbert Fitz-Matthew, who was said to have dreamt that bad things were in store for them, was killed by a stone hurled from an elevated position. Henry would have to go to Wales after all.[65]

By November 1244 the crown's financial situation was precarious enough for him to convene Parliament at the refectory of Westminster to ask for a tax. This was another historic occasion that came to define how that institution got to be where it is today. It was here that the king, as the head of state, addressed the assembly in person for the first time, hoping that the allure of majesty might win them over. All he got for his trouble was the establishment of a committee of twelve to consider his request, but this too was revolutionary in that it confirmed Parliament as a deliberative body with the power to grant or deny taxation.[66]

The barons and clerics probably spent most of their deliberations grumbling, because all they came back with were complaints about how the king had violated Magna Carta, although no specifics were given, and wasted all the previous taxes. They wanted him to revive the offices of justiciar and chancellor in order to clamp down on a growing, faceless bureaucracy, and they proposed constitutional checks reminiscent of the political crisis six years earlier, when they demanded unheard-of control over royal spending and the enforcement of liberties.[67]

They may have been sincere in wanting to impose a 'paper constitution' for the sake of more responsible government, but these were also men who saw something happening in England (and elsewhere in Europe) that they didn't like at all. They were being squeezed out of government by a bureaucracy that demanded a new type of councillor. Men from humble backgrounds, trained in the law and finance, were taking their place in royal councils. That summer Henry added four new members, each an Englishman, but none of them from the ancestral nobility.[68] He was coming to rely on men of this type, knights and clerks who had proven their ability in the chancery, exchequer and household, not on the tournament field. He wanted professional men like them to run his administration, not untrained landlords with pretensions to status. The barons and bishops, however, considered it a façade: Henry only wanted men he could bend to his will the way he was unable to with them.

Henry agreed to take their complaints under advisement but warned them he would do nothing under compulsion. He tried to lobby them separately, and in one speech to the bishops, spelt out plainly that they were all in this together: 'I am your prince and your king. Without you I cannot live, nor you without me. Your being depends on me and mine on you, for if I am rich, you are rich. If I am poor, you are poor.'[69] In case that wasn't plain enough, he sent Montfort and Peter of Savoy round to work on them, and finally produced a letter from the pope entreating them to act. William Raleigh, who had led the fight for the king's last tax, found himself in a position to exact revenge for Henry locking him out of Winchester, and pleaded with the other bishops to stand firm. He too used the plainest language possible: 'If we are divided, we shall immediately die.' But as he was saying this, he was busy levying his own tax on his newly acquired estates. The discussion dragged on into the following year but neither side gave ground. Henry decided to withdraw the request and fall back on his right to ask for a feudal aid for the marriage of his eldest daughter. This required no consent, but the magnates refused to offer more than a paltry £1 per knight's fee. The result was a disappointing yield of £6,000.[70]

The letter from the pope probably hardened the clergy's opposition to the tax. Earlier that year Innocent had sent a fellow by the name of Martin to make the rounds of English churches, abbeys and religious houses to press for his own subsidy. A materialist and braggart, Innocent IV decided to renew hostilities with the empire and wanted the rest of Europe to pay for it. It was all so unnecessary, because at the outset of his pontificate he got Frederick to make major concessions. They agreed to meet at a halfway point to iron out a treaty, but it turned out to be a ruse. Innocent was intent on crushing the 'dragon' and used a phony rendezvous to dash for the coast, where a squadron of galleys waited to transport him to his native Genoa. 'The wicked flee when no man pursueth,' joked Frederick, but he understood the danger of a pope on the loose and put together an army to march north against his implacable enemy. Learning that he was coming for him, Innocent crossed the Alps in November 1244.[71]

His flight westward had been made possible by the fifth Savoyard brother to enter the story. Philip was about Henry's age and had met the king when he escorted his sister Beatrice and niece Sanchia to Gascony. Like his brothers, he aspired to lead armies but had to settle for scrounging off church offices or courtly favours. As the Bishop of Valence, he convinced his brother Amadeus, the Count of Savoy, to allow the pope and his entourage to pass through his territory despite their allegiance to Frederick. The papal party settled in Lyon, which was then part of the empire but had always enjoyed a measure of autonomy under the local archbishop. Seeing that Philip was a man to get things done, Innocent forced the Archbishop of Lyon to step aside and put him in his place.[72] Since Philip was an uncle of the Queen of France, it was understood that Louis would offer the pope refuge if the emperor came after him there.

Like Henry and the rest of the ruling class, Louis wished the pope and emperor could somehow put this squabble behind them. Almost since it began, the Mongols had been sweeping through Eastern Europe, ravaging what is now Poland, Hungary and the Balkans. The fear and destruction they wrought made them seem like the horsemen of the apocalypse. They displaced whole peoples and empires before them, including the Khwarismian Turks from south of the Aral Sea. Wandering as far west as Syria, 10,000 of them fell on lightly defended Jerusalem at the encouragement of the sultanate in Egypt and sacked the city in August 1244. They then joined the Egyptians in Gaza and defeated a combined Frankish and Syrian army in October.[73] In a matter of months, Jerusalem had been lost and the crusader states pushed to the edge of the Mediterranean. Christendom in the Holy Land was on the verge of extinction, and all the pope could think of was his private vendetta against the man he dubbed the Antichrist.

There had still been no official word of the disaster when Louis fell ill before Christmas. Although he and Margaret had finally produced a son and heir that year, Louis had not been the same physically since contracting the disease that wiped out a good portion of his army in Poitou. At one point he was thought to be dying, and a desperate Blanche had the crown of thorns and other relics placed at his bedside. If they didn't do the trick, something else did, because Louis slowly came out of his delirium. Her joy soon turned to dread, however, when he decided that thanks were in order for his recovery and so he vowed then and there to go on crusade.[74] For all her pleas for him to reconsider, the news of the fall of Jerusalem coincided with his convalescence, and made him determined to sail. It took him to the age of 30, but he had finally stood up to his mother.

9

THE GARDEN OF OUR DELIGHTS 1245–1248

Of all the troubles beleaguering Henry during these years, he was most worried about the queen, now 21 years old and about to have their fourth child. Given the complications of her last childbirth, the king turned to prayer and supplication to ensure a safe delivery, culminating in the lighting of 1,000 candles before Beckett's shrine in Canterbury. On 16 January 1245 Eleanor gave birth to a healthy boy, and father and nation couldn't be happier. The royal couple had a love for all their children rarely matched in English history, but ensuring the succession was always a priority. Indeed, 6-year-old Edward became seriously ill that same year, making the addition of a younger brother to the family all the more timely.[1]

He was given the name Edmund, after the Saxon king martyred in 869 at the hands of the Vikings Ivar the Boneless and his brother Ubba. Henry venerated St Edmund second only to Edward the Confessor and had informed the Abbot of Bury St Edmunds that if he had a son, he would bear the name of their patron saint. But as the contractions began, another Edmund entered his thoughts, the former Archbishop of Canterbury who had died in France four years earlier. A movement was underway to canonise him after miracles were reported at his tomb and in England. Nicholas Farnham, Eleanor's doctor until he became the Bishop of Durham in 1241, was said to have been cured of a tumour by drinking a concoction made with trimmings from Edmund's beard. Two days before the birth, Henry asked Edmund's two sisters, nuns at the Cistercian priory of Catesby, to bring their brother's cloak, then thought to have the same healing powers as his beard trimmings, to the queen's bedside at Westminster, just in case complications arose.[2]

The safe delivery of mother and child made a believer out of Henry. Prior to the birth, he had opposed canonisation for Edmund on the grounds that it would be used against him politically. There was already talk going around about how the former archbishop had been driven out of the country by the king when everyone knew he was on his way to Rome to lodge another complaint against his own community of Canterbury. The monks were, in fact, against his canonisation, in part because their other tormentor, Simon Langton, was driving the process forward.[3] But bishops like Grosseteste and Raleigh were sure to forget all that and instead evoke the future saint as a reminder to all that Henry had once sworn an oath before Edmund to abide by Magna Carta. In choosing to embrace the emerging cult of Edmund of Abingdon, Henry was not only giving thanks where thanks were due, but also co-opting a potentially formidable symbol for his critics.

For a symbol of more lasting endearment, Henry embarked that year on a truly great achievement. Having settled on Westminster as the capital of the country, he wanted the abbey there to serve for coronations and royal burials, and the current building simply wouldn't do. The cathedrals recently built in Winchester, Canterbury and Salisbury rendered it obsolete with their high vaults, elegant arches, window traceries and flying buttresses, part of the gothic style then sweeping through northern France. Henry had never seen the cathedrals of Amiens, Chartres or Rheims, but there were enough masons at work in England who had and who could only shake their heads at the Norman monolith built by his idol Edward the Confessor. Pulling down his abbey and building a new one was an odd way of honouring him, but reconstruction plans went as far back as 1220, when Henry laid the foundation stone of the Lady Chapel. After more than twenty years, the monks had given up hope of ever completing the chapel and all but invited the king to do with the abbey what he would, but of course at his own expense.

Henry was pleased to step in and hired Master Henry of Rayne to oversee the initial phase. It was a huge project, with as many as 800 men working on it at one time and hundreds more supplying the tools, construction materials, logistics and administration. While he would have liked to have had the resources that allowed Louis to build Sainte-Chapelle in only five years, the new Westminster Abbey would be a work in progress to the end of his reign and beyond, mostly because of money. At least £18,000 was spent on it during the first eight years.[4] The financial crunch of the next decade made the work precarious after that, as another round of expensive, less tangible foreign policy initiatives consumed ever more revenue. These initiatives, however, would give Henry his first look at French architecture and ultimately inspire his final image of the abbey.

Much of that foreign policy arose as a result of the Council of Lyon convened in the summer of 1245. Innocent had called for the council, the first in thirty years, to deal with various problems besetting the Church, but the pope made no secret of what he was really after. He intended to 'lay the axe at the root of the tree' and depose the emperor. He avoided making it look like the political vendetta that it was and lambasted Frederick for the irreligious nature of his harem, heresies and heathen offspring. The imperial counsel Thaddaeus of Suessa skilfully rebutted the charges before the assembly, pointing out that, unlike the pope, the emperor did not allow usurers to have the free run of his administration. But the deed of deposition had been drawn up long before he began to speak. 'I have done my part,' proclaimed Innocent. 'God must do the rest.' Frederick reacted to the news by putting on his crown and writing a flurry of letters to the other rulers of Europe, warning them that they could be next.[5]

For Henry, the deposition marked the twilight of his efforts over the past decade to build a strong alliance between England and the empire. Despite the cajoling, expense and support, Frederick had always shied away from any confrontation with Louis. He preferred to pick fights with the pope, a far more dangerous opponent it turned out. Henry sympathised, but the English delegation to the Council did little to defend him beyond a token plea for fairness. Their more important business had to do with all the money being siphoned out of the country by the 'endless number' of Italians installed in church benefices, to the tune of £40,000 annually according to one royal inquiry. They also wanted something done about Martin, the papal agent. He had been snooping around the accounts of priories and monasteries for more than a year and that was long enough.[6]

In fact, he was just then being run out of the realm. A group of knights had gathered for a tournament in Dunstable and, upon hearing that it had been banned by the king, decided to take it out on Martin. He was visited at his lodgings at the New Temple and told he had three days to disappear or risk being cut to pieces. He fled to Henry for protection, but should have known he would receive the cold shoulder that awaited him. Henry had been furious over reports of his arrogant conduct and wrote him an indignant letter to desist or 'we shall put a rein upon you'. Martin seems to have left in genuine fear for his life and complained about his ill treatment to the pope. According to Paris, Innocent told him not to fret: 'Once the dragon has been crushed, all the little serpents will be trodden underfoot.'[7]

He said nothing like that to the delegation. Their ranks included Roger Bigod, Ralph Fitz-Nicholas, John Fitz-Geoffrey and Philip Basset, hardened warriors only too willing to crush a papal agent or two. Speaking for them was William of Powicke, one of Henry's clerks, and he made a good enough presentation of their grievances that Innocent asked to think about it. He was just buying time, as he had no intention of making allowances in his hour of triumph. He responded by pigeonholing each of the English bishops in Lyon, including Robert Grosseteste, Walter Cantilupe and Fulk Basset, and ordering them to affix their seals to a charter confirming King John's pledge to pay tribute to the papacy. Henry was enraged when he learned about it because he specifically warned the bishops not to let something like that happen. He denounced them for weakness and swore off any more payments.[8]

Excepting recent episcopal elections, Innocent had tried to curry Henry's favour. He exhorted the clergy to grant him a subsidy, confirmed his ecclesiastical rights and privileges, and gave permission to the queen and 'ten honest women' to enter certain monasteries for prayers. He even revoked his earlier agreement to make Wales a papal fief, which would have deprived the kings of England of their overlordship there. That had been a close call, but the message was clear. If Henry didn't want to pay tribute, Dafydd would. The payments were brought up to date and did not cease completely until 1366.[9]

Dafydd wasn't cowed in any case and continued to proclaim himself 'Prince of Wales'. The sporadic fighting left Henry no choice but to go there in August 1245 to deal with the uprising. His plan called for starving the Welsh into submission, but the general embargo he imposed made it a miserable time for both sides as provisions ran low and an early frost set in. Supplies and auxiliaries were requisitioned from Ireland, but they were slow in coming and ended up costing long-time justiciar Maurice Fitz-Gerald his job.[10] When the irregulars arrived, they ravaged the countryside while Henry supervised the building of a new castle at Degannwy. The situation was still unsettled when he left in October. Dafydd died childless the following February, technically leaving Henry as his heir and in a good position to pursue that claim. But unlike his patrimony on the Continent, his heart was never into conquering Wales, which was what assuming complete lordship of the land entailed. That was clear when Owain escaped his captors in Cheshire and scurried to his brothers 'like a hare'. Henry left Nicholas de Molis, his former seneschal of Gascony, to work out alliances with other Welsh lords to keep the pressure on the sons of Gruffudd to submit.[11]

While Henry was busy trying to pacify the north of Wales, Walter Marshal was on his deathbed in Pembrokeshire in the south. He died on 27 November 1245 and was buried at Tintern Abbey. His brother Anselm stood to succeed him and would have been the only Marshal son besides William II that Henry was prepared to receive without contention. But he was already stricken by the malady that killed him less than a month later and never got around to performing homage. Since he too died childless, Paris notes that the mother of the five Marshal boys had once foretold how all her sons would be earls one day, but of only one earldom. The story behind this misfortune had to do with their father and a dispute he got into with an Irish bishop over two manors Marshal helped himself to while 'indulging in slaughter and pillage'. When he refused to return them, the bishop excommunicated him and refused to release his soul from hell until he got his property back. Marshal's sons spurned Henry's efforts to make amends to the bishop, who responded by cursing them with extinction in one generation.[12]

Marshal also had five daughters. All but one, the eldest, Maud, would be dead within a year, and the task before Henry was how to divide up the estate among so many widows and grandchildren. Maud got the honorary office of 'Marshal' before passing it on to her son, Roger Bigod. She had three other children from her first marriage, plus a son, John, and daughter, Isabella, from her later marriage to William de Warenne, the Earl of Surrey. Second-born daughter Isabel was the mother of Richard de Clare, the Earl of Gloucester, who was knighted by Henry that year. After her came Sibyl, who had seven daughters with the Earl of Derby. The fourth daughter, Eva, became a widow with four daughters after William de Braose was hung by Llywelyn ap Iorwerth in 1230. The second of her daughters, Maud, was married to Marcher lord Roger Mortimer, himself a grandson of Llywelyn. The youngest Marshal daughter, Joan, had died in her twenties a decade earlier. Her daughter Joan Munchensi was about 15 and, after the death of her brother John two years later, she became the most eligible heiress in the land.

The most eligible heiress in all of Europe just then was Beatrice of Provence, the youngest of the four sisters, who inherited the county upon the death of her father in August 1245. In drawing up his will, Raymond Berenger figured that his three older daughters were set for life. Margaret was married to the King of France, Eleanor to the King of England, Sanchia to reputedly the richest man in Europe. It was probably because of Richard of Cornwall's wealth that Sanchia received a gratuity of only £3,333, while her older sisters got double that.[13] All three were unhappy that the youngest, who was only 13, got their homeland lock, stock and barrel, but the scramble to procure the heiress was on just the same.

There was Raymond of Toulouse, who had worked out another marital alliance with Raymond Berenger when they met at the Council of Lyon the previous month. Neither liked the other, but both wanted independence from the French monarchy more than anything. Raymond's nominal ally King James of Aragon had ancestral rights in the region and brought an army up to Aix to claim the girl for his son. Frederick had similar designs for his own son Conrad and sent a fleet to Provence for her. When no port would take his ships, he decided to march there in person. Understandably nervous at all the attention on her daughter, Beatrice of Savoy asked the pope to take her under his protection. He would have the final say in who she married anyway, since all the parties were related in some degree or another. That was fine with Frederick. He would take his army to Lyon to have it out with the pope about his deposition and get the dispensation for his son while he was at it.[14]

Throughout this time, Innocent led Raymond and James to believe that he was leaning towards them, but he already had somebody else in mind for Beatrice. On

25 November 1245 he took his court to Cluny, about 60 miles north of Lyon, to await the arrival of Louis, Blanche and her youngest son Charles. He was 19 years old, ambitious, athletic and completely full of himself. In the talks that emerged from their meeting, it was decided that Beatrice would marry Charles in return for Louis offering the pope protection from Frederick. Charles and Philip of Savoy left the meeting with an armed troop to get the girl, and the marriage was performed on 31 January 1246. The rushed, secretive nature of the ceremony made the conceited Charles complain that it lacked dignity, so Louis made sure he got plenty of pomp when he knighted him later that spring and gave him his appanage of Anjou and Maine, both former Plantagenet lordships.[15]

Henry was in Wales when he received word of his father-in-law's death. He sent strict orders that no announcement was to be made until he could break the news to Eleanor himself. Her personal grief aside, there was work to be done. Anticipating the French moves on Provence, they worked out a strategy with Peter of Savoy and Aigueblanche to gain some leverage if Henry and Eleanor were completely cut out of the settlement, particularly concerning the castles they held on lien. The plan they came up with was to acquire control over more castles and land, this time in Savoy. Count Amadeus would do homage to Henry in return for £666 and an annuity of £133, plus a marriage for one of his granddaughters to a future earl, either Edmund de Lacy, a royal ward, or John de Warenne, whose guardian was then Peter of Savoy.[16]

Under this arrangement, it would be Henry's decision to open the Alpine passes to Frederick, inviting the emperor to make that long elusive move against France and have at the pope. This allowed Amadeus to avoid the papal wrath should that happen and gain some material advantage in an alliance with England. The deal was sealed in Westminster on 16 January, but news of it was unlikely to have reached Provence before the wedding. It probably would have made no difference in any case. Innocent already had plans in motion to have the princes of Germany elect a new emperor, which would be enough to keep Frederick busy beyond the Alps for the time being. Assured of his safety, the pope could easily deny Henry and Richard of Cornwall's request to revisit Raymond Berenger's will. The only consolation he offered them was a personal inducement to Charles to respect the rights of his sisters-in-law in Provence.[17]

As the dowager countess Beatrice of Savoy had played her role in this shady business, all but inviting the malicious Matthew Paris to suggest that she washed her hands of Henry, Eleanor, Richard and Sanchia with contemptuous ingratitude. In truth, she was mortified by what Charles of Anjou was doing and didn't hide her disgust with him. With the drive and ruthlessness that marked the rest of his career, he fell on Provence with a team of French clerks and lawyers who promptly informed their counterparts that their day in the sun was over. She had naively acquiesced in the marriage as the surest way of maintaining her administration, but could do little as her new son-in-law proceeded to trample on everyone's rights, including her own. She managed to stir up enough local resistance to get the pope and Louis to lean on Charles as far as they dared, but she was still going to have to answer to Henry and Eleanor some day for her poor judgement. The same went for her brother Boniface. He not only knew about the wedding, he was there.[18]

Boniface could have reminded Henry that, before he called him an ingrate again, he had come to Lyon to be consecrated by Innocent and stayed on afterwards for the Council. He only attended the wedding because he was in the neighbourhood, because Beatrice was his niece just the same as Eleanor was, and his brother Philip was the master of ceremonies. As for the debt of gratitude he owed, the king had secured his election as the Archbishop of Canterbury all right, but the bishopric was heavily in debt. Boniface was forced to ask the pope for help in liquidating it, and Innocent's willingness to do so obliged him all the more to look favourably on the wedding.

The papal expedient, however, flabbergasted the clergy. Innocent decreed that the first year's revenues of all benefices that fell vacant in England should go to Canterbury for the next seven years, or until the £6,666 in debt listed by Boniface had been covered. The appointment of Savoyard bishop Aigueblanche to oversee the collection only outraged xenophobes like Matthew Paris more. He naturally blamed Henry for promoting these two 'freebooters' in the first place, and remained unmoved even after the king advised the bishops to ignore the decree and ordered the port wardens to bar anybody carrying a copy of it from entering the country. Presumably that applied to Boniface as well, but the archbishop was nowhere to be seen. Fearing the backlash, he hid out at the papal court in Lyon. He had his proctors do the dirty work and got the pope to threaten anybody who stood in their way.[19]

★ ★ ★

It had been three decades since England was engulfed in civil war, when Henry's crown and very life were at stake. He hadn't forgotten the role played by the papacy in reclaiming the kingdom for him and told Grosseteste as much after the bishop returned from Lyon:

> You may take it for certain that we shall show and observe, entirely and always, obedience, fidelity and devotion to the lord pope as our spiritual father, and to the Roman Church as our mother, and that we will firmly, constantly and truly abide by them in prosperity and adversity.

Grosseteste reported these words to the pope, intimating, 'I thought the response of the lord king should be written down for your holiness, to make you unambiguously aware of the kind of devotion this lord has for you and the Roman Catholic Church'.[20] Henry's own letter to the pope showed little of that obedience, fidelity and devotion. While still entertaining 'sincere affection' for the Church, he could not turn a deaf year to the 'unusual clamorous complaints' of the nobles, clergy and people of England. He wrote in response to a meeting of Parliament held on 18 March 1246 in Westminster to deal with papal greed. Three other letters were written, each one representing the barons, bishops and, last but not least, the abbots, whose religious houses were the main targets of the tax collectors. The idea was to coordinate their protests in a series of separate complaints bemoaning a common injustice. They were written in the same vein, like the barons telling their 'mother' that if she 'deprives them of their milk, she may be reputed to be a stepmother'. Not until these abuses were corrected, they added, would the danger pass, not only for the Church, but the king as well. The abbots seconded this notion that Henry's authority was on the line: 'The people are stirred up against the king and are ready to withdraw their fidelity from him unless by his royal power he stays this evil.' The only real grovelling in the three letters came from the bishops, who threw themselves 'at the feet of your holiness, and with tearful entreaties beg of you, giving heed to the fervour of faith in the English'.[21]

Some of the bishops had every reason to worry. A letter from the pope arrived at this time asking the prelates who attended the Council of Lyon, including Robert Grosseteste (Lincoln), William Raleigh (Winchester), Fulk Basset (London) and Walter Cantilupe (Worcester), what had become of the £4,000 subsidy they had agreed to collect on his behalf. Henry was astounded to find out they had entered into a secret covenant with the pope on taxation and rounded on them for presuming to act on their own authority.[22]

With pagan logic, Grosseteste refused to admit they had been caught red-handed. It was the pope's authority, he insisted, that compelled them to act as they had. To disobey his command would be 'like the sin of witchcraft, and refusing to obey it like the crime of idolatry'. The way he saw it, there should only be indignation if they hadn't collected the money, for the Church had been driven into exile and had no adequate means to support itself. Despite the bold front, Grosseteste knew they were in trouble. In the opening of his letter, he couldn't exalt the king highly enough: 'To his most excellent Lord Henry, by the grace of God illustrious King of England, Lord of Ireland, Duke of Normandy and of Aquitaine, and Count of Anjou: Robert, by divine mercy humble minister of the Church of Lincoln, sends greeting and both dutiful and devoted respect.'[23]

The bishop could appreciate the rebuke better when he next received a visit from a pair of English Franciscans. He had always welcomed the friars, seeing in their pastoral mission the cure for souls he long felt had been neglected in the papal obsession with money and power. His friend Adam Marsh, who was another close friend and adviser of Simon and Eleanor de Montfort, had given up a career path in the Church to join their order. It was therefore a bewildered and dismayed bishop who learned from these two particular friars that they had come for £4,000, the tax assessed for his diocese. Innocent had drafted the friars to preach the crusade and figured they might as well do some tax collection while they were at it. Calling their action dishonourable, Grosseteste completely reversed himself and insisted he could pay nothing until he had discussed the matter with the king and Parliament.[24]

That was fine by Henry, who wrote a letter to him and the other bishops to remind them, now for the fourth time, that he had prohibited all levies for Lyon. He was especially angry with them because they were supposed to proceed in unison with him and the nobles. They had all agreed during Parliament to suspend all collections until they had received the pope's response to their letters, and yet here the bishops were, still secretly engaged in the business. The king wondered at their lack of shame and warned them to desist immediately and on no account to send any money abroad. Should they persist, 'we will lay our heavy hand on your possessions to a greater extent than you may fancy'.[25]

In early July the embassy was back from Lyon and Parliament gathered at Winchester to hear what they had to say. According to Paris, they reported that Innocent had flown into a rage upon receiving their demands and hissed that Henry was 'playing the Frederick'. The pope dismissed the king's objections with a curt 'he has his opinion and I have mine' and tacitly stood by as the embassy was ostracised for the rest of their stay.[26] None of this anger showed in the letter he wrote to Henry at the same time. In it he apologised for the subsidy but insisted that it was necessary because the danger in the Holy Land posed a danger to all Christian countries. As for his appropriating benefices, he needed to reward the people working hard for him at the papal court (not a few of whom were his relatives) and he was asking for these revenues throughout Europe, not just in England. Henry was unappeased and ordered his ban on the tax collection read out publicly in every hamlet. He did give way on the annual tribute, but only after Innocent made a personal appeal for it.[27]

Henry went back to Winchester for Christmas, where the recent, bitter standoff between him and Raleigh was completely forgotten and the bishop rejoiced over the royal visit. He had been one of the bishops caught up in the papal scandal and so was eager to put on his best face before the king. Another bishop involved, Fulk Basset, was at the same time convening a meeting at St Paul's in London to discuss Innocent's latest demand, now one half of all ecclesiastical revenue from benefices. Hearing what was going on, Henry sent two of his most trusted advisers, John of Lexington and Lawrence of St Martin, to warn them against yielding. Basset and his officials settled for sending the pope a letter – nothing is more indicative of this crisis than the slew of letters that went back and forth – that reiterated all the abuses besetting the faithful because of the misguided papal policy. If the subsidy were paid, the monks, priests, deacons and canons would be reduced to begging, and charity for the poor would suffer. By their reckoning, the pope was asking for more than £40,000, and to give him an idea of the havoc that would wreak, they recalled how crosses, chalices and other instruments of public worship had been pawned or sold off to raise a similar amount to help ransom Richard the Lionheart more than half a century earlier.[28]

When Parliament met in February 1247 this issue was again at the top of the agenda. The bishops were not in attendance, doubtless to avoid the angry looks of the others for allowing Innocent to believe that England was indeed, as he believed, an 'inexhaustible well' and 'our garden of delights'. All that came out of it was more letters, this time from the clergy and community combined. The nobility was strangely quiet, which was not the case in France. There, a group of barons led by the usual malcontents Peter of Dreux and the Lusignans formed a mutual defence league against papal exactions and benefactions. Louis could no longer ignore the practices flourishing under his protection, especially now that the extortion was lumped together with his crusade fundraising. At a grand parliament held in Paris, it was decided to dispatch envoys to Lyon in May. Through them, Louis reminded Innocent that the absolute power enjoyed by the papacy came with the responsibility to use it wisely.[29] But unlike Henry, he did not challenge the pope's authority, only decried the state of Christendom languishing under his watch. The quarrel with Frederick was upsetting everything, he said, and since he had it on good information that the emperor was offering to spend the rest of his life in the Holy Land, he advised Innocent to give him one more chance.

The emperor was invited to appear at Lyon to make his case. With the Alpine passes opened to him, he arrived in Turin in May with an army, but insisted he was coming in peace and had with him his 10-year-old son Henry by Isabella so the pope could baptise him. But just as Innocent believed Frederick's intentions were no good, neither were his own. The previous year he arranged the election of Henry Raspe of Thuringia as the King of the Romans, the title conferred by German electors on their candidate for emperor, held just then by Frederick's eldest legitimate son, Conrad. After some initial success, things went badly for Raspe and he died after only nine months as the 'anti-king'. Under pressure from Louis, Innocent had to make a show of seeking reconciliation, but in fact he had other conspiracies in the works. He instigated an uprising in Parma that forced the emperor to abandon his march to Lyon. He was still besieging the city when William of Holland was elected to succeed Raspe.[30]

Innocent's brinkmanship finally paid off in England as well. In April 1247 Parliament met again, this time in Oxford, and Henry finally dropped his opposition to the subsidy and provisions. The united front of the king, nobility and clergy of the previous year had dissolved for good as the pro-papal bishops were joined by barons like Richard of Cornwall, who switched sides after Innocent renewed his grant to sell crusade indulgences, even though he had no intention of ever going back.[31] What clinched it was the pope's threat to put England under interdict, backed up by the report that he had empowered Walter Cantilupe, the Bishop of Worcester, to carry it out.

The last interdict, under King John, had been a disaster, resulting in the subjection of the kingdom to the papacy and the payment of the accursed tribute. More pious than his father to begin with, Henry simply could not contemplate being excluded from the Church. Putting on grand displays of devotion, whether in visiting shrines, feeding the poor or holding sumptuous feasts for the saints was part of the public consumption of his kingship, but at night, in his stately bed at Westminster, he peered through the squint in the wall into his private chapel and prayed for spiritual rejuvenation. Going to mass every day, even multiple times, was for him as compulsory as dining. By contrast, his father ate heartily during his excommunication, leading his subjects to joke, 'How fat that stag has grown without ever attending mass.'[32]

In the month following Parliament, Henry retreated 10 miles north of Oxford to his country palace at Woodstock. Had he been John, he would have taken off to hunt stag, but Henry preferred the quieter outdoor pursuits of landscaping and strolling in the garden. There was a beautiful park nearby at Everswell, full of pools, pavilions and orchards. The place had been built by his grandfather to evoke the popular romance of Tristan and Isolde, another tale of illicit love that Henry and Eleanor were certainly familiar with, but the real romance Henry II had had in mind was his affair with the Fair Rosamund, which began just before the birth of John in 1166.[33] The legend of their lovemaking in a labyrinth meant to confound the searches of his wife Eleanor of Aquitaine, who eventually succeeds and poisons Rosamund, was contrived centuries later, but tales about the affair were already widespread. Solid as their marriage was, Henry and Eleanor could afford to indulge in mischievous speculation about it, but chances were they preferred Tristan and Isolde.

Matters of state followed the king wherever he went, and at Woodstock he received Owain and Llywelyn ap Gruffudd from Wales. They had given up their stand against the crown after realising that the easiest way to share rule for the time being was to submit to the king. On 30 April they sealed a treaty that called for them to do homage, accept royal jurisdiction in their territories and essentially go back to the status of Henry as their lord as per the agreement of

1241. Neither was happy with the arrangement, but it kept the peace for the next decade.[34]

Another important visitor received at Woodstock was Peter of Savoy, who had arrived from the Continent with two young ladies in tow. One was Alice de Saluzzo, the granddaughter of Amadeus. As per the treaty with Savoy, she had come to marry Edmund de Lacy, the 17-year-old heir to the earldom of Lincoln. The other was another Alice, destined to marry Richard de Burgh, the heir to the Irish lordship of Connacht.[35] There was nothing new about the Savoyards scoring patronage in this fashion, but it was the arrival of a third Alice as the bride of an English noble that marked a watershed in Henry's reign.

She was his 23-year-old half-sister from Poitou, the daughter of Hugh and Isabella. The Lusignan fortunes had dwindled considerably since their ill-fated rebellion against Louis, and following the death of their mother Isabella the year before in 1246, Henry saw opportunities for them, and him, in England. He had just the match for Alice: 16-year-old John de Warenne, half-brother of Roger Bigod and heir to the earldom of Surrey. Warenne was actually a ward of Peter of Savoy, but Henry had retained the marriage rights to the boy.[36] Peter wouldn't have complained anyway, not if he wanted another ward to come his way. But much to his dismay, he could see, as could everybody else, that the Lusignans had arrived in England.

They could hardly miss them. Forever the master of the grand entrance, Henry didn't bring Alice over alone, but accompanied by three of his five half-brothers and a papal legate passing through on his way to crown the King of Norway. The oldest Lusignan son, Hugh XI, had succeeded their mother as Count of Angoulême. He was making plans to go on Louis's crusade with his brother Geoffrey and their father Hugh. The three who came over were led by Guy, who was also planning to go on the crusade, but made the trip to England to raise funds for it. The two other brothers were Aymer and William, both commonly known by their birthplace of Valence. Like their sister, they had come to stay. Aymer was sent to study at Oxford in preparation for a career in the Church and, although still in his twenties, Henry could easily see him as a bishop in the near future. For William de Valence, the incentive to remain in England was immediate and spectacular. On 13 August 1247 he was given Joan Munchensi, the Marshal co-heiress to Pembroke, in marriage.[37]

The marriages of both Lusignan siblings turned out to be happy and successful, but it was not to validate his matchmaking instincts that Henry arranged them. They were political unions first and foremost. Henry wanted to bind the earldoms of Pembroke, Surrey and Lincoln closer to his court, to have his and the queen's relatives watching out for their interests throughout the realm. He figured he could count on the loyalty of these relatives more than the traditional clans, especially in Pembrokeshire, where he had had all he could take from the Marshals. He was also binding to England the Savoyards, with their indispensable network of diplomacy, and the Lusignans, who were not an entirely spent force on the Continent, with a permanent landed settlement.[38]

Interestingly, this marked the third time that Henry disposed of three earldoms in quick succession. He had a slightly superstitious nature and, being the third Henry, liked doing things in threes. He may also have believed in the old adage that 'all good things come in three'. The earls of August 1231, however, had not panned out particularly well. Richard Marshal had rebelled and thrown the kingdom into turmoil; Richard of Cornwall had rebelled and put a stiff price on his loyalty; Simon de Montfort had taken advantage of him and insulted him in his hour of need. Henry had better luck with the earls of May 1233, although Roger Bigod would always be something of a wild card.[39]

Strictly speaking, William de Valence was never an earl. His position was the same as Peter of Savoy's, who had been given custody of the earldom of Richmond near the Scottish borderlands six years earlier. Apart from Montfort, the only foreigner elevated to the rank of earl was the non-descript John de Plessis, a Norman who had been in royal service longer than Simon. In 1242 Plessis was with Henry in Poitou when the king granted him the marriage of Margaret, a widow who succeeded her brother as the Countess of Warwick. The proximity of that earldom to the Marches made Henry eager to make sure it fell into the hands of a loyal supporter. Plessis became the Earl of Warwick by right of Margaret, but a prenuptial agreement drawn up with her, one of the first of its kind in England, suggests that she was married to someone else at her death in 1253.[40]

As Henry's immediate kin, William de Valence was a step up from Plessis, but he was still a landless newcomer. It was one thing to insinuate him into the nobility, quite another to give him the honorific but prestigious and wholly English title of earl, at least at the outset. The king was nevertheless determined to promote him and decided to use the annual feast of St Edward to knight him and several other young men. He was going to make it a magnificent occasion because he had a lot to be thankful for just then. He had turned 40, his son Edward had recently recovered from a serious illness and the building works on Westminster Abbey were in full swing.[41] He had, moreover, received a relic from the Holy Land that he intended to keep in the abbey. It was no ordinary relic, however, and getting it there with the requisite reverence and devotion meant devising an elaborate ceremony that only a natural showman could pull off.

★ ★ ★

The nobles and spectators who came to London to hear the 'agreeable news of a holy benefit lately conferred by heaven on the English' were not disappointed, neither by the relic nor Henry's performance. After spending the previous night in fasting and prayer, he emerged on the morning of 13 October 1247 barefoot and dressed in a simple hoodless cloak, ready to take his place at the head of a procession starting out from St Paul's Cathedral. He was handed the relic: drops of the blood of Jesus Christ contained in a crystal vial. Holding it in both hands high above his head, he led the procession towards Westminster some 2 miles in the distance. He kept his eyes fixed on the vial the whole way, even when they encountered uneven patches of road. He walked beneath a canopy held aloft by four men bearing lances and was supported by an attendant on each side propping up his arms as needed.

When he reached the palatial home of the Bishop of Durham in today's Whitehall, he was met by the monks of the abbey and a congregation of bishops, abbots and other clergy numbering more than 100. They carried lit tapers and sang praises of the Lord as they followed the king around Westminster Palace before entering the abbey, where Henry made an official gift of the blood to the holy brethren of the place. The Bishop of Norwich preached a sermon that exalted these few drops above all the relics collected by Louis in Saint-Chapelle and offered indulgences to all those who came to worship them. Afterwards Henry swapped his cloak for cloth of gold, and knighted William de Valence and the others, most of them Englishmen. He was wearing a small crown that may have been meant to recall the chaplet used in his first coronation, as the canopy he walked under was a reminder of Eleanor's.

Matthew Paris was an eyewitness to this event. Henry was already familiar with the chronicler and, seeing him in the crowd, summoned him to sit on the step beneath the throne in the great hall. He asked him if he was impressed by what he had seen. 'Yes, my lord, the proceedings of this day are indeed glorious,' the monk answered. The king ordered him to record everything for posterity in a 'plain and full account', as though aware of Paris's penchant for inflecting his work with diatribe and invective. He then invited him and three companions to join him for breakfast the next morning.[42]

The fullness of Paris's account is evident by the inclusion of the doubts voiced about the relic. It was a gift from the Patriarch of Jerusalem, who claimed that it came from the treasure of relics supposedly ransomed by Richard the Lionheart for £5,000. In witness whereof, the patriarch and several clergymen from the crusader states attached their seals to the vial. That wasn't good enough for the doubters, who logically wondered how Christ could have been resurrected whole if some of his blood were missing (actually all of it, considering the enormous number of blood relics being passed off). To answer that question, Henry turned to Robert Grosseteste. He was not only the most brilliant mind in England at that time, but the one person who could confound any critic with his tortuous logic.

Grosseteste began by explaining there are two types of blood. One is produced by nutrition, which is to say nourishment, and is lost through effusions like nosebleeds. Then there is the blood of the innermost chamber of the heart, vital for the 'consumption of essential moistures' and therefore human existence. Joseph of Arimathea, said to have retrieved and embalmed the body of Christ with Nicodemus, kept the blood he washed from the wounds suffered on the cross and gave it, mixed with water and sweat, to his friends to use as medicine. This blood was meant to stay behind on earth as a memorial of the Passion, but being only diluted nutritional blood, it was now in a 'superfluous' state, not exactly the best selling point for the Westminster relic. As for the true Holy Blood itself, it disappeared with the resurrection. Grosseteste recalls that this is all speculation, because the Lord works in mysterious ways and whatever of his body he chose to take with him or leave behind was his business.[43]

Despite Henry's performance and the promise of indulgences to worshippers, the relic failed to catch on. The doubts about its authenticity never went away, probably because one of the arguments used to defend it in the beginning ended up working against it. The blood was transmitted from the Holy Land to England without any money changing hands. It was untainted by the evil corrupting the Church and mankind, but that purity of thought itself was tainted by an adage just as relevant then as today: you get what you pay for.

Another problem was Westminster Abbey, which remained a building site until the end of Henry's reign. Shrines with firmly established pedigrees or set in the pastoral calm and serenity of the countryside naturally had greater appeal to pilgrims. Henry, however, appears to have taken it all in stride. The expense and care he lavished on the knighting ceremony suggests where his real interests lay that day. Also, the relic may have been a gift, but the patriarch enclosed a letter begging for the restoration of property in England once belonging to his Church of the Holy Sepulchre, an obscure monastic order beset by hard times. He didn't get it.[44]

For sure, Henry was happy to receive the relic. Grosseteste argued that the blood of Christ, even the superfluous variety, trumped the true cross, crown of thorns and other Passion articles in Louis's reliquary. The rivalry between these two first cousins once removed, married to sisters, had only intensified since their troops squared off in Poitou five years earlier. Henry might never have invited Paris to another breakfast had he known that the chronicler, in his account of the Holy Blood, referred to Louis as 'the most Christian king' and his own king as merely 'a most Christian prince'.[45]

Louis was also hogging all the glory with his noisy preparations for the crusade and well-publicised desire to do justice to everyone before departing. He had sent a commission of friars throughout the realm to investigate abuses by his officials, and the news they brought back wasn't good. The scale of grievances was huge, precluding any chance of enacting reform before he left, but Henry thought he might try to take advantage of the situation. He dispatched his brother Richard and brother-in-law Simon to see if Louis's desire for justice included returning his Angevin lordships. Louis reiterated that he wanted nothing more than to return them, but his nobles were against it. He did make a show of it by turning the matter over to a council of bishops to consider, but they too opposed any restitution.[46]

Receiving this news, Simon went home to be present at the St Edward's day festivities, but Richard opted for a pilgrimage to the shrine of Edmund of Abingdon at Pontigny. He attributed his recent recovery from a life-threatening illness to his invocation of Edmund, who had been canonised earlier that year. The translation of the relics of this first English saint in twenty years had taken place on 7 June. It was a huge affair with Louis and his mother in attendance.[47] If they hadn't meant it to be a deliberate affront to Henry, they were doubtless aware of the attempts to politicise Edmund at his expense. Henry, however, was now fully committed to the saint, and after Richard's return he probably spent more time quizzing him closely about Edmund's shrine than Louis's sincerity in resolving their territorial dispute.

Richard had resolved to pay for a quarter of the shrine, but might have noticed that his money didn't get him very far in France. English coins had become so debased by clipping and shaving the metal that Louis ordered those in his kingdom found of insufficient weight to be confiscated and melted down. Following up discussions held at Parliament in Oxford, Richard was contracted to oversee the complete reissue of the currency. He was chosen principally because he had the start-up capital to get the enterprise going. Cornwall was the richest earldom in the realm, yielding about £6,000 a year, at least a quarter of that coming from the tin mines of Devon.[48]

Royal mints were regularly operated in London and Canterbury to accommodate foreign trade. A merchant would bring silver ingot, plate or foreign coins to the exchange and get back their value in pennies minus six on the pound for the king's traditional farm, or profit, and another six or more for minting charges, depending on the quality of his silver. Typically one pound of silver yielded 242 pennies. Each was about the size of a fingertip and stamped with a crowned king on one side and cross with four pellets in each quarter on the other. With the bag of pennies he received for his silver, the merchant then purchased wool for export, the main commodity driving the English economy.[49]

To replace the more than £400,000 worth of coins in circulation, Richard put up £6,667 to purchase silver bullion and set up seventeen local mints to help with production. Once started, the operation funded itself, namely through the exchange of old money for new. During the official assay, or assessment of the silver content, it was found that the current penny was deficient by ten pence on the pound, due mostly to wear and not actual tampering. It was therefore agreed that ten pence on the pound should go for minting charges, while the king got his six pence. This represented a general loss of about 20 per cent for the owner of the old coins.[50] Richard's hoard was exempt. He got back just as many coins as he brought in, and Henry also agreed to split the farm with him as his incentive for coming on board and sticking with it for so long. His contract started on 1 November 1247 and ran for seven years, later extended to twelve.

The new coins were called Long Cross because they were stamped with all four ends of the cross now touching the edge, apparently to deter clipping, and with three pellets in each quarter instead of four. In the first three years some 138 million pennies were minted, valued at just over £550,000, which works out to a daily output of around 150,000 coins. By the time his minting operation was completed, more than 240 million pennies had been issued, generating £20,800 in profits. Richard got his half, £10,400, plus his entire investment back out of his brother's half. But this wasn't his only windfall from this business. He rigorously enforced his right of the exchange, which gave him a monopoly over these transactions. He set up inquiries into infringements all over the country and collected another £3,400 in fines.[51]

Another inquisition was launched to expose the people behind the debasement of the currency. Paris blames the Jews and foreign merchants, saying that the former were driven to desperation by Henry's taxation. The £13,334 paid in 1241 was tripled three years later to a new tallage of £40,000, spread out over the rest of the decade. The plutocrats bore the brunt of it, but inevitably the effects were felt throughout their communities. In the end eight Jews were fined for clipping coins, a far cry from the mass executions for the same offence that blighted the next reign. Louis was merciless with those found guilty of tampering with his money and ordered them to be 'suspended on gibbets and exposed to the winds', a polite way of saying they were strung up.[52]

Altogether Jewish taxation during the decade represented not quite two years of income for Henry, and yet by 1248 he was broke again. The expeditions to Poitou, Scotland and Wales were expensive enough, but his construction costs, typically about £2,500 a year, were now nearly doubled to accommodate the rebuilding of Westminster Abbey. His almsgiving also soared, and the defeat in Poitou did nothing to change his policy of paying fees, or foreign aid, for his Continental alliances. He had managed up until now through the deaths of several barons and bishops. At one point, he had five earldoms in his hands, including Arundel after the death of Hugh d'Aubigny in 1243, and Devon two years later when Baldwin de Redvers, who served with Henry in Poitou, died still not yet 30 years old. But it was his windfall from vacant bishoprics that provided much of the extra revenue. Nearly 20 per cent of Henry's income before 1245 came from this one source alone. It fell from £6,000 a year to less than a tenth of that as the new bishops took over.[53]

On 15 February he convened one of the largest parliaments of his reign, with nine bishops, nine earls and a multitude of barons, knights and clergy in attendance, and asked for a tax. He was not only rebuffed but rebuked for the state of the kingdom. In addition to the usual grievances about foreigners, his right of prise drew severe criticism. Apparently even the fishermen were wary of coming in with their catch for fear of getting robbed by his agents. The king was advised to appoint a chancellor and justiciar with their approval in order to correct these abuses and overcome the scandal he brought on himself and the kingdom.[54]

Our only reporter for this and the other parliaments of that era is Paris. He paints it as another stormy session ending with Henry holding his head in shame, but the writs that run parallel to the Parliament suggest plenty of cooperation at the assembly on a range of issues, including reversing a case of outlawry and defying the pope over the favoured status given to the still absent Boniface.[55] The decision on the tax, however, was adjourned until summer. If the prorogation was meant to give Henry time to make amends and therefore be in a better position to make the request again, the visit of Beatrice of Savoy and her brother Thomas indicated that little was going to change, at least with regard to foreigners.

Beatrice was there to consult with Henry before returning to Provence to work out a treaty with Charles of Anjou, but Thomas came to sponge. His wife Joanna, the Countess of Flanders, had died in 1244, and her sister Margaret, the new countess, was unable to keep up with his pension. He appealed to Henry, who agreed to seize Flemish merchandise and traders to compel Margaret to make up the arrears. He also paid the £333 fee owed to the countess for her homage directly to Thomas, plus the £133 annuity to Amadeus, the Count of Savoy.[56] Henry saw these subsidies as maintaining his Continental policy and said as much when Parliament reconvened in June. He needed the tax to recover his rights on the Continent, he told his subjects, and if it wasn't their concern, it should be. As for their conditions, he wasn't prepared to accede to the appointment of a chancellor and justiciar at their recommendation and approval. To do so would be to go against the entire structure of their society:

> Those who are considered as inferiors ought to be ruled and governed at the will and pleasure of their lord. For the servant is not above his lord, nor is the pupil above his master; and your king, therefore, would be no longer so, but would be, as it were, a slave, if he were thus to incline to your will.[57]

The lecturing tone suggests they had been down this road before, going back to the barons' attempts to straitjacket him a decade earlier. Henry wearied of trying to make them understand that they could expect no more power over their king than their own vassals might expect over them. They should stop grumbling and get on with the business of feudalism. They certainly couldn't object to his theory of kingship on ideological grounds. He was doing nothing more offensive than his predecessors. They too browbeat the clergy, played favourites, brought foreigners to court and scrounged for money, none of which, incidentally, was banned by Magna Carta. Even the foreigner argument was ringing hollow in the face of Henry's veneration of English saints and history and his reliance on Englishmen in his administration.[58] High-profile foreigners like Peter of Savoy and Peter d'Aigueblanche were not personally obnoxious, and they were the ones who had to do all the grinding work of his foreign diplomacy. While the arrival of the Lusignans was worrying, so far no major conflicts with them had ensued, apart from knightly bravado.

The problem was Henry's lavish open-heartedness and celebrations, his building works and Continental schemes. All of it cost a fortune, far more than he could afford. The kings before him had despaired of official ceremonies for the expenses they entailed, but Henry couldn't get enough of them. They had been a stingy lot, amassing and hording treasure, whereas he was forced to pawn his jewels just to make ends meet.[59] It hardly squared with all his talk about enhancing the majesty and dignity of the monarchy. The barons wanted control over the offices of chancellor and justiciar to save the king from his vanity, generosity and ambitions.

What they were really trying to save, however, was themselves, from an increasingly encroaching bureaucracy. It seemed as if the decade had been one of never-ending inquiry into rights and ownership. Henry was convinced that many lands of the crown had been lost during his minority and was eager to recover them to improve his stock of patronage and income. The forest again became a prickly issue, and anyone asserting their privileges had better have a charter backing them up. The exchequer had rolls of debts going back to John's reign and was still asking for payment. The people responsible for this harassment were led by his professional administrators, men like Robert Passelewe for the forest and John Mansel for everything else.[60] The keeper of the seal just then was John of Lexington, a very capable man who, like the other two, was a careerist beholden to Henry. The barons and bishops hoped that by supplanting these commoners with men of their own stamp and status, they could put an end to all these invasive inquests, all the king's grandiose dreams and flourishes, and finally put the crown on a secure financial footing.

Henry would have replied that he had heard it all before. Peter des Roches had promised him the same thing and look what happened. He also knew they were being disingenuous, because they had it good under him. He never harried them the way his father had. He gave them the best possible terms for paying their debts or else forgave them entirely. A case in point was John Fitz-Geoffrey. He owed nearly £670 to the exchequer, mainly in arrears for his time as the Sheriff of Yorkshire and Gloucestershire, but Henry pardoned a quarter of it and allowed him to pay off the rest at a ridiculously low £10 a year. If anything, he was too lax with them, allowed them too much princely authority. The old rebel firebrand Richard Siward died that year of 1248, but not before bringing suit against Richard de Clare for acting like a king in Gloucestershire.[61] In coddling the barons the way he did, Henry hoped to maintain the peace and win their support, but differences in personality and interest guaranteed his relationship with them would always be fraught with tension and misunderstanding. There was no better example than his brother-in-law Simon de Montfort. The king had a mission for him, and their history suggested that, whatever the success or failure of it, the outcome was going to be spectacular.

10

WEIGHED IN AN EVEN BALANCE 1249–1251

In the records of the time, the heir to the throne was known simply as the Lord Edward. He had spent most of his life until that point at Windsor Castle, growing up under the watchful eye of his mother and household of English and Savoyard staff. His parents constantly fretted over him, especially as he had recently survived two serious illnesses. The first befell him in 1246 when the family was at the dedication of Beaulieu Abbey, founded by his grandfather John. Eleanor insisted on remaining within the abbey confines for the three weeks it took for him to recover, she didn't care what the monastic rules were about women overstaying their welcome. When he fell ill again the following year, his father asked all the religious houses in and around London for their prayers. When it came to their children, no emergency was too small for Henry and Eleanor, whatever the distance. While in Gascony, Henry heard that the children at Windsor were being served an inferior wine (diluted to soft-drink form). He ordered the constable to replace it with two casks of the best he could find.[1]

Those children would have included Edward's playfellows. The two with whom he developed the closest bonds were his cousins, both called Henry, the sons of Richard of Cornwall and Eleanor de Montfort. Nothing is known about Edward's education, but in all probability he learned to read his native French, even some Latin, and spoke the English of his wet nurses and guardians. There's no evidence he learned to write, which was a far more challenging discipline in the days of quill and parchment. Henry de Montfort could write, very elegantly, but it was thanks to his later tutorship under the most challenging taskmaster of them all, Robert Grosseteste.[2]

Edward was at this time 9 years old, the same age as his father when he became king. In the barest of descriptions that have come down, they had few physical traits in common. Edward outgrew him by at least half a foot and his hair darkened quite considerably as he got older. Although reputedly possessed of eloquence, he had a lisp or stammer that kept him from becoming the master of the sharp-witted riposte that Henry was. The other big difference between the two was hunting. Edward took to it with enthusiasm and skill and was already at it in Windsor Forest by the time he was 8, later learning how to chase down a stag and butcher it with his sword.[3] He was clearly predisposed to aggression in a way Henry never was, but his predecessors were. It was an indication that the next reign would see a return to the hard-bitten, violence-prone style of kingship the country had been used to before Henry came along. It also meant Edward was well suited to become the lord of a place in need of crackdown, as was the case of Gascony.

Three seneschals had come and gone since Henry left Gascony in a relatively calm but troubled state. As much as they tried, they were unable to put an end to the private wars going on between feuding clans. The growing anarchy left the province vulnerable to outside forces, and there were plenty of those. The kings of Aragon and Castile were also descendents of Eleanor of Aquitaine through John's older sister Eleanor and could insist that the lordship of it rightfully belonged to one of them. Theobald of Champagne, now King of Navarre, took advantage of a dispute with Henry to cause trouble on the southern border, and Raymond of Toulouse held some territory in the east that Henry claimed. And there was of course a hostile France to the north, with the five-year truce about to come to an end.[4]

Jettisoning the province was not an option at this stage, but imposing order there was a job nobody wanted. That included Simon de Montfort when Henry offered him the post in the spring of 1248. He and Eleanor had taken the cross and were planning to join Louis's crusade. They were reluctant to abandon their vow, which may have been undertaken to atone for her broken vow of chastity. The preaching of the friars had convinced them that not even ten years of marriage, four children and the pope's absolution were enough to expunge that sin.[5] But Henry's latest seneschal lasted barely two months on the job. He turned to his brother-in-law in the hope that his military background, gained in that region, would give him an edge over his predecessors.

It wasn't just to keep from breaking another vow that Simon and Eleanor shrank from the assignment. Their relationship with Henry had never recovered from the incident of the queen's churching a decade earlier, when Henry had thoughtlessly humiliated them in front of everybody. It took another five years for him to make amends, and only then at the prodding of his mother-in-law. While he was characteristically generous, even granting them the castle of Kenilworth, Simon and Eleanor felt more aggrieved than ever, lately over the partition of the Marshal estate in May 1247. There were thirteen co-heirs among the grandchildren of William Marshal, including the earls Roger Bigod, John de Warenne and Richard de Clare. They were all now technically responsible for paying Eleanor her £400

Irish dower but felt little obligation to do so. The Montforts brought suit against them for redress, but for reasons unknown the case never came to verdict.[6]

With an income of £2,000 a year, the Montforts were among the most affluent of the nobility. At least half of that money, however, came from Eleanor's combined dower, which was generated by estates they could not pass on to their children. Once she died, there went the farm, and they had four boys to provide for. Henry had promised to convert part of that income into land, but his stock was dwindling and the queue for patronage got ever more muddled after the Lusignans arrived and began competing for what was left. He only exacerbated their feelings of injustice by giving William de Valence a Marshal heiress in marriage, together with her fifth of the estate.[7]

The queen was brought in to work on the couple. Despite an age difference of eight years, the two Eleanors were close, doubtless with much shared experience in being married to men as complicated as these two. Simon only agreed to go to Gascony after he was given assurance that he could finish the job he set out to do and would have the king's support. This meant full control over the province's revenues, £1,333 up front and fifty knights a year for service, and reimbursement for anything he spent on castles and fortifications. More importantly, his tenure was to run for seven years, a clear sign that he knew it was going to be a grind to restore order. Under these terms, he was no mere seneschal, an official easily removable at the king's will, but more like a viceroy, with the independence to make decisions on behalf of the king.[8] Knowing Henry's penchant for micromanagement, it's a wonder he thought it was ever going to work.

Simon's first task was to suppress external threats. Accompanied by Eleanor, he went to the court at Paris, again run by Blanche after Louis's crusade departed in the spring of 1248, and got an extension of the truce. The Montforts then proceeded south, where an agreement was worked out with Theobald to submit his dispute with Henry to arbitration. With the kings of Castile and Aragon still only observant at this stage, they went to Bordeaux and found the leading families, the Solers and Columbines, at relative peace, having just concluded a truce of their own.[9] This freed Simon and his troop of knights to move into the countryside to confront the local barons who were freely waylaying merchants and travellers. The more notorious he locked away, others he let off after paying a ransom. It was a crackdown in the fullest sense and earned him kudos when he returned to England for the Christmas court. 'If the king's pleasure were such,' says Paris, Simon would return to Gascony to 'crush his other enemies'.[10]

It was indeed Henry's pleasure, but the Montforts didn't start back until June 1249, in the company of an English contingent of crusaders led by William Longespee II. Simon was supposed to have led this force, and perhaps he and Eleanor felt a twinge of guilt for not continuing with them to Egypt, where Louis's army had just landed. Any hint that it was possible to join up with them later was dismissed soon after their arrival in Bordeaux. It was the eve of municipal elections, and they had retired for the night when news came that the two factions were rioting in the streets. With a small force he was able to put together at short notice, Montfort raced towards the trouble and ended up fighting alongside the Colombines against the Solers. The insurgents were overpowered, but not before he lost two knights and his standard-bearer in the melee.[11]

Simon moved against both parties in the aftermath, but it was the Solers who complained of their rough treatment at his hands. Their patriarch had died while in custody and the property of their adherents who failed to answer charges against them were seized. After hearing both sides, Henry decided that his viceroy had acted correctly but felt it necessary to send him a letter of advice and caution: 'Act energetically and unremittingly, see that no excessive indulgence encourages the criminals to begin again, but that the punishment be not greater than the offence, as befits a consistent and just judge.'[12]

The uprising in Bordeaux quickly spread, and Montfort found himself moving from stronghold to stronghold to enforce his authority, much like his father in Toulouse four decades earlier. By the end of the year, it appeared he had the province firmly under control, at least according to an eyewitness account made to Alphonse of Poitiers in Egypt. Raymond VII had died in September 1249, without begetting the son he had hoped for. As he feared, his county passed into the hands of his son-in-law Alphonse, who sent a chaplain to meet Simon and Eleanor to discuss matters of litigation. The chaplain noted that 'Montfort holds Gascony in good estate, and all obey him and dare undertake naught against him'.[13] Simon broached the idea of joining the crusade again, but even as he was speaking, everything began to unravel.

The chief culprit was Gaston de Béarn, whose lordship straddled the southern border with Navarre. Much of the depredation preceding Montfort's arrival had been carried out by him and his men. In the beginning, Simon managed to isolate him by coming to terms with Theobald and an aged countess named Perronelle. She held Bigorre, a strip of land coveted by Gaston by right of his wife, who was Perronelle's daughter by her fifth husband. Perronelle had two older daughters, both by her third husband, who was none other than Guy de Montfort, Simon's long deceased older brother. The elder Montfort had arranged the marriage when he was supreme during the Albigensian Crusade, but then he was killed and Guy died in captivity in 1220. Perronelle intended her grandson by her eldest daughter to succeed her, which didn't please Gaston at all, so she turned to her former brother-in-law for help. Simon agreed to take control of her county for a fixed sum and to use it as a base of operations in the south.[14] He captured Gaston and packed him off to England to receive judgement at Clarendon, where the royal family was staying. To his dismay, Gaston was pardoned, went home and picked up where he left off.

Montfort would bitterly recall what a serious miscalculation that was on Henry's part, but it's fair to wonder if he shouldn't have questioned himself for sending the robber baron to England in the first place, rather than keep him detained for ransom like all the other prisoners. Gaston's mother, whom Paris derides for her 'singularly immense size', was a sister of Raymond Berenger, making Gaston the queen's cousin. He was sure to have played on that connection and combined it with honeyed promises of homage to Henry to gain his release. The king, however, saw his carrot and Montfort's stick as the best approach to pacifying the rebels, for to disinherit a lord as powerful as Gaston could easily have ignited a full-scale rebellion. As it was, Montfort only had to busy himself with Gaston and other guerrilla bands.[15]

It was an exhausting ordeal and one Simon was bound to lose. In March 1250 he went to Paris, where Richard of Cornwall had led a delegation to renew the truce with Blanche. There he wrote a sober if depressing situation report to Henry that shows how far their fortunes had reversed since he was feted as a hero the last time they saw each other:

> Sir, I have heard for certain that some knights of Gascony have provided themselves with everything to demand their lands by war. And they are certainly leagued together, they and their friends; and I fully understand that they will begin soon to overrun the land; but what force they will have I cannot as yet be sure. And because the great men of the land bear me such ill will, because I uphold your rights and those of the poor against them, there will be danger and shame to me, and great damage to you, if I were to return to the land without instructions from you and without speaking to you.[16]

Simon's intelligence suggested they were planning to strike in groups of up to forty armed riders, burning and plundering and holding people for ransom. Harsher measures were needed to head them off and he wanted Henry to realise what that meant. But he also understood that the king had heard many 'sinister things' about his rule and was anxious for Henry to hear his side of the story in person. Finally, there was the pressing problem of funds. For obscure reasons, the local revenue on which Simon depended had been choked off by France. Cash-strapped as usual, Henry had already assigned him all his income from Ireland for the next two years, plus a grant of £660 in January. Now, after Simon arrived in May, he was forced to arrange a loan of £1,200 from Italian bankers to maintain three castles, in addition to scrounging up another £803 for the service of the knights he had promised. The money may have been a vote of confidence, but Henry clearly had his concerns. In the summer, he ordered two officials to go to Gascony to audit his accounts.[17]

Eleanor did not accompany her husband this time. She had become pregnant and had a daughter while in Bordeaux, but the infant died some time after birth.

But there were signs of strain in their marriage in these difficult years. The lone surviving daughter of King John, Eleanor was easily her husband's equal in terms of energy, ambition and insistence on her rights. Princess or no princess, medieval women were expected to be submissive and she seems to have totally failed in this task. Adam Marsh, a Franciscan lecturer who acted as a spiritual adviser to the couple and other members of the court, sent letters to her while she was in Gascony, sternly reprimanding her about her wifely duties. He had heard certain reports of 'marital insubordination' that were 'soiling your reputation not a little'. He urged her to support Simon and 'bring him gently, by your sweetness and good advice, to conduct himself more prudently in the future'. In another letter, he found her vanity unbecoming and admonished her that women should dress with 'modesty and sobriety, not with plaited hair, or gold, or pearls or costly attire'. Her outward appearance should profess 'godliness with good works'.[18]

Marsh also chided Simon for his temper, for acting imperiously when he all but kidnapped a local priest to serve with him in Gascony and for allowing his custodians to come down hard on his peasants:

> What does it profit to guard the peace of your own fellow citizens and not guard the peace of your own household? Better is a patient man than a strong man, and he who can rule his own temper than he who storms a city. I doubt not that your wisdom will understand what I mean by this saying.

Marsh referred Simon to Scripture for guidance, like Job 31: 'If I have walked with vanity, or if my foot hath hasted to deceit, let me be weighed in an even balance, that God may know my integrity.'[19]

* * *

The rivalry between the Plantagenet and Capetian dynasties began a few years before Henry II became king, when he married Eleanor of Aquitaine, the former wife of Louis VII. That Henry was almost driven to get the better of that Louis in everything, leading the latter to observe that the King of England has 'men, horses, gold and silk, gems and everything. But in France we have nothing except bread, wine and joy.'[20] Louis's son Philip II wasn't content with just having everything worth having and strived to make France rich and powerful at England's expense. He succeeded insofar as 100 years on, the Plantagenets were seen as playing catch-up. If Louis IX passed a law, Henry III passed a law. If Louis built a church, Henry built a church. There was obviously more than mere emulation at work here, but where Henry couldn't escape comparison concerned crusading. Louis VII (with Eleanor of Aquitaine) and Philip II had led armies to the Holy Land, but Richard I was the only English king to fulfil his vow. He may have accomplished more than both French kings combined, but Louis IX's departure in the summer of 1248 again made the Capetian look that much more 'the most Christian king'.[21]

The crusades had always been marred by mistrust, and the overly pious Henry and Louis were no different. On his march to the Mediterranean, Louis stopped at Lyon to ask the pope to make sure Henry did not try to reclaim his patrimony while he was away. Innocent could hardly refuse him, but he had never been thrilled about the thought of Louis leaving him at the mercy of Frederick should the emperor overcome his recent setbacks. Henry was equally worried, but that Louis stay on course with his crusading army and not use it like his father for local conquest.[22] The idea that he might have similar designs may have informed Henry's choice of Simon de Montfort to take charge of Gascony. The Montforts had been invaluable in the Capetian absorption of Toulouse. For Louis to express his gratitude to Simon's family by provoking a war with him next door was unthinkable.

By the end of summer, his army of 15,000 set sail. They would strike at Egypt, the main Islamic power in the region, but the logistics of the operation and internal feuds meant wintering on Cyprus first. While there, Louis warned the Sultan of Cairo that his army was 'poised against you like the sword of destiny. I put you on your guard.' The sultan was unimpressed: 'The day will dawn to our advantage and end in your destruction. Then you will curse yourself.'[23] A storm scattered Louis's fleet when it left Cyprus, but enough ships arrived off the Egyptian coast to launch an assault outside Damietta on 5 June 1249. The defenders were routed, with Hugh Lusignan among the few losses in the fighting on the beach, and the port city deserted. It had taken Louis only one day to capture Damietta as opposed to the seventeen months required by the Fifth Crusade four decades earlier.[24]

Never were the conditions better for an immediate march on Cairo. The River Nile was low and the sultan's court in turmoil over his impending death from tuberculosis. And yet Louis decided to wait for the ships that had been blown off course to arrive, then for his brother Alphonse of Poitiers, who had stayed behind to help Blanche run the regency. Not for six months, until the end of November, did the army begin to move towards Mansourah, 45 miles southwest of Damietta, where the main Egyptian line of defence was established. It took a month to get there, and then they wasted more time trying to cross a canal that separated the two armies. Futile attempts were made to build a causeway, which was destroyed by the opposing camp tossing flaming projectiles at the works or else widening their side of the canal to allow the weight of the onrushing water to do the trick.[25]

The crusaders kept at it in part because the sultan had died, and this was seen as a good sign. His Armenian-born widow had everything under control, however. She had delayed the news of his death long enough to consolidate her power with the Turkish warrior caste known as the *mameluks* and waited for her stepson to hurry home from his base in Mesopotamia. After six weeks wasted trying to cross the canal, some locals showed Louis a ford further upstream in return for 500 bezants, or £60. The Templars and contingents under Louis's brother Robert of Artois got over first and immediately fell upon the enemy forces that had kept them at bay all this time. They slaughtered them en masse, including their general, who was just stepping out of his bath, and put the survivors to flight. This was the kind of crusading Robert liked. Back at Damietta, he had spurned the other commanders' suggestion that they strike at a softer target like Alexandria instead of making the arduous push for Cairo. He convinced his brother that 'to kill the snake, you must crush its head'. Now defying Louis's order to wait for the rest of the army to cross, he gathered up his men and headed straight for Mansourah. In doing so, Robert obliged the Templars and English troops with him to follow.[26]

Finding the gates wide open should have deterred them, but they kept riding all the way up to the citadel. There the *mameluks* struck. Using the narrow streets to their advantage, they were able to throw the knights into disarray and unhorse them. With their superior numbers, they hacked to death all but five of the 290 Templars and most of the English troops, including Longespee. Robert and his men found shelter in a house, but were tracked down there and massacred. Peter of Dreux was one of the few to escape, but he barely had time to inform Louis of the disaster when the Egyptians sallied forth from the city and attacked.[27] The enemy arrows were so thick that Joinville, Louis's future biographer, claimed to have taken five and his horse fifteen. He somehow found a moment in the chaos to admire how the King of France 'towered head and shoulders over his people, a gilded helmet on his head, and in his hand a sword of German steel'. But the French crossbowmen were still on the other side of the canal and only after a pontoon bridge was quickly constructed were they able to join the battle and repulse the onslaught.[28]

It was clear the next morning that the crusade was lost, yet Louis could not bring himself to admit defeat, and so they lingered by the Nile for a month as supplies dwindled and disease set in. He seems to have hoped that by making a stand, he could revive the enemy's original offer to swap Damietta for Jerusalem, which he had scorned as fraternising with the infidel, and gain a free exit from the country. By the time he gave the order to retreat, he was sick from dysentery but insisted on enduring the hardships of his men instead of convalescing on a river barge. Charles of Anjou found his pride insufferable and berated him for putting the whole army at risk. The Egyptians and Turks made use of the pontoon bridge the French had failed to destroy behind them and pursued them relentlessly, killing Hugh Lusignan XI in one skirmish. Various units began laying down their arms, allegedly at the instigation of a madman or traitor named Marcel, and Philip de Montfort arranged the king's surrender on 6 April. Louis and his surviving brothers were put in chains while the Egyptians debated what to do with them.[29]

It might have come to a mass beheading had it not been for Queen Margaret. She had insisted on accompanying Louis on the crusade, no doubt to get away from her mother-in-law, and fell pregnant some time after the fall of Damietta. She was just days away from giving birth when the news of the catastrophe arrived. The Italian sailors who served as the garrison were ready to flee in order to save themselves, but she understood that holding the port city as a bargaining counter was the only way to keep her husband alive. She convinced them to stay at a cost reputedly as high as £90,000. The new sultan had hoped to retrieve Damietta without a fight because his own position was fragile and agreed to exchange what was left of the Christian army for the city and a ransom of 800,000 bezants, or about £85,000, half to be paid before their release. His fears came true when the Turkish warriors, allied with the Armenian widow, made a botched attempt to kill him at a banquet. Catching up with him at the river, they slew him and cut his heart out to show Louis as a demonstration of the way they did business.[30] Later, in the counting of the ransom money, Louis severely rebuked his men for trying to cheat their captors of several thousand pounds, perhaps not so much out of some innate sense of honesty, but rather the thought of his heart winding up in similar hands.

Relieved to escape, the French made for the crusader states, where Louis was reunited with Margaret and saw his newborn son for the first time. She called him John Tristan to reflect the sadness surrounding his birth. The name fittingly applied to Louis, who was inconsolable over the calamity he had wrought and the fate of the prisoners left behind as surety for the other half of the ransom payment. He disgusted his brothers by moping around and coming to life only to denounce them for gambling on board ship, which he found morally outrageous under any circumstance. When it came time to decide their next move, Alphonse and Charles were all for returning to France, gathering up another army if need be, but definitely going home. Louis couldn't bear the thought. He couldn't go back to his kingdom with only shame and humiliation to show for the £500,000 and thousands of lives lost under his direction. Needing to salvage something of his crusade, he wanted to pursue the hare-brained idea of teaming up with the Mongols against the sultanates.[31] The next month his brothers, their wives and children born to them overseas, and most of what remained of his once-powerful army, sailed away, Peter of Dreux dying en route. Louis and Margaret settled in for the next four years and had two more children.

On 6 March 1250, as Louis and his men were enduring appalling agony on the banks of the Nile, Henry stood before a packed gathering in Westminster Hall beside the Thames and took the cross from the Archbishop of Canterbury. Nobody knew anything of the disaster that had befallen the French army, only the success they had enjoyed in capturing Damietta almost without a fight. That obliged Henry more than ever to lead his own crusade and achieve whatever glory and prestige was left after Louis was done. He wouldn't be going any time soon, not for years judging by the time it took to organise the most recent crusades, and no collection for it could begin until he had set a date for his departure. Naturally he made a show of the occasion. Basking in penance, he asked the citizenry of London to forgive him for coming down hard on them lately, whether by taxing them or suspending their municipal rights.[32] They did, but little changed in their frosty relations, and they were about to get worse.

The news about Damietta had been brought to England by Boniface, who returned in September 1249 after an absence of five years. He seemed to be the worst example of the absentee foreign cleric, but he was ready to take up his duties in earnest. The tense climate should have warned him to proceed gingerly. He had created a lot of resentment with the way he fobbed off Canterbury's debts on the rest of the clergy and then threatened to excommunicate anybody who resisted him. But Boniface was impressed by the way Grosseteste had exerted his authority over his Lincoln diocese and decided to carry out some of his own inspections of chapters and religious houses, to 'visit' them in the parlance of the time.

He didn't confine himself to just Canterbury, however. As archbishop, he claimed the right to visit any clerical institution in his province. Visitations were touchy enough when an Englishman like Grosseteste harangued and penalised his monks and canons for slothfulness and debauchery, and it took years of litigation to get the papacy to back him up on the matter.[33] A foreigner like Boniface marching in and scolding them in like manner was bound to cause a riot, which was what allegedly happened at St Bartholomew's in London when he was informed by the canons that the right of visitation belonged to their bishop Fulk Basset only. Boniface flew into a rage, struck the sub-prior, and demanded a sword as if he was going to chop his head off right then and there. 'Thus it becomes me to deal with you English traitors,' he hissed. The canons rescued the sub-prior, and in the scuffle that followed it was revealed that the archbishop was wearing armour beneath his cloak. He had come there specifically to chop heads, only somehow forgot his sword. As word of the brawl spread, a mob gathered to seek out the archbishop and 'cut him to pieces'.[34]

It's a shocking, scandalous story, just as it was meant to appear from the tabloid sheets of Matthew Paris. The problem with his account is that Adam Marsh accompanied Boniface on his visitations and reported on them in a letter to Grosseteste. These visits were full of 'untold heartache and physical labour' but nowhere does he mention swords, armour or violence. There was plenty of contention to be sure as Basset attempted to block Boniface from usurping his authority, and the archbishop excommunicated him and his officials as a result.[35] In the end, it meant more litigation ahead, and in June, after no more than nine months back on English soil, Boniface left for the Continent to see the pope about it.

He couldn't know it, but on 13 May 1250, the exact day he was stirring up a fuss in London, Grosseteste was in Lyon doing the same about him. The Bishop of Lincoln had been part of a large party of bishops, nobles and knights that went first to Paris under Richard of Cornwall to arrange a longer truce with Blanche, then to the papal court, where Richard held secret talks with Innocent, presumably about how Henry was going to finance his crusade.[36] On behalf of his fellow suffragans, Grosseteste complained that Boniface had crossed the line in his demand that the clergy pay for the honour of his visits. When told that canon law supported the archbishop, he took matters all the way back to Aristotle, whose work he had translated, and drew a distinction between kingship and tyranny.

'It is as natural for a father to rule his children … as for a king to rule his subjects,' wrote the Greek philosopher, which Grosseteste interpreted to mean that kingship and, by definition, the papacy, was heavenly ordained. This was his way of assuring the pope that he was not challenging anyone's authority. His view is remarkably conservative given that Stephen Langton had led a school of thought in Paris a half-century earlier that held that all men were created equal. Kings and popes were merely being tolerated in the divine scheme of things. Grosseteste was decidedly old school in this regard and believed that rebellion against kingship was unnatural and therefore an affront to God. Even so, a good king should be able to harvest his resources for the purpose of expressing his majesty and dignity. The moment he imposes this burden on his subjects, he becomes a tyrant. He's only looking after his own welfare and not that of his people. The same holds true for a good archbishop or magnate endowed with the wealth of his rank or office. It was their duty to be self-supportive.[37]

Anybody listening to Grosseteste make that famous speech had to wonder if he did not have Henry more in mind. The king's financial situation had not improved overall, and at a Parliament held at Easter the year before, it was thought that he was ready to concede to the baronial demand that he appoint official ministers in return for a tax. For reasons unknown, Richard of Cornwall failed to show up, citing business in remote parts, and the meeting broke up with the king and barons back at square one. Now that Henry had taken the cross, Matthew Paris raised the suspicion that he might try to use the fundraising for his own purposes. The first response of this 'beggar-king with open mouth', as he derides him, was actually the opposite. He cut down on the expenditures of his household. But even here he couldn't get a break from the chronically dissatisfied chronicler, who accuses him of skimping on the trappings and hospitality befitting his court.[38]

Another bishop who didn't return with the party from the Continent was William Raleigh. He decided to stay on in France, supposedly to cut down on living expenses as well, but more likely because he was worn out by the cares of his office. There had been a great scandal the year before in Winchester after the robbery of several foreign merchants revealed a well-organised racket throughout his diocese. Henry was outraged that such lawlessness was allowed to flourish, especially in the city of his birth. At a speech given in the great hall of Winchester in March 1249, he declared, 'I am only one man, and do not wish, nor am I able, to support the burden of managing the whole kingdom without assistance.' When a twelve-man jury refused to say what they knew about the perpetrators, they were imprisoned and another jury assembled with a view to what happened to the first one. The mass arrests that then followed ended with thirty men going to the gallows, including several from the royal household who claimed they had been forced into a life of crime when their pay wasn't forthcoming.[39]

The affair could only have taken a toll on Raleigh, who had once been the chief justice of the land and head of the council. He died at Tours on 20 September 1250, just as Grosseteste was returning to England, and the king wasted no time in advising the monks on their choice of successor. They should have known he would in light of what happened the year before in Durham. There, Nicholas Farnham, old and in ill health, turned in his robes as the bishop of that place, and Henry immediately began lobbying for his half-brother Aymer de Valence to succeed him. Aymer had not yet reached the age of 30, considered the minimum for a bishop, and was said to be ignorant, which was a blunt way of saying he lacked solid theological training. Henry cast aside these objections, allegedly offering to hold the bishopric in his hands until Aymer was deemed acceptable by the monks. The horrified brethren moved fast to keep the youthful foreigner out of their midst and elected a northerner, Walter Kirkham, a former keeper of the wardrobe. Henry let it pass, but took his time about confirming Kirkham's election.[40]

His high-mindedness returned on 7 October 1250 when he walked into the exchequer to address an assembly of sheriffs. With his council in attendance, he exhorted them to bring swift justice to wards, orphans and widows, not to sell the right to hear complaints, not to punish peasants for the debts of their lords and to 'diligently and rightly inquire into how the magnates conduct themselves towards their men'. They should correct them insofar as it was in their power, or otherwise bring their cases before him. As much as Henry believed that ensuring peace and justice were the main priorities of kingship, the occasion for what was arguably his greatest speech was learning the full impact of Louis's failed crusade. There was a feeling that he had encountered disaster in Egypt because he had not set his kingdom aright before departing. He had left a land teeming with injustice and so brought the wrath of the Almighty down on himself and his men. With the help of his sheriffs, Henry hoped to avoid their misfortune.[41]

★ ★ ★

The word 'nepotism' has its origins in the provisions made by a bishop or other clergyman for a nephew (*nepos* in Latin) who, more often than not, was not his nephew but his illegitimate offspring. Peter des Roches, for one, was thought to have been the father and not the uncle of Peter de Rivallis, only one of the many kinfolk who were beneficiaries of his patronage as the Bishop of Winchester. His successor William Raleigh dispensed offices and favours to his own relations as well, as many as a dozen of them.[42] In neither instance was this unusual among medieval magnates. Like the king, they were naturally inclined to look after their own, for both bonds of affection and political concerns. A decade later Simon de Montfort came in for criticism for including his family's welfare in the reform movement, but the people voicing it would have probably looked askance had he not.

In setting up his family, Henry could argue that he was ensuring the stability of the realm much the way Louis had done by making his brothers potentates in France. This wasn't a case of imitation, just what a king does. Henry's grandfather had failed in a similar course because his sons and wife resented his ham-fisted attempts to manipulate their inheritances. Henry too had an initial rocky start with his brother Richard of Cornwall, but they reached an accommodation that they could both live with. He couldn't give him Provence and wouldn't give him Gascony, but his grants allowed Richard to accumulate enough wealth to go out and buy a principality on the Continent should one enter the market. Nobody complained there, as Richard was a senior baron and enjoyed a good reputation in Europe. Perhaps it had once been Henry's plan to endow his sister and brother-in-law in like fashion, but the disaster of the queen's churching changed everything with the Montforts.[43] But Eleanor too was a child of King John and deserved equal consideration. The problem was these other siblings.

There is no evidence that Richard or Eleanor felt any closeness to their Lusignan half-brothers Guy, Geoffrey, William and Aymer. The latter were much younger, by eight years and more, and grew up in distant Poitou. If anything, they were to be viewed as new rivals for their brother's favours. Henry may have been more family-oriented than them, but the Lusignans' promotion in England was primarily political, to continue his European strategy and strengthen his support from within the magnates. But where the Savoyards were a seasoned lot who knew how not to ruffle feathers, the Lusignans were loud and brash and sported chips on their shoulders despite their recent disgrace in France.

Upon first arriving, Guy challenged Richard de Clare, the Earl of Gloucester, to a tournament at Dunstable, but Henry cancelled it out of concern for his half-brother's life. His fear was justified, for at another tournament at Newbury, William de Valence was singled out by the opposing side, knocked to the ground and pummelled. He was injured both in body and spirit and demanded a rematch at Northampton after recovering. Henry prohibited that one as well, but William was ready to risk his anger; he wanted his revenge that much. It took a late winter storm to call it off, but he got his chance at Brackley near Oxford towards the end of 1249. In this contest, Clare joined the foreign party and helped William overcome an English knight, badly injuring him in the process.[44] Clare had nearly been married to one of the Lusignan sisters while he was Henry's ward, but his motivation here seems to have been his lifelong inability to choose one side or the other. Whatever his excuse, he aroused only more ill feelings towards the foreigners. When the two groups next met at Rochester in 1251, on the feast of the Conception of the Blessed Virgin (8 December), the English not only chased them off the pitch, but had another party of knights ready to pound them with sticks and staves as they sought refuge in the town.[45]

Henry did his part in stoking the resentment by trying to insinuate Aymer as a bishop, understandable as his intentions may have been. Durham was strategically important with its proximity to Scotland, and Winchester, he proudly proclaimed, was his birthplace. Of the post-Conquest kings, Henry I, Richard I and John were born in England, but such is the lack of certainty about where that none seems to have trumpeted that fact. Some of Henry's attachment to Winchester was ironically due to Peter des Roches. For all the bitter denunciations of the bishop's foreignness, Roches revered the Saxon saints and history associated with the city and no doubt passed it on to his pupil.[46]

As the election for the Bishop of Winchester neared, Henry sent Mansel and the keeper of his wardrobe Peter Chaceporc to lobby the chapter. The latter was a Poitevin whom Henry had unsuccessfully tried to make the Bishop of Bath in 1243 following the death of Jocelin of Wells, the man who dictated his coronation oath to him.[47] The monks of Winchester probably didn't need much convincing to accept Aymer. According to Paris, they felt they had paid dearly for their right to elect Raleigh over the king's wishes, because he turned out to be a beast of a bishop. 'We were imprisoned, dragged about, and beaten; we suffered from hunger, were bloodstained from our wounds, and were shackled like thieves.' Henry himself arrived at the chapter house in early November 1250 and, taking his place before the monks as if he were about to sermonise them, did just that with a line from Psalm 85: 'This day, because you have fortunately shown yourselves favourable to my request, as I have heard, and it is well for you that you have done so, Righteousness and Peace have kissed each other.'[48]

While reiterating that this was a special case because he had been baptised in that church, Henry may as well have been speaking to all the monks in the land, who numbered, together with nuns and friars, between 20,000 and 25,000 at that time. The brethren at Winchester had erred in defying him and he came down hard on them. They now had a chance to put that behind them and enjoy the fruits that came from seeking his pleasure. Otherwise, he would ruin them. Almost as an afterthought, he threw in a word about the man who would be their bishop.[49]

> If elected, he will for a long time, as we hope, enlighten this church, like the sun, with the rays of his noble and royal extraction, for which he is distinguished by reason of his mother, of his illustrious blood which he derives from his father, and of his most willing kindness and his youth, in which he is pleasing both to God and man.

Sufficiently cowed, the monks did not disappoint and postulated Aymer de Valence as the next Bishop of Winchester. Henry had made his point. He was the Vicar of God, as Bracton stated in the famous legal treatise he was in the process of compiling, and would have a say over who became bishop in his realm. The monks of Rochester, having lost theirs around the same time, showed how well they understood this dogma by electing Lawrence of St Martin, one of Henry's closest councillors, as their next bishop without any encouragement from the top.[50]

Final confirmation of episcopal elections rested with the Vicar of Christ, as the pope called himself, and a stripling like Aymer might normally have furrowed his eyebrows. But Innocent was being assailed just then by Alphonse of Poitiers and Charles of Anjou, who had arrived from the East with the full story of the destruction of their crusade. He bore some of the blame, they said, because his vendetta against Frederick had thrown all Christendom into disorder. The pope was sufficiently unnerved by their vehemence to ask Henry for permission to relocate his court to Bordeaux.[51] Before Henry had to make what would have been a very delicate decision, Frederick died on 13 December 1250.

Supposedly an earthquake marked the passing of this man called a wonder of the world by Matthew Paris. A charming intellectual fluent in six languages and tolerant in matters of religion and culture, Frederick's position had steadily deteriorated after his deposition. His siege of Parma ended disastrously when the population sallied forth while he was on a hunting expedition and routed his forces. His defender before the papal court, Thaddaeus of Suessa, was torn to pieces in the mayhem. Later his most trusted confidant, Peter de Vinea, was implicated in a plot to poison him and met a similarly horrific end, and his favourite natural born son Enzio was captured in a skirmish and spent the rest of his life, twenty-three years, in prison. Frederick's next favourite, Manfred, was by his side when a fever carried him away. The old Archbishop of Palermo, who had known him since his boyhood in Sicily, was there too and, for what it was worth, gave him absolution.[52]

For Innocent, the death of the dragon was cause to rejoice, but there was still his Hohenstaufen 'race of vipers' to deal with. They included Henry's namesake nephew, who was now the king's only hope of salvaging something of the marriage that cost so much and yet had yielded only this 15-year-old lad. Unlike Manfred, Henry was given nothing in his father's will except the empty titles to Burgundy and Jerusalem, but he stood in line to succeed the legitimate heir Conrad. In fact, Innocent thought the best solution for everyone was papal recognition of Conrad's power in Germany in return for the crown of Sicily going to his younger half-brother, thus avoiding another all-consuming force like their father emerging in the future.[53] In view of later developments, it would have been all Henry III could have hoped for.

Frederick's death meant the pope could forget about Bordeaux and slowly move his court back to Rome. After six years of sanctuary in Lyon, it was fitting for one of the cardinals to make some sort of speech to the citizenry. It went over well until he decided to end it with a jest that offended the women in attendance. 'When we first came here, we found three or four brothels. Now we leave behind only one, but it runs from the eastern gate of the city to the western one.' In England, Grosseteste committed a similar outrage when, on his visitations, he had the nuns fondled to check their chastity. Says Paris: 'He went to the houses of religious females, and caused their breasts to be squeezed, to try, like a physician, if there was any debauchery practised amongst them.'[54] Those found wanting to the touch were presumably turned out.

As far as the other bishops were concerned, it was still the Archbishop of Canterbury who was out of line during visitations. On 24 February 1251 they convened at Dunstable Priory under Grosseteste's direction and agreed to pool together £2,667 to send proctors to the pope to make a personal appeal against him. They figured their chances were good now that Innocent was no longer in Lyon and so under the influence of the Savoyard party. Fulk Basset, however, couldn't wait for the outcome of the episcopal mission. Boniface had excommunicated him and, although he believed the archbishop acted wrongly, he humbled himself before him to get the sentence lifted. It was distasteful and humiliating, but he needed a clean slate in order to defend Henry of Bath, a senior judge on the king's bench married into the Basset family. He was accused of bribery, literally stuffing his purse and receiving gifts from both parties to a suit. He was disgraced and fined £1,333, but Fulk, his brother Philip and their friend Richard of Cornwall intervened with Henry and got him rehabilitated.[55]

That summer, plans got underway to stage a royal wedding in York to coincide with the Christmas festivities. It would have been two years on 8 July 1251 since Alexander II of Scotland died suddenly at the age of 50 after moving north against one of his barons. The new king, Alexander III, was now 9 years old and betrothed to Henry and Eleanor's daughter Margaret in accordance with the treaty that had averted war in 1244. Archbishop Walter Gray would be the host, but there was no way Henry was going to miss out on the details of organising the first of his children's weddings. The nobility of England and Scotland would be there, as well as the French relatives of Alexander's mother Marie de Coucy. They had to be fed in lavish style. The orders that started going out included 60 oxen, 170 wild boar, 1,300 deer, 7,000 chickens, game birds and rabbits, 10,000 haddock, 60,000 herring, 68,500 loaves of bread to be baked, all of it washed down with 25,000 gallons of wine.[56]

Before the wedding, there was another great ceremony to perform, the dedication of Hailes Abbey, built by Richard of Cornwall in thanks for surviving his difficult voyage from Gascony nine years earlier. On 9 November 1251, the bishops gathered in force in Gloucestershire for the occasion, thirteen of them assisting Walter Cantilupe, the Bishop of Worcester, in the proceedings before the king and queen, while Grosseteste chanted mass at the main altar. Richard was proud of his work and wished he had spent the same amount, almost £6,667, as wisely in reconstructing his residence at Wallingford Castle.[57]

One voyage that didn't make it at this time was that of Simon de Montfort and Guy Lusignan. They had almost reached port from the Continent when the winds suddenly changed and blew them all the way back. Naturally Paris sees this as a symbol: even English weather rose up to keep the foreigners from coming ashore. They caught the next boat over and, while Henry was overjoyed to see his half-brother, he cold-shouldered Simon over the denunciations that continued to pour in from Gascony. At the beginning of the year, Montfort had returned 'ingloriously' from the province; perhaps he was even driven out. He told the king then that without money and men he could not be expected to put down the rebellion. Henry appreciated his commitment, but felt obliged to mention that the complaints coming in about him included throwing people into prison and sending them to their deaths. Such was the scale of their lies and treason, replied Montfort, that it was a wonder the king believed any of it.[58] Henry scraped together another £1,333 and sent him off. Simon succeeded in again quieting the situation, but aroused the fury of the locals, who went all the way up to the Archbishop of Bordeaux. Worse, Simon was now presenting the king with a bill of reimbursement for new castle work, some of which he said he had paid out of his own resources in Leicester. Henry had enough and refused to give him the money. Simon's answer amounted to, 'if you won't pay, somebody else will'. The queen then got involved through her sister-in-law and reminded her husband that those castles would one day be Edward's. Henry agreed to establish a commission to count up the costs, but refused to let Simon return until he had heard from his accusers. He wasn't angry enough to bar the Montforts from his daughter's upcoming wedding, but mistrust had again clearly crept into their relationship.[59]

As the end of 1251 approached, the court arrived in York, where the king and queen took up residence at the archbishop's palace. They did their entertaining there while Gray went out and about making sure everything was taken care of, from firewood for the guests to fodder for the horses. On Christmas day Henry, wearing silk garments trimmed with gold braid, knighted Alexander and twenty other youths. The young king then did homage for his lands in England, and Henry, never missing an opportunity, asked if he might not want to do homage for Scotland as well. Alexander understandably said he could not take such a decision without consulting his nobility first. Not wishing to cast a pall over the occasion or trouble the young couple, Henry let the matter drop.[60]

The wedding itself was held early the next morning, in secret to avoid the crush of people. Although the English, Scots and French were quartered in different parts of the city, fights inevitably broke out whenever parties crossed paths, starting off as fisticuffs but then reaching the point where swords were drawn. The marshals and attendants provided by the king and archbishop, and ample entertainment, mostly kept the situation under control. Finally, the time came for Henry and Eleanor to say goodbye to their 11-year-old daughter, with at least the same sadness and tenderness that must have accompanied the queen's own farewell at around the same age. The marriage was not to be consummated for four years, and Margaret would have as her guardian Matilda, the widow of William Cantilupe, brother of Bishop Walter, who like their father had served many years in the royal household. She seemed in good hands, but his sister Joan's loneliness as Queen of Scotland had left an indelible impression on Henry not to let the same fate befall his daughter.[61]

11

THREE TIMES LUCKY 1252–1254

Few words incited so much fury in this period as *non obstante*, literally 'notwithstanding'. It was the medieval equivalent of a loophole, a way of getting around rights and privileges protected by law and charter. The papal court had come to abuse it as a means of ordering English religious houses to provide for their clerks and relatives 'notwithstanding' the rights which these institutions already had on the books. Activist bishops like Grosseteste despised the practice, not just because it essentially disregarded their rights, but stuck them with a bunch of outsiders unable to communicate with their worshippers.

A case in point is the 'our father who art in heaven, hallowed be thy name' of the Lord's Prayer. A priest from the Continent, where the languages were bonded by their common Latin roots, would have been able to recite it in the Anglo-Norman French of the nobility and educated class. But this 'li nostre Pere, qui ies es ciels, saintefiez seit li tuens nums' wasn't even close to the 'oure fadir þat art in heuenes halwid be þi name' in the Middle English of his flock. Since it was his duty to care for the souls of people who had only their souls to live for, he and many like him didn't even bother showing up. They stayed at home and had their salaries sent to them, smug in the belief that the friars working the countryside for free were taking up the slack created by this unwholesome system of salvation.

But as much as *non obstante* was open to this abuse, it also corrected chinks in the law and kept litigation moving forward against the tide of delaying tactics. An example is the case of the Bishop of Carlisle. Walter Mauclerk had died in 1248 (along with Simon Langton) and was replaced by Silvester Everdon, who had loyally served Henry in the chancery. As the new bishop, Everdon petitioned a local landowner to warrant a charter, but the latter demurred, got letters of protection and went abroad in an attempt to thwart the proceedings. The case went forward anyway, notwithstanding his letters.[1]

Matthew Paris inadvertently brought up the issue with the king on one of his visits to St Albans. The abbey's right of free warren (hunting tract) conflicted with the same privilege granted to Geoffrey Childwick, a knight in Henry's household and brother-in-law of John Mansel. Henry admitted he had acted wrongly in granting Childwick the warren, but the abbey lost the case because it took action against the knight without first obtaining confirmation of its charter. Paris wasn't pleased and represents the king as dismissive of the sanctity of charters:

> When the writer of this book, namely brother Matthew Paris, reproached the king for these proceedings, the latter said, 'Surely the pope acts in a similar fashion, subjoining in his letters, "Notwithstanding any privilege or indulgence".' However, at length speaking more modestly, he added, 'Wait awhile, wait; we will think on the matter.' But all recollection of his words and promises passed away with the sound of his voice.[2]

That Henry took at least an exasperated view of charters can be seen in the exchange reported between him and Robert de Maneby, a prior of the Hospitallers who was involved in a dispute with forest justice Geoffrey Langley. The case had been postponed several times, lately after the prior was sent on a mission to Gascony. Apparently Maneby wanted his letters of protection renewed after he got back, and this led to an altercation with Henry. 'You prelates and religious men,' the king told him, 'have so many liberties and charters that your superfluous possessions make you proud, and from pride drive you to insanity.' Speaking rhetorically, he again mused on the pope's use of 'notwithstanding' to revoke grants he had come to question. 'I will also break this charter,' he warned the prior, 'and others too, which my predecessors and I have rashly granted.' Maneby scoffed at any such notion. 'As long as you observe the laws of justice, you will be a king; but when you infringe them, you will cease to be one.' To this implied threat Henry could only answer, 'You English wish to hurl me from the throne, as you formerly did my father; and, after dethroning me, to put me to death.'[3]

The prior is unlikely to have taken such a superior tone in the king's court, not if he wanted to win his case. Even less credible is the image of the king himself, ranting and paranoid in front of his judges, stewards and courtiers, calling them an alien race out to depose and execute him, all for a trivial matter. Paris evidently got carried away with dramatic dialogue of this sort, but his intention was to show that people like the prior felt free to talk down to the king because he inspired neither fear nor respect in his subjects. He hadn't bested or killed an opponent in combat, had forgiven everyone who abused his trust and authority. At a meeting of the council at this time, Henry planned to request a tax so he could manage both the affairs of Gascony and his crusade. Some of the barons began whispering among themselves that surely he was joking:

> What reasonable hope buoys up this petty king to suppose that he, who has never learned experience in chivalry, who has never mounted a horse, never drawn sword or shaken spear in battle, can triumph where the French king has been made prisoner, and the chivalry of France has succumbed?[4]

Writing in the safety of his shadowy monastery, Paris often uses words like 'womanish' or 'effeminate' to convey what he perceives as a lack of manliness. Another interview conducted after this council gave him the chance to drive the point home. It happened in the Painted Chamber, where Henry generally received guests, in this instance Isabella d'Aubigny, the Countess of Arundel. She had been left a childless teenage widow upon the death of her husband Hugh nine years earlier, and since then had devoted herself to religious works and looking after the extensive assets of her dower. One of these included a quarter of a knight's fee that had been recently taken into the king's hands upon the death of the lord who held it from her. When Henry granted the wardship of this quarter-fee to Peter Chaceporc rather than her, she used the influence of her younger brother John de Warenne, Earl of Surrey and brother-in-law to the king, to take her case all the way to the top.

The meeting began calmly enough, but when the countess persisted in her demand, Henry put her in her place. This gave Paris the opening for the speech he probably always wanted to put in somebody's mouth, and a feisty young woman squaring off against the king, now in his mid-forties, was all he could have asked for. Declares Isabella:

> Why, my lord king, do you avert your face from justice? One cannot now obtain what is right and just at your court. You are appointed a mediator between the Lord and us, but you do not govern well either yourself or us, neither do you fear to vex and trouble the church in many ways, which has been proved not only now, but often of old also: moreover, without fear or shame you oppress the nobles of the kingdom.

To this rebuke, the king supposedly flares his nostrils and laughs derisively, almost like an imbecile, but Paris doesn't deny him his typically sharp wit. 'And where,' he asks, 'is the charter that the nobles gave you to speak on their behalf?' Isabella is more than ready with the answer. 'They didn't give me a charter,' she replies. 'You did,' namely Magna Carta, which:

> you agreed and swore to observe faithfully, and to keep inviolate; and many a time have you extorted money from your subjects whilst promising to observe their rights and liberties, but you have always proved yourself to them a shameless transgressor of those liberties; whereby it is plainly proved that you have broken both your faith and your oath. Where are the liberties of England, so often granted, so often committed to writing, so often redeemed?

In front of whoever else was present at that meeting, the countess swore that the 'god of vengeance' would settle this and all his other acts of injustice. Then, without asking permission to leave or even waiting to obtain it, she left, apparently confident that nothing bad would happen to her for having just insulted the king, over a quarter knight's fee worth roughly £5 a year.

In fact, Henry never intended to deprive her of it. A further review of the rights connected to the wardship proved she was right, and he ordered Chaceporc to surrender it to her. The victory went to her head, however. She decided to press other claims that turned out to be false and was fined £20 for her presumption. Again, using her influence at court, she got Henry's pardon, but only on stipulation that she never again address him with the same language she used in his bedchamber. This suggests that she did indeed make a scene and bragged about it to Matthew Paris. The king was granting her this grace as an inducement to remember the decorum that befitted her station. As for what she really said to him that day, whether it was a great speech denouncing royal tyranny or a shrill lecture from a baroness determined to get her way, only the god of vengeance knows.[5]

Another bit of litigation with a woman running concurrently was markedly more painful for Henry. A decade earlier he had given the wardship of Roger de Tony to his wife, his way of giving her an independent income and patronage to bestow on her own behalf. The grant did not include the advowsons (the right to fill churches or benefices) that were in the gift of the ward. Just before the wedding celebrations at York the previous year, Henry presented such a church, at Flamstead, not far from St Albans, to Artaud de St Romain, a wardrobe clerk of his from Burgundy, only to discover it was already occupied. Eleanor had surreptitiously given it to her chaplain, William of London. Maybe she knew it wasn't hers to give, maybe she didn't. The king suspected the former and lashed out: 'How high does the arrogance of woman rise if it is not restrained.' Henry ordered the sheriff to throw William out, which mortified the queen, but since the church was within the diocese of Lincoln, Grosseteste got involved. Never one to side with foreigners in his parishes, he excommunicated the Burgundian and put the church under interdict, strange for a man so concerned with the spiritual welfare of his parishioners. Now it was the king's turn to feel mortified as the case inevitably wound up in the courts and took the better part of a year to resolve.[6] Eleanor's man apparently won, for he was the rector of Flamstead as late as 1274, but Artaud received the deanery of another church and was raised to be the keeper of the wardrobe at the death of Peter Chaceporc in 1254.[7]

The standoff with the queen was exacerbated by the situation in Gascony coming to a head. At the beginning of the year, Henry dispatched a fact-finding mission to ascertain the extent of the complaints against his viceroy. Simon de Montfort rightly suspected that it was meant as an inquiry into his conduct and protested, but Henry figured he should be happy to be vindicated: 'If everything is clear, what harm will the scrutiny do you? Indeed, your glory will be greater still.'[8] The commissioners reported that Montfort had treated certain persons there with 'great inhumanity', although recognising that they deserved it. He was allowed to return to the province in March, with another injection of £2,000, but no sooner had he arrived than he learned that the Archbishop of Bordeaux was already en route to England with a delegation to charge him in person before the king. Hurrying back, he found the king in a grim mood.[9]

Henry was appalled by the accusation that his viceroy had imprisoned people unjustly, committed fraud, had essentially driven the entire province up in arms through misgovernment. Should he continue, the Gascons threatened to look elsewhere for a new lord. Four years ago, the king had named Montfort to be his new administrator in the troubled land, had given him his full confidence and untold sums of money, but all he got for it was his lordship hanging by a thread. And yet as Simon had shrewdly foreseen, Henry's hands were tied by their agreement. Any move to dismiss him could be legally challenged. To make him walk away of his own accord, Henry needed to convict him in the eyes of his peers. That set the stage for Simon to face his accusers in front of a panel of magnates assembled in the refectory of Westminster Abbey in early May.[10]

It was a trial in the sense that witnesses were called, testimony heard and a verdict given. Lasting nearly a month, each side had at the other, but Henry tried to throw the weight of opinion against his brother-in-law. According to Adam Marsh, he heaped 'vociferous abuse' upon him, while Simon himself maintained 'self-restraint and meekness and magnanimity towards both his lord and adversaries. It must be a long time since any nobleman or private individual has been so harshly and insensitively treated.'

The king's efforts didn't sway the panel in the least. Instead they extolled Simon's 'splendid virtues, fearless loyalty, victorious energy, and the justice of his purpose'. Their reasons were hardly impartial, however. Richard of Cornwall felt that he himself had been robbed of Gascony by his brother and therefore wasn't going to do him any favours. Two other earls, Gloucester and Hereford, had served with Henry on his last expedition and seen first-hand how Gascon treachery nearly ruined them all. Simon could also count on his friends Walter Cantilupe and the bishop's nephew Peter de Montfort, a Marcher lord unrelated to him. Even Marsh was a good friend, hence the bias of his report.[11]

A greater blow to the king was Montfort's support from Peter of Savoy, who would have taken his decision in consultation with his niece the queen. This meant that she too supported staying the course in Gascony. Whatever the complaints, they had come this far, and since Henry had finalised the grant of the province to their son only the previous month, continuity was needed for one or two years until Edward could go there himself. But Eleanor's friendships with Marsh and Eleanor de Montfort suggest her motivations were likely also personal. It was all the same to Henry. He didn't have her backing, and since their squabble over the church in Flamstead was just then going to the courts, he doubtless felt his wife was taking an excessively independent line against him.[12]

With the nobility and clerics arrayed behind Simon, Henry had no choice but to pronounce him vindicated. The Gascons refused to accept the verdict, which Montfort figured was typical of their untrustworthiness, but he offered to go back and rule with mercy and to resort to force only if provoked. Otherwise, he would surrender his agreement in return for full compensation and exoneration. Some time during these talks, tempers flared to the point that, according to Paris, Henry declared Simon a traitor and as such he was free to break the agreement himself. Montfort furiously shot back that the only thing saving the king from getting a thrashing at that moment was his rank. He even taunted his piety, scoffing that it was a mere sham because he didn't take confession and penance seriously. Henry had the last word, however. 'I never repented any act so much as permitting you to enter England to gain land and honours and grow fat and insolent!'[13]

Cooler heads intervened to keep the war of words from landing Simon in the Tower. It was agreed that the king would make plans to go to Gascony, or else send his son there, to attend to these matters in person. In the meantime, both camps were ordered to return and observe a ceasefire. Henry forever embittered his brother-in-law with his interference and unwillingness to take his side against people he considered the real traitors. But as far as Henry saw it, Montfort's rule had turned into a classic case of destroying the village in order to save it. The contempt these two now felt for each other could be seen in their parting shots, with Henry telling Simon, according to Paris, 'Return to Gascony, you lover and fomenter of war. May you find the reward you deserve, just like your father.' His father, of course, found death, but Simon didn't let the jibe bother him: 'With pleasure, and, ungrateful though you are, I shall not return until I have them grovelling at your feet.'[14]

Crossing over with his eldest son, who was now 13, Simon fumed about what he considered the king's betrayal. He even suspected it was part of a plot to eliminate him so that Henry could bestow his earldom on a Savoyard or Poitevin supporter. In France, he gathered up a band of mercenaries who were 'greedier than bloodsuckers' and returned to exact his revenge. The Gascons were of the same mind.

Before leaving England, they rejoiced at the thought of confronting him again on home soil and immediately raised troops when they got back. He set an ambush for them, but they discovered it and his men were routed in the initial melee. He dashed headlong into the fight, was nearly taken prisoner but managed to regroup with his men and beat them off. Two royal commissioners, one of them Nicholas de Molis, the former seneschal of Gascony, then arrived to find the country at war. They ordered Montfort to desist, and when he said it was impossible with these ruffians attacking him, they formally relieved him of command. He refused to go, citing the terms of his agreement, so the king was forced to buy him out with £4,667, plus the payment of his debts.[15] It was extortion as far as Henry was concerned, but he was glad to be rid of him. Their sobering partnership, so hopeful and successful in the beginning, had ended in acrimony with the mission far from complete.

★ ★ ★

The two Eleanors in Henry's life did not let this latest estrangement of their husbands come between them. Eleanor de Montfort was 37 at this time and pregnant with her seventh child. Fearing for Simon and her own health, she turned to Marsh and Grosseteste for spiritual solace. As she reached the late stages, the queen began inquiring of her condition by messengers. Eleanor gave birth to her only surviving daughter, also named Eleanor, as autumn fell at Kenilworth. Her sister-in-law was so overjoyed at the news that she gave the messenger £2 and sent one of her nurses to attend her.[16] It's doubtful whether Henry joined her in this joy, not because he was taking his quarrel with Simon out on his sister, but because he had still not patched things up with his wife. They even got worse when he ordered the arrest of Robert del Ho, her clerk at the Jewish exchequer, on charges of corruption. This could have been connected to a similar scandal caused by the new treasurer Philip Lovel the previous year, but Robert's swift release and pardon suggests that Henry meant it as a warning to the queen about the company she kept and the opinions she harboured.[17]

Ho had only just been freed when a more serious rupture overtook the royal pair. It began with a confrontation that had been five years in the making. Few people had eyed the arrival of the king's Lusignan half-siblings with more suspicion than the Savoyards. Since then, William had become a major landowner, Aymer bishop-elect, and Geoffrey and Guy, while retaining their lordships in Poitou, were constantly hanging around court and collecting fees from the treasury. They were now an entrenched group, the 'king's men' as opposed to the 'queen's men'. Henry had so far shown no inclination to promote his brothers at the expense of the Savoyards because he needed both factions in order to achieve that elusive success on the Continent. But they were as much foreigners to each other as they were to the English, speaking different forms of French and having different ideas of where the king's best interests lay. It was in this atmosphere of wariness that the inevitable turf war between the two sides nearly became an all-out brawl.

It began when Aymer claimed the right to appoint the prior of the hospital of St Thomas in Southwark, opposite Westminster Palace. Boniface's permission was required, or so said his official, Eustace de Lenn. When Aymer ignored him, Eustace excommunicated the new prior, who also ignored him. Eustace then had the new prior seized and imprisoned at Maidstone pending the archbishop's return from the papal court, where Boniface had gone to defend his right of visitation. Aymer put together a posse from the various Lusignan households and sent them to rescue the prior. Breaking into the manor at Maidstone on 3 November 1252, they found neither him nor the official, but were informed they should try Lambeth. Off they rode towards London and found Eustace, but not the prior. They grabbed him with the intention of taking him to Winchester to hold in return for their man, but evidently thought better of it. Eustace was let go, but forced to walk back.[18]

The court was at Windsor when word about the raid arrived. Everyone naturally took sides, but Henry maintained a neutral stance by stopping payments to William de Valence, who supposedly had some part in the posse, and Peter of Savoy, for perhaps complaining too loudly on behalf of his brother Boniface. The queen, however, must have said something that really set him off, because Henry took control of her assets and packed her off to Winchester.[19] He was planning to take the court there for Christmas anyway, but there was no mistaking the meaning of putting her under house arrest within Aymer's dominions. His brothers were here to stay whether she and her uncles liked it or not, and they were going to gnaw and scratch over every bit of patronage just like the rest of them.

If we believe Paris, they were doing more than that. He cites examples: Guy Lusignan borrowing horses and servants from an abbey for a trip to London, but insulting the servants and failing to return the horses; William trespassing on the Bishop of Ely's property to hunt and then, cursing English beer, ransacking the bishop's wine cellar to quench his thirst; and Geoffrey insisting on being treated like a king when he showed up at an abbey seeking accommodation. In a notorious incident in the orchards of St Albans, Paris has Geoffrey's chaplain, an 'utterly ignorant Poitevin' who doubled as a court jester, pelt the king and his party with little green apples, apparently to the amusement of all, except Matthew Paris.[20] The Lusignans' arrogance and sense of entitlement were nothing unusual for their class, but their status as foreigners, related to the king no less, subjected them to greater scrutiny. The Savoyards had so far avoided unwelcome attention by always backpedalling in timely fashion. Unfortunately, in this case, Boniface was an exception, and no sooner had he returned in mid-November than he set out to put the much younger Aymer in his place.

His main weapon was excommunication, and to give it the maximum effect, he asked the Savoyard Bishop of Hereford, Peter d'Aigueblanche, and the Bishop of Chichester, Richard Wyche, a good friend of the queen, to join him in donning their pontifical robes and pronouncing sentence. Aymer responded by having his men publicly proclaim the sentence 'null, void and frivolous'. Henry ordered Peter of Savoy to put an end to the bickering, but when he claimed that it had gone too far for that, the king curtly told him that his presence at court was no longer needed. Meanwhile, the queen was restored to favour for the purpose of bringing about a reconciliation. She made the most of the seasonal gift giving by making presents of expensive belts to Geoffrey and William, and received valuable plate herself from Aymer. Finally, the antagonists exchanged the kiss of peace and the matter was officially closed. Beneath the surface, however, nothing was forgiven or forgotten.[21]

The affair seemed all the pettier now that Henry had plunged headlong into planning his crusade. Back in April 1252, he had declared his intention to depart within four years of 26 June and began sending out requisitions for ships to carry men, horses and supplies. Marseille, still an independent port city, was to be the point of embarkation, and agents were chosen to arrange provisions in advance.[22] Four years was a long time for Louis, who was playing power broker between the warring sultans of the region while waiting for a relief force to arrive. In a letter meant to be reassuring, Henry told him that the return of his Continental possessions would certainly expedite his sailing date. Louis seems to have given it some serious thought, but Blanche was his regent and if she didn't reject it outright as blackmail, there was no way she was going to undo all the work she had put into expanding and consolidating the French monarchy.[23]

But Blanche was worn out by the crusade she had tried to prevent. Her son Robert of Artois had been killed ingloriously, while another, Alphonse of Poitiers, had suffered a stroke after his return. The disaster prompted tens of thousands of shepherds and urban poor to mass together for a new crusade to rescue the king, and she was desperate enough to give them her support. But then they started rioting and ransacking everywhere they went, forcing her to order their dispersal and destruction. Her faith received a final blow when a ship carrying money to her son in the Holy Land sank to the bottom of the Mediterranean. On 29 November 1252, while Boniface and Aymer were calling each other out, she died at Maubuisson Abbey in Melun. When news of her death reached Louis at Sidon, he withdrew and didn't speak to anyone for two days. This outpouring of grief for his mother stood in contrast to the way he treated his wife, which even his admirer Joinville found appalling. Margaret arrived from Jaffa after giving birth to her third child born overseas, but Louis couldn't be bothered to go down to the dock to greet her and their children, an unthinkable act for Henry. Louis remained in the chapel and merely asked about their well-being.[24]

Alphonse and his brother assumed the regency, but Charles still had much pacification to do in Provence. It was perhaps because Alphonse had still not sufficiently recovered from his illness that the French council asked the 'bold and faithful' Simon de Montfort to help them run the government. They were impressed by his pedigree, fidelity and courage, and repeated the offer when he turned them down the first time. He again declined, declaring that no man could 'properly serve two masters opposed to each other'.[25] But the fallout with Henry rankled deeply, and Simon turned to his old friend Robert Grosseteste for solace. In the aftermath of the churching affair thirteen years earlier, the bishop had told him that suffering begets glory and so provided the occasion 'not for sadness but joy'. This time he advised him to do good for evil 'in the spirit of charity and humility'. He should forget the king's inopportune words and remember instead all the good things he had done for him, like giving him his earldom and sister in marriage.[26]

Grosseteste was not of a mind to practice what he preached. He took the lead in opposing Henry's request for 10 per cent of Church revenue for three years to finance his crusade, even though Louis had got the same. It was precisely because the French prelates had given their consent that he advised his colleagues to stand firm, otherwise it would become a customary tax. The king might have expected the bishops of Worcester (Cantilupe), London (Basset) and Chichester (Wyche) to side with Grosseteste as was their wont, but he was beside himself when he learned that Aymer had joined the protest. In the amusing scene depicted by Paris, Henry goes berserk and drives everyone from the room 'like a madman'. He then invites Hugh Northwold, the Bishop of Ely, for a private conference, flattering him to no avail against a long set speech about the need to resist the impoverishment of the Church and how all Louis got for his crusade money was disgrace. Hugh should have saved his breath, for Henry ordered his attendants to throw 'that peasant' out. 'Thus this bishop, who on being summoned had been received with courtesy, went away covered with reproaches and insults.'[27]

Since the pope had mandated the collection, the bishops were going to have to give way sooner or later, but not before they won some concessions. One was to demand stronger action against the Jews. Henry had always been apathetic about enforcing the anti-Semitic Langtonion canons of thirty years earlier, which among other things required the Jewish community to wear badges on their garments and barred them from regular intercourse with Christians. Fulk Bassett had sought to follow Stephen Langton's example by banning the sale of food to the Jews, but Henry intervened to allow the purchases to go forward. Now he needed Bassett and the other bishops' support and, since oppressing 'infidels' usually formed the backdrop to any crusade planning, he agreed to a new Statute of Jewry in the wake of the council of bishops in January 1253. The measures mostly reiterated past decrees, such as demanding the Jews provide some kind of service to the king, forbidding the employment of Christian wet nurses for their male infants, or denying Jews the right to eat or buy meat during Lent. Louis went further that year and issued an edict from the Holy Land for the Jews' expulsion, save those willing to work as mechanics, but Henry again doesn't seem to have applied himself to a concerted drive against them. But then he had already done enough damage by wrecking much of their financial network with tallages the previous decade. It's not surprising that, given all these pressures, his conversion home for the Jews was doing brisk business at this time.[28]

Another concession sought by the bishops, which they weren't going to get, was an end to royal encroachment in their affairs. In another conference that may have been a figment of Paris's imagination but is nevertheless worth retelling, Aymer joined his new friend Boniface, along with William of York, the Bishop of Salisbury, and Silvester Everdon, the Bishop of Carlisle, to ask the king to respect the liberties of the Church and stop manipulating episcopal elections. Henry acquiesced and invited the four of them to join him in remedying the situation. Since they each owed their bishopric to him, they should set the example and resign their cushy positions immediately. Do that, he said, and he will take care not to promote any man like them 'who is not worthy'. Boniface managed to rescue himself and the others from this embarrassing situation by telling the king that they were speaking about the future, not the past.[29]

At a similar council thirteen years earlier, the bishops had evoked Magna Carta as their basic protection against the king. They did so again now, with Grosseteste deploring what he considered Henry's lack of regard for the 'peace and tranquillity of the realm' as enshrined in the charter. Their intention was to rally the barons to their side since they too were being lobbied for a tax. But it was a feudal aid for Edward's knighting, which Henry had every right to levy, and at £5,956, it was a sum the barons could live with. They also considered the Church to be too privileged anyway, especially its demand for special treatment when it came to criminal justice.

Although Henry expressed remorse about the bishops' sense of aggrievement, he had conceded nothing by the time Parliament met to discuss the issue, and the prelates got no help from the barons. He did agree to their wish that he confirm Magna Carta, now for a second time, but only in return for their affirmation of the rights and liberties of the crown. Apart from inflicting further misery on the Jews, that was all the clergy got for granting Henry a subsidy of £30,000. But the confirmation of Magna Carta was still a grand ceremony in Westminster Hall. On 13 May 1253 Boniface led thirteen bishops (not including Wyche, who had died the previous month) in pronouncing excommunication against anyone who violated the charter of liberties:[30]

> The king, as he listened to the above sentence, held his hand to his breast, and preserved a calm, cheerful, and joyful look, and when at the end of it they threw down the candles, which on being extinguished sent forth a stench, and each and all had exclaimed, 'Thus perish and stink in hell all who incur this sentence,' the bells at the same time ringing, he thus spoke, 'So help me God, all these terms will I faithfully observe, as I am a man, a Christian, a knight, and a crowned and anointed king.'[31]

Taking no chances, Grosseteste gave the threat of excommunication the widest possible notice in his see. But his problems with Henry had always gone beyond Magna Carta to the essential divide between church and state. For example, he liked making people answer questions under oath, even when they didn't want to, and Henry would tell the sheriff to put a stop to it. When Grosseteste and Walter Cantilupe went further and set up an inquisition, the king put a stop to that too. He felt that forcing people to inform on the sins of their neighbours amounted to harassment and was an affront to all good Christians. Besides, it was bad for business, as it took them away from their everyday occupations. But the bishop was also an ungrateful wretch, because Henry tried to appease him at this time, forgiving him a fine of £100 imposed for one of his clerks for skipping bail, on top of pardoning two similar fines.[32]

Now well into his seventies, Grosseteste was coming to the end of his days and yet there was still much work to do. His pet peeve remained papal provisions, and he had an assessment drawn up showing that as much as £45,000 had been drained from the country by this unholy system. This figure was ridiculously inflated, for it represented nearly half of all ecclesiastical revenue. The real sum was closer to £10,000, and the pope offered to cap it at half that amount, plus require appointees to take orders and reside in England. But then, with spectacular impropriety, probably intentional, he asked for a benefice for his nephew Federico Lavagna and Grosseteste to provide it. The bishop was outraged. His belief in the plenitude of papal power was unabated, but only insofar as it was constructive. When it served a 'hateful thing', as these provisions were, particularly subjoined with *non obstante*, it was his duty to resist. 'I obediently decline to obey,' he thundered.[33]

It was his last great show of defiance. Grosseteste fell ill at the manor of Buckden and died in the early hours of 9 October 1253.[34] With his death, following those of Frederick and Blanche, three of the greatest personalities of the age had disappeared in the span of three years. Each had been a political animal who died in bed, properly blessed and confessed, but ill at ease with the state of the world they left behind. For a reforming zealot like Grosseteste, that was just the way to go, drawing his last breath with a fist pumped at the people and institutions he had hounded to the end. His self-righteousness must have aggravated many people besides the king and pope, but it also fired up plenty more in an era where the crusade ideal had long since abandoned the religious for the political. He himself, however, wouldn't have wanted that or anything else that abrogated absolute power. He was at heart conservative and would have despaired at the thought of revolution wrought from below. He liked the way the world was ordered simply because it was ordered from above. It was the veneer of corruption and falsity that made it unpalatable and stirred him into action. If he was uncompromising, it was because first principles demanded it, which in turn gave him the authority to hold others to account. Nowhere were these same convictions and contradictions more in evidence than in his most famous disciple, Simon de Montfort.

★ ★ ★

The greatest service Henry could do to the memory of the great churchman was not to interfere in the election of his successor. That just wasn't going to happen, but it was going to be a long process nevertheless because the king wasn't in the country. Following Parliament, he had made plans to sail to Gascony, but struggled to collect men and money for a campaign to a region that was coming to be viewed by his barons as a bottomless pit. He reached Portsmouth in July, then had to wait another month for the right wind. He embarked in early August after a touching scene with his son, recounted by Paris: 'The boy, Edward, after his father had kissed and wept over him at parting, stood crying and sobbing on the shore, and would not depart as long as he could see the swelling sails of the ships.'[35]

Henry arrived in a land plunged into civil war, but it had nothing to do with Montfort, who had been gone for nearly a year. Rather, it was Gaston de Béarn, the queen's cousin and Simon's mortal enemy, whom the king had released from custody after he reaffirmed his allegiance to the crown. The crown he now preferred belonged to Castile, the Spanish kingdom in the central, northern part of the Iberian Peninsula. King Ferdinand III became ill with dropsy and died on 30 May 1252, right in the middle of Montfort's trial. To his son and successor Alfonso he gave this remarkably simple advice: 'If you manage to hold all that I leave you, you are as good a king as I; and if you should enlarge it, you are better than I; and if you should lose any of it, you are not as good as I.' Alfonso, it turns out, was burning with ambition and decided to resurrect the old Castilian claim to Gascony through his great-great-grandmother Eleanor of Aquitaine. Gaston saw his chance to become his viceroy there in the vacuum left by Montfort's departure, and renounced his allegiance to Henry.[36] He began ravaging the countryside and brought the war to Bordeaux.

Although military intervention was inevitable, Henry shrewdly saw that the best way to get Alfonso to back off was to make him a part of the family. The King of Castile had a half-sister named Eleanor who was then about 12 years old, an ideal match for his slightly older son. If Henry had his way, all conflicts in Europe would be settled by marriage instead of war: 'Friendship between princes can be obtained in no more fitting manner than by the link of the conjugal trough.'[37] And this was no ordinary sister, either, but the daughter of Joan of Ponthieu, the woman Henry had legally married seventeen years earlier. In 1249, as Henry and Eleanor began contemplating their children's marriages, they decided to take no chances and asked Innocent to issue an official annulment of his marriage with Joan. Typical of medieval bureaucracy, a thorough investigation was launched with witnesses questioned and hearings held, and five years later an annulment comprising fifteen modern pages confirmed that Henry and Joan were related in the fourth degree and therefore required papal dispensation, which was never issued.[38]

In the midst of putting together resources for his latest Gascon campaign, Henry dispatched Mansel and the Bishop of Bath to treat with Alfonso for the marriage. He was open to the idea, but since he presumably held the advantage, he demanded two particularly stiff terms. The first was to knight Edward, which was not just a point of pride in the warrior tradition of Castile but made the presence of the young man at his court surety for the deal. Henry's heart must have dropped upon hearing this, for he had no doubt dreamt of the day of knighting his son on St Edward's day. Alfonso also expected a generous dower for his sister, without bothering to offer a marriage portion for her himself, and to ensure she was well provided for he wanted Edward to be endowed with lands worth £10,000 a year, an enormous sum that would make him the greatest landowner in the kingdom after his father. Daunting as the terms were, Henry gave his consent and everything seemed to be on course. And then Theobald I of Navarre died in July 1253.

His slice of a kingdom, wedged between the bigger Castile and Aragon and bordering Gascony to the south, was now ruled by his son, also named Theobald, who was Edward's age and another possible match for Eleanor. Going this route, Alfonso could get his hands on both Gascony and Navarre. But the queen dowager of Navarre rightly saw what he was up to and sought protection from Aragon, whose King James I was equally wary of Alfonso despite being his father-in-law.[39] Henry arrived in Gascony as Alfonso was making this latest move and, despite his marriage plans, he was determined to stamp out Gaston and his lot.

To this end, the king's half-brothers were instrumental. Geoffrey Lusignan had earlier helped Montfort put down one of the more serious rebellions. Now he, Guy and William pooled together to supplement Henry's force of 300 knights with another 100 from Poitou.[40] Henry even got some assistance from his brother-in-law Simon, which was surprising since he had planned to resume his trial there in Gascony. But after seeing for himself what the situation demanded, that sometimes you have to destroy vineyards and houses to put down a rebellion, he asked Simon to join him. The sharp words of their last encounter prevented his letter to him in early October from being anything other than official: 'We command and request you to come to Gascony and discuss matters with us; if you think that it befits neither our honour nor yours to remain with us, you can withdraw when you please, without incurring our indignation.' He closed by assuring him that 'throughout the time you remain with us, you shall have nothing to fear from those who wish you ill'.[41]

Simon came but, feeling both aggrieved and vindicated, he was ready to impose conditions for his return. The result was Henry's agreement to give the Montforts Kenilworth Castle for life, £500 to cover his latest costs and another £667 after Henry assumed the lordship of Bigorre from Esquivat, who owed that money to Montfort. All that in return for staying only one month, clearly a sign that Henry wanted to make amends with his sister and her husband. As it was, Simon didn't leave Gascony until early the next year, by which point their new reconciliation and partnership had allowed the king to bring most of the province back under control.[42]

There was still the problem of Gaston and Alfonso, but by February the Castilian marriage was back on and Mansel again went to the Spanish court. This time he was accompanied by Peter d'Aigueblanche, the Bishop of Hereford, Henry's most experienced diplomat. The urgency of the matter can be seen in the progress Peter made once he set out from Meilhan in Gascony. Toledo was about 400 miles away and he reached it in nine and a half days, having covered on average 42 miles a day on horseback or by carriage.[43]

On 1 April 1254 a treaty of alliance was announced that basically reaffirmed the original terms. Edward was to go to Castile to be wed and knighted, while Henry transferred £10,000 worth of holdings to him and provided a dower of £1,000 for his new wife. Paris sneers that Henry harmed his dignity by giving away so much land, as if his son wasn't going to inherit it anyway, but much of it was in Ireland and Wales, where Edward could assert the royal lordship Henry never had the inclination to do. Others were recent acquisitions, like the earldom of Chester, which came to the crown after Henry bought out the sisters of John the Scott. Significantly, he did not give the title of earl to Edward, and those of Duke of Aquitaine and Lord of Ireland he retained for himself.[44] In return, he got Alfonso to relinquish his claim to Gascony and cut ties of support to Gaston and other rebels. Henry could also be sure that the alliance between England and Castile would give Louis something to discuss after he arrived home, for he was just then wrapping up his crusade.

Back in England, the regent was charged with making the arrangements. In a major advancement for queenship, Henry had appointed Eleanor, then about four months' pregnant, to govern the realm, with any counsel as needed from Richard of Cornwall. The regency and pregnancy were signs that they had put their recent troubles behind them but, remembering the Flamstead incident, Henry authorised only Richard and the chancellor, William Kilkenny, to confer benefices.[45] Her powers included granting licences to elect bishops and abbots, but final approval rested with Henry. It was reported that the king wanted Aigueblanche to be the new Bishop of Lincoln, so Henry of Lexington, the dean who was elected, went nervously to Gascony in April to get his blessing. These nerves were likely to have been caused by the sea voyage, because as the brother of Robert of Lexington, one of Henry's trusted advisers, the new bishop should have been welcomed.[46]

On 25 November 1253 Henry and Eleanor's last child was born, a daughter named Katherine. It had been eight years since she gave birth to their youngest Edmund, suggesting there may have been miscarriages or stillbirths in the intervening years. She remained in firm control of the government between her confinement and purification, however, as can be seen in the disposition of the marriage rights and wardship of John de Vescy, the grandson of Eustace, one of the lords who instigated the rebellion against King John. William de Vescy had died while with the king in Gascony and, given that he held the key northern barony of Alnwick, Henry assigned the wardship of his heir to Peter of Savoy, who was in control of nearby Richmond. Knowing that the revolt against his father had started in the north, Henry's unstated policy was to keep that region under tight royalist control. The writs affecting the Vescy estate were all going out around the time of the queen giving birth.[47]

Eleanor's biggest challenge during her regency, as with the challenge of anyone connected to Henry's government, was keeping him solvent. She had to manage the final payoff of Montfort's original £7,000 settlement, and another £3,226 to Alphonse of Poitiers to settle damages incurred as a result of the conflagration affecting his adjacent counties.[48] While Henry was still treating for peace with Alfonso, Eleanor received a request from him to convene Parliament for the purpose of providing men and money for war against the Spanish king. Alfonso was engaged in troop movements at the time that, though later found to be a demonstration against Navarre and Aragon, could easily have been meant for Gascony. Eleanor was still waiting for her purification feast, scheduled for 6 January, when the summons went out for an assembly on 27 January 1254. In her report of the outcome sent on 14 February, the prelates promised either service or money if Alfonso attacked, but didn't think the lower clergy would do the same unless the terms for the crusade collection were modified. To avoid that looking like blackmail, they added that they would work on their brethren if the invasion did occur. The barons declared their willingness to come to the king's aid with their knightly tenants, but 'the other laity', that is those not subject to military service, were not disposed to approve any money until the sheriffs, at the king's behest, complied with Magna Carta. Apparently, his public confirmation and proclamation of the charter the year before had had little impact.[49]

Another Parliament was summoned for 26 April to make a direct appeal to these lower clergy and other laity, and in doing so Henry, Eleanor or one of their advisers came up with an innovation. For the first time on record, two knights from each county were to be elected to go to Westminster to represent their constituencies, joining representatives of the lower clergy who were summoned in like manner. Apart from the magnates, it was the first truly elected Parliament to meet in England. In fact, magnates like Richard of Cornwall may have taken a superior attitude about it, because they were late in coming. When they finally got down to business, Simon de Montfort suddenly appeared on the scene and informed them of the peace initiatives currently underway. According to Paris, the parliamentarians felt they had been deceived by the king and his regent, and left without voting any money.[50] Like many great innovations, this one got off to a rocky start.

It was, of course, an era when it took weeks or months for breaking news to arrive. The treaty with Castile was already a month old when Parliament gathered to discuss the war appropriations. Examining documents long after the event, Paris suspected that Henry had concocted the whole affair to get his hands on money he certainly needed. In financing his expedition, he had run through his entire gold treasure, nearly £19,000, and another £17,000 in addition to loans he had taken out locally. Henry's original letter to the regency council about the invasion was, moreover, simply too bizarre to be taken seriously. In it, he declared that Alfonso had an army of Christians and Moors ready to overrun Gascony, and once they were done there, England and Ireland were next.[51]

If anyone had an invasion to worry about, it was the Moors. Since before Louis left for Egypt, King Ferdinand III had tried to interest Henry in joining him on a crusade to North Africa. Alfonso was eager for his father's crusade to go forward, and saw the alliance with England as the best way to bind Henry to the adventure, promising him he could keep half of all they conquered. Wanting the treaty, and perhaps enticed by the idea of getting mixed up in that part of the world, Henry accepted, and in doing so committed himself to two crusades. Actually, it was three, as he had recently committed himself to another.[52]

In February, as the report complaining of infringement of Magna Carta was being prepared, Henry accepted an offer from Innocent that had been in circulation for two years. The pope, feeling that accommodation with Conrad was no longer possible, was prepared to offer the throne of Sicily, which also included southern Italy, to anyone willing to fight for it. There were two names on his shortlist, Richard of Cornwall and Charles of Anjou. Both were interested, but Richard considered the terms little better than offering him the moon. He was also uneasy about supplanting his teenage nephew Henry Hohenstaufen as successor to Conrad.[53] Charles was more receptive, despite protests from his mother and Louis, but his involvement in a succession crisis in Flanders took him out of consideration.

That was only a respite, for the ambitious Charles would surely be back. If the Plantagenets were intent on beating the Capetians to any part of Frederick's former empire, Sicily ought to be it. It was rich, cultured, just the type of kingdom Henry might have dreamt of for himself. When his nephew died in December 1253, he decided to accept Innocent's offer on behalf of his son Edmund, who had replaced Richard on the shortlist. Edmund was only 9 at the time, but Innocent didn't care as long as he had England behind him. He even hinted that Henry's crusading vow to the Holy Land should be commuted to Sicily to focus his efforts, but Henry himself was evasive on that point because, characteristically, he was looking at the big picture. Conrad had also inherited the kingdom of Jerusalem, so they may as well wrestle that from him in the process.[54]

As fate would have it, the 26-year-old Conrad died of a fever at the end of May 1254, and Innocent, now faced only with his enemy's infant son Conradin and half-brother Manfred, felt he had moved too hastily in making the offer to Henry. He still encouraged him to send Edmund and a well-financed army to 'strike thunder in these parts, as though a voice from heaven', but he nevertheless dispatched his envoy Albert of Parma to Gascony to size up the situation. Albert, who had met Henry in England while negotiating with Richard, left in disbelief that they had made the offer to him in the first place. This king, the nephew of Richard the Lionheart, was on his third attempt at military success on the Continent and completely broke. Albert didn't even have to do any due diligence. Henry told him flat out he had no money. The crusade tax was their only hope of getting Edmund to Sicily. When Henry asked for a re-confirmation of the grant, essentially committing the pope to what he had started, Albert refused, and the Sicilian business, as it came to be known, hung in limbo.[55]

With three crusades now on his plate, Henry made a push that summer to bring Gascony firmly under control. He was helped by a cash injection from Eleanor, who pawned the crown jewels to Richard in return for £6,667. Richard also got the regency when the queen left with the money at the end of May, taking Edward, Edmund and Boniface with her. Eleanor's growing confidence in her role as queen can be seen in her disregard of a last-minute order from her husband not to sail. Whatever complication had arisen, she decided to sail anyway because the arrangements had been made and the winds were right.[56] Henry was in the field when they arrived on 10 June, and Edward went to join him. The family was together in Bordeaux in August when his future mother-in-law passed through on her way to Ponthieu in the north. Joan had fallen out with her stepson Alfonso and decided not to stay for her daughter's wedding. Henry and Eleanor's impressions of the woman who was technically his first wife went unrecorded.

Edward's knighting had been scheduled for 13 October, but delays arose and he did not arrive in Burgos until five days later, with a noticeably smaller retinue than anticipated. His wedding to Eleanor took place at Las Huelgas on 1 November 1254, and three weeks later they were in Bordeaux, where he was expected to take up his duties as the new lord of the land. The province was finally quiet with the surrender of the last rebel stronghold in August, but there were still plenty of divisions to deal with and claims to settle, and next to no money for any of it. If he complained to his father about it, Henry would have replied that he became king under similar circumstances. Edward did have his bride by his side and, although he was 15 and she 13, they were definitely having a honeymoon. The first of their many children was born prematurely and died in May the following year.[57]

The royal couple was in a hurry to leave because Louis, back after nearly six years abroad, had given them permission to travel homeward through France. Henry couched his request in flattery, saying that it was his desire to see the cities and churches of the country, but that he also wanted to visit his mother's grave at the abbey of Fontevrault, and Louis could hardly deny him that. He never bore his mother a grudge for abandoning him, and routinely honoured her memory by having masses said for her soul. At Fontevrault, he had her remains moved from the churchyard to a proper tomb inside the abbey, next to his uncle Richard I and grandparents Henry II and Eleanor of Aquitaine. Feeling strangely at peace among these four stormy characters, he willed his heart to the abbey on that visit.[58]

On 24 November, they were at Orleans on their way to Pontigny to visit the shrine of Edmund of Abingdon, the man who married them. There, Henry and Louis met for the first time. It was natural and appropriate that these two kings should meet, and evidently they hit it off. They had much in common, both being pious, faithful, married to sisters and hopeless warriors. They also enjoyed the advantage of sharing the same language, although Henry's French, which betrayed the Poitevin dialect he grew up with and the Anglo-Norman of his court, must have had an odd ring to the ears of the Parisian court. The French couple had come to accompany Henry and Eleanor to Pontigny, but seeing how tired they still were after their crusade, Henry wouldn't hear of it. Once St Edmund was out of the way, they met up again at Chartres, where the cathedral would surely have caught Henry's eye, more so than others', and from there they rode the 56 miles to Paris together, the men and women in their own coaches.[59]

The city they entered on 9 December 1254 had a population of 160,000, perhaps three times that of London, and 5,000 students. Many of these were English, and throngs of them and Parisians turned out in their finest with candles and flowers in hand, singing and playing music as the royal cavalcade moved along. Henry was profoundly impressed by the architecture, large and small, from the exquisite Sainte-Chapelle, which he ached to take home with him, to the multi-storey houses that were actually plastered on the outside. The people leant out of their windows three or four floors above for a glimpse at him. From their lodgings at the Old Temple, the English threw open the doors on their first morning there to feed the poor, setting off a round of feasting that would dominate their stay. The highlight was a state banquet with twenty-five dukes and counts, eighteen countesses and twelve bishops in attendance. The kings went through the almost expected ritual of deferring the place of honour at the table to the other. 'No, you, sir. No, you, sir …'[60]

Afterwards Louis stifled Henry's objection that he stay in his grand palace, saying in jest that he was king and would decide. Henry was careful to be a gracious visitor and accepted. He is unlikely to have heard about the last visit by an English king to Paris, that of his father John in 1201. King Philip had given him the same palace to use, but when he got it back he discovered, rather amusingly, that the English party had emptied his cellars of all the bad wine and left the good stuff.[61]

The real public relations bonanza of the visit was the reunion of Beatrice of Savoy and her four daughters. Sanchia arrived from England with a magnificent entourage arranged by her husband Richard of Cornwall, who as regent had to stay behind. The Provencal sisters had not seen each other since they were children, but their difference in social rank and old quarrels likely kept them from falling into each other's arms. Sanchia should have been the most resentful, as she was neither queen nor had she received any inheritance, but she appears to have been quiet and unassuming and wanted more than anything to see her mother again.[62] Margaret was the most jealous of all, hating the way Beatrice and Charles had taken Provence for themselves and abandoned them on crusade. She took an instant liking to Henry, no doubt envious of the affection he showed to Eleanor. Her Louis had been neglectful enough before leaving on crusade. Since returning, he added a stern moroseness that came from feeling sorry for himself.[63] She may have hoped that during the course of the visit her husband would look to Henry as an example of how to treat a lady, if not a wife and queen, properly.

After nearly a week of festivities, the guests headed for the coast. Louis rode with them for part of the way, clearly much taken with Henry's company. In embracing and kissing him at their parting, he told him he wished they could be inseparable friends, but the twelve peers of France and his barons would not allow him to reach any accommodation about his patrimony. Henry had intended to hold Christmas court in England, but the winds kept them from sailing until 27 December. He was returning after nearly sixteen months abroad, having secured Gascony, a major alliance with Castile and the friendship of the French king. This marked the beginning of a new era that would see his foreign policy achieve the absolute highs and lows of his long reign. On his previous return from the Continent he had been much mocked, but this time even his most insatiable critic commended him. After making his customary complaint about the cost of the visit, Matthew Paris wrote, 'However, the honour of the king of England, and, in fact, of all the English, was much increased and exalted.'[64]

12

COLLAPSE 1255–1257

Gift giving was just as important as hospitality in medieval relations and diplomacy, and Henry made sure to distribute lots of silver cups, brooches and girdles to the guests at the banquet in Paris. A flirtatious Margaret gave him a bejewelled washing basin shaped like a peacock at full spread, whereas Louis's gift was far more rustic. It was an elephant he had taken back with him from the East. His one success in the Holy Land had been an alliance with his former captors against a rival sultan, earning him the repatriation of the remaining Christian prisoners, the forgiveness of the balance of his ransom and the elephant. Henry already had a zoo of sorts at the Tower of London, which he had set up after Frederick sent him a camel and the three leopards. A polar bear from Norway was added in 1251, tied to a long rope so it could catch fish in the Thames. The elephant arrived in February 1255 and was housed in a specially built pen measuring 40 feet long and 20 feet wide. The costs of feeding it and maintaining a keeper were enormous, about £30 a year, but it drew in the crowds in a land where such animals were known only from the bible and fables.[1]

The two sheriffs of London were given overall responsibility for the elephant, but the creature was the least of their worries. Upon his return, Henry was informed that a prisoner had escaped and fled abroad. He was a clerk suspected of inciting a crowd of fellow clergy to murder Bernard of Champagne, a prior in the service of the Bishop of Hereford. Bernard may have been an unpleasant fellow to work with, not helped by his foreign accent, but he was also a distant relative of the queen. At first, Henry wanted to hold the whole of London to account, but the aldermen banded together to pin the blame on the sheriffs who, after a month's imprisonment, were deposed and new ones elected.[2] But the city couldn't escape the tax bill to help defray the king's costs overseas. Of the £5,666 levied on the towns and shires by the council, London's share was £2,000. Doubtless few would have been pleased to think they were paying for the good time had by the royal party in Paris.[3]

In need of a lot more money, Henry again turned to his brother for a loan. Since he had already pledged the crown jewels to him, the security he offered was the Jews. On 24 February, Richard of Cornwall gave him £3,333 in return for the receipts of the Jewry until he had recouped the principal plus an extra £2,000. On 11 April, Henry convened Parliament again to ask for a tax, but it was more of the same never-ending saga. They would only grant his request if he gave them control over the justiciary, treasury and chancery, but he refused, and the session was adjourned until autumn.[4] The king didn't go into details about his debts, but the following month he assumed his most onerous one yet, a burden so heavy that the elephant may well be seen as a metaphor for the weight he was about to carry around his neck for the next few years.

The Sicilian business was back in play thanks to the events that unfolded while Henry and Eleanor were making their way north through France. On 2 December, near Foggia in southern Italy, Conrad's half-brother Manfred defeated forces loyal to the papacy as the pope lay ill in Naples. Innocent IV died five days later, spiritually crushed because it wasn't supposed to have ended this way. Manfred had agreed to his terms and even led his horse by the bridle as he re-entered Apulia, the mainland territory of the kingdom of Sicily. But then relations broke down because there were lots of people on both sides with their own opinions and agendas. The new pope, Alexander IV, tried to negotiate with Manfred, but as usual nothing came of it and he had no choice but to get on with the campaign. The problem was money, as Manfred had got to the imperial treasure first.[5] Alexander decided to revive the grant of the kingdom to Edmund, but seeing that Henry had not put much effort into their agreement after it was first made, he now imposed new terms.

First, the papacy offered to put up no money of its own, and demanded that Henry pay the entire amount of war debt so far accrued, around £90,400. Second, Henry's crusade to the Holy Land would be commuted to Sicily and the collection of the clerical tenth for that enterprise extended from three years to five. Third, Henry was to raise an army of 8,500 men for Sicily, and have them ready to fight in eighteen months. And, finally, failure to act would result in Henry's excommunication and England being placed under interdict. The terms were harsh, almost punitive, but Alexander wanted it understood that the enterprise, called 'the thing' by his predecessor, was now real. There could be no more delays. At that point Henry could have walked away at no loss to himself because he still had his original crusade ahead of him and no pope could hold a grudge against him for wanting to help the Holy Land.[6]

But he didn't walk away because he didn't want to. Conceived as a whole, the Sicilian business seemed like the opportunity of a lifetime. Henry had not been able to dislodge the French from his Continental patrimony because he never had any backing. The English lords who followed him on his earlier campaigns did so out of duty, but their hearts and purses were never in it. Here he would have the full backing of the papacy, whose economic and diplomatic power still counted for something. Switching his focus from France to the Mediterranean would earn him tacit support from Louis, at least freedom from interference as he marched an army to Italy. Louis may even have cooled Henry's ardour for the Holy Land with the tale of all the miseries he suffered there and the generally hopeless situation of the crusader states. The half a million pounds that Louis sank into that wasted venture, moreover, made this deal seem like a bargain. As for the technicality of what a crusade was for, it was well known that Manfred, like his father, employed Saracen soldiers, so there were infidels of some sort to conquer in the undertaking.[7]

Henry might also have believed that his recent successes with Gascony, Castile and France would free him to concentrate on the Sicilian business, but even before he returned from the Continent it looked as if Scotland was going to be his most immediate concern. Alan Durward, a Scottish nobleman forced out of government by the ruling Comyn faction, accompanied Queen Eleanor to Gascony and later Edward to Castile. Anxious to regain his position, he hinted that all was not well with Henry's selection of two Anglo-Scottish nobles John de Balliol and Robert de Ros as guardians for his daughter Margaret. This was confirmed when Eleanor's physician, Reginald of Bath, travelled north to check up on the 14-year-old queen in early 1255. He found her pale and distraught from life in the castle of Edinburgh, a 'sad and solitary place' by the sea. No sooner had Reginald kicked up a fuss about her mistreatment when he died suddenly – poisoned, suggests Paris, due to the timing.[8]

Clearly something was wrong, and in the summer Henry began moving his court north, arriving in Nottingham on 17 July. Prior to that, he dispatched Richard de Clare and John Mansel to see what they could find out. Claiming to be servants of Ros, they gained entrance to the castle and, like Reginald, found the girl in deep distress. She was not allowed to go anywhere, the castle's air was unwholesome and it lacked pristine views of green fields, her handmaidens were not of her own choosing, and she and her husband were not allowed to sleep together. Clare and Mansel did what they could to console her and putting the young couple in the same bed certainly helped. In the meantime, Henry reached Scotland, his one and only visit there, and while Margaret was brought south of the border to spend time with her mother at Wark in early September, he worked with Durward and Patrick Dunbar, the Earl of March, to purge the Scottish government of the Comyns. New ministers were put in place with a term of office until Alexander reached his majority.[9]

Next, Henry went after Balliol and Ros, holding them responsible for Margaret's misery. Balliol, called 'avaricious, rapacious, and tenacious' by Paris, compounded his difficulties by instigating an assault during that very month against the men of the Bishop of Durham. He was fined £500, a third of which was eventually pardoned. As the one in charge of Edinburgh Castle, Ros could argue there was nothing he could do about the air or lack of greenery, and in keeping the couple apart, he was following orders that the teenagers were not to enjoy conjugal relations until Alexander, the younger of the two, reached his fourteenth birthday. But he foolishly demanded to defend himself in a trial by battle, which was his way of saying he didn't trust the judgement of his peers. For that, the council fined him £666. When, unlike Balliol, he didn't pay up, Henry ordered the sheriff to seize his lands and sell off his goods. Ros too eventually received a pardon, but according to him the fine had actually been a thousand times higher, or £66,666. It was an outlandish figure that no one could pay, but by then it was November 1259 and Henry had lost control over his council to reformers. The whole point of the new council taking all power into their hands was to demonstrate that the king and his old 'fair-weather' councillors had not meted out justice fairly, and Ros's absurd claim sounded like a good example of this. There was no need to check it against the records.[10]

One person not involved in the affair was the man who married the Scottish royal pair, Walter Gray, the Archbishop of York. He had travelled to London for the spring Parliament, but was taken ill and died in nearby Fulham on 1 May. He was the last surviving magnate of John's reign, a witness to the inception of Magna Carta, but a loyal servant to the end. The canons elected their dean, Sewal de Bovill, to replace him, but Henry objected on the grounds that Bovill was born out of wedlock and maintained a retinue of knights. For Paris, the king was on the lookout for any such trifle in order to appropriate York's revenue while it was in his hands. He goes on to say that Henry stopped in Durham on the way home to pray at the tomb of Cuthbert, a seventh-century saint, and while there learned of an immense sum of money kept there on deposit. He ordered his attendants to break open the chests so that he might borrow it. He did pay the money back, but without any compensation for helping himself to it in the first place.[11]

While Henry was in Scotland he received a disturbing visit from a woman named Beatrice, who came from Lincoln some 150 miles to the south. She claimed that her 8-year-old son Hugh had been murdered by the Jews there. Hers was the latest anti-Semitic accusation fixated on the kidnapping of Christian boys, who were then allegedly subjected to a mock crucifixion. Known as 'blood libel', these cases were not uncommon in the superstitious and intolerant atmosphere of the day. Norwich alone accounted for at least three. During the latest, in 1240, the Jews of Norwich sought the protection of the king's court when charged, but the bishop at the time, William Raleigh, refused their request on the grounds that it was an ecclesiastical crime. Four of them ended up on the gallows.

Most medieval rulers put little stock in such charges, and so far neither had Henry. When Beatrice made her plea, he felt the grief of her loss, especially as she was a widow and Hugh her only child. He himself was a devoted parent, and before setting off to Scotland, he said it was his wish to see his daughter 'with the greatest desire' of his heart. But as for Beatrice's demands for justice, he told her that if what she said was true, then the Jews deserved to die. If, however, she was falsely accusing them, then she should suffer the same fate. In fact, all she knew was that her son was last seen playing with some Jewish boys, which gives an idea of the intermingling of faiths that existed despite the attempts to legislate against it.

What sealed it for her and many of the locals was the large number of Jews who had gathered in Lincoln from all across the country that summer. They were there to celebrate a wedding between two prominent families, but the disappearance of the boy at the same time fed the rumour that they were there for a more sinister purpose. It was almost inevitable that when the boy's body was discovered in a well on 29 August, nearly a month after he had gone missing, a convert was produced who verified the marks of crucifixion on his corpse, as if he had seen other cases before, or decomposition hadn't rendered any opinion in this particular case impossible. The canons of the cathedral quickly buried the boy, even before his mother returned. The shrines of martyrs were always big money-makers and there was clearly one in the making here.

When informed of this latest development, Henry ordered his senior justice Roger Thurkelby and steward Ralph Fitz-Nicholas to meet him in Lincoln on 23 September. In the event, the business in Scotland delayed his departure until two days before then. He was keen to get back to Westminster, where a glittering feast of St Edward had been planned for 13 October, but felt the situation in Lincoln demanded his presence. Upon his arrival on 3 October, all the male Jews were taken into custody for interrogation by Henry's other steward, John of Lexington, whose family came from the area. He was more than qualified for the unenviable task before him. One of his brothers was a royal justice, another an abbot, a third was the Bishop of Lincoln and John himself was described as 'prudent and discreet', an expert in canon law who also sat as a judge on the king's bench. In the course of his investigation, he arranged a plea bargain with a man named Copin. In return for his life, he confessed that it was a case of blood libel. Henry was so horrified when he heard the confession that he overruled his steward and ordered the wretch to be dragged and hanged. Since Copin had implicated his entire community, the other ninety-two Jews remained in prison to await trial.

In October they were taken to the Tower of London. Eighteen had refused to submit to a jury of Christians. This was taken as a confession of guilt and they were dragged and hanged on 22 November. With Beatrice still hounding them, the other seventy-four were reportedly convicted, but by May 1256 all had been released. The friars had intervened on their behalf, as did Richard of Cornwall, who was in the city at the time of the hysteria on a pilgrimage to Grosseteste's tomb. Even though two of his business agents were Lincoln Jews, he kept his head down throughout the inquiry. Despite his ambivalence, the possessions of those executed went to his profit under the terms of his loan to Henry. Lincoln Cathedral also benefited from the tragedy, certainly not the last to visit the Jews before their expulsion from the realm thirty-five years later. In November 1256, a year after the executions and a few months before John of Lexington's own death, the canons made plans to begin construction of what became the angel choir, so admired today, but no doubt funded in part from the proceeds left at the shrine erected for Little St Hugh, as the boy found down the well came to be known.[12]

Henry's anxiety about missing the feast of St Edward of 1255 was more than a matter of religious devotion. He had hoped to make it the occasion of presenting his new daughter-in-law to the English public, but her late arrival and lack of decent apparel scuttled those plans. He must have thought his son a cad for not furnishing her with a better wardrobe and dispatched £66 to Dover for her needs. The young Eleanor didn't arrive in London until 17 October, thrilled no doubt by the ornamental display put on for her at the king's urging, but less so by the cold, damp, squalid metropolis that invited little comparison to the sunny cities of her youth. Henry tried to ease the transition by decorating her rooms at Westminster with tapestries as they did in Castile, 'even on the floor' reports a disgusted Matthew Paris, not at all taken with this first instance of carpets being used in England. He has nothing good to say about the Spaniards in her retinue either, accusing them of adultery, fornication and murder among other things, but it was for two other foreigners present at the feast that he reserved most of his venom.[13]

They were an Italian, Cardinal Ubaldini, and a sub-deacon from Gascony named Rostand Masson. On 18 October 1255, Ubaldini formally invested Edmund with the kingdom of Sicily by placing a ring from Alexander on his finger. Since the boy was only 10, a year older than Henry when he became king, his parents would act for him until he turned 15 and could swear allegiance to the pope for himself. It was Rostand's job to formally commute Henry's crusading vow for that purpose.[14] The king and queen were naturally elated. Making provisions for a second son was always potentially troublesome in royal families, as Henry knew well from his relationship with Richard of Cornwall, and they had made glorious provisions indeed for Edmund.

Richard, however, was having none of it and denounced the business in the Parliament gathered for the occasion of the feast. Having turned down the offer of Sicily for himself, he may have been unwilling to see it go to anybody else, but he rightfully argued that Henry had not consulted them before agreeing to the terms. Other magnates chimed in with their complaints, citing the cost, distance, need to confront an entrenched enemy and an England exposed to danger with so many of them gone, as if none of these things would be an issue for a crusade to the Holy Land.[15] With that seemingly out of the way, Roger Bigod turned to other matters at hand and asked for leniency for Robert de Ros, whom he knew from his youthful days at the Scottish court. That was the last thing Henry wanted to hear, and in the sharp exchange that followed, he called the Earl of Norfolk a traitor for supporting Ros, hinting that he could lose his lands for it. Bigod scoffed at the presumed threat. 'If you are just, how can you harm me?' A later King Henry might have responded with 'off with his head', but here his reply was a decidedly tepid, 'I can seize your corn and sell it.'

By that, Henry was threatening to call in Bigod's debts. In the hope of fostering cooperation among his magnates, he had always been easy-going about the debts they owed the crown. The Earl of Norfolk alone owed as much as £1,000, but he warned he would chop off the head of anybody who seized his corn. Henry ordered it anyway until the money was made good. Bigod got the message and worked out a new repayment schedule with the exchequer.[16] He made no further attempt to intercede for Ros, not until the reform period turned the tables and put the king on notice.

At this same Parliament, but sitting apart from the baronage, the clergy was being put through the grinder by Rostand. He spelt out the terms of his mission, which was to oversee the collection of reliefs, exemptions, legacies, gifts and tenths earmarked for a crusade now redirected to Sicily. To facilitate that process, he was equipped with letters bearing *non obstante*, meaning no debate allowed. The bishops were especially dismayed to find that one of their own, Peter d'Aigueblanche (Hereford), was the prime mover behind it all. He was Henry's proctor for most of the business and had even devised a scheme, or rather was blamed for devising it, that allowed the papacy to borrow money secured with collections yet to be made. Fulk Basset (London) announced that they might as well chop off his head for all the cooperation they were going to get out of him in this affair, and he was seconded by Walter Cantilupe (Worcester), who declared himself poised for the scaffold.[17] Their resistance was futile, however, for neither had the stature of Grosseteste, now dead two years, and even the great prelate himself would probably have caved in the end. He had fought with his soul against secular rulers like Henry getting their hands on church money, but when it was the holy father who wanted it, as was the case here, he felt it was their duty to comply.[18]

In the age of Magna Carta, the barons were under no similar compulsion to aid the king and stood their ground for the month Parliament was in session. After it adjourned, Henry convened his council at Windsor in a belated attempted to seek consultation on Sicily. There are no surviving minutes, just a memorandum dated 30 November indicating those signing on to the undertaking. They include three earls, Gloucester, Surrey, and Warwick; three Lusignans, Aymer, William and Geoffrey; three royal justices, Thurkelby, Bath, and Bracton; and his three top advisers, Mansel, Fitz-Nicholas, and Robert Walerand, the last just then coming to fore in English politics. Edward arrived from Gascony around that time and got his father's permission to pledge himself on his brother's behalf.[19] He understood that giving Edmund his own island kingdom meant he was going to get everything else.

★ ★ ★

Just as he was getting consent of some sort, Henry's plans were dealt a major setback when Thomas of Savoy was imprisoned in Turin after his forces were routed by the commune of Asti on 23 November. He had become the regent of Savoy on the death of his brother Amadeus two years earlier and presumed to extend his authority east and southward into the Italian Piedmont. Henry had hoped to employ him as Edmund's regent as well and gifted him the principality of Capua within the kingdom of Sicily as an incentive. His capture also deprived Henry of the other Savoyards, as the two archbishops Boniface (Canterbury) and Philip (elect of Lyon) joined their brother Peter, who was then administering Gascony for Edward, in mobilising an army to either free Thomas, the oldest among them, or force the commune to come to terms for his ransom. Richard of Cornwall contributed £1,000 to the operation, but Henry was so strapped for cash at this time that Alexander sent him an angry reminder about falling behind on his payments for Sicily. The best he could offer the brothers was the note he held to the castles in Provence, worth £2,666, if they could collect it from their sister Beatrice.[20]

The events that brought Thomas back to Savoy had begun a decade earlier following the death of his wife Joanna, the Countess of Flanders. He cast his lot with Frederick in the papal-imperial cold war, but at the emperor's death, switched loyalties and married Innocent's niece. He had supported Charles of Anjou in his acquisition of Provence, but that didn't earn him any gratitude. Charles saw his imprisonment as an opportunity to extend his own power into Piedmont. He began working behind the scenes to make sure Thomas now had all the time in the world to think things over.

Charles had, in fact, only just returned to Provence after intervening in the civil war that erupted in Flanders after Thomas left. The childless Joanna had been succeeded by her sister Margaret, whose two sons from her first marriage, the oldest being John d'Avesnes, began fighting with their half-brothers from her second marriage, led by William of Dampierre. Margaret favoured her younger brood, as did Louis when, as the arbitrator of the dispute in 1246, he gave Flanders to William and the smaller county of Hainault to John. After William was killed in a tournament in 1251, John rose up again with the aid of his brother-in-law William of

Holland, King of the Romans, who had his own territorial dispute with Margaret. They captured Margaret's remaining Dampierre sons, but when John attempted to treat with her for their release, her response, according to Paris, was: 'I will not be turned from my purpose on their account. Put them to death and eat them, one boiled with pepper, the other roasted with garlic.' She invited Charles to join the toxic savagery, promising him Hainault as his reward. He did, and had conquered most of it by the time Louis returned from crusade and took up a new arbitration. His award in September 1256 was completely skewed in his brother's favour.[21]

John d'Avesnes had tried to interest Henry in these affairs while he was in Gascony, but the king avoided getting involved because Margaret held a fief of him and he was already too busy with the negotiations for Sicily. The situation suddenly changed two months after Thomas was imprisoned. On 28 January 1256 William of Holland was hacked to pieces after his horse got bogged down during a skirmish in Friesland. He had been a successful King of the Romans in that he gave the German principalities their freedom and didn't aggravate the pope. The seven electors charged with finding his replacement wanted more of the same policy. Whoever succeeded William had to be more interested in the title than any power that might be inherent in the job description.[22] This all but guaranteed a king from outside Germany, and Avesnes saw this as an opportunity to win English support for his cause in Flanders. Within a week of losing his ally, he was making overtures to Richard of Cornwall, offering to be his front man in the race for the crown.

Richard seemed like the ideal candidate. He was available, had an international standing and could speak English, which in those days was presumably similar enough to German to meet the language requirement. Perhaps the most important factor was his wealth. Paris was again wildly exaggerating when he estimated Richard's liquid worth at £243,000, but buying a majority of the electoral votes, followed by the coronation and lots of largesse, was going to be supremely expensive. Richard, now 47 and still longing to exalt his status, did a quick crunch of the figures and decided he was in. On 5 February, Avesnes was granted a pension of £200 at the exchequer by Richard's counsel.[23]

It goes without saying that Henry fully backed his brother in this endeavour. Plantagenet ties to Germany went back long before his attempts to establish a firm alliance with Frederick. Emperor Otto IV, who had been forced to abdicate in favour of Frederick in 1215, was the son of Matilda, the oldest daughter of Henry II and Eleanor of Aquitaine. This consideration aside, Henry needed a King of the Romans who would neither thwart nor usurp his Sicilian plans, and Richard, for all his bluster in Parliament, would drop all opposition once he realised that he too was going to be a king. Henry also had to check Capetian interest in this affair. He may have become friends with Louis, but their rivalry had not abated. Louis was even balking at the suggestion of allowing Henry passage to Sicily despite a renewal of the truce negotiated the previous summer.[24]

Finally there was a mystical element that only Henry could appreciate. The enthronement of his brother and son would make three English kings at the same time, not quite the three kings of the Bible, but an encouraging reference just the same to his pious nature and infatuation with the number three. He later permitted the Archbishop of Cologne, one of the electors with the right to crown the King of the Romans, to run collections in England for the construction of a cathedral in Cologne to replace the one destroyed by fire in 1248. In doing so, he helped restore the old cathedral's shrine of the three kings, said to hold the bones of the Magi themselves.[25]

The only other serious outside contender was the one who could just then make the most trouble. Alfonso of Castile had a better dynastic claim to the throne, being the grandson of Philip of Swabia, who had preceded Otto IV as King of the Romans. Relations with England had soured in the year after their accord, and the grievances were mostly on Alfonso's part. No second marriage, aid against Aragon or progress on an African crusade had been forthcoming. In January 1256 Henry sent Aigueblanche and Mansel to Castile to discuss these and other issues.

The sticking point was the marriage between Henry's daughter and Alfonso's brother. Margaret's plight in Scotland probably left Henry and Eleanor clinging more than usual to 13-year-old Beatrice, and they managed to stall the betrothal with a technical loophole. It was the understanding of the English court that in Castile a king like Alfonso could disinherit anyone on a whim, including his brother. Richard of Cornwall for one thought it would be degrading to marry Beatrice to a prince who could easily become a pauper the next day. Apparently they got that information from Alfonso's stepmother, Joan of Ponthieu.[26]

A further embassy in the summer conveyed the news that Henry would at least try to get Alexander to switch his crusading vow to Africa. But the new envoys lacked the distinction of the previous ones, probably because Henry was growing tired of the grumbling and his mind was on a more important diplomatic mission. On 12 June 1256, he accredited Richard de Clare and Robert Walerand to Germany to lobby for the election of Richard of Cornwall, Clare's stepfather. Alfonso was far from placated by the crusade offer and threatened to invade Gascony, but the marriage between Edward and Eleanor ultimately held him back. In any case, he had his own proctors at work in Europe to secure the crown for himself, and was already one step ahead when, also that June, he got the commune of Pisa to back him. How much each side knew of the other's intentions and willingness to go the distance remains obscure, but the race was definitely on.[27]

Henry's biggest row over Gascony at this time was with Edward. The young man had acquitted himself well as the lord of the region, and it was only at his parents' insistence that he moved on. They suggested he go to Ireland, to introduce himself to all his new domains, but the unspoken reason was to keep him separated from his wife for a while. They wanted to avoid her getting pregnant again while still so young, but he ignored them and followed her to England.[28]

His presence at the Christmas court in Winchester became intrusive when he went to his father with complaints from Gascon merchants about the seizure of their goods by customs officials. He wanted redress for them, and Henry gave it, but the king did not like the tone of Edward's 'I will not tolerate such proceedings on any account', as if he himself were the final court of justice. Henry wondered aloud whether his son was now presuming to imitate the struggle between Henry II and his rebellious sons. The 16-year-old Edward was far from it at this stage, but his year in Gascony had given him a taste for power. He aimed to show it off in England by riding around with a huge retinue of horsemen.[29]

These riders may have been a contingent-in-waiting for Sicily. In April 1256 Edward confirmed his commitment to back his brother's bid, and that same month Henry ordered what was referred to as the distraint of knighthood, whereby able-bodied men were compelled to become knights. Unlike the age factor of modern conscription, the threshold here was personal wealth, usually determined by possession of a knight's fee or land of similar value, roughly £20.[30] The distraint had been first implemented in 1224 in anticipation of sending a force to defend Gascony. Those failing to comply might find their possessions distrained by the sheriff until they went through the whole process of becoming a knight. Many demurred on account of the cost and inconvenience. The ceremony was expensive enough, but then came horses, armour, weapons, squires and maintaining all of them in condition. This consideration weighed against the honour, fraternity and dignity that went with knightly status. It was better to make money and buy those distinctions in some other form.

Sensing the mood, Henry had offered exemptions when the distraint was enforced in 1252 for Gascony and the preparation for his crusade. In 1256, exemptions were offered again, but the threshold was lowered to £15 in order to widen the pool of conscripts. Costing a little over £3, the exemptions weren't cheap and ran for just three years.[31] To make it look like a serious attempt at sustaining chivalry, and not some rank money-making scheme, Henry relaxed his opposition to tournaments and allowed one to proceed at Blyth near Nottingham in June. The novices included Edward, who came to relish the lists and tests of martial strength. He was unusually tall for that age (and sensitive – he didn't like his later nickname Longshanks) and eventually reached six feet two inches, which gave him a natural advantage in close-quarter combat. Just the same, the other participants were expected to keep it chivalrous for him. He emerged unscathed, but several nobles were trampled and crushed on the field. William Longespee III was among those who didn't survive.[32]

As his father wished, Edward began to visit his other dominions and reached Wales in July. He was the lord of the area known as the Four Cantrefs in the north of the country, adjacent to Cheshire, which was also under his control. He found a swell of resentment over the English practices of administration foisted on the

Welsh inhabitants. Following the Treaty of Woodstock in 1247, Henry insisted that their customs and liberties be observed and had restrained the justice of Chester, Alan la Zouche, in respect of them. The responsibility now passed to Edward's steward, Geoffrey Langley, who was in high favour with the queen. The high opinion Geoffrey had of himself can be seen in his boast that he had the Welsh in the palm of his hand. Contrary to his actions in Gascony, Edward took no notice of the local grievances, and in failing to do so, created an opening for Llywelyn in neighbouring Gwynedd. He had already defeated and imprisoned his brothers Owain and Dafydd on the way towards consolidating his position in the northwest part of the country. The peace that had held for the past nine years had begun to unravel.[33]

Edward caused his father further consternation when, on 9 September, he entered a pact with Gaillard de Soler in contravention of the policy of not playing favourites between the two political factions of Bordeaux. It was meant to be a secret, but Gaillard went back to Gascony and boasted about it. Henry was not amused and had him locked up.[34] The lecture he gave Edward this time is unrecorded, but it had to be worrying to think that his son was capable of such underhanded action. Little did he realise that Edward was only getting started.

Not quite a fortnight before that, Margaret and Alexander were entertained at a stately feast in Westminster thrown by John Mansel. The merriment belied the political grappling that continued unabated up north a year after English intervention. Henry tried to help by investing Alexander with the honour of Huntingdon and by dispatching Mansel to call out the troops if necessary. Some time during their visit, the King and Queen of Scotland were beseeched by the wife of the Sheriff of Northampton, who was facing the gallows for nearly torturing a herdsman to death in an effort to acquire the cattle he was tending. A commission composed of Clare, Montfort, Bath and Walerand confirmed that the sheriff, one William de Lisle, had committed this and other crimes. Henry was inclined to condemn him, but the entreaties of his daughter and son-in-law moved him to spare Lisle's life.[35]

The sheriffs were on Henry's mind when he went to the exchequer on 9 October 1256 to make a speech much as he had nearly six years earlier to the day. At that time he admonished his officers of the law to look after the vulnerable and ensure justice for all. This occasion, however, saw no similar exhortation of the sacred duties and integrity of the office, no action to prevent the misconduct of the likes of Lisle. His interest was now accountability, not responsibility. The sheriffs were consistently late settling their accounts, and he wanted something done about it. His own order was that for the first day they were late, they were to be fined £3, the second £7, then £10 and finally on the fourth day they were to be held at his pleasure.[36]

His retreat from high ideals reflects the toll the Sicilian business was taking on him and the country at large. Michaelmas, or the feast of St Michael, was the deadline to fulfil the papal terms, but that date of 29 September 1256 had passed with neither the army nor the full amount of money in sight, though not for want of trying. Rostand and his agents had come down hard on the clergy, collecting whatever sums they could from the various abbeys, monasteries and priories. There was £1,700 from Westminster, £500 from Durham, £50 from Dunstable. In many cases, the money had already been drawn from merchants in Italy. The religious houses were simply handed promissory notes and told to cover them.[37] Henry's support was enlisted for the more obstinate houses, and in an exchange reported by Paris, a Cistercian abbot told him that he should follow Louis's example and ask for prayers, not money. 'I require both,' the king replied. 'Your money and your prayers.' In trying to evade payment, the abbot and his brethren were described as blind men feeling their way along the wall, each for himself 'in the English way'.[38]

Henry knew back in the spring that he wasn't going to make the deadline and so, as was his wont, had begun exploring a way out through marriage. Manfred himself had been married in 1247 to yet another Beatrice of Savoy, this one the daughter of Amadeus, as part of the diplomacy between the count and emperor. They had one daughter, Constance, now 7 years old, and in June 1256 Rostand was empowered to negotiate a marriage between her and Edmund. It was part of the proposals he took back to discuss with Alexander.[39] For Henry, it was the only viable alternative. Perhaps he knew all along when he accepted the pope's terms that he had no chance of fulfilling them. It was a gamble, the hope that the papacy would get its act together and Sicily would just fall into his lap. When that happened, the money he owed would come from that island, not this one.

The pope was barely able to secure his own position in Rome, much less stop Manfred, but that didn't deter him. There would be no marriage alliance with the devil. Together they would defeat him. In the meantime, the bill was due. Since only a third of it could be generated through the crusade tax, Henry was faced with the unpleasant prospect of having to ask Parliament for help again. Without a victory to show for what he had spent so far, the barons, knights and freeholders were not likely to throw good money after bad.

It would do Henry no good to mention how the Sicilian business had come at the worst possible time. He would assume the debt himself if he could, but his income was at an all-time low, less than £20,000. His endowment for Edward cost him £6,000 in annual revenue, and he had received no major aid since his son's knighting.[40] He couldn't go to his demesne or the boroughs because they had been recently tallaged, and the Jews hadn't recovered from the extreme taxation of the 1240s. Henry was still expected to dole out patronage, only there was a dearth in the death of great landowners and the rich wards and heiresses they left behind. Wardships alone had brought in only £1,266 in the last four years, ten times less than a decade ago for the same period.[41] His predecessors could have taken harsh, one-off measures in the same situation, but Magna Carta put an end to that.

Henry had always been careful to stay within the constraints of the charter. His father's outrageous fees, like charging Nicholas de Stuteville £6,666 to succeed to his brother's lands, led to a cap of £100 in the charter, which is what Stuteville's daughter Joan paid when her turn came to succeed. The charter put no limit, however, on what the king could charge a wife to have custody of her husband's lands, her remarriage and the marriages of her children. When Joan found herself widowed in 1241, she had to pay £6,666, in instalments of £700 a year, to maintain control. She eventually married the man of her choice, Hugh Bigod, Roger's brother.[42]

With lawful windfalls like these now in short supply, the exchequer had to look elsewhere for extra revenue. An inquest into the crown's rights was undertaken in June 1255 to identify and recover missing sources of income, always an alarming development for those skimming off receipts to Westminster. The sheriffs were given ever higher targets to meet for the county farms. Their total in 1256 stood at £4,690, up from £3,850 fourteen years earlier. They also had to collect exemptions from the distraint of knighthood and fines imposed by the judicial eyres, both of which were looking suspiciously more like concerted fund-raising drives. Some £10,000 in fines had already been levied since the decade began.[43] Altogether these petty exactions amounted to harassment more than oppression, and were certainly nothing compared to what the Church was going through, but they engendered plenty of acrimony in the shires just the same.

Had everything gone according to the original plan, Henry would have been in the Holy Land at this point. The cost would have been far more crippling and the gains to Christendom practically nil, and not just because he was unwarlike to begin with. He could have ended up in captivity, chained and reeking of filth, but that fate had only enhanced the King of France's prestige. Never mind the incomparable calamity of his crusade, Louis had suffered for Christ and that was what counted. Henry couldn't lose even if he did lose. He would reap the glory of being a crusader king, just like his uncle Richard the Lionheart. As it was, he was stuck with an alternative enterprise that nobody liked or respected and which now hung around his neck like a millstone.

It's ironic that these troubles fell on the fortieth anniversary of his first coronation, when a few magnates stepped forward to protect his succession and very life. Now he felt completely isolated from the men who had replaced them. Whatever they thought of him getting into this mess in the first place, he needed their help, but they only stood by with their mealy-mouthed argument that they had not been consulted. That was the thanks Henry got for coddling them during the years of his personal rule. Following Marshal's insurgency, already nearly a quarter of a century past, Henry had cherished peace throughout the realm more than anything else. He deliberately backed away from leaning on his magnates the way his father had just to keep them happy, despite knowing they needed a firm hand at times. When he ordered another proclamation of Magna Carta the previous year, he had wondered aloud about their hypocrisy: 'Why don't these bishops and nobles of my kingdom observe towards their subjects this charter about which they make such outcry and complaint?'[44] Now, in 1256, he went further in an expression that evokes bitterness and wit in his relations with them. For his lavatory at Westminster Palace, he ordered a painting showing a king being rescued by his faithful hounds 'from the sedition plotted against him by his own men'.[45]

★ ★ ★

In early November, Llywelyn made his move and struck across the River Conway, overrunning all of the Four Cantrefs save for two castles. Edward planned to respond with a war of extermination and got a loan for it from Richard of Cornwall who, like Henry, preferred mediation. His men were hampered by poor weather from the outset, though it didn't stop Llywelyn from continuing his drive southward. Edward did not go there himself to direct operations, which was unlikely to have made a difference, but it was another indication of the lack of discipline that beset his household. Even while he was asking his uncle for the loan, his men were in a nearby priory, pushing the servants around, helping themselves to whatever they wanted and in general ransacking the place. In an even more infamous outrage reported by Paris, Edward ordered his men to maim a passing traveller just for the fun of it. It may have been only a rumour that reached the ears of the chronicler, for no charges were ever filed, but the heir to the throne was clearly worrying more people than just his parents about the kind of man he was turning into.[46]

The Christmas court at Westminster finally brought some good news with the arrival of envoys from Germany. Before a Parliament convened on 26 December 1256, they declared that the negotiations conducted throughout the year had been successful and Richard of Cornwall was the unanimous choice for the next King of the Romans. In fact, only the three votes of the northern electors were assured. The three southern electors were leaning towards Alfonso, and the wild card, King Ottokar II of Bohemia, wanted the crown for himself. Richard was aware of this, and that he would have to shell out £19,000 just for those three votes. But it was reckoned that the English magnates would be less likely to voice their disapproval of yet another foreign adventure if convinced it was a done deal and not hanging in the air like that other one.

Their biggest concern turned out to be Richard's well-being. Everyone knew what happened to the last two men who wore that seemingly accursed crown. In the ensuing discourse stage-managed by Henry, the envoys provided only reassurances. The pope had nothing to do with the election, a large sum of money was waiting for Richard in Germany and, speaking of well-being, everyone also knew of the sorry fate of William the Conqueror's son Robert after he refused the crown of Jerusalem, imprisoned by his brother the king until his dying days. With Richard's own brother the king encouraging him on, he stepped forward, humbly accepted the offer, and declared that he would rather burn in hell than let greed and ambition dictate his motives. The lie having thus come full circle, John d'Avesnes was duly empowered to make the final arrangements.[47]

On 13 January 1257, the new King of the Romans was proclaimed outside the walls of Frankfurt. The northern electors would have preferred to do it inside the city, but it was controlled by Alfonso's supporters. By the end of the month, Richard got a majority when Ottokar cast his vote for him. For his coronation in Aachen, where Charlemagne had reigned as emperor nearly five centuries earlier, he began putting together the entourage to accompany him, Sanchia, and their 7-year-old son Edmund. His 21-year-old son Henry would also be going and henceforth known as Henry of Almain (Allemagne being Germany) to trumpet a legitimate foreign title for a Plantagenet prince.[48]

This was all well and good, but as far as the pope was concerned, 11-year-old Edmund would also be going abroad for his own coronation if only his father showed more industry in the Sicilian business, or at least followed his own feverish example. In letter after letter, Alexander becomes a man possessed. He taxes the prelates, demands the fruits of vacant benefices, orders the goods of people dying intestate seized for the crusade. He gives advice to Henry on settling disputes over the priority of payments and indulges him with permission to eat meat on the feast of St Edward, even though it will fall on a Saturday. He extends the deadline once, then twice, and excommunicates all ecclesiastics who have not paid the tenth for the crusade.[49] This last was a clear message to Henry that he could be next.

There was nothing left to do but try again to finagle a tax out of Parliament. Buoyed by the successful presentation of Richard's German business, Henry decided to make this gathering also something of a show. Richard himself would set the mood by making a farewell speech.[50] Then there would be the other guest of honour, Giovanni Colonna, a Dominican friar since elevated to become the Archbishop of Messina. He had accompanied Rostand back to England for the purpose of bearing down on the uncooperative clergy, but would ultimately implore the assembly to back their king. His august presence in magnificent robes was sure to be eye-catching. Young Edmund would likewise make an appearance, dressed in Apulian attire to arouse sentimental support for his quest. Anyone still ready to deny the child such a God-given gift would only reveal himself to be heartless. A proper stage was needed to add a bedazzling effect, and this Henry had in the new Chapter House of Westminster Abbey. His beautiful house of houses had bowled over everyone who walked into it so far, even the grouch of grouches, Matthew Paris.[51]

But even if the setting and programme were just right, the parliaments of recent memory excluded the mere mention of a tax without offering political concessions. Any chance of getting one was going to require reform of some sort. Since hammering out a deal would be tedious and drawn out, not to mention unbecoming before the distinguished company, Henry opted for a reform of his council. He added two critics, Fulk Basset and Walter Cantilupe, and in February 1257 had all members take a new oath. They swore to receive no gifts from anyone involved in cases of the king's court. They were forbidden from receiving a gift from the king, and if he insisted on giving it anyway, they were to get the consent of the entire council in order to keep it. Anyone caught doing otherwise was to be dismissed, ordered to return the gift and pay a fine of £100. They were to take action against the misconduct of sheriffs and remove those and their bailiffs found abusing their office. Lastly, 'no letters, liberties, privileges nor anything else, by which the king or any other person may suffer prejudice or injury, shall be sealed without the consent or knowledge of the king and of the majority of the council present'.[52]

It's possible the oath would have been necessary regardless of the upcoming Parliament. The provisions specifically dealt with the breakdown of trust that had afflicted the court for the past decade. It started with the arrival of the Lusignans in 1247, followed by the onset of Montfort's governorship of Gascony and the creation of Edward's appanage. All three coincided with the exhaustion of the last great store of patronage, the lands of the Normans that were seized following the partition of 1204. The scramble for what was left put a severe strain on Henry's resources, inflaming tempers and jealousies between the various political factions. Calling it a problem of foreign favourites is again misleading, because in warily eyeing each other, the Lusignans and Savoyards had their own English allies, who would have been jostling for favours had there not been a single foreigner among them.

The worry now was the king having to fall back on his own lands for grants to keep everyone satisfied. This would unquestionably diminish the assets of the crown and endanger its one stable source of income. The councillors were therefore bound not to allow any alienations from the royal demesne.[53] If Henry, against his better judgement, tried to give one of his manors or castles to them or anyone, the grant was to be automatically revoked. It was not just a check on the king, but also on the men sitting around the table, who would take every opportunity to besiege him for handouts when the others weren't looking.

Typically, when Henry had something big in front of him, he made offers at shrines or religious houses in the hope of a favourable outcome. With much riding on this Parliament, he went to St Albans on 3 March with many splendid gifts, including a silver cup for use as an urn for some dust from a lately discovered tomb thought to be of St Alban himself, a fourth-century Christian martyr. The king spent a week at the abbey, which normally made his most inveterate critic grumble that he was only after free hospitality for his court. Henry, however, had Matthew Paris stay close to him throughout his stay, at the dinner table and in his chamber, and during that time performed the incredible feat of naming 250 baronies of the realm and all the sainted kings of England. If nothing else, the king showed he had an excellent memory.[54]

The religious aspect of the visit was of no avail in the end. As described in the Introduction, the full baronage that met in Parliament on 16 March 1257 again insisted that Sicily wasn't their problem and refused to offer any support. They no doubt appreciated the Chapter House and may have fawned over the archbishop and little Edmund in his costume. The theatricality of Henry's reign never ceased to impress them. But they wanted nothing to do with any chimerical schemes on the Continent. They, of course, had the luxury of refusing him. Magna Carta was their guarantee against reprisals, and there was nothing the king could do about it. The clergy, on the other hand, had no such protection from the holy father. The show over, Rostand and Colonna spelt out the new terms of taxation they were expected to provide. Left on their own by the barons, the bishops and abbots agreed to a settlement of some £52,000 to wipe the slate clean.[55]

The failure to get Parliament on his side forced Henry to wipe the slate clean as well. Not with Sicily, but with France. He and Louis would stop the endless renewals of the truce and seek a permanent peace. Louis had first mooted the idea to his brothers while he was in the Holy Land, doubtless in response to the new alliance forming between England and Castile. There were calls at that time for Henry and Alfonso to march through France together and take what was rightfully theirs.[56] Henry chose instead to meet Louis in person and found they got along well. That didn't stop him from wanting his lands back or ease French suspicions about Anglo-Castilian relations. Louis contracted to have his 13-year-old namesake heir marry Alfonso's eldest daughter just to make sure. Richard's projected enthronement in Germany caused him further angst about being flanked by Plantagenet power and moved him both to support Alfonso's bid for Germany and to fortify Normandy.[57]

But Louis was burdened by more than just national security upon his return to France in the summer of 1254. His defeat and imprisonment, the slaughter of so many of his men and squandering of the money taken from the poor for his crusade, had left him reeling. He blamed himself, not for the military bungling, but for not eradicating the sin and evil apparently flourishing in his realm. This was clear from the inquiry launched before his departure and manifested in the Shepherds' Crusade, which was as much a protest against the wretched conditions of the peasantry in France as it was any rescue attempt of the king. An example was the complaint of an orphan girl who leased her one field for the erection of the king's gallows. The rent had not only failed to provide her with the 'necessities of a miserable life', but the spectators trampled her grain, and the bailiffs left the bodies to rot on the end of the ropes. The gallows were 'against God and all reason' and she wanted them out.

In December 1254, as Louis and Margaret were entertaining Henry and Eleanor, his administration enacted the Grand Ordinance. It primarily regulated the conduct of his local officials, enjoining them not to accept gifts, excepting some fruit and wine, or to offer bribes. They were not to impose exactions to raise money, unlawfully detain people or terrorise them into making settlements. They were not to buy land in their assigned districts or marry off their relatives there, and had to remain behind for fifty days after their term of office ended to deal with any accusations against them. Since the Ordinance was all about sin, the private lives of his subjects were also scrutinised under the new legislation. Louis's officials were to desist from blasphemy, gambling and public carousing, and were ordered to expel all prostitutes from the fields, towns and other places where their trade was active.[58]

For all its noble character, the Ordinance was also about getting another chance. Louis's pride had been as wounded by the crusade as his conscience, and he was determined to go back and prove he could do it right. He needed to prove that he was a most Christian king before then and clean up both his realm and himself. He adopted a more ascetic way of life, eschewing royal garments and wearing a hair shirt until even his confessor found it unseemly for a man in his position. He watered his wine, didn't salt his soup and refused to eat meat on Wednesdays or Fridays. He prayed constantly, boring his chamberlains stiff, and might snap out of it at any moment while still on his knees and ask, 'Where am I?'[59]

All this soul searching worked in Henry's favour. Louis had been assured by his peers that the confiscation of Plantagenet lands in France had been just, and maybe it was if confined to what John had lost. But there was no way to justify his father using a crusade army to swipe the lordship of Poitou from the underage Henry. Louis VIII's early, untimely death, and Henry's persistence all these years were an indication that this matter was still awaiting final judgement. Louis couldn't give Henry all that he wanted, almost none of what he wanted in fact, but he could make amends elsewhere and together they could bring about the first sustained peace between their dynasties ever.

Henry would have absolutely no problem selling the idea to anyone. Alfonso, Alexander, the Savoyards all wanted it, and the English nobility could breathe a sigh of relief that their king had finally given up his hopeless endeavour to recover his Angevin inheritance. It would certainly be no loss to his honour. Even if his two forays to get them back had ended rather ingloriously, he did try, and it might be said that in doing so he made England safer by always staying on the offensive. The terms for surrendering his claims, however, were everything. Peace wasn't going to come overnight with all the haggling sure to ensue. But he was already exploring this option even at the time of restructuring his council, and had sent Montfort and Walerand to Louis for preliminary talks. It also allowed him to avoid giving Pope Alexander the bad news about no aid coming from Parliament.[60]

In the meantime, relations with France remained tense in the wake of Richard's departure for Germany. His flotilla of fifty ships left on 29 April 1257 and reached the mouth of the Rhine a few days later. He and Sanchia were crowned on 17 May, followed by a coronation feast of unrivalled excellence in his own estimate. Now styling himself 'the forever august Richard, King of the Romans', he boasted in a letter home that there were 3,000 knights, thirty dukes and counts, and ten bishops in attendance. What he didn't share was his apprehension over recent developments that greeted his arrival. The three other electors had got around to casting their votes for Alonso, and while doing so found themselves joined by Ottokar. The Czech king, still ambitious for the thrown himself, had no qualms about voting twice. That made two elected kings of the Romans. It would ultimately come down to the pope to decide, which didn't bode well for Richard. The whole point of carving up Frederick's empire had been to keep Germany and Sicily out of the hands of one family.[61] As far as Alexander was concerned, the only Plantagenet with the right to any throne in the area was Edmund. Richard was going to have to wait to see how that turned out before he got a proper hearing.

At home, Henry could never completely count on his brother for political support, but he had always been good for stopgap funding. With those resources now tied up in Germany, he had to undertake some financial discipline in order to stay afloat. On 10 April he ordered the treasurer not to pay out any receivables whatsoever until there was at least £13,333 on accounts for the royal household, plus an extra thousand for building work on Westminster Abbey. Should the king come to the exchequer in person and demand money, they were to refuse him.[62] In a way, he was building on his February 'reforms' by putting checks on his spendthrift approach to patronage, but it could only lead to explosive rows between claimants with money fees. Two of the more insistent in this group were brothers-in-law Simon de Montfort and William de Valence.

Montfort had a long-standing grudge against Valence ever since the younger man arrived in England. Through his wife Joan, William acquired lands from the Marshal estate that should have gone to his half-sister Eleanor de Montfort as the first Marshal widow. Eleanor was still arguing that she had been short-changed by Richard Marshal in their 1232 settlement, and her proof was the fourth Marshal widow, Walter's wife Margaret, who was previously the widow of John de Lacy, the Earl of Lincoln. As the niece of Ranulf of Chester, Margaret was the Countess of Lincoln in her own right, and marriage to Walter made her even richer. The dower settled on her just for the Marshal lands in Ireland was £572, far more than the £400 Eleanor got for Ireland and Wales together. Eleanor, moreover, had trouble getting the Marshal heirs to pay her even that. Margaret alone fell seven years behind in her payments, and it was only in the summer of 1256 that she caught up with her £1,066 in arrears. And she was a friend of the family.[63]

Henry was not only surety for his sister's fee, but owed various debts to Montfort himself. Simon preferred that he convert this money into land, thereby sparing them both the bother of dealing with it, and he resented the way Henry strived to make such a conversion for Valence but not for him and his sister. In those lean times, it would have been better for everyone to back off. But then an argument broke out over alleged trespasses made by Valance's men on Montfort's property. It grew heated to the point where William called Simon a traitor, who, in front of the king and nobles, rushed upon him. Allegedly he would have killed him had Henry not thrown himself between them.[64]

Much of William's ire came from the situation in Wales. Llywelyn's success put pressure on his lands and those of the other English barons in the region. Henry had hoped that his son would get everything under control, but Edward merely came to him to complain. The king, complaining himself that he was too busy, tried to goad him into action. 'The land is yours by my gift. Exert your powers for the first time, and arouse fame in your youth, so that your enemies may fear you for the future.'[65] Properly rebuked, Edward put together a force designed to break apart Llywelyn's coalition, but incredibly he stayed behind at Westminster while it marched forth in early June. They were forced to retreat, cornered and slaughtered. Most of the 3,000 men who fell at Cymerau were Welsh, but the victory was all theirs. Edward's failure left Henry no choice but to call out the feudal host to meet at Chester in August.[66]

There could never have been a good time for such news, but Henry was particularly distracted by the different course he resolved to take over Sicily. On 26 June an embassy was appointed to seek an amelioration of the terms. The envoys were to cite the fact that Manfred's gains had made Henry's task that much harder. They were even to inquire whether it might not be better to make peace through some sort of division of Sicily. Unless something were done, Edmund would have to withdraw his candidature. Artaud de St Romain, the keeper of the wardrobe, set out to deliver the instructions for this mission to Montfort and Peter of Savoy, who were in Paris to advise Walter Cantilupe, Hugh Bigod and Adam Marsh on the opening round of peace negotiations with Louis. For unknown reasons, Simon and Peter never set out for Rome. It's possible the presence of these two heavyweight diplomats wasn't required anyway. Rostand, who had come to fully sympathise with the English position, would be presenting the case to Pope Alexander himself and needed only a royal clerk and chaplain to accompany him.[67]

To fund his campaign in Gascony, Henry had had to spend the gold treasure he had accumulated for his crusade in the East. He started another treasure after returning, but the cash crunch constrained his purchases to the point where his officials asked that regular fines to the crown be made in gold. By the summer of

1257, he had only 600 marks of gold (£4,000) on hand, just a fifth of his earlier store. Since he would likely have to use some of it for Wales, he ordered the gold ingots, leaf and dust minted into coins to avoid reaping any losses if forced to dump them. Doubtless he wanted the gold coins for their own sake, the true expression of his majesty, and spent long hours on the design showing a king holding orb and sceptre, tellingly a sign of peace and not war. It was completely characteristic of Henry to issue a tangible, glittering reminder of the glory of kingship at one of the lowest points of his reign.[68]

It was precisely his sort of kingship that made the English clergy despair, and in August, as the army was mustering at Chester, they met at an assembly called a 'convocation' for the first time, to air their grievances. They deplored how their courts were being subjected to both the common law of the land and orders and writs from the chancery. The king was again manipulating their elections, promoting unworthy candidates and exploiting their assets. The latest example was at Ely, where at the death of their bishop, William Kilkenny, Henry's former chancellor, the monks chose their sub-prior Hugh Balsham to succeed him over the wishes of both Henry, who wanted his current chancellor Henry Wengham for the post, and Boniface, who favoured Adam Marsh. And last but not least, there was the papal taxation that had the full connivance of the king. For Henry, to be assailed by Parliament and now by convocation in less than six months was a bit much, and he tried to prevent the gathering, insisting he needed the clergy in Wales as well. But Boniface, the organiser, simply ignored him. If there was ever a lesson for the king against promoting his own candidates to become senior prelates, Boniface was definitely it.[69]

At Chester, meanwhile, the feudal host waited nineteen days as Henry attempted to negotiate a settlement with Llywelyn or else split apart his coalition. When that got nowhere, the army slowly set out in a two-pronged assault, with forces under Richard de Clare moving in the south. Paris says the king brought his royal standard with him 'like a dragon which knows not how to spare any one', but his heart was not in it, nor was Edward's if the report of his willingness to give up Wales altogether is accurate. When ships bearing provisions failed to arrive, the two met with the council and agreed to call the whole thing off. It was only early September, but any operation now could easily drag out until winter was upon them. In a letter to Clare, who had had some success, Henry said the decision was 'repugnant' to him, but he didn't need convincing. He certainly didn't want to celebrate his upcoming fiftieth birthday campaigning around Snowdonia, and if he left now, he would be back at Westminster in time for the feast of St Edward. Llywelyn took advantage of the English retreat to strengthen his position among the other Welsh lords and even opened negotiations for an alliance with Scotland. There the Comyns had kidnapped Alexander III in late October to reassert their authority, creating yet another worry for Henry.[70]

And the bad news kept pouring in. The rains that had plagued the realm since the start of the year ruined the harvest, guaranteeing future shortages. The threat of famine loomed, ironically, because all the peace and prosperity had led to a population explosion. There were now more mouths to feed than the land could handle even under normal conditions. The resulting glut of unskilled labourers stagnated wages at around a penny and a half per day. A surge in the price of bread would be catastrophic for them and their families.

The economic situation wasn't helped by the vast sums of money flowing out of the country to fund two crown-buying enterprises. The new gold coin, moreover, was so highly denominated that it kept a lot of working capital out of circulation. Valued at twenty silver pennies each, it was of no practical use to most people. On 1 November, Henry summoned the mayor and aldermen of London to the exchequer to ask their opinion about its viability as a new specie for the kingdom. They declared that it would cause irreparable damage and drive down the price of gold, which was happening as they spoke. As usual, naysayers all around. Henry declined to withdraw the new coin, but decreed that no one should be forced to take it, and anyone who wanted to could exchange it for nineteen and a half silver pennies.[71]

The news from abroad was not good, either. Alfonso was furious about Richard's election and demanded an explanation. In a letter dated 14 December, Henry told him that he had known nothing at all of his (Alfonso's) plans for the German throne, but as far as he could tell, Richard had been elected and crowned properly. As they were bound by treaty, he would look into the matter.[72] And the word from Rome was also worrying. Pope Alexander offered no change in his terms for the Sicilian affair, only an extension until next summer. The clearer picture of the situation provided by Rostand made no difference to him at all. In fact, it only infuriated him, and Rostand suddenly found himself accused of taking bribes. He wasn't dismissed, but was forced to return to England in a reduced capacity. The pope sent a new envoy in his place, armed with papal bulls to threaten the king and clergy to make good the rest of the money or face excommunication.[73]

It couldn't have been a cheerful Christmas at Westminster for Henry and his family. On 3 May 1257, his 3-year-old daughter Katherine had died. She seems to have been afflicted with a disorder early on, for Paris describes her as mute and incapable, 'but possessing great beauty'. Losing the only toddler left in their family, born of their middle years together, was a severe blow for Henry and Eleanor. Grief-stricken, they both took ill, with the queen likely bed-ridden for much of that summer. Her condition compounded Henry's own distress until, beleaguered on so many fronts, he collapsed with a fever that may well have been part of a nervous breakdown.[74]

PART III

REFORM AND RESTORATION

13

THE MARCH ON WESTMINSTER 1258–1260

The long years of Henry III's personal rule came to an end abruptly and dramatically, almost as if it were staged for theatre, which, if nothing else, at least he could appreciate. Parliament was in session in the spring of 1258 when, on 27 April, he formally asked his barons for their help with the Sicilian business. It was his third try, and three was his number. The barons replied that they would give him an answer in three days' time. They not only kept their word, but arrived at Westminster Palace as the 'third hour' (after sunrise) approached. A good omen all around. And yet Henry would have heard a fearsome racket outside his bedchamber as the barons and knights removed and stacked their swords and daggers. They had come to him fully armed. Wearing chain mail, they walked in and 'saluted him as their lord king in devoted manner and fitting honour'. However alarmed he may have been by this demonstration, Henry's response was one of wry bemusement: 'What's this, my lords? Am I your prisoner?'

Their spokesman was Roger Bigod. He was not known as an orator, but his status as the honorary Marshal of England after his grandfather William made him the best choice to address the king. He assured Henry that no menacing intent was meant, but he got right to the point: 'Let the wretched and intolerable Poitevins and all aliens flee from your face and ours as from the face of a lion!' Bigod was just then part of a sworn confederation that included two aliens, so this scene, reported by the Tewkesbury annalist, should be treated with caution.[1] But their anger towards the Poitevins, especially the Lusignans, was real enough. The latest outrage had occurred on 1 April when Aymer's men got involved in another brawl over a church appointment, leading to the death of a priest sponsored by John Fitz-Geoffrey. At the opening of Parliament some time after 7 April, Fitz-Geoffrey demanded that

Henry do something about it, but the king asked him not to cause a scandal. Fitz-Geoffrey was a brother-in-law of Roger, who had his own dispute with Aymer over a wardship.[2] Together with Roger's brother Hugh Bigod, they entered an oath of alliance with four other nobles with their own grievances against the Lusignans.

One of these, of course, was Simon de Montfort. His long-standing quarrel with William de Valence had carried over into this Parliament. Valence decried the poor response to Welsh incursions as the work of traitors and singled out Montfort, even going so far as to sneer that he was the son of a traitor too. The fury rising in him, Simon shot back, 'No, William, I am neither traitor nor son of a traitor. Our fathers were nothing alike.' Not content to leave it at that, he rushed at him much as he had the year before, and Henry again had to interpose himself. In turning to Simon, the Bigods and Fitz-Geoffrey knew they were getting a man of action, one not afraid to back up his words. He also brought to their confederation Peter de Montfort, a Marcher baron who served Henry intermittently as an envoy.[3] These two unrelated Montforts had drawn closer during Simon's turbulent tenure in Gascony, and Peter was also a nephew of Walter Cantilupe, who had become Simon's spiritual mentor following Grosseteste's death.

The other alien in their confederation was Peter of Savoy. His problem with the Lusignans went back to Aymer's earlier confrontation with his brother Boniface in 1252, but the situation had now become critical. It all had to do with Edward, who had been firmly under Savoyard control throughout his upbringing. Initially, after becoming a lord in his own right, Edward too viewed the Lusignans as unscrupulous land-grabbers. Henry tried several times to make provisions for his half-brothers Guy and Geoffrey in Ireland, but Edward saw the grants as an encroachment of his rights there and obstructed them.[4] Everything changed, however, with the crisis in Wales.

Edward was now 18 years old, was married to a loving wife, and was one of the largest landowners in the kingdom. Although his income of £6,000 rivalled Richard of Cornwall's, he had proved to be an impossible spendthrift like his father. Henry tried to help by giving him nine wardships, the most of anyone after the queen.[5] Hard up for cash, Edward sold the lucrative Ferrers wardship to his mother and Peter of Savoy for £4,000, and Boniface lent him another £1,000 on security of one of his manors. Despite this, he resented all the Savoyard money and effort going towards ransoming Thomas in Turin.[6] Steeped in humiliation over Wales, he turned to his Lusignan uncles and found them not only willing to lend him money, but ready to excuse his brash and unruly behaviour. They were clearly on the same page. His drift into their orbit was perhaps the worst of all scenarios for the Savoyards. Their allies like the Montforts and Fitz-Geoffrey, who was serving on Edward's council, could only feel the same apprehension.

The last of the confederates was Richard de Clare, the Earl of Gloucester. At 36, he was also the youngest, richest and most unexpected addition. He had long been friendly with the Lusignans and rode with them on the tournament circuit. In 1252, he contracted to marry his heir Gilbert, then 9 years old, to Alice Lusignan, the daughter of the late Hugh (XI) and Yolanda of Dreux, in return for £3,333 provided by William and Aymer. The match infuriated Matthew Paris, who railed at Henry for mixing the 'noble blood of Englishmen with the scum of foreigners'.[7] In 1257, the queen tried to counter that match with one of her own, between Clare's daughter Isabel and her cousin, the Marquis of Montferrat (more scum). According to the Dunstable annalist, Clare actually left the southern front during his drive against the Welsh to discuss the matter with Eleanor at Tutbury. In his speech in Parliament denouncing traitors, Valence identified only Clare and Montfort by name. Henry tried to win his former ward back by standing surety for the money Clare owed for his daughter's marriage, but to no avail.[8]

If the confederates and their followers asked the king for the expulsion of the Lusignans during their march on Westminster, a royal letter three days later, on 2 May, made no mention of it. Instead, Henry announced that he would undertake to reform the realm based on the good and faithful advice of his barons, and they in turn agreed to do their best to secure a tax for Sicily, conditioned on better papal terms. In another act that day, he decreed that the reforms were to be drawn up by a committee of twenty-four, half named by Henry, half by the barons.[9] The prospect of the Lusignans going anywhere fast was dispelled by their appearance among Henry's twelve nominees. Other political notables on his side were Fulk Basset, Henry of Almain and John de Warenne (Earl of Surrey), both friends of the Lusignans, John de Plessis (Earl of Warwick) and Mansel. For their twelve, the barons elected six of the confederates and five who would play major roles in the upcoming period: Walter Cantilupe, Humphrey de Bohun (Earl of Hereford), Roger Mortimer, Hugh Despenser and Richard Grey.[10]

Conspicuously absent from either list were the Savoyards. After all Henry had done for Peter, it's unlikely he ever trusted him again after this stunt, and if it was the queen who put him up to it, the atmosphere in the royal family was going to be chilly that week. The other confederates had welcomed Peter's support against the Lusignans, but all things considered, he was worse than they were in terms of the patronage he had scored. In fact, the Savoyards as a whole were far better off than the Poitevins. Of the 170 who came to England, thirty-nine got land from the king and forty pensions worth at least £66. By comparison, only eight of the 100 Poitevins got land and twenty-eight similar pensions.

The difference was in the timing. The Savoyards had migrated to England a decade before the Poitevins, when Henry still had a lot to give. They were generally savvy enough not to flaunt their good fortune, but had to know their position was now equally tenuous if Bigod was serious about getting rid of all aliens. Peter of Savoy, for one, was much more a foreigner than somebody like Simon de Montfort or even William de Valence, who also had an English wife, children and retainers.

Peter rarely employed Englishmen, spent half of his time abroad (mostly on Henry's business) and invested no small part of his English revenues in his homeland, where his wife and daughter remained.[11]

As for Boniface, he and the rest of the clergy had withdrawn from Parliament soon after it convened, for fear of the king, says the Tewkesbury annalist, though no explanation is given. Since the main talking point was baronial aid for the Sicilian business, the clerics decided to hold another convocation at Merton Priory in June. It was a spectacular case of poor timing. Their meeting was completely overshadowed by the reform work then already in progress. By the time they produced their fifty articles bemoaning the 'evil state of the church of England', nobody cared.[12]

Meanwhile, the peace negotiations with France got an unexpected boost from the papacy. Since Henry still had no army to send to Sicily, Louis was persuaded to compensate him for his lost lands with money equivalent to the cost of 500 knights for two years. The rest of the force would come from the aid Henry was expected to get from his barons. On 8 May, Montfort, Bigod, Peter of Savoy, and Geoffrey and Guy Lusignan were dispatched by Henry to conclude a treaty with Louis including this concession. In mixing the confederates with his half-brothers, he may have hoped that everybody would get along for the sake of peace and reform. Whether or not the men were actually on speaking terms during the course of their mission, they were successful. In a draft treaty of 28 May 1258, Louis agreed to concede the money and certain lordships on the Continent which Henry might not have recovered otherwise. This was good news going into the prorogued Parliament summoned for 11 June.[13]

The venue was Oxford, chosen because it was on the way to Wales. Back in March, the knightly service had been ordered to muster in Chester on 17 June in response to Llywelyn's latest move, a pact of alliance with Scotland, where the Comyns were still holding the young king Alexander III in 'unwilling detention'.[14] The presence of these knights and lesser barons in Oxford, armed and ready for war, completely changed whatever programme the committee of twenty-four had planned to introduce after Parliament convened at the Dominican friary. They wanted their own say about reform, particularly in matters that affected them locally. The magnates may have intended to have these retainers there as a show of force against the Lusignans, but seeing their mood, a core group of them thought they might be equally effective in intimidating the king. Henry was still at nearby Woodstock when they began circulating a petition that included the grievances of these minor barons. By the time he arrived, the push for reform had gone beyond the politics of Westminster and was now aiming to take the entire realm into account. But in going after the king, the magnates had to wonder if they weren't leaving their own rights and privileges open to scrutiny.[15]

Unable to cope with reforming the entire realm in one Parliament, the committee of twenty-four settled for various provisions to regulate the machinery of government at the top. A new council of fifteen was to be elected and empowered with unprecedented authority for a term of twelve years. It would have oversight over the appointment of ministers and any major grant going out over the king's seal. The office of justiciar, vacant since 1234, was to be revived with full judicial control and answerable only to the council. The most far-reaching provision was the establishment of Parliament as an institution of state. No longer would it be the king's prerogative to decide when and where it met. It would convene three times annually, at fixed dates, and discharge the business of the realm through the council working together with a standing committee of twelve.[16]

None of these Provisions of Oxford, as they came to be known, was enshrined in a constitution. They were memoranda that guided the committee in their deliberations. Henry doesn't appear to have been vexed or perplexed at the direction they were taking. On 22 June, he ordered the committee to continue their work, promising they need fear no future retribution. Finding themselves free to act with impunity, the majority then pounced with three provocative decrees. In a move to restore the finances and security of the crown, they declared that all aliens must give up any royal lands and castles granted to them by the king. Second, all bailiffs and estate managers found to be oppressive were to be punished and their lords required to make reparations. Lastly, they were all to swear to observe the Provisions of Oxford, and anyone who failed to take the oath or moved against them was to be declared a public enemy.[17]

Henry must have now wondered what he had got himself into. The reforms were supposed to be about cooperation, not coercion. The new, sinister tone was clearly meant to goad the Lusignans into resistance, since they had the most to lose, and they fell for it. They refused to take the oath, with William de Valence protesting the loudest. He was especially angry because they were supposed to be subduing the Welsh, but instead the English barons were trying to subdue him and his brothers. Montfort finally had enough and warned him to either give up his castles or his head.[18] In this grim atmosphere, the Lusignans decided to run for it and took with them Edward and their brother-in-law Warenne, who had remained close to them after his wife Alice died in 1256. They made for Aymer's castle in Winchester, thinking that if they holed up there long enough, they could win some concessions. In fact, they only rallied the whole of Parliament to pursue them and lay siege. Not until Edward and Warenne reluctantly came out did they agree to take the oath, but by then the barons, as was probably their plan all along, were clamouring for their expulsion.

Through Henry's intervention, it was agreed that William and Aymer could remain because they were settled in England, but they were to be remanded in custody to face charges. They naturally preferred exile with their brothers and left with the other Poitevins on 14 July. They were allowed to take £3,000 with them to their stopover point in Boulogne, but such was the enmity they had aroused that Simon de Montfort's son Henry, now 19, crossed over with a group of young nobles and besieged them there. Louis eventually intervened and allowed the Poitevins to proceed to Poitou over the objections of Margaret, who was incensed that they had defamed her sister. Apparently the Lusignans had discovered the role of Queen Eleanor in their demise and were saying nasty things about her.[19]

One of the jeers would have been to question her intelligence. In throwing the gates open to reform, she put her herself in a straightjacket. Under Eleanor of Provence, queenship flourished in England for the first time, and she owed it all to Henry. Before, the consort was expected to dedicate herself only to bearing children and pleading mercy for somebody in deep disfavour. Henry allowed Eleanor to play an independent role at court and made it possible by empowering her household with patronage. He granted her a total of eleven wardships, which she either profited from personally or distributed among a loyal following. Now, nuggets like these, as well as marriage rights and even her 'queen's gold', which was a 10 per cent surcharge on fines made to the crown, were in the council's gift, not her husband's.[20]

The first test case came with the death of 28-year-old Edmund de Lacy at the end of May. Henry had intended to sell the wardship of Edmund's young son, the future Earl of Lincoln, to his widow Alice, a Savoyard émigré. But reforms intervened in the meantime, and it was no longer Henry's decision alone. It was up to king and council to decide whether Alice or her English mother-in-law, Margaret de Lacy, got custody of the heir.[21] One Savoyard did manage to get to the king in time. It was Thomas, finally free after nineteen months' captivity. He came to England just as the April Parliament opened, naturally looking for a handout, and Henry gave him £666 despite the financial crunch. It was an act of charity and gratitude in his mind, a complete waste of money in others'. Not that Thomas had been of much use before, but he was now in such a bad way that he had to travel in a litter. He died the following year, long after reforms were put in place to end Henry's open-hearted generosity to spongers like him.[22]

For now, all the vehemence towards foreign relatives was directed at the Lusignans. A letter drafted by the barons to the pope, explaining why they had expelled one of his bishops, indicated that the brothers were gone for good. They even begged him to depose Aymer from his bishopric and so spare everybody the scandal of what might otherwise ensue. They might have helped their case by saying what it was they found so offensive about him. As a group, the Lusignans were accused of being 'assassins and bandits' who delighted in the 'tears of the poor and nakedness of orphans', but Aymer at least seems to have been an able manager at Winchester and was on friendly terms with respected clerics like Grosseteste and Marsh. Probably what sank it for them was their influence over Edward. Having failed to turn Henry against reform, they found their nephew pliable and persuaded him to stand firm against the oath.[23] They even got him to grant Guy the Isle of

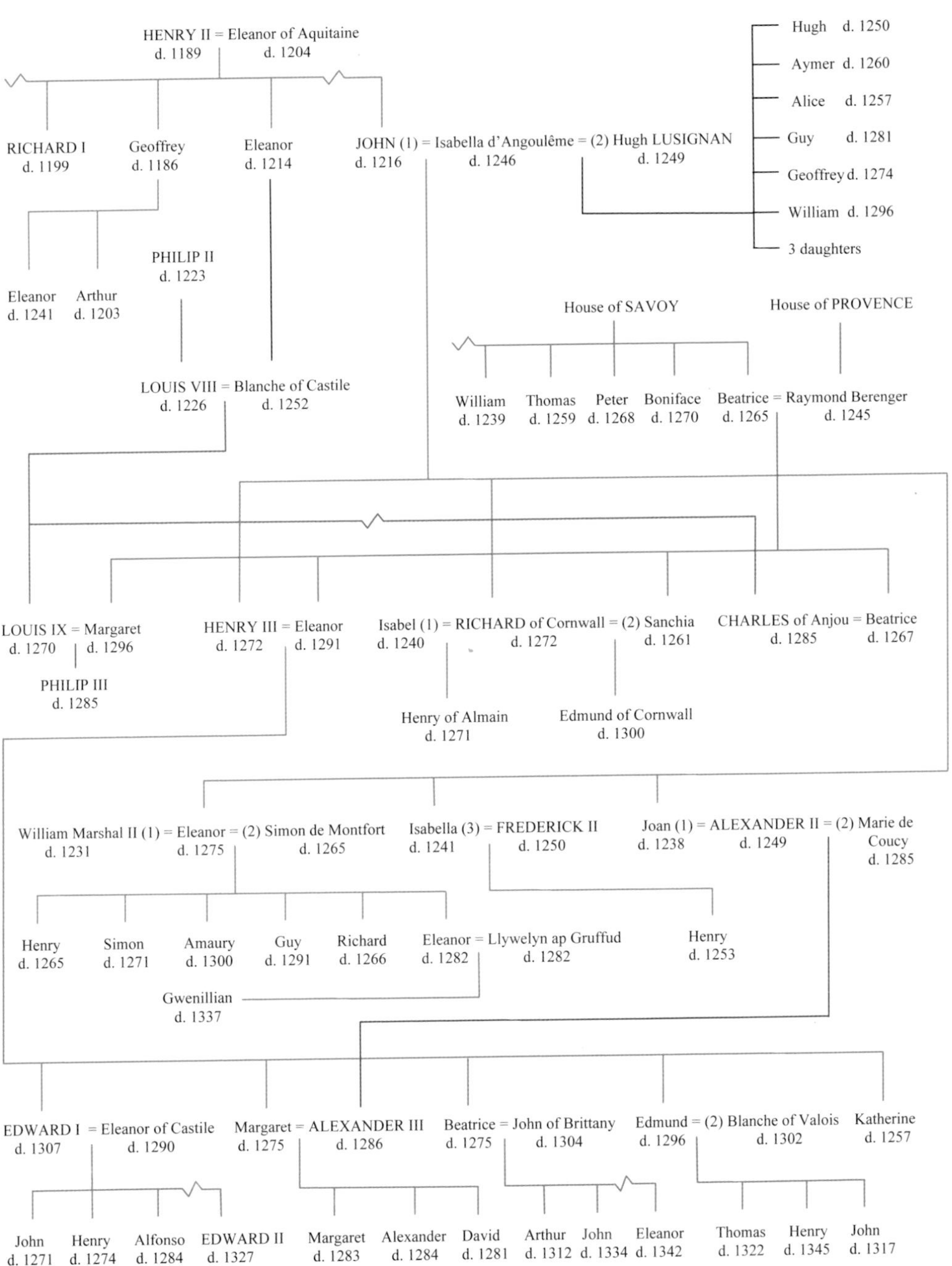
HENRY II = Eleanor of Aquitaine
d. 1189 d. 1204
RICHARD I d. 1199
Geoffrey d. 1186
Eleanor d. 1214
JOHN (1) = Isabella d'Angoulême = (2) Hugh LUSIGNAN
d. 1216 d. 1246 d. 1249
Hugh d. 1250
Aymer d. 1260
Alice d. 1257
Guy d. 1281
Geoffrey d. 1274
William d. 1296
3 daughters
Eleanor d. 1241
Arthur d. 1203
PHILIP II d. 1223
House of SAVOY
House of PROVENCE
LOUIS VIII = Blanche of Castile
d. 1226 d. 1252
William d. 1239
Thomas d. 1259
Peter d. 1268
Boniface d. 1270
Beatrice = Raymond Berenger
d. 1265 d. 1245
LOUIS IX = Margaret
d. 1270 d. 1296
PHILIP III d. 1285
HENRY III = Eleanor
d. 1272 d. 1291
Isabel (1) = RICHARD of Cornwall = (2) Sanchia
d. 1240 d. 1272 d. 1261
CHARLES of Anjou = Beatrice
d. 1285 d. 1267
Henry of Almain d. 1271
Edmund of Cornwall d. 1300
William Marshal II (1) = Eleanor = (2) Simon de Montfort
d. 1231 d. 1275 d. 1265
Isabella (3) = FREDERICK II
d. 1241 d. 1250
Joan (1) = ALEXANDER II = (2) Marie de Coucy
d. 1238 d. 1249 d. 1285
Henry d. 1265
Simon d. 1271
Amaury d. 1300
Guy d. 1291
Richard d. 1266
Eleanor = Llywelyn ap Gruffud
d. 1282 d. 1282
Henry d. 1253
Gwenillian d. 1337
EDWARD I = Eleanor of Castile
d. 1307 d. 1290
Margaret = ALEXANDER III
d. 1275 d. 1286
Beatrice = John of Brittany
d. 1275 d. 1304
Edmund = (2) Blanche of Valois
d. 1296 d. 1302
Katherine d. 1257
John d. 1271
Henry d. 1274
Alfonso d. 1284
EDWARD II d. 1327
Margaret d. 1283
Alexander d. 1284
David d. 1281
Arthur d. 1312
John d. 1334
Eleanor d. 1342
Thomas d. 1322
Henry d. 1345
John d. 1317

Family trees.

The luckless King John, who died in 1216 in the middle of a war to despose him. His son and successor Henry III had this effigy made for his tomb in Worcester Cathedral in 1232.

Effigies of Henry's mother Isabella of Angoulême and his uncle Richard the Lionheart at Fontevrault Abbey in France. Isabella returned to her homeland while her son was still a minor and died in 1246 after a spectacular fall from grace.

Ruins of Wolvesey Castle in Winchester, where Henry was likely brought up after his birth in the city on 1 October 1207. The castle belonged to the Bishop of Winchester, who at that time was John's confidant Peter des Roches.

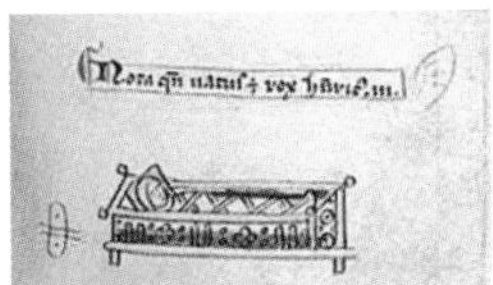

Matthew Paris's sketch of the infant Henry in his cradle.

This genealogical membrane shows the five children of King John and Isabella of Angoulême: Henry; Richard, later King of Germany, who had two sons; Isabella, Empress of the Holy Roman Empire, whose son and daughter are not shown; Eleanor, who had six children with Simon de Montfort who survived to adulthood; and Joan, Queen of Scots, who died without issue.

Illuminated depiction of the civil war in England in 1216. When John repudiated Magna Carta in 1215, rebel barons invited Crown Prince Louis of France to become their king.

Gloucester Cathedral, where the 9-year-old Henry was crowned on 28 October 2016 under the protection of William Marshal and papal legate Guala Bicchieri.

A second coronation was arranged for Henry in 1220 in Westminster Abbey, with Stephen Langton, the Archbishop of Canterbury, depicted here placing the crown on his head. Henry is the only English monarch to be crowned twice.

Hubert de Burgh, the minister who guided Henry through most of his minority. He is shown here seeking sanctuary after he was banished from government in 1232 on corruption charges.

This image shows Edmund of Abingdon, the third Archbishop of Canterbury during Henry's reign, reconciling the king and Gilbert Marshal in 1234 following the disastrous insurgency of Gilbert's brother Richard.

The 28-year-old Henry and his 12-year-old bride Eleanor of Provence in 1236. Their marriage was affectionate and enduring, and queenship flourished under her thanks to Henry, but the chroniclers found her influence and alien status threatening.

Delighting in interior design, Henry had his elongated bedchamber at Westminster Palace painted with wall murals throughout, thus giving rise to its name The Painted Chamber. Artist William Capon painted it in 1799, thirty-five years before it was destroyed by the great fire at the palace.

Winchester Hall, completed by Henry in the 1230s. The famous round table hanging there dates from his son Edward's reign, but could easily represent a wheel of fortune Henry had painted on the eastern gable of the hall as a reminder that charity exists precisely because of life's ups and downs.

Two historic antagonists, Henry III and Simon de Montfort, shown in these modern renderings. The charismatic Montfort was the son of a famous crusading family, became a good friend and confidant and married Henry's youngest sister. The relationship between king and subject waxed hot and cold for the next three decades until the reform period split them apart for good.

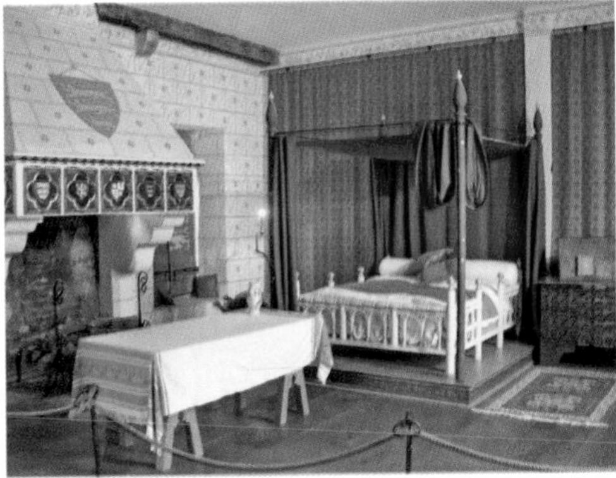

Tower of London and Henry's bedchamber inside the fortress. The whitewash dates from his improvements begun in 1238 to make the Tower a secure bastion for times of political crisis. At the top in the image at left is London Bridge, where in 1263 a mob harangued Queen Eleanor as she attempted to flee the city during the baronial uprising.

Robert Grosseteste, the remarkably learned and dynamic Bishop of Lincoln, who tussled with Henry over a variety of issues until his death in 1253. He was the spiritual mentor of Montfort and other future radical reformers.

Holy Roman Emperor Frederick II, who was called the 'wonder of the world' in his time. Henry hoped that the marriage of his sister Isabella to Frederick in 1235 would create an alliance against France, but the emperor had too many troubles elsewhere to be of much use.

Henry and Eleanor in a boat returning from Gascony in 1243, with Nicholas de Molis, one of his best field commanders, in the smaller craft.

Left: Edward the Confessor, the Saxon king of England whose death in 1064 led to the Norman Conquest two years later. Henry considered the pious and peaceful Confessor a kindred spirit and hoped to make him the patron saint of England.

Below: Westminster Abbey depicted in 1245, the year Henry undertook to rebuild the Romanesque church in an English and Gothic style more in tune with the age. To the right is Pope Innocent IV convening the Council of Lyon for the purpose of deposing Frederick. His interference in secular politics proved calamitous for the Church and Europe.

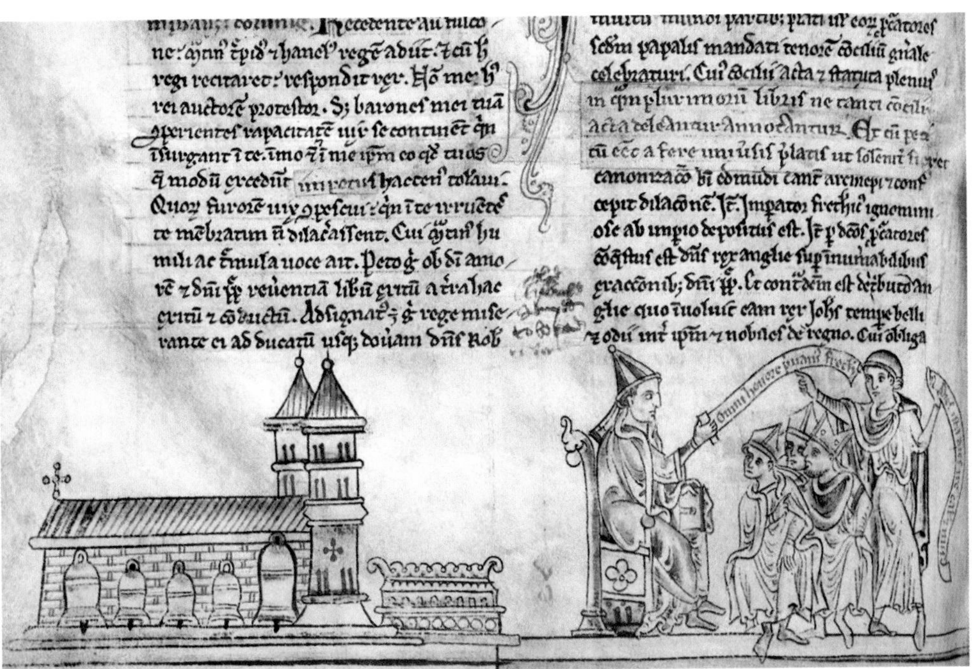

Henry was a master showman who enjoyed organising and putting on theatrical feats. In a dazzling ceremony in 1247, the king carried a vial of the Holy Blood barefoot from St Paul's in London to Westminster Abbey.

Henry and Eleanor had five children, shown here in this genealogical membrane. From left the future King Edward I; Queen Margaret of Scotland, married to Alexander III; Edmund, who for several years as a boy was the king-designate of Sicily; Beatrice, actually the third child, was married to John of Brittany, the future Earl of Richmond; and Katherine, whose death at the age of 3 left her parents distraught.

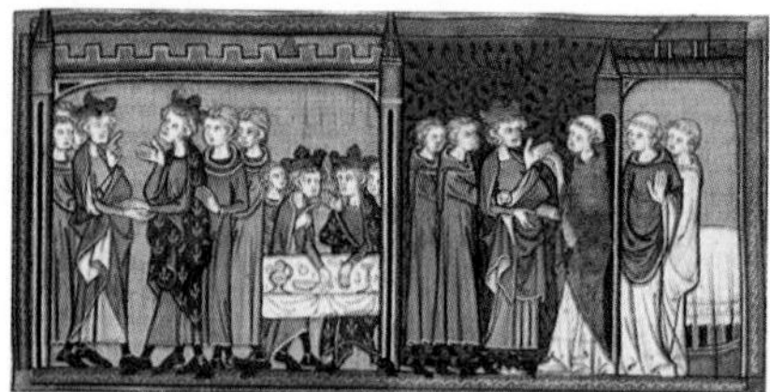

Henry visiting Louis IX and Saint-Denis just north of Paris. The friendship between these two former boy kings, who were brothers-in-law, was one of the great political achievements of the Middle Ages.

The Chapter House at Westminster Abbey. Although meant as a meeting place for the monks and canons of the abbey, Henry had it built and decorated as a venue for future parliaments.

This floor tile from the Chapter House shows the three leopards of Henry's coat of arms. The leopards were probably lions when the design was conceived for Richard I at the end of the twelfth century.

This image shows two knights fighting over a hound. Conflict and litigation over ownership was a common theme in the Middle Ages.

While the men tended their knightly and feudal duties elsewhere, the women protected and provided for the home.

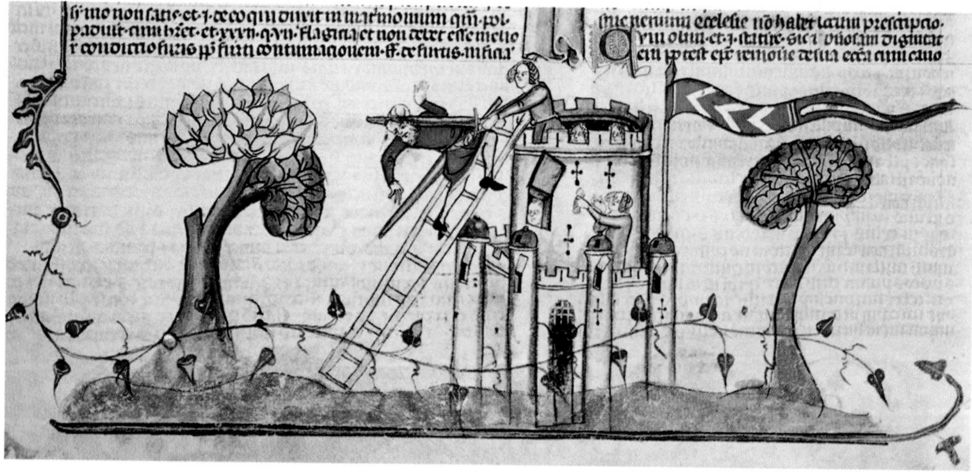

Above: Warfare in medieval Europe was mostly about avoiding large-scale battles, instead concentrating on taking the enemy's castles one by one.

Left: Inspired by Simon de Montfort, the leading bishops opposed the king as the country drifted towards war.

Civil war broke out in the spring of 1264 between Montfort's baronial and clerical faction and men loyal to the king. On 14 May Montfort assembled his forces at dawn on the ridge overlooking Lewes in Sussex. The battle was fought where the houses stand today.

Defeated, Henry was a captive of his own government for the next fifteen months. He attended council meetings and issued letters, but Montfort, at the head of a parliamentary state, was the real power in the land.

Edward's escape from captivity led to a royalist resurgence and decisive battle at Evesham on 4 August 1265. Here on Greenhill, north of the town, Henry barely escaped the slaughter that claimed Montfort and most of his knights. The butchery, thunderstorm and pathos of an aged king forced to fight against his will anticipate Shakespearean tragedy like *King Lear.*

A lone slab marks the spot where Montfort's remains, such as they were, were buried in Evesham Abbey. Some reports indicate they were disinterred and disposed of elsewhere, but in any event, the abbey, save for the bell tower, was destroyed during the Tudor era.

Montfort's former castle of Kenilworth in Leicestershire became the organised centre of resistance of the Disinherited. It was finally surrendered in December 1266 under the terms of the dictum named for it.

The Cosmati pavement at the high altar of Westminster Abbey, one of the wonders of the medieval world. Henry sought to represent the creation of the universe in these intricate shapes and swirls, and also foretell its demise.

Henry scrounged and laboured for a quarter of a century to rebuild Westminster Abbey into the form we know it today. He spent more than £40,000 on it, at least £40 million in today's money, but, as a major tourist attraction, it has returned that investment many times over.

Henry III in all his majesty. The likeness of the effigy crafted for his tomb in Westminster Abbey in 1291 is probably genuine, but shows few careworn features one might expect after more than half a century on the throne. Apparently he aged well thanks to a mostly peaceful and prosperous reign, a loving and affectionate family, and the charity, humility and forgiveness that guided his beliefs.

Oléron in Gascony and appoint Geoffrey his seneschal of the province. Both were sneaky attempts to pre-empt reforming legislation. The grants were discovered, revoked and Edward put under close surveillance by a new princely council of four that included John Balliol.

At the end of July, Richard de Clare and his brother William sat down for breakfast with Edward to discuss these and other matters. The brothers fell ill afterwards, with William dying and Richard losing all of his hair and nails. They were in all likelihood victims of an epidemic that had broken out in Winchester and claimed other lives, including Henry's friend the Abbot of Westminster, but panic soon spread of a mass poisoning arranged by the Poitevins in the event that they were proscribed. Paris reports that certain jars of a blue liquor were discovered that proved fatal to dogs when mixed with their food. Clare's steward, who happened to be Edward's tenant, was accused of taking part in the plot. Terrified, he fled for his life but was caught and executed in Winchester the next year.[24]

The epidemic forced Parliament to adjourn early. The government was now in the hands of the council, which had replaced the committee of twenty-four as the executive body of the realm. The fifteen councillors had been chosen by four members of the committee, two from each side, who were themselves chosen by their opposites. Seven were from the baronial side, including all but Hugh Bigod of the confederates, but only three were king's men. They met daily at the New Temple and elsewhere, arguing long into the night and immersing themselves in a 'furious orgy of activity'.[25]

The only departmental shake-up was in the wardrobe. When keeper Artaud de St Romain died in September 1257, Henry named as his replacement an old hand, Peter de Rivallis, who had re-entered government service in the early 1250s. Ousted by the revolt of 1234, he was now ousted again, but it had nothing to do with his chequered past. He was at least 70 and would die in 1262. Rivallis in his early tenure had been responsible for turning the wardrobe into what it was now, a mini treasury that kept the king in ready funds while the exchequer plodded along. By 1258 more than 80 per cent of its revenues were coming from outside the exchequer, not all of them accounted for. The council wanted to get their hands on the wardrobe to stop the uncontrolled flow of money through it. The point was to get a grip on crown finances, but everyone knew it would cost the king a tremendous amount of his independence.[26]

Henry himself had sworn to abide by this and 'whatever the council or the greater part of them should do'. He remained at Westminster until 4 August and then headed upcountry for the next two months, visiting favourite haunts like Windsor, Reading, Woodstock and the shrines of East Anglia. He made twenty-five stops in all, unusually hectic for him, but this was no ordinary royal progress.[27] In his train was Hugh Bigod, newly appointed to the resurrected office of justiciar at a salary of £666, meant to keep him from taking bribes. Although he had been a councillor and envoy for Henry, he was no judge and had had no legal training, but both were considered of secondary importance to having somebody of baronial rank who could get the job done. His task was to go from county to county, hearing complaints compiled by local knightly commissions and dispensing justice on the spot. It was essential to show that reform had Henry's blessing, and there was no more visible evidence of that than having Bigod accompanying the court and discharging this function from the king's bench itself.[28]

The first tangible results came at the Parliament of October 1258 and the passage of the Ordinance of the Sheriffs, which closely regulated the most contentious office in the land. The sheriffs were ordered to treat rich and poor alike, take nothing but food and drink as gifts, and lodge only with people making at least £40 a year, and then only once a year 'or twice at most'. They were to be local knights, given salaries instead of profits and serve for one year only. Nineteen of the twenty-two sheriffs were dismissed, some of them, like the notorious Lisle, convicted and imprisoned for various offences, and replaced by men who had never held the job before. Their nominal boss at the exchequer, Philip Lovel, was also disgraced and replaced. He had never been popular as treasurer, and it was Henry himself who moved against him. In a folksy touch, he grabbed Lovel by the arm one day and told him he was under arrest. Finally, the remaining Poitevins were proscribed. They were identified, expelled and their lands seized for the profit of the new order.[29]

On 18 October, Henry himself conveyed these and other glad tidings in a proclamation of his support for all that the council and Parliament had done. He admitted that progress was slow, but that was because things had 'gone amiss for so long'. To ensure the widest possible audience, the proclamation was drawn up in three versions: Latin for the record, French for the nobility and clergy, and Middle English for everybody else. This marked the debut of English as an official language, another of the many firsts of Henry's reign. The content of the proclamation also reflected the attitude of the more militant members of the council, as evident in a line towards the end. Henry was never comfortable with it, and in his mind and others', it was the beginning of the end for the whole experiment: 'And gif oni other onie comen her onghenes we willen and hoaten thæt alle ure treowe heom healden deadlice ifoan.' (And if anyone should oppose this decree, we will and command our faithful subjects to treat them as our mortal enemies.)[3]

* * *

Even at this stage, the political reforms that had been carried out were so profound and radical that nothing like them would be undertaken in England for another 400 years. And that king ended up losing his head. By contrast, the success in 1258 was due in no small measure to Henry's cooperation. Had he turned his back once the council got started, the whole thing might have collapsed into confusion and war. Why he didn't is a matter of debate, because for twenty years he had warded off all attempts by the barons to share in his government. Suddenly, he's handing the whole thing over to them and assuming what appears to be a diminished role. Something must have happened during that eventful year to cause him to have this change of heart about kingship and seemingly surrender it without a fight.

The logical explanation is that he gave in to the barons because this time he really needed their money. The pope was threatening to excommunicate him for constantly missing deadlines, and the new papal emissary, Arlotus, was equipped to do just that. King John had weathered his excommunication well, even grew rich out of it, but Henry was far more pious and less cynical than his father. Expulsion from the Church would have been devastating for him. The problem was that where John had been defiant, Henry was compliant. He laboured endlessly on the Sicilian project because he wanted it as much as the pope. Alexander could hardly impose ecclesiastical penalties on him in the circumstances, especially now that peace between England and France was close at hand. When Arlotus left with Rostand in mid-August, another deadline was about to come and go, but no thought was given to putting the king's soul at risk.[31]

The barons had been far more menacing with their armed protest, but despite being caught off guard, Henry didn't cave in to their demands. He agreed to reform only as a potential trade-off for aid and made it clear that he was sticking by his brothers. Once at Oxford, however, everything changed. The petition of grievances, indicating widespread anger and discontent across the realm, coincided with a spectre that truly unnerved him. Two consecutive harvests had failed on account of the atrocious weather, spreading famine throughout a land where the peasants depended on bread, pottage and ale for 75 per cent of their calorie intake. At the famine's peak that summer, Paris describes the dead lying everywhere, 'swollen up and rotting, on dunghills, and in the dirt of the streets, and there was scarcely any one to bury them'. His estimate of 15,000 dead in London alone would represent one-third of the population, but many had probably come there from the barren countryside in search of food.[32]

For Henry, feeding the poor was a divine duty, and this disaster must have led him, like Louis after his crusade, to identify himself as the cause because his house was not in order. He had allowed Sicily to distract him and warp his sense of priorities. Indeed, the Ordinance of the Sheriffs evokes the Grand Ordinance enacted by Louis four years earlier. While their injunctions against official misconduct were generally timeless in principle, and Grosseteste had drafted similar rules for Margaret de Lacy's estate back in 1241, the French connection between the two ordinances was obvious.[33] Henry was no great lawmaker; he had professional jurists for that. But he had a sincere desire to make things right, and far from fearing his barons' intervention, he may have welcomed their willingness to shoulder the burden with him. The sacrifice of his half-brothers was surely a small price to pay.

He said as much in a letter addressed to the pope on 1 August, which opens with the declaration that the best ordered city is the one where 'each forgets his own personal interests':

> This saying receives today striking confirmation in the reform and reorganisation of our kingdom, for our barons, neglecting their own affairs for ours, are working with all their power upon our business and the business of our kingdom. Today we have a constitution prepared by them, one most profitable to us and our heirs.[34]

That was his official attitude, but a deeper, more personal testament to his feelings can be heard in an oration drawn up to accompany the baronial letter to the pope denouncing the Lusignans. Where the tone of the letter was arrogant and defensive, the oration expressed the remorse and hopefulness of a penitent who has seen the light and rejoices in a new beginning. Possibly drafted by John Clarel, one of Mansel's clerks, it began with the bold announcement that peace had been made. Like the three kings of old, the kings of France, England and Germany were offering the three gifts of devotion, charity and peace. It was almost not to be, however, because the King of England had neglected his duty to give 'very much to his country, much to his kinsfolk, nothing to the alien'. His brothers had seduced him from his people, but they had been punished and the barons had helped Henry rediscover his royal dignity. Together they sought the reform of the realm because such was God's work, but because self-seekers abounded in their ranks, and change naturally brings enmity and discord, the pope must send a legate to restore the king and Church to their glory and ensure peace at home and abroad. Unity would reign supreme again under the legate's guiding hand. Thus implored one 'speaking with the overflowing bitterness of a full heart, in unrestrained heat and with fluent tongue'.

Henry would have remembered how, as a boy, the legates Guala and Pandulf had done as much as anyone, even William Marshal, to save his throne. The third legate, Otto, had helped him win back the power and prestige lost through the insurrection of Marshal's son. The situation was different now though. Reforms were proceeding harmoniously and to good effect. The barons did not seek to subject the king to their control, still less to humiliate him, rather to work together in a partnership for the benefit of all. And yet, truth be told, 'some will seek cause or occasion to desert the fellowship'.[35] Henry knew these men were grumblers by nature who saw no reason to put aside their own interests while everybody else was receiving justice. A good example was John Fitz-Geoffrey, whose quarrel with Aymer had started it all. Their case was the first one heard by the justiciar when he set up his special eyre. As might be expected, Bigod ruled completely in favour of Fitz-Geoffrey, his brother-in-law, who went to his grave in November of that year assured that the system worked.[36]

Then there was the king's own brother-in-law. The reforming committee of twenty-four had only recently been established when Simon de Montfort pressed them to hear his complaints about the money and land owed to him and his wife. He had to know nothing would come of it. Committee members like Clare, Warenne and the Bigods were Marshal grandsons, and other barons like Roger Mortimer were married to Marshal heirs. They stood to lose anything the Montforts gained by revisiting the settlement. Since divisions like these were bound to arise, Henry was counting on the outside authority of a legate to keep them and the other barons focused on their combined agenda, to remember they were a community in this endeavour. He especially had his eye on Simon. Ambitious and able, Montfort had an intensity of purpose that made him a host in himself. Once he latched onto a principle, there was no stopping him. Simon was, in fact, the one baron who inspired fear in him, and Henry let him know it one afternoon in late July.[37]

Matthew Paris recounts that the king had decided to have dinner while boating on the Thames. His barge got caught in a thunderstorm and he quickly ordered the crew to put in at the nearest landing. It belonged to the palace of the Bishop of Durham, who had lent it to the Montforts for that summer. Alerted that the royal party was docking at the water gate, Simon came out to greet his distinguished guest and was surprised to find him trembling. He assured him that the storm had passed, but Henry just looked at him sternly and said, 'The thunder and lightning I fear beyond measure, but by the head of God, I fear you more than all the thunder and lightning in the world.' Simon protested that he had him all wrong. He was the king's firm and faithful friend. There were others, false flatterers, he ought to fear.[38]

Henry certainly wasn't alone in seeing Montfort as the one individual willing to use force if it came to it. Simon had proved in Gascony that he had the martial zeal to impose his will in a cause he felt was right. He took the lead in expelling the Lusignans, threatening to chop their heads off if need be, and seemed to be present at every crucial turn of reform, whether bringing the city of London on board or communicating with the papacy. His promotion of men on the council and as castellans who were friendly to his way of thinking made it clear that he was planning to see the reform process through to the end.

It was therefore all the more surprising when Simon hesitated before taking the oath to preserve and protect the Provisions of Oxford. A well-heeled story has this born and bred Frenchman claiming to know the English too well, that the minute things didn't go their way, they turned and ran for it. If in the end the Provisions had to be fought for, there was no guarantee that the men taking the oath with him would still be there.[39] On the other hand, forcing the others to plead with him to take the oath accentuated his importance and compelled them to recognise his leadership. He was still one among many equally capable men, but his connections in France gave him an especially important role with the peace treaty now imminent. It was the occasion of that treaty, however, that first stirred disillusion in Henry with the reformers, and his brother-in-law in particular.

In late November 1258, the kings of England, France and Germany were supposed to meet at Cambrai in northern France to ratify the Treaty of Paris. As Henry stated in his oration, peace between the three kingdoms, between him, Louis and Richard, all of whom were married to sisters, was something now dear to him. But the council had second thoughts about him going. There was an unspoken fear that trouble might ensue from allowing him to go abroad this early into reform. In deciding to send a delegation instead, they deeply embarrassed and humiliated him. The delegation, moreover, was headed by Montfort, the councillor who seemed to be everywhere. It's possible that Montfort planted suspicions about Henry in his colleagues' minds so that he could bask in the glory of the occasion alongside his good friend the King of France. If so, he overestimated his importance. Louis was well disposed to him and the other delegates, but didn't see the point in attending the conference without Henry, and so stayed away.[40]

Then, on 18 December, the pope responded to events in England. Outwardly he rejoiced that the 'profit and tranquillity of the kingdom' was the ultimate objective of reform, but in truth he knew it could only make it harder for the king to prosecute the Sicilian business. He may have even been inclined to think it all part of one big conspiracy, because Manfred was crowned in Palermo in August, just as the baronial letter to him was being written. Angry that it had come to this, he declared that since Henry had not fulfilled the terms of their agreement, Alexander was free to offer the Sicilian throne to someone else.[41]

This didn't mean Sicily was lost, but close. The barons didn't try to hide their disgust with the business in their letter, and their promise to work for an aid for it in return for reforms proved empty. They had set up a committee to consider it, but it was full of the same names and doubters and in the end, it never even met. The pope behaved no better. After all Henry had endured, he took the £40,000 invested in the affair so far and ran. He did suspend penalties against Henry for the missed deadlines 'with our accustomed kindness', but then further disappointed him by declining to send a legate despite the exalted appeal of his oration. Not enough cardinals were available, he claimed.[42]

The important issue for the barons was keeping Aymer out of the country, but here Alexander deferred judgement until the bishop-elect had a chance to defend himself. In fact, the pope had already decided that they had acted unjustly and secretly made plans to dispatch a papal chaplain to plead for Aymer's return. As if sensing he might try something like that, the council moved in January 1259 to nominate the chancellor Henry Wengham for the new Bishop of Winchester. The king had nothing against Wengham and was used to rewarding his civil servants in this manner, but he refused to give his licence. It was nonsense to postulate a bishop before the other one had been deposed, he told them. The awkward impasse lasted until June, when Wengham was elected Bishop of London at the death of Fulk Basset.[43]

The paranoia that had begun with the blue liquor was now becoming a common feature of the council. Fear of the Poitevins still topped the list of concerns. In an effort to deny William de Valence support from his wife Joan, they put her on an allowance rather than give her control of her Marshal inheritance. When she went to join her husband in December, however, she managed to smuggle out an undisclosed sum of money stashed in sacks of wool. Then word came that Richard of Cornwall, who was the only king to show up at Cambrai, had decided to return to England. The council was worried he would accuse them of persecuting his brother and driving his half-brothers into exile 'as though they had been guilty of the greatest crimes whilst they themselves were innocent'. That would give him a pretext to bring the Lusignans back with him and cause all kinds of commotion.[44]

Richard had good reason to be disturbed by the baronial takeover of government. His confirmation as the King of the Romans ultimately depended on his wealth at home, which no longer seemed secure. When his son Henry of Almain demurred from taking the oath to the Provisions of Oxford without securing his permission first, the young man was warned to get it within forty days or lose his lands. The aborted peace conference was another blow, because Richard needed a treaty with France to isolate Alfonso's position against him in Germany. These troubling events made it imperative that he visit England, but the barons were alarmed by the prospect that he might try to do more than look after his own interests. It was agreed through an embassy that he would be allowed to land, but with only a modest retinue and if he promised to take the oath forthwith. On 28 January 1259, he and Sanchia were met at Dover by Henry, who led them to Canterbury and the banquet Boniface had arranged in their honour. The next day Richard took the oath, as recited by his stepson Richard de Clare.[45]

His arrival was followed by Simon de Montfort's, who had remained on the Continent following Cambrai to take care of personal matters. In leaving the council guessing as to his whereabouts, he had given them something else to worry about. But Simon's commitment to reform was as strong as ever, as is evident in the will he drew up while abroad. He had been an exacting lord as the Earl of Leicester and was now anxious to make provision for the 'poor people' of his lands.[46] That was just the kind of spirit needed for the business of Parliament that opened at the New Temple on 9 February. It was now the turn of the barons to hold themselves to account. In an ordinance sealed not quite a fortnight later, they agreed to subject themselves and their officials to the same restraints placed on the crown and to allow judicial inquiry and action into the management of their estates. Privileges like forcing their tenants to attend their manorial courts when they had better things to do would also be restricted. This effectively broadened the scope of reforms to include everyone at the top. Clare, however, had doubts about where this might lead and sought to delay publishing the legislation until it was amended to offer magnates like him more protection. This drew an angry response from Montfort, who reminded him that as one of the richest landowners, he had a special obligation to observe the new 'wholesome statutes'. Clare relented under pressure from him, Bohun and other peers, and ordered his officials to abide by the new reforms.[47]

But it wasn't long before he and Montfort fell out again. In April, they were in France as part of the delegation to conclude the peace treaty. The last item was the official renunciation of Plantagenet family claims to their former lands. Henry did his on 24 February, his son Edmund, Richard of Cornwall and Henry of Almain a little before that. Edward refused to renounce because he didn't like the treaty at all. As king, he figured he might like a go at winning those ancestral lands back. His aunt Eleanor also held out. Nothing had been done to advance her outstanding claims in all the time her renunciation had been part of the treaty. Simon of course stood by her, causing Clare to accuse him of using peace with France as a bargaining tool for his own enrichment. After trading venomous insults, they nearly came to blows in front of their French counterparts, who found their behaviour both infantile and amusing. Simon wisely stayed behind while Clare and the other envoys went back to England to discuss the Montforts' demands with Henry and the rest of the council.[48]

The first of the Montforts' three complaints, the money still owed for the buyout of Gascony, was satisfied on 7 May. Two weeks later, the Montforts received nine manors to fulfil Henry's promise to convert their annual fee into land. Finally, there was the problem nobody wanted to deal with: whether Eleanor had received a fair dower settlement. In July, an arbitration panel was named to issue a ruling by November, but it was hamstrung from the start by the Montforts' insistence that her dower lands were worth £933 more than the £400 she had been receiving. Considering the twenty-six years going back to the original agreement, she claimed the fantastic sum of £24,258 in arrears. Even asking for half that amount, which was probably closer to what she was due, was beyond what Henry could or was willing to pay. The panel consisting of the earls of Norfolk and Hereford and Philip Basset had to rule on their claim by 1 November, but Henry was not hopeful. He sent Louis a draft of the treaty that omitted his sister's renunciation and offered to indemnify him for any action she brought in the matter.[49]

By this point, Eleanor's stonewalling was the only thing holding up the treaty. Edward made his renunciation by 20 May, prompting Henry to make preparations to leave for France. Suddenly he was informed that Louis had rejected the draft. No renunciation from Eleanor, no treaty. Henry was beside himself. He suspected that his brother-in-law had used his personal acquaintance with Louis to convince him not to accept anything less than her full cooperation. It was all the more galling because at the beginning of the peace negotiations, he had authorised Simon to pursue any historic claims his French kinfolk might still have. Simon denied any ill intent or deviousness, but Henry never forgave him or his sister for jeopardising what had become a project dear to him.[50]

★ ★ ★

The success of the reform programme would ultimately come down to whether people like the Montforts felt their grievances had been properly addressed. From the outset, the reformers realised that the justice system was not up to the task. For starters, there were too many jurisdictions to navigate: the courts of the king's bench, common pleas, eyres, counties, boroughs, subdivisions, manors and the Church. And it was expensive for most people. Just a standard writ to initiate a judicial action cost six pence, easily a day's salary for a skilled artisan. It was an era, moreover, of the strictest technicalities, where a case could be thrown out instantly for an error in the writ. The process was also made needlessly cumbersome thanks to England's special language situation. Whenever a jury was required to give evidence, the judges presented their questions in French, the jurors answered in English and the clerk wrote it all down in Latin. Any misinterpretation of the facts could easily land somebody in jail.[51]

To get around this morass, the reform committee appointed four knights in each county to collect complaints and bring them to Westminster. This material was then forwarded to Hugh Bigod, who would hear the cases when he arrived in each county. But he also welcomed any grievance not on the rolls read out by the clerk. These were *querelae*, or oral complaints, and they were popular because they cost only the time it took to stand in the queue, and judgement was given practically on the spot. They ranged from civil cases like lords obstructing roads or streams and exacting tolls from villagers to criminal offences like assault, theft and extortion. The main point of the *querelae* was to give peasants the opportunity to seek redress, but knights and patricians took advantage of them too. In one year, up to July 1259, Bigod heard 268 cases and was praised for treating 'rich and poor with equal justice, yielding to the prayers and promises of no man, not even the mightiest'.[52]

Of course, not everyone was happy. *Querelae* could also reveal some uncomfortable truths. For instance, there were twice as many complaints against Boniface, a member of the council, than against Aymer, who had been exiled by the council. Some serfs got the idea that a revolution was in the works and thought Bigod could improve their lot. In one case in Oxfordshire, a group of them complained that their lord, a local knight, was making them do extra services and taxing them at will. The knight responded that he was doing just that, because it was his right. The serfs were technically unfree, so he could do with them as he pleased. The serfs confirmed that they were indeed unfree peasants, forcing Bigod to find for the defendant and ordering them held at his mercy for making a false complaint.[53]

There were people and institutions who feared something like this would happen when the doors to justice were thrown wide open. Without writs and bureaucracy, the disenfranchised would get it into their heads to get uppity and try to upset the whole balance of feudalism. Rich landowners like Richard de Clare naturally liked it when the justiciar tackled abuse and corruption committed by foreign lords and royal officials, decidedly less so when their own bailiffs came under investigation. In fact, Bigod had mostly avoided holding the higher nobility to account, and the perception that they were getting off scot-free set the stage for another political march. Some time after Parliament opened on 13 October 1259, a group calling themselves the 'bachelors of England', probably young knights fed up with the great lords' oppressions, told Clare and the other councillors that the king had done all he had promised to do, but they themselves were doing little more than profiting from it. Either they submit to reform as well or the bachelors would see to it that they did.[54]

Clare listened because they had found an ally in Edward. He and the heir to the throne hated each other. They were fighting over the castle of Bristol, and there was of course the breakfast the year before when Clare was disfigured by something in the food but Edward somehow escaped unharmed. Things had got so bad back in March that barons on both sides got them to make what amounted to a non-aggression pact. But as Clare drifted further towards reaction, Edward embraced reform. He was more or less forced to, because the *querelae* had identified him as an oppressive landlord. He also had his reputation to rebuild after sulking over his uncles' exile and the peace treaty. The bachelors may have turned to him only as an afterthought, but he willingly took up their cause. He had been late to the game, he admitted, but was ready to stand by his oath to the Provisions of Oxford to the death.[55]

That caught the attention of Clare's other enemy, Simon de Montfort. In one of those flash appearances that became his trademark, Montfort showed up from France in time for the opening of Parliament but left before it ended. He was still a radical for reform and took the opportunity of his godson's change of heart to bind him to the movement he dubbed 'the common enterprise' with a pact of their own. The two were ideally suited to aid each other because both had stores of energy and were ready to use force to get what they wanted. But they were also equally focused on themselves, and one of the reasons why Montfort showed up for Parliament was because Louis had decided to accept the treaty without Eleanor's renunciation. Montfort's only hope now was the award of the arbitrators, and he wanted Edward's support to make sure the Marshal heirs disgorged if and when ordered to do so. In return, Edward was hoping Simon could help him win greater freedom from the council and his parents.[56]

The threat of the bachelors, backed up by these two malcontents, was enough to move Parliament and the council to enact legislation that made reform more comprehensive. They included provisions that exempted a tenant from attending a manorial court unless his lord could prove that the obligation existed by charter. *Querelae* were now given official status in the general proceedings and could be backdated seven years. Since that increased the scope of the special eyre well beyond what one man like the justiciar could handle, seven circuits under the direction of other councillors were set up to cover more ground. They were charged with investigating all abuses, but one article explicitly mentioned the conduct of baronial officials and 'the rich men themselves'. In building on the progress made since the previous year, these Provisions of Westminster, as they became known, were the high-water mark of the reform period. King and nobility were now both answerable to their subjects. But it was also going to be downhill from there, as seen in the provision that nobody was to come to Parliament armed. This was meant to avoid a repeat of the coercive atmosphere in which these provisions were promulgated, but it hinted that open conflict between reformers was a possibility, especially with the king set to depart for France.[57]

Recognising the dissension, Henry left Edward at home and took Clare with him as a councillor accompanying the court abroad. Simon was still technically part of the council, but he went to France on his own and was already there with his wife when the royal party arrived. They kept their distance, however, because the arbitrators failed to publish their award on her dower by the 1 November deadline. It is not clear why, but it meant they were all back to square one. The Montforts were more determined than ever not to let the treaty go forward until they received some satisfaction. Simon had even informed the French side that if it came down to it, Eleanor would activate her claim to Plantagenet lands. This alarmed Louis to the point that it was uncertain whether there woud be a treaty to ratify when Henry arrived in Paris on 26 November 1259. Prior to his departure, Henry had tried to placate his sister with little favours, but she refused to budge. This left him clawing at the air in frustration. In his mind, she and her husband were acting in bad faith, if not treacherously.[58]

In the old days, friends like Robert Grosseteste and Adam Marsh were able to exert a calming influence over Simon and Eleanor, but both were gone now following the death of Marsh a week earlier on 18 November. Stepping up in their place were Louis and his chief negotiator Eudes Rigaud, the Archbishop of Rouen, who was a good friend of Simon. After arranging a pension for the Montforts in France worth £110, Louis decreed that £10,000 of the money owed to Henry under the treaty would be withheld until their claim was settled. With pressure now on them from all sides, Eleanor finally renounced on 4 December, the day Rigaud formally read out the treaty in Louis's apple orchard before a distinguished gathering. Henry's claims to Normandy, Anjou, Maine, Touraine and Poitou were officially extinguished, and he was required to do homage to Louis for Gascony. In return, he received three conditional land grants of South Saintonge, Agenais, and Quercy, all adjacent to Gascony, and Louis's holdings in the three dioceses of

Limoges, Cahors and Périgueux. Lastly, Louis agreed to pay him the cost of 500 knights for two years.[59]

To the peers of France, their king seemed to have lost his mind in giving away so much, but he explained that he desired peace between their children, who were after all first cousins (as Henry and Louis's mother Blanche had been). The treaty achieved just that for the next thirty-five years. In more practical terms, he had made the King of England his liegeman, thus putting the French monarchy in a position to influence affairs across the Channel, a boast that turned out to be more prophetic than anyone could have realised. The ceremony of homage itself was a mere formality. Henry knelt before Louis, put his hands between those of his new lord and became his 'man' as the Duke of Aquitaine.[60]

On 6 December, Henry honoured the new relationship between England and France with a huge feast at his lodgings in Saint-Germain-des-Prés on the outskirts of medieval Paris. The kings and their nobilities, sitting strictly according to rank, dined in the hall together with the 150 paupers whom Henry fed every day. Outside the hall of the monastery, Parisians flocked to collect the 5,000 loaves of bread baked for distribution. Louis doesn't seem to have emulated Henry's passion for great feedings. The most he fed on special occasions was 300, while with Henry the number reached well into the thousands. On 5 January, the anniversary of the death of Edward the Confessor, he fed 1,500 French paupers. He also washed far more paupers' feet, something which Joinville admitted would make him sick if he had to do it. Presumably he turned away when Louis told him that Henry not only washed the feet of lepers, but kissed them as well.[61]

Henry and Queen Eleanor had intended to return after Christmas, but treaty business and diplomacy, which included the marriage of their 17-year-old daughter Beatrice to John of Brittany, the grandson of Peter of Dreux, postponed their departure. The wedding was scheduled for 14 January 1260. Grief intervened after Louis and Margaret's first-born son Louis died unexpectedly at 15 and was buried that day. Henry helped bear his coffin for half a mile of the funeral procession, an act of grace and kindness immortalised to this day on the lad's tomb chest. The wedding took place eight days later at Saint-Denis, doubtless an agonising experience for Margaret, who had been behind the match.[62]

The English royals then left for the coast. Since they could not reach London in time for Parliament on 2 February, Henry wrote to the justiciar, who was the head of the regency council, to delay it until his return. The council was to take measures instead against an unexpected attack by Llywelyn on 10 January on the castle of Builth. Hugh Bigod, his brother Roger and Philip Basset were ready to obey, but Simon de Montfort was still committed to the supremacy of the council and Parliament. Back in France, he had told the Duke of Brittany as much when he took him aside during the negotiations over Beatrice's marriage portion. No matter what the king might promise him, he warned, the council had final approval.

He then further undercut Henry's authority by leaving the court without asking his permission first.[63]

Montfort returned to England specifically to hold Parliament. Failure to do so would undermine the Provisions of Oxford, he claimed, which he suspected to be the point of the king's delay abroad. Since Henry was in need of money, Simon advised the council against sending him any as a way of forcing him homeward. He not only had the backing of the other radicals on the council, Bishop Cantilupe, Peter de Montfort, Humphrey de Bohun and Richard Grey, but also Edward, who had come to London with an armed retinue. Now 20 years old, he despaired of being subjected again to his parents' control. With his uncle, whose drive, knightly prowess and improbable mix of idealism and selfishness clearly appealed to him, he could win the respect and independence he craved. Henry must have learned they were up to no good, for he suddenly cancelled plans to cross the Channel for the Parliament rescheduled to 24 February. That made Edward wonder if he hadn't gone too far. He sent his father a note of reassurance, which Henry said greatly pleased him, but he was still sending someone over to see if the young man's 'deeds matched his words'.[64]

That person was Clare, who found the situation truly alarming. Simon had engineered the dismissal of Peter of Savoy from the council and was working with Edward to bring in foreign troops, under the Lusignans of all people. The Earl of Gloucester suggested they were out to depose the king and recommended they bring in retainers of their own to counter the threat. The moderates now urged Henry to raise troops abroad, even sending him money for it, but Montfort scoffed that if they came, he would give them 'such a welcome that none would wish to follow them'. Henry moved to isolate the radicals by ordering Parliament to meet on 25 April, but leaving their names off the list of people to invite. Under Montfort, the radicals decided to hold their own rogue parliament, which could have easily erupted into a riot in the tense atmosphere in London at that time. Just the previous year, three Italian clerks were chased down and murdered by a crowd in broad daylight outside St Paul's. With Simon and Edward's men camped to the west of the city and Clare's to the south, it looked as if they might clash at any moment. Richard of Cornwall, who had lain low for most of the year since his return, appeared on the scene and, working with the mayor and moderates, closed the gates and put the city on lock-down. Now everyone waited for the king's next move.[65]

He was then at St Omer near the coast enlisting French and Flemish mercenaries. Louis helped him with a down payment of £5,690 from the treaty money. He nevertheless told Henry that he thought it was shameful for him to linger away from home for so long. It was strange that he should rebuke him in such a manner after Henry had volunteered to be a pallbearer at his son's funeral, stranger still that Henry should share it with anyone, but that's what he did in a letter to Clare. Either he was forever burdened by the need to confess unflattering judgements of himself or he was hinting that the shame was, in fact, the council's for having let things get out of hand. Since the council was incapable of maintaining the peace and harmony of the realm in his absence, he began giving out specific instructions on how to handle the situation. He was particularly worried about Edward and ordered Bigod to keep him and others 'of whom suspicion of evil might be entertained' out of the city.[66]

At last, Henry crossed over with a force of foreign knights and arrived in London on 30 April. He invited Clare and his men to accompany him inside the city walls, but pointedly refused to see Edward. He was furious at him but, being Henry, admitted that if he were to see him, he wouldn't be able to resist embracing him. He let Edward stew for two weeks, then had him arraigned before a gathering of magnates at St Paul's. Edward denied any evil intentions, and managed to save face by declaring that none could judge him but his father or uncle Richard. A king, in other words. Reconciliation with his family followed, but he had to purge his household to their liking and submit his quarrel with Clare to arbitration. He was then sent abroad to work out his restlessness and disappointments on the tournament pitch.[67]

Meanwhile, Henry aimed to destroy the one he held responsible for leading his son astray and inciting sedition. He ordered Simon to stand trial before the magnates, reasonably sure he would not find the same support that had got him off in 1252. Clare, worried that his attempt to turn Henry against Edward might be exposed in the process, managed to get the trial postponed, but a panel of bishops was convened to conduct a discovery phase. Montfort turned in a brilliant performance, parrying nearly every charge with a wry aloofness bordering on insolence.[68] The trial was to take place at Parliament in July, but was postponed once more after Llywelyn made another attack on Builth, this time overrunning and destroying the castle on 20 July. In ordering the feudal host to muster in September, Henry named Montfort one of the commanders. He was clearly hoping that his military skill would lead him to either victory or death in the field. As it was, a truce was arranged before any fighting broke out and the king prepared to go forward with the trial at Parliament in October.[69]

His worry was that his son was still plotting with Montfort. When Walter Kirkham, the Bishop of Durham, died on 9 August 1260, both the king and queen wanted Mansel to succeed him and went to great lengths to get the monks to accept him. Edward got word of this and, eager to thwart his mother's influence, promoted his own candidate, Hugh Cantilupe, a nephew of the Bishop of Worcester and leading Montfortian radical. The monks ended up choosing one of their own, as they probably would have done in any case.[70] Just days before St Edward's day, when Edward personally knighted his two elder Montfort cousins, he assented to another cousin, Henry of Almain, serving as steward for the feast in place of Simon. It was the steward's duty to hold a vessel of water at the table for the king to wash his hands, and the earls of Leicester had traditionally performed this service. Montfort was keen to retain the title of steward for political purposes, but anxious to avoid being seen in a subservient role to the king. He got the council to appoint Almain as his deputy to do it for him.[71]

Simon had another surprise in store for Henry when Parliament opened after the feast. Despite his disruptive actions and long absences from the council, he got his trial postponed indefinitely. He did it by striking a deal with Clare to roll back reforms. The special eyre, which was meant to root out baronial and crown abuses, had been halted in June by Henry, officially because of the ongoing famine, but also as a reward to Clare and other supporters for their loyalty. It was now revived at Parliament as planned, only without special provisions for redress and enforcement. It was to be a general eyre as in the days before reform. The move could have been linked to the strain on judicial resources caused by the deaths of senior justices Thurkelby and Bath in late summer, but was ominously accompanied by an amendment that allowed any baron cited for abuse to correct himself without oversight.[72]

It wasn't as if Montfort had sold out to save his skin. Since in his mind the key to reform was control over the king, he and the other radicals relinquished the direction of legislation to the reactionaries in return for naming their own adherents as ministers. This was made easy by Wengham's decision to retire in order to become the Bishop of London full-time, and by the death of treasurer John Crakehall. Nicholas of Ely became chancellor and John de Caux, the Abbot of Peterborough, treasurer. The only minister turned out of office was Hugh Bigod, who was now seen as compromised because he had put his loyalty to the king above the Provisions of Oxford. His job as justiciar went to Hugh Despenser, a rising Montfortian and member of Edward's household. While Henry found the appointment of Caux particularly unpalatable since he had helped fund Edward's run at rebellion, he objected to all three on the grounds that he had not been consulted. The council had foisted upon him men of their own choosing and expected him to accept them.[73]

His brother was just then facing a similar affront to his kingly dignity. After superficially reconciling Edward and Clare in mid-June, Richard of Cornwall left for Germany again, this time in the hope of going all the way to the pope to be crowned emperor. By the time he reached Worms in August, however, support for him had cooled, and Alfonso was again advising the papacy against making any rash decisions. Fed up, Richard went home and never again presumed that his title meant anything more to him than it did to others. He was in London on 29 October 1260 to celebrate in state with Henry and Alexander III, visiting from the north. It was a three-kings deal that greatly pleased Henry, but his enthusiasm on this occasion was probably tempered by the knowledge that his 19-year-old son-in-law, having recently reached his majority in Scotland, enjoyed the most power among them.[74]

It was odd that Edward should ever confer legitimacy on restrictions that diminished the English throne he would some day occupy, but all he could think about was his independence and enjoying the limelight as his own man. Having conspired in this humiliation of his father, he and his entourage of young knights, including his two Montfort cousins, left to tourney on the Continent. In Paris, he met up with his Lusignan uncles before going to Gascony for Christmas. He appointed Guy de Lusignan as his seneschal of the province and confirmed him in possession of his family's ancestral land, the Isle of Oléron. These were provocative acts that, in the days before Montfort and Clare took over, would have elicited a stern rebuke from the council followed by an order to revoke them.[75] As it was, there was no longer any council to speak of. The success of their October surprise had depended on Edward and the muscle he could bring with his militant, idealistic retinue. But his departure in November left the position of both his partners exposed. By early December, neither Montfort nor Clare was witnessing any more charters, and the rest of the council, caught up in the whole shabby business, drifted towards the king or went home. In the absence of an advisory body, Henry went about fashioning a court around men whose company he preferred and whose loyalty he could count on, including his brother Richard, John Mansel and Robert Walerand. Among those receiving Christmas robes from him at Windsor that year, Philip Basset, James Audley, Roger Mortimer, Hugh Bigod and Hugh Despenser were welcomed as his *familia*, the men he would listen to now that the council had ceased to exist.[76]

Tellingly, they were all Englishmen. Peter of Savoy had recently returned from the Continent, but was probably retained more as an adviser to the queen. It was an anxious period for Eleanor. Her daughter Margaret was expecting her first child and had doubtless talked her husband Alexander into making the trip south so that she could have her beloved mother nearby as the birth approached. Since the Scottish nobility naturally opposed that plan, the young king provided the ruse that he planned to wrest Margaret's dowry of £2,666 out of the exchequer, now ten years in arrears. In the event, no money was forthcoming, and Alexander returned home alone while his queen stayed at Windsor for her confinement.[77]

But, as usual, Eleanor's biggest worry was Edward. She knew what he was up to on the Continent, plotting to reinstate her enemies the Lusignans. While she was in France earlier that year, she had Henry write to the pope to ask him not to proceed any further on Aymer's behalf. The entire realm was against him ever coming back, the letter said, which for good measure contained the jibe that he was only 'pretending' to be the Bishop of Winchester.[78] The pope decided to show them all, and on 16 May, he consecrated Aymer as bishop. His petulant response only served to unite the different factions at court, for keeping the Lusignans out was the only thing they could all agree on, the whole reason why reform got started in the first place. As long as there was the threat of their return, and Aymer's in particular, they would always stand together. Then, on 4 December 1260, Aymer died in Paris, and everything changed.[79]

14

WERE IT NOT FOR ONE MAN 1261–1263

The reforming partnership between king and council was stamped for eternity in the building of Westminster Abbey. By 1258 the eastern end of the abbey, containing today's main altar, transepts and chapter house, was nearly finished and joined to the remaining portion of the Romanesque church built by Edward the Confessor. Far from leaving it as a hybrid hulk, the council agreed that work should proceed, and in February 1259 adopted a funding measure that could only have been initiated by the king. It involved assigning the valuable wardship of 8-year-old Henry de Lacy, the future Earl of Lincoln, to his mother Alice for £326 per year, payable directly to the project. This not only ensured long-term support, but gave the wardship of the boy to the person Henry originally had in mind for it. He showed his gratitude when the next phase of construction began and the adjoining section of the Confessor church was demolished. In the wall arcades of the choir to be erected there, the armorial shields of the great baronial families were installed, including those of the earls on the council. In commemorating them in this fashion, it would seem that reform had finally allowed Henry to be at one with his nobility. It was an elusive desire that went at least as far back as 1243, when he commissioned a painting for the great hall of Dublin Castle to show a 'king and queen sitting with their baronage'.[1]

But even within the abbey project itself there were signs that this unity wasn't going to last. In September 1259, the king had to write a begging letter to Hugh Bigod to remind him of his promise to pay £100 to the keepers of the works. While in France, he again had to press for funds to be released for construction.[2] The council's habit of ignoring his requests was hugely frustrating considering how the councillors would have jumped just a few years before. Then came Simon and

Edward's open defiance of Henry's authority and the council's lukewarm response to it. Far from holding Montfort to account, the councillors allowed him back into government, where he and Edward forged an unholy alliance with Clare. The result was essentially a coup d'état, for by putting the king's household and ministers under their control, the barons had all but forced a second minority on him. What had started out as a common enterprise under his lordship had become a tyranny of the council with the king as little more than a figurehead.

While the council brought about its own demise soon enough, Henry was forever burdened by the fact that after two years of intensive activity, reform and the institutions associated with it were firmly ingrained in the national consciousness. No matter how far the council overreached, no matter how much his authority had been impinged upon in the process, any attempt to take power back would be construed as bad faith and provoke a reaction. His situation was especially exasperating because the reforms that affected the most people, the Provisions of Westminster, had his full support. The problem was the Provisions of Oxford, which gave rise to the supremacy of the council and Parliament. They were never meant to subject him to the indignity of baronial tutelage, but that's what they had become in the hands of people like Montfort, Clare and, of all people, his son and heir. Now 53 years old, Henry knew that if he was ever going to breathe freely again as king, the Provisions of Oxford had to go.

Of course, there was the matter of his oath to uphold them, which he had willingly given when they were enacted. The only way out was to ask the pope for a bull of absolution. Arlotus and Rostand, who were witnesses to the inception of reform, could surely help him procure it from Alexander, particularly since Henry gave every sign that he was still eager to pursue a successful outcome to their Sicilian project. At the end of January 1261, John Mansel's namesake nephew was secretly dispatched to Rome for this purpose.[3] In the meantime, the king and his advisers would put through a plan which, with skill and adroitness, would catch the barons off guard much the way they had caught him with their march on Westminster.

The unexpected death of Aymer before Christmas made this possible. While Henry grieved the loss of his half-brother, he ever had his eye on the main chance, and this was it. With the least desirable of the Lusignans no longer a factor, he wanted his queen and the Savoyards to understand that they were going to have to put their pride aside and accept his other brothers back into the realm. This would help them win back Edward and isolate Montfort and Clare as dangerous inciters of discord. They understood, but wanted assurances that the Lusignans would be on their best behaviour and would receive no more special favours or protection.[4] Henry's response, we can imagine, was probably something like 'leave that to me'.

It was Montfort himself who gave Henry the next opening. Apparently complacent that his coup would stick, Simon followed Edward across the Channel to support his wife in a lawsuit against her half-brothers for a share of their mother Isabella's inheritance. It was a surprising move, because earlier in the spring of 1260 Edward had got Simon to end his quarrel with William de Valence in the expectation they could call in his help against the king and council. Edward also worked out an arrangement that had the Lusignans protecting Montfort's interest in Bigorre now that Gaston de Béarn and Esquivat had teamed up to try and take the county from him. But Eleanor soon dropped the case against William and eventually narrowed her focus on her nephew Hugh XII.[5]

This suit paled in comparison to the grievance that really bothered the Montforts: Eleanor's by now ancient Marshal dower. It had been over a year since it was agreed that £10,000 of the treaty money would be withheld until the issue was settled, but so great was Henry's anger over their conduct that he was willing to leave the money safely stored in the Paris Temple rather than work for their satisfaction. Montfort turned to the King of France to break the deadlock, and on 11 January 1261, Henry agreed to a request from Louis that he let the French royal couple and their chamberlain arbitrate their dispute. Simon was likely counting on the fact that he and Louis had much in common besides friendship and family history. Both had been on crusade, had an austere approach to religion and Queen Margaret herself had been cheated out of her own dower. But as much as all that might work in Simon's favour, Henry didn't see how any king, much less one that was his friend too, and brother-in-law, could condone Montfort's sedition and general contempt for a fellow monarch. Montfort himself did not accept the arbitration until 14 March, an indication that he might have had second thoughts about asking one king to rule on a case involving another.[6]

The most important element of Henry's plan to recover power was to project the image of business as usual. Since the Provisions of Oxford decreed that Parliament should meet every February, the summons went out for the gathering to take place on the twenty-third of the month. Two weeks before that, on 9 February, he left Windsor and took up residence at the Tower of London. Though he had upgraded the comforts of the Tower two decades earlier, he never stayed there. The last time he was in residence was when the barons rose up against him in 1238 on account of, oddly enough, the marriage he had arranged between his sister Eleanor and Simon.[7] For him, the Tower was all about the potential for conflict, to which he hinted further on 13 February by ordering the gates of London closed and guarded, and requiring all men and boys over the age of 12 to give their oath of fealty to him and Edward. Four days later he wrote to twenty-seven barons unconnected to recent events to come to Parliament armed.[8] He clearly expected trouble. In all this anxiety, Henry became a grandfather for the first time when his daughter gave birth to a girl, also named Margaret, at Windsor on 28 February 1261.[9]

Parliament was likely held at the New Temple, as no baron was ever keen on meeting the king at the Tower. Montfort returned from France for it, but he and

Clare were powerless as Henry let loose a tirade accusing them and the council of making a mess of things. His grievances, which were put down in writing on 9 March and subsequently amended, charged them with going well beyond the mandate of their reforming partnership. The council met without him, took decisions in his absence or else ignored him when he was present, and failed to pay off his debts as agreed. The country had become so impoverished and lawless under their rule that even the king's own baggage train was robbed. Their foreign policy was woefully negligent. They had done nothing for Sicily despite their promise, Wales was as good as lost and the Treaty of Paris lacked full implementation. He turned his ire on Montfort for seducing Edward away from his father's 'friendship and obedience'. He summed up his disappointment with the accusation that the magnates had 'stripped him of all honour and dignity, against their first oath, that of homage, and against their second oath, that of preserving the king's rights'.[10]

Parts of the indictment seem petty at first glance, but actually deal with the issue of feudal structure and authority. For example, Montfort deputising Henry of Almain, to act as steward for the feast of St Edward in October 1260, was more than just a presumed slight to one's lord. Simon got permission to do it from the council, as if the king's recognition of hereditary offices like steward and marshal was of no consequence. The way Henry saw it, if the current steward didn't want to minister his will, he should ask to be excused by the king, who would then appoint another baron to fill the office.[11]

Henry neither expected nor wanted the barons to reply to his grievances on the spot. He was aiming for arbitration, which would drag out, like all arbitrations of that period, and so allow young Mansel time to return with the papal bulls. Henry was also waiting for Edward to return with William de Valence. He had put up the pretence of ordering his son to disengage from the Lusignans, but plans were already underway to receive William. Valence was required to see Queen Margaret beforehand, perhaps to swear an oath to refrain from any more attacks on her sister, a prospect he found degrading but nevertheless undertook.[12] When he and Edward arrived on 24 April, the barons agreed that Valence could stay if he took the oath to the Provisions of Oxford. He did so, but with his usual tough-guy front that he was ready to answer anyone who complained about him. That was presumably a warning shot to the Savoyards, but here Henry stepped in and made it clear to William that their feud simply had to end. Within a week, he was fully restored to favour together with two other Poitevins.[13]

The wild card was still Edward. Despite getting his uncle William back into the realm, he knew that dropping his opposition meant crawling back to his parents. But it was either Edward's tutelage or his father's. In the end, he had no choice. Playing the big man abroad, he had nearly bankrupted himself with all the grants he made with abandon. Henry agreed to bail him out by providing him with funds and repaying his large loan of £1,000 from Louis. But he also took Peter of Savoy's advice and made several grants of his own to members of Edward's retinue, promising them positions in any forthcoming shake-up. This allowed his son to save face and end his rebellion once and for all. The London chronicler attributes Edward's defection to his mother's 'flattery', which probably means she said something nice for the first time about the Lusignans.[14]

All this was going on around the time arbitration ensued at Easter. There were indications that the king had something in the works besides the return of the Lusignans and remaining behind the protective walls of the Tower. In March, he deprived the barons of a potential ally in Llywelyn by confirming the truce reached the previous autumn without demanding any customary payment. That same month he ordered the sheriffs to arrest anyone spreading rumours that he might levy a tax. But the barons seemingly suspected nothing as talks got underway because Henry came ready to moderate his position, even dropping his personal charges against Montfort. He reassured them that he intended to stand by his oath to the Provisions of Oxford.[15] He may have been telling the truth, because he and his advisers had to know that annulling them would be explosive in any scenario. The papal absolution of his oath was likely meant to be deployed as a last resort.

Had the barons seized the moment and recognised that his grievances were justified, an accommodation might have been reached that restored to the king his basic rights and renewed their original spirit of cooperation. But their answers, although tinged with embarrassment, denied any blame and merely promised to amend whatever faults could be proved. They even missed the tenor of Henry's whole argument that they no longer showed him the respect and obedience due to him as their lord, as can be seen in their reply to his complaint that they ignored his opinion in discussions when it ought to prevail. Yes, they said, he should have his way, 'but only when he talks sense'.[16]

Reconciliation impossible, Henry put into action the boldest part of his plan. On 2 May 1261, he appeared before Dover and ordered Hugh Bigod to hand over custody of the castle to Walerand. Bigod had served the king well over the past year, but Henry knew that could easily change once the annulment of the Provisions was announced.[17] He took possession of other castles in Kent, then went back to London and installed Mansel as the keeper of the Tower in place of Despenser. In doing all this, he secured passage for foreign mercenaries, who were being funded with another sizeable advance from Louis. Henry was just in time, for Montfort was on to him and making arrangements to bring over mercenaries of his own. The king ordered the bailiffs of the Channel ports to be on the alert for them and to prevent their landing.[18]

On 25 May, Mansel's nephew was back from Rome. It was on that very day that Pope Alexander died after a pontificate of seven years, but news of his death wouldn't reach England for weeks. Henry being Henry, the publication of the bulls had to be done with flourish and ceremony. In early June, he moved to his birthplace of Winchester, where thirty years earlier Peter des Roches had exhorted him to be a real king. At his side were the mercenaries, probably several dozen strong, plus a strong contingent of English knights provided by Edward and baronial supporters like John Balliol, Robert de Ros and the earls of Warwick and Devon. Henry may have had as many as 100 knights standing by when the feast of Whitsun arrived on Sunday 12 June 1261, which he marked by distributing shoes to the poor and feeding 500. Some time during the rituals of the day, a papal bull was produced that declared that no oath used for the 'depression of royal liberty' or 'depravity or perfidy' was valid. The king was therefore absolved of his oath to uphold the Provisions of Oxford. A second bull absolving everybody else in the realm was also published.[19]

Officially free of baronial control, Henry's first act was to dismiss Nicholas of Ely and Hugh Despenser from their offices as chancellor and justiciar. It was not personal, but they had both been appointed without his consent, and he could not accept any plan of government that denied him the right to choose his own ministers. The choice of their replacements nevertheless showed that he meant to be conciliatory. The new chancellor Walter Merton had served as vice-chancellor under the council and could count men like Clare as friends. The justiciar Philip Basset came from one of the most distinguished families in the land and was the father-in-law of two Montfortians, Despenser and John Fitz-John, the son of Fitz-Geoffrey.[20]

Simply by not abolishing the offices, Henry signalled to his opponents that there was nothing to fear, that this was no return to personal rule. They began preparing armed resistance just the same. Mansel appeared two days after the bulls' publication to urge Henry back to the Tower, both to play it safe and save on the costs of maintaining his foreign knights. No protests had materialised by the time he returned to London more than a week later, nor by 8 July when he went about dismissing castellans and sheriffs and replacing them with his own appointees. The barons were outraged by his overthrow of the Provisions but, short of war, they could see no effective response other than to co-opt the arbitration set to begin between Henry and Simon. The French arbitrators backed out, however, leaving them no one to turn to except Louis, but he too chose not to get involved.[21]

The essential problem for the barons was Henry's Tower diplomacy. It had neutralised any chance of intimidating him with a show of strength. Unable to confront him in person, they dared not force their way into the stronghold. That would constitute rebellion and give him every right to disinherit them. Edward's desertion left Montfort the only militant leader among them anyway. He was willing to take the risk because, unlike them, he could always start life anew in France. But they did have one advantage denied to their fathers and grandfathers when King John was absolved of obedience to Magna Carta more than forty-five years earlier. The Provisions and ordinances of the reform period had been promoted widely throughout the land. People were well aware of what had been going on over the past three years. They couldn't care less who the chancellor was, but their sheriff was a big deal. He hadn't been replaced after one year in the job as promised by reform. The eyres, moreover, were no longer of the special *querelae* type, but the old burdensome money-making judicial circuits. To the peasants and freeholders, it felt like the days before 1258 all over again.[22]

Since the barons couldn't go to the king, they went to the countryside and exploited this resentment. Their charge that Henry had been duplicitous in claiming to adhere to the Provisions while seeking to annul them resonated well, but they naturally made no mention of their own failure to renew the special eyre or change the sheriffs. Instead, they supported the locals in their resistance to the itinerant judges and installed their own anti-sheriffs in most counties.[23] These 'keepers of the peace' as they were called generally avoided direct confrontation with royal officials, but in Gloucester, William de Tracy ran afoul of Sheriff Matthew Bezill and his men when he attempted to hold court. He was grabbed, run through the mud and hauled off to jail. Henry thought Bezill was justified in his action, but it was a public relations disaster. Bezill came from Touraine originally, and although he had lived in England for nearly three decades and had an English wife, he was still seen as an alien. He had, moreover, risen through the queen's circle, which basically made him a Savoyard, and people like Montfort were working hard then to label that group the new Lusignans.[24]

Henry tried to allay local fears in a proclamation of 16 August 1261 from Windsor. All the discord, he said, was caused by evil-doers out to alienate him from the affections of his subjects. It wasn't true that he was out to oppress them with his new sheriffs. Quite the contrary, he was appointing household knights or magnates like the Earl of Warwick to protect the people from the barons, who had chosen mediocre sheriffs specifically so they could overawe them and so do what they liked in the counties. For forty-five years his reign had given the country peace and justice unlike any other time in its history, and he wasn't about to let a few troublemakers undermine it.[25]

He added that just the year before he had had to bring in mercenaries when the barons fought among themselves, and he might have to do so again to calm the situation. Simon went abroad to do some recruitment of his own, forcing Henry to warn Louis about what he was up to and ask him not to do the earl any favours. But where Montfort posed the biggest threat turned out to be in Rome. A new pope, Urban IV, was elected on 29 August, and Henry and his advisers felt it necessary to ask him to confirm Alexander's bull of absolution. Little did they realise that the Earl of Leicester had beaten them to it. With incredible speed and facility, he had an unnamed English clerk procure a bull from the papal court that actually confirmed Henry's oath to abide by the Provisions of Oxford. By the time royal proctors made their request for its annullment, Urban seemed angry and confused about what was going on. They had to explain that for a while the king did not have control of his seal, and that 'a certain earl' was working against him. It took several months for the proctors to sort it out, but by that time the damage had been done.[26]

Montfort had less luck trying to interest Llywelyn in an alliance, but upon his return to England, he joined Clare and Cantilupe in what was their most audacious act of defiance yet. They summoned three knights from every county to meet them in St Albans on 21 September 1261 for their own parliament, a rogue assembly to decide on their next course of action. But Henry bested them when he heard by summoning the same knights to meet him that very same day at Windsor. He had undercut his opponents again. While there is no record of a meeting taking place in St Albans, some local business was transacted with the king at Windsor during the last week in September.[27]

At the same time he was laying plans for the real Parliament to meet. On 18 October he ordered 150 tenants-in-chief to meet him by the end of the month with their full military service. The sheer number suggests he felt he had the majority of barons on his side. Among those left off the list were four earls, Montfort, Clare, Warenne and Bigod, but the Earl of Hereford could now be counted as loyal, as could Hugh Bigod. Yet by then Clare figured he had had enough. Through his stepfather, Richard of Cornwall, he arranged a peace conference between the king and recalcitrant barons. Some say it was Montfort's ever-growing radicalism that caused him to desert, others that it was the promises or favours of the queen.[28]

Whatever did it, negotiations were begun at Kingston-on-Thames, the ancient coronation site of Saxon kings located 10 miles southwest of London. A treaty was drawn up on 21 November 1261 that allowed each county to nominate four men for sheriff, and Henry would choose one of them. This was to be a provisional arrangement while a committee of three royalists and three barons arbitrated the contentious issues between them. Those who shunned the talks would have two weeks to seal the document, in person or by proxy, in order to receive a pardon. Simon de Montfort was the only one known to have refused. His stalwart companions Peter de Montfort and Walter Cantilupe not only went along with the treaty, but helped draw it up. In disgust, Simon left for France, saying he preferred to die without a country than abandon the truth.[29]

* * *

In the midst of this bickering, Richard's wife of nineteen years, Sanchia of Provence, died at Berkhamsted Castle aged about 35. Hardly the family man his brother was, Richard showed no signs of bereavement and put her executors to work on disposing of her property as the end drew near. He was not at her side when it came on 9 November 1261, ten years to the day after the dedication of the grand abbey he built at Hailes in Gloucestershire. It was fitting that she should be buried there, six days later, with her uncles Boniface and Peter of Savoy in attendance. Her husband, however, skipped the funeral to attend other matters, including securing the wardship and marriage of their 12-year-old son Edmund.[30]

Henry and Eleanor paid to have mass said daily for Sanchia's soul at the Tower, where they had again retreated on 14 October prior to the talks at Kingston. They did not emerge again until 9 December, four days after the treaty was ratified. All in all, they spent more than 170 days at the Tower in 1261, perhaps the least comfortable of their residences but vital to overthrowing the revolution of 1258. In his own standoff with the barons, King John would have gone insane cooped up there for so long. But his son got what John hadn't, victory over his opponents – and he achieved it without bloodshed, something unheard of in medieval England.[31]

It was nevertheless a relief to get back to Westminster for Christmas. Henry had been there for only two days throughout his Tower diplomacy, one of them naturally the feast of St Edward.[32] Edward was expected to join them. He had left the country in July as tensions began to mount, most likely to avoid the angry looks and contempt of Montfort and his cohorts. He did not arrive until late February, but could claim he had been working hard managing his duchy. A letter to the king that autumn indicated as much: 'Our lord Edward is in good and prosperous state, and by God's grace his affairs in Gascony are going well.' An audit of his accounts, however, showed there was going to be a reckoning when he got back. Several members of his household, purged during the upheaval of the previous summer, were charged with misusing his money or outright stealing it. They happened to be the same violent men whom the queen considered a bad influence on her son. In revealing them as shameless embezzlers, she hoped to sever his ties with them once and for all.[33]

The accused included Edward's former steward, Roger Leybourne. There was no denying he was a dangerous man. In 1252, he had killed another knight in a joust at the Waltham Round Table. Since the dead man had broken Leybourne's leg during a previous contest, he was suspected of not blunting his lance, which Clare, who was there, found out to be the case. Leybourne had avoided trial for murder by taking the cross and winning a pardon from the king.[34] Now, a decade later, Henry ordered him to pay back £1,820 missing from Edward's accounts. In April, Edward himself revoked the grant of a manor made to Leybourne eighteen months before. As Eleanor hoped, Leybourne's disgrace severed her son's relationship with him and the other men that formed their circle, including Henry of Almain and John de Warenne.[35]

Then it was Edward's turn. To avoid him running up debts and squandering his grants again, he was persuaded to hand over a large portion of his estates in England and Wales for three years in return for loans arranged by his mother from Italian merchants. The idea seems to have been to keep him busy with his overseas holdings until Henry could be sure of the political situation at home. Edward also agreed to swap his honour of Hastings for some manors held by Peter of Savoy up north in Richmond. Given the strategic importance of Hastings, the arrangement showed that the royal family did not yet have complete trust in him.[36]

Trust, of course, was the challenge facing Henry. He had overthrown the council, but not necessarily restored trust in his government. The arbitration certainly didn't help matters. When no agreement was reached, Richard of Cornwall stepped in as stipulated by the treaty and ruled that the king alone had the authority to name and remove the sheriffs. It was perhaps in anticipation of this outcome that Henry ordered the sheriffs, in May 1261, to publish in all the counties the bull of absolution he finally received from Urban and to arrest anyone caught preaching against it. But they were remiss in their duty, for Mansel noticed how woefully active this preaching was on a visit to Sussex. He could only wish the king enjoyed similar support from the friars.[37]

This was a sign that the grass-roots movement inspired by reform, and the clergy's role in it, was as strong as ever. Bishop Cantilupe remained a fervent advocate of the Provisions of Oxford despite his ratification of the Treaty of Kingston, and his friend Simon across the water was identified as their unrelenting champion. Henry understood better than anyone what a threat Montfort still posed to his rule and hoped to mollify him somehow, like continuing to pay his annual fees at the exchequer. Since no political settlement with him was likely without settling his private grievances first, Henry asked Queen Margaret to arbitrate their dispute. She agreed, and the English royal couple made plans to cross to France in the summer.[38]

It wasn't just for a single disgruntled baron that the king proposed to leave the country while political unrest remained. There were unresolved matters concerning the Treaty of Paris he was anxious to work out. The failure of the baronial council to do just that had been one of his bitterest complaints against their administration.[39] But perhaps the real reason was the desire of both couples to see each other again. Henry didn't hide that fact when Louis offered him one of two residences for his stay. He chose the one that allowed him and Eleanor to 'more easily enjoy your conversation and presence'.[40]

The visit was nevertheless awkward and ended up almost killing him. It started off with a bad omen when Richard de Clare died near Canterbury on 14 July 1262, just as they were sailing. He was not quite 40 years old at the time, giving rise to suspicions of poisoning again, but it was probably a chronic illness since he had been absent from court for most of the year. Clare's ginger-haired heir Gilbert crossed over after the royal party, and beseeched Henry of Almain and William de Valence to get him in to see the king. Although technically underage, he seems to have expected Henry to confirm him right away in his inheritance, to wave his hand and say, 'All right, it's yours.' But the king had already entrusted the Clare estate to custodians in order to keep others from doing what Boniface had done, moving in and seizing possessions held of them by the Earl of Gloucester. He also wanted to identify and reclaim all the assets Clare had appropriated from the crown during his ascendancy on the council. All this was within Henry's rights, but Gilbert was a touchy 18-year-old with a supreme sense of entitlement. Convinced he deserved more respect, he fumed and went home in a fit.[41]

There was also a problem when the two kings met again, although it was entirely Henry's fault. As the Duke of Aquitaine, he was summoned to *parlement* in Paris, but arrived too late to get any work done. The excuse he gave is that he passed many lovely churches on the way and couldn't resist stopping to hear mass at each of them. Louis kindly asked him to be on time the next day, but he was late again and for the same reason. Despairing of getting any work done with him like this, Louis ordered all the churches on his route closed until the King of England was safely out of sight. When later queried by Louis why he attended so many masses, Henry replied that it was for the same reason his French counterpart liked to hear so many sermons: it was just that he also liked to see his creator (elevation of the host) and not only hear about him.[42]

Presumably Henry was on time as the arbitration with Montfort got underway before Queen Margaret in August. Simon recounted the story of what brought him to England, his marriage to Eleanor and Henry's outburst at the churching twenty-three years earlier, when the king used 'ugly and shameful words which it would be painful to recall'.[43] He showed no gratitude at all for the fact that he owed his earldom and marriage to Henry, something Grosseteste had admonished him never to forget. For his part, Henry neglected to commend Simon for his service. Instead, he recalled the insults and insolence he had to put up with and how he almost lost Gascony on account of Montfort's tyrannical government there. He even ordered Gaillard de Soler to proceed to Paris with all speed to give evidence to that effect.[44]

Hearing all this from two men with strong ties to the French royal family, who were both eloquent even in their petulance, couldn't have been easy for Margaret, but she was probably more on Henry's side at the outset. An undercurrent of humour and affection characterised their relationship, and she could only admire her sister for having a husband willing to let her become a part of his life and reign. Her situation with Louis was still hopeless. He would never allow her to be regent the way Henry had empowered Eleanor. He didn't even trust her judgement to run her own household. Despairing for her future, she undertook to bind her son Philip, now heir to the throne, with an oath to listen to no one but her until he was 30. If he became king before then, he would be under her thumb the way Louis had been under Blanche's.[45]

In the event, she did not have to render a decision because an epidemic struck the English court in Paris. Henry, his son Edmund and Mansel fell gravely ill, and some sixty other members succumbed. The bishop-elect of London, who replaced Henry Wengham after his death in July, arrived to get confirmation of his election, but caught the disease and died. Not until 30 September was Henry able to get out of bed.[46] By then, Montfort was rumoured to be on his way to England to sow discord. On 8 October, Henry warned the regency council to be on the lookout for him. Simon appeared four days later, just as the barons were gathering for the feast of St Edward, and in defiance of the justiciar Basset, announced the papal bull acquired by his agent in Rome that seemingly confirmed the Provisions of Oxford. He then immediately returned to France, both to add a flourish to this propaganda ploy and to avoid detainment by Basset.[47]

He found much discontent in the land during his brief appearance. Roger Leybourne felt he had been framed in the investigation over Edward's finances and refused to accept Henry's order of distrainment against his lands. Originally from Kent, he sought shelter in the northern Marches from his brother-in-law Roger Clifford, whose sadistic uncle was once fined £666 for forcing a messenger to eat a letter from the king.[48] Clifford had also been purged from Edward's household and was eager to avenge himself on the queen and Savoyards, the people widely blamed for their dismissal. They began organising resistance and creating enough of a fuss for Basset to ban all tournaments. Other Marcher lords not involved in their transgressions made matters worse by conducting raids and reprisals against their Welsh neighbours. The death of Clare, who if nothing else had been a dominant force in the region, left several of his castles in South Wales vulnerable to attack should Llywelyn decide to retaliate.[49]

Henry was kept abreast of these developments, but upon regaining his strength he decided to make a pilgrimage to Reims. Mansel was stunned and urged him to return to England. He continued to urge him by letter after he had left the king's party.[50] But Henry persisted. He was not just travelling to discover new shrines and see new places; this was Reims, the great cathedral city where the Capetian kings were crowned, where Louis had been crowned. He knew he might not ever get another chance to see it, and since the cathedral was, like Westminster Abbey, undergoing reconstruction, it was also something of a fact-finding mission. He reached it on 10 November, managed to linger there for about ten days before heading towards the coast. He met Louis in Compiègne, where he implored him to get more involved in the dispute between Montfort and him. Simon had disturbed the kingdom of England for too long now, he told him.[51]

On 20 December, Henry and Eleanor returned to England after an absence of more than five months. They came home to a land enjoying its first bountiful harvest in six years, but a troubled land nevertheless. The inevitable war in the Marches had broken out three weeks earlier when the Welsh subjects of Roger Mortimer revolted and seized his castle of Cefnllys. Mortimer and his men were attempting to retake it when they found themselves surrounded by Llywelyn and his army and told to just walk away. They did, and after that Llywelyn overran other strongholds. From his Christmas court at Canterbury, Henry exhorted the

Marchers to take effective action, but save for the efforts of Peter de Montfort, their overall response was weak and uncoordinated. As the situation deteriorated, Henry wrote a heated letter to Edward about his responsibilities.[52]

> These things should cause you great concern. This is no time for laziness or boyish wantonness. It is a disgrace to you that Llywelyn spurns the truce which he promised to maintain with us, for I am growing old, while you are in the flower of early manhood; and yet, instigated by some men of my realm, he dares to do it.[53]

There was no question of Henry going there. He was again in ill health, and it was so cold that winter that the Thames froze from bank to bank. Henry would not leave Westminster for the next three months, even after a fire broke out at the palace on 7 February 1263. It caused extensive damage to his chamber and other buildings, but naturally he wanted to supervise the repairs and decorations himself.[54] This work offered a distraction from the growing disquiet that had compelled him to reissue the Provisions of Westminster on 22 January 1263. He took pains not just to give them the maximum publicity, but to declare that he was doing it of his own 'free will and power'. This was meant to show that he completely supported the reforms that affected the common people, and always had. Unlike the Provisions of Oxford, there had never been any hint of coercion. In addition, he agreed to observe 'other things to be provided' by Basset, the Bigods and, interestingly, Montfort. It's unclear what these things were, but on that same date he accredited two envoys to Louis to see if he might not, one last time, try to reconcile the Earl of Leicester.[55]

The envoys were instructed to meet Margaret first, who arranged to be present when they discussed their embassy at court. A few days later, Louis had a long talk with Simon, but on 22 February he reported to Henry that he was unable to bring him round. Simon had told Louis that he believed Henry wished him well, but there were people around him who were of a different mind. Since they were unwilling to procure peace, Simon was no longer able to do the same with honour. He therefore asked Louis to avail himself no more, but the King and Queen of France did make a last-ditch effort by having him meet the envoys himself. That conference too failed, and the envoys wrote to Henry that they were coming home. They would tell him in person 'certain things' that were bothering his adversary the most.[56]

The end of their mission coincided with the return of Edward, who was accompanied by a large troop of foreign knights. Henry had been putting together a force for him to lead against the Welsh, but was also trying to bring Llywelyn around to negotiation. Most of the Marchers were willing and peace talks were scheduled, but Mortimer wanted to avenge his humiliating surrender and pressed for an attack. Edward agreed, but got next to no support from the other Marchers. This had nothing to do with the Welsh, rather all those foreign knights he had with him.

Leybourne and Clifford had reckoned that Edward would turn to them for help and they would all be friends again. But he ignored them. He had new friends now and, making matters worse, they were aliens, just like the queen and the people around her who had engineered their disgrace. So the Marchers ignored him, but that didn't stop Edward. He left them to sulk and went ahead with his offensive. He had made little progress when, in May, had to break it off in response to events in England.[57]

Simon de Montfort was by then back in England. He had arrived on 25 April 1263, but Henry didn't find out for nearly a fortnight. That's when he reprimanded the bailiffs at Dover for allowing 'certain persons' to enter the country with horses and arms without permission. 'Don't let it happen again,' he warned them, but of course it was too late. Simon had come to make war, despite Henry's ongoing attempts to conciliate his opponents. After baronial treasurer John de Caux died in March, he had been replaced by another popular reformer, Nicholas of Ely. This was irrelevant to Montfort. It was not for the king to make official appointments. The Provisions of Oxford gave that power to the council, and Simon had sworn to defend them. As he saw it, his oath obliged him to make the Provisions the law of the land, regardless of what the king or pope thought, and that's what he aimed to do. Around 20 May, he convened a meeting of other disaffected nobles to devise a strategy to force the king to accept their tutelage.[58]

The location was Oxford, symbolic as the birthplace of reform five years earlier. Simon found many men there who never had anything to do with the movement, nor were they likely to be converts now. Leybourne, Clifford and Gilbert de Clare were only there because avenging themselves on the royal family was all they could think about. The same was true of others at the meeting, particularly Henry of Almain and John de Warenne. It will be remembered how the oath to the Provisions of Oxford had to be wrung out of these two but, like the Marchers, they had been abandoned by Edward and blamed the queen and Savoyards for it. But then everyone knew that Montfort himself had made sure to keep his own personal affairs at the forefront of his commitment.[59]

There was, however, a new aggrieved element in this, arguably, the first political party in English history, one that added legitimacy to their attempt to resurrect the Provisions. These were the young lords at the heart of what many barons felt was Henry's misguided policy over wards and marriages. Contemptuously called 'boys' by Thomas Wykes, another irascible chronicler in the vein of Matthew Paris, they included Henry Hastings and John de Vescy, who had been wards of Guy Lusignan and Peter of Savoy respectively. Robert de Ferrers, the new Earl of Derby, was given to Edward when his father died, even though they were the same age. Ferrers was also married to one of Henry's Lusignan nieces, as was Gilbert, who hated his wife Alice. Warenne loved his deceased Lusignan wife, but complained that he spent seventeen years as a ward, under Peter of Savoy.

The bitterness of these men guaranteed that a few scores were going to be settled before it was through, and they all but said so when, in renewing their oath together, they reiterated the special provision that declared anyone who opposed them a mortal enemy. Save the king and his family, naturally.[60]

★ ★ ★

Simon and Peter de Montfort were all that was left of the seven confederates who helped launch the reform movement. Richard de Clare and John Fitz-Geoffrey were dead, Hugh Bigod and Peter of Savoy were solidly behind the king and Roger Bigod had retreated to his estates in Norfolk. They still had the backing of veterans like Hugh Despenser and Richard Grey, and clergymen like Walter Cantilupe were as faithful as ever. And yet the letter sent to Henry demanding that he restore the Provisions of Oxford and proscribe his court of their enemies bore the seal of Roger Clifford, probably to remind Henry that the last war on English soil had broken out in the Marches. The letter was a formality in any case. They expected him to refuse, but wanted the semblance of justification for the assault they were now prepared to unleash.[61]

Their first target was carefully chosen. Apart from some diplomacy with the Welsh, Peter d'Aigueblanche, the Bishop of Hereford, had kept a low profile since the reform movement began. Paris claims he had a disfiguring skin disease, but it was really a matter of saving his own skin because, as one of the alleged masterminds of the Sicilian business, he was as hated as any of the Lusignans. He had little to do with the Savoyards' intrigues that had earned them such infamy of late, but that was beside the point. On 7 June 1263, he was seized in his cathedral, imprisoned in one of Clifford's castles and his lands ransacked. In Gloucester, Marcher henchmen attempted to mete out the same treatment to Matthew Bezill, the sheriff from the queen's circle who had run his baronial counterpart through the mud. He put up a good fight, though, and it took four days to overpower him at the castle and pack him off to join Aigueblanche.[62]

The lands of high-profile royalists were targeted next, including those of Mansel, Walerand and Simon Walton, the Bishop of Norwich, who had been instrumental in securing Henry's papal absolution. The spontaneity and speed at which the disorder spread across the realm suggest superb planning and coordination on Montfort's part. Henry was quick to respond, but other than securing Dover, he could not hope to stop the blitzkrieg.[63] He tried to get Simon to come to London to talk, telling him to bring the family, unarmed of course, but he was already en route to his main objective. His plan was to take control of the southern counties separating London and the ports, thereby denying Henry any chance of calling in help from the Continent. On 24 June, Montfort sent a letter of his own addressed to the people of London, asking where they stood in this conflict, and included in it a petition that spelled out what his party wanted. The Provisions of Oxford were to be 'strictly and inviolably' observed, though subject to possible concessions, and only 'trusty and skilful natives' were to run the country. That's the way it was done in other kingdoms and they wanted the same for England.[64]

London at that time was controlled by an oligarchic class. The *querelae* introduced by the reformers posed the first significant challenge to their privileges, but they had managed to retain their hold on the offices of the mayor and aldermen. The approach of Montfort's army now galvanised the city. Groups of horsemen were hired by the oligarchs to patrol the wards, but they attracted crowds who took to looting wherever they went. The mayor was Thomas Fitz-Thomas, who came from a wealthy family of drapers. Quite unexpectedly, he went over to the Montfortians and began ruling through the populist folkmoot, the medieval equivalent of a town hall meeting. He led a group of aldermen to the Tower to inform Henry that they intended to welcome the re-establishment of baronial rule.[65]

They found the king with Eleanor, Edward, Richard of Cornwall and Robert Walerand. The news about their change of political affiliation was bad enough, but neither they nor the other rich merchant families of the city would now lend the crown any money. Provisions were running low and Edward's mercenaries were not there for free. In anticipation of trouble, Henry had ordered payments to be made to the wardrobe, but they had yet to arrive and the money from the jewels pawned in May was already gone. What happened next was a mark of their plight, although who knew what and when about it is still a matter of debate.[66]

On 29 June 1263, Edward and Walerand left the Tower, picked up Edward's troop at Clerkenwell and left the city. This was what the Londoners wanted, for they didn't like foreign mercenaries hanging around. Once outside the gate, they turned south towards the river and came to the New Temple. Henry, who in his youth had expressed a desire to be buried there, had often used its vaults as a bank for making deposits and withdrawals. The cash crunch of the previous decade can be seen in his withdrawals of £9,500 against deposits of barely £300. Edward told the custodian at the treasury that he would like to check up on his mother's jewels on deposit there. It was a lame excuse, but seeing the glowering look on his face and those of his compatriots, the custodian handed him the keys and looked away. Having gained access to the vaults, Edward and his men produced hammers and went to work on the chests indiscriminately, taking as much coinage and valuables as they could carry off. In all, this first great bank robbery in English history yielded a little over £1,000, worth about £900,000 in today's money, which the gang took with them to Windsor.[67] From there they planned to intercept Montfort's advance.

That same day, Richard of Cornwall informed Henry that he was going to intercept Montfort himself. Presumably he said he wanted to try and talk some sense into him, but his own position at this time was suspect. The previous summer he had left again for Germany just before Henry's trip to France, but admonished him beforehand to make peace with Simon. Returning to England in February 1263, Richard found his brother still convalescing amidst growing discontent. Since it seemed like he might never recover, all men were ordered to swear fealty to Edward, which Gilbert de Clare pointedly refused to do. On 23 March, the Tewkesbury annalist heard that the king had died and wrote up an obituary for him. It was probably an honest mistake, but it was in this atmosphere that a rumour began to spread that Richard had in fact come home to England to succeed his brother. The Dunstable annalist even goes so far as to place him at the Oxford meeting with Montfort. Now, in his attempt to seek out Simon, he specifically asked Henry not to let Edward attack him. Simon's whole strategy depended on avoiding direct military confrontation, as open warfare before he had captured the government could only work against him. Maybe Richard knew this, maybe he didn't, but in any event Simon sent his messenger back with a note saying he had no time to talk.[68]

In the meantime, the situation in the Tower had become desperate. Hearing of the attacks on Savoyards and other courtiers, flight was the order of the day. Also on 29 June, as Edward and Walerand set out to rob the New Temple, Mansel fled the country while he still could. With Edmund, now 18 years old, he led a party of 'ladies from overseas' to Dover. There, Edmund took charge of the castle while Mansel and the ladies crossed over. The minute word of his escape reached the Montfortian ranks, Henry of Almain got it into his head to go after him, as if to bring him back in irons to stand trial. Mansel was much too clever to let that happen. When Almain arrived in Boulogne, a Savoyard knight was waiting and slapped irons on him instead.[69]

Almain's release was one of the terms brought to Henry by a coterie of bishops he had empowered on 4 July to sue for peace. The other terms included the transfer of castles to the barons, observance of the Provisions, rule by natives and the new, more ominous demand that all aliens be expelled from the realm 'never to return' save those found to be acceptable. The Montfortians originally wanted only the Savoyards and foreign mercenaries out, but discovered that the common people, in joining their uprising, were venting their own frustrations and resentment against Italian clerks, French moneylenders, Flemish merchants, basically anyone in their neighbourhood who couldn't speak English. The Jews spoke English, but were attacked just the same. If the Montfortians hadn't initially planned to arouse nationalist sentiment on this point, they were quick to exploit it. It was no longer enough to kick the aliens out of government, they had to be kicked out of the country entirely. By appealing to the masses in this manner, Montfort set himself up as the first populist leader in English history. The 'acceptable' clause was only added because passions were likely to die down at some point. When that happened, everyone would be able to see that some aliens were useful, starting with Montfort himself.[70]

The Archbishop of Canterbury likely fell into this category, but Boniface didn't wait to find out. He fled for the Continent with his brother Peter, whose estates were also in the path of Montfort's army. On 12 July, Simon completed his sweep when he reached Canterbury. There he was informed that London stood behind him and, more importantly, the king had accepted the barons' terms two days earlier. Henry had procured the release of Almain and dispatched the Bishop of London to take custody of Dover Castle from Edmund. All that was left for the rebellious barons to do was march into London in victory.[71]

The next day, 13 July 1263, the queen emerged from the Tower and boarded the royal barge at the wharf with various attendants. Her plan was to join Edward 27 miles upriver at Windsor, but as the boat approached London Bridge half a mile away, they could see an angry crowd of onlookers jeering at them. They were shouting 'whore' at her, which she probably didn't understand in English but the crew did. The worst was to come as the boat came into range and the people began pummelling them with rocks, debris, any objects they could get their hands on. Edward's actions had inflamed them and other inhabitants of the city beyond measure. They had already sacked several properties belonging to prominent royalists, aliens, anybody who made a convenient target. Try as the oarsmen might, there was no way to get under one of the narrow arches of the bridge with the hailstorm of missiles and filth raining down on them.

Mayor Fitz-Thomas was alerted to the disturbance at the bridge. Knowing it was his head if any harm came to the queen, he hastily organised a rescue party with the militia he kept close at hand. They managed to escort her boat back to the wharf, only to find that the king, according to the Dunstable annalist, had given orders not to admit them. Taken together with the claim of the *Flores* annalist that the queen had left in the first place because she refused to accept the peace terms, it might appear that the royal couple had had a spat and she had abandoned him to his fate. Now he was having his revenge by leaving her to the mob. The more probable scenario is that they both decided she should leave the Tower for her own safety. There was no telling what the people of London were capable of now that their fury was worked up. Perhaps watching the outrageous spectacle from the ramparts, Henry realised that any attempt to dock back at the wharf would only draw in the crowds and cause a riot, so he ordered Fitz-Thomas to find an alternate landing point and conduct her to the relative calm of St Paul's.[72]

She had rejoined him at the Tower by the time the Montfortian army entered the city two days later on 15 July, and Henry formally accepted the peace agreement the following day. Simon must have been delighted as the king and queen left the Tower and took up residence at Westminster. He had learned his lesson from the way Henry used the fortress against them in 1261. This time, when Henry retreated to it as expected, he was welcomed to stay there, out of harm's way, while Simon went about isolating him from the rest of the realm. Once that was done, all he had to do was wait for Henry to come out of his own accord. So it was, making Simon's victory in 1263 every bit as impressive as Henry's had been two years earlier.

The difference, however, was that Henry had won his victory without violence. The pillaging and destruction that accompanied Simon's had forever tarnished the Provisions of Oxford. The provision that sanctioned the use of force against opponents had never been tried until now, and the result was mayhem and a pathological hatred of foreigners. And yet Montfort was aware it would come to this before setting out. They were on a crusade as he saw it, with men he likened to 'the army of God'. As the son of the most famous and ferocious crusader of their time, he might have justified it all by saying that God's work was never easy or pretty.[73]

For now, he still had to deal with Edward who, after missing his chance to ambush the Montfortians, had led his forty foreign knights westward to exact revenge on his former Marcher friends. But the inhabitants of Bristol rose up and besieged them in the castle. Edward asked Walter Cantilupe to rescue them, promising he would go to London and make peace with his uncle. This was arranged, but Edward broke his word and led his men back to Windsor to continue the resistance. Montfort gathered troops to take the castle by force if need be, and Henry came along to prevent the talks between these two hotheads from erupting in violence. According to *Flores*, the day was won by a trick concocted by Montfort and Cantilupe. Edward came out to treat for peace and they simply didn't let him go back inside. His knights surrendered on 1 August 1263 and were escorted to the coast, where they caught passage over. As unwanted aliens, they were asked to swear they would never return 'unless summoned by the whole community'.[74]

The first order of business for the new Montfortian government was to pick up where the last reform administration left off. Their campaign seemed frightening and radical, but in the end what they wanted was to go back to 1258. That was hardly possible with so many members of the original council dead, neutral or hostile. Of the fifteen, only Simon, Peter de Montfort, Richard Grey and Walter Cantilupe were ready to take up their posts again. The offices of chancellor and justiciar were easier to settle. Merton and Basset were replaced by the men who had held the posts under the barons, Nicholas of Ely and Hugh Despenser.[75] Henry's sheriffs were not removed, just given a new job description. They were now to act as agents of the exchequer and collect money. Actual law enforcement would be done by keepers of the peace, local Montfortians who had stirred up trouble during the uprising. This could be seen as a concession, but the truth was that the council wanted to avoid further violence breaking out. The old sheriffs would slowly be eased out over time.[76]

There was one sheriff who wouldn't be coming back, though. Matthias Bezill, the alien bruiser who had proved more than a match for an any single Marcher, was released along with Peter d'Aigueblanche by resolution of the first Montfortian Parliament. The Bishop of Hereford wisely left the country, but Bezill had nowhere else to go. He had been in England as long as Montfort and had his family there. Bezill was more than qualified for the job, but Clifford wanted his reward and weaselled his way into the post of Sheriff of Gloucestershire.[77]

As in the first reform period, the regime was set up as a parliamentary state. All 'common business' of the government was subject to review by the representative body of the nation. The assembly met at St Paul's on 9 September 1263 and got off to a good start by approving the peace terms, but the discussion turned acrimonious when the restitution of confiscated estates was brought up. Owners deemed suspect had been allowed to reclaim their lands after swearing to observe the Provisions, but this didn't mean they all got them back. The new occupants saw nothing in their oaths that said they had to surrender their estates or provide compensation. For all his skills as an orator and operator, Montfort couldn't make the men who had brought him to power disgorge their spoils. He had made a pact with the devil, and the devils were holding him to it.[78]

He played his own part in Parliament's failure to allay suspicions and resentment. He was acknowledged as the undisputed leader of the government, but felt he needed a title that evoked more authority than simply the Earl of Leicester. His earldom provided the solution, for it conferred the ancestral title of 'steward' on him. He now aimed to make it more than honorary, certainly with more authority than waiting on the king at the banquet table. It would signify him as first among equals, akin to a modern prime minister. But his intention struck some as boastful and unscrupulous, and because the office of steward was hereditary, it would go to Henry de Montfort after him. This naturally aroused concerns over his real agenda.[79]

The move that most enraged the king and queen was Simon's appointment of two deputy stewards for the royal household. One was Leybourne, who by this act 'was made Paul from Saul', noted one chronicler. He was the man Eleanor hated above all others. He had led her son astray with his corrupt, sinister ways, then masterminded Montfort's return and the orchestration of attacks on her relatives and other Savoyards. Simon wasn't deliberately trying to make her more miserable by insinuating him into her life, however. Like Clifford, Leybourne wanted his reward, and the Montfortians were still dependent on the Marchers for support. But it was a matter of principle for Henry. He didn't want Simon or anyone else naming his officials for him, least of all in his household. Yes, the lord king deserved more respect, they answered, but measures had to be taken to make sure he brought no more aliens into government. That's what he had agreed to.[80]

This was essentially another great departure from 1258. The baronial regime now had to work with a distinctly hostile monarchy. Montfort made efforts at reconciliation by banishing no aliens and permitting Henry to make personal gifts, notably the marriage rights of Isabel de Forz, the richest widow on the wedding market, to his son Edmund. Walerand even received a pardon for his part in the robbery of the New Temple, but the indignities inflicted on the queen ruled out any chance of these two families, who had once been close, ever coming together again for Christmas breakfast.[81] And the same might well apply to his brother Richard of Cornwall. The baronial army was just then encamped at his private park in London, almost as if by invitation, and he was given a valuable wardship by Montfort. The pope for one thought Richard was at least complicit in the 'boisterous fluctuation of the storm' that was engulfing England and told him so in a scathing letter. The rebellion was raised 'with your tacit permission, perhaps even stirred up by you'. Urban believed that with his wealth and influence Richard could have stopped it had he wanted to.[82]

Henry got a letter at that time too, a response to his efforts to revive the Sicilian business with Urban. It took more than a year for the pope to reply, but his decision of 28 July 1263 was devastating. The offer was withdrawn. The vendetta against Manfred was still on, it's just that Henry had had more than nine years and nothing had come of it. Edmund was already a grown man, for heaven's sake. But just so there were no misunderstandings, the king's original crusading vow was switched back to the Holy Land.[83]

Henry could at least count on the pope to condemn Montfort's coup, but Urban was a man who needed time to act. On the other hand, there was Louis, who was a friend, brother-in-law and like-minded king. At Henry and Eleanor's prompting, Louis summoned Henry, as his lord for Aquitaine, to appear before him. Simon saw that no good would come from Louis getting involved at this stage and tried to put him off with two separate diplomatic missions, but Louis was insistent. Parliament agreed that the entire royal family could go abroad upon their oath to return and sent Montfort ahead of them with a baronial delegation.

The conference held in Boulogne on 23 September 1263 attracted wide attention. Charles of Anjou and many leading French nobles and bishops were there, as was Beatrice of Savoy, who expressed her outrage over the London mob's treatment of her daughter. A belligerent audience of Savoyard exiles and their families tried to arraign the Montfortians for inciting rebellion against their king, but Simon rejected any notion that the affairs of England were subject to outside jurisdiction. He made the case for the regime and managed to convince Louis of the merits of the Provisions. No official judgement was given, but the King of France sympathised with Simon's cause and agreed that England should be run by natives. His only condition was full restitution for the despoiled. Simon and his team went home rejoicing, but Henry didn't rage or call Louis an apostate and imposter. He might have thought he was more than a little foolish, but the fact that Montfort had been forced to defend his actions was victory enough. It broke up his momentum. Leaving Eleanor and Edmund in France, Henry returned with the intention of keeping Simon on the defensive.[84]

Events moved quickly after that. At the Parliament held in October, Henry refused to countenance the council naming his household personnel and demanded that restitution be made before any other business went forward. As the debate grew heated, Edward left to see his wife Eleanor of Castile at Windsor. By this time, they had been married for nearly nine years, had an infant daughter and were as famously close as his parents. The next day, Henry joined him with a large retinue.[85] It was a well-planned operation, for suddenly Simon was deserted by many of his followers. He should have known it was coming. In August, Edward won Henry of Almain and John de Warenne back to his side with several grants from his wife's dower. These two then went to work on the Marchers, who had never been advocates of the Provisions, and persuaded them to be Edward's friends 'in all things', with the promise of forgiveness and patronage. Edward had to proceed cautiously, however, knowing as he did that his mother would freak out to learn that these ruffians would be both forgiven and reinstated. It was for this reason that Henry left Eleanor behind in France with Edmund, contrary to their oaths.[86]

Distasteful as this wholesale accommodation of traitors was, it proved effective. Simon was still supported by London, the clergy and the younger crowd, but now even the formally neutral earls of Norfolk and Hereford joined Henry at Windsor. It wasn't an easy decision for some to blatantly switch sides so soon, and Henry of Almain felt compelled to go to Simon in person and explain his reasons. He simply did not have it in him, he said, to continue to oppose his father, Richard of Cornwall, who had seemingly learned his lesson and rejoined his brother, or the king himself. But he wanted Montfort to know that he would never take up arms against him. By this time, Simon was in a right sour mood and had just ejected Hugh Bigod from London for prevaricating too long about his loyalty. When his nephew Almain, whom he generally seems to have liked, gave him this set speech, he just laughed and told him to come with all the arms he pleased. He wasn't afraid of them. If he had had anything to fear in the young man, it was his inability to stand by his principles. He seemed the worst example of the Englishman turning tail when adversity set in. Montfort then made a set speech of his own to the world:

> I have been in many lands and among many nations, Christian and pagan, but nowhere have I found such infidelity and deceit as I have met in England. Even if everyone falls away from me, I with my four sons will stand by fearless for the just cause which I have already sworn to uphold, to the honour of the church and the utility of the realm, nor will I fear to undergo war.[87]

It was a righteous declaration that didn't sit well with some who weren't necessarily for the royalists. A circular going around at this time criticised Montfort for promoting his family, for favouring some aliens over others and, at 55, for being old. It was probably written by someone connected to Gilbert de Clare, who considered himself the type of young, vigorous leader the reform movement needed if it hoped to survive. The circular also accused Montfort of leaving England vulnerable to interdict and the coming of a legate.[88] This follows action taken by Urban, who expressed his dismay over all the disturbance and sent letters to various personages, including the 'chief disturber of the realm' Simon de Montfort. On 22 November, he appointed a legate to go to England and sort out the mess.[89]

This was not good news for the bishops, who were now mostly committed to Montfort. Some of it was personal. Cantilupe and Richard Gravesend, the Bishop of Lincoln, were friends of his and devotees of Grosseteste, but others were simply opposed to the business of provisions for foreigners and the king interfering in their affairs.[90] They looked first to Magna Carta for protection, now to the Provisions. As archbishop, Boniface had stood up to Henry, but he was likely lost after being driven from the country, and if he came back with a legate, it would only make life worse for them.

It was best to achieve peace before then, and a trio of bishops led by Cantilupe arranged for both sides to submit their dispute to Louis for arbitration, each taking an oath to observe whatever he decreed. Simon withdrew to Kenilworth after that, but Henry went about reclaiming the machinery of government. With a large force of men, he went to Oxford and recovered the chancery. On 3 December, he appeared in front of Dover. The garrison professed their loyalty to him, but said they could not turn over the castle without the permission of the castellan, Richard Grey, who was absent.

Unwilling to storm the place just yet, Henry learned that his move against Dover had brought Simon back to London with a small army. He ordered the city authorities to throw them out and marched back in that direction. When he reached Croydon, he was informed by four wealthy Londoners that the Montfortians were camped outside the city in Southwark, on the south bank. That was 10 miles to the north of his position. What's more, these same citizens had hatched a plan to bar the gates of London Bridge to them. If the king moved on them, they would be trapped in the bend of the Thames. On 11 December, Simon found that was indeed the case. With Henry advancing on him, he refused his call to surrender; rather, he told his men to confess their sins and make ready to fight to the last. The plot, however, was discovered in time. A mob broke open the gates, swarmed into Southwark and escorted the Montfortians within the safety of London's walls.[91]

It was a bitter disappointment for Henry, for all his troubles seemed to come down to this one man. He had no choice but to agree to a truce in preparation for the arbitration. On 16 December, he sent his letters to Louis, three days after Montfort had done likewise. His list of supporters was far more impressive, with at least three earls (Norfolk, Warenne and Hereford) and two major barons (Basset and Hugh Bigod). Simon had no one of comparable rank save for Peter de Montfort and Hugh Despenser. Robert de Ferrers, the Earl of Derby, had joined him in Southwark but, like Gilbert, was unstable and kept aloof. He did have two bishops on his side, Cantilupe and Henry of Sandwich (London), while no clerics stood by the king.[92]

Although Henry enjoyed the advantage at this point, he was still losing the propaganda war. He had tried to retake Dover, it was preached, so he could bring in an alien force. On 20 December, he issued a manifesto from Windsor denying this and ordering an end to unauthorised taxes being collected locally for a home guard. He went on to declare that most of the barons were now on his side and those still defying him would soon be repressed. And make no mistake about it, he would always be willing to keep the oath he made at Oxford. He followed up four days later with the appointment of senior royalists to serve as military governors in the counties where he was strongest. He didn't bother in the Midlands and adjacent areas, where Montfortian anti-sheriffs were still in control.[93]

If the king's professed willingness to respect his oath rang hollow, another move of his at this time was seen as positively scandalous. The experience in Boulogne had shown that Montfort was the key to his opponents receiving another favourable ruling from Louis. Since Henry had failed to capture him at Southwark, he devised a scheme to prevent him from attending the arbitration. It involved Roger Mortimer, who had been on the fence for much of the reform period because he was angry at both Henry and Simon. His attempt to recover a manor called Lechlade had been thwarted when the king gave it to Richard of Cornwall. The council turned a deaf ear to his pleas, but in 1259 they gave Montfort nine manors for his wife's settlement, and three of them edged up against Mortimer's lordship in the Welsh Marches. Henry was never happy about this grant, and now saw a way to get his revenge on Montfort while simultaneously winning over Mortimer. He told him to forget about Lechlade, he could have the three neighbouring manors instead. The only condition was that it had to be now. It would drive Simon west to take them back and away from the arbitration.[94]

Mortimer seized the opportunity, but Montfort didn't take the bait. He knew too much was riding on the outcome of the meeting at Amiens, where Louis was to render his decision. His cohorts were counting on his prestige, persuasiveness and friendship with the King of France to win them the outside support and legitimacy they needed. Some time around Christmas, he left Kenilworth to catch a boat over, but 25 miles into his journey he turned off to visit Catesby Priory, where two of Edmund of Abingdon's sisters had been nuns. If he was hoping to evoke a miracle at one of his relics there, he got exactly the opposite when his horse tumbled. Simon was thrown to the ground and broke his leg in the fall. He would not be making the case after all.[95]

15

IN THE YEAR OF OUR LORD 1264

This would be Henry's fifth trip to France but, like Simon, he almost didn't make it. Leaving England on 2 January, his ship encountered a storm so violent and terrifying that, according to the Dunstable annalist, Edward panicked and poured forth prayer after prayer. It took a toll on Henry too. He was ill on arrival in Boulogne and had to cancel his initial appearance in Amiens for the arbitration. On 8 January, Walter Merton made the case for him before Louis. The barons, he declared, had usurped the king's authority over appointments and wreaked havoc throughout the land. He was seeking nullification of the 'constitutions' at the heart of the discord and £433,000 in damages. Merton had been brief and to the point, and for his efforts was granted the privilege of taking 'one or two deer' from any forest he passed through in England for the rest of his life.[1]

Even without Montfort, the baronial side had a very able advocate in Thomas Cantilupe, the nephew of Walter and cousin of Peter de Montfort. He was lately the chancellor of Oxford and had met Louis during his studies in Paris. His argument was six times longer and read like an indictment. The king oppressed the Church, favoured aliens, squandered resources, cheated merchants, sold or denied justice and ravaged all the lands that fell into his hands. He had done all this in violation of Magna Carta, and so provisions had to be enacted, with his blessing it must be remembered, to remedy these abuses. As for damages, the money wasted on the Sicilian business alone exceeded the figure cited.[2]

On 23 January 1264, Louis gave his decision. He began by reminding everyone that all parties to the arbitration had sworn to abide by whatever award he issued, 'high and low'. In going through the formalities, he repeated their oath twice more, a clear sign that a bombshell was ahead, and it was:

> In the name of the Father, and of the Son, and of the Holy Spirit, by our award or ordinance we quash and invalidate all these provisions, ordinances, and obligations, or whatever else they may be called, and whatever has arisen from them or has been occasioned by them.

He also nullified the statute that reserved the right of rule to natives only and banned aliens from the realm. All castles and appointments were to be restored to the king, and he was to have the 'full power and free authority' that he enjoyed before the time of the Provisions. The King of France concluded by calling on both sides to renounce all malice and ill feeling arising from their dispute. Despite receiving no damages, Henry signalled his full acceptance of the award the next day by declaring a general amnesty.[3]

Given that Louis had approved the Provisions only a few months earlier, it might seem that the horse that buckled beneath Simon de Montfort had changed the course of history. In fact, it's doubtful that even Simon could have made a difference. Louis had been under sustained pressure from his wife and the exiles at court to reverse himself. The Tewkesbury annalist says that Eleanor was particularly effective in 'beguiling and deceiving him with the serpentlike fraud and speech of a woman'.[4] But the arrogance and overkill of Cantilupe's case didn't help. He wasn't so much defending the Provisions as attacking the king. Whatever Henry's faults, he wasn't an oppressive ruler in any sense of the word. There was nothing in the charges about him hounding his opponents or locking them up, God forbid, even executing them. He certainly deserved more respect than being called plain 'king' in the same sentence where Louis was addressed as 'illustrious king'. Louis may also have suspected that Cantilupe was trying to bind his hands by linking the Provisions to Magna Carta, as if to declare the former untouchable by virtue of its association with the latter. He was having none of it, but played it safe by adding the proviso that all charters and liberties in existence before 1258 were unaffected by his ruling. Magna Carta would remain enshrined for all time, but the Provisions of Oxford were history.

In nullifying the Provisions, Louis noted that he was doing no more than two popes had done before him. This attempt to hedge his decision belied a new common cause between the papacy and French monarchy that couldn't have made Henry very happy. While he had been trying to revive the Sicilian business, Urban was busy wooing Charles of Anjou to become the new papal champion against Manfred. He would be the King of Sicily and not Edmund. Louis struggled over whether to give his consent, knowing how bad it would look to Henry and Eleanor. Urban told him to forget about his conscience, the Church came first.[5] In disposing of Henry's baronial problem once and for all, Louis may have thought he was making it up to him. He and Margaret had already taken a step in that direction after the conference in Boulogne by asking the pope to dispatch a legate to

England. He was Guy Foulquois, an intimate who had served the Capetian brothers well in his days as a secular administrator, but Louis's lobbying for any legate was a sign that the Montfortian case was lost long before Simon got up on his horse.[6]

As to why the Montfortians had risked his unofficial verdict in favour of the Provisions in the first place, they were hoping to break up Henry's momentum much as he had done theirs at Boulogne. They knew they were a spent force militarily, with no way to impose any terms found unacceptable by the king, which were likely to be all the ones that counted. They may have had their doubts about whether Montfort could pull off another convincing performance and win them international recognition from a man widely admired, but in preparing such an elaborate case, they were at least hoping that Louis would see the need for an itemised approach to the problem. They certainly didn't expect him to sweep away the reform programme in the blink of the eye, as if, in the words of one historian, Henry had drafted the award himself.[7] The shock of the chroniclers bears this out. The Dunstable annalist declares that Louis was 'unmindful of his own honour', adding, 'he had neither God nor the truth before his eyes when he made his pronouncement.' Even the anti-Montfortian Wykes questions whether the King of France exercised the proper wisdom and foresight required for the task.[8]

The uncompromising nature of the Mise of Amiens, as the award is known today, led London, the Channel ports and 'nearly all the middling men of the kingdom' to reject it out of hand. Montfort and his immediate followers did the same despite their pledge to abide by whatever Louis decided. To avoid the charge of perjury, they convinced themselves that to accept it would violate their oath to the Provisions, which was a sacred, if not superior oath. They could also add their relatively new claim that the Provisions of Oxford and Magna Carta were inextricably linked. It was impossible to confirm one and invalidate the other in the same breath. Seen in terms of political evolution, there was much to commend this argument. By appropriating the executive functions of the crown, the Provisions became the instrument of enforcement that Magna Carta had always woefully lacked.[9] But it was too late to get into theory now. The whole point was to find an excuse to make war with a good conscience.

It's unlikely that Montfort would have retired from the scene in any case. Mortimer had provoked a war with him prior to Amiens. Still laid up at Kenilworth, he now sent his older sons and a troop of men to give him all the war he wanted. Richard of Cornwall, acting as regent from Windsor, learned of their advance on 4 February and ordered the bridges over the River Severn broken. Three days later he was in Oxford, where Edward had returned ahead of his father. Together they set out to help Mortimer, but he had already fled when the Montfortians appeared and began pillaging and burning his lands and castles. Lacking the strength to drive them out, Edward and Mortimer found an easier target in the Earl of Hereford's namesake son Humphrey de Bohun. He had refused to follow his father back to the king's side, but for Mortimer it was personal. He and the younger Bohun were married to sisters, Marshal granddaughters, and were feuding over their wives' inheritances.

Henry had stayed behind in France to settle the money Louis owed him under the Treaty of Paris. Finally fixed at £33,500, a balance of £14,500 was still outstanding. This allowed him to redeem the crown jewels that were pawned in Paris in 1261 and build up the war chest he was going to need upon his return home. Arriving in Dover on 15 February, he was again refused admittance to the castle. He moved on to Canterbury, where he spent nine days recuperating from his journey and managing a very delicate affair concerning the archbishop. Boniface had drawn up a list of perpetrators he planned to sue for their recent destruction of church property during the summer offensive. The Montforts were included, which was welcome, but so too were Leybourne and the other Marchers, who had since switched sides. While in France, Henry promised Boniface that they would answer for their crimes. Now, needing Leybourne's support in his native Kent, particularly against Dover and the Channel ports, Henry gave him a full pardon on 28 February, declaring that he would answer for him. On that same day in Rochester, where his court had since moved, he received news of the birth of his second grandson, a future Alexander IV of Scotland, it was hoped. His first grandson incidentally had been born to Beatrice and John of Brittany in July 1262 and was poignantly named Arthur. As one who believed in laying old ghosts to rest, Henry could only have approved of the choice.[10]

He reached Windsor on 4 March. Two days later, he summoned the feudal host to muster at Oxford, adding that 'those against the king' need not bother. Officially, they were to move against Llywelyn, who had lately made a pact of alliance with the Montfortians but had so far not intervened in the escalating hostilities in the Marches. At the end of February, the strongly royalist Worcester was sacked by combined forces under Robert de Ferrers, the Earl of Derby, Peter de Montfort and Henry de Montfort. They then moved on towards Gloucester, which had fallen to Marcher lord John Giffard after he and some of his men slipped in through the gate disguised as wool merchants. The castle still held out, and on 5 March, Edward and Henry of Almain fought their way inside to bolster the garrison. The foolishness of that move became apparent when Ferrers and the Montforts arrived on the scene with their forces. Realising he was trapped, Edward asked Walter Cantilupe for help and the bishop arranged a truce that called for both sides to withdraw and enter peace talks. Henry de Montfort complied, but no sooner were he and his allies gone than Edward turned on the townspeople for allowing themselves to be duped by Giffard. He robbed and terrorised them before leaving to continue the war in the countryside. Simon upbraided his son for allowing Edward to escape, knowing that he had pulled a similar stunt the year before, again with Cantilupe as intermediary. Ferrers was also furious, for he and Edward loathed each other. As in any civil war, the two of them used the fight over the Provisions as an opportunity to settle their personal scores.[11]

The king arrived in Oxford on 8 March. Four days later he ordered the chancellor of the university to leave and take his students with him. They had engaged in another spring riot and, given their youthful inclination towards the Montfortians, he was concerned that war might break out right there in the town with so many of his armed supporters pouring in. The next day, 13 March, he empowered proctors to treat for peace at a conference in nearby Brackley. The initiative came from Louis, who sent an experienced diplomat personally known to both Henry and Simon to see if he might not succeed where he had failed. Now able to get around by coach, Montfort arrived with his trusted friend Walter Cantilupe and two relatively new bishops, John Gervais of Winchester and Stephen Berksted of Chichester. These last two had shown no overt sympathy for Montfort before recent events but, as with many others, there was something about the man himself that drew them into his circle.[12]

Henry would have seen it in more cynical terms. It was exactly thirty years ago that a different set of bishops had all but ganged up on him in defence of Richard Marshal's irrational and destructive war against aliens at court. Indeed, Montfort and his bishops now surprisingly offered to accept the Mise of Amiens if the king agreed to get rid of the foreigners and rule through native men only. Like that, the Provisions would be abolished to everyone's satisfaction. But again, his brother-in-law, that consummate political animal, was being too clever by half. Simon wasn't making the offer to Henry, but to Louis, to show him that he wished to abide by his judgement, and to his base, to reassure them that he was all about England for the English. The offer was rejected, as it was meant to be, because it restricted the king's right to name whoever he wanted as his ministers.[13]

This impasse made conflict inevitable. Perhaps to steel himself for it, Henry first set out to dispel a curse. According to an ancient Saxon legend, a lustful king intent on ravishing a noble abbess was struck blind after he pursued her to Oxford. For 500 years, no other king had dared go anywhere near her tomb, or even enter the town for that matter, for fear of meeting the same fate. On 25 March, Henry walked barefoot into the convent named after her, St Frideswide, to make his devotions and celebrate mass. Before leaving in good health, he gave the church a pension of £5 to employ a chaplain and pay for candles. By this time, Edward had joined Henry in Oxford, but declined to make the visit with him, nor would he during his own many years as king.[14]

Meanwhile, the Londoners were itching for a fight. At the tolling of the great bell of St Paul, a mob followed the constable, the marshal and Hugh Despenser, who was in charge of the Tower, on a tour of properties belonging to Richard of Cornwall, Philip Basset and other prominent royalists. At each stop, they ransacked the homes, uprooted the orchards, even emptied Richard's prized fishpond.

Officials of the court and exchequer were then rounded up and imprisoned. If the point was to impress the king with a show of strength, it certainly aroused his fury. He broke off the peace talks and, unfurling his dragon standard, marched his men out of Oxford on 3 April.[15]

His brother would have preferred to descend on London to exact revenge. Simon had, in fact, gone there in expectation of the king doing just that. Henry, however, merely sent out orders to secure the surrounding castles in the event the Londoners attempted to ravage the neighbouring countryside. His course was 40 miles northeast to Northampton, which was the gateway to the Montfortian-held Midlands. The city had been reinforced with men who had recently fought in the Marches and was seemingly in a good position to defy the king when he appeared outside the walls two days later and ordered them to surrender. Somehow word had reached Henry beforehand that the prior of St Andrews had weakened the wall adjacent to the priory's garden near the north gate. As one royalist force began battering the south gate on 5 April, the main body was able to breach this section of the wall. The younger Simon de Montfort, who was in command of the garrison, twice drove them back, but he was then thrown from his horse and captured. The city was stormed up to the castle, which Peter de Montfort surrendered the next day. The prisoner haul included the two Montforts and nearly sixty barons and knights along with their foot soldiers.[16]

The king moved on to Leicester which, like Oxford, was another town no king had dared to enter on account of superstitions associated with the place. Just the fact that it was home to Simon's earldom was enough for Henry to shrug off that spell as well. The townspeople paid him £333 for his grace and entertained him in great style before he continued north to Nottingham, where he was expecting reinforcements from the northern barons. Edward wasn't with him. He turned west towards Derbyshire to continue his feud with Ferrers, burning his manors as he went and capturing his castle at Tutbury. Henry de Montfort scored a victory for his father when he and Giffard, working out of Kenilworth, took and destroyed the castle belonging to William Maudit, who had become the Earl of Warwick at the death of John de Plessis in early 1263.[17]

Informed that Northampton was under siege, Simon headed that way with a relief force, but only got as far as St Albans, 20 miles out, when word came that it had fallen. Panic now gripped London as rumours spread that the city was about to be given up to the king through treachery. The Jewish community was accused of having made replica keys to the gates and storing up incendiaries to set off in various parts of the city. During the night of 9 April, a mob set upon them and massacred more than 500 before dawn. Those who survived were given shelter in the Tower by Despenser and Fitz-Thomas, but Despenser's brother-in-law John Fitz-John was said by Wykes to have personally killed the most distinguished Jew in the city, Cok the son of Abraham. Wykes also implicates Simon in this atrocity by his order to Fitz-John and the other perpetrators to turn over most of their plunder for the sustenance of his army.[18]

The Jews of Canterbury were also despoiled at this time by men under Gilbert de Clare. The Earl of Gloucester had finally committed himself to the Provisions party and came up from his castle at Tonbridge for a joint operation against Rochester, which lay 30 miles to the east of London. Simon had chosen Rochester because, as a royalist stronghold, it could cut off his links with Dover and the Continent. He also needed to make a move that would draw Henry's forces south, where his odds were much better. The initial assault on 17 April was easily repelled thanks to an ingenious defence devised by the garrison of Rochester. After pulling down the bridge that stood on the rebel side of the River Medway, they used their own half of it, now well fortified, to beat off Montfort's attacks before he got close to the gate. The next day Montfort deployed his own trick by having boats filled with pitch, coal and pork fat set alight and sent down the river into this jutting section of the bridge. It caught fire, and in the confusion and destruction that followed, he and his men crossed the river and took the town. Although it was Good Friday, hordes of them sacked the cathedral and other parts of the town. Montfort and Clare were probably unaware of the sacrilege as they pushed their assault right up to the great tower, where Warenne, Leybourne, Almain and the rest of the garrison were holed up with plenty of fish and wine.[19]

Henry at last reacted as planned and began moving his forces south, but the speed and vigour of his march again caught Montfort off guard. Even going the long way around London, the royalists covered the 150 miles between Nottingham and Croydon in six days. Worried about being cornered and hearing reports of more treacherous activity in London, Montfort and Clare left behind a skeleton force to continue the siege of the tower and retreated to London during the night of 25 April. When Henry learned of their withdrawal, he broke off his march long enough to take Clare's castle at Kingston before reaching Rochester on 28 April. The remnants of the rebel force were easily overwhelmed, and some of them had their hands and feet mutilated as punishment for defiling the town. Henry next headed south towards the coast, seizing Gilbert's castle at Tonbridge along the way.[20]

It wasn't all easy going for Henry's men, however. Archers lying in ambush picked them off as they walked in a column along the forest roads, and on 2 May his favourite cook, Thomas, was killed in such an attack. After taking counsel with Richard, Henry ordered the beheading of the insurgents captured during a skirmish in the village of Flimwell in reprisal. Flimwell belonged to the abbey at Battle, and when the king arrived there next, he let his men have a go at the place while he harassed the abbot and fined him £66 pounds for his favour. He then turned east to Winchelsea where, on 4 May, representatives of the Channel ports arrived to do fealty to him. With their fleets now available to him, he planned to blockade

London while he mustered up a force at Canterbury to launch an assault on the city. He returned to Battle on 8 May in full confidence, but received disturbing news the next day. Three days earlier, on 6 May, Simon de Montfort had gathered up his army and left London. All indications were that he was coming after him.[21]

* * *

Since seizing and maintaining the initiative a month ago, the king had conducted a masterful campaign. Montfort's bold move now forced him to alter his plans and adopt a more cautious approach. He and his troops got into their armour, those who had some anyway, and headed 20 miles west to Lewes, where Warenne had a well fortified castle. Until Henry could determine what his adversary was up to, his army would stay encamped in and around the town while he took up lodgings at the priory just south of the walls. Around that same day, 11 May, Montfort's men reached his manor at Fletching, about 8 miles north of Lewes. The first sign that they were nearby was the appearance of a scouting party reconnoitring on the ridge that ran along high ground, called the Downs, to the west of the town. Royalist troops were sent up to confront them, and when they reached the 400-foot summit of today's Mount Harry, they spotted the rebel army below in a grassy plain between the edge of the high ground and a woodland north of it. Apart from a skirmish with foragers, they did not descend to attack, rather posted sentries and returned to Lewes.[22]

It's possible that had the entire army come up, they could have stormed down the hillside and destroyed or at least dispersed Montfort's forces. But nobody was willing to take that chance because this was the Middle Ages, an era when direct conflict between opposing armies was generally avoided. Crossing swords for real, away from the tournament pitch, was a terrifying prospect. Warfare was won by laying siege to castles and hounding the other side until they gave up out of isolation or exhaustion. There hadn't been a single battle fought in England since Lincoln in 1217, when Henry was still a boy king, and that was more street-fighting than anything else. Although Montfort had little choice but to gamble everything on one, all-out confrontation, the fact that he was taking such a risk was unnerving, more so when the royalists considered that Simon's father had done the same thing at the battle of Muret in 1213 and won a spectacular victory. His followers clearly had faith in his ability to pull off a similar miracle.

Another reason no action took place was because two separate peace missions arrived at the priory that day, 12 May. First came Stephen Berksted, the Bishop of Chichester, with a group of friars. The king had to understand that they could not go back on their oath to the Provisions, but they were willing to see them subjected to arbitration by an expert panel of clerics. They were followed by the bishops of Worcester and London, who offered £30,000 in damages for the spoliations. Henry was inclined to accept the deal. Apart from staking his reputation on peaceful outcomes, he appreciated better than most what it meant to square off against somebody like Montfort.[23] Legends and superstitions he could handle, but his brother-in-law was a real-life curse that would not go away, who emerged from every scrape unscathed and stronger than ever. But his brother and son convinced him to dismiss the overtures, Richard reminding him that the Provisions in any form represented a 'depression of power' for him and his heirs. The bishops were probably stunned to hear him talking the king out of peace, even if his political argument was sound. The offer of money was made specifically with Richard in mind, but so greatly did he feel aggrieved about the destruction of his properties that revenge was his priority of the moment.[24]

The next day, 13 May, Montfort moved his men closer to Lewes, near a bend in the Ouse before the river runs south behind the town lying on its west bank. The terrain in front of him was marshy and would work to his advantage if he could provoke the king into attacking him there.[25] In any case, he sent a letter to 'the most excellent lord Henry' explaining the rebels felt no ill will towards him personally:

> As it is plain from much experience that those who are present with you have suggested to your highness many falsehoods respecting us; intending all the mischief that they can do, not only to you but also to us, and to your whole kingdom, we wish your excellency to know that we wish to preserve the safety and security of your person with all our might.

They insisted that they were not making war against the king, rather his advisers, who were the source of all the trouble. This, of course, implied that he was some helpless stooge in need of rescuing. In his reply, Henry did not bother to return greetings to 'Simon de Montfort and Gilbert de Clare and their partisans':

> It is distinctly visible that you do not preserve the fidelity which you owe to us, and that you have in no respect any regard for the safety of our person … Since our faithful subjects are manfully standing by us and maintaining their fidelity in opposition to your disloyal conduct, we do not care for your safety or your affection, but defy you, as our enemies and theirs.[26]

Richard and Edward understood they were the ones being accused of giving Henry false counsel. They sent their own letter to Montfort, Clare and all their 'accomplices in treason', warning that they would do everything in their power to 'injure' their persons and property. Edward was said to have boasted that the Montfortians would have no peace whatsoever unless they put halters around their necks and surrendered themselves 'for us to hang or draw, as we please'.[27]

Some time after receiving these letters, Montfort led his men through the ritual of withdrawing their homage and fealty to the king. They marched back to the grassy plain south of the woodland, and during the night began to ascend the Downs from the rear side, undetected by the sentinels posted on the ridge. It happened that only one was on duty that night and he was asleep. On a stretch of level terrain below the ridge, Montfort knighted Gilbert and some of the other young nobles and addressed the troops, reminding them that theirs was a struggle for the honour of God and kingdom. The men prayed, were absolved by the bishops and painted white crosses on their outer garments, both to profess their crusade-like fervour and to identify each other in battle. They stretched out into formation and, some time before dawn, crossed over the crest and began their descent on the town.[28]

No special precautions against such a surprise attack had been taken in and around Lewes. If the report of a certain friar can be believed, Henry and Richard were carousing the night away in the priory, as doubtless Edward and his retinue were doing in the castle. The king did, however, make time for one official act that suggests he knew battle was imminent. Some time in the early morning hours, while Montfort was making his dispositions, Henry dictated an acquittance to Louis for the rest of the treaty money he owed him. This followed his order the day before that £500 of the balance should go for the upkeep of the Holy Land. He was evidently worried about falling in battle with his crusader vow unfulfilled and wanted to make a show of good faith.[29]

The date was 14 May 1264, the forty-fifth anniversary of William Marshal's death. As Henry's unwilling regent, the famed warrior had spent his last years putting the country back together after a destructive civil war. His dying wish was for the young king to be a good man and avoid the example of 'any evil ancestor', meaning his father John. He would not have been disappointed, yet nor would he have been surprised that the country was again plunged into civil war. As he lamented on his deathbed, no people in any land were more divided than the English.[30]

Dawn broke around four o'clock that morning. About then, a party out foraging for men and horses spotted the advancing troops and raised the alarm. There seems to have been enough time for Henry and Richard to array their forces outside the priory and march out to the clearing in front of the city walls with the dragon standard before them. Henry commanded the left, on the southernmost portion of the field, with Humphrey de Bohun, the Earl of Hereford, in his van. Richard took the centre with his son Henry of Almain. Edward, staying in the castle north of the priory, was the last to get his men into formation. He had the right wing with William de Valence, John de Warenne, Roger Mortimer and Hugh Bigod. Altogether their line stretched for a little over half a mile. The king's army may have numbered as many as 9,000, a quarter of them mounted.

Facing them on the rebel right were Henry and Guy de Montfort and the younger Bohun. The centre was under Clare and Fitz-John, and on the left were

John Giffard and Henry Hastings. Ferrers's failure to turn up as summoned left them under-strength, with a little over half the troops the king had, and the left was comprised mostly of Londoners. They were not soldiers, rather rabble-rousers armed with anything they could find, perhaps some tool or stave looted from Richard of Cornwall's estate. Nevertheless, Montfort found enough men to form a fourth division, which he placed behind his centre corps. With his excellent view of the movements below him, he would be able to deploy it wherever a weak point developed in Henry's lines.[31]

It was Edward who charged first. Somehow realising that he was facing a mob of Londoners, doubtless some of the same people who had stoned and insulted his mother at London Bridge, he gave the order forward at around five o'clock. He and his several hundred knights completely scattered the opposing cavalry, easily capturing Giffard in the initial rush. The shock sent the Londoners screaming and running for safety. The royalist infantry that followed mopped up any who dared remain on the field. Montfort's left wing had completely collapsed within minutes. All Edward had to do was call a halt to his knights, get them back into formation and drive headlong into his uncle's exposed flank. It could soon be over after that.

Montfort knew the young man as well as anyone, knew he was brave and fearless, but also rash and undisciplined. If he had deliberately baited him with the Londoners, inviting him to indulge in a killing spree, then the royalist right wing would also disappear from the field. And so it was that Edward couldn't help himself. Given the chance to take his revenge, he and his men chased their fleeing, panic-stricken opponents for up to 4 miles. They trampled them, cut them down with mace or sword, or forced them into the river to drown.[32]

Back on the battlefield, Henry's and Richard's divisions were making far slower progress, both because of the steeper elevation and the volley of stones from enemy slingers pummelling them. Once Edward's wing was out of action, Simon ordered his centre and right divisions to charge. With the speed they were able to obtain from going downhill, they barrelled into the royalist front lines with great impact. Richard's men had barely absorbed it when Montfort threw his fourth division against them. The royalist centre began to crumble as the men were forced back towards a hospital for lepers. Those who took flight at that point still had to cover half a mile of ground to reach the castle. Their commander wasn't one of them. Two hundred yards behind the hospital stood a windmill and Richard decided it was as good a place as any to seek shelter from the mayhem.[33]

Montfort could now deploy all the men he had left on the field against Henry's division. The ferociousness of the personal combat here can be seen in the twenty wounds suffered by Philip Basset alone. The king himself fought bravely. He took blow after blow from sword and mace and lost two horses beneath him. His line managed to hold long enough to make an orderly retreat to the priory, where his household knights took up positions around the gate. Meanwhile, Montfort's men were thrown into disarray as the fighting spilled into the town. He managed to get them back into formation, presumably for a coordinated assault on the castle, when he was alerted to a large group of horsemen approaching from the west.[34]

It was Edward and his knights. At the end of their pursuit of the Londoners, they had spotted Montfort's baggage train and standard at the top of the hill. Driving their horses up the slope, they found only his rearguard there under the command of William Blund, whom they slew along with the rest of his men. They surrounded the special coach Simon had been using to get around in with his injured leg, but which he had lately turned into a mobile jail for some citizens of London trying to rally the city for the king. The hapless occupants tried to explain all that to them, but were slaughtered just the same and the coach set alight. Only then did Edward redirect his attention to the battle below and saw that it was lost. He tried to salvage what he could, but Montfort's men chased his off before any real action took place. Warenne, Bigod and Valence fled for Pevensey Castle on the coast, and from there to France, while Edward, Leybourne and Mortimer chose to fight their way into the priory.[35]

In doing so, they blundered for a second time that day. Henry was trapped, but by no means beaten. He could easily have held out long enough for his son's contingent to withdraw to Tonbridge or other nearby garrisons, reform into an effective fighting force, then return and strike at Montfort again, allowing the king to break out. Perhaps conscious that his misconduct on the field had cost his father the battle, if not his kingdom, all Edward could think of was reaching his side. Henry was unlikely to have known the particulars at that point and would have been overjoyed to see that he was safe. Montfort was certainly glad he had chosen this option, for the death of either the king or his son in the battle would have been a serious blow to his prestige and authority. He had won a great victory, but in order to make it complete he had to take both of them alive.

By noon the battle itself was over. Over 2,000 men fell that day, nearly all of them foot soldiers. Richard of Cornwall was still safely ensconced inside the windmill, but the steadily growing calls for the 'bad miller' to come out made him realise he had no chance of escape or rescue. The jeers and howls that greeted his surrender doubtless made him regret the boastful threats he had issued the day before. Elsewhere, pockets of royalist resistance were stiffening. The castle easily repelled an initial assault and the defenders responded by setting several townhouses ablaze with flaming arrows. Since storming the priory was unlikely to be any more successful, Montfort sent a group of friars to negotiate with Henry. They came and went throughout the night until both sides gave ground and a peace treaty, the Mise of Lewes, was worked out. In it, the king undertook to observe the Provisions of Oxford under a caretaker government, but Montfort agreed to submit them to arbitration with more French involvement.[36] Henry had to give up Richard, Edward and Henry of Almain as hostages for his compliance, at least until the arbitration was implemented, but he won freedom for the captured barons, most importantly the Marchers and northerners. Letting implacable enemies like Mortimer loose was a risk, but one that Montfort felt he could afford as long as the royal family remained captives.[37]

As a point of pride, Henry made the formal act of surrender to Gilbert de Clare and not Simon. The court left Lewes on Saturday 17 May and reached Canterbury three days later. Edward and Henry of Almain were taken to Dover by their cousin and custodian Henry de Montfort while the two kings remained together. After arriving in London on 30 May, they were separated, with Richard going to the Tower and Henry to St Paul's. Richard and the two princes were then placed under the care of his sister Eleanor de Montfort at his castle of Wallingford, 14 miles southeast of Oxford. Henry remained at the bishop's mansion for most of the summer, comfortable lodgings to be sure, but the idea was to keep him securely behind the walls of London as opposed to the more open environment of Westminster.[38]

His household was reduced and handpicked for him, but he was kept in state. Expenditures for luxuries like cinnamon, figs and almonds were actually increased, although this would have only reminded him that these were the same items he used to send his cousin Eleanor of Brittany to alleviate the loneliness of her long confinement. Montfort may have thought that no amount of special treatment was going to make the king any less hostile to the complete appropriation of his government, but he needed to maintain appearances as a way of imposing his own authority throughout the land. To that end, keepers of the peace were appointed in the counties on 4 June, and various edicts were issued that month with provisions for protecting the Jews.[39]

Other orders that went out under the king's seal demanded the surrender of royalist castles. Some, like Pevensey, Nottingham and Bristol, still held out, but Windsor was vacated, forcing one of the occupants, Eleanor of Castile, to seek shelter in Westminster for herself and her daughter Katherine. Having become pregnant during one of Edward's furloughs before Lewes, she likely ended up attached to Henry's household for the duration of these events. Bereft of his immediate family, he would have welcomed the proximity of his daughter-in-law and granddaughter, who sadly died later that summer, aged twenty months.[40]

In addition to restoring some semblance of order, the keepers of the peace also supervised the election of four knights from each county to attend Parliament, which hadn't met in nine months. This first of Montfort's two great parliaments was dominated by the crafting of an ordinance to serve as the constitution of the land until the Mise of Lewes was implemented. It encompassed the principles of the Provisions, but with stricter control of the crown than before. A triumvirate of three electors, Montfort, Clare and Berksted, were empowered to choose nine councillors, whose consent was required for all appointments and other routine business of the realm. Three of the councillors, whose numbers included Peter de Montfort, Thomas Cantilupe and the younger Humphrey de Bohun, were always to be in attendance at court in order to prevent Henry from slipping through their grasp as he had done during the first Montfortian government. Under the Ordinance, the king was essentially deprived of all executive authority and independent action, thus creating the first constitutional monarchy in the modern sense of the term. Henry had no more power than any one of the Nine, who were themselves subordinate to the Three. The Ordinance was sealed on 28 June 1264 with the consent of the assembly and witnessed among others by Roger Bigod, who was named a keeper of the peace for Norfolk and Suffolk. Henry naturally found the whole scheme abhorrent and refused to cooperate until he was told that the only alternative was his deposition and the election of his successor, which likely would have meant Edward's incarceration for life and Edmund's banishment from the realm.[40]

The only escape clause for Henry was the implementation of the Mise of Lewes. Whatever came out of the arbitration on the Provisions was supposed to supplant the Ordinance, and Louis was specifically given the role of convening the French panel. He had received the mise shortly after the battle, followed by a letter from Henry on 25 May urging him to act. He refused to get involved, however, because to do so would be to admit that his decision at Amiens had been wrong. It would also confer legitimacy on a regime where the king was essentially held captive. Montfort probably expected Louis to respond in this manner and had deliberately included him in the process to ensure that nothing came of it. This way, the Ordinance would remain in effect indefinitely. So sure was he of this outcome that, once the king and his son gave themselves up at the priory, Montfort never bothered to enrol the mise in the chancery, as if it didn't even exist. Henry was determined to try just the same and sent more letters to Louis, on 6 July and again on the 10th, this time reminding him that Edward was a hostage for the fulfilment of the mise. Of course, nobody in their right mind believed Montfort would chop off the head of the heir to the throne because the negotiations were failing to move forward. Hostage diplomacy had long since become obsolete by that time. In demanding custody of Edward following the battle, Simon was principally concerned with keeping him locked up and therefore in no position to upset the peace.[41]

★ ★ ★

One person who certainly didn't believe Edward's life was in peril was his mother. Queen Eleanor's first knowledge of the disaster at Lewes probably came from Warenne and the other fugitives from the battlefield. Although they had been at odds with her for most of the reform period, they now clung to her 'waiting for happier times'. She had already been engaged in building up a fleet and force of men for her husband, to the point of annoying Alphonse of Poitiers with requests that he illegally seize English shipping in his ports in Poitou. Now this 'most gallant woman' aimed to put together an invasion force. On 1 June, she was at the French court collecting an instalment of the treaty money. With assistance from exiles like Mansel, her son Edmund and Savoyard relatives, she used it to hire knights and men-at-arms from various parts of Europe to muster in Flanders under the command of Peter of Savoy.[42]

By early July, the threat was real enough for Montfort to call out the feudal host but, never one to do things by halves, he went further and ordered every village to send as many men as possible. A letter dispatched under the king's seal on 7 July, certainly drafted by Simon, declared: 'we know for a fact that a great horde of aliens is getting ready to invade the land.' The army that amassed on the southeast coast that summer was probably the largest seen in England since the Conquest two centuries earlier. Most were peasants armed with the sickle they would otherwise be using to cut the wheat, but the letter declared that the invaders were thirsting for English blood, so no one should plead the harvest as an excuse to stay at home.[43]

The alien argument was meant for the benefit of the lordly class and clergy, who were still convinced that all foreigners were spongers and oppressors. On the other hand, the peasants had such restricted, toilsome lives that practically anyone not from their village was an alien. The reform movement changed that by opening up a whole new world of opportunities to them, from seeking redress through *querelae* to enjoying the adventure and plunder that came with civil strife. But in a nobler sense, it had also stirred their political consciousness. They recognised that they too were part of the community of the realm just as much as the lords and clerics (who were the real spongers and oppressors). They mustered in force on the south coast not just to defend England, but also the principles espoused by the man so completely identified with them. Under Simon de Montfort, life for the peasant could only get better, even if it meant going hungry that winter.[44]

The man himself was not there to organise the troops. After Parliament adjourned, he and Clare marched west to deal with the Marchers, who had shown only contempt for the new government since their release. They not only refused to hand over the prisoners they had captured at Northampton, but had seized several castles in the Severn Valley. An attack by these two earls, coordinated with Llywelyn striking from Wales, quickly brought the Marchers to heel. The castles were surrendered, and Mortimer and Audley were forced to surrender a son each as hostage for their future behaviour. Montfort doubtless would have liked to stay until Mortimer at least had been thoroughly thrashed, but the impending invasion demanded his presence in the southeast.[45]

The invasion force had yet to sail, in part because Cardinal Foulquois was in Amiens seeking permission to enter England to discharge his duties as papal legate.

Since his powers of excommunication and interdict made him as big a threat as Eleanor's army, he was advised by the council to stay where he was and work instead on disbanding the mercenaries. He was also asked to remind Louis that the Treaty of Paris specifically prohibited the use of the money pledged in the agreement for the benefit of anything other than God, church and England. He wrote back on 26 July that he had already tried but failed to get the queen to stand down, but if anyone needed reminded of anything, it was the English of the good service legates had done them in the past, most notably Guala saving them from the French in the first years of Henry's reign. Louis finally intervened at this point to propose a peace conference in Boulogne and moved there in early August with the legate.[46]

Hopeful at last, Henry sent off a flurry of letters. He thanked Louis and promised that envoys would be sent to Boulogne, then asked Montfort and Clare to make sure of it. He urged them to return as soon as possible and bring the royal hostages with them. He wrote to them again the next day, 31 July, surprised to learn that his son and nephew were being held further away than he thought, at Kenilworth in the Midlands, where Montfort thought it prudent to keep them while he was away in the Marches. That forced Henry to write to Louis again to postpone the conference until mid-August, adding that he should do everything in his power to keep the invasion from launching. It could only lead to a further depression of his status, he warned him. Henry sent similar appeals to various French prelates and peers, including Charles of Anjou, who was said to be Simon's 'brother', bound to him by an oath of fidelity.[47]

On 12 August, the English court moved to Canterbury to facilitate the speed of negotiations. Edward and Henry of Almain were brought there as a sign of good faith, but by then the legate's patience had run out. On that same day in Boulogne, he ordered the Montfortian council to restore the king to power, release the hostages and admit him to England by 1 September, or else suffer the full weight of ecclesiastic penalties. They should also forget the Mise of Lewes. Louis hadn't bothered to forward it to the nominated panel of arbitrators, who in any case declared that they wanted nothing to do with it. At that point, Montfort arrived. Having counted on the rejection of the mise, he had a backup plan ready to dispatch to Boulogne. Called the Peace of Canterbury, it reiterated the rule of the Three and the Nine with the caveat that, should the mise be a dead letter, the Ordinance would remain in force until some undetermined point in Edward's reign, which would all but finish Henry as a real king. Some concessions were made, namely in clauses that called for reform of the Church and the readmission of aliens for any purpose other than serving as officials of state.[48]

Three envoys left on 15 August with the peace document. Two days later, the legate wrote to the bishops to express his outrage that they were party to any plan that subjugated the kingdom to a triumvirate. He was furthermore aghast that they expected him to sell the idea to Louis, whose own reaction when informed of the Peace of Canterbury was to declare that he would rather look at the rumps of oxen in the fields all day than rule under such restraints. The legate went on to demand that the bishops appear before him to explain their conduct. He had already summoned them, but they had made excuses because they knew they would either be detained in France or sent back with letters of excommunication. Instead, they stood surety for the enormous sum of £13,333 to release Henry of Almain on 4 September so he could go to France to promote the offer of arbitration on the Peace of Canterbury. This got nowhere because the Montfortians both tried to stack the panel in their favour and insisted that the prohibition against alien councillors was non-negotiable.[49]

A delegation of barons and bishops followed with a second scheme on 24 September, creating more cross-Channel traffic as amendments were proposed by both sides. Tempers began to flare, and on one occasion Almain's party was set upon by a mob in Boulogne that left nine of them dead. On 3 October, the bishops of Worcester and London arrived back in England with both the latest proposal and letters of excommunication and interdict to publish if no agreement were reached within fifteen days. Their letters were seized at Dover during a random search (instigated by the bishops themselves, suggests Wykes), torn up and tossed into the sea. The legate was worried something like that could happen and so demanded in his new proposal that the council turn over Dover and the hostages to him in return for Edmund and an equivalent castle in France. He got a reply on 11 October when a single English knight rowed up to the shoreline and dropped a chest into the water containing a formal rejection of his proposal, the Peace of Canterbury and the Ordinance. Nine days later, the legate published the bull of excommunication, but in Flanders, where it had no impact on the Montfortian regime. Henry nevertheless thought he was being vindictive and wrote to him to suggest he 'act graciously in the matter' because experience had taught him that kindness worked better than coercion. In any event, it was the legate's last act in the office, for word arrived that Urban IV had died earlier that month, on the 2nd. The legate's mandate expired with him and he had to return to Rome for the election of a successor.[50]

The legate wasn't the only one to leave the scene at that time. The queen's army had largely dispersed by then due to a lack of funds. She was already running short of money when negotiations began in August and had again turned to Louis for help. With counsel from the exiles, she sold him her husband's rights in the three French bishoprics ceded to him under the Treaty of Paris for £5,000. It was a delicate move, given Henry's touchiness about his rights, and when he learned of it in November, he wrote to her, Louis, Margaret and Peter of Savoy in some heat about making deals 'against his will and knowledge'. She had anticipated him reacting in this manner and so had wisely insisted on a buy-back clause, which Louis conceded but with a 50 per cent penalty attached.[51]

Eleanor had likely held back the invasion in the hope that the legate would at least procure Edward's freedom and was bitterly disappointed when the hostages didn't even figure in the final peace proposal made by the Montfortians. In November, she somehow encouraged Robert Walerand, who had been holed up in Bristol Castle since Lewes, to embark on an attempt to rescue the prisoners at Wallingford Castle, where her son and Henry of Almain were again detained with Richard of Cornwall and his other son following the breakdown of talks. Walerand led Warin Bassingbourne and several other former knights of Edward's household 80 miles to Wallingford and, striking before dawn, succeeded in fighting their way into the inner courtyard of the castle. They broke off only after the warden threatened to catapult Edward to them from a mangonel, and had him brought up to the ramparts to tell them that he was dead serious. The prisoners were then moved to more secure detention at Kenilworth.[52]

Walerand's daring expedition coincided with another outbreak of mayhem among the Marchers, led by a notorious plunderer named Hamo Lestrange. Montfort called out the feudal host and took Henry with him to Worcester to confront them, but according to *Flores*, 'it appeared that the king's heart and that of his friends were inclined to them, because they had stirred up war and sedition among the people on behalf of the king, who was, as it were, in confinement'. Outnumbered and threatened by the Welsh in their rear, Mortimer and the other two Rogers, Clifford and Leybourne, again yielded to 'that most sagacious warrior Simon de Montfort'.[53] The new terms for their submission were severe. They had to relocate to Ireland for a year and a day, leaving their lands in Montfort's hands, and Edward was forced to swap the rump palatine of Chester which he received from his father in 1254, along with two castles, for a dozen of Montfort's manors scattered elsewhere. By clearing Edward out of the Marches before his eventual release, Simon aimed to put some distance between him and his strongest allies. The Rogers were given safe conducts to Kenilworth to hear Edward tell them himself that that was the deal and they had better abide by it.[54]

The conditions for his freedom were one of the main talking points for Parliament scheduled early the next year. Writs for the assembly started going out on 14 December 1264 while the court was still in Worcester. Unlike the first of Montfort's great parliaments, this second one gained famed for who was summoned rather than what was actually accomplished. Although the men of the towns had likely sat in Parliament before, this was the first time on record that these 'burgesses' were officially invited to deliberate on the affairs of state, in this case two each for York, Lincoln and other unnamed constituencies. It was the same with the Channel ports, four men from each were summoned. Together with two knights representing each county, they would far outnumber the twenty-three barons invited.[55]

Apart from the localities, the Montfortian base was strongest among the clergy, which can be seen in the 120 bishops, abbots, priors and other men of the cloth asked to attend. He needed them for more than the moral and spiritual support they gave his cause. For the defence of the realm, they had provided armed men or money worth a tenth of all their revenues.[56] Just how they had come to back Simon against the king is difficult to explain at first glance. Henry was deeply pious, revered mass and other rituals, supported saints, religious houses and universities, exalted clerks in his administration, fed and clothed the poor, and was generous in almsgiving all around. He had interfered in their elections and exploited their resources, but so had his predecessors and that hadn't provoked rebellion. It's also true they had been taxed mercilessly to fund his Sicilian scheme, but they would have ended up paying much more had he gone on a real crusade.

What seems to have turned them against the king was bad timing. The papacy's overreaching demand for benefices coincided with the politicalisation of the English clergy begun by Stephen Langton during John's reign and continued by Edmund of Abingdon and Robert Grosseteste, even if the latter two insisted they were against it. While a lot of their struggles had to do with infighting and turf wars among Englishmen, it was the presence of so many foreign clerics that united them in radicalisation. It was nothing personal against their foreignness, but an Italian, Frenchman or Spaniard in their midst meant one less cosy position for a nephew or son or relative of a benefactor. The king's determination to create an international nobility in their island nation fit only too well with this intolerable diversification of their ranks and strain on their purses, both of which were interpreted for their parishioners as the subjugation of Englishness.

But not even the great churchmen had dared to defy their superiors to the extent the bishops were doing now in supporting the Montfortians. Again, it was partly a matter of timing.[57] There was a baronial rebellion and they latched on to it. If the clergy hadn't joined the earlier revolt against John with equal zeal, it was because there had been no leader comparable to Montfort. His background and piety imbued him with religious fervour, his commitment and friendship elicited their trust, his charisma and speechmaking inspired them to act, and his organisational and military skills got things done. Indeed, his miraculous victory at Lewes was proof that their combined cause was divinely ordained. An anonymous friar in Berksted's household glorified it as such in the *Song of Lewes*, a poem composed at this time to praise the new order:

> Now England breathes again, hoping for liberty, to whom may God's grace grant prosperity … We give first place to the commonalty. We say that law rules the dignity of the king; for we believe that law is a light, without which we infer that the guide goes astray … Therefore let the community of the realm take counsel, and let that be decreed which is the opinion of the commonalty.[58]

The author did not have the commons in mind for his audience. He wrote the poem in Latin specifically for other clergymen as defence and justification of a form of government condemned by their pope. He didn't even have Henry in mind when he talked about kingship as subordinate to both the law and the community of the realm. Rather, he was looking to the future and rule under the devious Edward:

> The treachery or falsehood whereby he is advanced he calls prudence; the way whereby he arrives, crooked though it be, is regarded as straight; wrong gives him pleasure and is called right; whatever he likes he says is lawful … O Edward! You wish to become king without law; they would be wretched who were ruled by such a king![59]

Truth be told, there were doubts about Montfort's character too. It was no secret he had been pursuing his family's personal grievances throughout the reform period. Now, at the height of his power, authorisation was given to Despenser, Peter de Montfort, and the bishops of Worcester and London, all personal friends of his, to rectify his wife's Marshal dower, including the losses incurred by her in the thirty years she had disputed the original settlement.[60] The author praises Montfort, but feels compelled to dispel rumours of anything untoward in his intentions:

> The faith and fidelity of Simon alone is become the security of the peace of all England … If it was his own advantage … he would set before him the advancement of his own friends, would aim at the enrichment of his sons, and would neglect the safety of the community, and would veil the poison of falsehood with the cloak of duplicity.[61]

These doubts weren't going away, however. The treachery of the Marchers had taught Montfort to rely only on people he knew he could trust. Stalwarts like Despenser as justiciar and Peter de Montfort on the council of nine were expected, but questions were raised about the appearance of his older sons in key positions at the Channel ports, where rampant piracy was hampering recovery of the wool trade and the economy as a whole.[62] The war had wrecked government finance, and it wasn't until after the threat of invasion melted away that the exchequer, which had closed during the London riots, reopened in October. For the whole year, the sheriffs only accounted for £139 in receipts. The keepers of the peace had made little headway in quelling disorder. Reports of 'rapine, homicides and plunderings' were common, and the order forbidding the carrying of arms was impossible to enforce. Not even the threat of decapitation prevented the ongoing desecration of religious properties and assaults on their caretakers.[63]

Nobody could remember things being as bad as they were now. It was against this background of an inverted legal order that the chroniclers described the inverted political order. One noted how nothing of importance was done without Montfort's control, leaving Henry with only the shadow of his name. Another said that Montfort was less willing to treat for peace now that he had the whole kingdom at his disposal.[64] Then there is Wykes, whose critique of the situation was scathing: 'He was not ashamed to rule the king, to whom he should be rightly bound; and he acted above himself, it was as though the name of the earl completely overshadowed the royal highness. What shameless things of unheard evil, such that he exceeded the pride of arrogant Lucifer!'[65] But there was no denying that 'fortune smiled' on all that Simon had conceived. The Montforts spent Christmas at Kenilworth, where he had gathered around him at least 140 knights, more than twice as many as Henry ever had. Doubtless Edward, Richard of Cornwall, and his sons Henry of Almain and Edmund joined in the festivities, if only to relieve the boredom of their captivity.

Meanwhile, the king was spending Christmas just over 42 miles to the south at Woodstock. His daughter-in-law Eleanor of Castile was the only family with him and she was in confinement with her third child expected any day. But he certainly didn't want for company. Thirty oxen, 100 sheep, five boars and six caskets of new wine were provided for the feast. He didn't mope about, either, rather he cast his eye about for repairs to be made, and had 100 pear saplings planted in the orchard of nearby Everswell.[66] The splendour of their springtime blossom would make a nice gift for the queen after her return from France. And she would be returning, for faith had never failed him before. It had been his greatest comfort and security in the uncertain days of his youth and the first civil war he lived through. It delivered him then and would do so again. He had been on the throne for nearly half a century, surviving everything adversity had thrown at him. This was doubtless his toughest trial yet, Montfort by far his toughest opponent, but he would survive them, too.

16

THE RECKONING 1265–1267

The Parliament that opened on 20 January 1265 became the best-remembered of Henry's reign because, for the first time, the burgesses were sitting alongside the knights, clerics and barons in a national assembly. For that reason, Simon de Montfort was later credited with creating the House of Commons, but nobody then thought about it in terms of history. Since it was popular support that swept him into power, Montfort needed the broadest representation possible to approve a general settlement for the realm. The nobility was mostly marginalised because they held aloof or were opposed to his revolutionary principles. Henry was his lord, and if he treated him that way, they could be next. Wykes for one believed that was his agenda. He wrote that Montfort deliberately set out to 'put down the mighty and ruin their power, to break the horns of the proud, that he might more freely and easily subdue the people'. But the chronicler admits that the barons had only themselves to blame. They were an untrustworthy lot, ready to switch sides at a moment's notice to suit their interests.[1] It almost seemed fitting that this particular Parliament was summoned to discuss the fate of Edward, who epitomised their unchivalrous behaviour *par excellence*.

There is no record of the proceedings, but there must have been a lot of ill will. Not until 14 February, St Valentine's Day, was there any progress to show, none of it to Henry or Edward's liking. That's when Parliament was informed that the king and heir had sworn not to seek retribution against Montfort, Clare, the people of London or anybody else who helped put them in their present state. Henry also ordered the strictest observance of Magna Carta, the Forest Charter and, more importantly, the Ordinance.[2] No reason was given for his endorsement of constitutional monarchy. Likely it was that or Edward's imprisonment until he came around. It was probably because he was being stubborn that Montfort had the announcement made in the Chapter House of Westminster Abbey. With its glazed tiled floor bearing his coat of arms, Henry had envisioned it as the home for future parliaments, his majesty enhanced by the beautiful surroundings.[3] All that was being enhanced now was his own debasement. If he wished to preserve what was left of his majesty, he had better cooperate.

Further aggravating the royal gloom at this time was a personal loss. As Parliament was getting underway, John Mansel died in exile, reportedly in great poverty. He had been a boy when the king took him under his wing, eventually rising to become his ablest and most trusted adviser and diplomat. Henry valued the widely travelled soldier and clerk for his hard work and loyalty, but his wealth from preferment made him as divisive a figure at court as any foreigner.[4] Of the many benefices made vacant by his death, the office of treasurer of York was by far the most lucrative. Normally it was up to the Archbishop of York to choose his successor, but he had died a week before Mansel. The decision thus fell to the king, and on 7 February he appointed his 22-year-old nephew Amaury de Montfort to the post. It was a clear case of nepotism, but not of Henry's doing. He later claimed that his brother-in-law Simon acted against his will and used the royal seal to make the gift to Amaury, his third son. It wasn't the first time he had acted in this manner to advance his family.[5]

All of Simon and Eleanor's six children had been taken care of under his administration, whether with herds of deer or custody of confiscated lands and castles. Gilbert de Clare had also done well, appropriating the large estates of Warenne and Valence for himself, but Montfort's monopolisation of all the fame and glory rankled him. It could hardly have been otherwise given Clare's youth, inexperience and failure to join the cause until the last possible moment, but he felt slighted nonetheless. He and his brother Thomas also resented the high positions granted to Henry, Simon and Guy de Montfort, who were on average a few years older. As the enmity between them grew, they decided to have it out on the tournament pitch with their followings, and announced one for Dunstable on 17 February.[6]

Montfort couldn't believe it. Here they were in the middle of an important Parliament and they were going to adjourn for a melee that, given the undercurrent of jealousies, could well turn into clan warfare. He had no trouble convincing Henry to ban it, then warning his sons that if they ever tried a stunt like that again he would 'put them in such place that they would no longer see the light of sun or moon'. Clare was furious with Simon because of the money he had spent organising the tournament and openly denounced his partner in the triumvirate.[7] He added it to a growing backlog of grievances that included the failure to release Richard of Cornwall, allegedly because the Montforts were enjoying a big payday off their custody of his lands. Richard was Clare's step-grandfather, but it was because he wanted his own payday that he was demanding his release. As the one who officially captured the King of the Romans in battle, Clare was entitled to a huge ransom, as much as £17,000 in silver and £5,000 in gold – a 'sum worth having,' commented the Melrose chronicler.[8]

On a political note, Clare even accused Montfort of flouting the anti-alien platform of the Provisions by garrisoning castles with foreign mercenaries. Simon being an alien himself made it easy for him to assume an air of indignity. 'It's ridiculous that this foreigner should presume to put the whole realm under his yoke,' he was heard to declare. Some time after 23 February he'd had enough and left Parliament, although more out of fear than temper. On that day, Robert de Ferrers, the Earl of Derby, was arrested and sent to the Tower. He had used Edward's imprisonment to ransack and occupy his lands and Henry was demanding his suppression. Others put a different spin on his arrest. Montfort was soon to come into possession of those very lands in the swap forced on Edward and this was the easiest way to remove Ferrers before then. Clare got the idea that he too could end up in the Tower alongside his fellow earl and sought safety in Gloucestershire.[9]

The other member of the Three, Bishop Berksted, didn't have similar reservations about Montfort's political integrity, nor did any of the Nine. The moral authority of their government, such as it was, even got a boost on 25 February when Thomas Cantilupe was named chancellor. He replaced Henry's hand-picked official John Chishull, who had been retained after Lewes to bolster the appearance of continuity. Cantilupe's unimpeachable credentials were meant to dispel doubts that the use of the king's seal did not reflect the royal will. He was so prickly about his conscience and reputation that when the council voted him an expense account of £333 annually, he asked Henry to fold the authorisation writ himself.[10]

A peace agreement was finally reached and solemnised at a grand ceremony in Westminster Hall on 11 March 1265. Nine bishops wearing pontifical robes and holding lighted tapers excommunicated transgressors of Magna Carta and the Ordinance establishing the new government. The most demeaning moment for Edward had to be when he was handed over to his father by Henry de Montfort. Even then he wasn't free, because a troop of minders, again under his cousin's watch, was assigned to keep him under close surveillance. One concession was made to Clare in bringing in his brother Thomas as a companion for the future king. Gilbert had been vocal in demanding Edward's release, although not out of any innate sense of decency. He was as young as Montfort was old and would likely be alive for much of the next reign. Edward's vengeance against the Londoners at Lewes, which got him into the current mess, suggested he was going to make a lot of people pay for his humiliation some day.[11]

The final major business of that historic Parliament was to order Boniface to return and resume his duties as Archbishop of Canterbury. He was sure to ignore it, as he was also ordered to annul the sentence of excommunication against the

Montfortians first. Even if he wanted to, there was no way he could do it without displeasing the new pope, Clement IV, previously known as Guy Foulquois, the former legate. Foulquois's failure to reach England still gnawed at him and he blamed Montfort for it. When his permission was sought for a marriage contract, he told the supplicant he could have whomever he wanted as a bride so long as it was no relation of 'that pestilent man'.[12]

All that was left to signal the country at peace again was to renew the oath of fealty to the king. On 17 March, Mayor Fitz-Thomas led the aldermen of London to St Paul's to perform this act and surprised many there with his conviction that the new order was here to stay. Addressing Henry in front of the people, he declared, 'My lord, so long as you will be a good king to us, we will be faithful and devoted to you.'[13] The mere thought of making fealty conditional on the behaviour of the lord, to say nothing of the king, was an astounding reflection of just how radical some of these reformers were. Doubtless there were plenty there besides Henry who were sure that Fitz-Thomas would regret those words one day.

The king endured an even more distasteful episode three days later when Cheshire was officially transferred to Montfort. Few acts of the captive monarchy drew his ire as much as this one. He had gone to great expense and trouble acquiring the lands of the former earldom of Chester to create an appanage for his son. Now Montfort was all but swiping it from him for his own son. Considering how Simon had first been set up in England by the Earl of Chester himself, he was probably even congratulating himself for coming full circle. And if that weren't enough, it was at this point that he began referring to himself as 'steward of England'. He was presuming to legitimise his supremacy and rub it in at the same time. Henry had to acquiesce in order to obtain Edward's freedom, but he didn't have to like it and showed that he didn't in the charter itself. His custom had always been to 'give' such grants himself, but he refused in this case. He left it to Cantilupe to give it instead as the chancellor.[14]

All Montfort had to do to make his victory complete was satisfy Clare somehow. He had announced a tournament at Northampton for 20 April to make up for the one cancelled in Dunstable and took the whole court there for it. Clare's failure to show up coincided with the Marchers again delaying their departure for Ireland. Clare and John Giffard, who had his own grievances about prisoner ransoms, were evidently forging an alliance with them. Montfort realised he had to go to Gloucestershire to win them back or destroy them all together. Packing up the court again, he arrived in Gloucester on 27 April and called out the local militias.[15]

Clare and Giffard withdrew their forces to the nearby hills and entered negotiations, but only to buy time for Warenne and Valence to land at Pembroke with a force of 120 mounted men. Learning of their collusion, Montfort moved to Hereford on 8 May to prevent this force from linking up with Mortimer and the other Marchers, but an agreement reached with Clare several days later convinced him he had the situation under control. He was so confident that he allowed Clifford, Leybourne and other Marcher lords to visit Edward. This allowed his enemies to plot their next move, which occurred on 28 May. While out riding, Edward dashed for freedom with Thomas de Clare and several minders, a knight and four squires to be exact. A concealed party of horsemen led by Mortimer was waiting to fend off any attempt to retrieve them. They took Edward to Ludlow Castle for talks with Gilbert, who demanded the observance of the 'good old laws', whatever they were, and the banishment of aliens as the price for his support. Edward readily agreed.[16]

For Montfort, to retreat at this point would be to admit defeat. He sent out letters in Henry's name denouncing Edward as a disinherited public enemy and urging the bishops to excommunicate the lot of them. He summoned his son Simon to raise levies as fast as he could and march westward while he himself sought reinforcements from the Welsh. In a treaty drawn up at Pipton on 19 June, Llywelyn agreed to give him military assistance and £20,000 paid in instalments in return for recognition of his territorial gains, overlordship of Wales and the title 'Prince of Wales' to go with it. He was also allowed to demolish Painscastle, where Henry had bestowed the earldom of Leicester on Montfort while building the castle in 1232. Since the treaty went against Henry's entire Welsh policy, a codicil was added that if the king acted against the terms, he could be deposed under the covenant he had recently made in Parliament.[17]

By this time Edward's forces had isolated the Montifortians from the rest of England by seizing the line of the River Severn from Worcester to Gloucester. Montfort's bid to cross the Bristol Channel to link up with his son in early July was thwarted when Clare's men destroyed the boats meant to ferry them across. Confronted by a now much larger army, Montfort was forced inland and spent two weeks on a circuitous route back to Hereford. Desertions were rampant as provisions ran low. His men longed for bread in a region where the people subsisted off meat and milk.[18] They got a respite when the arrival of young Simon's army at Kenilworth sent Edward back to Worcester to avoid getting caught between the two opposing forces. But Edward's spies informed him that his cousin's men were camped mostly in the town and not in the castle. He and the Marchers gambled on a quick cavalry strike to take them out of action. Covering 34 miles in the night, they surprised them at dawn, most of them stark naked in their beds, and captured several leading barons like Richard Grey and Robert de Vere, the Earl of Oxford. The raid was hardly an unqualified success, however. Young Simon and most of his troops were able to get away and regroup, and Montfort got his men across the Severn in the meantime. They were only a few miles south of Worcester, but when Edward's men returned, they were too exhausted to force a battle. Montfort then slipped away overnight. Instead of marching southeast for Oxford and London, he turned north, hoping to join his son's still substantial force. With their combined strength, they would turn on Edward and crush him.[19]

It too was a gamble, because once they crossed the River Avon at Evesham, they were committed. They reached the abbey of the town in the early hours of 4 August 1265, and halted to rest and have breakfast despite speed being of the essence. Henry also insisted on attending mass. News soon reached Montfort from the front lines that the delay had cost them nothing. An army was seen approaching from the north, and the banners they were flying belonged to their adherents. It seemed his son had finally arrived. But the lookout in the bell tower quickly dashed those hopes. Spies had kept Edward abreast of their progress throughout the night. He tracked them there, then deployed the banners captured at Kenilworth to lure them into a false sense of security. The hearts of the Montfortians sank, but their leader was nevertheless impressed with Edward's troop movements. He couldn't help boasting that his nephew had learned them from him.[20]

All would not be lost if young Simon was making good time, but Montfort was under no illusions and advised his associates to flee while they could. All refused, with Despenser declaring: 'Today we shall all drink from one cup, just as we have in the past.' The sky eerily darkened as they moved forward, intending either to break through or keep the loyalists occupied until help arrived, but they were soon hemmed in by superior numbers. Montfort was determined to fight to the end, and Edward was ready to hasten that outcome. He had waited more than a year for this moment, to exact his revenge for all the humiliation heaped upon him. Before the battle, he assigned a death squad, eagerly led by Mortimer, to find his godfather and cut him down. He might have claimed that Montfort deserved it for all the discord he had caused over the years, but he also wanted total revenge. His men were to forget about collecting future ransoms and kill as many of the enemy as they could.[21]

'More murder never was before in so little time,' lamented Robert of Gloucester of the massacre unleashed. Forty knights were hacked to death in a slaughter of the nobility not seen since the Conquest. One of the first to fall was Henry de Montfort. Then came the justiciar Hugh Despenser and councillors Peter de Montfort and Roger St John. Simon de Montfort put up a good fight for a man in his late fifties. It was said that he fought with such vigour against the death squad that it took a blow from behind to bring him down. As the battle moved past him into the town, where the carnage was no less horrific, his lifeless body was chopped up into trophies, with Mortimer taking the head and testicles as gruesome tokens for his wife Maud.[22]

A new, terrifying page in English history had been turned and Henry was subjected to the full horror of it. He had been accoutred for battle in plain armour, without any crest to distinguish his royal rank, and for all the Edwardians knew he was just another Montfortian knight to cut down. As the butchery closed in around him, he desperately tried to make himself known above the violence and fury on the ground and the thunderstorm raging overhead. Parrying the blows that fell upon him, he repeatedly cried out, 'For the love of God, I am Henry of Winchester, your king. Don't kill me!' He was wounded in the shoulder before his attackers halted and removed his helmet.[23] Realising he was indeed the king, they led him off to safety, doubtless before Mortimer and his minions went about desecrating Montfort's corpse.

Given his personal and religious sensibilities, Henry could only have been appalled by their savagery, but his anger at his fallen adversary lingered long after he had been restored to power. Montfort had appropriated his kingdom, dragged him around Wales in his bid to survive, and as a final indignity forced him to fight incognito against his son and supporters. There's no record of any last words to pass between these two historic antagonists as they rode off to meet their fates that morning. Probably there weren't any. After thirty years of sharing the world stage together, they had nothing more to say to each other.

* * *

Henry's wound was slight. Within three days he was 13 miles away in Worcester reviving the chancery, which had been suspended on 28 June after the fugitive court reached Monmouth. The chancellor was no longer with them at this time. For reasons unknown, Cantilupe had handed in the seal on 7 May and left while the court was still in Gloucester.[24] Although his departure was treated as temporary, he could forget about resuming his duties now that the king was again naming his own ministers. Henry appointed Walter Giffard, the son of Edward's former childhood guardians and currently the Bishop of Bath, as chancellor.[25] One of the first orders to go out was to rescind the grant of the York treasuryship to Amaury de Montfort and to give it to Mortimer's son. Henry then moved on to Gloucester for three weeks, revoking other grants made while he had been 'in the keeping of Simon de Montfort' and making new ones to his supporters. For the first week of September he was at Marlborough, where he showed he was the same old Henry by ordering repairs to be made in and around the castle. He then arrived in Winchester for the first parliament following his restoration.[26]

In the month after the battle, there had been a mad scramble among loyalists to seize the properties of the vanquished rebels. Not surprisingly, it was the two main defectors who led the way: Clare's men occupied 160 homesteads and John Giffard's nearly forty. Parliament urged the king to get in on the act, both to punish the rebels for their treason and to reward loyalists for restoring him to power. Other considerations in favour of wholesale confiscation was the chance to recover royal lands and rights alienated during the late reform period and to generate much needed income for the empty exchequer that would flow from the reliefs paid by the new owners. But Henry was always inclined to mercy, and the quick surrender of castles like Windsor and the Tower of London made clemency a real possibility. Taking advice from Edward, he wrote to the men of the Channel ports on 26 August that he was 'willing to show mercy and grace instead of vengeance', and to the garrison at Kenilworth on the same day that due to his 'inborn benevolence' he saw fit to spare them their inheritances and lives on condition that they hand over the castle without delay.[27]

The nominal commander at Kenilworth was the younger Simon de Montfort, who blamed himself for the disaster that had befallen them, and rightly so. His troops had got to within miles of Evesham when he called a halt that morning, also to have breakfast. He reached the battlefield in time to see his father's head silhouetted in the distance, pitched up on a lance. The young man couldn't touch a thing for breakfast for days after that. Back at Kenilworth, he had to stop his men from butchering Richard of Cornwall in retaliation for the treatment of his father's body. He released his captives on 6 September, hoping it would obtain him and his family some much-needed goodwill. He then went to Winchester under safe conduct to negotiate with Henry and Edward. Apparently he found their terms unacceptable and went back to the castle to continue resisting with the garrison.[28]

That settled it for Henry. On 17 September 1265, he had Walerand proclaim the peace, meaning that the lands of anyone still in rebellion at that point were forfeit to the crown pending a review conducted by independent commissioners in each county. It was more complicated working out a start date of the rebellion, whether to go all the way back to the summer of 1263 or just the Evesham campaign. The assault on Northampton on 4 April 1264 was eventually chosen, which put turncoats like Clare and Giffard in jeopardy. They wisely sought and got exoneration from the king on 9 October.[29]

By then Parliament had moved to Windsor, where Henry summoned the feudal host in preparation for a siege of London. Mayor Fitz-Thomas and the aldermen were anxious for a peaceful settlement and agreed to submit fully to the king. On 4 October, Leybourne brought a delegation of them and other prominent citizens to Windsor, where they were forced to wait outside until evening. Once admitted, they were locked up in the tower despite their letters of safe conduct. Henry forwent the opportunity to make Fitz-Thomas squirm for his impudent words to him at the spring Parliament. There was no, 'Ah, my lord Mayor, we meet again'. There was no meeting at all, in fact. Henry handed him and four others over to Edward to decide their fate and left without seeing any of them. He went to London and called the citizens his enemies. Remembering their infamous treatment of the queen at London Bridge, he gave control of the bridge to her. He then demanded the entire city fine for his grace, which meant punishing the innocent with the guilty, but he showed he was in no mood to quibble by expelling sixty families, presumably among the guilty, and granting their homes to his supporters.[30]

This adoption of disinheritance as policy was announced at the feast of St Edward on 13 October 1265, which Henry also marked by wearing his crown, as had King Stephen in 1141 and Richard the Lionheart in 1194 following their captivities. Although his majesty 'shone forth gloriously' for the occasion, he faced opposition to his drive to deprive the Montfortians of their estates. Richard of Cornwall and Philip Basset were against it, probably for family reasons. Richard had promised to help his sister Eleanor, whose family stood to lose most, and Philip was the father-in-law of both Fitz-John, the only leading Montfortian captured intact at Evesham, and the now-deceased Despenser. Both men eventually partook of the spoils, however. Roger Bigod was also opposed to the scheme despite initially seizing four manors himself. As a collaborator with Montfort's government, he could expect to gain little from the final settlement and got little.[31]

The whole concept of disinheritance suggested that it was going to be a messy, bitter affair, and the initial seizures made sure of it. In swarming over as many rebel properties as they could, the loyalists were out for plunder. They hauled away livestock, grain and tools, anything they could get their hands on. In some cases, they had to contend with other loyalists who showed up with the same agenda. The commissioners had to deal with this and other obstacles put in their way by rebels and loyalists alike. Despite all the haste and complications, Henry got on with the business as soon as the reports came in. He tried to make the process as humane as possible in making provisions for the families of the Montfortians. The womenfolk were not only allowed to keep their marriage portions, but their dowers as well, which were normally forfeit under the law for treason. A sliding scale between a fifth and the nominal third was used to spare them total confiscation, as in the case of Edith, the widow of Thomas Astley of Warwickshire. He had been an adherent of Montfort for years and served as a keeper of the peace before his death at Evesham. Of his estate valued at £150, she received lands worth £34. Bassingbourne got the rest.[32]

There was one widow for whom Henry was not likely to show much sympathy. Although he owed all the fine food and clothes he received during the captive monarchy to Eleanor de Montfort, she never believed that that act of duty and kindness would alone restore her and her children to favour if things went awry for them. The first thing she did after learning of Edward's escape was to go to Dover and secure it for a possible escape later on. She could have sought mercy like so many other relatives, but her position was exceptional, being both the sister of the king and widow of his enemy. She opted for exile in France and sent her sons Amaury and Richard ahead of her with £7,333 in cash.

Edward then arrived ready to lay siege to Dover Castle if necessary, but hoping his aunt would give it up without a fight. He was most considerate of her plight, as well he might be after the disgraceful mutilation of her husband's body. He may not have condoned it, but it still made him look bad in front of her and his foreign relatives and in-laws, and he had to reckon with a blood feud now between the Plantagenets and Montforts, who were still a powerful clan in France and the Holy Land. He immediately tried to make amends by attending the funeral of her son at Evesham Abbey, even openly weeping at it. They may only have been crocodile tears, for Henry de Montfort had been his jailer, and Edward's reputation for deceit was by now legendary, but when Eleanor asked him to pardon the members of her household, he not only promised he would, but actually did.[33]

On 28 October, she left England with her young daughter Eleanor. Ironically, her departure coincided with the arrival of her sister-in-law and former friend, Queen Eleanor, who disembarked at Dover the next day after two years of her own exile, the latter part of it spent lording over Gascony. Edward greeted his mother and brought her to Canterbury, where Henry was waiting with the court to receive her in state. He had evidently shared his eagerness to see his wife again with Queen Margaret. In a jocular letter that underscored the warm and flirtatious relationship between the King of England and Queen of France, she assured him that she would speed her sister along. She had heard that the dowager Countess of Gloucester was in his neighbourhood, and, taking a playful dig at Henry's well-known impulsiveness, claimed she was afraid he might marry someone like her in the meantime.[34]

The reunion between Henry and Eleanor, he now 58 and she 41, was doubtless an affectionate one. The extent to which the trials of the past couple of years had strengthened the intimacy between them can be seen in a letter which Henry wrote to Louis three years later. He was anticipating another trip to France, but since it was supposed to be strictly for business, he asked if he might not bring the queen with him, 'so that we may be cheered by the sight of her, and by talking with her'. Of course, it's also possible to read into this a hint that Louis, whose own marital relations were more frigid than ever, should make sure Margaret was there as well.[35]

Accompanying his mother homeward was 20-year-old Edmund. He didn't realise it, but he stepped off the gangplank as the new Earl of Leicester. Four days before, on 25 October, Henry had granted him 'all the lands late of S. de Montfort, the king's enemy' in a charter witnessed by Basset and Hugh Bigod. This could have been the point of contention that kept the younger Simon, the earl-designate after his father, from reaching a settlement at the Winchester Parliament. The king might not confiscate other estates, but this one he would for sure because he had given it to Montfort based on the most tenuous of claims and Montfort had repaid him with civil war and usurped his power. Besides, Henry needed to set up Edmund now that the throne of Sicily was truly gone for good, thanks in no small part to the reform period. On 28 June 1265, as Montfort was preparing to take the court on his desperate run through the south of Wales, Charles of

Anjou was formally invested with the kingdom of Sicily in preparation for his fight against Manfred.[36]

There were bound to be complaints that Edmund didn't deserve Leicester since he had played no part in defeating the Montfortians. And yet he did his father a great service simply in being abroad the whole time. Simon de Montfort had always been dogged by rumours that what he was really after was the English throne, if not for himself, then for his son Henry, who was a grandson of King John.[37] But Henry de Montfort was sixth in line after Edward, Edmund, Richard of Cornwall, Henry of Almain and Edmund of Cornwall. Four of these five Montfort was holding as hostages, and presuming he had it in him to make them all disappear, there was no way he could get his hands on Edmund Plantagenet in order to clear the dynastic path for his son. As for just seizing the throne for himself, Simon would have had to get rid of the king first, and his supporters, principally the bishops, would have drawn a line there.

These bishops were a nervous lot in the wake of the defeat. Walter Cantilupe had travelled with Montfort's army on its final trek to Evesham and preached to the men before the battle 'so that they had less fear of death'. Already in his seventies, he took to his bed while Henry initiated a suit against him and six of his colleagues for their role in the captive monarchy. The king lacked the authority to actually turn them out of office, but the fine gentleman who also accompanied the queen homeward did. He was Ottobuono Fieschi, a cardinal in his fifties who was known to Henry through the Sicilian business. Fieschi had been appointed legate for England before Evesham and was given explicit instructions by Pope Clement not to seek any treaty of 'false peace' until Montfort and all his progeny were 'plucked out of the realm of England'. Running scared, the bishops avoided him after his arrival, but in due course Ottobuono was able to determine the worst offenders among them, namely the hardcore Montfortians. Cantilupe topped the list, but he died on 12 February 1266, before any action could be taken against him. The other four, Sandwich (London), Berksted (Chichester), Gravesend (Lincoln) and Gervais (Winchester), were suspended later that spring and ordered to appear before the papal court.[38]

About a month after the king granted away the estate he was set to inherit, the younger Simon de Montfort moved to the Isle of Axholm in Lincolnshire to join another pocket of resistance. Edward took part of the feudal host summoned to lay siege to Kenilworth and marched against this new threat. He had little trouble forcing the rebels to submit, and in January led his cousin to Northampton, where the court had spent Christmas, to receive judgement. Simon was to abjure the realm, promise not to work against the crown's interests and in return would receive a yearly income of £333. He was taken to London, but suspected treachery and fled to Winchelsea. After the briefest of careers as a pirate, he caught a boat to the Continent. In April, his brother Guy, who had been wounded at Evesham, also reached France. Imprisoned at Windsor, he was transferred to Dover, whence he escaped after bribing his gaoler.[39]

They crossed just in time, because Edward and Leybourne next set out to pacify the strongly Montfortian port cities. The last of them capitulated on 24 March 1266, thanks in part to the carpet clemency they received. Henry then named Edward their lord protector with full authority to regulate all trade going in and out, thus establishing a commercial alliance that would serve the future king well. The people of London were none too happy about the arrangement, however. Here the king was letting these pirates off the hook, but earlier, on 10 January, he had slapped them with a fine of £13,333 for their trespasses in the late conflict. The sum was enormous, about £12,000,000 in today's money, but despite them paying it, their mayor and the others handed over to Edward remained imprisoned. In the week before the election of a new sheriff at Guildhall on 6 May, crowds began demanding the release of Fitz-Thomas. Leybourne was standing by with troops to put down any riot and ended up hauling away more than twenty protesters.[40]

The fine was meant to include the £5,000 needed to redeem the three French bishoprics sold by the queen to Louis, which took place on 20 March. The city balked at paying the £2,500 penalty as well, so the king told them to pay it to Edward instead, who would then answer to Louis if he really wanted it (apparently he did). Eleanor had contracted other debts abroad during the troubled years, as much as £15,000. To pay them off, and to alleviate the general insolvency of the crown brought on by the conflict, Pope Clement ordered religious institutions to contribute a tenth of their revenues for three years.[41] This was bound to create the usual resentment, but he probably felt he owed it to Henry for reasons other than failing him during his tenure as legate. On 26 February 1266, Charles of Anjou defeated and killed Manfred at the battle of Benevento, bringing the papacy that much closer to achieving its objective in Sicily. The island kingdom should have gone to Edmund, whom Clement likely met during the standoff with Montfort. He would have seen first-hand that this naturally congenial prince was the imported king they were looking for. Had the previous popes treated his candidature with more respect and been less motivated by greed, they might not now be stuck with the ruthless Charles, who was already showing signs of becoming another Frederick, only without the stellar charm or cultivation.[42]

Edmund was finding his position as the new lord of Leicester difficult enough. Kenilworth fell within his domains, but he was unable to contain the garrison and keep them from plundering the surrounding countryside. They spurned all attempts to negotiate, and in one brazen act of cruelty, chopped off the hand of a royal messenger. Nothing infuriated Henry more than his messengers being maltreated. He called out the feudal host to attack the stronghold, but found his resources depleted by the need to reduce other centres of resistance.[43] On 15 May 1266, Henry of Almain and John Balliol routed a force of Montfortians, now collectively called the Disinherited, at Chesterfield in Derbyshire. Five days later, Edward caught up with a different guerrilla band operating around Alton Pass in Hampshire. In the heat of the moment he went berserk and engaged their leader Adam Gurdon in single combat. He had bitten off more than he could chew, because Gurdon was an immensely strong career soldier. Edward managed to wound him, but it was all he could do to hold him off until his men came up and helped overpower him. His pride injured, Edward ordered all the bandits strung up from the surrounding trees, but Gurdon himself he had loaded down in chains and dispatched to his mother at Windsor.[44]

Gurdon was the second high-profile prisoner to arrive that week. One of the insurgents captured at Chesterfield was Robert de Ferrers, who had spent the collapse of Montfort's regime still locked up in the Tower of London. On 5 December 1265, he received a pardon from Henry in return for a gold drinking cup and £1,000. Ferrers got off without being deprived of his earldom because he hadn't been at either Lewes or Evesham and his crimes were more personal than political. It also helped that he was married to one of the king's Lusignan nieces. It was probably his everlasting hatred for Edward that got him mixed up with the Disinherited. Since he had cast his lot with them, Henry decided he should share their fate and gave his lands to Edmund. Wykes notes that Gurdon was sent to Windsor specifically to keep Ferrers company in the dungeon there.[45]

By late June, troops, equipment and nine siege engines were in place around Kenilworth. Henry, Edward, Edmund and Mortimer each took a side of the castle and began pounding away at it relentlessly. They had their work cut out for them. The massive outer walls encompassed an area of more than nine acres, with a lake protecting the approach on two sides. The garrison was said to number more than a thousand and it sallied forth from time to time to drive back the loyalists. Ottobuono arrived with Boniface, who had finally returned to England that spring, but their entreaties fell on deaf ears. Even their sentence of excommunication was met with scathing mockery when a clerk dressed up in priestly robes appeared on the ramparts and retorted, 'The same to you.' The rebels could thank the previous owner for having turned the castle into an impregnable fortress, but from where the king was standing, it was just one more gift to Simon de Montfort that he had come to regret.[46]

* * *

The best news that summer came on the night of 13–14 July 1266, when Eleanor of Castile gave birth to a baby boy at Windsor. The child, who was now second in line to the throne, was named John. Whatever anyone else might think of the previous king, Henry always respected the memory of his father and doubtless urged his son to do the same. The name also made a handy political statement. The era of baronial revolutions that had begun with John was officially over and the folk at Kenilworth might want to take heed. The people of London certainly did. They declared a holiday the next day and celebrated with a fanfare that recalled Edward's own birth twenty-seven years earlier.[47]

The garrison continued to hold out, buoyed by the expectation that the younger Simon de Montfort was gathering troops on the Continent for an invasion. When a new centre of resistance arose on the Isle of Ely under the firebrand John Deyville, Henry faced increased pressure from a group around the legate to reverse the whole disinheritance scheme. At the same time, he was being advised to stand firm by hardliners like Mortimer, who was the second largest recipient of confiscated lands after Edmund. He opted for a twelve-man committee under Ottobuono and Henry of Almain to find a way out. On 31 October 1266, three days after the little-noticed fiftieth anniversary of Henry's coronation in Gloucester, they issued the Dictum of Kenilworth, an ordinance covering the state of the kingdom since the restoration. Politically it marked a defeat for the Disinherited. It reaffirmed royal authority as it had been in the old days and repudiated the conciliar control at the heart of Montfortianism. The king was only asked to choose men of integrity for his officers and to respect the rights and liberties of his subjects and the Church. But the Disinherited were offered total amnesty and the chance to redeem their lands by paying a fine based on the gravity of their rebellion. Those forced to support Montfort had to pay the annual value of their lands, those who willingly supported him twice that value and those who fought for him five times. The idea was that since land was worth roughly ten times its annual value, the hardcore rebels could take possession of half of their estates by selling the other half. Two were singled out to pay seven years' income: Henry Hastings for his part in mutilating the messenger, and Robert de Ferrers for just being stupid.[48]

The lone exception to the redemption policy were the Montforts. In France, Louis had kept an eye on the younger Simon to stop him gathering an invasion force, but he wanted Henry to make peace with him and the rest of the family. Pope Clement had already done so himself when, on 15 September 1266, he removed the sentence of excommunication from Montfort at the behest of his son Amaury. Ten days later, Henry wrote to Louis to say he would stand by any award he might issue on their behalf, including restoring Leicester to them. He only asked that they be prepared to sell it to him at a price set by the King of France, minus the damages he had suffered on account of their revolt. He agreed to pay his sister a pension of £500 for her dower or allow her to come to England to sue for a better deal if she wanted. Her son could also return but, naturally, would have to answer for his actions in a court of law. Simon found the terms too stiff and left for Italy, where he and his brother Guy found service under their father's old friend Charles of Anjou.[49]

Another clause dealing with the late Simon de Montfort had to do with the miracles reportedly worked by him at Evesham, presumably at the spot where the monks had buried what remains they could find, next to his son and Despenser near the high altar of the abbey. Since he died an excommunicate, such talk of miracles was blasphemous, and the Dictum of Kenilworth forbade it under pain of corporal punishment. There was no loosening Montfort's grip on the imagination of his followers, however. John de Vescy returned to his barony of Alnwick near Scotland with one of Montfort's feet, retrieved from the battlefield, he said. He gave it to the local canons who, seeing how well preserved it was several months later, had it encased in silver to work a few miracles for them.[50]

So anxious was Henry to reach a settlement that the men of Kenilworth and Ely were consulted in the drafting of the Dictum. They found much to dislike in the final version, but the struggle after Evesham had been going on for more than a year and many just wanted a return to normal life. That was especially true for the garrison at Kenilworth, which had been reduced to a shell after the constant bombardment. With food running low and winter setting in, it was time to call it a day, but they asked for and received, as a point of honour, forty days to see whether a relief force really wasn't on the way. It was a wonder they held out that long, for when they finally emerged on 14 December, they left behind a stench so foul that it nearly floored the first occupants after them. They were free to go and do whatever they pleased as long as they kept the peace and abided by the Dictum.[51]

Some had no intention of doing so and followed their commander Henry Hastings to Ely, where they found like-minded men still ready to resist. What bothered them most about the deal was the steepness of the fines and the lack of a provision for them to take possession of their lands before paying it off. They signalled their definitive rejection of the Dictum by riding into Norwich on 16 December and sacking the town. Despite this and other depredations, their cause was taken up by Clare, who demanded they receive their lands first and pay their fines afterwards. He was an unlikely defender of the people whose defeat he had helped orchestrate, but he always claimed he defected because Montfort had lost his way and become corrupted by power. He wanted it understood that he went over to Edward as matter of principle.[52]

Like Edward, however, he had a credibility problem. Everyone knew he was driven to betray Montfort by his jealousy of him and his sons. He felt he had not been adequately rewarded with wealth and power and the same thing was happening again. His share of the spoils fell far short of the number of properties he had seized in his rush to enrichment after Evesham. His influence with the king, moreover, was negligible compared to loyalists like Mortimer, who were dead set against going back on disinheritance. They felt they had sacrificed much in remaining consistently loyal to the king, whereas all Clare could really claim was that he had always been on the winning side during the recent war. He and Mortimer were also quarrelling over two castles that had belonged to the younger Humphrey de Bohun before he succumbed to his wounds from Evesham. As neighbours in the Marches, things were bound to get personal between them, and Clare suddenly left the siege of Kenilworth for fear that Mortimer was out to murder him. Henry failed to reconcile them at the Christmas feast held in Oxford, and when he summoned the magnates to meet again at Westminster at the start of the year, Clare sent messengers instead to demand that Edward keep his promise about getting rid of the foreigners and resurrecting all the good old laws. It was more tiresome justification for turning against the Montfortians, but this time he hinted he would take action if he was not appeased.[53]

To the court, it seemed as if Gilbert 'the Red', as Clare was called, was simply full of himself. He had been on the committee of twelve that drew up the Dictum, which by most accounts was working. Disinherited from all over the country were coming in, including Robert de Vere, the Earl of Oxford. He was in the five-year class of offenders because he had fought at Lewes and was captured at Kenilworth. Mortimer was undoubtedly unhappy to have to give him his lands back. Fiercely ambitious, he may even have fancied himself becoming the Earl of Oxford some day. But since he had defended his hard line on loyalty to the king, he went along and worked out a private agreement with Vere. Although liable for £2,000 based on the £400 annual value of his estate, Vere eventually got it back for £1,667.[54]

But there were others who had second thoughts after initially accepting the Dictum. The lands of Evesham survivor John de Vescy, worth £500 a year, had been granted to the Count of St Pol, a French nobleman who had always supplied Henry with mercenaries whenever he needed them. The king had to know he was playing with fire in making a grant to a foreigner. Only the year before he had to quell rumours that he was planning to seize Roger Bigod's earldom for this very purpose. Like Clare and Ferrers, Vescy was married to a foreigner by arrangement of the royal couple, but he was also impulsive like they were and probably would have taken the action he did regardless, which was to form a league with other Disinherited to reoccupy their ancestral estates.[55]

Vescy's renewed disaffection was a severe blow to Henry. He had summoned Parliament to meet on 9 February 1267 at Bury St Edmunds as a prelude to investing the rebel stronghold on the Isle of Ely. If he could not get the malcontents to surrender, he would throw the full weight of the feudal host against them. Vescy's uprising now forced him to change plans and dispatch Edward with a large force 240 miles to the north to bring him to heel. It was in a churlish mood that Henry reminded Deyville and his belligerents that they had been justly deprived of their lands for raising rebellion against their lord, as they would have been anywhere in the Christian world at that time. They replied that they had fought with the king at Evesham, not against him, and so were technically not guilty in that sense. Ottobuono's appeal to their religious sensibilities was similarly snubbed, so Henry moved to Cambridge to begin operations against them. He threw himself into it with vigour and personally led an assault on a group of rebels plundering a nearby village. His overall plans were elaborate, from encircling them with a ditch to sending a fleet against them, but Deyville was equally resolute. He struck back at every encroachment made by the loyalists and drove away the fleet in confusion. It was shaping up to be a long, arduous slog just like Kenilworth.[56]

The men at Ely were encouraged to fight on because they were engaged in secret negotiations with Clare. He had gathered a large army in the Marches to pummel Mortimer; now he was taking it to London instead. Deyville was supposed to slip through the blockade and meet up with him on the outskirts of the city, only he had to scurry back after Henry discovered his movements and sent Leybourne to intercept him. London was thrown into panic when Clare arrived on 8 April, but Ottobuono assured city leaders he had come in peace and convinced them to let him set up camp in Southwark. Even more incredibly, Ottobuono arranged for Clare and his men to have passage over the bridge to have talks with him directly in London. In the meantime, Deyville and his men had given Leybourne the slip a second time and appeared in Southwark on 11 April. It was when the people of London asked Clare for help in expelling them that he revealed his true intentions. He took control of all the city gates, allowed the rebels access to the city and basically declared that it was under his occupation.[57]

Almost instantly London was again transformed into a Montfortian commune. The aldermen were replaced by 'keepers', the city jail was thrown open and those banished after Evesham came back. Although Clare gave orders for his men and the rebels to be on their best behaviour, the inevitable looting and depredations also included Westminster Palace. Ottobuono took himself and most of the Jewish community to the safety of the Tower and put the city under interdict. Clare demanded that he give up the fortress, and when he refused, laid siege to him there. He still insisted there was nothing to be afraid of and showed that he was serious about maintaining order by having four of his men caught in the act of pillaging bound up and tossed into the Thames.[58]

Not until the arrival of his son's forces from the north did Henry have enough manpower to do something about Clare's latest betrayal. Edward had not only put down Vescy and his adherents, but earned their everlasting loyalty by giving them a pardon for their trespass (though not for their redemption fines). With these reinforcements, including a Scottish contingent, Henry marched to Windsor at the end of April, reorganised his forces there, then moved on to the abbey of Ham to the east of London. Feeling bold, the rebels challenged the loyalists to meet them in open battle on a plain called Hounslow. The king came with his men, but Clare was worried about escalating the standoff and restrained Deyville. Henry now moved to Stratford to edge up against the city walls close to the Tower. From this position, he was able to help the legate and his staff make their escape. He remained there for the next month while Leybourne was on the Continent recruiting mercenaries, from the Count of St Pol among others. Lacking money to pay for them, Henry was forced to pawn the jewels set to go in the new shrine for Edward the Confessor.[59]

Clare had made preparations for the coming siege by digging a ditch around the walls and fortifying Southwark. He turned to his friends outside the city for help, but they spurned him and joined the king instead, including his brother Thomas. By the time the mercenaries arrived at the end of May, negotiations were already underway to end the occupation. The Earl of Gloucester was now distancing himself from the rebels, and on 4 June sent a delegation under John Fitz-John to meet Fitz-John's father-in-law Philip Basset, Richard of Cornwall and other moderates in the king's camp. Eleven days later, a deal was reached for their evacuation. Clare and his men were to receive a pardon for everything except the damages they caused to the merchants they had despoiled. He was required to reconcile with Edward, which he did later at Windsor, and to post security of £6,666 for his future good behaviour. On 15 June, he left the city, apparently satisfied he had made his voice heard. Three days later, Henry entered London for the third time in his reign following the surrender of the city.[60]

Deyville and the rebels were left to make their own separate peace. They didn't get the remission of their redemption fines as hoped, but the king promised to 'diligently ask' the beneficiaries of their lands to allow them to take full possession immediately. For his part, Ottobuono got the Church to make a contribution of a twentieth for the relief of the Disinherited. On 1 July, Deyville and his men in Southwark were pardoned and departed, but their compatriots on Ely still held out. Two weeks later, Edward was able to get them to submit using reconnaissance from former rebels and the threat to hang them. The war of the Disinherited was over, marking an end to the struggle between the king and barons that had begun nearly a decade ago. The appalling weather that helped bring it on back then now gave way to a beautiful spring and summer. Bread, fruit and wine were abundant, and the trees, flowers and fields blossomed like they hadn't in living memory. Most of the Montfortians eventually got their lands back, though not without plenty of hardship, but their reintegration into society was so fast and remarkable that the miracle cult of Simon de Montfort was soon largely extinguished.[61]

There was one more act of the captive monarchy left to undo, the compact made with Llywelyn at Pipton. In early August, Henry began moving his court in the direction of Wales. Negotiations for a new accord began in Shrewsbury at the end of the month, but little progress was made because Llywelyn understandably resisted giving back all that Montfort had conceded to him. Henry put the whole matter in Ottobuono's hands and within a week the legate got both sides to agree to what were essentially the existing terms, only with the tribute lowered to £16,666. Llywelyn's territorial gains, his overlordship and status as 'Prince of Wales', for him and his heirs, were again recognised in the new Treaty of Montgomery. He had achieved the supremacy that evaded his ancestors, including his namesake grandfather, but the King of England still remained his lord. This could only mean future interference in disputes between the prince and his brothers and the Welsh barons owing him homage. More ominously, the treaty was unable to resolve all the encroachments and acquisitions made by Llywelyn during the years of strife. They had come at the expense of the Marchers, the most aggrieved and quarrelsome faction of the English nobility. It was only a matter of time before they set out to reverse them.[62]

Two days after the treaty was ratified on 29 September 1267, Henry celebrated his sixtieth birthday. He spent it at Ludlow, the castle 23 miles north of Hereford where Edward, Mortimer and Clare had agreed to destroy Montfort. As with his golden jubilee the year before, the occasion wasn't marked by any known anthems or festivities, probably at his own insistence. He had stopped in Evesham on the way to Wales, nearly two years to the date after the battle, and revisiting the scene of that apocalyptic horror would have reminded him of the remorse and humility needed in the wake of his salvation. It would also have made him more aware than ever of the need to strive for permanent reconciliation throughout the land, and so in November he summoned a Parliament 'of the higher as well as the lower estate' to Marlborough to provide for speedier justice and better administration of the realm, 'as belongeth to the office of a king'.[63]

Parliament's work was enacted on 18 November 1267 as the Statute of Marlborough, a series of provisions embodying three basic principles of law enforcement. The first takes aim at those who distressed their neighbours or anyone else, which is to say they sought 'redemption' through acts of vengeance carried out during and after the recent disturbances. Malefactors caught taking the law into their own hands in this fashion, and the evidence suggests Henry had loyalists more in mind, were to be punished by paying a redemption themselves. The second part stipulates strict compliance with the charter of liberties, which incidentally took on the name Magna Carta fifty years earlier that very month with the co-issue of the Forest Charter. Of greater importance was the article stipulating that writs regarding the charter were to be granted for free, much like the *querelae* under the Provisions of Oxford. The poor were thus guaranteed access to the courts whenever their basic rights were infringed.

Lastly, the Statute incorporates many of the clauses of the Provisions of Westminster, particularly those that protect tenants from their lords. This was the part of the reform movement that Henry always supported and had perhaps envisioned when he joined his barons in reforming the realm in 1258. Since then, the country had been to hell and back. There was plenty of blame to go around over how such good intentions got so out of control, and each would have to answer for his own actions when his day of reckoning came. But at least for now, it looked as if they might all get that behind them and again enjoy the peace and tranquillity Henry had always hoped would be his lasting legacy.[64]

17

BY GIFT OF THE THIRD HENRY 1268–1272 …

As the final years of his reign began, Henry III was a king in a hurry. The reconstruction of Westminster Abbey had been going on for more than two decades, but the fraught years of reform had slowed the pace considerably. Annual expenditures on the works had fallen to nearly half compared to the period before 1258. The Montfortian government kept the construction site in funds, but at the time of Evesham, there were only 100 tradesmen, from masons and marblers to carpenters and polishers, labouring on it, down from a high of 800. Not until the struggle with the Disinherited ended was Henry again able to devote his energies to the abbey, and the proverbial clock was running. He was planning to translate the remains of Edward the Confessor to a new tomb and shrine and had just two years to have everything ready for the projected date of 13 October 1269. He had chosen this particular feast day because the liturgical calendar for that year was the same as in 1163, when the Confessor was first translated. In both years, all the dates fell on the same days of the week, with the feast day, like Easter, falling on a Sunday. He would grieve to miss the opportunity to highlight the ceremony with such elegant spiritual symmetry.[1]

The most spectacular of the new works was the sanctuary pavement before the high altar. Named after the Cosmati family of craftsmen who did similar floors, the idea to replicate their technique came from the Abbot of Westminster, Richard de Ware. He had been to Italy and knew the king would appreciate splendour of this sort in the abbey. Henry had probably made it known to him that he was after more than just any mosaic for the pavement, and he certainly got it in the design elaborated by the team brought over from Rome by Ware. The nearly 25 square feet of embedded stones, more than 50,000 of them harvested from ancient ruins, starts at the centre with a bright disc of porphyry showing randomly swirling lines and colours. Four bands run along its perimeter, each weaving around to encircle their own discs. These five spheres are enclosed within a square whose sides devolve into four more circles, and on and on the shapes and patterns continue until the work as a whole hints at something far more intricate than just an ornamental floor to enhance coronations and state occasions.[2]

Henry did not have the brilliant education of his grandfather, nor did he own a great library like his father. The only books he is known to have possessed were liturgies in Latin and romances in French.[3] He was always more at home with the visual arts, and it was in the building, painting and craftsmanship of others that he sought to express his thoughts, which were typically nothing if not big. Given the prominent location of the high altar, he decided to reach for the biggest of them all and have the floor in front of it paved with a depiction of the universe. Indeed, the nebulous cloud in the centre roundel looks like formless matter at the heart of the creation. It swirls in a circle, the shape that has no end or beginning, while the four sides of the square around it represent the basic medieval elements of earth, water, air and fire, or to put it in larger perspective, the earth, sun, moon and stars.

Anyone not sure of that interpretation only has to read the words inscribed in the central square enframing the first nine spheres. It tells beholders that, having taken it all in, what they were actually seeing was the end of the universe. A bizarre formula using a factor of three was provided to calculate when that was going to happen. The lifespan of a hedgerow is reckoned to be three years. Multiplying that by three gives the life of a dog (9), by three again that of a horse (27), that of a man (81), and on it goes until giant sea serpents are presumed to live for 6,561 years. Finally, that number is multiplied by three to get the life of the world/universe, which works out at 19,683 years. Everything will come to an end when that age is reached, and the souls of everyone, including all future monarchs crowned on that very spot, will be called to account.[4]

It's impossible not to see Henry's sense of humour in all this, but he took the end of the world seriously. Some of his devotion to Edward the Confessor had to do with finding a saint who embodied the virtue and goodness needed to help get him and the rest of the nation through the Last Judgement, something they all dreaded. But he was equally concerned with his place in the world while it lasted. The central inscription mentions him first among the creators of the pavement, and marks the year that it was made with a calculation that's all about him. It gives the backdated form 1,000 + 200 + 12 + 60 – 4 to indicate it was installed four years before he died (1272 – 4 = 1268). Apparently, Henry had foretold his own end much the way he had the universe, and he threw in the number of years he reigned (60 – 4 = 56) for good measure. These predictions could have been added after his death to add some mystery, but they nevertheless reflect the same mysticism that led him to astrologers and magic stones back in his early days on the throne. Considering how far he had come since then, through what seemed like an endless number of trials and tribulations, he probably felt he was destined for a happy ending and so could indulge in an excursion or two off the straight and narrow path of piety.[5]

Back in the real world, there was still the problem of paying for it all. Work on the shrine was interrupted the previous year when he was forced to pawn the rubies, emeralds, sapphires and gold figurines meant to adorn it, some of them worth as much as £200 each.[6] He got them back, but a new national enterprise was guaranteed to keep him scrounging for funds well into the next year. In addition to restoring peace to the land, Ottobuono's mission included preaching a new crusade. He had had little luck with it, and his decision to allow Clare to enter London with an army may have been a sign of his presumption that he could convert it to this purpose. After hostilities ceased, Edward jumped at the chance to go, but his father opposed it. He was counting on his son and his circle to fill the political vacuum caused by age and the late turmoil. Basset and Walerand were all that was left of the old advisers. Mansel was dead, Hugh Bigod had died in 1266, as had Peter of Savoy and Peter d'Aigueblanche in 1268, although they hadn't bothered to come back to England. Richard of Cornwall still had clout, but he was about to go abroad himself, for a third and final trip to Germany.[7]

Of greater concern, however, was the state of the country. It was only just getting back on its feet, and an enormous amount of money would have to be diverted from reconstruction and reconciliation to prop up a hopeless cause, for that is what the crusader states had become. They had steadily lost ground to the Egyptian sultanate until they were literally pressed up against the sea. Clement naturally didn't see it this way, but he agreed that the leader of the English expedition should not be Edward. He wanted Henry, who had vowed to go eighteen years earlier. Given his age, the pope was willing to allow Edmund to go as his proxy, but he denied him a clerical tax to help fund it.[8]

Edward would not be deterred. He was now 29 years old, had a wife and son, and they added another in May 1268, whom they named after Henry. But he was restless, not at all looking forward to the tedium of governing which was what being a king was really all about. He needed an outlet for his aggressive impulses and Henry tried to give him one by lifting the ban on tournaments following the return of peace to the land.[9] The problem neither could overcome, however, was Edward's ego. Crusading was a badge of honour for life, even for those who experienced no fighting, like Richard of Cornwall, or those who failed at it miserably, like Louis IX. The thought of his brother and friends going without him and winning such easy laurels was unbearable. He could imagine them all in the future, he recalling some mighty feat of prowess in the field, and the crusading veterans patronising him with a grin that could only mean, 'Sure you did'.

Plainly, if an English expedition left, he was going be a part of it, and an English expedition was going to leave because a French one was. Louis was still haunted by his previous fiasco, and in March 1267 vowed to go again, against the wishes of almost everyone. Crusades were now regarded with contempt in many quarters. Their violence and incompetence not only hurt the faith but drained away resources that could be better spent on good works at home. But for all his protestations of humility, Louis had an ego as big as any aristocrat in that age and was determined to try again. Since that would give him two crusades under his belt, Henry had no option but to start planning to go himself. That would really leave Edward fuming and perhaps liable to do something they would both regret. The king finally relented and gave him permission to take the cross, which he did at a big event staged by Ottobuono in Northampton in June 1268. Satisfied he done all he set out to do, the legate left England the next month.[10]

Now the hard part began, because there was simply no money for a crusade. Normally the Church would provide the major funding, and Ottobuono attempted to revive the request for a tax with Clement, but the pope died in November 1268, and the college of cardinals, more divided than ever, could not agree on a successor. Not that the English Church had much to give even if it wanted to. It was still contributing a tenth of its revenues to the crown and a twentieth for the relief of the Disinherited, both grudgingly. The only alternative was a tax on the laity, but there hadn't been one in thirty years on account of the political wrangling between the king and barons. That issue had since been settled in the king's favour, and the barons were willing to approve the tax because many of them were planning to crusade and could use the subsidy. But Parliament was no longer the same club that it had been before the reform period. Following up on Henry's earlier initiatives, Montfort had revolutionised its membership, turned it into the first real commons, where the voice of the burgesses, gentry and knights had as much say as the nobility. They had financial problems of their own and wanted something done about them before a national tax made them even worse.[11]

Their biggest difficulty was how to keep the debts they owed to Jewish creditors from falling into the hands of other Christians. They serviced these debts with annual payments called 'rentcharges', which worked well enough until the lender needed to call in the loan to raise immediate cash, whether to pay his own taxes or for other reasons. Since the debtor couldn't pay up, the lender was forced to sell the bond at a discount. The buyer was typically a speculator tied to the court with no interest in assuming the loan, rather in seizing the land used to secure it. Small landowners faced eviction under this unscrupulous practice, which involved nearly every member of the royal family. Reformers promised relief, but nothing was done, and the violence inflicted on the Jews in this period was as much a mark of economic anger and opportunism as religious intolerance. Many of the perpetrators had been Montfortians who, ironically, were now turning to the Jews for credit to pay their redemption fines. Worried about being disinherited a second time, they joined other indebted landowners to demand an end to the trade in Jewish bonds. Henry of Almain and Edward, himself a former speculator, began promoting legislation to abolish rentcharges and outlaw the transfer of debts to Christians except with the king's permission, and then without any interest tacked on. No agreement on it was reached at parliaments held in January and April 1269, which was a disappointment because, in order for the tax to yield the most revenue, the assessment had to be performed in the autumn when the barns were full after the harvest.[12]

Meanwhile, Edward and Almain helped Edmund concoct a scheme to disinherit one particular landowner forever. The time had come to set Robert de Ferrers, the Earl of Derby, free after three years in prison. Under the Dictum, he should have been allowed to redeem his lands from Edmund for seven times their value, or about £9,000, but together with the fine for his transgressions, the amount was raised to £50,000, which he had no chance of finding. Since Almain and other peers offered to stand surety for the money, the king ordered him released on 1 May 1269. Ferrers, however, was taken under guard to a meeting with John Chishull, who was again the chancellor. There Chishull asked him if he agreed with all that had been arranged, including the part about Almain and the other sureties giving his lands to Edmund until he paid up. Once enrolled, he warned him, there was no going back on the deal. Desperate to get out of prison, Ferrers told him he agreed. He was nevertheless detained in Edward's custody for another three weeks before being released, as a landless, former earl. He had been swindled, but could take no legal action until Edmund got back from the crusade. His later argument that he had acted under duress when he gave his consent to the chancellor was of no avail because he was technically a free man at the time. The swindlers had it all figured out, and Ferrers never got a fair hearing in the decade remaining to him.[13]

If Henry didn't know about the scheme in advance, he certainly condoned it. Ferrers was the kind of unstable magnate he could do without, and besides, it had become a priority for him and Eleanor to increase the landholdings of their youngest son. In July 1267, Henry granted him the revived earldom of Lancaster, later to become the duchy of that name made famous in history. Together with Derby and Leicester, that brought the number of earldoms in Edmund's possession to three, and he was set to make it five when, on 9 April 1269, he married 10-year-old Aveline de Forz, the heiress of the dowager Countess of Devon and Aumale. As the prime mover behind the match, the queen undertook to pay the £2,000 for the marriage rights, half for the girl's mother, half for her grandmother. She also spearheaded the wedding that took place six weeks later between Henry of Almain and Constance de Béarn in Windsor. The bride was the heiress of Gaston, the lord based in the Pyrenees who had given Simon de Montfort and the king so much trouble in Gascony. The marriage had the full blessing of Edward, who would have to deal with Gaston some day. Almain's father, Richard of Cornwall, was in Germany at the time and apparently not consulted on it, but he was busy getting married himself. On 16 June, he took as his third wife Beatrice of Falkenburg, who was described as incomparably beautiful. She was 15 to his 60.[14]

In August, Edward led a delegation to France to discuss the crusade with his uncle the King of France. He got a substantial loan from him, £17,500, but had to agree to send a third of it to Gaston for his part in the crusade. He also had to promise to depart with the French expedition in a year's time, to serve under Louis as a subordinate and to surrender one of his sons as a hostage for the deal. His submission to the surprisingly onerous terms was an indication that he needed the money because the tax was still far from assured.[15] Their best hope of securing it would come at the Parliament summoned for the traditional feast of St Edward on 13 October 1269, which would also see the translation of Edward the Confessor to his new shrine at Westminster Abbey, right on schedule. Twice before Henry used pageantry of this sort to overawe his parliaments. In 1247 it was the Holy Blood, which ultimately failed to catch on. Ten years later, the new Chapter House and little Edmund dressed as an Italian prince also flopped. This would be his third attempt, again the magical number three, and for extra support his brother Richard and son-in-law Alexander of Scotland would be there to make it another stately occasion with three kings present.[16]

The feast was going to be lavish, with plenty of venison and new knighthoods to go around. Henry originally thought about wearing his crown, but decided against it because it would be like exalting himself after the most solemn of ceremonies. That was when his sons and brother helped him bear the remains of the Confessor to his new place of eternal interment. Bassett, Warenne and a host of others crowded them for a touch of the relics, and two Irish onlookers, said to be possessed by the devil, were cured on the spot. All those watching marvelled at the spectacle of the translation and splendour of the new church, with the mysterious pavement in front of the high altar and gold shrine behind it glittering with precious stones. This was Henry's statement for the ages, a temple of wonder and adoration to evoke pride, devotion and all that was best about the English nation.[17]

And yet, as William Marshal cautioned him fifty years ago, no people were more quarrelsome than these very English, and they refused to put aside their gripes and grievances to stand by the king on this his finest hour. First, the citizens of London and Winchester got into a scrape over who was going to have the honours of serving the royals during the feast. Then it was the bishops in a temper because the Archbishop of York presumed to be the officiating primate in place of the ill Boniface. He was Walter Giffard, the former Bishop of Bath and chancellor who was elevated to the post in 1266. Protocol demanded that his cross not be carried before him in the province of Canterbury, but he was a total show-off and insisted on doing it this way as he incensed the shrine. The bishops considered it provocation and refused to join him. They just sat in their stalls sulking, all thirteen of them.[18]

Another great sulker was Gilbert de Clare. His relations with Edward had again deteriorated, and he stayed away from the ceremony for fear that he would try to have him imprisoned. Rumour had it that it involved Clare's wife Alice, who was Edward's cousin, but a more likely reason was the crusade. He had also taken the cross at Northampton, and Edward signalled their new brotherhood by getting the king to forgive the extra security imposed upon him by the pope following his takeover of London. But since that time, Clare had come to feel that Edward was hijacking the crusade all for himself, which was an affront to his self-importance, and he began to balk at going. Without the men and resources he could provide, the English expedition would be severely hampered. Clare went to Paris to lay their dispute before the crusade commander, but Louis refused to humour him and he came home dissatisfied as ever.[19]

Henry had heard it all before. No matter who the person or what the reason, somebody was going to grumble. He might have hoped they would all forgo it for this one glorious occasion, to get past their complaints and join him in the spirit of reconciliation. A walk around the newly completed choir of the abbey would show that he had. Some time after that section was started in 1258, it was decided to place the armorial shields of some of the earls in the main spandrels together with those of monarchs like him, Louis and Alexander. One of the shields depicted a lion with a forked tail on a red surface, which everyone knew was the coat of arms of Simon de Montfort. Henry could have had it excised and replaced with the arms of a loyal supporter, but he didn't. Here in this abbey, his gift to the people, he wanted forgiveness to be the order of the day.[20]

★ ★ ★

The building, ceremony and feast had drew the 'admiration and wonder of all', says the hard-to-please Wykes, but in the Parliament that followed, approval of the tax 'hung in suspense', which is to say that Henry was only half successful. The nobles and bishops were willing to concede it, but the commons and lower clergy continued to resist. In the end, a twentieth on movables was granted, but only insofar as assessing it was concerned. Approval for actually collecting it was put off until another Parliament, which gathered on 27 April 1270. This time the two main points of contention were ironed out. The king ordered enforcement of the legislation restricting the trade in Jewish bonds, and Clare agreed to submit his quarrel with Edward to arbitration by Richard of Cornwall. Henry also confirmed Magna Carta, but this wasn't so much a concession as a redundancy. The Statute of Marlborough now made observance of the charter of liberties the law of the land. The commons then fell in line with the lords, and the tax, worth

£31,000, was passed on 12 May. Two weeks later, Richard of Cornwall published his award, which obliged Clare to keep the peace and set out after Edward within a year.[21]

This successful outcome spurred Henry into making representations that he was going on the crusade as well, but Parliament declared that it was 'neither expedient nor safe' for both the king and his son to leave at that time. In June, a violent scene in Westminster Hall was testament to the unrest that still disturbed the realm. Loyalists John de Warenne and Alan la Zouche were quarrelling over a matter that went back to the spoils of the Disinherited. As they waited for their case to come up before the justices, Warenne's men suddenly attacked Zouche and his son. Warenne, who had only recently come to blows with Henry de Lacy over a bit of pasture land, fled the scene, but Edward quickly gathered up a posse to bring him to justice. He was fined £6,666 for his unpremeditated outburst and ordered to do penance. He was pardoned on 4 August, the same day Henry resigned the 'business of the cross'. Zouche died of his wounds later that month.[22]

By this time, the expedition was hopelessly behind schedule. It would take them more than a month to make it to the Mediterranean and the French had resolved to leave by mid-August. The delay had to do with collecting the first proceeds of the tax, the poor winds along the coast, and news that Boniface, who had returned to his native Savoy, died on 18 July. Edward raced up to Canterbury to work for the election of his favourite clerk, Robert Burnell, as the new archbishop, but the monks looked aghast at all his illegitimate children (at least five) and rejected him. As for his own children, Edward and his wife Eleanor, who was going with him, committed them to the care of Richard of Cornwall. The choice of Richard as guardian over their grandmother was probably due to political concerns. The queen's reputation never recovered from the anti-alien innuendo spread during the conflict. The dim view of her as 'the root, the originator, and the sower of all the discord' still fed a lot of resentment, and all the uncertainty about the xenophobic Clare's stability made it imperative not to take any chances. On 20 August they left Dover.[23] Father and son said their goodbyes earlier in Winchester. In view of the perils ahead, doubtless it was an affectionate parting.

The men left behind to help the king rule were an able lot. There were the old intimates Richard, Basset and Walerand, together with Edmund, who delayed his departure for half a year, Mortimer, Archbishop Giffard and newcomer Burnell. They were immediately confronted with the threat of war in Wales. Relations between Llywelyn and Clare were already bad before Edward's departure. On 11 October, the prince stormed the fortress built by the Earl of Gloucester in Caerphilly and destroyed it. The council reprimanded him, but Clare took matters into his own hands and began building an impregnable castle in its place. Llywelyn vowed to destroy it as well, but with artificial lakes inspired by Kenilworth and a concentric design that was wholly new to Britain, Caerphilly was a great contribution to the military architecture of the age and a portent to the future subjugation of Wales. The mistrust and confrontations between them dragged on for years to come.[24]

Clare forgot about going abroad after that, which turned out to be his good fortune. When Edward's party set sail from the south of France, they learned that the crusade had been launched in Tunis. Louis and Charles of Anjou had decided it worked to their advantage to strike at the local emir there. Charles was working on building a Mediterranean empire and wanted to neutralise any potential threat to his underbelly from North Africa. Louis was looking for an easy victory. The *mameluks* were even more fearsome than when they defeated him two decades earlier, and since then they had even turned back the Mongols. The emir was not only a softer target, but it was rumoured he was ready to convert to Christianity. In his eagerness to start, Louis found himself outside the ruins of Carthage smack in the middle of summer. The heat and dysentery brought on by foul sanitary conditions quickly ravaged his army. His son John Tristan, named for the debacle of the earlier crusade, was one of the first to die. Louis lingered in agony for three weeks before dying on 25 August 1270, only hours before Charles finally arrived with his forces. He salvaged what he could of the operation and got the emir to accept terms favourable to the crusaders. He didn't, however, convert.

This was in November, when Edward arrived. He thought it was disgraceful to make peace with the infidel, but had no choice but to follow Charles back to Sicily for the winter. After a storm wrecked the French fleet, Louis's son and successor Philip III, who had nearly died in Tunisia himself, figured it was wiser to head home to be crowned and have his father's bones interred at Saint-Denis (Charles got the heart and entrails for entombment near Palermo). Edward was expected to follow suit. On 6 February 1271, the council wrote to him that the king had just recovered from a serious illness and urged him to come home without delay. But he despaired of returning with his vow unfulfilled and began making plans to sail east. He swore to revive the crusade even if all others deserted him, eerily echoing Simon de Montfort at the lowest ebb of the reform movement.[25] He detached Henry of Almain to go look after his affairs in Gascony before heading to England to help run things there. Since he was going through Italy with the French party, Edward asked him to accomplish a little mission along the way if possible.

Back on 23 August 1268, Charles of Anjou had become the undisputed King of Sicily when he defeated Conradin, the last of the Hohenstaufen heirs, at the battle of Tagliacozzo. He owed his victory in no small part to Guy de Montfort, who proved himself just as capable a soldier as his father. Charles valued him enough to make him his vicar-general in Tuscany, prompting Edward to seek reconciliation with the Montforts through Almain, who was also their cousin. What, if any, preliminary steps were taken is unknown, just that on 13 March 1271, while Almain was worshipping in an obscure church in Viterbo, Guy and his brother Simon pounced on him at the altar and stabbed him to death. They then fled north to evade capture. It was revenge for their father at Evesham. Almain wasn't at the battle, but he turned his back on Montfort and married the daughter of his mortal enemy. His death would do. As with Louis, his body was boiled to remove the flesh from the bones, which were then taken to England and buried at Hailes Abbey next to his stepmother Sanchia.[26] He was 35 years old at the time, childless and the only descendent of both King John and William Marshal.

All of Europe was shocked by the murder, Edward especially since the rapprochement with the Montforts had been his initiative. He didn't alter his plans, however, and sailed for the crusader states that spring. His departure coincided with his father falling seriously ill again. The monks of Westminster were so concerned that they walked barefoot in the rain to the New Temple to celebrate mass for him. Recovering after all hope had been extinguished, Henry renewed his vow to go on crusade. On 16 April, he told his council to institute an austerity programme to help him pay off his loans and raise the money he needed to go abroad. They were to cut down his gift-giving to only £120 pounds a year, all in pennies (28,800 of them) to distribute to the knights, sergeants, yeomen and grooms of his household, who have had 'little or nothing for their service'.[27] Even though his sons were fulfilling his obligation to the cross, he felt keenly that the vow he made twenty-one years earlier would always hang over his legacy. Louis had only misery and calamity to show for his two crusades, but dying on the second one had made him a martyr in a twisted sort of way. If Henry also died on crusade, in the Holy Land no less, as his boyhood tutor Philip d'Aubigny had, it would secure his place in history. There were also the selfish reasons of every crusader, in his case seeing his sons and many new places, perhaps Sicily even, before he left this world.

The state of affairs at home, however, would not allow him to leave. The Countess of Flanders was feistier than ever and started a destructive trade war over the payment of back fees she claimed Henry owed her. Like the dispute in Wales, it occupied the rest of his reign. The lawlessness and robberies brought on by four years of armed conflict had not fully abated four years after its end. One chronicler writes how the barons took advantage of Henry's infirmity to oppress the poor and each other. In one notorious case, Matilda Longespee, to whom Henry refers as his 'baroness', charged John Giffard with abducting and marrying her in order to get his hands on her fortune. In all likelihood, it was a scheme concocted by the two of them to avoid seeking the king's permission to marry and paying him a fine.[28] Richard of Cornwall was still reeling from the murder of his son when the royal family was struck by a fresh blow. On 3 August 1271, Edward and Eleanor's oldest son John, aged 5, died in his care at Wallingford. He brought the child's body to Westminster Abbey for burial in front of his grief-stricken grandparents. In October, Philip Basset died, depriving Henry of his most trusted confidant. Then, in December, Richard suffered a stroke that left him speechless and bedridden in Berkhamsted. Returning to London after spending Christmas at Winchester, the king was confined to the Tower of London for three weeks, probably because he was nearby when he too was overcome by a severe illness.[29]

In February 1272, Henry emerged from the Tower a man of 64, now into the fifty-sixth year of his reign. Nearly all of the generation that had gone with him on his three military expeditions to the Continent were gone now. He had survived everyone, including, with the death of Roger Bigod two years earlier, all seven confederates who had conspired against him in 1258. Another passing was marked on 2 April 1272 when the one he had known the longest, his brother Richard, died without recovering from his stroke.[30] Their relationship had never been easy. Richard was too close in age, too covetous of power, glory and money to ever be content as the number two prince. He had raised rebellion against him, or did little to stop others from doing it, and was really loyal to Henry only insofar as it affected his bottom line. He had used little of his vast fortune to build anything of lasting beauty with the exception of Hailes Abbey, which is where he was buried, next to his son and second wife. Like many of England's spiritual gems, it was later destroyed by the Tudors.

By this point it was clear to Edward that nothing would come of his intervention in the east. With too few men to launch a major offensive, he revived Louis's dream of an alliance with the Mongols, but the crusader states themselves took what they could get and accepted a ten-year truce with the Sultan of Egypt. Edward's rejection of it was followed by an elaborate ploy to assassinate him in his tent on 17 June. He killed his Muslim attacker, but was seriously wounded with what may have been a poisoned dagger. The infected flesh was cut away, he convalesced in the summer heat, and by the end of September he, his family and his remaining contingent left. In all, his crusade had cost the crown alone £100,000, at least twice what had been spent on the Sicilian business.[31]

His presence at home was sorely missed that month. In the middle of August a full-scale riot broke out between the priory and citizens of Norwich. The source of the trouble was the prior and monks, or rather their grooms, who threw their weight around in the town and did as they pleased. As a crowd gathered to do something about it, the prior unleashed a gang of thugs he had brought in for protection. The scuffle led to a mob attacking the priory, and the cathedral was sacked and burnt in the resulting mayhem. Henry was appalled by the news and went there with the council to deal with the 'sons of blasphemy'. The perpetrators were put on trial and thirty-two were condemned to drawing and hanging. Their bodies were afterwards burnt as the punishment for arson. The prior was also convicted of homicide but, being a churchman, was handed over to the bishop for judgement. He got off, but became an outcast and died in wretched circumstances within six months.[32]

Disheartened by the tragic affair, Henry sought solace at his favourite shrines, like Bromholm, on the way back to Westminster. He celebrated the feast of St Edward by knighting Richard's heir Edmund of Cornwall, Henry de Lacy and other youths. Dissension in the land continued to stalk him, however. On 28 October, London was thrown into an uproar when the aldermen and leading citizens elected Philip the tailor as the new mayor. The people wanted to keep their current mayor, Walter Hervey, who had declared that the £13,333 fine levied on the city by the king in 1266 had been unfairly imposed. In fact, it was Henry who started it all when, in July, he ordered an investigation to find out who had paid too much or too little. Hervey told the people that collecting 'arrears' from certain privileged individuals would put less burden on them. Both sides marched to Westminster Hall to protest, but Hervey was a populist in the Montfortian mould and brought along hundreds of noisy demonstrators. He was told to bring a dozen at most the next day, but a crowd again followed him, filling the courtyard and causing the king distress across the way in his bedchamber. He had taken ill again, but apparently it was nothing serious. On 5 November, he ordered the feast for Christmas, to be spent at Winchester. His fondness for the city of his birth was as strong as ever.[33]

The council didn't know how to proceed on the matter as a legal issue and they didn't want to disturb Henry, so the demonstrations continued day after day. Not until 11 November did they take affirmative action and appoint a royal warden for the city to serve for one month while they tried to bring the two sides together. That ended all the racket and hollering and gave the king some peace, because by then he had grown alarmingly weak. It was now certain that he was dying. On 15 November, he issued his last order from the chancery, to settle the debt he owed his wine merchant for purchases made on his behalf. The total was 1,372 pounds, 9 shillings, and 6 1/2 pence, or about £1,000,000 in today's money. He did love his wine.[34]

On the morning of 16 November 1272, Gilbert de Clare was summoned to his bedside. In front of a gathering of magnates and bishops, he swore to the king that he would preserve the peace and keep the realm in good order until Edward's return. Henry confessed his sins, remitted ill will to all and received absolution. He died late in the day, doubtless with Eleanor, his wife and companion of thirty-six years, at his side. He was 65 and had been king for fifty-six years and twenty-four days, a record that stood until the modern era. There were few people alive that day who knew any other king but him. No matter what the hour or season, what the fortune or mishap, what the prayer or damnation, there was always the third King Henry somewhere. Going back to the beginning of his reign, there were perhaps even fewer then who believed that the fair-haired boy knighted by William Marshal would make it that far, but as usual he had them all fooled.[35]

He had probably made the funeral arrangements himself. It was held on Sunday 20 November, the feast day of St Edmund the martyr, which coincided with his death on the feast day of St Edmund the archbishop. Henry always appreciated symmetry of that sort. In the first will he made in 1246, he left his body to Westminster Abbey, just so there was no confusion over his earlier desire to be buried in the New Temple next to Marshal. He was laid out in the red samite vestments of his coronation regalia, holding only a dove-topped staff, not a sceptre or sword like his ancestors, so that the onlookers who gathered there could see that a man of peace was being borne before them by the great men of the kingdom. He was placed in the grave near the high altar that had formerly held his idol Edward the Confessor. It was only temporary until a permanent tomb could be constructed for him near the shrine, which he had intended to become the royal mausoleum of English monarchs. Afterwards the nobles stood before the high altar and swore fealty to Edward, 'though they were wholly ignorant whether he was alive'. Henry's great seal was then produced for all to see and broken. His reign was officially over.[36]

★ ★ ★

The obituaries were mostly mixed. The monk writing in *Flores* said: 'How great was this king's innocence, how great his patience, how great his devotion to the service of his Saviour.' But the author of the *Oseney Annals* frowned about how he 'loved aliens above all Englishmen, and enriched them with innumerable gifts and possessions'. Rishanger thought he was 'strong and vigorous but precipitous in his actions', which he nevertheless brought to 'lucky and happy conclusions'. The Dunstable annalist ventured no assessment at all, whereas Wykes tactlessly noted that he shined with more splendour dead than alive. Chroniclers writing in a later generation repeated what by then were the usual refrains about his character. 'He was an ingenuous man, of peaceful not warlike ways,' said Walter of Guisborough. 'He was simple in affairs of the state, but his largesse to the poor was to be admired.' Added Nicholas Trivet: 'He was strong in build but rash in behaviour.' Inasmuch as Henry loved a good joke, he might have been amused to learn that the only truly glowing tribute came from the Tewkesbury obituary mistakenly written about him in 1263, when he was still very much alive: 'He was a strenuous ruler of his kingdom, restorer of peace, generous giver of alms, and supporter of widows and orphans.'[37]

Henry's final will had been made back in 1253, prior to his departure to Gascony. Most of the executors named in it had predeceased him, men like Richard, Boniface, Aymer, Peter of Savoy and John Mansel. Among the outdated items is a bequest of £333 to finish the shrine of Westminster Abbey. His last keeper of the wardrobe, Peter of Winchester, felt that this money should now go to the poor members of the household. Provisions for Eleanor had already been made in 1262, when Henry and the rest of the court were struck down by plague in France. Her dower settlement was increased from the original £1,000 to £4,000 annually, a very handsome pension. His concern for his widow couldn't be more different from Louis and his shabby treatment of Margaret. He left her a paltry lump sum of £1,000 in his will compared to £5,000 for his sister.[38]

In the days that followed the royal funeral, Clare finally stepped up with some statesmanlike craft and helped resolve the mayoral conflict in London. Hervey was retained as mayor, but the aldermen received certain protections. Merton became the new chancellor while the council continued to rule, only now in Edward's name, and with a seal they had made for him. In December, Edmund returned from the crusade to assist them, but his brother only learned of their father's passing the following month, when he made landfall in the kingdom of Sicily. Charles of Anjou was surprised to find Edward relatively unconcerned about the loss of his son John, but completely distraught over his father. He could always have more sons, he told Charles, but his father was irreplaceable. There was probably some guilt behind that reaction. Henry would have had far fewer problems in his life had his son been a consistently loyal and dutiful heir. Although king now, Edward didn't rush back to be crowned. He felt England was secure enough to allow him to take care of business on the Continent while he was there. This also allowed him to make a subtle dig at his cousin Philip III and the way he had bailed out of their crusade when his own coronation beckoned.[39]

The ceremony took place on 19 August 1274. It had all the grandeur that Henry admired, and the family reunion occasioned by it, with Margaret and Beatrice there with their husbands, would have moved him to tears. He would have been proud to see that Edward could be every bit the showman he himself had been, but less so by the actual display of it. After the crown was placed on his head, Edward took it off and swore not to put it back on until he had reclaimed all that his father had given away, particularly the lands and rights enjoyed by aliens. It put the realm on notice that he wasn't going to be the same open-hearted king. A firmer, more discreet hand could now be expected.[40]

Tragedy then befell the royal family over the next several months. The 6-year-old grandson named after Henry, who was then heir to the throne, died on 16 October. Less than a month later Edmund's wife Aveline died in childbirth at 15, along with the twins she was carrying. Early the following year Eleanor was devastated when both her daughters died within a month of each other, still in their thirties. Their husbands were equally broken-hearted. Alexander III of Scotland only remarried a decade later because his three children with Margaret had died and he needed an heir. He didn't succeed before falling off his horse one stormy night in 1286 and breaking his neck. He was 44. John of Brittany, now the Earl of Richmond, remained a widower until his accidental death in 1305. He was taking part in the coronation of a new pope in Lyon when a wall collapsed on top of him. Edmund, who remained loyal to Edward in a way Henry could only have dreamt of from his own brother, remarried and had children. But the later conflict and bloodshed between his son Thomas of Lancaster and Edward's son Edward II made the political tolerance of Henry's reign a thing of the past.[41]

On 11 May 1290, Henry's remains were moved to an exquisite tomb which Edward had commissioned for him, also fashioned in the Cosmati style. There was little ceremony or advance notice, which must have disappointed his widow. Eleanor had hoped a cult of personality would flourish around her husband much as one had for Louis in France.[42] Canonisation was unthinkable without one, and Henry certainly deserved it for all the poor people he fed and the peace he fostered. But miracles more than anything were wanted for future saints, and here he couldn't compete, not even with the likes of Simon de Montfort. More than 200 miracles were recorded at Simon's gravesite in Evesham before that cult started to wither. A nondescript knight did claim that his eyesight was restored after a visit to Henry's tomb, but Eleanor's attempts to convince Edward of it led to a tense interview. 'I knew my father's justice well,' he was reported to have said, 'and am sure he would have gouged out the eyes of that scoundrel rather than restore his sight to him.'[43]

Six months after Henry's translation, Eleanor of Castile suddenly died and was buried in Westminster Abbey at the foot of his tomb. Her marriage to Edward had also been one of endearing affection and, in addition to memorialising her with crosses that marked the stops of her funeral cortege, he had a beautiful gilded effigy cast for her tomb. He ordered one for his father's as well, both crafted by William Torel. The king represented on Henry's effigy, crowned and bearded with wavy locks, was meant to exude noblesse, and does so perfectly. As for whether it actually looks like him, no complaint from that age has survived.

By that time, Eleanor of Provence was in retirement at Amesbury Abbey, several miles north of Salisbury, in the company of two of her granddaughters. Edward paid a last visit to her in February 1291, and it was probably then that he told her she wasn't going to be buried next to her husband in Westminster as both of them had wished. Her tomb had to be appropriated for her daughter-in-law, but Edward didn't want her there in any case. As much as he loved and respected his mother, her exalted queenship had been reviled by her subjects. There was no sense in reminding people of it in the most high-profile location in the country. He was happy to have her tucked away at Amesbury, where she died on 24 June 1291.[44]

She had chosen to retire there because it was a daughter house of Fontevrault Abbey in France, which she visited with her husband in 1254. Henry was moved on that occasion to will his heart there, to be closer as it were to his mother and grandparents, but Eleanor would not allow it to leave England while she was alive. With her death, the Abbess of Fontevrault braved a rough passage over in order to receive 'that most excellent treasure', which had been placed inside a lead container. The ceremony took place on 11 December 1291 in the presence of Edmund and the aged William de Valence. The abbess had hoped that since Eleanor was not to be interred in Westminster, they might have her as well. The queen, however, had already been buried at Amesbury, in the land of her destiny, on 8 September. She was fortunate, because five centuries later Fontevrault Abbey was decimated during the French Revolution. The remains of the occupants were all dispersed, although Henry's heart was reportedly whisked away to safety. It came into the possession of a convent in Edinburgh, where it can still be found today.[45]

Margaret, the oldest of the four fabled sister queens of Provence, died five years after Eleanor. Always amiable to everyone except Charles of Anjou, she became good friends with Eleanor de Montfort after the latter withdrew to the abbey of Montargis, south of Paris. Simon's widow died there in 1275, the last of King John and Isabella's children. She and her brother were never reconciled, but Edward made sure to visit her when he was nearby, and even lent her money. He was hostile to her children on account of the murder of Henry of Almain and pressed the new pope to take action. The younger Simon died the same year as the murder, but Guy got off with the briefest of excommunications and confinements. He went back into service for Charles, was captured in a sea battle with the Aragonese and died in prison in 1291.

Edward believed that Amaury had also been involved in the murder and had him and his sister seized as they made their way to Wales for her marriage to Llywelyn, a match previously arranged by their father. Despite entreaties from his aunt Margaret, Edward did not free Amaury for six years, and he allowed young Eleanor de Montfort to marry Llywelyn only after the Welsh prince came to new, harsher terms. She died in childbirth in 1282, Llywelyn at the end of that same year in an ambush by Marcher troops. Two years later, Edward moved in to conquer Wales, which his father had declined to do when the chance was open to him forty years earlier. His prestige among English chroniclers soared, but the cost was enormous, upwards of £120,000, and it was never really more than an occupation enforced by a line of castles.[46]

After that, reversals set in. Relations with France deteriorated to the point where Edward, supposedly so canny, was hoodwinked into surrendering Gascony. He needed a decade and another fortune to get it back. Edmund died there in 1296, worn out by the crisis, leaving Edward the last of Henry and Eleanor's children. It was a bleak time for him and the realm as he struggled to find money for his military campaigns, now exacerbated by the Scottish bid for independence. In these years alone, he imposed five times more taxation than Henry had throughout his entire reign.[47] But he never faced opposition on the same scale because everyone was afraid of him. He had shown at Evesham that he was ready to use vengeance and violence to deal with people and problems that wouldn't go away. His humiliation and execution of his foreign opponents ushered in a new barbaric age of English politics, one that would have shocked and appalled his father. He was furiously off to pound the Scots again when he died at a barren outpost in 1307, leaving behind massive debts and a wholly incapable successor. He was buried in Westminster Abbey close to the saint he was named after, but for whom he otherwise had no use. He was placed in an austere marble box that couldn't contrast more with his father's tomb, probably as it was meant to be. The two were pious family men with a flair for drama and temper, but in the end, one wanted to be remembered for conceiving beautiful works of art, the other for hammering his enemies into submission.[48]

And yet it was Edward who was feted as the greater of the two, because he represented the heroic tradition of the warrior king. He was another Richard the Lionheart, if not a King Arthur. He was strong, courageous, single-minded, sitting tall in the saddle, spurring men on to great deeds, building castles and turning his court into a regular Camelot. It all seemed so glorious from afar. As later generations latched on to the warrior cult as the true fixture of greatness, it was inevitable that St George and the dragon should be insinuated over St Edward the Confessor and the dove as the patron perfectly suited to inspire the English nation.[49]

There was no place for Henry in this new ethos of kingship. Although he was that rare English king to actually fight in battle, he could never be forgiven for Simon de Montfort's victory at Lewes. It didn't matter that he lost it through no fault of his own or that the only other king (Charles I) to face such a supremely masterful opponent (Oliver Cromwell) lost his head in the end. The fifteen months of the captive monarchy were a stain which, to borrow a phrase from Shakespeare, not all the water in the rough rude sea could wash away. In searching for how it could have happened, the pundits believed the answer was there all along. Henry never outgrew the innocence of the boy who became king. Without the right minders, he drifted from one problem to the next until he found himself isolated from his people. So common was this theme that Dante picked up on it in his *Divine Comedy*: 'There you see Henry of England, the king of the simple life, sitting alone.'[50]

Henry would have been profoundly perplexed by this crude image of his place in history, not to mention the afterlife. He gave his people peace and prosperity, regularly fed thousands of the poor, engaged in no unseemly scandals with mistresses and sired no illegitimate offspring. Whenever he was called to account, he humbled himself and welcomed a new spirit of cooperation. He didn't emerge from his difficulties blaming others and swearing retribution. Misfortune didn't embitter or corrupt him. An example was his stubborn pursuit of restitution in France. With the honour of the Plantagenets at stake, he kept at it for three decades. He didn't succeed in the end, but it's unlikely anyone could have. Henry V came closest, but the slaughter and misery he left behind ensured his gains came to nothing after his untimely death. Indeed, his march through Paris as a foe and conqueror in 1420 pales in comparison to 1254, when his four times great-grandfather was welcomed by the cheering crowds as a guest and admirer.[51] The friendship that ensued from that visit between Henry III and Louis IX easily ranks as one of the great political achievements of the Middle Ages.

Lacking a strong knightly resume, Henry's best chance to be judged a great king was through sainthood. His piety, charity and pacifism clearly qualified him, but it was Louis who got the honour. His disastrous crusades, abysmal family life and other ills were quickly forgotten as an almost cartoonish figure of goodness and godliness seeped into the historical record. A St Henry would have enjoyed the same fate, but Edward declined to make the effort. His father had been caring and devoted, certainly more loving and tolerant of him than he was of his own son, but as with his mother, he drew a line between his parents as people and as king and queen. Their status as a power couple was no more to his liking than it was to the rest of the country. With Eleanor of Castile, he set things right again. He ruled, and she was at his side, supportive but quiet. His father as saint would only confuse the issue.[52]

Most assessments of Henry inevitably come down to comparing him to his father and son. Since he seemed like a buffer between the evil John and dynamic Edward, he was deemed to be neither wicked nor worthy, a decent man but woefully not up to the rigours of kingship. At least he fared better than either of them in the monikers they were given. 'Henry the Builder' may not excite the imagination, but it's certainly more flattering than 'John Lackland' or 'Edward Longshanks'. He also escaped the indignity inflicted on both when their tombs were opened in the eighteenth century. Thousands came to gawk at John's dusty remains on display in Worcester Cathedral, and one of the antiquarians present at the opening of Edward's coffin was suspected of stealing a finger from the corpse. A body search showed that he had indeed nicked it. In 1871, another group of antiquarians set out to expose Henry as well. After removing the effigy, nine workmen were required to lift the three marble slabs underneath it. An oak coffin was revealed, completely covered in gold cloth, but the tomb raiders suddenly lost their nerve and left him in peace.[53]

It would be the last peace he got. The Victorian era saw little in the man to appreciate and created an image of him that has lasted until this day. He was weak and inept, and a bit lazy to boot. He let himself be ruled by his wife and her relatives, then by his own relatives, and the result was calamity. England prospered in spite of him, not because of him, which must be a record given how long it went on. Although he outlived three kings of France, seven popes and countless magnates, including sixty bishops, the sheer vastness of his reign was not taken into account. The reason for this narrow interpretation was what the country itself had become in the intervening centuries – the largest empire the world had ever seen. The British, as the English were now called, went out and conquered, ruled the aliens instead of letting the aliens rule them. It was the zenith of the warrior cult (now including intrepid seamen) and there was no fitter way to symbolise it than by raising a statue of Richard the Lionheart. It didn't matter that he was an alien king who, in dying without securing the succession, had failed in the one duty expected of every monarch. You couldn't beat that moniker.

But it was the glorification of another warrior that sealed it for Henry. The Victorians were also proud that theirs was the oldest constitutional government in Europe, dating back to the rise of Parliament. It was during Henry's reign that Parliament evolved from the royal councils of old into an institution of state that sat elected representatives and passed legislation. What made this possible was Magna Carta. Because the king could no longer use strong-arm tactics to make up shortfalls in his spending, he needed the kind of taxation that only the barons and clergy sitting in assembly could provide. Their refusal to grant one to Henry for more than twenty years has been interpreted as an indictment of his personal rule, ultimately leading to the reform period and civil war.

It's an impossibly simplistic and misleading argument. No king of England was crowned and came of age under more harrowing circumstances. Henry survived the rebellion against his father, then one against himself, and in between was pulled in different directions by his regents and magnates. His personal rule, which saw him create a new court with professionals running his administration, was more of an indictment of the barons and clergy. The reforms of his late reign came at a time when famine fuelled the growing resentment and political awareness of local communities. There was some idealism in it at the start, an attempt by the crown and nobility to do right by the rest of the realm. It unravelled as ambitions, grievances and radicalism turned it into another ordeal of survival for the king, with the Jews, foreigners and peasants caught in the crossfire.

The constitutionalists knew all this, but couldn't resist the irony and glamour of Simon de Montfort. He was a charismatic figure, a crusader who embodied all the highs and lows of the age, and his alien status saved them from charges of being chauvinistic at heart. To make him the hero of the piece, however, Henry had to become a villain more like King John. And so William Stubbs, the leading Victorian historian, declared that he failed to 'unlearn' the evil ways of his father and that his character only deserved analysis 'as a contrast to his brilliant rival'. Those following Stubbs in the early twentieth century were equally contemptuous. James Ramsay found Henry to be 'vain, false, and shifty', a monarch inevitably 'born to provoke opposition to authority'. Reginald Treharne, whose research was otherwise commendable, viciously heaped on the scorn. 'He was a negligible, contemptible figure, selfish, mean, cowardly, foolish and wholly unreliable.' Maurice Powicke brought things back on track before the current age of scholarship began, but even his sober view sometimes makes him seem more jester than king. 'The simplicity which could by turns amuse and madden those who had to deal with him maintained him in the end.'[54]

It was back to him being a simple fellow who just happened to be lucky. And yet the lucky one, it might be said, was England. The success of Magna Carta would ultimately come down to the first monarch obliged to rule under it, and Henry had, as David Carpenter has suggested, the ideal temperament for it.[55] A different sort of king, one inclined to bullying, debauchery and megalomania, might have viewed restraints foisted on him by the misdeeds of his father as a personal affront and seek to nullify them. How well Henry actually observed the charter of liberties after his initial missteps is arguable, but three times he gave it his official blessing.[56] By the end of his reign, it was enshrined as the bedrock of English values.

Posterity, however, has taken little note of this and other achievements, even in Winchester, the place most identified with Henry outside of Westminster. Despite the impressive ruins of Wolvesey Castle, where he was likely born, and the great hall built by him that stands intact today, the city trumpets no association with its most famous son. It did erect a prominent statue to a great king, but he goes by the name of Alfred, who ruled when Winchester was one of the capitals during the Saxon era. Needless to say, he looks like a fearsome warrior with sword and shield in hand.

As the first king to rule in the age of Magna Carta and Parliament, Henry III underwent some tough lessons to find the right balance between liberties, laws and the crown. When he died, he was at the height of his power and all three had a secure hold on the political landscape. The kingdom was far grander and stronger than the one he inherited, and he left it to a successor well-equipped to receive it. If these reasons alone don't make him a great king, they show that at least he was blessed, and he would take that over greatness any day. They also show that his reign, when compared to all the violent and degenerate monarchies that followed it, was easily the high point of medieval England.

His remarkable grasp of destiny, moreover, anticipated the modern age. In embracing both Saxon and Norman traditions, he set the groundwork for diversity and experience, and his exaltation of pageantry practically invented the concept of royalty as we know it today. And then there is his singular legacy, Westminster Abbey, where he has lain on the north side of the shrine for more than seven centuries. With its tracery, transepts and wondrous pavement, all evoking the finest in English and Continental design, it still infuses the spirit of the nation with faith, beauty and mystery.

NOTES

Introduction: Theatre Royal

1 Steane, *Archaeology of the Medieval English Monarchy*, p. 147.
2 Paris, *Matthew Paris's English History Vol. III*, p. 225.
3 Carpenter, *Reign of King Henry III*, pp. 204–05.

1 Reclaiming a Scarred Kingdom

1 Carpenter, *Struggle for Mastery*, pp. 199, 258.
2 Vincent, 'Isabella of Angoulême', pp. 172–75.
3 King, *Medieval England*, p. 99.
4 Strickland, *Lives of the Princesses*, p. 50; Wendover, *Roger of Wendover's Flowers of History*, pp. 205–06. John had his prisoners, including Hugh Lusignan, chained in carts and hauled to Normandy by oxen.
5 Carpenter, *Magna Carta*, pp. 210–11; Turner, *King John*, p. 95.
6 Vincent, *Peter des Roches*, p. 92; Carpenter, *Magna Carta*, p. 207.
7 Warren, *King John*, p. 190; Vincent, 'Isabella of Angoulême', p. 197.
8 Wendover, pp. 248, 255; Bradbury, *Philip Augustus and King John*, p. 53.
9 Carpenter, *Struggle for Mastery*, p. 247.
10 Seel, *King John*, pp. 67–69.
11 Wendover, pp. 259–60.
12 Bettenson, *Documents of the Christian Church*, pp. 163–64.
13 Davis, *Gothic King*, pp. 21–22.
14 Carpenter, *Struggle for Mastery*, p. 272; Warren, *King John*, pp. 223–24.
15 Wendover, pp. 302, 276–78. Wendover's account of how Langton lit the fire under the barons, as it were, has come in for severe scrutiny by modern historians, although he himself admits that his report of the scene at St Paul's is hearsay. See Carpenter, *Magna Carta*, pp. 311–13; Clanchy, *England and its Rulers*, pp. 209–10. In 'Archbishop Langton and Magna Carta: His Contribution, his Doubts and his Hypocrisy', Carpenter describes how Langton, 'like a great salmon from the water', snatched at a deal engineered by John that involved extortion of the Mandeville family (p. 1059).

16 Wendover, pp. 303–06.
17 King, *Medieval England*, p. 107.
18 Carpenter, *Magna Carta*, pp. 36–69. Carpenter provides the complete text of Magna Carta in parallel Latin-English translation.
19 King, *Medieval England*, p. 109; Wendover, pp. 333–34.
20 Brooks, *Knight Who Saved England*, p. 164–65.
21 Wendover, pp. 377–79. John supposedly made his condition worse by eating too many peaches and drinking new cider. This obituary was added by Paris: 'King John reigned eighteen years five months and five days, during which time he caused many disturbances and entered on many useless labours in the world, and at length departed this life in great agony of mind, possessed of no territory, yea, not even being his own master.' But, he goes on to add, he did found a monastery and, when dying, gave another one land worth ten pounds.
22 Ibid., p. 337.
23 Carpenter, *Struggle for Mastery*, p. 301; Wendover, p. 365.
24 Davis, *Gothic King*, p. 35.
25 Crouch, *William Marshal*, pp. 125–26.
26 Wendover, pp. 379–80; Powicke, *King Henry III*, p. 4. Marshal had already dubbed another young king, John's oldest brother Henry, more than four decades earlier.
27 Norgate, *Minority of Henry III*, pp. 4–5.
28 Ibid., pp. 6–7.
29 Vincent, 'Isabella of Angoulême', pp. 174–75.
30 Wendover, p. 207.
31 Vincent, 'Isabella of Angoulême', pp. 196–97.
32 Vincent, *Peter des Roches*, pp. 18–19.
33 Ibid., p. 70.
34 Carpenter, *Struggle for Mastery*, pp. 301–02.
35 Carpenter, *Magna Carta*, pp. 426–27; Norgate, *Minority of Henry III*, p. 12.
36 Powicke, *King Henry III*, p. 6.
37 Ramsay, *Dawn of the Constitution*, pp. 6–7.
38 Turner, *King John*, p. 103. During the seizure of Normandy in 1203, Fitz-Walter and Quincy had surrendered a vital fortress to Philip without a fight. While they did so on John's orders, the two endured much humiliation and the expense of having to ransom their own freedom.
39 Brooks, *Knight Who Saved England*, p. 211.
40 Vincent, *Peter des Roches*, pp. 137–40.
41 Vincent, 'Isabella of Angoulême', p. 177.
42 Powicke, *Thirteenth Century*, p. 12; Wendover, pp. 391–97.
43 Ellis, *Hubert de Burgh*, pp. 40–45; Wendover, pp. 398–400.
44 Norgate, *Minority of Henry III*, pp. 54–59.
45 Carpenter, *Minority of Henry III*, p. 45; Norgate, *Minority of Henry III*, p. 78; Powicke, *King Henry III*, pp. 17, 29; Vincent, *Peter des Roches*, p. 152. The city that had been so strongly for Louis greeted their young king with fanfare and glory, and citizens from all walks, including many 'reverted perverts', did fealty and homage to him.
46 Ramsay, *Dawn of the Constitution*, p. 15.
47 Carpenter, *Minority of Henry III*, p. 69.
48 Vincent, *Peter des Roches*, p. 185–87.
49 Carpenter, *Minority of Henry III*, pp. 54, 125–26.
50 Ibid., p. 76.
51 Wendover, p. 405.

Pages 37–47

52 Norgate, *Minority of Henry III*, p. 102. Walter the goldsmith was paid £2 for his work creating the seal.
53 Carpenter, *Minority of Henry III*, pp. 93, 99.
54 Facaros and Pauls, *Italy*, p. 126. Henry expressed his gratitude for all Guala had done for him by giving him the revenues of the Abbey of St Andrew in Chesterton near Cambridge, which the cardinal used to build the Basilica di Sant'Andrea standing in Vercelli today.
55 Norgate, *Minority of Henry III*, pp. 104–07; Carpenter, *Minority of Henry III*, pp. 105–06.

2 Coming of Age

1 Clanchy, *England and its Rulers*, p. 45.
2 Carpenter, *Struggle for Mastery*, pp. 403–13.
3 Carpenter, *Magna Carta*, pp. 38–41.
4 Carpenter, *Minority of Henry III*, p. 123.
5 Wilkinson, *Eleanor de Montfort*, pp. 9–10.
6 Russell, Heironimus, *Shorter Latin Forms*, p. 19.
7 *CR, 1231–4*, p. 25; Paris II, p. 209.
8 Ramsay, *Dawn of the Constitution*, p. 23.
9 Norgate, *Minority of Henry III*, pp. 148–49. Henry asked Fawkes de Bréauté to come to Nicola's aid against the encroachment of his 'beloved uncle' William.
10 Warren, *King John*, p. 219.
11 Norgate, *Minority of Henry III*, pp. 134–39; Stephens, *Joan Makepeace*, p. 304. Based on a record in the Norman exchequer, Stephens suggests that Joan was born in 1203, four years before Henry, which would have made her 17 at the time of her mother's marriage to her fiancé.
12 Rymer, *Foedera*, p. 25.
13 Carpenter, *Minority of Henry III*, p. 193.
14 Norgate, *Minority of Henry III*, p. 127.
15 Wilkinson, *Eleanor de Montfort*, p. 8.
16 Carpenter, *Minority of Henry III*, pp. 196, 221.
17 Norgate, *Minority of Henry III*, p. 146.
18 Powicke, *King Henry III*, pp. 54–55; Wendover, pp. 428–29.
19 Wilkinson, *Eleanor de Montfort*, p. 19. Marshal's first wife, Alice, was the half-sister of Forz.
20 Ramsay, *Dawn of the Constitution*, pp. 25–26.
21 Wilkinson, *Eleanor de Montfort*, p. 21.
22 Carpenter, *Minority of Henry III*, pp. 249–50. The falseness of the charge was evident in Maulay's quick release.
23 Ellis, *Hubert de Burgh*, pp. 14–16.
24 Carpenter, *Minority of Henry III*, p. 251.
25 Ellis, *Hubert de Burgh*, pp. 63–65. Following earlier historians, Ellis says that Hubert and Margaret were married on the same day as Joan and Alexander, 19 June 1221, a double wedding in fact, but not even Hubert would have dared so much pretension. Their wedding took place later in the autumn, on 3 October.
26 Carpenter, *Minority of Henry III*, p. 254. Even Langton had to admit that Pandulf had served Henry well, namely in taking a leading role in restoring his finances, often with loans of money, and maintaining pressure on the magnates to surrender their castles. His reward was to be made Bishop of Norwich, but since that meant he was now subordinate to Langton, he spent most of his time on missions abroad. He died in Rome in 1226, but arranged to have his body brought back to Norwich for burial.

27 Vincent, *Peter des Roches*, pp. 112, 204, 207. Peter was also working on his own behalf, inasmuch as he was the guarantor for the money Maulay owed for the barony that came with his marriage to Isabella of Thurnham in 1214.
28 Clanchy, *England and its Rulers*, p. 201.
29 Norgate, *Minority of Henry III*, p. 182.
30 Carpenter, *Minority of Henry III*, p. 272.
31 Norgate, *Minority of Henry III*, p. 181.
32 Wendover, pp. 439–41; Ellis, *Hubert de Burgh*, pp. 69–73. The Abbot of Westminster sought refuge from Henry's former tutor Philip d'Aubigny, who was in the city after returning from crusade, but he ended up having to escape by boat under a hail of stones.
33 Ramsay, *Dawn of the Constitution*, p. 29.
34 Carpenter, *Struggle for Mastery*, pp. 32, 41.
35 Tolan, *First Imposition of a Badge*, pp. 145–66.
36 Wendover, p. 443; Norgate, *Minority of Henry III*, 215–16. Norgate believes that Wendover should have dated this event to the following January, in 1224, smack in the middle of the crisis to come. Carpenter refutes this argument in depth in a note in his *Minority*, p. 297.
37 Powicke, *King Henry III*, pp. 67–68; Carpenter, *Minority of Henry III*, pp. 264–65.
38 Carpenter, *Minority of Henry III*, p. 283.
39 Ibid., pp. 301–04.
40 Rishanger, p.75; Trivet, pp. 280–1. Writing in a later generation, chronicler William Rishanger said that one of Henry's eyelids drooped to covering part of the pupil, but his predecessor at St Albans, Matthew Paris, makes no such mention. Paris not only knew Henry well but never shied from making physical descriptions of him. Rishanger's contemporary Nicholas Trivet provides the same account of Henry's eyelid, word for word, in his annals. He claims Edward I also had a drooping eyelid and so must have inherited it from his father.
41 Carpenter, *Minority of Henry III*, p. 305.
42 Ramsay, *Dawn of the Constitution*, pp. 31–32.
43 Ellis, *Hubert de Burgh*, pp. 75–76.
44 Carpenter, *Minority of Henry III*, pp. 321–22. The reasoning here was that Hubert and his allies wanted to avoid the impression that they were expecting to carve up the kingdom the moment Henry got the free use of his seal.
45 Wendover, p. 449–50; Carpenter, *Minority of Henry III*, p. 326.
46 Vincent, *Peter des Roches*, pp. 212–13.
47 Everard, *Brittany and the Angevins*, pp. 156–57.
48 Carpenter, *Minority of Henry III*, pp. 326–27.
49 Vincent, *Peter des Roches*, p. 215.
50 Carpenter, *Magna Carta*, pp. 208, 410.
51 Carpenter, *Minority of Henry III*, pp. 328–29.
52 Norgate, *Minority of Henry III*, pp. 216–17.
53 Wilkinson, *Eleanor de Montfort*, pp. 27–28; Carpenter, *Minority of Henry III*, p. 354.
54 Wendover, pp. 450–52. Wendover says that Henry was 'highly incensed at this deed, and asked the advice of the clergy and people assembled as to what ought to be done to punish such offence. They all unanimously gave it as their opinion that they should without delay, putting off all other business, proceed with a strong armed force to the aforesaid castle, to punish such audacity; this opinion meeting the king's views, he gave the order.'
55 Carpenter, *Minority of Henry III*, p. 355.
56 Ibid., pp. 349, 358.
57 Norgate, *Minority of Henry III*, pp. 238–44.

Pages 56–70

58 Ellis, *Hubert de Burgh*, pp. 80–83.
59 Maurice, *Stephen Langton*, p. 264.
60 Powicke, *King Henry III*, p. 66; Carpenter, *Minority of Henry III*, p. 363.
61 Mitchell, *Studies in Taxation*, p. 159.
62 Carpenter, *Minority of Henry III*, pp. 372–73.
63 Wendover, pp. 455–56.

3 Silky White Gloves

1 Clanchy, *England and its Rulers*, p. 83.
2 Warren, *King John*, pp. 149–50.
3 Carpenter, *Minority of Henry III*, p. 385–86.
4 Carpenter, *Magna Carta*, p. 420.
5 Ramsay, *Dawn of the Constitution*, pp. 39–40; Norgate, *Minority of Henry III*, p. 262.
6 Denholm-Young, *Richard of Cornwall*, pp. 4–5.
7 Wendover, pp. 457–58.
8 Norgate, *Minority of Henry III*, p. 254.
9 Wendover, pp. 466, 468.
10 Wilkinson, *Women as Sheriffs*, pp. 120–22.
11 Ellis, *Hubert de Burgh*, pp. 98–99.
12 Wendover, pp. 475–76.
13 Powicke, *King Henry III*, pp. 274–75.
14 Wendover, p. 472.
15 Ramsay, *Dawn of the Constitution*, pp. 42–43.
16 Mueller, pp. 124–26.
17 Powicke, *King Henry III*, pp. 177–78.
18 Labarge, *Saint Louis*, p. 25.
19 Ibid., p. 22. Urraca ended up becoming the Queen of Portugal, where she died just into her thirties in 1220.
20 Rymer, *Foedera*, p. 29.
21 Clanchy, *England and its Rulers*, pp. 219–20.
22 Ramsay, *Dawn of the Constitution*, p. 47.
23 Wendover, p. 485.
24 Ibid., p. 486.
25 Powicke, *King Henry III*, pp. 176–79.
26 Wendover, pp. 487–88.
27 Denholm-Young, *Richard of Cornwall*, p. 13.
28 Wendover, p. 489.
29 Clanchy, *England and its Rulers*, p. 37.
30 Aberth, *An Environmental History*, p. 101.
31 Carpenter, *Minority of Henry III*, p. 290.
32 Denholm-Young, *Richard of Cornwall*, pp. 12–13.
33 Ellis, *Hubert de Burgh*, p. 115.
34 Wendover, pp. 509–11.
35 Prestwich, *Plantagenet England*, p. 146.
36 Ellis, *Hubert de Burgh*, pp. 91–93.
37 *Dunstable*, p. 107.
38 Wendover, pp. 459–60.
39 Ibid., pp. 508–09.
40 Ramsay, *Dawn of the Constitution*, pp. 51–52; Wendover, p. 519.
41 *Dunstable*, p. 116.

42 Wendover, p. 499.
43 Ibid., pp. 528–30.
44 Ibid., p. 512. Wendover says Henry was dithering 'in his simplicity' and turning to Hubert, his 'only councillor', to tell him what to do.
45 Powicke, *King Henry III*, pp. 179–80.
46 Labarge, *Saint Louis*, pp. 44–45.
47 Powicke, *King Henry III*, p. 181.
48 Wendover, p. 531–32. Wendover puts the amount at £3,500 but doesn't say where Henry got this information.
49 Powicke, *Thirteenth Century*, p. 94; Denholm-Young, *Richard of Cornwall*, p. 16.
50 Wilkinson, *Eleanor de Montfort*, p. 30. Wilkinson follows up a suggestion by Michael Ray that Eleanor may in fact have been pregnant and suffered a miscarriage during the voyage.
51 Labarge, *Saint Louis*, p. 40.
52 Ellis, *Hubert de Burgh*, pp. 18–19.
53 Wendover, pp. 536–37.
54 Labarge, *Saint Louis*, p. 41.
55 Ramsay, *Dawn of the Constitution*, p. 55.
56 Vincent, *Peter des Roches*, p. 264.
57 Wendover, p. 538.
58 Ellis, *Hubert de Burgh*, pp. 116–17.
59 Ramsay, *Dawn of the Constitution*, p. 57.
60 Vincent, *Peter des Roches*, p. 268.
61 Powicke, *King Henry III*, p. 183; Wendover, p. 538.
62 Labarge, *Montfort*, p. 30.

4 Exchanging the Old for the Old

1 Vincent, *Peter des Roches*, pp. 267–68. Raymond was survived by his wife Christina, the widowed Countess of Essex, and his father-in-law Robert Fitz-Walter.
2 Mortimer, *Honour of Clare*, p. 121. Tonbridge didn't exist during the compilation of Domesday Book, the great nationwide survey commissioned by William the Conqueror in 1087 to see how much England was really worth.
3 Ellis, *Hubert de Burgh*, p. 118.
4 Wykes, p. 72.
5 Carpenter, *Magna Carta*, pp. 40–41. Isabel de Clare's mother was also Isabel de Clare before she married William Marshal. Her ancestors and those of her son-in-law Gilbert came from different branches of the Clare family that emerged a century earlier.
6 Vincent, *Peter des Roches*, p. 272; Wendover, p. 542. Rymer's *Foedera*, p. 32, reports the estates in Ireland had been seized by 25 May 1231.
7 Davis, *Gothic King*, pp. 80–81.
8 Ellis, *Hubert de Burgh*, pp. 95–96. The wardship of Braose's lands was first given to William Marshal II and after his death to Richard of Cornwall, who then had a falling out with Henry, probably over Cornwall siding with Richard Marshal in their dispute.
9 Wendover, pp. 539–41; Dunstable, p. 127.
10 Wendover, p. 543; Ramsay, *Dawn of the Constitution*, pp. 57–58. Matthew Paris adds a note to Wendover's account that some thieves broke open Grant's coffin during the night to steal his ring and other jewellery, but were unsuccessful for all their force and skill. They fled, worried they had conjured up some supernatural spell.
11 Vincent, *Peter des Roches*, pp. 251–54.
12 Ibid., p. 273.

Pages 79–85

13 Denholm-Young, *Richard of Cornwall*, p. 21.

14 Maddicott, *Montfort*, pp. 8–9; Eales, 'Henry III', pp. 106–07.

15 Labarge, *Montfort*, pp. 17–26; Dunstable, p. 34. According to the Dunstable annalist, a group of disaffected barons gathered in 1210 to elect Simon III their king. Beaumont's wife Loretta was a Braose and aunt of the executed William. She was caught up in John's personal vendetta against the family, which saw her mother and brother starved to death in Windsor Castle. Although eventually given her marriage portion, she took a vow of chastity and became a recluse. The youngest Beaumont sister, Margaret, was already a countess by her marriage to Saer de Quincy, the Earl of Winchester.

16 Maddicott, *Montfort*, pp. 11–13.

17 Vincent, *Peter des Roches*, pp. 274, 277. The contested grants were 'lands of the Normans', over which Henry had given Ranulf control in 1227. While the council was still in session, Henry again reversed himself in favour of Hubert's side. He was probably worried he was giving too much to Montfort too early. When he gave Simon control over the 'lands of the Normans' in Leicestershire in the summer of 1232, one of Simon's first acts was to confirm the charter for Hubert's side.

18 Morris, *Bigod Earls*, pp. 5–6. Henry's uncle, William Longespee, originally got the wardship, but he died shortly afterwards.

19 Vincent, *Peter des Roches*, p. 276. Neither Margery nor her sister Isabella would have any children. In 1227, Richard of Cornwall went north to ask for Margery's hand. Eighteen years old at the time, he was overly conscious of his status as an earl with little land or financial security. He was looking for both, as well as social enhancement by taking a princess bride, but left empty-handed when his terms for Margery's dowry proved exorbitant for Alexander. The Scottish nobility saw him as a gold digger, anyway.

20 Wendover, p. 543; Vincent, *Peter des Roches*, p. 278.

21 Dunstable, p. 117.

22 Wendover, pp. 552–53.

23 Vincent, *Peter des Roches*, pp. 281–82.

24 Mundill, *England's Jewish Solution*, p. 135; Vincent, *Peter des Roches*, pp. 188–89.

25 Grosseteste, *Letters*, pp. 65–69.

26 Stacey, *Conversion of Jews*, pp. 267–69; Fogle, *Domus Conversorum*, p. 2. The gender pay gap already existed then, as male converts received an allowance of ten pence a week and women eight. The home generally accommodated about seventy converts in a monastic environment where the men referred to each other as 'brother' and whole families lived there, sometimes all their lives. Conversions during Henry's reign numbered around 300 in a community of up to 5,000, and the home survived into the seventeenth century.

27 Wendover, pp. 549–51.

28 Vincent, *Peter des Roches*, pp. 292–99. Rivallis was also given lifetime custody of the king's privy seal to allow him to act independently of the chancery, where Neville had just received lifetime custody of the great seal.

29 Ellis, *Hubert de Burgh*, pp. 120–21.

30 *CChR, 1226–57*, pp. 164–65.

31 Carpenter, *Reign of Henry III*, pp. 52–54.

32 Ibid., pp. 64–69. Two other members of the court, treasurer Walter Mauclerk and steward Ralph Fitz-Nicholas, got their own oaths but were not present at Bromholm.

33 Vincent, *Peter des Roches*, pp. 283–84.

34 Wendover, pp. 544–46.

35 Dunstable, p. 128; Wendover, p. 551.
36 Wendover, pp. 552, 562–65; Powicke, *King Henry III*, p. 79.
37 Vincent, *Peter des Roches*, pp. 303–08.
38 Paris I, pp. 237–39. Paris does have the king declare that Hubert 'deserved not only to be hung with a halter, but also to be torn to pieces' for the attack.
39 Ellis, *Hubert de Burgh*, p. 134.
40 Wendover, pp. 553–54.
41 Vincent, *Peter des Roches*, pp. 311–12.
42 Ellis, *Hubert de Burgh*, pp. 204–05.
43 Wendover, pp. 554–55. For more about Godfrey, see Carpenter, 'The Career of Godfrey of Crowcombe'.
44 Wendover, pp. 555–59; Ellis, *Hubert de Burgh*, pp. 134–40.
45 Clanchy, *England and its Rulers*, p. 230; Vincent, *Peter des Roches*, p. 315.
46 Knox, *Studies in Taxation*, p. 205. This was the only tax throughout Henry's fifty-six years on the throne that was approved without a quid pro quo.
47 Vincent, *Peter des Roches*, p. 323.
48 Ellis, *Hubert de Burgh*, pp. 140, 206–07.
49 Wendover, pp. 561–62.
50 Vincent, *Peter des Roches*, pp. 317–18. Article 39 of Magna Carta states: 'No freeman is to be arrested, or imprisoned, or disseised, or outlawed, or exiled, or in any way destroyed, nor will we go against him, nor will we send against him, save by the lawful judgement of his peers or by the law of the land.'
51 Ellis, *Hubert de Burgh*, pp. 141–42. The four earls were Richard of Cornwall, William de Warenne (Surrey), Richard Marshal (Pembroke) and the new Earl of Lincoln, John de Lacy.
52 Eales, 'Henry III', pp. 100–12.
53 Vincent, *Peter des Roches*, pp. 319–20.
54 Ibid., pp. 316–17.
55 Wendover, pp. 565–66.
56 Clanchy, *England and its Rulers*, pp. 198–202. Clanchy offers the instructive premise that Marshal and Montfort, coming from north of the Loire, would have spoken a French closer to the English barons than 'Poitevins' like Roches, who were from south of the river, and therefore would have seen the latter as foreign. This raises the intriguing question of what kind of French Henry actually spoke, inasmuch as he was born to a Poitevin mother and raised by Roches.

5 Henry's Harsh Lesson in Kingship

1 Carpenter, *Struggle for Mastery*, pp. 36–43.
2 Clanchy, *England and its Rulers*, pp. 86–88.
3 Vincent, *Peter des Roches*, p. 320.
4 Wilkinson, *Eleanor de Montfort*, pp. 38–42.
5 Crouch, *Acts and Letters of the Marshal Family*, p. 22. Paris has Henry reacting to William's death by tearing his clothes and wailing, 'Woe is me! Will there ever be satisfaction for the blood of Thomas the martyr!'
6 Vincent, *Peter des Roches*, pp. 332–33.
7 Holt, *Magna Carta*, p. 160.
8 Vincent, *Peter des Roches*, p. 318.
9 Wendover, pp. 566–67.

Pages 94–98

10 Vincent, *Peter des Roches*, pp. 373–75. The situation in Wales was vulnerable due to the untimely deaths of Marcher lords William Marshal II, Gilbert de Clare and William Braose all in the span of one year. Another lordship was vacated when John Braose, William's cousin, was killed in a horse riding accident and left behind minors.
11 Carpenter, *Struggle for Mastery*, pp. 41–42.
12 Ibid., pp. 251–52.
13 Vincent, *Peter des Roches*, pp. 363–64.
14 Rothwell, *English Historical Documents*, p. 350.
15 Dunstable, p. 134. Roger had actually excommunicated the ruffians *en masse*. The rift between Peter and his fellow bishops was also personal after the way they connived with Langton and Hubert to oust him from favour in 1224.
16 Vincent, *Peter des Roches*, pp. 365–70.
17 Wendover, p. 567. Blund's candidacy was officially doomed by his holding of multiple benefices without licence and the pope's worry that the Bishop of Winchester had too much control over affairs in England. According to Wendover, Gregory encouraged the monks who accompanied Blund to Rome to elect Edmund of Abingdon right there in front of him. They only agreed to take up his suggestion upon their return to Canterbury.
18 Powicke, *King Henry III*, pp. 20–23.
19 Barker, *Tournament in England*, pp. 25–26.
20 Crouch, *Acts and Letters*, p. 22. William Marshal himself had been made a hostage as a 5-year-old boy during the civil war of King Stephen's reign and was nearly launched from a trebuchet when his father failed to comply with the agreement, and even mocked Stephen that he could have plenty of other sons. Fortunately for William, Stephen was a much kinder man than his father John Marshal.
21 Wendover, p. 567; Ramsay, *Dawn of the Constitution*, p. 37. He was Robert Bacon, a friend of Edmund of Abingdon.
22 Powicke, *King Henry III*, p. 133. They planned a tournament at Northampton as the staging point, but it had been banned at the council meeting in Oxford precisely to keep something like this from happening.
23 Vincent, *Peter des Roches*, pp. 386–87; Wendover, p. 569. The story Wendover concocts is that Marshal arrived to attend the Westminster council, but was warned by his sister Isabel that it was a trap to imprison him. He therefore mounted his horse in the night and didn't stop until he reached Wales.
24 Vincent, *Peter des Roches*, pp. 390–91. The castle was Hay-on-Wye.
25 Wendover, pp. 570–71. The chronicler insists that Henry was making no headway and had to beg for the castle of Usk's surrender because his honour was at stake, but Marshal was clearly losing the war and allies.
26 Morris, *Bigod Earls*, pp. 10–11.
27 Vincent, *Peter des Roches*, pp. 401–02.
28 Ellis, *Hubert de Burgh*, pp. 146–47.
29 Wendover, p. 570; Rymer, *Foedera*, p. 34. Bishop Roger also complained about the rough treatment of Walter Mauclerk he had witnessed in August. It happened at Dover, when Roger was returning from Rome and Walter was trying to make his way there, presumably to complain to the pope about all the royal harassment he had to endure. Since he didn't have the king's permission to leave, the garrison turned him back. Roger was indignant over the way they manhandled Walter and excommunicated the lot of them. Henry forbade him to pronounce the sentence, but agreed that Walter could go into exile abroad if that was one less problem to deal with.
30 Clanchy, *England and its Rulers*, p. 231.

31 Wendover, pp. 572–73.
32 Ellis, *Hubert de Burgh*, pp. 147–48.
33 Vincent, *Peter des Roches*, pp. 417–18.
34 Wendover, pp. 573–74. The chronicler says Marshal refused to attack the king, implying an ingrained loyalty prevented him from doing so. Interestingly, Marshal's nephew the Earl of Norfolk is also listed as one of the witnesses, but is given the name of his father, Hugh Bigod.
35 Ibid., pp. 575–76.
36 Vincent, *Peter des Roches*, pp. 417–18.
37 Powicke, *King Henry III*, pp. 132–34.
38 Wendover, pp. 576–80. Philip Augustus called William Marshal the most loyal man he ever met. Much of what Richard Marshal tells the friar seems to be a figment of Wendover's imagination, like Roches supposedly bragging that he could get his good friend Emperor Frederick to come to England in person to help put down the rebellion.
39 Dunstable, p. 139; Wendover, p. 581.
40 Vincent, *Peter des Roches*, pp. 427–28.
41 Costain, *Magnificent Century*, pp. 109–12.
42 Vincent, *Peter des Roches*, p. 429.
43 Powicke, *King Henry III*, p. 135.
44 Wendover, pp. 583–85.
45 Vincent, *Peter des Roches*, p. 425; Ellis, *Hubert de Burgh*, pp. 146–50. Henry named Hubert's archenemy Peter de Maulay as the new warden of Devizes just so the fugitive knew what to expect when his days on the run were over.
46 Wendover, p. 585. During his previous pilgrimage to Bromholm twenty months earlier, Henry made the controversial oath to Margaret and others that their grants would be protected for life. A combination of pity, piety and the pope's interest in her welfare probably moved him to regret that occasion and much of what followed.
47 Ibid., p. 586.
48 Vincent, *Peter des Roches*, pp. 435–36.
49 Wendover, pp. 588–89; Vincent, *Peter des Roches*, pp. 37–38. She was Gervasia de Dinan, a Breton heiress.
50 Dunstable, p. 137.
51 Vincent, *Peter des Roches*, pp. 430, 438–39.
52 Wendover, p. 594.
53 Vincent, *Peter des Roches*, pp. 443–57.
54 Wendover, p. 592.
55 Ellis, *Hubert de Burgh*, p. 152. Warin Basset was killed in the skirmishing.
56 Carpenter, *Reign of Henry III*, pp. 41–42.
57 Vincent, *Peter des Roches*, p. 443.
58 Wilkinson, *Eleanor de Montfort*, pp. 45–46.
59 Powicke, *King Henry III*, p. 157–58.
60 Wilkinson, *Eleanor de Montfort*, pp. 11–12. Eleanor and her former governess, Cecily Sandford, literally became brides of Christ.
61 Vincent, *Peter des Roches*, p. 444.
62 Wendover, pp. 594, 596, 602; Vincent, *Peter des Roches*, p. 445.
63 Wendover, p. 595; Vincent, *Peter des Roches*, pp. 448–49.
64 Vincent, *Peter des Roches*, p. 451.
65 Carpenter, *Struggle for Mastery*, p. 316.
66 Vincent, *Peter des Roches*, p. 445.

Pages 109–117

6 A Complete Makeover

1 Vincent, *Peter des Roches*, p. 436.
2 Weiler, *Gregory IX, Frederick II*, pp. 201–02. Roches was accused of scheming to marry off Isabella to his good friend Frederick, but the negotiations for the marriage did not begin until after he was in disgrace.
3 Wendover, pp. 607–08.
4 Powicke, *King Henry III*, pp. 144–45; Vincent, *Peter des Roches*, pp. 470–73.
5 Labarge, *Saint Louis*, p. 58; Cockerill, *Eleanor of Castile*, pp. 34–35. Joan's father Simon had fought for John at Bouvines in 1214, forcing him to flee to England while his wife Marie remained on the Continent. They managed to see each other often enough to produce Joan in 1220, followed by three more daughters. Not until 1230 was Simon allowed to come home, but with the caveat that Joan not marry an enemy of the kingdom.
6 Howell, *Eleanor of Provence*, p. 11; Rymer, *Foedera*, p. 36. Eleanor of Aquitaine was Henry's grandmother through her second marriage to Henry II and Joan's great-grandmother through her first marriage to Louis VII.
7 Labarge, *Saint Louis*, pp. 54–55.
8 Cox, *Eagles of Savoy*, p. 44.
9 Wendover, pp. 608–09; Wild, *Empress's New Clothes*. Henry's wardrobe and interior decorating were dominated by green, which Wild notes could suggest various interpretations in the observer, whether 'youthfulness and vigour', 'chaos and disorder' or even justice dispensed 'out in the open'.
10 Wendover, p. 610; Strickland, *Lives of the Princesses of England*, pp. 12–18. The English seal of three leopards facing right to left became standard under Richard I, though they almost certainly started off as lions.
11 Rymer, *Foedera*, p. 36; Cockerill, *Eleanor of Castile*, p. 36.
12 Howell, *Eleanor of Provence*, p. 7; Denholm-Young, *Richard of Cornwall*, pp. 18–19.
13 Cox, *Eagles of Savoy*, pp. 46–48.
14 Pollock, *Scotland, England and France*, pp. 124–26; Paris I, p. 37.
15 Powicke, *King Henry III*, pp. 740–59.
16 Cox, *Eagles of Savoy*, p. 44.
17 Howell, *Eleanor of Provence*, p. 14.
18 Ibid., pp. 4–6.
19 Paris I, pp. 7–8.
20 Howell, *Eleanor of Provence*, pp. 15–16.
21 Paris I, pp. 8–10.
22 Howell, *Eleanor of Provence*, pp. 17–18.
23 Labarge, *Saint Louis*, p. 56.
24 Stanley, *Historical Memorials*, p. 70.
25 Bémont, *Montfort*, pp. 9–15, 51.
26 Paris I, pp. 10–11.
27 Ibid., pp. 12–14.
28 Powicke, *King Henry III*, pp. 148–51. A council meeting had been convened in Tewkesbury in October 1234 to resolve the matter, but became deadlocked over the issue of wedlock and legitimacy.
29 Grosseteste, *Letters*, pp. 117–18.
30 Carpenter, *Reign of Henry III*, p. 382.
31 Dunstable, pp. 145–46. The annalist bemoans that 'perjury' would be the likely outcome of their deliberations.
32 Cox, *Eagles of Savoy*, p. 15.

33 Carpenter, *Reign of Henry III*, pp. 166–69; Stacey, *Politics*, pp. 84–89. The royal demesne, which formed the greatest part of that revenue, was removed from their control and given to the exchequer to farm out separately.
34 Paris I, p. 29.
35 Vincent, *Peter des Roches*, pp. 348–49.
36 Paris I, p. 34; Dunstable, p. 144; Powicke, *King Henry III*, p. 141.
37 Paris I, p. 30; Powicke, *King Henry III*, p. 153; Stacey, *Politics*, pp. 96–100. Stacey finds no evidence to corroborate the story that Henry tried to take the seal away from Neville. It was perhaps another case of Paris reading later events backwards to suit his narrative and propaganda.
38 Howell, *Eleanor of Provence*, p. 7.
39 Morris, *Great and Terrible King*, p. 163.
40 Paris I, pp. 36–37.
41 Nelson, *Henry Fine Rolls Project*, May 2011.
42 Folda, *Crusader Art*, p. 162; Paris I, p. 41; Vincent, *Peter des Roches*, p. 473.
43 Powicke, *King Henry III*, pp. 760–63. Clare went into the care of Peter des Roches before becoming the king's ward.
44 Carpenter, *Henry III and Edward the Confessor*, pp. 876–77.
45 Ibid., p. 870.
46 Huntington, *Edward the Celibate*, pp. 119–33.
47 Wilkinson, *Eleanor de Montfort*, p. 29.
48 Steane, *Archaeology of the Medieval English Monarchy*, p. 73.
49 Hyams, *Henry III in Bed*, pp. 93–97. 'Ke ne dune ke ne tine ne prent ke desire.'
50 Carpenter, *Reign of Henry III*, p. 209.
51 Powicke, *King Henry III*, p. 155.
52 Stacey, *Politics*, pp. 111–15; Paris I, pp. 42–46. Fitz-Geoffrey got his manor back.
53 Mitchell, *Studies in Taxation*, pp. 214–18; Tewkesbury, p. 102 (*civium et burgensium*); Wykes, p. 83 (*populo*).
54 Paris I, p. 49.
55 Ibid., pp. 53–54.
56 Ibid., pp. 47, 54–55, 68.
57 Above, p. 74.
58 Above, p. 103.
59 Paris I, pp. 61–62.
60 Ibid., pp. 69–70; Watt, *Medieval Church Councils*, pp. 49–51. The council was held on 19 October 1239 in Holyrood Abbey.
61 Paris I, p. 54; Ramsay, *Dawn of the Constitution*, p. 83.
62 Nelson, *Henry Fine Rolls Project*, May 2011.
63 Paris I, pp. 71–93.
64 Ibid., p. 117.
65 Nelson, *Henry Fine Rolls Project*, May 2011.
66 Paris I, p. 68.

7 *Waxing Hot and Cold*

1 Bémont, *Montfort*, pp. 53–54. Joanna was the widow of Ferrand, son of the King of Portugal, who was a notorious sore loser at checkers and used to beat Joanna when he lost to her.
2 Maddicott, *Montfort*, p. 19.
3 Wilkinson, *Eleanor de Montfort*, pp. 51–56.
4 Paris II, p. 442.

Pages 128–139

5 Baker, *With All for All*, p. 58.
6 Above, p. 46.
7 Paris I, p. 117.
8 Powicke, *King Henry III*, pp. 158, 764–65. It was decided in the council that a match should first be proposed between Clare and one of Henry's half-sisters in the Lusignan clan, but Hugh and Isabella failed to respond by the deadline.
9 Paris I, pp. 121–22.
10 Powicke, *King Henry III*, pp. 291–92; Paris II, pp. 11–13.
11 Paris I, p. 123; Denholm-Young, *Richard of Cornwall*, p. 35.
12 Gee, L., *Women, Art, and Patronage*, pp. 30–31; Oram, *Alexander II.*
13 Paris I, p. 124; Maddicott, *Montfort*, p. 25.
14 Paris I, p. 129.
15 Cox, *Eagles of Savoy*, pp. 65–66.
16 Paris I, pp. 126–29.
17 Ibid., pp. 132–33.
18 Ibid., pp. 135–36; Cox, *Eagles of Savoy*, pp. 69–71.
19 Ibid., pp. 136–37; Vincent, *Peter des Roches*, p. 48.
20 Ward, *Saint Edmund*, pp. 117–27.
21 Paris I, pp. 138–39.
22 Prestwich, *Plantagenet England*, p. 83; Powicke, *King Henry III*, pp. 751–59. William's father Geoffrey fled to Scotland at the time of his son's execution, but was later forced to leave at Henry's insistence, and this former justiciar of Ireland ended his days in 1245 a miserable wretch.
23 Paris I, p. 155.
24 Vincent, 'Master Alexander of Stainsby', pp. 614–40.
25 Paris I, pp. 158–60.
26 Kjær, 'Matthew Paris and the Royal Christmas', pp. 141–54.
27 Labarge, *Montfort*, p. xi.
28 Powicke, *King Henry III*, pp. 270–71.
29 Paris I, pp. 162, 167–69; Shepard, *Courting Power*, p. 68.
30 Weiler, 'Gregory IX, Frederick II', pp. 199–200.
31 At Vaucouleurs, see above p. 122–23.
32 Labarge, *Saint Louis*, p. 57.
33 Paris I, pp. 172–73; Howell, 'Children of King Henry III', pp. 57–72. Henry and Eleanor are mentioned as having only five children during their lifetime. Starting in the next century, four more children appear, all sons who died in infancy, none of whom appear in contemporary chronicles, and all lacking prayers for their souls, which Henry would surely have had done as he did for even the grandchildren who predeceased him. Margaret Howell provides the most thorough examination of this topic.
34 Carpenter, Kantner, 'King Henry III and Windsor Castle', pp. 25–35.
35 Howell, *Eleanor of Provence*, pp. 20, 27; Morris, *Great and Terrible King*, pp. 5–6.
36 Paris I, p. 172.
37 Carpenter, *Struggle for Mastery*, p. 348.
38 Paris I, pp. 237–39. Hubert had retreated from view since being the only notable magnate to support Henry during the crisis over the Montfort marriage. The charge about Poitou claimed he had sent the garrison of La Rochelle caskets filled with sand instead of silver.
39 Ibid., p. 194.
40 Maddicott, *Montfort*, pp. 24–25.

42 Cox, *Eagles of Savoy*, pp. 71–77.
43 Paris I, pp. 236, 241. Paris adds that Henry tore his clothes, threw them into the fire and refused all solace.
44 Stacey, 'English Jews under Henry III', pp. 41, 47–48.
45 Novikoff, *Medieval Culture of Disputation*, pp. 191–93; Perry, *Saint Louis*, p. 101.
46 Rokéah, 'An Anglo-Jewish Assembly', pp. 71–73.
47 Powicke, *King Henry III*, p. 311.
48 Paris I, p. 290; Harvey, *Episcopal Appointments*, p. 89; Grosseteste, *Letters*, pp. 283–85.
50 Powicke, *King Henry III*, p. 271; Harvey, *Episcopal Appointments*, pp. 115–16.
51 Ward, *Saint Edmund*, pp. 131–32; Creamer, 'St Edmund and Henry III', pp. 137–38. Edmund was incensed by the election of a new prior in his own diocese and excommunicated all seventeen electors involved in it.
52 Carpenter, *Magna Carta*, p. 409.
53 Paris I, pp. 264–65.
54 Ibid., pp. 267, 269–72, 280–87.
55 Ibid., pp. 175, 245–46; Powicke, *King Henry III*, pp. 772–83. Years later, when compiling his work, Paris added that Simon the Norman had aroused the king's anger by refusing to seal the writ authorising payment to Thomas of Savoy for the wool tax. Simon supposedly did so out of conscience, believing that such business was against the interests of the crown. But given the earlier payments he sealed to Thomas, it seems likely that Paris recast him as a conscientious objector to embarrass the king. Geoffrey the Templar, another councillor despised by Paris, was also discredited at this time, allegedly for the same act of conscience, but he was principally involved in the collection of the Third from the Jews and had probably ran afoul of somebody during the course of it.
56 Denholm-Young, *Richard of Cornwall*, pp. 40–42. Baldwin was married to the daughter of Richard's wife Isabel.
57 Maddicott, *Montfort*, pp. 29–30; Labarge, *Montfort*, p. 57.
58 Creamer, 'St Edmund and Henry III', pp. 131–33.
59 Howell, *Eleanor of Provence*, p. 30; Hamilton, *Plantagenets*, p. 22.
60 Paris I, pp. 318–19; Kjær, 'Matthew Paris and the Royal Christmas', p. 151.

8 Not the Usual Retirement and Pleasures

1 Cox, *Eagles of Savoy*, p. 108–09; Paris I, p. 320.
2 Paris I, pp. 322–23.
3 Clanchy, *England and its Rulers*, p. 260; Crouch, *Acts and Letters of the Marshal Family*, pp. 30–31; Paris I, pp. 360–61.
4 Maund, *Welsh Kings*, pp. 201–03; Paris I, pp. 371–73.
5 Carpenter, *Reign of Henry III*, p. 203.
6 Crouch, *Acts and Letters of the Marshal Family*, pp. 33–34; Paris I, pp. 378–79.
7 Seabourne, *Imprisoning Medieval Women*, pp. 67, 82.
8 Paris I, pp. 323, 392.
9 Ibid., 388–89.
10 Ibid., pp. 382–83; 384–85. Paris puts his skills as a gossip to good use here, naming all those cardinals who voted for Celestine, and those who voted for Romulus, the former legate during Louis's minority who 'was said at one time to have debauched Blanche'.
11 Ibid., pp. 334–36. Paris says Henry had a glowing recommendation sheet of Boniface's qualities drawn up and passed around to other prelates to add their seals.

Pages 148–158

Some refused for fear of bearing false witness, others did so out of fear of the king. Since no names are given here, this is likely another of Paris's fabrications.

12 Stacey, *Royal Taxation*, pp. 188–204.
13 Clanchy, *England and Its Rulers*, pp. 56–57.
14 Carpenter, *Reign of Henry III*, pp. 170–73.
15 Carpenter, *Struggle for Mastery*, p. 469.
16 Ibid., p. 267.
17 Barratt, 'Counting the Cost', pp. 31–33.
18 Labarge, *Saint Louis*, pp. 63–65.
19 Perry, *Saint Louis*, pp. 103–04.
20 Wall, *Shrines of British Saints*, pp. 228–31; King, *Medieval England*, p. 123.
21 Paris I, pp. 362, 368.
22 Ibid., p. 359.
23 Strickland, *Lives of the Princesses of England*, pp. 39–41.
24 Labarge, *Montfort*, p. 60.
25 Perry, *Saint Louis*, pp. 107–09.
26 Paris, pp. 396–402.
27 Rymer, *Foedera*, p. 40; Denholm-Young, *Richard of Cornwall*, p. 46; Stacey, *Politics, Policy and Finance*, pp. 160–200. Stacey's is one of the best and most thorough accounts of Henry's Poitevin and Gascon policies.
28 *Royal Letters*, pp. 25–29; Paris, pp. 404, 414–16.
29 Rymer, *Foedera*, p. 41; Edbury, 'The de Montforts in the Latin East', pp. 23–26. Philip had been born in the Holy Land during the Third Crusade of 1204 and returned there after his father Guy was killed during the second phase of the Albigensian Crusade in 1228.
30 Maddicott, *Montfort*, pp. 31–32. Henry forgave the £1,565 he had lent Montfort for his trip to Rome for the marriage dispensation.
31 Denholm-Young, *Richard of Cornwall*, p. 47.
32 Paris I, pp. 422–23. Paris makes sure to report that Henry was the first to flee: 'King Henry, then, did not spare the spur, or the sides of his horse, but fled without stopping to the city of Blaye, hungry and fasting as he was, and troubling little as to who of his troops followed him.'
33 Perry, *Saint Louis*, p. 119.
34 Paris I, p. 432; Howell, *Eleanor of Provence*, p. 35.
35 Perry, *Saint Louis*, p. 120–21.
36 Sibly, *Chronicle of William of Puylaurens*, p. 105.
37 Paris I, pp. 453–54; Vincent, 'Isabella of Angoulême', p. 212.
38 Powicke, *Thirteenth Century*, p. 100. The couple had not lived together since the birth of their daughter in 1220.
39 Sibly, *Chronicle of William of Puylaurens*, pp.100–04.
40 Rymer, *Foedera*, p. 42; Paris I, p. 437; Bémont, *Montfort*, p. 66; Powicke, *King Henry III*, p. 215. In a note, Powicke says Simon apparently denied making the crack about locking up the king in one of the barred houses of Windsor.
41 Denholm-Young, *Richard of Cornwall*, pp. 48–49.
42 Paris I, pp. 385–86; Howell, *Eleanor of Provence*, pp. 33–34.
43 Denholm-Young, *Richard of Cornwall*, p. 50.
44 Mitchell, *Studies in Taxation*, pp. 238–39; Paris I, pp. 445–46.
45 Howell, *Eleanor of Provence*, pp. 37–38; Rigg, *History of Anglo-Latin Literature*, p. 198.
46 Marsh, *English Rule in Gascony*, pp. 96–97.
47 Carpenter, *Minority of Henry III*, p. 378. By the end of the century, Edward was collecting upwards of £6,000 in annual duties at Bordeaux.

48 Carpenter, *Fine of the Month: November 2011*, access at http://www.finerollshenry3.org.uk/content/month/fm-11-2011.html. Carpenter also relates a story of how Henry ordered one of his household clerks to cut the hair of the other clerks before the king picked up the scissors and gave him a cut.
49 Stacey, *Politics*, pp. 106–08.
50 Paris I, pp. 455–56, 459–60.
51 Strickland, *Princesses of England*, pp. 43–44; King, *Medieval England*, p. 107; Carpenter, 'Meetings of Kings', p. 18; Stacey, *Politics*, pp. 241–42.
52 Paris I, pp. 437, 478.
53 Howell, *Eleanor of Provence*, pp. 39–40; Stacey, *Politics*, p. 241. Beatrice received a gold eagle that cost more than £100.
54 Maddicott, *Montfort*, pp. 32–33.
55 Powicke, *King Henry III*, pp. 271–72. Another version of the story has some canons from Lincoln telling Innocent that Raleigh was a good friend of the king, who wanted him in Winchester. That could only mean that Robert Grosseteste, the Bishop of Lincoln and a good friend of Raleigh's, had resorted to an underhanded move to check the king's constant interference in church elections.
56 Paris I, pp. 462–64, 480–81, 487–88; 530–36.
57 Stacey, *Politics*, pp. 221–22; Powicke, *King Henry III*, p. 273.
58 Grosseteste, *Letters*, pp. 290–92; Harvey, *Episcopal Appointments*, pp. 85–86.
59 Young, *Royal Forests*, p. 77.
60 Howell, *Eleanor of Provence*, pp. 41–42; Harvey, *Episcopal Appointments*, p. 102; Mayr-Harting, *Religion, Politics*, p. 263.
61 Grosseteste, *Letters*, pp. 367–73; Clanchy, *England and its Rulers*, p. 234.
62 Paris I, pp. 487–88; Smith, *Llywelyn Ap Gruffudd*, pp. 47–50.
63 Blaauw, *Barons' War*, p. 190; Vincent, 'Leopards, Lions and Dragons'; Powicke, *King Henry III*, p. 459.
64 Paris I, p. 406; Paris II, pp. 5; 23–26; Oram, *Alexander II*.
65 Paris II, p. pp. 27–28, 46; Stacey, *Politics*, p. 245. The foreign contingent consumed much of the £4,000 in outlays.
66 Maddicott, *Montfort*, p. 34.
67 Paris II, pp. 7–9. It is to this Parliament that Paris assigns the historic 'Paper Constitution', the terms of which are described in the crisis of 1238 on p. 130.
68 Clanchy, *England and Its Rulers*, pp. 237–38; Prestwich, *Plantagenet England*, pp. 90–91.
69 Maddicott, *Origins of the English Parliament*, p. 174.
70 Paris II, pp. 10–11; Vincent, *Politics of Church and State*, p. 165; Mitchell, *Studies in Taxation*, p. 243.
71 Allshorn, *Stupor Mundi*, pp. 209–18.
72 Cox, *Eagles of Savoy*, pp. 144–45.
73 Runciman, *History of the Crusades 3*, pp. 224–27.
74 Perry, *Saint Louis*, pp. 131–32.

9 The Garden of Our Delights

1 Howell, *Eleanor of Provence*, pp. 44–45.
2 Creamer, 'St Edmund and Henry III', pp. 129–39.
3 Ward, *Saint Edmund*, pp. 179–94.
4 Powicke, *King Henry III*, pp. 569–75; *CR, 1242–47*. Henry also undertook to have a new throne constructed at this time. He wrote to Edward of Westminster, his keeper of the works, to go ahead with his idea to have the two leopards depicted on either side of the high-backed chair cast in bronze rather than made of marble or carved

Pages 168–178

directly into it, and the steps of the approach were to be made of stone. The idea was to imitate the throne of Solomon, with the leopards, already used in the Plantagenet coat of arms, taking the place of the lions of biblical times. See Steane, *Archaeology of the Medieval English Monarchy*, pp. 37–38.

5 Allshorn, *Stupor Mundi*, pp. 223–41.

6 Paris II, pp. 73–77.

7 Ibid., pp. 56–58; Powicke, *King Henry III*, pp. 354–55.

8 Paris II, pp. 107–08, 164; Gasquet, *Henry III and the Church,* pp. 230, 241–42.

9 Rymer, *Foedera*, pp. 43–44; Solt, *Church and State in Early Modern England*, p. 4.

10 Paris II, pp. 109–12, 114–16; Powicke, *King Henry III*, pp. 303, 314–15; Knox, *Studies in Taxation*, pp. 245–46. To fund the expedition, Henry pawned his jewels at the New Temple to his brother for a loan of £2,000, and tried to shake down the foreign merchants active in the country for more. He had ordered their expulsion from the kingdom on 15 June for charging interest on their transactions, then said they could stay if they made him a gift of £2,666 or at least loaned him the money.

11 Paris II, pp. 104–11; Smith, *Llywelyn Ap Gruffudd*, pp. 49–64.

12 Paris II, pp. 119–22; Crouch, *Acts and Letters*, pp. 35–36.

13 Howell, *Eleanor of Provence*, pp. 40, 46–47.

14 Cox, *Eagles of Savoy*, pp. 146–53.

15 Labarge, *Saint Louis*, pp. 89–90.

16 Paris II, pp. 113–14; Rymer, *Foedera*, p. 45.

17 Denholm-Young, *Richard of Cornwall*, pp. 52–53.

18 Paris II, p. 130; Cox, *Eagles of Savoy*, pp. 159–61.

19 Paris II, pp. 133–35; Gasquet, *Henry III and the Church*, pp. 258–62. Boniface was consecrated on 15 January 1245. Henry's actions might have earned him some respect from Paris, but the chronicler is ashamed to say that the English are wretched because they knew 'the slippery disposition of the king, and had learned by frequent experience that he was dissuaded from any resolution with the same facility as he was induced to make it'.

20 Grosseteste, *Letters*, pp. 356–57. Henry added: 'The day when we shall not do all this, we will give our eyes to be plucked out and our head to be cut off.'

21 Paris II, pp. 148–56. Henry addressed a separate letter to the cardinals urging them to use their influence lest the 'outcries against oppressions' grew only worse.

22 Paris II, pp. 133–35; Gasquet, *Henry III and the Church*, pp. 251–53.

23 Grosseteste, *Letters*, pp. 358–59.

24 Paris II, pp. 178–79, 207–09; Gasquet, *Henry III and the Church*, pp. 270–71. Paris says the friars had the king's permission to carry out these exactions.

25 Paris II, p. 173.

26 Ibid., pp. 175–76.

27 Gasquet, *Henry III and the Church,* pp. 253–54; Rymer, *Foedera*, p. 45.

28 Paris II, p. 199; Gasquet, *Henry III and the Church*, pp. 264–65.

29 Paris II, pp. 164–65; Labarge, *Saint Louis*, pp. 91–92; Powicke, *King Henry III*, pp. 359–60.

30 Paris II, pp. 144–46; Weiler, *Henry III and the Staufen Empire*, pp. 113–14; Allshorn, *Stupor Mundi*, pp. 252–57.

31 Paris II, p. 176.

32 Carpenter, *Struggle for Mastery*, p. 276.

33 Steane, *Archaeology of the Medieval English Monarchy*, p. 120; Howell, *Eleanor of Provence*, pp. 74–75.

34 Smith, *Llywelyn Ap Gruffudd*, pp. 49–64.

35 Howell, *Eleanor of Provence*, p. 53.
36 Cox, *Eagles of Savoy*, p. 172.
37 Paris II, pp. 230–31.
38 Ridgeway, 'Henry III and the "Aliens"', pp. 82–85.
39 See above, p. 79.
40 Ridgeway, 'Henry III and the "Aliens"', p. 90; Waugh, *Lordship of England*, pp. 86–87; *CPR 1247–58*, p. 76; Butler, *Divorce in Medieval England*, p. 96.
41 Paris II, p. 238.
42 Ibid., pp. 239–43.
43 Vincent, *Holy Blood*, pp. 22–23, 88–92; Bynum, *Wonderful Blood*, pp. 98–101.
44 Vincent, *Holy Blood*, pp. 17, 24–29.
45 Paris II, p. 240.
46 Ibid., pp. 243–44; Labarge, *Saint Louis*, pp. 105–06; Denholm-Young, *Richard of Cornwall*, p. 60; Bémont, *Montfort*, p. 71.
47 Paris II, pp. 232–33; Ward, *Saint Edmund*, pp. 195–200. The canonisation took place on 7 January 1247.
48 Dunstable, p. 172; Denholm-Young, *Richard of Cornwall*, pp. 57–60. Richard was also still in the scandalous business of redeeming crusade vows. In one unscrupulous case, his agent won £17 from the estate of a man he swore had taken the cross, even though that was news to everyone who knew the man.
49 Cassidy, 'Exchanges, Silver Purchases', pp. 107–18.
50 Allen, *Mints and Money in Medieval England*, pp. 171–72.
51 Mayhew, *New History of the Royal Mint*, pp. 107–13; Cassidy, 'Richard of Cornwall and the Royal Mints', pp. 137–56. Henry was left with £3,733 and had to pay back his old loans from Richard, plus his annual fees.
52 Paris II, pp. 215, 233–34, 262–63; Hillaby, *Palgrave Dictionary of Medieval Anglo-Jewish History*, pp. 104–05; Stacey, *Politics*, p. 154.
53 Stacey, *Politics*, pp. 219–22.
54 Paris II, pp. 254–57. Later in his chronicle for that year (pp. 284–86), Paris describes a mission he undertook to Norway to settle the affairs of a monastery fallen on hard times. He was chosen for his 'wisdom and fidelity' and, as he himself says, because he was a 'most particular friend to the king'.
55 Powicke, *King Henry III*, pp. 339–40.
56 Cox, *Eagles of Savoy*, pp. 161–62, 169–70.
57 Paris II, pp. 266–67.
58 Clanchy, *England and its Rulers*, pp. 232–38.
59 Paris II, pp. 267–68. Having failed to get his tax, Henry was forced to pawn whatever treasure he had and lashed out at his councillors for having brought him to this state. According to Paris, they soothed him with honeyed speech like, 'As all rivers flow back to the sea, so everything which was now sold will at some time return to you in remunerative gifts.'
60 Stacey, *Politics*, pp. 238–39, 250–53.
61 Carpenter, *Reign of King Henry III*, p. 93; Prestwich, *Plantagenet England*, p. 144.

10 Weighed in an Even Balance

1 Prestwich, *Edward I*, pp. 5–6.
2 Clanchy, *From Memory to Written Record*, p. 232.
3 Powicke, *King Henry III*, pp. 686–87.
4 Bémont, *Montfort*, pp. 73–75.
5 Paris II, p. 252; Maddicott, *Montfort*, pp. 86–87.

Pages 189–200

6 Wilkinson, *Eleanor de Montfort*, pp. 78–79.
7 Maddicott, *Montfort*, pp. 47, 135–36.
8 Ibid., pp. 108–09.
9 Labarge, *Montfort*, pp. 111–12.
10 Paris II, pp. 288–9.
11 Labarge, *Montfort*, pp. 112–13.
12 Bémont, *Montfort*, pp. 82–85.
13 Maddicott, *Montfort*, p. 112; Labarge, *Montfort*, p. 114.
14 Labarge, pp. 131–33.
15 Paris I, p. 431; Paris II, pp. 331–32.
16 *Royal Letters*, pp. 361–62.
17 Labarge, *Montfort*, pp. 115–16. Half of the money was from Jewish tallages, half from London rents.
18 Maddicott, *Montfort*, p. 44; Bémont, *Montfort*, p. 38; Wilkinson, *Eleanor de Montfort*, pp. 12–13.
19 Hutton, *Montfort and his Cause*, pp. 19–20; Maddicott, *Montfort*. Maddicott provides this section from Job as the epigraph to his biography.
20 Reuter, *Medieval Polities*, p. 451; Clanchy, *England and its Rulers*, p. 254.
21 Lloyd, 'King Henry III', pp. 103–06.
22 Above, pp. 54–55
23 Gabrieli, *Arab Historians of the Crusades*, p. 178.
24 Tyerman, *God's War*, pp. 787–88.
25 Labarge, *Saint Louis*, pp. 120–21.
26 Perry, *Saint Louis*, pp. 172–77.
27 Runciman, *A History of the Crusades*, pp. 266–70.
28 Joinville, *Crusade of Saint Louis*, pp. 413–18.
29 Labarge, *Saint Louis*, pp. 123–25.
30 Tyerman, *God's War*, pp. 796–98.
31 Goldstone, *Four Queens*, pp. 182–88.
32 Paris II, pp. 329–30.
33 Cox, *Eagles of Savoy*, pp. 175–76.
34 Paris II, pp. 344–49.
35 Lawrence, *Letters of Adam Marsh I*, pp. 93, 147.
36 Denholm-Young, *Richard of Cornwall*, pp. 73–74.
37 Ambler, *On Kingship and Tyranny*, pp. 115–22.
38 Paris II, pp. 289–91, 308–09, 340; Powicke, *King Henry III*, p. 304. The cash crunch at this time was due to the high outlays for Gascony.
39 Paris II, pp. 294–98; Clanchy, *Did Henry III Have a Policy*, p. 210.
40 Paris II, pp. 292, 293–94, 316. Huw Ridgeway has shown that Aymer was in fact quite a serious churchman. He was university-educated and had a higher proportion of graduates in his household than even Grosseteste.
41 Clanchy, *Did Henry III Have a Policy*, p. 216; Sabapathy, *Officers and Accountability*, p. 118.
42 Vincent, *Politics of Church and State*, p. 168.
43 See pp. 138–39
44 Paris II, pp. 234, 264, 293, 316; Barker, *Tournament in England*, pp. 48–49.
45 Paris II, pp. 466–67.
46 Vincent, *Peter des Roches*, pp. 246–47.
47 Harvey, *Episcopal Appointments*, p. 78. Henry withdrew his nomination for reasons unknown.

48 Paris II, pp. 395–98; Clanchy, *Did Henry III Have a Policy*, p. 211. The sermon Paris attributes to Henry is ambiguous enough to stir debate as to whether he arrived on the date of the election (4 November 1250) and therefore attempted to influence it, or the day after and mingled his gratitude with a warning for future elections.
49 Harvey, *Episcopal Appointments*, pp. 81–82; Harding, *England in the Thirteenth Century*, p. 233.
50 Paris II, p. 400.
51 Ibid., pp. 402–04.
52 Ibid., p. 404; Allshorn, *Stupor Mundi*, pp. 261–63, 266–69, 276–77.
53 Runciman, *Sicilian Vespers*, pp. 26–31.
54 Paris II, pp. 433–35, 443.
55 Dunstable, p. 181; Paris II, pp. 418, 424–26, 431–33; Powicke, *King Henry III*, p. 335. Paris puts the arraignment of Bath before a meeting of Parliament in February, where the king flies into such a rage over both the charges and Bath's attempts to use his family's influence that he declares before the assembly that he will pardon anyone who kills the judge. The *Close Rolls* indicate that Bath made his appearance before the king some time after May.
56 Hammond, *Food and Feast*, pp. 127–28.
57 Paris II, p. 464; Denholm-Young, *Richard of Cornwall*, p. 76.
58 Paris II, pp. 420–21, 464–65.
59 Bémont, *Montfort*, pp. 91–97.
60 Paris II, pp. 467–71; Howell, *Eleanor of Provence*, pp. 77–78.
61 Ramsay, *Dawn of the Constitution*, pp. 131–32.

11 Three Times Lucky

1 Powicke, *Reign of King Henry III*, pp. 324–25; Paris II, pp. 422. Paris suspected that the *non obstante* clause had been invoked for an entirely unsavoury purpose, but the record offers no clue one way or the other.
2 Carpenter, *Reign of Henry III*, p. 78; Crook, 'Charters of Free Warren', pp. 45–46; Paris II, pp. 351–53.
3 Clanchy, *Did Henry III Have a Policy*, pp. 8–9; Paris II, p. 531. Paris was not in the habit of giving the outcome of cases like these. Langley was dismissed from office a month later and Maneby ultimately received the renewal of his letters of protection.
4 Paris II, p. 528.
5 Carpenter, *Reign of Henry III*, p. 80; Waugh, *Lordship of England*, p. 254; Annesley, *Henry Fine Rolls Project*, August 2009; Paris II, p. 528.
6 Howell, *Eleanor of Provence*, p. 65–66; Paris II, pp. 494–95.
7 Tout, *Chapters in Administrative History*, pp. 278–79.
8 Bémont, *Montfort*, pp. 98–102; Paris II, pp. 476–77.
9 Maddicott, *Montfort*, pp. 114–15.
10 Paris II, pp. 486–87.
11 Lawrence, *Letters of Adam Marsh I*, pp. 79–91. In his letter, Marsh says he approached members of the panel and they 'did not hesitate to promise help and advice to protect the earl from danger, loss or disgrace. Really, in such constant expressions of goodwill he experienced very rare and genuine friendship'.
12 Howell, *Eleanor of Provence*, pp. 63–64.
13 Maddicott, *Montfort*, pp. 116–17; Paris II, pp. 487–88.
14 Prothero, *Montfort*, pp. 101–02. Paris II, pp. 507–08.
15 Labarge, pp. 122–23; Bémont, pp. 113–15; Maddicott, pp. 118–19; Paris II, pp. 508–10.

Pages 211–221

16 Wilkinson, *Eleanor de Montfort*, p. 90.
17 Howell, *Eleanor of Provence*, p. 66; Paris II, pp. 536–37.
18 Paris III, pp. 1–3.
19 Howell, *Eleanor of Provence*, p. 67.
20 Paris II, pp. 417, 534–36.
21 Howell, *Eleanor of Provence*, p. 68–69; Paris III, pp. 3–6.
22 Lloyd, 'King Henry III', p. 99.
23 Jackson, *Seventh Crusade*, pp. 179–97, 202–03.
24 Joinville, *Crusade of Saint Louis*, pp. 502–03.
25 Paris III, pp. 21–22.
26 Grosseteste, *Letters*, p. 265; Paris III, pp. 56–57.
27 Paris II, pp. 518–20, 523–25.
28 Watt, *English Episcopate*, pp. 140–44; Tolan, 'First Imposition of a Badge', pp. 159–66.
29 Paris III, pp. 22–25.
30 Carpenter, 'Magna Carta 1253', pp. 179–83; Maddicott, 'Pre-reform Parliaments of Henry III', pp. 34–35; Mitchell, *Studies in Taxation*, p. 257.
31 Paris III, pp. 26–27.
32 Carpenter, *Magna Carta* 1253, pp. 186–87.
33 Grosseteste, *Letters*, pp. 441–46; Powicke, *King Henry III*, pp. 278–79; Paris III, pp. 7–8.
34 Paris III, pp. 44–51. Paris had always been a severe critic of Grosseteste on account of his visitations but admired him for standing up to what he called Roman avarice. He tells a story of how Fulk Basset, staying close to Buckden, heard the most agreeable melody of a bell in the distance. When the others in his party claimed to have heard nothing, it was taken as a sign that Grosseteste was just then leaving for the heavens. He was indeed dead when their party arrived to investigate.
35 Ibid., pp. 30–31.
36 Cockerill, *Eleanor of Castile*, pp. 41–43, 77.
37 Morris, *Great and Terrible King*, p. 18.
38 D'Avray, *Dissolving Royal Marriages*, pp. 42–49.
39 Cockerill, *Eleanor of Castile*, pp. 78–79.
40 Ridgeway, 'Henry III and the "Aliens"', pp. 83–84.
41 Bémont, *Montfort*, pp. 119–20.
42 Maddicott, *Montfort*, pp. 121–24, 133–35. Henry also forgave Montfort's annual payment for the Umfraville wardship, which had offset the fee he and Eleanor were given as her marriage portion. The exchequer commenced paying that fee, now upped to £400.
43 Barrow, 'Peter d'Aigueblanche's Support Network', p. 36.
44 Powicke, *King Henry III*, pp. 788–89; Cockerill, *Eleanor of Castile*, pp. 79–81.
45 Howell, *Eleanor of Provence*, pp. 114–15.
46 Paris III, pp. 60–61.
47 Ridgeway, 'Henry III and the "Aliens"', pp. 85–86; Howell, *Eleanor of Provence*, pp. 117–18.
48 Howell, *Eleanor of Provence*, pp. 118–19.
49 Maddicott, *Origins of the English Parliament*, pp. 210–14.
50 Paris III, pp. 61–63, 75.
51 Powicke, *King Henry III*, pp. 234–35. Maddicott; *Montfort*, p. 125.
52 Gonzáles, 'Lope Fernández', pp. 106–10.
53 Paris III, pp. 89–92. Paris presents the pope accusing Conrad of poisoning Henry Hohenstaufen.
54 Lloyd, 'King Henry III', pp. 111–13.

55 Carpenter, 'Henry III and the Sicilian Affair', pp. 1–4.
56 Howell, *Eleanor of Provence*, pp. 126–27.
57 Cockerill, *Eleanor of Castile*, pp. 82–90.
58 Paris III, pp. 97–98, 104.
59 Carpenter, 'Meetings of Kings', pp. 1, 11, 14–15.
60 Labarge, *Saint Louis*, pp. 189–90; Paris III, 105–09.
61 Carpenter, 'Meetings of Kings', p. 10; Paris III, p. 109.
62 Goldstone, *Four Queens*, pp. 126, 254.
63 Labarge, *Saint Louis*, pp. 208–12.
64 Paris III, pp. 109–10.

12 Collapse

1 Prestwich, 'Wonderful Life', p. 164; Cassidy, 'Henry III's Elephant'; Paris III, p. 115. Louis also received a zebra.
2 Barrow, 'Peter d'Aigueblanche's Support Network', pp. 32–33; *Mayors and Sheriffs*, pp. 23–24; Paris III, p. 115.
3 Powicke, *King Henry III*, pp. 308–09; Paris III, pp. 113–14.
4 Ramsay, *Dawn of the Constitution*, pp. 151–2; Paris III, pp. 119–20.
5 Runciman, *Sicilian Vespers*, pp. 32–33.
6 Carpenter, 'Henry III and the Sicilian Affair'. Innocent had offered £25,000 up front.
7 Cazel, *History of the Crusades*, pp. 144–46.
8 Paris III, pp. 128–30.
9 Ramsay, *Dawn of the Constitution*, pp. 157–58; Dunstable, p. 198; Paris III, p. 181. Following up a suggestion made by Paris, Ramsay insinuates that Henry pursued the two barons because their fathers were among the Northerners who had been active in the rebellion against his father John.
10 Carpenter, 'Vis et voluntas of King Henry III'; Paris III, p. 148. There are no surviving records of the fine besides an entry made at the time by chronicler John of Wallingford, a contemporary of Matthew Paris at St Albans, that it was 1,000 marks (£666). Carpenter believes that Henry did in fact amerce Ros 100,000 marks (£66,666) in a fit, citing the case against Gilbert Marshal (see above p. 146) as an example of his emotions getting the better of him, but that his council reduced it to the amount documented by Wallingford.
11 Dunstable, p. 196; Paris III, pp. 121, 130–31, 138.
12 Carpenter, *Crucifixion and Conversion*, pp. 129–48; Stacey, *King Henry III and the Jews*, pp. 125–27; Paris III, pp. 138–41; *Mayors and Sheriffs*, p. 25.
13 Cockerill, *Eleanor of Castile*, pp. 97–101; Paris III, pp. 135–36, 151.
14 Ramsay, *Dawn of the Constitution*, pp. 152–53; Paris III, pp. 133–35, 137–38.
15 Dunstable, pp. 199–200; Paris III, pp. 144–47.
16 Morris, *Bigod Earls*, pp. 50–51; Paris III, pp. 150–51. Bigod's debts were £576 on fees owed for scutages and aids and £427 in arrears for Eleanor de Montfort's dower payments.
17 Paris III, pp. 141–42, 144–47.
18 Powicke, *King Henry III*, pp. 367–69.
19 Bémont, *Montfort*, pp. 130–31; Rymer, *Foedera*, p. 55.
20 Cox, *Eagles of Savoy*, pp. 252–61; Howell, *Eleanor of Provence*, p. 144; Rymer, *Foedera*, p. 59; Carpenter, 'Henry III and the Sicilian Affair'. Henry assigned the money for the castles to Peter of Savoy on 3 February 1257, more than a year after Thomas's capture, and nothing had come of the brothers' military attempt to free him. He had

Pages 233–239

just sent Beatrice a letter of condolence for her troubles with Charles of Anjou and may have decided at that point that he would never see the money again.

21 Labarge, *Saint Louis*, pp. 151–53; Paris III, pp. 69–75. Countess Margaret had to pay Charles £40,000 for his military intervention, and John d'Avesnes and his brother Baldwin were required to do homage to him for Hainault.

22 Huffman, *Social Politics of Medieval Diplomacy*, pp. 272–75.

23 Denholm-Young, *Richard of Cornwall*, p. 86; Paris III, p. 213, 228. Paris says he has it from the royal chamberlain himself that since Henry commenced plundering and wasting the wealth of the kingdom, he spent £633,000, easily twenty years' worth of revenue.

24 *Royal Letters*, pp. 107–08; Weiler, *Henry III and the Staufen Empire*, p. 162. The extension of the truce was negotiated by Montfort and Peter of Savoy.

25 Huffman, *Social Politics of Medieval Diplomacy*, p. 290.

26 Cockerill, *Eleanor of Castile*, pp. 104–05; Carpenter, *Reign of King Henry III*, p. 80; *Royal Letters*, pp. 109–14. Before sending the embassy to Castile, Henry had received an offer of an alliance from James of Aragon, but demurred from giving him an answer.

27 Denholm-Young, *Richard of Cornwall*, pp. 87–88; Weiler, *Henry III and the Staufen Empire*, p. 167.

28 Morris, *Great and Terrible King*, p. 22.

29 Paris III, pp. 156–57.

30 Rymer, *Foedera*, p. 56.

31 Carpenter, 'Between Magna Carta and the Parliamentary State', pp. 21–23.

32 Paris III, pp. 172, 174–75.

33 Smith, *Llywelyn Ap Gruffudd*, pp. 77–84; Howell, *Eleanor of Provence*, pp. 125–26; Dunstable, pp. 200–01. Langley was a forest official who had supplanted his mentor Robert Passelewe in courtly favour before the latter died in 1252. Langley's rise prompted Passelewe to quit royal service altogether and become a priest. When he was given a church that Henry wanted for Aymer, he found himself under investigation for abuse of his former office and, as with his earlier fall from grace, had to pay a fine to be restored to favour in December 1250.

34 Prestwich, *Edward I*, p. 15; Paris III, p. 186.

35 Paris III, pp. 187–91. The grant to Alexander in *Royal Letters* is dated 16 August 1256. The ubiquitous Mansel also appealed on behalf of Mrs Lisle. He was in the company of the Scottish royal couple on their way homeward to deal with the still unsteady situation up north.

36 Carpenter, *Reign of King Henry III*, pp. 137–50; Paris III, p. 197.

37 Ramsay, *Dawn of the Constitution*, p. 155; Dunstable, p. 198.

38 Paris III, pp. 151–52, 169–70. This would seem to contradict what Henry said to a Dominican friar, William of Abingdon: 'Brother William, there was a time when you used to speak of spiritual things; now all you can say is "give, give, give"'.

39 Weiler, *Henry III and the Staufen Empire*, pp. 169–70. Runciman, *Sicilian Vespers*, pp. 35–38.

40 Maddicott, *Montfort*, p. 125; Jobson, 'John of Crakehall', p. 90.

41 Ridgeway, 'Foreign Favourites', p. 592; Waugh, *Lordship of England*, p. 163.

42 Carpenter, *Magna Carta*, pp. 213–14; Stacey, *Politics*, pp. 217–18.

43 Cassidy, 'Bad Sheriffs', pp. 35–47; Waugh, 'Origins of the Articles of the Escheator', pp. 94–95.

44 Paris III, p. 125.

45 Clanchy, *England and its Rulers*, p. 236; Hamilton, *Plantagenets*, p. 45.
46 Paris III, pp. 200–01, 204–05.
47 Denholm-Young, *Richard of Cornwall*, pp. 88–89; Paris III, pp. 207–09.
48 Huffman, *Social Politics of Medieval Diplomacy*, pp. 287–89.
49 Rymer, *Foedera*, pp. 57–58.
50 Paris III, pp. 224–25.
51 Carpenter, 'King Henry III and the Chapter House', pp. 32–39.
52 Powicke, *King Henry III*, pp. 336–38.
53 Ridgeway, 'Foreign Favourites', pp. 598–99.
54 Paris III, p. 220.
55 See Introduction; Powicke, *King Henry III*, p. 375.
56 Powicke, *King Henry III*, p. 239.
57 Procter, *Curia and Cortes in León and Castile*, p. 126; Paris III, pp. 132, 227.
58 Labarge, *Saint Louis*, pp. 186–88.
59 Ibid., pp. 207–08.
60 Maddicott, *Montfort*, p. 140; Rymer, *Foedera*, p. 59.
61 Denholm-Young, *Richard of Cornwall*, pp. 90–95.
62 Ridgeway, 'Foreign Favourites', pp. 604–05.
63 Wilkinson, *Eleanor de Montfort*, pp. 78–79, 112.
64 Paris III, pp. 233–34. Paris calls anger a short madness, indicating that temporary insanity was known even in those days.
65 Ibid., pp. 217–18, 243–44.
66 Smith, *Llywelyn Ap Gruffudd*, pp. 97–99.
67 Bémont, *Montfort*, p. 133; Maddicott, *Montfort*, p. 140; Paris III, p. 244.
68 Carpenter, *Reign of Henry III*, pp. 107–30.
69 Storey, *The First Convocation*, pp. 151–59; Paris III, pp. 215, 222, 234–35.
70 Paris III, p. 245; Smith, *Llywelyn Ap Gruffudd*, pp. 102–05; *Henry III's Fine Rolls Blog*, 19 August to 8 September 1257, access http://blog.frh3.org.uk/?cat=393&paged=2
71 Paris III, p. 212; *Mayors and Sheriffs*, pp. 31–32; Carpenter, *Struggle for Mastery*, pp. 26–27.
72 Denholm-Young, *Richard of Cornwall*, pp. 95–96.
73 Powicke, *King Henry III*, pp. 374–76.
74 Paris III, pp. 232, 241. Maddicott, *Montfort*, p. 139; *Henry III's Fine Rolls Blog*, access http://blog.frh3.org.uk/?tag=merton-priory. Henry gave his almoner £51 for Katherine's funeral, suggesting that 10,000 paupers were fed for the occasion.

13 The March on Westminster

1 Tewkesbury, pp. 163–64; Carpenter, *Reign of Henry III*, pp. 187–88; Bémont, *Montfort*, pp. 152–54. According to the *Annals of Tewkesbury*, the only chronicle to record this scene, Henry asked, 'Wretched me, am I your prisoner?' The Latin (*Captivus ego a vobis ne captus sum*?) contains a pun that suggests wit rather than fear, but the annalist also says the king was 'disturbed in mind'.
2 Carpenter, *Reign of Henry III*, pp. 183, 192; Paris III, pp. 296–97.
3 Rymer, *Foedera*, pp. 56–57; Paris III, pp. 267–69.
4 Ridgeway, 'Lord Edward and the Provisions of Oxford', p. 90.
5 Waugh, *Lordship of England*, p. 243.
6 Howell, *Eleanor of Provence*, pp. 147–48.
7 *CChR, 1226–57*, pp. 438–39; Paris III, pp. 14–15.

Pages 252–257

8 Dunstable, p. 203–04; Bémont, *Montfort*, p. 133; Carpenter, *Reign of Henry III*, p. 190. The marriage contract was formalised in the queen's chamber at Westminster on 18 December 1258 with Montfort as one of the witnesses. Clare and Valence also seem to have had a falling out over a manor.

9 Paris III, pp. 278–80; Powicke, *King Henry III*, p. 378. Paris describes the king again as remorseful standing before such accusations and swearing on the altar and shrine of St Edward to mend his ways: 'But his frequent transgressions previously rendered him entirely unworthy of belief and as the nobles had not yet learned how to keep their Proteus in check (for it was an arduous and difficult matter), the parliament was prorogued … '

10 Another member of the king's twelve was John of Darlington, a Dominican friar who served Henry as both councillor and confessor. The only surviving list of the reform committee, provided in the *Annals of Burton*, is missing the twelfth member of the king's side. This would be Geoffrey Lusignan if the barons' claim that all of Henry's half-brothers served on the committee. But in the patent rolls dated 22 June 1258, when the move against the Lusignans was being formulated in Parliament, Henry addresses Richard de Clare, the Earl of Gloucester, as a member of his side, even though *Burton* names him as one of the baronial twelve. Powicke unconvincingly dismisses this as a 'curious official error' but it fits nicely into the intrigues that were definitely in motion by this stage.

11 Ridgeway, 'Henry III and the "Aliens"', pp. 81–82.

12 Tewkesbury, p. 163; Burton, pp. 409–13.

13 Powicke, *King Henry III*, pp. 249–52.

14 Ibid., pp. 380–81.

15 *DBM*, pp. 77–91. There is no known author of this 'Petition of the Barons', which lists 29 grievances pertaining to the sheriffs, marriages, castles, fees and amercements, attending manorial courts, etc.

16 Ibid., pp. 97–113.

17 Treharne, *Baronial Plan*, pp. 75–76.

18 Paris III, pp. 285–88.

19 *DBM*, pp. 91–97; Howell, *Eleanor of Provence*, pp. 158; Paris III, pp. 291–92. Louis denied Aymer permission to continue his studies in Paris.

20 Waugh, *Lordship of England*, p. 243; Powicke, *King Henry III*, p. 402.

21 Howell, *Eleanor of Provence*, p. 156.

22 Carpenter, 'Between Magna Carta', p. 20; Paris III, p. 324; *CPR, 1258–66*, pp. 16, 30. The reforming council was generous to Thomas's heirs and paid them £2,000 arrears of his fee. Paris considered all the money that went to him wasted like 'seed sown on the seashore'. He puts his death down to poisoning, the same fate as his older brother William.

23 Ridgeway, 'Ecclesiastical Career of Aymer de Lusignan', pp. 155–60; Bémont, *Montfort*, pp. 163–65.

24 Prestwich, *Edward I*, pp. 25–27; Paris III, pp. 296, 329–30; *Winchester*, p. 98. The steward was Walter de Scoteny. The *Winchester Annals* say he was actually pulled apart by wild horses. His possessions went to Edward after his execution, which incidentally was the subject of the last entry Paris made in his massive chronicle. He died in June 1259, bringing to an end his entertaining eruptions and fulminations in a colourful chronicle of 1,700 pages.

25 Powicke, *Thirteenth Century*, p. 136; Treharne, *Baronial Plan*, pp. 89–90; Ramsay, *Dawn of the Constitution*, pp. 172–73.

26 Treharne, *Baronial Plan*, pp. 26–30.

27 *Royal Letters*, p. 129; Treharne, *Baronial Plan*, p. 383.

28 Treharne, *Baronial Plan*, pp. 91–92, 112–13. Given the prestige attached to the office of justiciar, it's a wonder the earls and other senior barons like Fitz-Geoffrey didn't angle for the job. In fact, they probably did, until it was decided to make the position itinerant, requiring them to travel all around the country doing the hard work of reform. It could even have been Henry's idea to have the justiciar act in this way. It would keep him out of Westminster, put the magnates under closer surveillance and do justice to the poor, all advantages for the king.

29 Ramsay, *Dawn of the Constitution*, p. 177; Treharne, *Baronial Plan*, p. 118; Paris III, p. 302. Lovel died shortly after Christmas.

30 *DBM*, p. 177; Ramsay, *Dawn of the Constitution*, p. 186.

31 Carpenter, *Reign of Henry III*, pp. 183–87; Paris III, pp. 241–42, 274–78, 281–82. Pope Alexander already made good on a similar threat against Sewal de Bovill, the Archbishop of York, when he refused to have one of his Italians in a deanery at the church. The sentence had been lifted by the time Bovill died on 2 May 1258, but he was broken by the experience. Even as he lay on his deathbed, Arlotus was prowling around with a list of chapels to place under interdict unless more money was forthcoming. Henry wearily sent his clerk Simon Passelewe, a 'degenerate Englishman', to induce several of them to stand surety for loans on this basis, but he was rebuffed in a series of hilarious exchanges ('What does this mean? Am I to go away empty-handed?').

32 Sharp, *Famine and Scarcity*, pp. 33–36; Keene, 'Crisis Management', pp. 54–57; Paris III, pp. 283, 291. The crisis could have been even more devastating had Richard of Cornwall not sent fifty ships from Germany full of corn and bread in March, and other imports of food from the Baltic region followed.

33 Maddicott, *Montfort*, pp. 167–68.

34 Bémont, *Montfort*, p. 166.

35 Powicke, *King Henry III*, pp. 388–89; Treharne, *Baronial Plan*, pp. 104–05; Burton, pp. 461–66. Scholars have long ascribed the oration only to the baronial council, but the motif of the three kings and above all the request for the legate clearly make it more Henry's work.

36 Treharne, *Baronial Plan*, p. 113. To get an idea of how big the brawl must have been, some sixty of Aymer's men were pardoned for their role in it.

37 Maddicott, *Montfort*, p. 154.

38 Paris III, pp. 294–95. Vincent, 'Inventory of Gifts', pp. 134–35. The king was known to be afraid of thunder, doubtless for religious reasons. In 1235 he was given a 'stone against thunder' to hang from his neck by one Peter the surgeon.

39 Maddicott, *Montfort*, pp. 161–62.

40 Labarge, *Montfort*, pp. 155–56. Paris III, pp. 306–07.

41 Bémont, *Montfort*, pp. 166–67; Paris III, pp. 307–08.

42 Treharne, *Baronial Plan*, pp. 142–43; Carpenter, *Reign of Henry III*, pp. 185–86; Runciman, *Sicilian Vespers*, pp. 63–64.

43 *CPR, 1258–66*, pp. 35–42; *CR, 1256–9*, pp. 484–85; *Royal Letters*, pp. 138–40; Treharne, *Baronial Plan*, p. 132. In what was one of the strangest episodes of this period, the council next had Prior Andrew elected as Bishop of Winchester and Henry gave his assent on 29 July 1259. But on that same day, he issued a safe conduct to a papal nuncio named Velascus, who was sent by Alexander to plead for Aymer's return. A Parliament was gathered to hear Velascus, who threatened the country with interdict unless Parliament rescinded his exile, but he was told to get lost. The man who escorted him to London on Henry's orders was Richard Grey, the

Pages 263–268

constable of Dover. On 8 September, Grey was relieved of duty and ordered to turn the castle over to Hugh Bigod. On 23 September, Henry explained the affair to the pope in a letter that has the tone of 'better luck next time'.

Treharne suggests this was a sneaky attempt by Henry to get Aymer reinstated. He waited for chancellor Wengham to be absent to approach his subordinate Walter Merton to have him seal the writ for Grey, somehow unbeknownst to the council despite the official enrolment of the documents. Grey was a member of the council, however, and even Treharne admits it is baffling that he doesn't know what's going on in the government. In all likelihood, there was some intrigue at work between Henry and the council, because Grey was a close ally of Montfort, who was still on the Continent and in disfavour over his obstruction of the treaty with France. In the meantime, the council gave the supposedly absent Wengham, the newly elected Bishop of London, 5,000 sheep, 200 cows and ten bulls from Winchester's stock with the proviso that he should answer for them to Aymer if the latter managed to get his bishopric back.

44 Paris III, pp. 314–16.

45 Denholm-Young, *Richard of Cornwall*, pp. 98–99; Paris III, p. 287.

46 Maddicott, *Montfort*, pp. 173–77; Bémont, *Montfort*, pp. 276–78; Paris III, p. 316. Bémont provides a facsimile of the will, drafted in French in the hand of Henry de Montfort, as an appendix to his work.

47 Powicke, *Thirteenth Century*, pp. 147–48; Paris III, pp. 326–27. A *Provisions of the Barons*, drafted in French, formed the basis for the ordinance.

48 Rymer, *Foedera*, p. 63; Paris III, p. 327.

49 Maddicott, *Montfort*, pp. 52–53, 182–84; Wilkinson, *Eleanor de Montfort*, pp. 97–98.

50 Chaplais, 'The Making of the Treaty of Paris', p. 244; *DBM*, pp. 195–97; Maddicott, *Montfort*, pp. 141, 183–84. Montfort had in fact been busy elsewhere trying to profit from the Treaty of Paris. In 1256, his grandnephew Esquivat had ceded him the county of Bigorre near the Pyrenees because he was unable to pay his debts to him and defend it against his neighbour Gaston de Béarn. Henry wanted control of the county for himself for the security of Gascony, and on 27 July 1259 obtained it from Montfort in return for £1,000 or lands elsewhere.

51 Clanchy, *Memory to Written Record*, pp. 207–09; Moore, 'Expansion of Royal Justice', pp. 55–71. England also had jurisdictional subdivisions known as Hundreds and Honours.

52 Hershey, 'Hugh Bigod and Judicial Reform', pp. 65–87; Carpenter, *Struggle for Mastery*, p. 370; Treharne, *Baronial Plan*, p. 156.

53 Ridgeway, 'Henry III and the "Aliens"', p. 87; Carpenter, *Reign of Henry III*, pp. 329–31. The knight was Roger de Oilly and the eyre took place in January 1260.

54 Treharne, *Baronial Plan*, p. 154.

55 Powicke, *King Henry III*, pp. 397–98.

56 Carpenter, *Reign of Henry III*, pp. 241–51; Maddicott, *Montfort*, p. 186.

57 Prestwich, *Plantagenet England*, p. 107; Treharne, *Baronial Plan*, pp. 157–212.

58 Powicke, *Thirteenth Century*, pp. 154–55; Maddicott, *Montfort*, pp. 185–87; *DBM*, pp. 201–03. Henry later accused Montfort of learning in advance that the arbitration had gone against him and used his friends on the council Walter Cantilupe, Peter de Montfort and Richard Grey to prevent its publication. It would be surprising if the panel had ruled in his favour given that one of the three, Roger Bigod, was a Marshal grandson and beneficiary of the estate.

59 Maddicott, *Montfort*, pp. 187–90; Wilkinson, *Eleanor de Montfort*, pp. 100–01, 179–80; Bémont, *Montfort*, pp. 179–80.

60 Labarge, *Saint Louis*, pp. 195–96.

61 Carpenter, 'Meetings of Kings', pp. 12, 16–19. Joinville is the only source for this information about Henry interacting with lepers.

62 Howell, *Eleanor of Provence*, p. 161; Carpenter, 'Meetings of Kings', pp. 19–20.

63 *DBM*, p. 169; Howell, *Eleanor of Provence*, pp. 161–62; Strickland, *Princesses of England*, pp. 232–41. Simon only compounded the insult by claiming he had Louis's permission to leave instead. The whole point of the marriage between Beatrice and John of Brittany was to resolve the problem of the Honour of Richmond, to which the dukes of Brittany had an ancestral right but which had been forfeited to the crown because Peter of Dreux's final treachery in 1234. Peter's son Duke John proposed the marriage as a way of reviving his claim. Richmond, however, had been given to Peter of Savoy in 1241 and he was not keen to give it up. The deal worked out by Henry had Beatrice and John receiving an annual payment of £1,333 until Peter, who had no male heirs, vacated the earth. To avoid unwelcome scrutiny from the exchequer and the council, that money was to come from what Louis owed Henry as money-rent for Agenais. The way Simon saw it, that money represented royal revenue and therefore the deal required the approval of the council. But Louis changed his mind even before the wedding, and on 5 January told Henry the arrangement was none of his affair and he wasn't paying. The young couple had to wait two years until Henry recovered full power and paid them the money out of the exchequer.

64 Treharne, *Baronial Plan*, pp. 220–23; *DBM*, pp. 175–57.

65 Dunstable, p. 214; *DBM*, pp. 207–09; Prestwich, *Edward I*, pp. 32–33; Treharne, *Baronial Plan*, p. 225; Howell, *Eleanor of Provence*, p. 160. The split between Montfort and Peter of Savoy went back a year to 16 March 1259, when Montfort refused to stand surety for late payments to be made to various Savoyards. He probably considered it an affront that their claims should be satisfied and not his. Then in the summer, the transfer of the nine manors to his wife Eleanor involved displacing other Savoyards, creating another point of contention between these former allies. The final break was the negotiation for Beatrice's marriage portion and Simon's protest that Peter was protecting his own interests at the expense of the realm.

66 Carpenter, 'Meetings of Kings', p. 22; *DBM*, p. 185; Treharne, *Baronial Plan*, pp. 224–28. Henry had spent all of the £2,400 earmarked for the trip by the council, plus another £670 from a loan contracted in Paris. He had also taken hordes of his gold penny with him and raised £2,181 by selling off more than 20,000 of them (twelve gold pennies roughly equalling one pound). He received £1,000 from the justiciar on 9 March 1260 and sent orders for £1,000 more by 19 April. Another £2,000 was to be sent to Dover to be ready for payment to the foreign knights.

67 Dunstable, p. 215; Treharne, *Baronial Plan*, pp. 232–33. The arbitrator was Richard of Cornwall.

68 Maddicott, *Montfort*, pp. 197–99; *DBM*, pp. 195–211. Montfort could afford the brave front because Archbishop Rigaud and a Norman companion, John de Harcourt, were just then in England. They had been dispatched by Louis on unnamed business, but their presence was clearly intended to ensure the proceedings were fair. They were hardly impartial observers, however. Rigaud was a friend of Simon and had conferred a position in his cathedral on 17-year-old Amaury Montfort, who was slated for a career in the Church. Simon returned the favour by restoring an ancestral manor in Warwickshire to Harcourt (part of the confiscated 'lands of the Normans' given to Montfort by Henry in 1236) and granting certain rights to the archbishop for his own holdings in England.

Pages 270–277

69 Ridgeway, 'Henry III's grievances', pp. 231–32; Labarge, *Montfort*, p. 188. Builth was one of Edward's castles but was taken from him following his ill-conceived rebellion and entrusted to Roger Mortimer, an ally of Clare. Mortimer was absent at the time of the attack, attending Parliament, but Edward saw it as blatant treason. Mortimer was later fully exonerated.

70 Howell, *Eleanor of Provence*, pp. 172–74. See above p. 198.

71 Ridgeway, 'Henry III's Grievances', p. 230. Henry knighted his son-in-law John of Brittany and two dozen other men on this occasion.

72 Treharne, *Baronial Plan*, pp. 232, 247–48.

73 Maddicott, *Montfort*, pp. 171, 200–03. Montfort was probably behind John Crakehall succeeding Philip Lovel as treasurer in 1258. They were connected by their friendship with Grosseteste, and action was taken on the money owed to Montfort at the exchequer just after Crakehall's appointment.

74 Denholm-Young, *Richard of Cornwall*, pp. 104–06.

75 Howell, *Eleanor of Provence*, pp. 175–76; *CPR 1258–66*, p. 141.

76 Powicke, *King Henry III*, p. 419; Maddicott, *Montfort*, p. 204.

77 Strickland, *Princesses of England*, pp. 201–06.

78 *CPR 1258–66*, p. 113.

79 Ridgeway, 'Ecclesiastical Career', pp. 148–49.

14 Were it Not for One Man

1 Carpenter, 'Westminster Abbey in Politics', pp. 50, 52–53; Carpenter, *Reign of Henry III*, p. 96; *CPR 1258–66*, pp. 12–13. See p. 256. Alice was awarded two-thirds of the wardship, including the castle of Pontefract, minus the other third for her dower. Over the next decade, she would pay £3,754 towards building the abbey. David Carpenter makes the plausible suggestion that it was the barons themselves who imposed the addition of their shields on what had been the king's pet project up until that time.

2 Carpenter, 'Westminster Abbey in Politics', pp. 53–54.

3 Rymer, *Foedera*, p. 66; Howell, *Eleanor of Provence*, p. 178.

4 Howell, *Eleanor of Provence*, p. 179.

5 Labarge, *Montfort*, pp. 200, 204–05.

6 Maddicott, *Montfort*, pp. 205–06; Treharne, *Baronial Plan*, p. 258.

7 Carpenter, *Reign of Henry III*, pp. 201–02; 'Henry's Residence at the Tower of London in 1261', Henry Fine Rolls Project, access at http://blog.frh3.org.uk/?p=409.

8 Treharne, *Baronial Plan*, p. 251.

9 *Flores*, p. 391; Strickland, *Princesses of England*, pp. 205–06. The valet who brought him the news received a pension for life.

10 Treharne, *Baronial Plan*, pp. 252–54; *DBM*, p. 219.

11 Ridgeway, 'King Henry III's Grievances', p. 230.

12 Morris, *Great and Terrible King*, pp. 48–49; Howell, *Eleanor of Provence*, p. 180.

13 Ridgeway, 'What Happened in 1261?', p. 97. So complete was the reconciliation of the Lusignans and Savoyards by the summer of 1261 that Geoffrey Lusignan welcomed Henry and Eleanor's daughter Beatrice on her first visit to Brittany in the company of Henry Wengham and a Savoyard knight.

14 Ibid., p. 96; Prestwich, *Edward I*, p. 36; *Mayors and Sheriffs*, p. 57. *Flores*, pp. 466–67. The *Flores Historiarum* claims that Edward made a show of his opposition upon returning by denouncing the men then advising Henry.

15 Ridgeway, 'What Happened in 1261?', p. 94; Ridgeway, 'King Henry III's Grievances', pp. 236–37; Treharne, *Baronial Plan*, p. 252.
16 *DBM*, p. 223.
17 Morris, *Bigod Earls*, p. 84.
18 Maddicott, *Montfort*, p. 209; Ridgeway, 'What Happened in 1261?', p. 94; *CPR 1258–66*, pp. 152, 185. In all, Henry received nearly £7,500 before the summer was over.
19 Treharne, *Baronial Plan*, pp. 260–62; *DBM*, pp. 239–47; *Flores*, pp. 393–94. The *Flores Historiarum* says that Edward responded by renewing his oath to the Provisions, but the chronology is confused.
20 Ridgeway, 'What Happened in 1261?', p. 99. Just before his death, Clare made a bequest to the college set up by his 'most dear friend' Merton in Oxford.
21 Labarge, *Montfort*, pp. 196–97.
22 Maddicott, *Montfort*, pp. 209–11.
23 Dunstable, p. 217; Treharne, *Baronial Plan*, pp. 260–62. The barons also refused to surrender the castles under their command. Hugh Bigod, sorry he had turned over Dover so easily, refused to relinquish the two he still held, but they were inconsequential fortresses.
24 *CPR 1258–66*, p. 220; Ray, 'Three Alien Stewards', pp. 52–53, 59. Bezill's wife was Beatrice, the widow of John de Bassingham. It seems she preferred another man, and after Bezill's death in 1268, went back to using the name Bassingham.
25 Powicke, *King Henry III*, p. 424.
26 Treharne, *Baronial Plan*, pp. 275–77; *Royal Letters*, pp. 188–92.
27 Ridgeway, 'What Happened in 1261?', pp. 105–06; Maddicott, *Montfort*, pp. 212–13; *Royal Letters*, p. 179.
28 Dunstable, p. 217; Labarge, *Montfort*, p. 198; Treharne, *Baronial Plan*, pp. 270–71.
29 Maddicott, *Montfort*, pp. 214; *Royal Letters*, p. 196.
30 Denholm-Young, *Richard of Cornwall*, pp. 112–13.
31 Ridgeway, 'What Happened in 1261?', pp. 106–08; Carpenter, *Reign of King Henry III*, pp. 202–04.
32 Carpenter, *Reign of King Henry III*, p. 206.
33 Prestwich, *Edward I*, p. 37.
34 Barker, *Tournament in England*, p. 48; Paris II, pp. 512–13.
35 Morris, *Great and Terrible King*, p. 52; Prestwich, *Edward I*, pp. 37–38.
36 Howell, *Eleanor of Provence*, pp. 186–89; *CPR, 1258–66*, p. 161.
37 *Mayors and Sheriffs*, p. 53; Maddicott, *Montfort*, pp. 215–16; Powicke, *King Henry III*, pp. 426–27.
38 Treharne, *Baronial Plan*, p. 282.
39 *DBM*, pp. 217, 233.
40 Carpenter, 'Meetings of Kings', p. 24.
41 Treharne, *Baronial Plan*, pp. 284–86.
42 Carpenter, 'Meetings of Kings', p. 27.
43 Bémont, *Montfort*, p. 61.
44 Maddicott, *Montfort*, pp. 217–18; Powicke, *King Henry III*, p. 428.
45 Labarge, *Saint Louis*, pp. 162, 211. Louis was naturally horrified when he learned about the oath and had Urban quash it in July 1263. The pope cited Philip's youth (18) for his folly in agreeing to the compact.
46 Treharne, *Baronial Plan*, p. 288.
47 Powicke, *King Henry III*, pp. 429–30.
48 Paris II, pp. 324–25.

Pages 285–291

49 Treharne, *Baronial Plan*, p. 286.
50 Carpenter, 'Meetings of Kings', p. 29.
51 *CPR, 1258–66*, pp. 240–41; Treharne, *Baronial Plan*, p. 290.
52 Treharne, *Baronial Plan*, pp. 291–95. Mortimer was a grandson of Llywelyn ap Iorwerth.
53 *CR, 1261–4*, p. 273; Powicke, *King Henry III*, p. 430.
54 *Mayors and Sheriffs*, pp. 54–55.
55 Ibid., p. 56; Maddicott, *Montfort*, p. 221.
56 *Royal Letters*, pp. 242–43; Hutton, *Montfort and his Cause*, pp. 111–13; Treharne, *Baronial Plan*, p. 300. The envoys had no thought for posterity to write down what these certain things were, but their offer involved the manors of the royal demesne that were given to Eleanor to facilitate the peace treaty with France. Simon and Eleanor were willing to return them, but apparently in exchange for something Henry found equally outrageous.
57 Burton, p. 500; Treharne, *Baronial Plan*, pp. 298–300.
58 Treharne, *Baronial Plan*, pp. 296, 301; *Royal Letters*, pp. 245–46.
59 Howell, *Eleanor of Provence*, p. 192.
60 Wykes, pp. 133–34; Labarge, *Montfort*, p. 214. The Montfortians made exceptions for the king and his family because they were not prepared to revoke their fealty to him and so risk disinheritance if they lost.
61 *Mayors and Sheriffs*, p. 56; Dunstable, p. 221.
62 *Flores*, pp. 479–81; *Mayors and Sheriffs*, p. 57; Dunstable, p. 222; Maddicott, *Montfort*, pp. 226–27.
63 Maddicott, *Montfort*, pp. 227–8.
64 *Mayors and Sheriffs*, p. 57.
65 Powicke, *King Henry III*, pp. 446–47; Treharne, *Baronial Plan*, p. 327; *Mayors and Sheriffs*, p. 62. Fitz-Thomas was first elected in 1261, then re-elected the following year. He won a third term in 1263 based solely on popular support. That was a precedent, as was his taking the oath of office directly from the people. He nevertheless went to the exchequer for sanction as was customary, only on 28 October 1263 the officials were ordered by Henry not to admit anyone as mayor who did not have his licence first. Fitz-Thomas didn't, but remained in office.
66 *Mayors and Sheriffs*, p. 58; Treharne, *Baronial Plan*, pp. 300–01; *CPR, 1258–66*, p. 257. There were 130 items in total, various silver bowls and cups, valued at 637 pounds, 13 schillings and 4 pence.
67 Dunstable, p. 222; *CPR, 1258–66*, p. 279; Lord, *Knights Templars*, p. 227. The conversion was done on the website https://www.measuringworth.com/ppoweruk.
68 *Royal Letters*, pp. 247–48; Dunstable, p. 221; Denholm-Young, *Richard of Cornwall*, pp. 114, 119–20; Carpenter, *Reign of Henry III*, pp. 219–24, 253–59. An oath of fealty marked Henry's very first public act. He was not even 2-years-old in September 1209 when his father John, feeling under threat, demanded his subjects swear the oath to him and his son at Marlborough.
69 Dunstable, p. 223; *Flores*, p. 406; Treharne, *Baronial Plan*, p. 305.
70 *CPR, 1258–66*, p. 270; Carpenter, *Reign of Henry III*, pp. 261–75; Maddicott, *Montfort*, pp. 230–32.
71 *CPR, 1258–66*, p. 269; Treharne, *Baronial Plan*, pp. 306–07.
72 Dunstable, p. 223; *Flores*, pp. 406–07; Wykes, p. 136.
73 Maddicott, *Montfort*, pp. 232–33, 235–38; Carpenter, *Reign of Henry III*, pp. 205–06.
74 *Flores*, pp. 407–08; Howell, *Eleanor of Provence*, pp. 197–98, 205. Following up an assertion made by Powicke, Howell suggests Henry had been forced to accompany

Simon in his plan to eject Edward and the knights from Windsor, calling it 'inhumane humiliation'.

75 Maddicott, *Montfort*, pp. 239–41.

76 Treharne, *Baronial Plan*, pp. 315–16.

77 Ray, 'Three Alien Stewards', pp. 58–59. James Audley was also removed for being an unreconstructed royalist and because Hamo Lestrange wanted his job as sheriff.

78 Maddicott, *Montfort*, pp. 242–43; Dunstable, p. 224.

79 Wykes, pp. 123, 131; Labarge, *Montfort*, pp. 212–13. Wykes claims that in blocking the Treaty of Paris in 1259, what Montfort was really after was the throne of England for his son.

80 Maddicott, *Montfort*, p. 240; Howell, *Eleanor of Provence*, p. 199.

81 *CPR, 1258–66*, pp. 275, 279. Interestingly, Walerand's pardon says that if he had transgressed against the Provisions of Oxford, it was at the king's command and will.

82 Denholm-Young, *Richard of Cornwall*, p. 122. Urban was moved at the same time to declare that Richard would henceforth be merely king-elect of the Romans, the same as Alfonso. Both were to be in Rome on 2 May 1265 and he would tell them then who would be king.

83 Ramsay, *Dawn of the Constitution*, p. 208.

84 Dunstable, p. 225; *Flores*, p. 409; Tewkesbury, p. 176; Maddicott, *Montfort*, p. 243.

85 Cockerill, *Eleanor of Castile*, pp. 130–31.

86 *CPR, 1258–66*, p. 278; Ridgeway, 'The Lord Edward and the Provisions of Oxford', pp. 97–98.

87 Bémont, *Montfort*, p. 209; Labarge, *Montfort*, pp. 217–18.

88 *CPR, 1258–66*, p. 273; Tewkesbury, p. 179–80; Treharne, *Baronial Plan*, p. 334. The charge of Montfort promoting his family's interest principally concerns committing all of John Mansel's lands to his second son Simon.

89 Powicke, *King Henry III*, p. 454.

90 Maddicott, *Montfort*, p. 233.

91 Dunstable, p. 226; *Flores*, pp. 409–10; Treharne, *Baronial Plan*, pp. 330–34.

92 Maddicott, *Montfort*, pp. 248–49.

93 *CPR, 1258–66*, pp. 357–58; Maddicott, *Montfort*, pp. 256–57.

94 *CPR, 1258–66*, pp. 302–03; Dunstable, p. 226; Carpenter, 'A Noble in Politics', pp. 198–200.

95 Dunstable, p. 227.

15 In the Year of Our Lord 1264

1 Dunstable, p. 227; *DBM*, pp. 253–57; *CPR, 1258–66*, pp. 376–77.

2 *DBM*, pp. 257–79; Maddicott, *Montfort*, pp. 259–60. Henry actually gave two figures: £300,000 and 200,000 marks (£133,333). The barons cite only the latter in their brief.

3 *DBM*, pp. 281–91; *CPR, 1258–66*, p. 378.

4 *Tewkesbury*, p. 177; Howell, *Eleanor of Provence*, p. 205.

5 Runciman, *Sicilian Vespers*, pp. 66–69.

6 Powicke, *King Henry III*, pp. 453–54.

7 *DBM*, p. 46.

8 Wykes, p. 139; Dunstable, p. 227.

9 *Mayors and Sheriffs*, p. 65; Maddicott, *Montfort*, pp. 261–62.

10 *CPR, 1258–66*, pp. 189–90, 300, 317, 378–79, 381–82; Dunstable, p. 227; Melrose, p. 214. Alexander was born on 21 January 1263, but died in his twentieth year, two years before his father.

Pages 301–302

11 Dunstable, pp. 227–28; *Flores*, pp. 410–11; Robert of Gloucester, pp. 743–46; Powicke, *King Henry III*, pp. 456–58; Prestwich, *Edward I*, p. 42.

12 *CPR, 1258–66*, pp. 307–08; *Flores*, p. 412; Labarge, *Montfort*, pp. 227–28; Maddicott, *Montfort*, pp. 265–66; Powicke, *King Henry III*, pp. 458–59. The envoy was John Valentinis, who played a leading part in organising Louis's crusade and was his intermediary with the pope on the Sicilian business.

13 Ramsay, *Dawn of the Constitution*, pp. 213–14.

14 *CPR, 1258–66*, p. 308; Wykes, p. 143; Blaauw, *Barons' War*, p. 121.

15 *Mayors and Sheriffs*, p. 65; *Flores*, pp. 411–12; Wykes, pp. 140–41; *CPR, 1258–66*, p. 310; Dunstable, p. 229. The disruption of the peace talks was sudden, for Peter de Montfort was given a safe conduct on 2 April to continue the negotiations at least until 13 April. Prior to the bishops' departure, the king had them and twenty-four priests excommunicate all those against the Provisions (of Westminster presumably, although the Dunstable annalist says they were the nullified Oxford provisions).

16 Dunstable, p. 229; Wykes, pp. 144–45; *Flores*, p. 412; Ramsay, *Dawn of the Constitution*, p. 215.

17 Dunstable, p. 230; Wykes, p. 146; *Flores*, p. 413; Maddicott, *Montfort*, p. 267.

18 Wykes, pp. 141–43; *Mayors and Sheriffs*, p. 66; Dunstable, p. 230.

19 Wykes, pp. 146–47; Dunstable, pp. 230–31; Prestwich, *Edward I*, pp. 43–44.

20 Labarge, *Montfort*, pp. 230–1, Blaauw, *Barons' War*, pp. 131–33.

21 *CPR, 1258–66*, p. 316; Wykes, pp. 147–48; *Mayors and Sheriffs*, p. 66; *Flores*, p. 414; Jobson, *First English Revolution*, p. 111; Maddicott, *Montfort*, p. 269.

22 Carpenter, *Battle of Lewes*, pp. 18–20.

23 See pp. 210, 270.

24 Wykes, pp. 148–9; Wright, *Political Songs*, p. 69.

25 *Mayors and Sheriffs*, pp.67–69; Carpenter, *Battle of Lewes*, p. 24. The London annals provide all three letters, but dates the royal letters to a day earlier, to 12 May, which Carpenter shows would render the peace negotiations 'unintelligible'.

26 *Flores*, pp. 414–15; *Mayors and Sheriffs*, pp. 67–69.

27 *Flores*, pp. 415–16; *Song of Lewes*, pp. 38, 69–71.

28 Prothero, *Montfort*, pp. 274–76.

29 *CPR, 1258–66*, p. 317; Powicke, *King Henry III*, p. 458. The money was to be paid to John Valentinis, who had come to England not only as a peace envoy but also to raise funds for the Holy Land, where he spent many years and was the lord of Haifa until 1261.

30 See pp. 209–10, 277–80.

31 Carpenter, *Battle of Lewes*, pp. 27–31; *Flores*, p. 416; Dunstable, p. 232.

32 Carpenter, *Battle of Lewes*, p. 32; Wykes, pp. 150–51.

33 Carpenter, *Battle of Lewes*, pp. 28–30; Wright, *Political Songs*, p. 69; Hutton, *Montfort and his Cause*, pp. 127–28.

34 Carpenter, *Battle of Lewes*, p. 33; *Flores*, pp. 417–18; Ramsay, *Dawn of the Constitution*, p. 224.

35 *Melrose*, pp. 216–19. The chronicler gives a full account of this coach and represents some captured Londoners enticing Edward's men into attacking it, claiming that Montfort was hiding within. The loyalists spent so much time and effort in breaking open the iron-caged vehicle, all the while shouting for Simon to come out, that a great many Londoners were saved by the diversion. In their anger and disappointment on not finding him among the occupants, the loyalists burnt alive the two men they found inside instead.

36 Maddicott, *Montfort*, pp. 272–75. In the first instance of arbitration, a panel of four Englishmen would consider amendments to the Provisions. If they failed to agree,

two French nobles, Charles of Anjou and Hugh V, Duke of Burgundy, both friends of Montfort, would decide. The second instance called for three French nobles and three French prelates to be empowered by Louis to choose two other Frenchmen, who would then come to England and choose an Englishman to form a three-man arbitration panel. The essence of their mission would be to revisit the Mise of Amiens, which as a legal ruling stood in the way of the Provisions of Oxford regaining legitimacy.

37 Carpenter, *Reign of Henry III*, pp. 284–91; Sadler, *Second Barons' War*, pp. 66–69; Rishanger, pp. 37–38. Other terms of the mise included purging the council of 'traitors', pardoning the Montfortians, releasing those captured at Northampton and restoring their lands. One contemporary claim has it that Montfort threatened to chop off the heads of Richard of Cornwall, Philip Basset and other barons and stick them on pikes unless the king came to terms. Interestingly, on the day of the battle itself, Henry issued safe conducts for Mortimer, Balliol and other barons to go back to their lands (*CPR, 1258–66*, p. 318).

38 Dunstable, pp. 232–33; *Mayors and Sheriffs*, p. 67; Wykes, pp. 152–53; Wilkinson, *Eleanor de Montfort*, pp. 105–06.

39 *CPR, 1258–66*, pp. 320–23; Wild, 'A Captive King', pp. 47–48.

40 *CPR, 1258–66*, pp. 324–25, 328; Cockerill, *Eleanor of Castile*, pp. 137–38. Another pregnant occupant of Windsor was Valence's wife Joan, but because her term was approaching, she was advised to withdraw to a nearby convent. On 18 July, she was granted six manors for the support of her family (*CPR, 1258–66*, p. 337).

40 *DBM*, pp. 295–301; *Mayors and Sheriffs*, pp. 69–71; Maddicott, *Montfort*, pp. 285–87. A two-thirds majority was necessary to pass acts of the council. If the Nine were unable to achieve this, a two-thirds majority of the Three would decide, although the elector representing the prelates had to be part of the majority in matters affecting the Church. If any of the Nine misbehaved, he was to be replaced by the king with the advice of the Three, who themselves were to be replaced with the advice of the great men of the realm, meaning Parliament without the lesser folk.

41 Powicke, *King Henry III*, pp. 468, 473; *Royal Letters*, pp. 257–59; *CR, 1261–64*, pp. 390–91.

42 Howell, *Eleanor of Provence*, pp. 211–17; Labarge, *Montfort*, pp. 238–39; Wykes, p. 154; *Flores*, pp. 420–21; Dunstable, p. 233.

43 *CPR, 1258–66*, pp. 360–62; Maddicott, *Montfort*, pp. 290–91; Powicke, *King Henry III*, pp. 475–76.

44 Carpenter, *Reign of Henry III*, pp. 328–38; Powicke, *King Henry III*, pp. 509–10.

45 *CPR, 1258–66*, p. 362; Powicke, *King Henry III*, pp. 476–77.

46 Powicke, *King Henry III*, p. 479; Maddicott, *Montfort*, pp. 292–93.

47 *Royal Letters*, pp. 261–69; *CR, 1261–64*, pp. 396–99; *Flores*, p. 422; Powicke, *King Henry III*, p. 477.

48 Maddicott, *Montfort*, pp. 293–94, 304; Powicke, *King Henry III*, pp. 478–79, 484–85. The reform of the Church principally involved making restitution for damages incurred during the conflict and taking action against clerks who had borne arms.

49 Maddicott, *Montfort*, pp. 295–96; Dunstable, p. 234. Nominated to serve on the panel to consider amendments to the Peace of Canterbury were two staunch Montfortians, Henry of Sandwich, Bishop of London, and Hugh Despenser, the justiciar, and for the French side Montfort's friend Charles of Anjou and the Abbot of Bec. Another close friend of Montfort's, Eudes Rigaud, the Archbishop of Rouen, was to break any deadlocks. There were two conditions attached: only natives were to hold office

Pages 314–318

and all quarrels between Henry and Simon were to be settled before any final peace. Maddicott points out that Montfort was trying to safeguard his interests in the event he was swept from power.

50 *CPR, 1258–66*, pp. 370–71, 474; Maddicott, *Montfort*, pp. 297–301; Powicke, *King Henry III*, pp. 481–82; Wykes, pp. 156–57. The arbitrators for the new scheme were to be Sandwich, Despenser, Rigaud and Peter le Chamberlain, with the legate now given the casting vote. They were to choose the king's councillors, who were again to be exclusively English, but the same did not necessarily apply for other officials of state, and no mention was made of the council's power over appointments. The legate tried to entice Montfort into the swap of castles and hostages by offering to include a settlement of his grievances in the proposal.

51 Howell, *Eleanor of Provence*, p. 213; *CPR, 1258–66*, p. 474.

52 Howell, *Eleanor of Provence*, pp. 224–25; *Flores*, p. 423; *CPR, 1258–66*, p. 374. The Montfortians removed the inclusion of the hostages in the peace negotiations after the Marchers commenced a siege of one of Clare's castles in Worcestershire. They were obviously unaware that Clare, as Henry pointed out to them on 6 October, was just then insisting on Edward's release, and their wrongheaded strategy had put it in jeopardy. Says Robert of Gloucester of Edward's possible deliverance to his rescuers: 'hii wolde Sir Edward vawe out to hom sende ilithered with a mangenel' (II, 752).

53 *Flores*, pp. 422–23; Dunstable, pp. 234–35.

54 *CPR, 1258–66*, pp. 394–95, 397; Maddicott, *Montfort*, pp. 321–22.

55 *DBM*, pp. 301–03; Rymer, *Foedera*, p. 72; Maddicott, *Montfort*, p. 317.

56 Powicke, *King Henry III*, p. 483; *Flores*, p. 420; Dunstable, p. 233.

57 Some of the difference to the earlier revolts was also due to leadership. In the rebellion against John, the legate (Guala) was in the field while the archbishop (Langton) was detained abroad. No papal censure had been brought in for Marshal's rebellion, allowing the archbishop (Edmund) and his suffragans to throw their weight against the king. Lastly, Richard Marshal was no Simon de Montfort.

58 *Song of Lewes*, pp. 33 (lines 9–10), 49–51 (764–66, 849–51).

59 Ibid., pp. 42–43 (439–43, 450–51).

60 *CPR, 1258–66*, pp. 388–89.

61 *Song of Lewes*, pp. 38 (265–66), 40 (329–32).

62 *CPR, 1258–66*, pp. 393, 399; Wykes, pp. 158–9; *Mayors and Sheriffs*, pp. 77–78; Maddicott, *Montfort*, pp. 325–26; Blaauw, *Barons' War*, pp. 231–32; Powicke, *King Henry III*, pp. 707–08. Henry de Montfort was made the warden of the Channel ports, and on 8 December he was authorised to seize all wool shipments to prevent marauders and pirates from getting their hands on them. Wykes acidly notes that he was changed from a 'bold knight to a wool merchant' and other chroniclers hinted at a family racket at work. The London chronicler, for one, had heard rumours that the Montforts, including the father, were allowing piracy to flourish as long as they got a third of the loot. Such a racket was best illustrated in the case of the younger Simon de Montfort. After Mansel's flight in 1263, he was then given custody of his estates, which were then plundered by royalists under Marcher lord William de Braose. A stacked tribunal consisting of Henry de Montfort and Hugh Despenser ordered Braose to pay Simon the wildly excessive £6,666 in damages. Until the money was made good, his young son was to remain in the guardianship of Eleanor de Montfort.

63 Maddicott, *Montfort*, p. 283; Rishanger, p. 29; *CPR, 1258–66*, pp. 325, 327, 476. Montfort alone was exempt from the order against carrying arms.

64 *Flores*, p. 424; *Rishanger*, p. 30.

65 Wykes, pp. 153–54.

66 *Flores*, p. 424; Cockerill, *Eleanor of Castile*, pp. 139, 144; Howell, *Eleanor of Provence*, pp. 74–75; *Henry Fine Rolls Project* '28 December 1264', access http://blog.frh3.org.uk/?p=1536. Eleanor of Castile's presence in Henry's household is inferred from the presentation of robes made for her and her staff at Christmas and also the lack of any record of a gift being made to a messenger bearing the news of the birth, which occurred around the turn of the year. She may also have been at Westminster at this time, where Henry himself had returned by 4 January 1265. Her purification occurred there on 3 February. Henry's purchase of medicine for her in that month suggests a difficult delivery and therefore the improbability that she would have moved about between her confinement and purification. The baby was a daughter named Joan, who died around 1 September 1265. Although this was after Evesham, Edward went to Cheshire following the battle and likely never saw her.

16 The Reckoning

1 Wykes, pp. 159–60.

2 *Mayors and Sheriffs*, pp. 75–76; Dunstable, pp. 236–38.

3 Carpenter, 'King Henry III and the Chapter House', pp. 32–39.

4 Powicke, *King Henry III*, pp. 294–95; Melrose, p. 235. The *Melrose* chronicler reports that Mansel said of one benefice paying £20 a year, 'This will provide for my dogs,' but he also claims that he enjoyed the impossible sum of £12,000 in church revenues, or 600 benefices worthy of his dogs. Even the master inflator Matthew Paris assigns him less than a fourth of that amount.

5 *CPR, 1258–66*, p. 404.

6 *CPR, 1258–66*, pp. 406, 479; Dunstable, p. 238; Maddicott, *Montfort*, p. 324. Montfort and Clare were also disputing possession of seventeen manors located in ten counties.

7 Rishanger, p. 31.

8 *CPR, 1258–66*, p. 394; Melrose, p. 219; Maddicott, *Montfort*, pp. 309–10; 394; Denholm-Young, *Richard of Cornwall*, p. 130.

9 *CPR, 1258–66*, p. 409; Rishanger, p. 31; Wykes, pp. 160–61; Maddicott, *Montfort*, pp. 322–24.

10 *CPR, 1258–66*, pp. 409–10, 416; Carpenter, *Reign of Henry III*, pp. 299–301. The salary was voted a month later, on 26 March. This only known record of Henry holding and folding a writ with his own hands suggests that he at least perused it beforehand and therefore could read Latin.

11 *CPR, 1258–66*, pp. 412, 414; *Mayors and Sheriffs*, p. 76; Powicke, *King Henry III*, pp. 488–89; Maddicott, *Montfort*, pp. 319–20. Edward's probation called for him to maintain the current government and forswear any reprisals against the Montfortians. He was not to leave the realm for three years or bring in any aliens, otherwise he risked disinheritance. He had to sign over Cheshire to Montfort, and the five royal castles to be transferred to him by his father, including Dover and Corfe, were to be held by the council for five years as surety for his good behaviour.

12 *CPR, 1258–66*, p. 413; Powicke, *King Henry III*, p. 492; Bémont, *Montfort*, p. 226.

13 *Mayors and Sheriffs*, p. 77.

14 *CPR, 1258–66*, p. 416; Maddicott, *Montfort*, pp. 326–27; Carpenter, *Reign of Henry III*, pp. 302–03. See Carpenter for a more in-depth analysis of the authorisation of charters under Cantilupe's keepership.

15 Powicke, *King Henry III*, pp. 492–94; Maddicott, *Montfort*, pp. 331–32.

Pages 323–327

16 *CPR, 1258–66*, pp. 423–25; Prestwich, *Edward I*, pp. 48–49; Robert of Gloucester II, 752–57; Howell, *Eleanor of Provence*, pp. 228–29. Montfort suspected a far-reaching conspiracy at work to free the royal family. He had sent Henry of Almain to France the previous month to work out a peace deal with Louis, and then just ten days before Edward's escape reluctantly granted his request to extend his stay there. Not taking any chances, he sent orders to Kenilworth to put Richard of Cornwall and his son Edmund in chains.

17 *CPR, 1258–66*, pp. 429–34; Smith, *Llywelyn Ap Gruffudd*, pp. 165–70; Maddicott, *Montfort*, pp. 337–38.

18 Wykes, pp. 167–69; Blaauw, *Barons' War*, p. 265.

19 Wykes, pp. 170–71; *Mayors and Sheriffs*, p. 79; Melrose, p. 222; Blaauw, *Barons' War*, pp. 268–69.

20 Rishanger, p. 45; Robert of Gloucester II, 763; Ramsay, *Dawn of the Constitution*, pp. 244–45. Presumably Montfort was suggesting that Edward had copied his troop deployment at Lewes.

21 Laborderie, Maddicott and Carpenter, 'The Last Hours of Simon de Montfort', p. 403; Prestwich, *Edward I*, p. 51; Morris, *Great and Terrible King*, pp. 68–69.

22 Robert of Gloucester II, 764–65; Wykes, pp. 173–74; Blaauw, *Barons' War*, p. 276.

23 Melrose, p. 223; *Flores*, p. 438. Walter of Guisborough (p. 201), writing forty years later, identifies the knight who attacked Henry as Adam de Mowhaut.

24 *CPR, 1258–66*, pp. 423, 434; Carpenter, *Reign of Henry III*, pp. 303–04; Knowles, *Disinherited (III)*, p. 103. There may have been a political reason behind Cantilupe's departure. He had refused to seal some letters and was too earnest in his righteousness and independence. The strict guidelines for his enrolment of writs in the presence of councillors, however, suggests that Cantilupe's departure was expected to be only temporary. The seal was entrusted to Ralph of Sandwich, the keeper of the wardrobe, who was captured at Evesham, pardoned in November 1266 and rose to high office during Edward's reign, eventually serving as the constable of the Tower of London.

25 *CPR, 1258–66*, pp. 319, 328, 343, 443; Wykes, p. 164; Howell, *Eleanor of Provence*, pp. 221–22; Powicke, *King Henry III*, p. 461. Giffard was elected the Bishop of Bath and Wells within weeks of Lewes, but wasn't content to remain bishop-elect like Aymer. Since Boniface refused to return to England or delegate his duties as archbishop, Giffard crossed over to obtain consecration, which he received from Aigueblanche in Paris. According to Wykes, Boniface obliged Giffard to publish the letters of excommunication against Simon and his adherents upon his return. He evidently didn't, because he received the temporalities for his diocese in September 1264 and was one of the nine excommunicating bishops in Westminster Hall for Edward's release. Giffard received the seal some time before 22 August 1265, when Cantilupe was issued a safe conduct.

26 *CPR, 1258–66*, p. 436; Powicke, *King Henry III*, p. 503.

27 *CPR, 1258–66*, pp. 488–89; *Royal Letters*, pp. 289–90; Knowles, *Disinherited (III)*, pp. 4–5, 10–11.

28 Wykes, p. 175; *Robert of Gloucester* II, 762; Denholm-Young, *Richard of Cornwall*, p. 131.

29 *CPR, 1258–66*, p. 460; Knowles, Disinherited, (III), p. 11; Powicke, *King Henry III*, p. 507.

30 *CPR, 1258–66*, p. 459; *Mayors and Sheriffs*, pp. 82–84; Wykes, pp. 176–77.

31 *Robert of Gloucester* II, 768; Wykes, p. 172; Knowles, Disinherited, (III), p. 14; Morris, *Bigod Earls*, pp. 94–95.

32 *CPR, 1258–66*, p. 533; Knowles, Disinherited, (III), pp. 6–7, 13–15, 32–35.

33 Wykes, pp. 178–79; *CR, 1264–68*, p. 136; Rishanger, p. 26; Wilkinson, *Eleanor de Montfort*, pp. 114–16, 124–25. Henry wrote to Louis and advised him to seize the money from her and apply it towards his countrymen who had claims against English pirates during the recent troubles. There's no evidence that Louis did, nor any sign of what became of the money.

34 Howell, *Eleanor of Provence*, pp. 231–32.

35 *CR, 1264–68*, p. 552; Howell, *Eleanor of Provence*, p. 241.

36 *CPR, 1258–66*, p. 470; Powicke, *King Henry III*, p. 518; Runciman, *Sicilian Vespers*, p. 85. Powicke takes *Foedera* as his source and dates the grant to 26 October, although it is Edward who is listed there as the recipient, at least in the syllabus.

37 Wykes, p. 123.

38 Robert of Gloucester II, 763; Dunstable, pp. 240–41; Wykes, p. 185; Powicke, *King Henry III*, pp. 492, 528–29; Ambler, *Bishops in the Political Community*, pp. 184–89. The other bishops sued by Henry were Hugh de Balsham (Ely) and Robert Stitchill (Durham). Gervais died shortly after reaching the papal court in January 1268, but had received absolution. Gravesend got his absolution and returned in 1269, dying a decade later. Pope Clement died in 1268, before Sandwich and Berksted got their hearing, forcing them to wait three years until the election of a new pope. Sandwich then got absolution from Gregory X in May 1272, returned to England early the next year and died that September. Unlike Sandwich, Berksted did not have royal backing and had to wait until November 1272 to receive forgiveness. He remained a committed Montfortian to the end and died in 1287.

39 *Mayors and Sheriffs*, p. 87; Wykes, p. 190; Rishanger, pp. 50–51; Bémont, *Montfort*, pp. 252–53, 264. The fate of the younger Simon de Montfort was decided by Richard of Cornwall, Basset and the legate. Jealous as ever of the Montforts, Clare prevented him from being restored to full favour. Simon made his escape on 10 February 1266, Guy de Montfort his on 23 April (Gervase) or 16–23 May (Wykes).

40 *CPR, 1258–66*, pp. 530–31, 575–76; *Mayors and Sheriffs*, p. 89–91; Powicke, *King Henry III*, pp. 521–22. Fitz-Thomas was not released until 1268 and then had to pay a fine of £500. He died in 1276.

41 *CPR, 1258–66*, pp. 658–59, 662, 667–68; Howell, *Eleanor of Provence*, pp. 236–37. The pope's grant to the queen was dated 15 July 1267. Other sums were to be used to bring the English tribute to Rome up to date.

42 Runciman, *Sicilian Vespers*, pp. 87–95.

43 *CPR, 1258–66*, p. 664; Powicke, *King Henry III*, p. 531.

44 Wykes, pp. 189–90; *Mayors and Sheriffs*, p. 91; *Flores*, pp. 443–44; Ridgeway, 'Adam Gurdun at Dunster', pp. 39–45. The *Flores Historiarum* says that Edward wounded Adam, Rishanger that Edward asked Adam to surrender and he agreed. However it happened, his lands were forfeited to Queen Eleanor, but he later redeemed them, became a public servant under Edward and lived to over 80.

45 Wykes, p. 189; *CPR, 1258–66*, pp. 517, 522, 665, 672; Powicke, *King Henry III*, p. 523.

46 *Flores*, p. 444; Dunstable, pp. 241–42; Robert of Gloucester II, 771; Ramsay, *Dawn of the Constitution*, p. 256.

47 *Mayors and Sheriffs*, p. 92; Knowles, *Disinherited (III)*, pp. 22–23; Cockerill, *Eleanor of Castile*, pp. 145–46. Edward and Eleanor also participated in the spoils of the Disinherited. He received lands belonging to ten rebels, she four, but when a fifth grant was withdrawn from her, she wrote a famous letter trying to get it back, which concludes with her telling the addressee to 'deal with this matter in a way which ensures that they shall not set it down to covetousness'.

Pages 332–337

48 Dunstable, pp. 242–43; *Mayors and Sheriffs*, pp. 92–94; Powicke, *King Henry III*, pp. 532–35; *DBM*, pp. 316–37. Prior to the publication of the Dictum of Kenilworth, Magna Carta was read out before the people at Guildhall and copies of it were sent to all the sheriffs to do likewise in the counties.

49 *CPR, 1258–66*, p. 678; *CPR, 1266–72*, pp. 130, 140–41; *Royal Letters*, pp. 304–05, 315; Powicke, *King Henry III*, pp. 535–36. Louis's arbitration between Henry and the younger Simon was conducted over the course of a year between the spring of 1267 and 1268.

50 *DBM*, pp. 322–23; Melrose, pp. 226–27; Prothero, *Montfort*, pp. 371–73.

51 Wykes, pp. 195–96; *Mayors and Sheriffs*, p. 94; Powicke, *King Henry III*, p. 539.

52 Dunstable, p. 244; *Mayors and Sheriffs*, p. 94; Ramsay, *Dawn of the Constitution*, p. 259.

53 Knowles, *Disinherited (III)*, pp. 35–36; *CPR, 1267–72*, p. 56. Bohun held the castles in right of his wife Eleanor Braose, who was a sister of Mortimer's wife Maud. Another of Clare's grievances concerned the size of his mother's dower from his late father's estate. He claimed that it was far too generous and Henry moved to rectify the situation. She was the Countess of Gloucester whom Queen Margaret teased Henry about marrying.

54 Knowles, *Disinherited (III)*, pp. 61–62.

55 Knowles, *Disinherited (II)*, p. 27, *(III)* p. 71; *CPR, 1258–66*, p. 653; Howell, *Eleanor of Provence*, p. 236. The count, Guy de Castillon, also held a note from Queen Eleanor for £267 she contracted while overseas. Vescy ultimately fined for £2,467 to get his lands back from him, which he did by the time of his death in 1289.

56 *Flores*, pp. 445–46; Wykes, pp. 196–97; Dunstable, p. 244; Knowles, *Disinherited (I)*, pp. 41–43.

57 *Mayors and Sheriffs*, p. 95; Wykes, p. 198; Dunstable, p. 245; Knowles, *Disinherited (I)*, pp. 45–50.

58 *Flores*, p. 446; *Mayors and Sheriffs*, pp. 96–97; Wykes, p. 201.

59 *CPR, 1266–72*, pp. 64–65; Wykes, pp. 197–98; *Flores*, pp. 447–48; Wykes, p. 202; Dunstable, pp. 246–47. According to the Dunstable annalist, it was Clare's wife Alice, who was Henry's niece, who came to warn the king about an imminent attack from Deyville.

60 *CPR, 1266–72*, pp. 70–72, 144–45; Wykes, pp. 204–06; *Flores*, pp. 446, 448; *Mayors and Sheriffs*, p. 98–100; Knowles, *Disinherited (III)*, p. 72; Powicke, *King Henry III*, p. 554. Fitz-John's £340 worth of lands were granted to Clare, but the settlement between them is unknown. Basset held the redemption fine for the lands of his other son-in-law Despenser. He willed it to his daughter Aline, Hugh's widow, who bequeathed it to their son, making this younger Despenser, infamous with his own son in the reign of Edward II, heir to both his father's lands and the fine to redeem them.

61 *CPR, 1266–72*, pp. 73–74; Wykes, pp. 206–07, 209–11; *Mayors and Sheriffs*, p. 100; Dunstable, pp. 246–47; Knowles, *Disinherited (I)*, pp. 58–67; Valente, 'Simon de Montfort', pp. 27–49. As an incentive to stand down and get the men of Ely to surrender, Deyville was given immediate possession of his lands. It was a delicate issue for Henry, because he had granted them to his wife Queen Eleanor. He knew she was going to be even more disappointed to learn that he also remitted Deyville's first-year payment of the £600 fine he now owed her, but relied on her 'spirituality' to understand. In the letter informing her of this, he 'lovingly' requested her to accept it for reasons he would explain at their next meeting. Another of the rebel leaders, Nicholas Seagrave, who together with his mother helped Edward force the surrender of Ely, also got to take possession of his lands, which had been granted to Edmund.

62 *Royal Letters*, pp. 312–14; *CPR, 1266–72*, p. 111; Smith, *Llywelyn Ap Gruffudd*, pp. 177–81; Morris, *Great and Terrible King*, pp. 132–33.

63 *CPR, 1266–72*, pp. 98, 114.
64 *The Statutes*, pp. 6–15; Powicke, *King Henry III*, pp. 547–49.

17 By Gift of the Third Henry

1 Carpenter, 'Westminster Abbey in Politics', pp. 49–58; Powicke, *King Henry III*, pp. 572–74. Carpenter writes that in late 1263 Henry earmarked £333 of Clare's £1,000 fine for inheriting his father's estate for the project. Clare ignored the order, and the king hounding him to pay up may have helped pushed the deadbeat earl to side with Montfort before Lewes.
2 Wander, 'Westminster Abbey', pp. 138, 142–43; Binski, 'Cosmati at Westminster', pp. 7–9. Porphyry ('purple' in Greek) was used for the stone roundel in the centre because it evoked the colour of royalty from ancient times.
3 Clanchy, *Memory to Written Record*, pp. 161–62.
4 Wander, 'Westminster Abbey', pp. 141–45; Binski, 'Cosmati at Westminster', pp. 22–25. The inscription reads: 'If the reader prudently considers all that is set down, he will find here the end of the *primum mobile*. The field (hedge) lives three years; add dogs and horses and men, stags and ravens, eagles, huge sea serpents, the world: whatever follows triples the years of the foregoing. The sphere shows the archetype, this globe shows the macrocosm. In the year of Christ one thousand, twice one hundred, twelve, with sixty, taking away four, King Henry III, the city (Rome), Odoricus, and the abbot joined together these porphyry stones.' *Primum mobile* is literally the prime mover, which ordered the universe through its movement in and around all heavenly bodies. The abbot, of course, was Richard de Ware, and Odoricus was the Roman artist responsible for the design of the pavement. He could have also been the father of Peter the Roman, who later made Henry's tomb.
5 Clanchy, *England and its Rulers*, pp. 281–82; Wander, 'Westminster Abbey', pp. 151–56; Binski, 'Cosmati at Westminster', pp. 10–11.
6 *CPR, 1266–72*, p. 338; Scott, *Gleanings*, pp. 134–35. The king owed the abbot £50 for the pavement, the abbot owed the Bishop of Worcester £50 for his temporalities in the bishopric as part of collecting the clerical tenth and the bishop owed the king £50 for his own temporalities. This triangular convenience made it possible to acquit all three claims in one fell swoop.
7 *CPR, 1266–72*, p. 362; Howell, *Eleanor of Provence*, pp. 242–43. Peter of Savoy willed the honour of Richmond to the queen, but inasmuch as Henry had been promising it to their son-in-law John of Brittany, an annual buyout of £1,333 had to be arranged with her.
8 Morris, *Great and Terrible King*, pp. 84–85.
9 Wykes, p. 212; Cockerill, *Eleanor of Castile*, p. 154.
10 Labarge, *Saint Louis*, pp. 226–30; Prestwich, *Edward I*, p. 67; Morris, *Great and Terrible King*, p. 83.
11 Maddicott, 'The Crusade Taxation', pp. 94–95.
12 Ibid., pp. 101–02.
13 *CPR, 1258–66*, p. 336; Powicke, *King Henry III*, pp. 523–26; Denholm-Young, *Richard of Cornwall*, p. 144; Knowles, *Disinherited (II)*, p. 26. Ferrers eventually recovered only the manor of Chartley. His Lusignan wife Mary died while he was in prison and he married again, to Eleanor, daughter of the dead Montfortian Humphrey de Bohun, and begot a son, Robert, with her who rose high in royal service.
14 *CPR, 1258–66*, p. 275; *CPR, 1266–72*, p. 100; Wykes, p. 222–24; *Mayors and Sheriffs*, pp. 113–14; Howell, *Eleanor of Provence*, pp. 244–45; Powicke, *King Henry III*, pp. 707–09. Aveline's mother was Isabella de Forz, born in 1237 to Baldwin de Redvers, the Earl

of Devon, and Amice de Clare, sister of Richard. In 1249, she was married to William de Forz, the Count of Aumâle. The deaths of her father, brother and husband by 1262 left her the richest widow on the marriage market. Henry granted the rights to her remarriage to Edmund on 22 August 1263, interestingly after Montfort came to power the first time, but when he came to power the second time the grant was redirected to his own second son Simon for £333. She balked at the deal, and Eleanor de Montfort's apparent campaign to soften her up came to nothing (Wilkinson, *Eleanor de Montfort*, pp. 107–08). At some point the younger Simon attempted to abduct Isabella, as she claimed in a later lawsuit, and she was forced to flee to Wales for safety.

15 *Mayors and Sheriffs*, pp. 115–19, 127; *CPR, 1258–66*, p. 412.

16 See pp. 235, 271; *CPR, 1258-66*, p. 365.

17 *Flores*, p. 450; Wykes, pp. 226–27;

18 *Mayors and Sheriffs*, p. 121–2; Weiler, 'Symbolism and Politics', pp. 34–36.

19 Prestwich, *Edward I*, pp. 60–61; Morris, *Great and Terrible King*, p. 90; Powicke, *King Henry III*, pp. 545, 579. As additional security, the pope decided that Clare should commit either his eldest daughter to the care of the queen or his castle at Tonbridge to Henry of Almain, in both cases for three years. Among Clare's other reasons for dissatisfaction were the Treaty of Montgomery, which he felt gave away too much at his expense, his continuing feud with Edward over Bristol, the treatment of Ferrers, and claims and counterclaims between him and the crown over losses during the recent war. His visit to Louis took place in February 1270.

20 See p. 273.

21 Wykes, pp. 227–28; Prestwich, *Edward I*, pp. 70–71; Maddicott, 'The Crusade Taxation', pp. 105–10; Powicke, *King Henry III*, p. 565–66. Mitchell, *Studies in Taxation*, pp. 295–99.

22 *CPR, 1258–66*, pp. 452, 625; Wykes, pp. 234–5; *Flores*, pp. 449–50; Powicke, *King Henry III*, pp. 584–85.

23 Prestwich, *Edward I*, p. 73; Howell, *Eleanor of Provence*, pp. 249–50; Cockerill, *Eleanor of Castile*, pp. 161–62; *Mayors and Sheriffs*, pp. 146–47; *Melrose*, p. 215. The queen admittedly had done little to try to win over her subjects. Even the royalist chronicler of London complains how she used all the tolls and proceeds from her control over London Bridge for her own purposes and allowed the bridge to fall into disrepair. The complaints grew so loud in 1270 that she agreed to relinquish control of the bridge, only to change her mind within two weeks and reinstall her own wardens.

24 Smith, *Llywelyn Ap Gruffudd*, pp. 347–54; Powicke, *King Henry III*, pp. 580–81.

25 *Mayors and Sheriffs*, pp. 137–38; Tyerman, *God's War*, pp. 808–13; Labarge, *Saint Louis*, pp. 239–46; *Edward I*, pp. 73–74. Others who died without making it back from the crusade included Alphonse of Poitiers and his wife Jeanne of Toulouse; King Theobald II of Navarre and his wife Isabel, who was Louis's daughter; Philip III's wife Isabella; and five counts, including Henry's nephew Hugh (XII) Lusignan. That makes three generations of Lusignans who died on Louis's crusades.

26 Wykes, pp. 241–44; Blaauw, *Barons' War*, pp. 336–53.

27 *CPR, 1258–66*, pp. 531, 622; *Flores*, pp. 452–53; Powicke, *King Henry III*, p. 582.

28 *CPR, 1258–66*, pp. 520–21; Dunstable, pp. 249–51; *Mayors and Sheriffs*, pp. 147–49; Lloyd, *English Wool Trade*, pp. 28–32. Giffard finally answered the charge after being summoned several times, saying she went on her own free will and he offered to pay the king £200 for the marriage rights. Henry agreed only if Matilda withdrew her complaint, but she deferred from appearing before him on account of illness. Some good news for Henry at this time was the capture of Roger Godberd, who led a gang of outlaws in the Midlands after the disinheritance of his former lord, Robert

de Ferrers. Godberd and his followers were apprehended in Sherwood Forest, and the Robin Hood ballads that began to appear two centuries later may have been partly inspired by their exploits. *CPR, 1267-72*, p. 622; Holt, *Robin Hood*, pp. 97-99.

29 Wykes, p. 246; Carpenter, *Reign of King Henry III*, p. 206.

30 Wykes, pp. 247–48; Denholm-Young, *Richard of Cornwall*, pp. 152–53. Richard's widow Beatrice survived him by five years, dying at the age of 23.

31 *Flores*, p. 453; Wykes, pp. 247–50; Prestwich, *Edward I*, pp. 78–81.

32 *Mayors and Sheriffs*, pp. 150–53; Rishanger, p. 73.

33 *CPR, 1258–66*, p. 705; *Mayors and Sheriffs*, pp. 153–57.

34 *CPR, 1258–66*, p. 715; Powicke, *King Henry III*, pp. 590–91. The conversion was done on the website http://www.nationalarchives.gov.uk.

35 *Mayors and Sheriffs*, p. 160; Powicke, *King Henry III*, p. 588. Henry's contemporary James I of Aragon ruled longer, sixty-three years, having come to the throne in 1213 at the age of 5 after his father was killed in battle by Simon de Montfort's father.

36 *Flores*, p. 454; *Mayors and Sheriffs*, p. 159; Carpenter, *Reign of King Henry III*, pp. 428–34; Church, *Henry III*, p. 93.

37 Carpenter, *Reign of King Henry III*, pp. 255–60; Flores, p. 454; Wykes, p. 252; Dunstable, p. 254; Rishanger II p. 75; Guisborough, pp. 212–13; Osney, p. 254; Trivet, pp. 279–80. Rishanger goes on to say that Henry's lucky turn of fate led many to believe he was 'the one designated by Merlin as the lynx penetrating all'.

38 Ramsay, *Dawn of the Constitution*, p. 281; Howell, *Eleanor of Provence*, p. 190; Carpenter, *Reign of King Henry III*, p. 420; Labarge, *Saint Louis*, p. 235. Louis also decided not to name Margaret as regent in his absence as Henry had done with Eleanor when he went abroad in 1253.

39 Powicke, *King Henry III*, p. 591; *Mayors and Sheriffs*, pp. 158–59; Rishanger, p. 78; Morris, *Great and Terrible King*, pp. 103–04.

40 Prestwich, *Edward I*, 90–91, Morris, *Great and Terrible King*, p. 115.

41 Howell, *Eleanor of Provence*, pp. 89, 103, 291.

42 Binski, 'Cosmati at Westminster', pp. 13–21; Carpenter, *Reign of King Henry III*, pp. 423–24; Howell, *Eleanor of Provence*, p. 306.

43 Prothero, *Montfort*, pp. 371–73; Trivet, p. 302.

44 Steane, *Archaeology of the Medieval English Monarchy*, p. 48; Howell, *Eleanor of Provence*, pp. 308–11; Cockerill, *Eleanor of Castile*, p. 348.

45 Carpenter, *Reign of King Henry III*, p. 428; Howell, *Eleanor of Provence*, pp. 304–05.

46 Wilkinson, *Eleanor de Montfort*, pp. 128–35; Bémont, *Montfort*, pp. 260–73; Morris, *Great and Terrible King*, p. 188. Guy de Montfort was the only child of Simon and Eleanor to create a line of descendents through his Italian-born daughter Anastasia.

47 Ramsay, *Dawn of the Constitution*, pp. 295–96; 536–37.

48 Morris, *Great and Terrible King*, pp. 377–78.

49 Morgan, *St George*, pp. 93–106.

50 *Richard II*, Act 3 Scene 2; *Purgatorio*, canto 7, lines 130–31.

51 Seward, *Warrior King and the Invasion of France*, pp. 152–8.

52 Labarge, *Saint Louis*, pp. 246–48; Howell, *Eleanor of Provence*, p. 273.

53 Carpenter, *Reign of King Henry III*, p. 427; Steane, *Archaeology of the Medieval English Monarchy*, p. 48.

54 Stubbs, *Constitutional History Vol. II*, pp. 107–08; Ramsay, *Dawn of the Constitution*, pp. 281–82; Treharne, *Baronial Plan*, p. 48; Powicke, *Thirteenth Century*, p. 19.

55 Carpenter, *Struggle for Mastery*, p. 340.

56 Confirmations in 1237, 1253 and 1265 of the 1225 version of the charter. It is this Magna Carta, issued under Henry's seal, that remains on the books today.

BIBLIOGRAPHY

Primary Sources

Bettenson, H. and C. Maunder (eds), *Documents of the Christian Church* (Oxford, 1963).

Burton, *Annales Monastici: The Annals of Burton*, Vol. I, ed. H.R. Luard (London, 1864).

Calendar of Charter Rolls, Henry III, 1903. (**CChR**)

Calendar of the Patent Rolls, Henry III, preserved in the Public Record Office, 1913. (**CPR**)

Chronicon de Lanercost, ed. J. Stevenson (Glasgow, 1839).

Close Rolls of the Reign of Henry III, preserved in the Public Record Office, 1932. (**CR**)

Documents of the Baronial Movement of Reform and Rebellion, ed. R.F. Treharne, I.J. Sanders (Oxford, 1973). (**DBM**)

Dunstable, *Annales Monastici: The Annals of Dunstable*, Vol. III, ed. H.R. Luard (London, 1866).

Flores Historiarum, trans. C.D. Yonge (London, 1853).

Gervase, *The Historical Works of Gervase of Canterbury, Vol. II*, ed. W. Stubbs (London, 1880).

Gloucester, Robert, *The Metrical Chronicle of Robert of Gloucester*, ed. W. A. Wright (London, 1887).

Grosseteste, Robert, *The Letters of Robert Grosseteste, Bishop of Lincoln*, ed. F.A.C. Mantello and F.M. Goering (Toronto, 2010).

Guisborough, Walter, *The Chronicle of Walter of Guisborough*, ed. H. Rothwell (London, 1957).

Joinville, John de, *Crusade of Saint Louis* (London, 1903).

Manners and Household Expenses of England in the Thirteenth and Fifteenth Centuries, ed. T.H. Turner (Roxburghe Club, 1841).

Marsh, Adam, *The Letters of Adam Marsh, Vol. I*, ed. and trans. C.H. Lawrence (Oxford, 2006).

Oseney, *Annales Monastici: The Chronicle of Oseney*, Vol. IV, ed. H.R. Luard (London, 1869).

Paris, Matthew, *Matthew Paris's English History from 1235 to 1273, Vols I, II, III*, trans. J.A. Giles (London, 1854).

Puylaurens, William, *The Chronicle of William of Puylaurens: The Albigensian Crusade and its Aftermath*, ed. and trans. W.A. Sibly and M.D. Sibly (Woodbridge, 2003).

Rishanger, William de, *The Chronicle of William de Rishanger*, ed. J.O. Halliwell (1840).

Royal Letters, ed. W.W. Shirley (London, 1866).

Rymer, Thomas, *Rymer's Foedera Vol. I*, ed. T.D. Hardy (London, 1869).
St Edmund, Archbishop of Canterbury, His Life, As Told by Old English Writers. arr. B. Ward (St Louis, 1903).
Tewkesbury, *Annales Monastici: The Annals of Tewkesbury*, Vol. I, ed. H.R. Luard (London, 1864).
The Chronicles of the Mayors and Sheriffs of London, 1188–1274, ed. H.R. Riley (London, 1863).
The Chronicle of Melrose, trans. J. Stevenson (London, 1856).
The Political Songs of England, ed. T. Wright (London, 1839).
The Shorter Latin Forms of Master Henry of Avarances Relating to England, ed. J.C. Russell and J.P. Hieronimus, The Medieval Academy of America (Cambridge, 1935).
The Song of Lewes, ed. C.L. Kingsford (Oxford, 1890).
The Statutes. Revised edition, Vol. I, Henry III to James II (London, 1870).
Trivet, Nicholas de, *Annales*, ed. T. Hog, Historical English Society IX (London, 1845).
Wendover, Roger, *Roger of Wendover's Flowers of History, Vols I, II,* trans. J.A. Giles (London, 1859).
Winchester, *Annales Monastici: The Annals of Winchester*, Vol. II, ed. H.R. Luard (London, 1865).
Waverley, *Annales Monastici: The Annals of Waverley*, Vol. II, ed. H.R. Luard (London, 1865).
Wykes, Thomas, *Annales Monastici: The Chronicle of Thomas Wykes*, Vol. IV, ed. H.R. Luard (London, 1869).

Secondary Sources

Aberth, J., *An Environmental History of the Middle Ages: The Crucible of Nature* (London, 2013).
Abulafia, A.S., *Christian Jewish Relations 1000–1300: Jews in the Service of Medieval Christendom* (London, 2011).
Allen, M., *Mints and Money in Medieval England* (Cambridge, 2012).
Allshorn, L., *Stupor Mundi, The Life Times of Frederick* (London, 1912).
Ambler, T.S., *Bishops in the Political Community of England, 1213–1272* (Oxford, 2017).
——, 'On Kingship and Tyranny: Grosseteste's Memorandum and its Place in the Baronial Reform Movement', *Thirteenth Century England XIV*, ed. J. Burton, P. Schofield and B. Weiler (Woodbridge, 2013).
Baker, D., *With All for All, The Life of Simon de Montfort* (Stroud, 2015).
Barker, J., *The Tournament in England 1100–1400* (Woodbridge, 1986).
Barlow, F., *Edward the Confessor* (Berkeley, 1985).
Barratt, N., 'Another Fine Mess: Evidence for the Resumption of exchequer Authority in the Minority of Henry III', *The Growth of Royal Government under Henry III*, ed. D. Crook and L.J. Wilkinson (Woodbridge, 2015).
——, 'Counting the Cost: The Financial Implications of the Loss of Normandy', *Thirteenth Century England X*, ed. M. Prestwich, R. Britnell and R. Frame (Woodbridge, 2005).
Barrow, J., 'Peter d'Aigueblanche's Support Network', *Thirteenth Century England XIII*, ed. J. Burton, F. Lachaud, P. Schofield, K. Stober and B. Weiler (Woodbridge, 2001).
Bémont, C., *Simon de Montfort* (Oxford, 1930).
Binski, P., 'The Cosmati at Westminster and the English Court Style', *The Art Bulletin*, Vol. 72, No. 1 (1990).
Blaauw, W.H., *The Barons' War* (London, 1871).
Bradbury, J., 'Philip Augustus and King John: Personality and History', *King John: New Interpretations*, ed. S.D. Church (Woodbridge, 1999).

Brand, P., *Kings, Barons and Justices: The Making and Enforcement of Legislation in Thirteenth-Century England* (Cambridge, 2008).

Brooks, R., *The Knight Who Saved England: William Marshal and the French Invasion, 1217* (Oxford, 2014).

Butler, S.M., *Divorce in Medieval England: From One to Two Persons in Law* (New York, 2013).

Bynum, C.W., *Wonderful Blood: Theology and Practice in Late Medieval Northern Germany and Beyond* (Philadelphia, 2006).

Carpenter, D., 'A Noble in Politics: Roger Mortimer', *Nobels and Nobility*, ed. A. Duggan (Woodbridge, 2000).

——, 'Archbishop Langton and Magna Carta: His Contribution, his Doubts and his Hypocrisy', *English Historical Review*, Vol. CXXVI, No. 522 (2011).

——, 'Between Magna Carta and the Parliamentary State', *The Growth of Royal Government under Henry III*, ed. D. Crook and L.J. Wilkinson (Woodbridge, 2015).

——, 'Crucifixion and Conversion: King Henry III and the Jews in 1255', *Laws, Lawyers and Texts, Studies in Medieval Legal History in Honour of Paul Brand* (Leiden, 2012).

——, 'Henry III and the Sicilian Affair', *Fine of the Month* (November 2012): www.finerollshenry3.org.uk/redist/pdf/fm-02-2012.pdf

——, 'King Henry III and the Chapter House of Westminster Abbey', *Westminster Abbey Chapter House: The History, Art and Architecture of 'A Chapter House Beyond Compare'*, ed. W. Rodwell (London, 2010).

——, 'King Henry III and Saint Edward the Confessor: The Origins of the Cult', *English Historical Review*, Vol. CXXII, No. 498 (2007).

—— and J. Kanter, 'King Henry III and Windsor Castle', *St George's Chapel Windsor: History and Heritage*, ed. N. Saul and T. Tatton-Brown (Stanbridge, 2010).

——, *Magna Carta* (London, 2015).

——, 'Magna Carta 1253: The Ambitions of the Church and the Divisions within the Realm', *Historical Research*, Vol. 86, No. 232 (2013).

——, *The Battles of Lewes and Evesham* (Keele, 1987).

——, 'The Career of Godfrey of Crowcombe: Household Knight of King John and Steward of King Henry III', *War, Government and Aristocracy in the British Isles, c. 1150–1500*, ed. C. Given-Wilson, A. Kettle and L. Scales (Woodbridge, 2008).

——, 'The Meetings of Kings Henry III and Louis IX', *Thirteenth Century England X*, ed. M. Prestwich, R. Britnell and R. Frame (Suffolk, 2005).

——, *The Reign of Henry III* (London, 1996).

——, *The Struggle for Mastery, Britain 1066–1284* (London, 2004).

——, 'The *vis et voluntas* of King Henry III: The Downfall and Punishment of Robert De Ros', *Fine of the Month* (November 2012): www.finerollshenry3.org.uk/redist/pdf/fm-08-2012.pdf

——, 'Thomas Fitz-Thomas', *Oxford Dictionary of National Biography* (2004).

——, 'Westminster Abbey in Politics, 1258–1269', *Thirteenth Century England VIII*, ed. M. Prestwich, R. Britnell and R. Frame (Woodbridge, 2001).

Carr, A.D., 'Anglo-Welsh relations, 1066–1282', *England and her Neighbours, 1066–1453: Essays in Honour of Pierre Chaplais*, ed. M. Jones and M. Vale (London, 1989).

Cassidy, R., 'Adventus Vicecomitum and the Financial Crisis of Henry III's Reign, 1250–1272', *English Historical Review*, Vol. CXXVI, No. 520 (2011).

——, 'Bad Sheriffs, Custodial Sheriffs and Control of the Counties, Authority and Resistance in the Age of Magna Carta', *Proceedings of the Aberystwyth and Lampeter Conference, 2013*, ed. J. Burton, P. Schofield and B. Weiler (Woodbridge, 2015).

—— and M. Clasby, 'Matthew Paris and Henry III's Elephant', Henry III Fine Rolls Project, 2012.

——, 'Richard of Cornwall and the Royal Mints and Exchanges, 1247–59', *The Numismatic Journal*, Vol. 172 (2012).
——, 'The Exchanges, Silver Purchases and Trade in the Reign of Henry III', *British Numismatic Journal*, Vol. 81 (2011).
Cazel, F.A. Jr., 'Financing the Crusades', *A History of the Crusades Vol. 6: Impact of the Crusades on Europe*, ed. H.W. Hazard and N.P. Zacour (Madison, 2006).
Chaplais, P., 'The Making of the Treaty of Paris (1259) and the Royal Style', *EHR*, Vol. 67 (1952).
Church, S., *King John: England, Magna Carta and the Making of a Tyrant* (London, 2015).
——, *Henry III: A Simple and God-Fearing King* (London, 2017).
Clanchy, M.T., 'Did Henry III Have a Policy', *History*, Vol. 53 (1968).
——, *England and its Rulers, 1066–1307* (Chichester, 2014).
——, *From Memory to Written Record: England 1066–1307* (Oxford, 1979).
Cockerill, S., *Eleanor of Castile, The Shadow Queen* (Stroud, 2014).
Cohn, S.K., *Popular Protests in Late Medieval English Towns* (Cambridge, 2013).
Costain, T.B., *The Magnificent Century* (Garden City, 1951).
Creamer, J., 'St Edmund of Canterbury and Henry III in the Shadow of Thomas Becket', *Thirteenth Century England XIV*, ed. J. Burton, P. Schofield and B. Weiler (Woodbridge, 2013).
Crook, D., 'The Petition of the Bearings and Charters of Free Warren', *Thirteenth Century England VIII*, ed. M. Prestwich, R. Britnell and R. Frame (Woodbridge, 2001).
Crouch, D., *The Acts and Letters of the Marshal Family* (Cambridge, 2015).
——, *William Marshal: Knighthood, War and Chivalry, 1147–1219* (Harlow, 1990).
Davis, J.P., *The Gothic King: A Biography of Henry III* (London, 2013).
D'Avray, D., *Dissolving Royal Marriages: A Documentary History, 860–1600* (Cambridge, 2014).
——, *Medieval Christianity in Practice* (Princeton, 2009).
Denholm-Young, N., *Richard of Cornwall* (New York, 1947).
Eales, R., 'Henry III and the End of the Norman Earldom of Chester', *Thirteenth Century England I*, ed. P.R. Coss and S.D. Lloyd (Woodbridge, 1985).
Edbury, P.W., 'The De Montforts in the Latin East', *Thirteenth Century England VIII*, ed. M. Prestwich, R.H. Britnell and R. Frame (Woodbridge, 2001).
Ellis, C., *Hubert de Burgh, A Study in Constancy* (London, 1952).
Everard, J.A., *Brittany and the Angevins: Province and Empire 1158–1203* (Cambridge, 2004).
Fogle, L., 'The Domus Conversorum: The Personal Interest of Henry III', *Jewish Historical Studies*, Vol. 41 (2007).
Folda, J., *Crusader Art in the Holy Land: From the Third Crusade to the Fall of Acre* (Cambridge, 2005).
Gabrieli, F., *Arab Historians of the Crusades* (Berkeley, 1984).
Gasquet, A., *Henry III and the Church* (London, 1905).
Goldstone, N., *Four Queens: The Provencal Sisters Who Ruled Europe*, Orion Books (London, 2009).
Gonzáles, O.C.M., 'Lope Fernández, Bishop of Morocco: His Diplomatic Role in the Planning of an Anglo-Castilian Crusade into North Africa', *Thirteenth Century England XIV*, ed. J. Burton, P. Schofield and B. Weiler (Woodbridge, 2013).
Gransden, A., *Historical Writing in England* (Abingdon, 1996).
Griffin, E., *Blood Sport: Hunting in Britain since 1066* (New Haven, 2007).
Hamilton, J., *The Plantagenets: History of a Dynasty* (London, 2010).
Hammond, P., *Food and Feast in Medieval England* (Stroud, 1993).
Harding, A., *England in the Thirteenth Century* (Cambridge, 1993).

Harvey, K., *Episcopal Appointments in England, c. 1214–1344: From Episcopal Election to Papal Provision* (Farnham, 2014).
Hershey, A., 'Success or Failure? Hugh Bigod and Judicial Reform during the Baronial Movement', *Thirteenth Century England V*, ed. P.R. Coss and S.D. Lloyd (Woodbridge, 1995).
Hillaby, J., *The Palgrave Dictionary of Medieval Anglo-Jewish History* (Basingstoke, 2013).
Holt, J.C., *Magna Carta* (Cambridge, 2015).
——, *Robin Hood* (London, 1982).
Howell, M., *Eleanor of Provence* (Oxford, 2001).
——, 'The Children of King Henry III and Eleanor of Provence', *Thirteenth Century England IV*, ed. P.R. Coss and S.D. Lloyd (Woodbridge, 1992).
Huffman, J.P., *The Social Politics of Medieval Diplomacy: Anglo-German Relations (1066–1307)* (Ann Arbor, 2000).
Huntington, J., 'Edward the Celibate, Edward the Saint: Virginity in the Construction of Edward the Confessor', *Medieval Virginities*, ed. A. Bernau, R. Evans and S. Salih (Toronto, 2003).
Hutton, W.H., *Simon de Montfort and His Cause, 1251–1266* (London, 1907).
Hyams, P., 'Henry III in Bed', *Anger's Past: The Social Uses of an Emotion in the Middle Ages*, ed. B.H. Rosenwein (Ithaca, 1998).
Jackson, P., *The Seventh Crusade, 1244–1254: Sources and Documents* (Farnham, 2009).
Jobson, A., 'John of Crakehall, the "Forgotten" Baronial Treasurer, 1258–60', *Thirteenth Century England XIII*, ed. J. Burton, F. Lachaud and P. Schofield (Woodbridge, 2011).
——, *The First English Revolution: Simon de Montfort, Henry III and the Barons' War* (London, 2012).
Johns, S.M., 'Loretta de Briouze, Countess of Leicester, Noblewoman and Recluse', *Oxford Dictionary of National Biography* (2004).
Keene, D., 'Crisis Management in London's Food Supply, 1250–1500', *Commercial Activity, Markets and Entrepreneurs in the Middle Ages: Essays in Honour of Richard Britnell*, ed. B. Dodds and C.D. Liddy (Woodbridge, 2011).
King, E., *Medieval England, 1066–1485* (Oxford, 1988).
Kjær, L., 'Matthew Paris and the Royal Christmas: Ritualised Communication in Text and Practice', *Thirteenth Century England XIV*, ed. J. Burton, P. Schofield and B. Weiler (Woodbridge, 2013).
Knowles, C.H., *The Disinherited, 1265–1280: A Political and Social Study of the Supporters of Simon De Montfort and the Resettlement after the Barons' War*, Doctoral Thesis, University of Wales, 1959.
Kushner, T., *The Jewish Heritage in British History: Englishness and Jewishness* (Abingdon, 1992).
Labarge, M.W., *Saint Louis: The Life of Louis IX of France* (London, 1968).
——, *Simon de Montfort* (London, 1962).
Laborderie, O.D., D.A. Carpenter, D.A. and J.R. Maddicott, 'The Last Hours of Simon de Montfort: A New Account', *English Historical Review*, 15 (2000).
Langmuir, G.I., 'The Knight's Tale of Young Hugh of Lincoln', *Speculum*, 47 (1972).
Lloyd, S., 'King Henry III, the Crusade and the Mediterranean', *England and Her Neighbours, 1066–1453: Essays in Honour of Pierre Chaplais*, ed. M. Jones and M. Vale (London, 1989).
Lloyd, T.H., *The English Wool Trade in the Middle Ages* (Cambridge, 1977).
Lord, E., *The Knights Templar in Britain* (Harlow, 2004).
Loveday, L.G., *Women, Art, and Patronage from Henry III to Edward III: 1216–1377* (Woodbridge, 2002).
Maddicott, J.R., 'Politics and the People', *Thirteenth Century England XIV*, ed. J.E. Burton, P.R. Schofield and B. Weiler (Woodbridge, 2013).
——, *Simon de Montfort* (Cambridge, 1994).

——, 'The Crusade Taxation of 1268–1270', *Thirteenth Century England II*, ed. P.R. Coss and S.D. Lloyd (Woodbridge, 1988).

——, *The Origins of the English Parliament, 924–1327* (Oxford, 2010).

——, 'The Pre-Reform Parliaments of Henry III', *Thirteenth Century England VII*, ed. M. Prestwich, R. Britnell and R. Frame (Woodbridge, 1999).

Marsh, F.B., *English Rule in Gascony, 1199–1259* (Ann Arbor, 1912).

Maund, K., *The Welsh Kings: Warriors, Warlords, and Princes* (Stroud, 2006).

Maurice, C.E., *Stephen Langton* (London, 1872).

Mayhew, N.J., 'From Regional to Central Minting, 1158–1464', *A New History of the Royal Mint*, ed. C.E. Challis (Cambridge, 1992).

Mayr-Harting, H., *Religion, Politics and Society in Britain 1066–1272* (New York, 2011).

McLean, T., *Medieval English Gardens* (New York, 2014).

Menache, S., 'Matthew Paris's Attitudes toward Anglo-Jewry', *Journal of Medieval History*, Vol. 23, No. 2 (1997).

Mitchell, S.K., *Studies in Taxation under John and Henry III* (New Haven, 1914).

Moore, T., 'The Fine Rolls as Evidence for the Expansion of Royal Justice during the Reign of Henry III', *The Growth of Royal Government under Henry III*, ed. D. Crook and L.J. Wilkinson (Woodbridge, 2015).

Morris, M., *A Great and Terrible King* (London, 2009).

——, *The Bigod Earls of Norfolk* (Woodbridge, 2005).

Mortimer, R., 'The Beginnings of the Honour of Clare', *Proceedings of the Battle Conference on Anglo-Norman Studies: 1980*, ed. R.A. Brown (Woodbridge, 1980).

Mueller, J., *A Companion to Clare of Assisi: Life, Writings, and Spirituality* (Leiden, 2010).

Mundill, R.R., *England's Jewish Solution, Experiment and Expulsion, 1262–1290* (Cambridge, 1998).

——, *The King's Jews: Money, Massacre and Exodus in Medieval England* (London, 2010).

Novikoff, A.J., *The Medieval Culture of Disputation: Pedagogy, Practice, and Performance* (Philadelphia, 2013).

Oram, R., *Alexander II: King of Scots 1214–1249* (Edinburgh, 2012).

Park, D. and R. Griffith-Park, *The Temple Church in London: History, Architecture, Art* (Woodbridge, 2010).

Perry, F., *Saint Louis* (New York, 1900).

Pollock, M.A., *Scotland, England and France after the Loss of Normandy, 1204–1296* (Woodbridge, 2015).

Power, Daniel, 'The French Interests of the Marshal Earls of Striguil and Pembroke, 1189–1234', *Anglo-Norman Studies XXV*, ed. J. Gillingham (Woodbridge, 2003).

Powicke, M., *King Henry III and the Lord Edward Vols I, II* (Oxford, 1947).

——, *The Thirteenth Century* (Oxford, 1962).

Pratt, H.M., *Westminster Abbey, its Architecture, History and Monuments* (New York, 1914).

Prestwich, M., *Edward I* (Berkeley, 1988).

——, *Plantagenet England* (Oxford, 2005).

——, 'The "Wonderful Life" of the Thirteenth Century', *Thirteenth Century England VII*, ed. M. Prestwich, R. Britnell and R. Frame (Woodbridge, 1997).

Procter, E., *Curia and Cortes in Leon and Castile 1072–1295* (Cambridge, 1980).

Prothero, G.W., *The Life of Simon de Montfort* (London, 1877).

Ramsay, J., *The Dawn of the Constitution* (London, 1908).

Ray, M., 'Three Alien Royal Stewards', *Thirteenth Century England X*, ed. M. Prestwich, R.H. Britnell and R. Fram (Woodbridge, 2005).

Reuter, T., *Medieval Polities and Modern Mentalities*, ed. J. Nelson (Cambridge, 2006).

Ridgeway, H., 'Adam Gurdun at Dunster (c.1263–1265): An Unknown Rebellion of the Community of the Realm in Somerset', *Proceedings of the Somerset Archaeological and Natural History Society*, Vol. 159 (2016).

——, 'Henry III (1207–1272)', *Oxford Dictionary of National Biography* (2004)

——, 'Henry III and the "Aliens", 1236–1272', *Thirteenth Century England II*, ed. P.R. Coss and S. Lloyd (Woodbridge, 1988).

——, 'King Henry III's Grievances against the Council in 1261', *Historical Research*, Vol. 61 (1988).

——, 'The Ecclesiastical Career of Aymer de Lusignan, Bishop Elect of Winchester, 1250–1260', *The Cloisters and the World: Essays in Honour of Barbara Harvey*, ed. J. Blair and B. Golding (Oxford, 1996).

——, 'The Lord Edward and the Provisions of Oxford (1258)', *Thirteenth Century England I*, ed. P.R. Coss and S.D. Lloyd (Woodbridge, 1986).

——, 'What Happened in 1261?', *Baronial Reform and Revolution in England, 1258–1267*, ed. A. Jobson (Woodbridge, 2016).

Ridpath, George, *The Border History of England and Scotland* (Berwick, 1810).

Rigg, A.G., *A History of Anglo-Latin Literature, 1066–1422* (Cambridge, 1992).

Rokéah, Z.E., 'An Anglo-Jewish Assembly or "Mini-Parliament" in 1287', *Thirteenth Century England VIII*, ed. M. Prestwich, R.H. Britnell and R. Frame (Woodbridge, 2001).

Rothwell, H., *English Historical Documents, 1189–1327, Vol. 3* (London, 1995).

Runciman, S., *A History of the Crusades, Vol. 3* (Cambridge, 1987).

——, *The Sicilian Vespers: A History of the Mediterranean World in the Later Thirteenth Century* (Cambridge, 1992).

Sabapathy, J., *Officers and Accountability in Medieval England 1170–1300* (Oxford, 2014).

Sadler, J., *The Second Barons' War: Simon de Montfort and the Battles of Lewes and Evesham* (Barnsley, 2008).

Scott, G.G., *Gleanings from Westminster Abbey* (Oxford, 1863).

Seabourne, G., *Imprisoning Medieval Women: The Non-Judicial Confinement and Abduction of Women in England, c.1170–1509* (New York, 2011).

Seel, G., *King John: An Underrated King* (London, 2012).

Serjeantson, R.M., *A History of the Church of St. Peter* (Northampton, 1904).

Seward, D., *The Warrior King and the Invasion of France: Henry V, Agincourt, and the Campaign that Shaped Medieval England* (New York, 2014).

Sharp, B., *Famine and Scarcity in Late Medieval and Early Modern England: The Regulation of Grain Marketing, 1256–1631* (Cambridge, 2016).

Shepard, L., *Courting Power: Persuasion and Politics in the Early Thirteenth Century* (New York, 1999).

Shepherd, R., *Westminster: A Biography: From Earliest Times to the Present* (London, 2012).

Sibly, W.A. and M.D. Sibly, *The Chronicle of William of Puylaurens: The Albigensian Crusade and its Aftermath* (Woodbridge, 2003).

Silvestri, A., *Power, Politics and Episcopal Authority: The Bishops of Cremona and Lincoln in the Middle Ages (1066–1340)* (Newcastle upon Tyne, 2015).

Singman, J.L., *Robin Hood: The Shaping of the Legend* (Westport, 1998).

Smith, J.B., *Llywelyn Ap Gruffudd: Prince of Wales* (Cardiff, 2001).

Soden, I., *Ranulf de Blondeville: The First English Hero* (Stroud, 2009).

Solt, L.F., *Church and State in Early Modern England, 1509–1640* (Oxford, 1990).

Stacey, R., 'King Henry III and the Jews', *Jews in Medieval Christendom: Slay them Not*, ed. K.T. Utterback and M.L. Price (Leiden, 2103).

——, *Politics, Policy, and Finance under Henry III, 1216–1245* (Oxford, 1987).

——, 'Royal Taxation and the Social Structure of Medieval Anglo-Jewry: The Tallages of 1239–1242', *Hebrew Union College Annual*, Vol. 56 (1985).
——, 'The Conversion of Jews to Christianity in Thirteenth-Century England', *Speculum*, Vol. 67, No. 2 (1992).
Stanley, A., *Historical Memorials of Westminster Abbey* (Philadelphia, 1899).
Steane, J., *The Archaeology of the Medieval English Monarchy* (New York, 1999).
Stephens, G.R., 'The Early Life of Joan Makepeace', *Speculum*, xx (1945).
Storey, R.L., 'The First Convocation, 1257?', *Thirteenth Century England III*, ed. P.R. Cossand S. Lloyd (Woodbridge, 1991).
Strickland, A., *Lives of the Queens of England* (London, 1840).
Strickland, A., *Lives of the Princesses of England* (London, 1857).
Stubbs, W., *The Constitutional History of England*, 3 Vols, 5th ed. (Oxford, 1891–98).
Tolan, J., 'The First Imposition of a Badge on European Jews: The English Royal Mandate of 1218', *The Character of Christian-Muslim Encounter*, ed. D. Pratt (Leiden, 2015).
Tout, T.F., *Chapters in the Administrative History of Medieval England: The Wardrobe, the Chamber and the Small Seals, Vol. 1* (Manchester, 1920).
Treharne, R., *The Baronial Plan of Reform* (Manchester, 1932).
Turner, R.V., *King John: England's Evil King* (Stroud, 2009).
Tyerman, C., *God's War: A New History of the Crusades* (Harvard, 2008).
Valente, C., 'Simon the Montfort, Earl of Leicester, and the Utility of Sanctity in Thirteenth-Century England', *Journal of Medieval History*, 21 (1995).
Vincent, N., 'Inventory of Gifts to Henry III, 1234–5', *The Growth of Royal Government under Henry III*, ed. D. Crook and L.J. Wilkinson (Woodbridge, 2015).
——, 'Isabella of Angoulême: John's Jezebel', *King John: New Interpretations,* ed. S.D. Church (Woodbridge, 1999).
——, 'Leopards, Lions and Dragons: King John's Banners and Battle Flags', The Magna Carta Project, April 2015: http://magnacarta.cmp.uea.ac.uk/read/feature_of_the_month/Apr_2015_4
——, 'Master Alexander of Stainsby, Bishop of Coventry in Litchfield, 1224–1238', *Journal of Ecclesiastical History*, 46 (1995).
——, *Peter des Roches: An Alien in English Politics, 1205–1238* (Cambridge, 1996).
——, *The Holy Blood: King Henry III and the Westminster Blood Relic* (Cambridge, 2001).
——, 'The Politics of Church and State as Reflected in the Winchester Pipe Rolls, 1208–1280', *The Winchester Pipe Rolls and Medieval English Society*, ed. R.H. Britnell (Woodbridge, 2003).
Wall, J.C., *Shrines of British Saints* (London, 1905).
Wander, S.H., 'The Westminster Abbey Sanctuary Pavement', *Traditi*, Vol. 34 (1978).
Warren, W.L., *King John* (Berkeley, 1978).
Watt, D.E.R., *Medieval Church Councils in Scotland* (Edinburgh, 2000).
Watt, J.A., *The English Episcopate, the State and the Jews* (Woodbridge, 1987).
Waugh, S.L., *The Lordship of England: Royal Wardships and Marriages in English Society and Politics, 1217–1327* (Princeton, 1988).
——, 'The Origins of the Articles of the Escheat', *Thirteenth Century England V*, ed. P.R. Coss and S.D. Lloyd (Woodbridge, 1995).
Weiler, B., 'Gregory IX, Frederick II, and the Liberation of the Holy Land, 1230–9', *The Holy Land, Holy Lands, and Christian History*, ed. R.N. Swanson (Woodbridge, 2000).
——, *Henry III and the Staufen Empire, 1216–1272* (Woodbridge, 2006).
——, 'Henry III's Plans for a German Marriage and their Context', *Thirteenth Century England VII,* ed. M. Prestwich, R. Britnell and R. Frame (Woodbridge, 1999).

——, 'Image and Reality in Richard of Cornwall's German Career', *English Historical Review*, Vol. 113, No. 454 (1998).
——, *Kingship, Rebellion and Political Culture England and Germany, c.1215–c.1250* (Basingstoke, 2007).
——, 'Symbolism and Politics in the Reign of Henry III', *Thirteenth Century England IX*, ed. M. Prestwich and R. Britnell (Woodbridge, 2003).
Westerhof, D., *Death and the Noble Body in Medieval England* (Woodbridge, 2008).
Wild, B., 'A Captive King: Henry III between the Battles of Lewes and Evesham', *Thirteenth Century England XIII*, ed. J. Burton, F. Lachaud, P. Schofield, K. Stöber and B. Weiler (Woodbridge, 2011).
——, 'The Empress's New Clothes: A *Rotulus Pannorum* of Isabella, Sister of King Henry III, Bride of Emperor Frederick II', *Medieval Clothing and Textiles VII*, ed. R. Netherton and G.R. Owen-Crocker (Woodbridge, 2011).
Wilkinson, L.J., *Eleanor de Montfort: A Rebel Countess in Medieval England* (London, 2012).
——, 'Joan, Wife of Llywelyn the Great', *Thirteenth Century England X*, ed. M. Prestwich, R.H. Britnell and R. Frame (Woodbridge, 2005).
——, 'Women as Sheriffs in Early Thirteenth Century England', *English Government in the Thirteenth Century*, ed. A. Jobson (Woodbridge, 2004).
——, *Women in Thirteenth-Century Lincolnshire* (Woodbridge, 2007).
——, 'Women, Politics and Local Government in the Thirteenth Century', *Henry III Fine Rolls Project, Related Papers*, July 2013: www.finerollshenry3.org.uk/redist/pdf/Wilkinson_Women_Politics_Local_Govt.pdf
Young, C.R., *The Making of the Neville Family in England, 1166–1400* (Woodbridge, 1996).
——, *The Royal Forests of Medieval England* (Philadelphia, 1979).

LIST OF ILLUSTRATIONS

INDEX